Lecture Notes in Computer Science

Lecture Notes in Artificial Intelligence   15562

Founding Editor

Jörg Siekmann

Series Editors

Randy Goebel, *University of Alberta, Edmonton, Canada*
Wolfgang Wahlster, *DFKI, Berlin, Germany*
Zhi-Hua Zhou, *Nanjing University, Nanjing, China*

The series Lecture Notes in Artificial Intelligence (LNAI) was established in 1988 as a topical subseries of LNCS devoted to artificial intelligence.

The series publishes state-of-the-art research results at a high level. As with the LNCS mother series, the mission of the series is to serve the international R & D community by providing an invaluable service, mainly focused on the publication of conference and workshop proceedings and postproceedings.

Oskar Palinko · Leon Bodenhagen ·
John-John Cabibihan · Kerstin Fischer ·
Selma Šabanović · Katie Winkle ·
Laxmidhar Behera · Shuzhi Sam Ge ·
Dimitrios Chrysostomou · Wanyue Jiang ·
Hongsheng He
Editors

Social Robotics

16th International Conference, ICSR + AI 2024
Odense, Denmark, October 23–26, 2024
Proceedings, Part II

Springer

Editors
Oskar Palinko 🆔
University of Southern Denmark
Odense, Denmark

Leon Bodenhagen 🆔
University of Southern Denmark
Odense, Denmark

John-John Cabibihan
Qatar University
Doha, Qatar

Kerstin Fischer
University of Southern Denmark
Sønderborg, Denmark

Selma Šabanović
Indiana University
Bloomington, IN, USA

Katie Winkle
Uppsala University
Uppsala, Sweden

Laxmidhar Behera
IIT Mandi
Mandi, Himachal Pradesh, India

Shuzhi Sam Ge 🆔
National University of Singapore
Singapore, Germany

Dimitrios Chrysostomou
Aalborg University
Aalborg, Denmark

Wanyue Jiang 🆔
Qingdao University
Qingdao, China

Hongsheng He 🆔
The University of Alabama
Tuscaloosa, AL, USA

ISSN 0302-9743   ISSN 1611-3349 (electronic)
Lecture Notes in Artificial Intelligence
ISBN 978-981-96-3518-4   ISBN 978-981-96-3519-1 (eBook)
https://doi.org/10.1007/978-981-96-3519-1

LNCS Sublibrary: SL7 – Artificial Intelligence

Preface

The 16th International Conference on Social Robotics (ICSR) + AI 2024 took place in Odense, Denmark as an in-person event from October 23–26, 2024. This was the first time for the conference to be hosted in Denmark and Scandinavia. The theme of this year's conference was "Empowering Humanity: The Role of Social and Collaborative Robotics in Shaping Our Future". Empowering Humanity means recognizing how social robotics and AI can help push the boundaries of creative expression and interactive experiences. This year's conference welcomed contributions that engage social robotics and AI across the domains of the visual and performing arts, including design, music, live performance, and interactive installations. ICSR + AI 2024 was organized as part of the Global Robotics, Arts, and Science Synergies (GRASS) event. GRASS hosted the 16th International Conference on Social Robotics (ICSR) across three locations: ICSR + BioMed in Singapore, ICSR + InnoBiz in Shenzhen, China, and ICSR + AI in Odense, Denmark.

This book comprises the peer-reviewed proceedings of the conference. From a total of 182 submitted manuscripts, rigorously reviewed by an international team of Senior Program Committee and Program Committee members, 128 regular papers were selected for inclusion in the proceedings and presented during the technical sessions.

ICSR + AI 2024 featured four Plenary Speeches, seven regular sessions, two special sessions, four teaser talks, four poster sessions, and one robot design competition. The first plenary speech, titled "The Role of Imagination in Social Robotics," was delivered by Giulio Sandini, the Founding Director at the Italian Institute of Technology and full professor of bioengineering at the University of Genoa. The second plenary speech, titled "Moral Interaction with Social Robots," was delivered by Takayuki Kanda, a professor in Informatics at Kyoto University, Japan. The third plenary speech, "Robot as Urban Flâneur," was delivered by Wendy Ju, an Associate Professor of Information Science at Cornell University. The fourth plenary speech, "Good Bedside Manner for Medical Robots," was delivered by Elizabeth Broadbent, a Professor of Health Psychology in the Department of Psychological Medicine at the University of Auckland.

The conference brought together researchers and practitioners working on the interaction between humans and intelligent robots and on the integration of social robots into our society, including innovative ideas and concepts, new discoveries and improvements, novel applications on the latest fundamental advances in the core technologies that form the backbone of social robotics as well as distinguished studies and projects pertaining to social robotics and its interaction and impact in our society.

We extend our sincere gratitude to all members of the Organizing Committee and the volunteers for their dedication, which made the conference a resounding success. We are also deeply indebted to the Senior Program Committee and the Program Committee members for their rigorous review of the papers. Finally, we are immensely grateful for

the continued support from the authors, participants, and sponsors, without whom ICSR
+ AI 2024 would not have been possible.

October 2024   Oskar Palinko
                                             Leon Bodenhagen
                                           John-John Cabibihan
                                              Kerstin Fischer
                                             Selma Šabanović
                                               Katie Winkle
                                            Laxmidhar Behera
                                             Shuzhi Sam Ge
                                          Dimitris Chrysostomou
                                              Wanyue Jiang
                                              Hongsheng He

Organization

General Chairs

Oskar Palinko   University of Southern Denmark, Denmark
Leon Bodenhagen   University of Southern Denmark, Denmark

General Co-chair

John-John Cabibihan   Qatar University, Qatar

Standing Committee Chair

Shuzhi Sam Ge   National University of Singapore, Singapore

Program Chairs

Kerstin Fischer   University of Southern Denmark, Denmark
Selma Šabanović   Indiana University, USA
Katie Winkle   Uppsala University, Sweden
Laxmidhar Behera   IIT Mandi, India

Special Session Chairs

Ross Mead   Semio, USA
Séverin Lemaignan   PAL Robotics, Spain

Workshop Chairs

Katrin Solveig Lohan   Eastern Switzerland University of Applied
                              Sciences, Switzerland
Mohammad Obaid   Chalmers University of Technology, Sweden
Kutluk Bilge Arikan   TED University, Turkey

Competition Chair

Amit Kumar Pandey   Rovial Space, France

Publication Chairs

Hongsheng He   University of Alabama, USA
Dimitris Chrysostomou   Aalborg University, Denmark
Wanyue Jiang   Qingdao University, China

Sponsorship Chair

Patrick Holthaus   University of Hertfordshire, UK

Publicity Chairs

Filippo Cavallo   University of Florence, Italy
Birgitte Østergård Sørensen   Danish Technological Institute, Denmark
Oliver Bendel   University of Applied Sciences and Arts
                                   Northwestern Switzerland

Communications Chair

Heather Knight   Oregon State University, USA

Local Arrangements Chairs

Karina Therkildsen   University of Southern Denmark, Denmark
Conny Heidtmann   University of Southern Denmark, Denmark

Exhibition Chair

Dražen Brščić   Kyoto University, Japan

Young Leaders Chair

Alva Markelius   University of Cambridge, UK

Sustainability Chair

Franziska Kirsten   Blue Ocean Robotics, Odense, Denmark

Robotics and Art Chairs

Hooman Samani   University of the Arts, London, UK
Elizabeth Jochum   Aalborg University, Denmark
Dylan Cawthorne   University of Southern Denmark, Denmark
Chen Li   Aalborg University, Denmark

Awards Chair

Evgenios Vlachos   University of Southern Denmark, Denmark

Events and Social Media Coordinator

Gulsabah Palinko   University of Southern Denmark, Denmark

Standing Committee

Oussama Khatib   Stanford University, USA
Maja Mataric   University of Southern California, USA
Haizhou Li   Chinese University of Hong Kong, China
Jong Hwan Kim   Korea Advanced Institute of Science and
                                     Technology, Korea
Paolo Dario   Scuola Superiore Sant'Anna, Italy
Abderrahmane Kheddar   LIRMM Montpellier, France and CNRS-AIST,
                                     Japan
Tianmiao Wang   Beihang University, China

Associate Editors

Matous Jelinek
Glenda Hannibal
Malene Damholdt
Aurelie Clodic
Silvia Rossi
Mike Ligthard
Eduardo Sandoval
Ronald Cumbal
Guy Laban
Yo-Yo Hou
Nik Martelaro
Amit Kumar Shukla
Paul Robinette
Daniel Rea
Katharina Rohlfing
Denise Geiskovitch
Anara Sandygulova
Ravi Prakash
Tom Ziemke
Yunchong Zhang
Jonas Frei
Giulia Belgiovine
Anna Dobrovovestnova
Elmira Yadollahi

Astrid Rosenthal von der Pütten
Johanna Seibt
Christina Vestergaard
Kerstin Haring
Frank Bu
Heerin Lee
Takayuki Kanda
Patrick Holthaus
Rebecca Stower
Hadas Erel
Mary Ellen Foster
Amit Bharadwaj
Drazen Brscic
Britta Wrede
Nils Tolksdorf
Pieter Wolfert
Zhi Tan
Kristina Tornbjerg Eriksen
Dimitris Chrysostomou
Miguel Vasco
Christoph Landolt
Stine Johannsen
Elena d'Aquilla
Casey Bennett

Contents – Part II

Should Robot Arms Be Thicc or Thinn? Examining the Impact of Shape Characteristics on Human Perceptions of Robot Arms

Rhian C. Preston[✉], Stayce Mockel, and Naomi T. Fitter

Oregon State University (OSU), Corvallis, OR 97331, USA
{prestonr,mockels,fittern}@oregonstate.edu

Abstract. The appearance of a robot is generally understood to affect human perception of the robot, yet the majority of investigation into the impact of robot form has focused on humanoid robots and robot size. To better understand the impact of less anthropomorphic morphological characteristics, we present an exploratory study on the impacts of variations in concavity and edge roundness on human perception of robot arms. We systematically varied robot arm stimuli to span three levels of concavity and three levels of edge roundness, before conducting an online, survey-based, within-subject study ($N = 157$) to investigate the impact on perceptions of social characteristics, safety, and expected price. The results show that concavity significantly impacts discomfort and price sensitivity, with participant preferences split on whether "thick" or "thin" arms are preferable for in-home use. The results of this work can inform roboticists and designers looking to develop new systems or when choosing robot systems for in-home tasks.

1 Introduction

Robot appearance is broadly understood to impact human perception of and willingness to use a system, but research on robot appearance has predominantly focused on humanoid systems and facial characteristics. However, non-humanoid systems are becoming more common for home use as research explores tasks such as bathing or feeding, where individuals could prefer a non-humanoid appearance due to social norms. Yet, little work has investigated how the appearance of these robots impacts perceptions and acceptance within this sphere. To this end we present an exploratory investigation into how aspects of curvature impact perceptions of a robot arm for assistive feeding tasks.

Explorations of robot form have prioritized humanoid robots and their anthropomorphic attributes (such as eyes) for improved perception of social characteristics such as warmth or competence compared to non-humanoid systems [2,5,9,11,13,16]. However, as robots grow in usage, and more systems are developed for in-home and human-centered use, *non-humanoid* robots have become more common in these spaces, especially for crucial but sensitive tasks

© The Author(s), under exclusive license to Springer Nature Singapore Pte Ltd. 2025
O. Palinko et al. (Eds.): ICSR + AI 2024, LNAI 15562, pp. 1–12, 2025.
https://doi.org/10.1007/978-981-96-3519-1_1

such as bathing or feeding [3,15,19,20]. Assistive feeding systems, while not necessarily social actors, have social impacts, as dining can be a communal or shared activity. Existing investigations and frameworks for determining the requirements and needs of assistive feeding robots prioritize the operational requirements, including shared autonomy level and non-verbal communication [3,4,15]. These same investigations also highlight the importance of minimizing attention drawn to assistive feeding systems, to minimize the user's self-consciousness and improve their sense of belonging, but the past works present few recommendations related to visual characteristics [3,15].

Investigations of non-humanoid robot forms are sparse, with much of the work surveying existing robots [10,17,18], as non-humanoid systems pose a challenge for formal investigations due to the myriad set of possible structures determined by their required capabilities. There is also difficulty in quantifying many non-anthropomorphic visual characteristics, such as "curvy" or "angular." While researchers have begun more concerted efforts to categorize and define the range of attributes for non-humanoid systems [12], controlled examinations of non-anthropomorphic characteristics have still prioritized humanoid robots [9,13].

Adding to the complexity is the importance of use context in shaping how the form of a system is perceived [8], which could be particularly true for systems that are less inherently social such as non-humanoid robots. Our previous work showed that in the absence of context for robot form, participants seek to define a context [17]. Our past pilot work included assistive feeding as the use context, as the form of a robot arm could potentially be important due to the social dining element, as well as the close level of both physical and cognitive involvement with the human user [14].

The presented work combines the idea of studying non-anthropomorphic features of non-humanoid robots with the professed use context of assistive feeding. Specifically, to investigate the role of more nuanced characteristics in shaping human perceptions of robots, we performed an online within-subject study with images of robot arms that varied across two factors related to curvature: link concavity and edge roundness. We primed participants with the idea that this arm was to be used in an assistive feeding context, and checked that they recalled this at the end of the survey. This work focused on the impact of the two selected visual characteristics on human perceptions of a robot's social characteristics, safety, and price valuation. We present the stimulus design and arm characteristics as part of our methods before presenting our results, discussion, and conclusions. The main contribution of this work is supporting the idea that even seemingly subtle differences in robot visual form can have a measurable impact on perceived social characteristics.

2   Methods

This work investigated the impact of changes in the visual form of robot arms, specifically the concavity and roundness of the robot arm links, on human perception of the robot. We employed an exploratory within-subject online survey

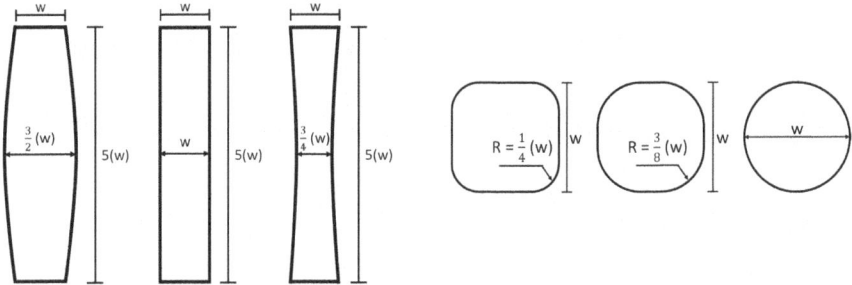

Fig. 1. *Left:* Lengthwise link profiles for the concavity variations. From left to right: convex, straight, and concave. *Right:* End of link cross-sections of the three roundness conditions. They each have a corner curvature radius, R, which is proportional to end width, w. From left to right: squared, rounded, and round.

to investigate perceptions of the robot arms, built upon a previous pilot investigation [14]. We presented assistive feeding as a mock use context for the arms to participants, based on previous work highlighting use context in initial perception formation [17]. Assistive feeding is a more social and intimate use case for a robot arm, and so we anticipated this as a use case where visual form might be an important consideration. Responses were collected with the approval of our university ethics board under protocol #IRB-2019-0172.

2.1   Stimulus Design

Our presented stimuli are a modification of the stimuli from [14], based on participant feedback about the strength of the lower link, compared to the upper link. Visual form can be broken into categories using visual descriptors, such as "geometric" or "organic," but these descriptors are difficult to operationalize, and they are often associated with multiple underlying components of a system's form. To operationalize form characteristics associated with "curviness," our stimuli consisted of controlled variations to the *concavity* and *roundness* of each link of a robot arm model. All other features such as pose, size, number of links, color, and texture were kept consistent for all arm stimuli. The proportions, colors, and finish of the models were selected to mimic a Kinova Jaco arm. The stimuli were modeled in Autodesk Fusion 360, rendered with a neutral background to minimize distraction, and posed at a three-quarter view to effectively display each arm's form. We defined three levels of concavity, and three levels of roundness to span each characteristic, as well as dimensions for each of these levels. The dimensions of our variations are presented as proportions of the end of the link cross-sectional width, w.

Concavity: The three concavity levels were convex, straight, and concave link bow. The work of [14] included convex and concave variation along only one dimension of the square joints, as well as a more extreme concave bow. For this work, the curvature variations were applied to both edges of the square links,

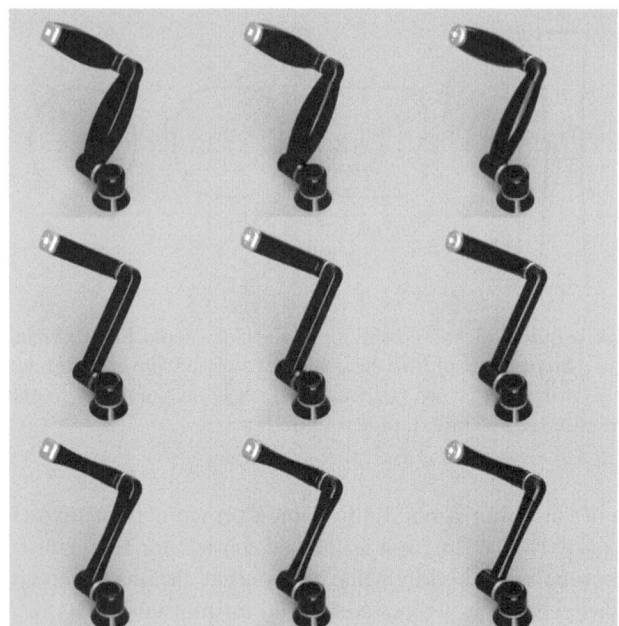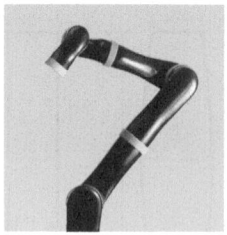

Fig. 2. *Left:* The nine stimuli used in the study. Concavity varies top to bottom: convex, straight, and concave. Roundness varies left to right: squared, rounded, and round. *Right:* The Kinova Jaco arm image we used as a baseline comparison point for price sensitivity estimation.

and the concave bow was adjusted to be less extreme. A profile view of each variation is presented in Fig. 1. All variants had a link length that was five times the link end width, $5 \times w$. The *convex* shape had an outward-arching curvature along the length, and the center width was $\frac{3}{2} \times w$. The *straight* shape had no curvature, so the width in the middle was the same as the width on the ends. The *concave* shape had an inward-arching curvature along the length, with a center width that was $\frac{3}{4} \times w$.

Roundness: The roundness variations were unchanged from those presented in [14], and included three levels of corner roundness: squared, rounded, and round. The end-of-link properties of each variation appear in Fig. 1. All roundness variants maintained the same end-of-link cross-sectional width. The *squared* variant cross-section was square-shaped with corners rounded at a radius of $\frac{1}{4} \times w$. The *rounded* variant cross-section was square-shaped with corners rounded at a radius of $\frac{3}{8} \times w$. The *round* variant cross-section was circular-shaped with a diameter equivalent to the end width, w.

Resulting Stimuli: The full factorial combination of these two independent variables resulted in nine arm stimuli, as presented in Fig. 2.

2.2   Measures

We gathered participant perceptions of social attributes, safety, and price valuation of each robot arm stimulus using self-report questions. We used the Robotic Social Attributes Scale (*RoSAS*) to measure social perceptions of warmth, competence, and discomfort on 9-point Likert scales [6], as well as a subset of the *Godspeed questionnaire* to measure perceived safety on a 5-point semantic differential scale [1]. To gauge *price sensitivity* we asked participants to estimate the cost of each arm, as well as the Kinova Jaco arm (Fig. 2) to use as a baseline comparison point. Additionally, we asked participants to provide *free-response* data about what they felt stood out or influenced their responses for each arm with the question: "What part(s) of the robot arm stood out to you most or most strongly influenced your responses?" At the end of the survey, we asked participants an additional free-response question: "What part(s) of the individual robot arms stood out to you most or most strongly influenced your responses throughout the survey?" We also asked respondents to reiterate the intended use of the robot arms (assistive feeding), as an understanding check. We looked for participants to include some reference to food, eating, utensils, dining, or home use within their answer. Finally, we collected *basic demographic information* on participant age, gender, ethnicity, nationality, and hometown.

2.3   Participants

Based on previous work examining robot morphology, we used a small effect size of $f^2 = 0.10$ in an *a priori* power analysis using G-Power 3.1.9.7 [7] with power set to 0.80 and error probability $\alpha = 0.05$, which resulted in an overall suggested sample size of 126. We collected a larger participant sample as we planned to exclude data from participants who failed to complete the study or who did not include some reference to food, eating, utensils, dining, or home use in a context-based manipulation check.

We distributed the survey to undergraduates through an introductory psychology course, over two terms. We obtained 243 responses, of which 182 completed the survey. Of the completed surveys, 157 correctly answered the end-of-survey context check question. Participant ages ranged from 18 to 54, with a median of 19, and the participants predominantly identified as female (112 female, 39 male, 4 genderfluid, & 2 non-binary).

2.4   Procedure

The study was a self-contained Qualtrics survey lasting approximately 30 min. Participants first confirmed the ability to view the images within the survey, and next they provided informed consent to participate. We then informed participants that the robot arms were being designed to provide assistance in feeding users. Subsequently, we presented a Kinova Jaco arm image, shown previously in Fig. 2, as a price sensitivity baseline comparison point, asking participants about what they believed the arm would cost.

Participants were shown each individual arm in a randomized order, and they were asked to complete the RoSAS, Godspeed safety, and cost questions for the presented arm image, in addition to providing free-response feedback.

Once participants had answered questions for all nine robot arm stimuli, the participants were asked to complete an open-ended question about their overall experience and opinions on the stimuli. As a context check, we asked participants to summarize the intended use context of the arm (assistive feeding). Lastly, participants answered the demographic questions.

2.5   Analysis

The Likert and semantic differential scale results were analyzed using repeated-measures analysis of variance (rANOVA) tests, with factors of concavity and roundness. For the price sensitivity analysis, we normalized the price values indicated by each participant for each stimulus against the baseline Kinova Jaco arm, as presented in Eq. 1, and then performed an rANOVA test, with factors of concavity and roundness, for the normalized prices.

$$P_{normalized} = \frac{P_{stimuli} - P_{kinova}}{P_{kinova}} \tag{1}$$

The significant p-value for main effects was adjusted to $p = 0.01$ after a Bonferroni correction to account for multiple analyses with the three RoSAS scales, one Godspeed scale, and price sensitivity scale. In the case of a significant main effect, we performed post hoc pairwise tests with a Bonferroni correction.

A thematic analysis was conducted on the responses to the open-ended questions. A second trained coder reviewed approximately 10% of the data to confirm inter-rater reliability; the Cohen's kappa value was 0.82, which indicates near perfect agreement.

3   Results

We present the results of our analysis of both the self-report scale-based ratings and the open-ended responses.

3.1   Self-report Ratings

The self-report ratings are presented below, first for the concavity factor and then the roundness factor.

Concavity. Figure 3 presents the participant ratings and significant post hoc pairwise comparisons for the three levels of concavity. There were no significant within-subjects effects found for the *warmth* ($F(2, 312) = 2.91$, $p = 0.056$, $\eta^2 = 0.001$) or *competence* ($F(2, 312) = 1.24$, $p = 0.292$, $\eta^2 = 0.001$) RoSAS subscales. A significant effect was found in the *discomfort* RoSAS subscale

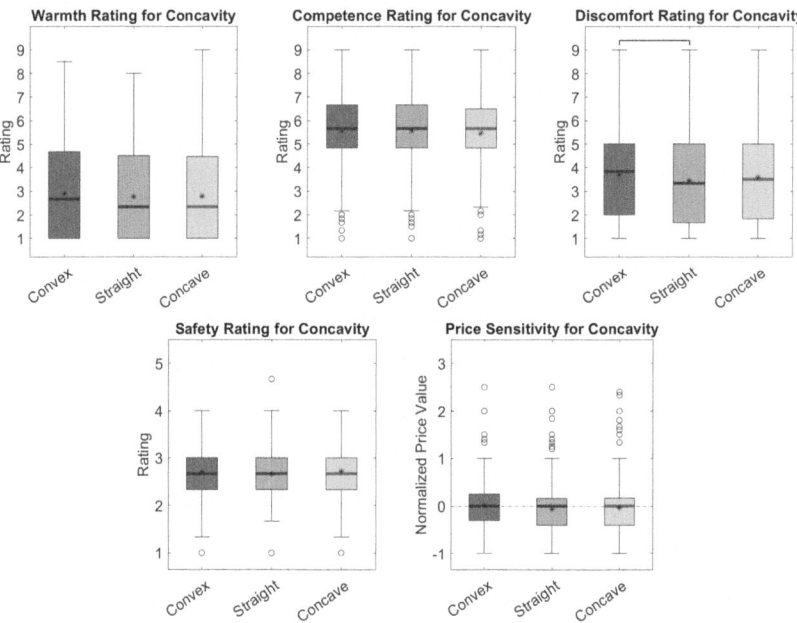

Fig. 3. Box plots of participant ratings of warmth, competence, discomfort, safety, and price sensitivity for the three levels of concavity. Price sensitivity outlier values greater than three have been excluded from the presented plot for visibility, but were included in the analysis.

$(F(2, 312) = 4.703$, $p = 0.010$, $\eta^2 = 0.002)$, with the post hoc tests showing that the convex arms were more discomforting than the straight arms $(M_{diff} = -0.236$, $t = -2.83$, $p = 0.016)$. There was no significant effect found in the *safety* Godspeed subscale $(F(2, 312) = 3.621$, $p = 0.028$, $\eta^2 = 0.003)$. The price sensitivity comparisons had a significant effect $(F(2, 312) = 4.799$, $p = 0.009$, $\eta^2 = 0.004)$, but the post hoc tests showed no significant pairwise comparisons.

Roundness. The participant ratings for the three levels of roundness are presented in Fig. 4. There were no significant within-subjects effects found for the *warmth, competence,* or *discomfort* RoSAS subscales. There were also no significant within-subject effects found for the *safety* Godspeed subscale or the price sensitivity comparisons (*p* value range: 0.30–0.90).

3.2   Open-Ended Responses

Key themes that arose from participant free-response input included the "thickness" or "thinness" of the arm links (with varying opinions about each), the arm material, and the end-effector mounting plate.

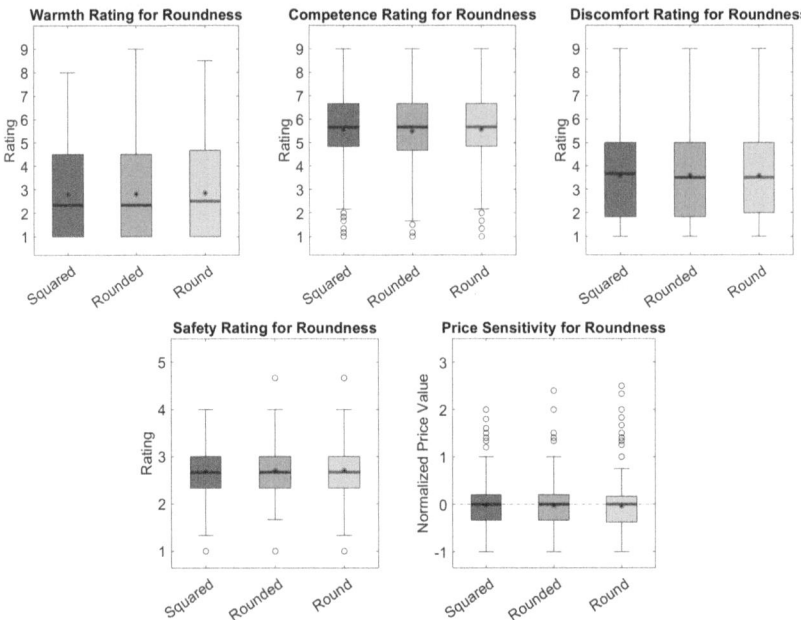

Fig. 4. Box plots of participant ratings of warmth, competence, discomfort, safety, and price sensitivity for the three levels of roundness. Price sensitivity outlier values greater than three have been excluded from the presented plot for visibility, but were included in the analysis.

Participants repeatedly described the arms as "thick" ($n = 70$) or "thin" ($n = 61$), and these descriptors were predominantly linked with specific positive or negative associations. Neither "thick" nor "thin" characteristics were solely positive or negative, and the alignment is presented in Fig. 5. Some participants mentioned *both* thick and thin characteristics ($n = 43$), most of which were contrasting the two characteristics ($n = 32$). About half of the participants who contrasted the characteristics mentioned "thick" characteristics as positive and "thin" characteristics as negative ($n = 15$), while the remainder attributed "thick" characteristics negatively and "thin" characteristics positively ($n = 17$).

Although the materials and colors were consistent throughout the baseline Kinova and all following arm models, a third of the participants ($n = 53$) mentioned material or color as influencing their perceptions of the arms in their free response feedback. When participants mentioned materials, they generally mentioned metal, however at least one participant noted they believed the material was a "cheap plastic." About half of the participants noting material or color expressed no opinion. Participants who expressed a negative impression used descriptors such as "cold," "harsh," "dull," and "unfriendly" or "unsafe." Participants who expressed a positive impression used descriptors such as "personable," "sleek," and "professional" to describe the material and color of the arm models.

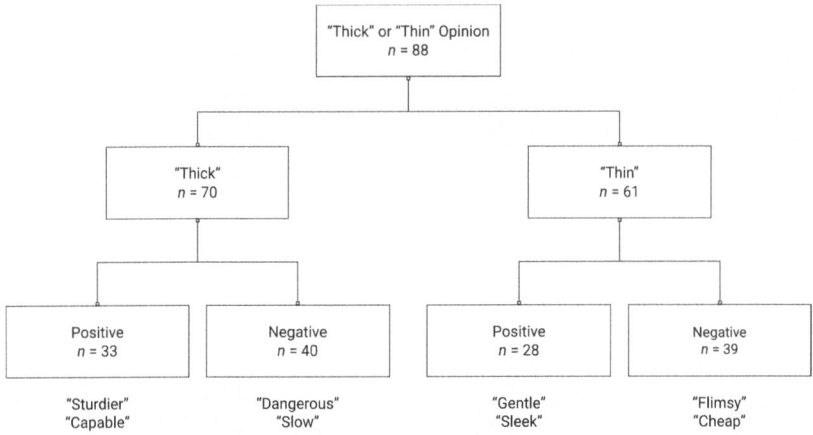

Fig. 5. Breakdown of "thick" and "thin" descriptors in the free response feedback, with sample descriptors for each category at the bottom.

While none of the arm models had a physical end-effector pictured for feeding (e.g., a hand, gripper, or other attachment), the models did have a visible silver mounting plate, whose shape matched the edge roundness condition cross-section. Squared and rounded models had a more square attachment point, while round models had a circular shape. Multiple participants ($n = 87$) noted the attachment point shapes in their free-response feedback.

3.3   Exploratory Participant Grouping

As a result of the large subset of participants highlighting opinions on "thickness" vs. "thinness" of the arms, we performed an exploratory repeated measures analysis of covariance (rANCOVA) with participant groups determined based on stated opinions related to arm thickness or thinness. The participants were grouped into those who stated no opinion, those who stated positive statements on thick arms, those who stated positive statements on thin arms, and those who stated positive statements on both thick and thin arms.

Concavity. There were no significant main effects found for the *warmth, competence,* or *discomfort* RoSAS subscales. There were also no significant within-subject effects found for the *safety* Godspeed subscale or the price sensitivity comparisons (p value range: 0.024–0.59).

There were significant interaction effects between concavity and participant groups, however. A significant interaction effect was seen for the *warmth* RoSAS subscale ($F(6, 306) = 3.78$, $p = 0.001$, $\eta^2 = 0.004$). The post hoc tests showed that participants who made positive statements about thick arms rated the convex arms higher than the concave arms. A significant interaction effect was also seen for the *discomfort* RoSAS subscale ($F(6, 306) = 5.05$, $p < 0.001$,

$\eta^2 = 0.007$). The post hoc tests showed participants who made positive state-ments about thin arms rated the convex arms as more discomforting than both the straight and concave arms.

Roundness. There were no significant effects found for the *warmth, compe-tence,* or *discomfort* RoSAS subscales. There were also no significant within-subject effects found for the *safety* Godspeed subscale or the price sensitivity comparisons (p value range: 0.17–0.99). There were no significant interaction effects between roundness and participant groups.

4   Discussion and Conclusions

Our goal was to investigate how specific aspects of visual form (namely concavity and roundness) impact perceptions of robot arms for home-use tasks such as assistive feeding. We found that participant opinions changed when the concavity of the links were varied, but not when the roundness of the edges were varied.

In our planned analysis, the convex arms were rated as significantly more discomforting than straight arms, which could be related to the use context. For example, one participant noted that bigger arms would have "more weight getting thrown around" when coming near the face for food delivery. On the other end of the spectrum, the concave arm ratings trended more safe than the straight arms. This tendency could be related to the perceived power of the arm, as thinner arms were sometimes referenced as "flimsy" by participants, with one participant in particular noting they preferred the thin robots because "if worst came to worst I could snap it" in the event of a malfunction. Ultimately, participants were split with their free response answers on whether thick or thin arms were preferable, referring to thick arms as "sturdy" or "reliable," and thin arms as "sleek" or "high-quality." This split led us to do an exploratory follow-up analysis which showed characteristic differences within groups who preferred one arm vs. the other, in alignment with the content of the free-response input.

It is noteworthy that there were no significant differences in self-reported competence ratings between the models (for either factor). Participant free-response comments did refer to and discuss the "capability" and "reliability" of the arms, using terms such as "strong," "sturdy," or "flimsy" to discuss the different arm characteristics, but there was no clear consensus across the group on visual characteristics that impacted competence. Together, these results could indicate that participants view all the models as more or less equally *competent* in performing the task regardless of visual form, or that another latent grouping variable could exist among users that impacts perception of robot capability.

Key *design implications* of this work include the lack of impact of edge round-ness, and the possible association between limb "thickness" and system quality assumptions. The lack in significant findings for edge roundness effects informs designers that while it may be important to add fillets around edges to make for a physically safer robot, the specific radius is not the most visually critical element. Participants anecdotally associated thicker limbs with sturdiness, as well as thinner limbs with sleekness, which aligns with design theory guidance related to assumed capabilities.

A strength of this work is that we utilized controlled variation of robot appearance to robustly isolate visual form characteristics that merit further exploration. Compared to past work that took a broader approach or focused on anthropomorphic robots, our efforts were able to further explore how these characteristics impact human perceptions. One key limitation of our work is in our participant population, which consisted of undergraduate college students at a single university in the United States. Owing to the interaction between visual design and cultural context, these results might change with a different or broader set of participant demographics.

Our work succeeded in exploring the relationship between human perception of a robot and its visual form characteristics. The results of this work show that the concavity of visual elements impact perceptions and expectations of the robot, while aspects such as edge roundness are perhaps less impactful on overall perceptions. This work can provide insights to designers and roboticists developing systems for assistive in-home use.

Acknowledgements. This work was supported by NIH award 1R01AG078124-01. We would like to thank Jessica Herring for her work developing the initial 3D models, and Dr. Chris Sanchez for assisting with participant recruitment.

References

1. Bartneck, C., Kulić, D., Croft, E., Zoghbi, S.: Measurement instruments for the anthropomorphism, animacy, likeability, perceived intelligence, and perceived safety of robots. Int. J. Soc. Robot. **1**, 71–81 (2009)
2. Bernotat, J., Eyssel, F., Sachse, J.: Shape it – the influence of robot body shape on gender perception in robots. In: Kheddar, A., et al. (eds.) ICSR 2017. LNCS, vol. 10652, pp. 75–84. Springer, Cham (2017). https://doi.org/10.1007/978-3-319-70022-9_8
3. Bhattacharjee, T., Cabrera, M.E., Caspi, A., Cakmak, M., Srinivasa, S.S.: A community-centered design framework for robot-assisted feeding systems. In: Proceedings of the International ACM SIGACCESS Conference on Computers and Accessibility (ASSETS), pp. 482–494. Association for Computing Machinery, New York, NY, USA (2019)
4. Bhattacharjee, T., et al.: Is more autonomy always better? Exploring preferences of users with mobility impairments in robot-assisted feeding. In: Proceedings of the ACM/IEEE International Conference on Human-Robot Interaction (HRI), pp. 181–190. Association for Computing Machinery, New York, NY, USA (2020)
5. Carpenter, J., Davis, J.M., Erwin-Stewart, N., Lee, T.R., Bransford, J.D., Vye, N.: Gender representation and humanoid robots designed for domestic use. Int. J. Soc. Robot. **1**(3), 261–265 (2009)
6. Carpinella, C.M., Wyman, A.B., Perez, M.A., Stroessner, S.J.: The robotic social attributes scale (RoSAS) development and validation. In: Proceedings of the ACM/IEEE International Conference on Human-Robot Interaction (HRI), pp. 254–262 (2017)

7. Faul, F., Erdfelder, E., Lang, A.E.A.: G*power 3: a flexible statistical power analysis program for the social, behavioral, and biomedical sciences. Behav. Res. Methods **39**, 175–191 (2007)
8. Giard, J.: The Contextual Nature of Design and Everyday Things. Kendall Hunt (2016)
9. Hwang, J., Park, T., Hwang, W.: The effects of overall robot shape on the emotions invoked in users and the perceived personalities of robot. Appl. Ergon., 459–471 (2013)
10. Kunold, L., Bock, N., Rosenthal-von der Pütten, A.: Not all robots are evaluated equally: the impact of morphological features on robots' assessment through capability attributions. J. Hum.-Robot Interact. **12**(1) (2023)
11. Kwak, S.S.: The impact of the robot appearance types on social interaction with a robot and service evaluation of a robot. Arch. Des. Res., 81–93 (2014)
12. Liberman-Pincu, E., Parmet, Y., Oron-Gilad, T.: Judging a socially assistive robot (SAR) by its cover; the effect of body structure, outline, and color on users' perception. J. Hum.-Robot Interact. (2022)
13. Lucas, H., Poston, J., Yocum, N., Carlson, Z., Feil-Seifer, D.: Too big to be mistreated? Examining the role of robot size on perceptions of mistreatment. In: Proceedings of the IEEE International Symposium on Robot and Human Interactive Communication (RO-MAN), pp. 1071–1076 (2016)
14. Mockel, S., Preston, R.C., Herring, J., Fitter, N.T.: A pilot investigation of human preference for robot arm visual form. In: Companion of the ACM/IEEE International Conference on Human-Robot Interaction (HRI) (2024)
15. Nanavati, A., Alves-Oliveira, P., Schrenk, T., Gordon, E.K., Cakmak, M., Srinivasa, S.S.: Design principles for robot-assisted feeding in social contexts. In: Proceedings of the ACM/IEEE International Conference on Human-Robot Interaction (HRI), pp. 24–33. Association for Computing Machinery, New York, NY, USA (2023)
16. Phillips, E., Zhao, X., Ullman, D., Malle, B.F.: What is human-like?: Decomposing robots' human-like appearance using the anthropomorphic roBOT (ABOT) database. In: Proceedings of the ACM/IEEE International Conference on Human-Robot Interaction (HRI), pp. 105–113 (2018)
17. Preston, R.C., Raghunath, N., Sanchez, C.A., Fitter, N.T.: "Armed" and dangerous: how visual form influences perceptions of robot arms. In: Cavallo, F., et al. (eds.) ICSR 2022. LNCS, vol. 13818, pp. 529–539. Springer, Cham (2022). https://doi.org/10.1007/978-3-031-24670-8_47
18. Reeves, B., Hancock, J., Liu, X.: Social robots are like real people: first impressions, attributes, and stereotyping of social robots. Technol. Mind Behav. **1**(1) (2020)
19. Werner, C., Dometios, A.C., Tzafestas, C.S., Maragos, P., Bauer, J.M., Hauer, K.: Evaluating the task effectiveness and user satisfaction with different operation modes of an assistive bathing robot in older adults. Assist. Technol. **34**(2), 222–231 (2022)
20. Zlatintsi, A., et al.: I-Support: a robotic platform of an assistive bathing robot for the elderly population. Robot. Auton. Syst. **126**, 103451 (2020)

Humanoid Robots, A Future Health Care Service?

Linda Sørensen[1,2](✉) [iD], Magnhild Kaarstad[3] [iD], Maren Eitrheim[3] [iD],
Alexandra Fernandes[3] [iD], and Kine Reegård[3] [iD]

[1] Sunnaas Rehabilitation Hospital, Nesodden, Norway
linda.sorensen@sunnaas.no
[2] University of Agder, Kristiansand, Norway
[3] Digital Systems, Institute for Energy Technology, Halden, Norway

Abstract. In this paper we discuss the possible use of humanoid robots within the healthcare services context. Recently, new technologies such as robotics have been further developed and are currently being assessed for use within healthcare services. A research project was carried out to explore whether the humanoid robot EVE can enhance healthcare services in rehabilitation and home assistance settings. In the project we carried out empirical studies to investigate the possible functionalities and use of a robot such as EVE for healthcare personnel and patients. In this paper, we took a step further and asked: What will it take to implement the robot EVE as a healthcare service? We conducted two workshops and a focus group interview with a total of 21 participants (healthcare staff and management representatives) where we discussed possible impacts, requirements, and strategies for a sustainable implementation of humanoid robots. Based on our findings, we discuss key topics such as contextual specificities, robot control paradigms, and the concepts of robots as a service/as a product. We conclude by listing recommendations for future implementations of humanoid robots in healthcare.

Keywords: Healthcare · Humanoid Robots · Service Design · Innovation · Implementation

1 Introduction

Norwegian healthcare prioritizes equity and universal access, ensuring all residents receive necessary services, regardless of socio-economic status [1]. However, in the years to come, the World Health Organization (WHO) has emphasized global staffing challenges, forecasting a possible shortage of 10 million healthcare workers by 2030 [2]. To alleviate this shortage, the healthcare sector is increasingly investigating the potential use of different types of welfare technologies [3] as well as robotics and artificial intelligence.

Welfare technologies aim to improve the lives of those in need by supporting independent living, and is typically developed collaboratively by government, municipalities,

O. Palinko et al. (Eds.): ICSR + AI 2024, LNAI 15562, pp. 13–24, 2025.
https://doi.org/10.1007/978-981-96-3519-1_2

research institutions, and private companies with a procurement process to ensure cost-effectiveness and compliance [4]. Examples of welfare technologies include remote monitoring and consultation services for at-home care, as well as devices enhancing safety and independence for elderly and disabled individuals [5].

Recently, the assistive robot market has experienced a significant growth driven by the increasing elderly population and the rising demand for support in daily activities, mobility, and companionship. Assistive robots can support patients, older people, as well as relatives and professional caregivers [6–9]. They may provide physical assistance, such as transportation of items, cognitive aid, like helping recognize and organize items, and emotional support, by fostering emotional closeness [3].

However, robots designed to physically assist users have not yet reached the market despite extensive trials and numerous research studies [10]. A study by Bedaf and collaborators [11] identified 106 types of care robots, but only six of these were successfully deployed and available on the market. Sørensen and collaborators [10] found nine robots capable of physical tasks such as retrieving objects, assisting with transfers, performing household chores and supporting self-care tasks, such as medications, covering with a blanket, feeding, wiping the mouth, and shaving.

In the Human Interactive Robots for Healthcare (HIRo 2020–2024) project, we investigated to what extent the humanoid robot EVE could enhance healthcare services in rehabilitation and home assistance settings through four phases: 1) identification of expectations among stakeholders and staff, 2) empirical study of staff interacting with a humanoid robot, 3) empirical study of patients interacting with a humanoid robot, and 4) identification of recommendations for developing an innovation plan.

In the first part of the project, we analyzed current work processes in the hospital and home assistance services to identify tasks suitable for the humanoid robot. Interviews with key stakeholders, including hospital, municipal, and robotics company representatives, helped align needs and expectations. Talk-through techniques and surveys were used to gather staff input on daily tasks, priorities, and preferences. Staff showed positive attitudes towards the robot, particularly for non-clinical, time-consuming, or physically demanding tasks. However, challenges were noted regarding the robot's technical limitations, safety, privacy, and concerns about job displacement. These results have been presented in [12, 13].

The findings of the initial study informed the second phase, which involved demonstrations and pilot studies to test the robot's capabilities in performing selected tasks. *Health personnel*, (eight nurses, physio and occupational therapists) working at a rehabilitation hospital participated in a first empirical study. The robot EVE assisted participants in a variety of tasks, such as fetching medical equipment, delivering a meal to the patients and assisting patients through the hospital facilities. Using video analysis and the NASA TLX workload assessment, results showed that EVE's assistance reduced perceived workload, improved performance, and decreased time pressure amongst the health personnel [8]. Participants noted fewer interruptions and improved task quality when supported by the robot (ibid.)

The third phase included a second empirical study where we explored *patient* perceptions of humanoid assistive robots in a rehabilitation hospital. Eight patients participated in the study. The robot EVE performed assistive tasks such as bringing a bottle of water and picking up an item from the floor, and participants were interviewed afterwards. Overall, patients were open to the concept, appreciating its potential to aid daily activities. However, concerns were raised about the robots' suitability for individual needs and recovery phases, as well as safety, privacy, and implementation challenges. These results have been presented in [9] (Fig. 1).

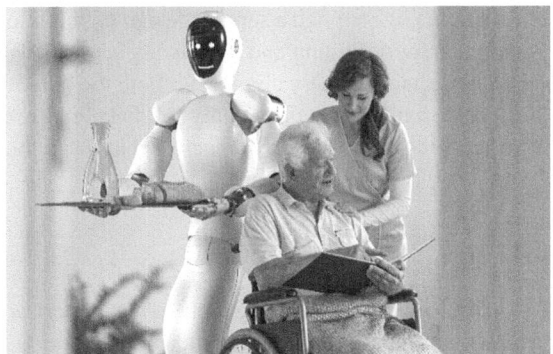

Fig. 1. Illustration of the 1X Technologies robot Eve in a healthcare context

This paper presents the fourth and final phase of the HIRo project, focusing on the innovation realization. Through workshops and a focus group interview, as suggested by [14], we examined secondary stakeholders' perspectives on the key requirements and considerations needed to develop a tailored innovation plan for implementation/deployment of the robot within these specific healthcare services.

There is an increasing interest in the use of assistive robots in healthcare, primarily centered on their ability to support patients and healthcare staff. However, integrating these robots into healthcare systems presents significant challenges. While care robots can enhance existing services, they may also need to evolve into standalone services. This requires the development of detailed service models that outline care pathways, delivery methods, and the alignment of robot functions with the roles of healthcare professionals. Additionally, ethical considerations, safety protocols, and privacy protections must be carefully addressed, as these robots will interact with vulnerable populations and collect large amounts of data, including video, audio, and user behavior patterns.

Introducing new health technologies requires more than just medical approval; it demands a well-coordinated, multidisciplinary approach. Stakeholders, including healthcare professionals, patients, technology developers, and regulatory bodies, must be involved throughout the process [14]. Successful implementation relies on methods such as user-centered design, iterative testing, and real-world pilot studies, all of which ensure the technology's usability, effectiveness, and ethical alignment with safety and regulatory standards.

While user experiences and expectations are important, they are insufficient for successful robot integration. A comprehensive approach should consider both the robot's functionality and how it integrates into existing workflows. Institutions must also evaluate their technical infrastructure and physical environment to ensure compatibility with robotic systems. Although many studies focus on robot functionality and user acceptance, there is a lack of attention to the organizational challenges that are critical for successful deployment.

2 Methods and Materials

In this part of the HIRo project, we applied a service design methodology [15], which is a multidisciplinary approach for designing and optimizing services to improve the user experience and ensure that service delivery aligns with both the potential users' and the providers' needs. Service design considers not only the front-end user experience but also the behind-the-scenes processes such as the factors that make the service possible [16].

2.1 Data Collection

Between 2021 and 2024, two workshops and one focus group interview were conducted: two workshops at a rehabilitation hospital and one focus group interview at a municipal health service. Workshops and group interviews are valuable in service design, as they allow for real-time feedback, discussion, and consensus-building, uncovering insights that may not arise in individual interviews or surveys. The central theme across these sessions was, "What will it take to implement the robot EVE as a healthcare service?" This included discussions on organizing a robot service and strategies to encourage change.

The first workshop, held in late 2021, included 11 participants responsible for planning new services at a rehabilitation hospital. Participants held various roles, including Property Manager, Head of Innovation, Head of Digitalization, and Head of Procurement. The two-hour session, moderated by the first author, featured a project presentation with videos of the robot and allowed participants to brainstorm thoughts and concerns, which were recorded and categorized.

The second workshop, in autumn 2022, took place shortly after a demonstration of the robot and lasted one hour. It included five participants, mainly experts in privacy and information security. Key roles included the Head of Digitalization, the Head of Safety and Security, and the Privacy Counselor. The workshop focused on privacy and security issues, with the first author taking notes of shared insights.

The third data collection, held in late 2022, included five participants from the municipal service's welfare technology implementation section. Participants included home service coordinators and an e-health nurse. This session was structured as a focus group interview and moderated by a counselor specializing in home service technologies. Participants were shown videos of the robot and engaged in discussions on pre-defined topics related to the research question.

2.2 Analysis Approach

We conducted a content analysis by first collecting all notes from the workshops and focus group interviews. These notes were then deductively coded in alignment with the roadmap for welfare technologies for Norwegian municipalities [17]. The coding was manually performed by the first author, followed by a collaborative discussion with the municipality's Home Service Technology Counselor to gain further insights and reach consensus. This process resulted in the development of four key themes: functional requirements, economic prospects, infrastructure and organizational needs, and recommendations for the implementation of the robot.

3 Views on a Humanoid Robot as a Healthcare Service

3.1 Specification of Functional Requirements

During the workshops, it was suggested that to address future challenges related to personnel shortages, it is conceivable that a humanoid robot, such as EVE, could support with certain tasks. While logistic robots and Autonomous Intelligent Vehicles (AIVs) already are in use in hospitals for transporting goods, participants were open towards a humanoid robot, like EVE, for tasks directly related to assisting patients and supporting healthcare staff.

A first step for implementing a robot in a hospital or in private homes, is to identify how it can support the needs of staff and patients. The participants in the workshops identified a range of tasks that would be desirable and feasible for a robotic assistant to perform. For patients in the hospital these tasks included e.g., guidance to their respective departments and rooms, escorting patients to appointments within the hospital, deliver a glass of water or a meal, pick up items that patients may drop on the floor, alert staff if a patient has fallen or is in distress, provide reminders for appointments and daily routines, and instruct patients on physical therapy exercises, ensuring they perform them correctly. The results from the municipality differed somewhat from those of the hospital, possibly reflecting the differing patient populations each serves. For example, home services frequently encounter a high number of patients with cognitive difficulties, such as dementia, which influenced their feedback and priorities. It was suggested that in municipalities, the robot could serve as a secondary caregiver for patients living at home, assisting with tasks such as hygiene and showering. For cognitive assistance, they highlighted the potential for the robot to help orient patients to time and place, engage in personalized small talk, and provide reminders or prompts for daily activities.

For clinical health personnel in the hospital, it was considered useful if a robot could assist with fetching medical equipment and supplies from a storage or other departments, deliver meals to patients, retrieve and deliver objects and perform simple tasks in contagion isolation rooms to minimize exposure for staff. It was also considered that a robot could support logistic personnel in managing and distributing linen to the appropriate storages, and handle waste management tasks, as well as locating and managing medical equipment throughout the hospital. Property management found it useful for a robot to conduct regular patrols to monitor safety within the facility, as well as to measure and report on temperature, CO_2 levels, and other indoor climate factors, for technical staff to take appropriate action if needed.

Strict hygiene standards are crucial in managing hospital-acquired infections, including methicillin-resistant staphylococcus aureus (MRSA). Therefore, both physical design of the robot and its adherence to disinfection protocols are critical. Protocols for the robot's hygiene routines, including sensors for contamination detection and logging cleaning activities, must be developed and monitored to ensure compliance.

Participants suggested the robot should feature both automated and remote operation modes to navigate large hospital spaces and tight home environments, catering to diverse patient needs. In hospitals, the robot should autonomously perform tasks like replenishing supplies, handling linen, and removing waste, particularly at night. During the day, staff could request tasks via a mobile app, and patients could use a call function for practical tasks like bringing water. The robot should also respond to verbal commands. For municipal home services, the robot may have preprogrammed tasks like tidying and responding to verbal commands. In emergencies, the municipal call center could connect to the robot, allowing the home services team to operate it remotely, and to send staff when needed.

A humanoid robot, like EVE, in a hospital or home setting must further comply with all privacy regulations, including the General Data Protection Regulation (GDPR), as care robots equipped with audio and video capabilities can capture and store patient data. In Europe, new technologies storing patient information undergo thorough Risk and Vulnerability Analysis. Participants highlighted several steps that would have to be considered before implementation of a novel technology like EVE. First one must make sure that the technology aligns with GDPR and other national regulation regarding privacy. Potential unwanted events and risks would need to be identified and assessed, utilizing existing risk registers and patterns where possible. For each identified risk, potential consequences should be analyzed. The analyses should be presented to the risk owners and decision-makers for approval, ensuring that residual risks are formally accepted or further mitigated.

3.2   Evaluating Potential Labor and Cost Savings

Given the constraints of hospital and municipality budgets, integrating a humanoid robot should result in cost-efficient task automation. In hospitals, an evaluation should be made focusing on how much it relieves staff of routine tasks, enabling them to dedicate more time to direct patient care. In patient home care, the cost-benefit analysis would consider the robot's ability to support independent living, potentially delaying the need for more expensive institutional care. Robot functionalities such as assisting with daily activities and providing medication reminders, could further reduce the burden on human caregivers.

The financial stability of the supplier of the robot technology is crucial to ensure reliable support and service for both settings. If the decision is made to procure a robot, the acquisition process must adhere to standard procurement procedures for medical equipment in Norwegian hospitals and in municipal healthcare settings. This process involves not only evaluating the initial purchase cost but also considering long-term maintenance, training, and support costs. The overall aim is to ensure that a humanoid robot, such as EVE, is a financially viable solution that enhances the efficiency, quality and effectiveness of healthcare delivery in both hospitals and home care environments.

3.3 Infrastructure Considerations

The infrastructure of a hospital can be very complex. For a humanoid robot as EVE to be effectively integrated into such a hospital setting, several key requirements must be met. First, EVE must be able to traverse areas in old and more modern buildings, accommodating different types of elevators, doors and hallways. Storage rooms in the hospital vary in size and feature different types of door handles and openers. EVE must be capable of handling various locking mechanisms to effectively access and navigate these storages. Since some hallways can be narrow, EVE should move at a natural speed that does not obstruct the access of patients or staff, ensuring smooth and unobtrusive navigation.

Additionally, EVE's software would have to be integrated with current hospital systems. These include the patient journal system, the mobile digital system for healthcare personnel, time-scheduling systems for staff and patients, and the indoor navigation system. For both hospitals and home settings, EVE needs to be compatible with existing digital infrastructure to maintain reliable connectivity for its operations and communication. In home environments, the size of the EVE robot poses a significant challenge. Many users live in small apartments with numerous obstacles, complicating the robot's maneuverability. It was noted by the workshop participants, that ideally, home services should be provided by a smaller, more compact robot better suited to moving around in confined spaces.

3.4 Organization and Implementation

When implementing new technology in healthcare, motivation and willingness to change are critical for successful adoption. Five areas were highlighted throughout the workshops to be essential for initiating humanoid robots as a future healthcare service: communication, training, leadership, advocacy and support.

Effective communication was mentioned as essential to help all stakeholders understand the purpose, scope, and benefits of the of a humanoid robot assisting in the hospital or home. The participants suggested various strategies to support this effort. Transparency helps to reduce uncertainty and build trust, making the change more acceptable. Spending time to inform the organization at all levels providing information on the innovation can be done by conducting educational meetings. By emphasizing how the new technology can improve job performance and patient outcomes, healthcare professionals can see clear, practical benefits and will be more likely to embrace the change. Highlighting the technology's potential to streamline workflows and reduce workload can be a strong motivator for adoption. Demonstrating tangible improvements in efficiency and patient care quality can reinforce positive attitudes towards the change.

The participants stated that staff are not familiar with robots and that they need adequate training throughout the implementation period. Comprehensive training on the new technology would help users feel competent and confident. This could significantly impact their willingness to adopt and integrate the robot into their daily routines. Participants suggested using educational methods that staff are already familiar with, featuring a combination of theoretical material and practical training. The training should focus on tasks like learning how to request assistance from the robot, how to operate it, how to resolve minor technical issues and who to contact if technical issues arise.

Furthermore, a leadership that advocates for the change and demonstrates commitment to the new technology can influence organizational members' attitudes and behaviors. It was suggested that leaders should model positive attitudes towards change and actively support their teams through the transition. The rehabilitation hospital shared how they had organized a course to foster an organizational culture to support innovation and continuous improvement. By cultivating a mindset in the leaders to view change as an opportunity rather than a threat, leaders can empower champions within the organization who can further advocate the new technology among their peers.

It was also seen as essential to build a project-team responsible for the implementation. The team should include a project manager, technical operation representatives, persons responsible for educating staff and representatives from the supplier. Providing resources for troubleshooting and learning can alleviate fears and frustrations associated with the new technology. Also, for a robot service to be successful, continuous technical support must be available.

The participants recommended an incremental implementation approach. They proposed that tasks should be introduced and tested one at a time. Initially, the robot would perform a limited number of automated operations, gradually expanding its capabilities as it becomes familiar with the specific context and tasks. The participants from the hospital had several suggestions regarding a pilot phase of introducing EVE before implementation and upscaling. The ideas for piloting a humanoid robot in the hospital setting are as follows:

- Interdisciplinary collaboration: The piloting phase is conducted through close interdisciplinary collaboration between the hospital or municipal healthcare service, the robot supplier and the ICT service provider
- Project-based piloting: The piloting operates on a project-based model, led by a project manager with experience in change management, over a specified timeframe
- Role of champions: Selected super users/champions play a crucial role in the piloting process. Their training occurs concurrently with the piloting, enabling them to become proficient in using and overseeing the technology
- Initial departmental implementation: The piloting begins in a single department, preferably one which has previous experience with the humanoid robot
- Key piloting elements: Essential elements of the piloting include identifying and automating the most relevant tasks, testing and quality assurance of operational control mode functions, and evaluating which tasks that are more effectively managed by each mode
- Ongoing communication: Continuous information about the project, piloting progress, and implementation phases is provided to employees via the Intranet and department meetings to prepare and motivate staff for full-scale implementation
- Follow-up research: Research based on Implementation Science is conducted throughout the piloting and subsequent implementation phases to evaluate the effectiveness and impact of the service and to inform the further development of the robot and its service integration

4 Discussion

The integration of humanoid robots into healthcare services has the potential to enhance the efficiency, effectiveness, and accessibility of care. Our study identified views among healthcare administrative and service staff towards deployment of humanoid robots, both in a rehabilitation hospital and in a home care setting. Key topics included the specification of functionalities, potential labor- and cost savings, infrastructure needs, and implementation strategies.

Riek [14] addresses deployment issues in a broad context, without focusing on any specific setting or technology. In addition to discussing usability and acceptability, she emphasizes the importance of investigating users' technological literacy, cost efficiency, safety, and reliability. Other authors have also explored deployment challenges. For instance, Mettler et al. [18] included both technical and service personnel in a study on service robots. Similar to our findings, participants expressed concerns about hospital implementation, particularly regarding privacy, safety, cost, infrastructure, and IT integration. Participants highlighted potential privacy issues, such as the risk of unauthorized data access or breaches, often focusing on general considerations rather than specific robot projects. Bartosiak et al. [19] reported positive outcomes from the rapid implementation of an assistant robot during the COVID-19 pandemic.

Although deployment factors have been studied in various contexts, we argue that these findings are not easily transferable across settings, facilities, or robotic services. We found markable differences in both requirements and expected impact in the two contexts we investigated: the rehabilitation hospital and municipal homecare services. It is crucial to understand the specific environment for deploying the robot. Healthcare services vary from hospitals to nursing homes, clinics, and homecare contexts. The expectations, relevance, and appropriateness of using robots depend on these contextual boundaries.

An important task for robot suppliers in the future is therefore to tailor robotic solutions for the various settings. This will be critical for robots´ usefulness, acceptance, and overall successful deployment. Some companies, such as Diligent Robotics (Texas, USA), have experimented with personalizing each robot to the specific hospital/department where it is to be used, before deployment. Such a solution focuses on introducing robotics as a service, not as a product, in healthcare [12], and may potentially lower initial adoption costs by providing a safer context for users to test the service, with available technical support and minimal training required for local staff.

In addition to a seamless adaptation of the robotics technology to actual needs, the design of the robots should reflect the tasks and environment for which they are intended to be used. In the workshops, as well as in previous work exploring patients' first impressions of humanoid robots [9], it was noted that the use of humanoid-shaped robots in these contexts is not necessarily obvious. The robot's appearance could rather be tailored towards specific user groups (hospital or homecare staff, patients, etc.) and healthcare contexts (e.g., rehabilitation hospital vs. home care). A common argument from humanoid/android robot companies is that this appearance allows the robot to navigate and interact in the human world smoothly, performing human tasks and leveraging human-human interaction paradigms for communication design. However, the validity of these statements can be questioned. For tasks like picking up and delivery, tidying, cleaning, and navigation, there may be a mismatch between the apparent simplicity of the tasks and the sophisticated appearance of a humanoid robot.

Another crucial aspect in any implementation project will be the actual control paradigms for the robots. Currently a high percentage of the existing robots' abilities are guided by human operators who control the robots live, usually through virtual reality (VR) headsets. To transition to a real-world context, it will be necessary to re-think this control paradigm. The higher goal might be to have fully autonomous robots, but as we have seen through the workshop findings, that might not be an option for many everyday situations. Familiar and user-friendly low interaction control systems such as applications in a phone or tablet could be a good starting point, at least for a few pre-defined actions that might be more common or cumbersome for the robot controllers – this would entail a hybrid automation/manual control systems that would surely require several iterations.

5   Conclusion

A robot within healthcare must be developed in close alignment with its context of use. Our study provides valuable insights into healthcare representatives´ perspectives on implementing humanoid robot healthcare services, emphasizing a real-world focus on both hospital and home care environments. It highlights the importance of understanding the needs and concerns within healthcare settings. While piloting, testing and developing a robot solution in an institution or hospital may seem quicker and less complex than in home care, each environment presents unique challenges. Homes vary in design and present different obstacles, whereas in hospitals, robots operate in fixed areas with more consistent tasks. Additionally, hospitals offer a more structured environment for establishing routines, developing training programs, and ensuring maintenance. It is also easier to implement robust safety and security measures for vulnerable patients in a hospital setting.

As key takeaways from this study and discussion we emphasize the relevance of:

- Robot capabilities and task performance: the robot must be capable of executing the prioritized and relevant tasks effectively.
- Cost saving potential: The innovation should demonstrate a significant reduction in time spent on routine tasks by healthcare personnel, enabling them to focus more on patient care and thereby improve the utilization of resources.
- Privacy and GDPR compliance: The robot's operations must address privacy concerns and be fully compliant with GDPR regulations.
- Infrastructure compatibility: Any issues related to infrastructure must be manageable and solvable to ensure seamless integration. The robot's software must integrate seamlessly with existing hospital systems, which could result in a possible economical investment.
- Training and implementation: The implementation process must include comprehensive training for staff to facilitate smooth adoption, which also should be included in the overall economic considerations.
- Flexible task expansion: There should be a step-by-step approach to increasing the robot's responsibilities, allowing for a flexible and scalable solution.

By considering context specificity, enhancing the characteristics of humanoids, integrating robotics into service delivery models, and optimizing human-robot interaction, we could unlock the full potential of humanoid robots to transform healthcare and improve patient outcomes.

Moving forward, we plan to conduct a long-term study with the next version of the robot. This will allow us to gather comprehensive data and refine our approach, ensuring that the implementation of humanoid robots in healthcare settings is both effective and sustainable. Our roadmap outlined in this study provides valuable guidance for these next steps.

Acknowledgments. The authors would like to thank the Norwegian Research Council for funding the HIRo project in the period between 2020 and 2024 (#309409) and Espen Joris Gottschal.

Disclosure of Interests. The authors have no competing interests to declare that are relevant to the content of this article.

References

1. Forskrift om kvalitet i pleie-og omsorgstjenestene for tjenesteyting etter lov av 19. November 182 nr. 66 om helsetjenesten i kommunene og etter lov av 13. desember 1991 nr. 81 om sosiale tjenester m.v. FOR-2003-06-27-792
2. WHO: World Health Organization. Global strategy on human resources for health: workforce 2023. World Health Organization (2016)
3. Johansson-Pajala, R.-M., Thommes, K., Hoppe, J.A., Tuisku, O., Hennala, L., Pekkarinen, S., et al.: Care robot orientation: what, who and how? potential users' perceptions. Int. J. Soc. Robot. **12**(5), 1103–1117 (2020)
4. Helsedirektoratet. Velferdsteknologi i omsorgstjenesten. Helsedirektoratet (2023)
5. Sørensen, L., Johannesen, D.T., Melkas, H., Johnsen, H.M.: Care-receivers with physical disabilities' perceptions on having humanoid assistive robots as assistants: a qualitative study. BMC Health Serv. Res. **24**(1), 523 (2024)
6. Hoppe, J.A., Tuisku, O., Johansson-Pajala, R.-M., Pekkarinen, S., Hennala, L., Gustafsson, C., et al.: When do individuals choose care robots over a human caregiver? Insights from a laboratory experiment on choices under uncertainty. Comput. Hum. Behav. Rep. **9**, 100258 (2023)
7. Glende, S., Conrad, I., Krezdorn, L., Klemcke, S., Krätzel, C.: Increasing the acceptance of assistive robots for older people through marketing strategies based on stakeholder needs. Int. J. Soc. Robot. **8**(3), 355–369 (2016)
8. Eitrheim, M., Kaarstad, M., Sørensen, L., Berg, K.: Workload of rehabilitation healthcare personnel when assisted by a robot. In: Proceedings of the 33rd European Safety and Reliability Conference (ESREL) (2023)
9. Reegård, K., Eitrheim, M., Kaarstad, M., Fernandes, A., Sørensen, L.: Beyond acceptance. Patients perspectives on humanoid assistive robots in healthcare. Accepted for IEEE, Roman (2024)
10. Sørensen, L., Johannesen, D.T., Johnsen, H.M.: Humanoid robots for assisting people with physical disabilities in activities of daily living: a scoping review. Assist Technol. (2024)
11. Bedaf, S., Gelderblom, G.J., De Witte, L.: Overview and categorization of robots supporting independent living of elderly people: what activities do they support and how far have they developed. Assist. Technol. **27**(2), 88–100 (2015)

12. Fernandes, A., Reegård, K., Kaarstad, M., Eitrheim, M., Bloch, M.: Humanoid robots in healthcare: lessons learned from an innovation project. In: Proceedings of the IEEE International Symposium on Robot and Human Interactive Communication. IEEE (2023)
13. Kaarstad, M., Fernandes, A., Eitrheim, M., Reegård, K.: What will it take to hire a robot? Views from health care personnel and managers in a rehabilitation hospital. In: The 33rd European Safety and Reliability Conference (ESREL) (2023)
14. Riek, L.D.: Healthcare robotics. Commun. ACM **60**(11), 68–70 (2017)
15. Schneider, J., Stickdorn, M.: This is Service Design Thinking: Basics, Tools, Cases. Wiley (2011)
16. Stickdorn, M., Hormess, M., Lawrence, A., Schneider, J.E.: This is Service Design Methods: A Companion to This is Service Design Doing (2018)
17. SINTEF and NOVA: Roadmap for Welfare Technology Implementation, KS/SINTEF (2013). www.KS.no
18. Mettler, T., Sprenger, M., Winter, R.: Service robots in hospitals: new perspectives on niche evolution and technology affordances. Eur. J. Inf. Syst. **26**(5), 451–468 (2017)
19. Bartosiak, M., et al.: Advanced robotics as a support in healthcare organizational response: a COVID-19 pandemic case study. Healthc. Manage. Forum **35**(1), 11–16 (2021)

Reaching and Grasping with NAO Robot

N. Alberto Borghese$^{(\boxtimes)}$ (ID) and Eleonora Chitti (ID)

Laboratory of Applied Intelligent Systems, Department of Computer Science, University of
Milan, Milan, Italy
{alberto.borghese,eleonora.chitti}@unimi.it

Abstract. In this paper we propose a robust approach that combines classical
computer vision with a smart setup that enables a NAO humanoid robot to play
with children. Blocks are adopted as playing objects as they are widely used
and are a highly versatile support. This approach addresses the challenges of
object reaching and grasping, by allowing the robot to approach the table over
which activity is carried out, orient appropriately, plan the reaching movement
that is executed partly through direct and partly through inverse kinematics, grasp
the block, moving it over the table and releasing it into its target position. By
integrating visual information provided by the robot cameras into a closed-loop
control system, no additional sensors are required. This approach enables not only
children to play with a Humanoid robot in a richer way, but also to be used to treat
cognitive / motor deficits inside what is termed Robot Assisted Therapy.

Keywords: NAO humanoid robot · reaching · grasping · Human-robot
interaction · Robot Assisted Therapy (RAT)

1 Introduction

Recently, humanoid robots, and NAO robot in particular, have been successfully proposed as an effective companion especially for children with cognitive or social disabilities. These children generally find NAO enjoyable and non-threatening possibly due to
its human-like shape and its predictable movements [1–3]. Such type of intervention, that
goes under the generic name of Robot Assisted Therapy (RAT), is still at an initial stage
and mainly relies on a Wizard of Oz approach in which NAO interacts through gestures
and voice [2]. This is quite far from traditional interventions, in which the therapist plays
with children with toys or table-top games.

We show here how combining classical computer vision methods with a smart set-up
enables NAO to play with children in an interactive way. To the aim we have selected
blocks as these are the most used and versatile playing objects and a robust methodology
to reach and grasp them on the playground, typically a table, and to move them to their
target position over the table is described.

2 Related Work

The ability to grasp objects of different sizes and shapes is one of the most important skills for a humanoid robot. A variety of reaching and grasping approaches has been described for NAO robots in different scenarios [4]. Proposed an adaptive grasping for the RoboCup[1] competition by replacing NAO's fingers with a flat gripper on both hands with a force sensor embedded. The grasping task is performed with both hands approaching the object from both sides through vision. Once the hands are positioned at the two sides of the object, grasping is obtained moving the two hands one towards the other until the required target force is measured by sensors. In [5] objects are recognized through stereo-vision obtained introducing two cameras inside NAO's eyes. Stereo-vision is used also to plan robot motion. These approaches are based on a modification of the hardware and firmware that makes them less attractive. [6] proposes a solution based on deep learning and NAOmarks [7]. The latter are azure markers on a white background (cf. Fig. 1). Each marker has its own shape and it is recognized robustly by NAO basic software. In [6] one NAOmark is placed frontally on the opposite side of a table with respect to NAO. The robot first moves towards the NAOmark thus walking towards the center of the table. Once arrived close to the table, object to be grasped is recognized through Yolo3 computer vision model and the 3D position of the object with respect to the robot is computed.

Fig. 1. A table covered with a checkerboard is used as playground (left) here. Blocks with a cylindric handle are positioned and moved over the checkerboard squares (right). The borders of the checkerboard are marked with a thick black line and a thick red line is drawn centrally. These lines are used for fine centering and orienting NAO. On the table side three different NAOmarks are attached and are used by NAO to approach the table and for gross orientation. Pose data are expressed in NAO *RobotFrame*, centered between the two feet, with the Z axis vertical, the Y axis in the sagittal plane and the X axis in the coronal plane.

---

[1] http://www.robocup.org.

3   Method

We have created a playground constituted of a table, with the child at one side and the NAO robot at the opposite side of the table. A checkerboard is painted over the table and the blocks have to be positioned inside its squares (Fig. 1). Given its limited workspace, NAO will be able to reach blocks in the first two lines. On one side of the table three different NAOmarks are attached.

Reaching and grasping by NAO can be subdivided into the following subtasks; A) move towards the table center. B) orient parallel to the table and raise right or left arm to get the hand over the table. C) Now NAO is ready for grasping: position the hand over the chosen block, orient the hand properly to have a stable grasp and close the fingers. D) translate the block to its target position and release it there, and E) get back to the starting position.

All these tasks are mostly based on vision information captured by the two NAO's cameras, thus realizing a closed-loop control of robot movement (cf. [7]).

3.1   Moving Towards the Table Center and Orienting Parallel to It

As suggested in [6, 7], NAO computes its 3D position with respect to the central NAO-mark from the images of its upper camera, and moves towards it. At each time step NAO measures its actual 3D position with respect to that of the marker and recomputes its path thus realizing a closed-loop gait control. The 3D NAO *Robot Frame* solid with the feet (cf. Fig. 1) is used here as this is the reference frame most frequently used for gait. Closed-loop control can be used until the marker can be viewed by the NAO camera, until a distance of about 300 mm from the table. Afterwards, the marker cannot be seen anymore and from then on the movement control becomes open-loop: the robot walks towards the last 3D position computed for the NAOmark. To avoid hitting its feet against the table, the robot stops at a distance of 150 mm from the marker, that is the length of its feet with respect to the NAO *Robot Frame* plus a margin.

To avoid hitting the table during subsequent arm reaching, NAO raises its arms above the table level, when it switches from closed to open-loop control gait. To this aim it moves arms from parallel to the body to the NAO *StandInit* position, with arms slightly folded (Fig. 2a, shoulder roll = 45° and shoulder pitch = 15°). From there, direct kinematics is applied to reach a final pose with shoulder roll = 45° and shoulder pitch = 70° to center the hands with respect to the working space (Fig. 2b).

The two lateral markers on the table side are used to orient the robot parallel to the table. To this aim, the yaw rotation angle (around z axis) is computed as $\theta = \arctan\left(\frac{x_R - x_L}{y_R - y_L}\right)$ where $\{x_R, y_R\}$ is the position of the right marker and $\{x_L, y_L\}$ the position of the left one. This rotation is applied to NAO before starting moving forward towards the table to start as parallel as possible with respect to the table.

To increase the accuracy of the final 3D position of the robot with respect to the table the stride length in the open-loop phase of gait is reduced by setting a maximum forward translation of 20 mm for each step.

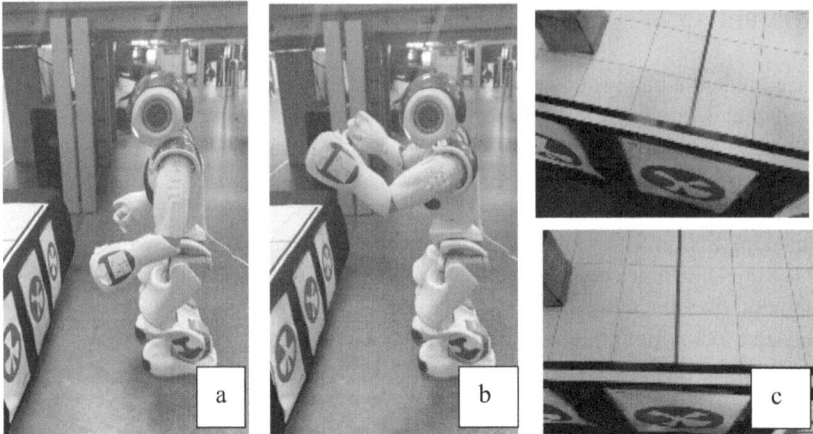

Fig. 2. NAO raises its hands at the end of its closed-loop walk from the NAO *StandInit* position (a) to the final position well over the table (b). When NAO is not parallel to the table it sees the checker-board at an angle (left). NAO rotates around the vertical Z axis to bring the thick horizonal line parallel to the horizontal axis on the image provided by its lower camera (column c). This allows orienting NAO parallel to the table.

3.2　Pose Adjustment

Once the table has been reached the parallelism between NAO and the table may has got lost, so we perform a final adjustment of NAO orientation. To this aim, we first filter the image provided by the lower camera by a Canny edge detector [8]. We then apply the Hough transform to the edges detected to calculate the tilt angle of each line on the image. In this process we filter out all the lines close to vertical (a threshold of 50° was used). We compute the NAO rotation as the median angle of the remaining lines and we rotate the robot around the vertical z-axis by this angle (Fig. 2c). After this rotation, the line becomes parallel to the horizontal axis and the robot becomes oriented correctly in front of the table and it can proceed with grasping.

3.3　Grasping

We start from the observation that given a 3D point on the checkerboard and the checker-board 3D orientation, the 3D position of all the squares is defined. Therefore, the grasping and the release position of a block can be defined simply specifying the raw and column of the desired square. To design an effective grasping, the structure of the NAO hand has to be taken in consideration; this has three fingers: a shorter thumb and two longer fingers. It has only one motor that allows opening and closing synchronously the fingers, thus enabling a grasping that can be classified as Power grasp through palm opposition [9]. To allow a firm grasp, we have also worked on the design of blocks. These are generic blocks that mount a cylindrical handle on their upper face, slightly longer than the NAO hand width (Fig. 3).

To grasp a block, NAO first opens its fingers maximally, it than reaches the handle and positions its thumb and the two fingers on the opposite sites of the handle, and lastly it closes them around the handle. To grasp the handle, NAO hand is positioned with fingers and thumb parallel to the plane on the opposite sites of the handle. Such pose allows tolerance for height position error of the hand as the block can be grasped at any height of the handle. It is also tolerant to errors parallel to the plane on hand position as fingers are spaced apart 50mm before starting to close.

Grasping is planned and executed using the NAO *Frame_Torso* reference frame, located in the NAO torso, with axes parallel to the NAO *Robot_Frame*, as this is stable reference frame for arms and hands.

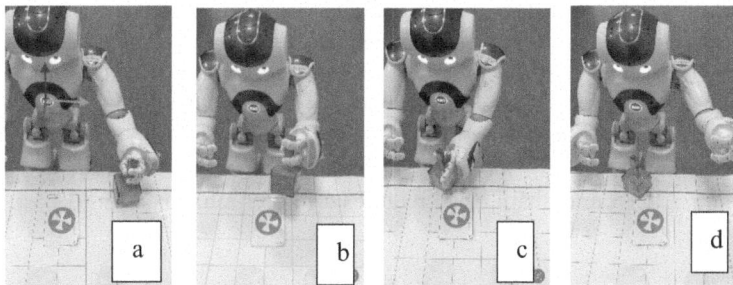

Fig. 3. Grasping a block (a). Raising the block (b). Translating it to the target position (c), and releasing it there (d). Afterwards NAO raises again its hand and moves it away from the playground. NAO *Torso Reference Frame*, shown in panel (a), is used to control this movement. The handle has a height of 50 mm and a radius of 10 mm

To get robust grasping we need to refine the position of the robot with respect to the block. In particular, the robot position can be offset laterally with respect to the table center at the end of gait. To correct this such offset has to be identified. This is the role of the thick vertical red line (Fig. 1), whose offset on the Y axis represents exactly such offset. Its detection is carried out with the same procedure used above to detect the thick horizontal border.

3.4   Translate the Block in Its Target Position and Release It and Go Back

After the block has been grasped, NAO first raises it vertically, on the Z axis, by raising its hand 40 mm above the table plane and then moves the hand laterally on the X axis and Y axes to the target position using inverse kinematics. The vertical position remains constant in this latter phase.

When the target position has been reached, NAO lowers its hand by the same 40 mm to put the block over the table and opens it to release the block. After the block has been released, NAO raises its hand again, this time higher to get above the handle of the block, translating it vertically by 80 mm on the Z-axis. Afterwards, it translates the hand externally in the X and Y directions by 20 mm to move the hand away from the block. From this position the arm, through inverse kinematics, is brought back to its starting position, memorized before grasping was initiated.

4 Results

We tested this reaching and grasping approach with a NAO robot V6 and a host PC Dell with Intel core i7-1255U and 16 GB of RAM, and Windows 11 Pro.

The NAO robot was positioned on the floor approximately at 1 m from the table at a small angle (<20°) with respect to the table side. The table has a height of 25 cm and a 8 × 8 checkerboard with squares of 5 cm was printed on an A3 sheet attached over its surface. The block prototype was realized with cardboard and can be positioned in any square of the first two rows of the board, as NAO is not able to reach further.

A total of 20 experiments were carried out. The robot succeeded in reaching and grasping a block 100% of the times. The mean error in hand grasping position was of 13,76 mm ± 23,1 mm in the lateral, Y, direction that is the most critical direction, that explains the success rate and shows the robustness of the method.

Before final refinement of its orientation, NAO was rotated with respect to the table of an average angle of −4,68° ±6,45°. Open-loop gait started at an average distance of 347,3 mm ± 13,5 mm, that indeed requires a further refinement of its position and orientation.

5 Discussion

The methodology described here opens the door for enabling NAO to play with blocks in a robust way. This is particularly important as blocks are a very flexible playing tool that is also widely used in cognitive/physical treatment in clinical domains [2]. Their faces can show symbols or colors that call for ordering, matching or composition. They can also be put in an ordered sequence to represent a sequence of actions typical of everyday life. Blocks can also work as cover for objects or tiles and be therefore used in a memory like games [10].

Enabling children to carry out these tasks with a robot would allow them to decrease the stress level often induced in the interaction with a Human partner [11] on one side, and on the other side allows the therapist on concentrate on the direct interaction with the child. Lastly, as the children have shown large appreciation for NAO [2]; this would possibly raise the engagement level in the therapy session, that is a critical factor for therapy success [11]. Lastly, when carrying out these tasks with a NAO robot, we can also envisage a cooperative and/or competitive playing modality that allows addressing different interaction modalities [10].

The decomposition of the reaching and grasping task in sub-tasks over which we have full control allows to modulate each component of robot action to match actual task needs. We can for instance, increase / decrease the walking or reaching speed, we can insert pauses between one sub-task and another and so forth. This can be fundamental to match the state of the child [12], and in particular his/her stress level to provide an adequate challenge level [13].

The number of blocks that can be used is limited by NAO arms structure and size. Given a working space with a radius of 265 mm, we could design a 8 × 4 checkerboard, with squares of 50 × 50 mm, so that NAO reaches with each if its arms, 4 × 2 different positions on its side of the table and the child will reach 8 × 4 position on his/her own side. Given this, blocks side is set to 40 mm. This is a compromise between blocks side length and their number: blocks of a smaller sizes would allow for more blocks, but their face area would be smaller and images attached on them more difficult to be understood.

Particular care has been put in obtaining a robust alignment of the robot with the table. In [6] this was obtained by putting one marker over the table but this would be intrusive as the marker would lay inside the checkerboard, the play area. We have thus preferred to put the markers on the side of the table and work open-loop from a certain distance onwards. Indeed, a drift in NAO position can take place as it approaches the table (we consistently measured a pitch of approximately 6° when approaching the table for our NAO robot), but we can correct the error obtained through robot vision of the checkerboard when NAO reaches the table, as the path length of the open-loop walk is limited. We prefer to use the two thick lines for refining orientation and the lateral pairs of NAOmarks for orienting the robot parallel to the table for two reasons: NAOmarks can be detected only at a distance and the accuracy is limited. Nevertheless, this has allowed the robot to walk more easily towards the table center. Moreover, computation of the orientation through lines is most accurate when the lines cover a large portion of the NAO camera image and therefore are seen from a close distance. Accuracy was verified for a reasonable large set of NAO initial positions and orientations.

A critical issue is represented by charge level. A careful control of this level is required before the task is started to avoid that the robot shuts down before the end of the task or performs poorly: when NAO has low charge, it does not stand up completely. This would decrease the success rate and, in turns, the level of trust between the child and the robot [14].

6 Conclusion

This work proposes a robust approach for carrying out activities with blocks between a child and a humanoid robot, like NAO, without requiring to add special and costly hardware. However, this approach is not limited to this kind of applications but can be extended to all tasks that require interaction through objects that can mount a handle and use a board. It could be applied for instance to chess playing or to classical any board games, thus enlarging the domain of application and the users population.

It presently requires that the robot approaches the center of the table and from there it reaches and grasps different blocks. As the NAO arms are quite short, the working space is limited and thus few blocks can be used. This approach could be enhanced setting multiple starting position besides the table and allowing the robot to move laterally from one position to the other, thus increasing its working space.

Acknowledgment. This work was partially supported by H2020 project ESENCE (grant n. 101016112) and by PRIN2022 MIUR Italian project AIRCA (grant n. G53D23002860006).

References

1. Bainbridge, W.A., Hart, J.W., Kim, E.S., Scassellati, B.: The benefits of interaction with physically present robots over video-displayed agents. Int. J. Soc. Robot. **3**(1), 41–52 (2011). https://doi.org/10.1007/s12369-010-0082-7

2. Bartl Pokorny, K.D., et al.: Robot-based intervention for children with autism spectrum disorder: a systematic literature review. IEEE Access **9**, 165433–165450 (2021)
3. Baron-Cohen, S.: The hyper-systemizing, assortative mating theory of autism. Neuropsychopharmacol. Biol. Psychiatry **30**(5), 865–872 (2006)
4. Mellmann, H., Scheunemann, M., Stadie, O.: Adaptive grasping for a small humanoid robot utilizing force-and electric current sensors **1032** (2013)
5. Müller, J., Frese, U., Röfer, T.: Grab a mug-object detection and grasp motion planning with the NAO robot. In: Proceedings IEEE-RAS International Conference on Humanoid Robots (2012)
6. Zhang, L., Zhang, H., Yang, H., Bin Bian, G., Wu, W.: Multi-target detection and grasping control for humanoid robot NAO. Int. J. Adapt. Control Sig. Process. **33**(7), 1225–1237 (2019). https://doi.org/10.1002/acs.3031
7. Liu, H., Luo, C., Zhang, L.: Target recognition and heavy load operation posture control of humanoid robot for trolley operation. In: 2018 IEEE-RAS 18th International Conference on Humanoid Robots, pp. 280–283 (2018)
8. Gonzaled, R.C., Woods, E.R.: Digital Image Processing, 4th edn. Person (2019)
9. Feix, T., et al.: The GRASP taxonomy of human grasp types. IEEE Trans. Hum. Mach. Syst. **46**(1), 66–77 (2016)
10. Brok, J.C.J., Barakova, E.I.,: Engaging Autistic children in imitation and turn-taking games with multiagent system of interactive lighting blocks. LNCS, vol. 6243. Springer, Berlin (2010)
11. Rudovic, O., et al.: Measuring engagement in robot assisted autism therapy: a cross-cultural study. Front. Rob. AI **4** (2017)
12. Pirovano, M., Mainetti, R., Baud-Bovy, G., Lanzi, P.L., Borghese, N.A.: Intelligent game engine for rehabilitation. IEEE Trans. CIAIG **8**(1), 43–55 (2016)
13. Brambilla, S., Boccignone, G., Borghese, N.A., Ripamonti, L.: Between the buttons stress assessment in video games using players' behavioural data, pp. 59–69 (2022)
14. Luperto, M., et al.: Seeking at-home long-term autonomy of assistive mobile robots through the integration with an IoT-based monitoring system. Rob. Auton. Syst. **161**, 104346 (2023). ISSN 0921-8890

Theory of Mind Assessment
in Human-Robot Interaction

Luigi Marino[1], Lorenzo D'Errico[2] , Marco Matarese[1,3] ,
Angelo Cangelosi[4] , and Mariacarla Staffa[1(✉)]

[1] University of Naples Parthenope, Naples, Italy
luigi.marino003@studenti.uniparthenope.it, marco.matarese@iit.it,
mariacarla.staffa@uniparthenope.it
[2] University of Naples Federico II, Naples, Italy
lorenzo.derrico@unina.it
[3] Italian Institute of Technology, Genoa, Italy
[4] University of Manchester, Manchester, England
angelo.cangelosi@manchester.ac.uk

Abstract. Theory of Mind (ToM) is a crucial inferential system in
human communication, allowing individuals to attribute mental states
to themselves and others, and predict behaviors based on these attributions. While it is probable that ToM plays a significant role in interactions with non-human agents displaying similar cues, it remains unclear
if humans apply ToM to mechanical agents that exhibit intelligence and
social characteristics. To address this gap, we designed an experimental
setting to assess ToM in Human-Robot Interaction (HRI). This study
investigates the influence of robots' social attitude on users' ToM and
their performance in False Belief Tasks. We examine how the behavioral
programming of robots affects human perceptions and the accuracy of
verbal and non-verbal ToM assessments.

Keywords: Human-Robot Interaction · Socially Assistive Robotics ·
Theory of Mind · Behavioral Programming · False Belief Task

1 Introduction

Human-robot interaction (HRI) focuses on developing robots that can seamlessly integrate into everyday environments [1], presenting unexpected technical
challenges due to the dynamic and complex nature of the social rather than the
physical interactions with humans [2]. Creating meaningful cognitive connections
between humans and robots is essential for achieving social interactions. With
the aim of constructing such cognitive models facilitating these connections, HRI
started to rely during the last decade on Theory of Mind (ToM) principles. ToM
refers to the ability to understand others by ascribing mental states - such as
beliefs, intentions, and desires - to them [3]. People use ToM mechanisms to make
sense of others' behavior by analyzing and inferring it. If robots could develop a
ToM, they could connect with humans socially in unprecedented ways [4]. They

© The Author(s), under exclusive license to Springer Nature Singapore Pte Ltd. 2025
O. Palinko et al. (Eds.): ICSR + AI 2024, LNAI 15562, pp. 33–42, 2025.
https://doi.org/10.1007/978-981-96-3519-1_4

would learn from human observers using common social cues, much like young children do, without needing additional training [5]. To engage effectively, social robots should so understand not only human mental states, including users' emotional states [6] to coordinate their behaviours accordingly [7], but also facilitate humans to ascribe mental states to the robot itself by using appropriate verbal and non-verbal communication. This would enable humans to form accurate mental models of a robot's capabilities and intentions based on both its appearance and behavior. However, differences in how humans and robots perceive the world can complicate these interactions, making such assumptions risky [8]. Additionally, a robot's embodiment and behavior can significantly influence ToM development.

In this work, we focused on robot's social attitude, interpreted as the tendency to respond to others, shaped by experiences and opinions. Unlike specific actions, social attitude is an abstraction from consistent reactions and plays a key role in intergroup dynamics, affecting acceptance, harmony, or competition among society members and, in turn, ToM [9]. By modelling the social attitude of a humanoid robot, we aim to examine the impact on users' perceptions, focusing on how these changes affect their understanding of others' mental states. This approach addresses key questions about the role of robots' appearance and behavior in shaping perceptions and ToM development.

2   Related Works

Assessing ToM, namely the ability to attribute mental states to others, is crucial for understanding social cognition. While traditional methods rely on human intervention, advancements in robotics provide new research opportunities. This study aims to validate the use of robots in ToM assessment and explore how robots' social attitude influences users' ToM and performance on False Belief Tasks (FBT) [10], which tests one's ability to ascribe to others correctly. Originally proposed by Wimmer and Perner (1983) [10] and adapted across various contexts, the FBT is a central tool for measuring the ability to interpret mental states, particularly false beliefs. This test focuses on scenarios where there is a contradiction between reality and a character's belief, such as in the famous Sally and Ann task [11]. FBT can be replicated in HRI because it is based on simple narrative scenarios that robots can enact or facilitate. Moreover, the use of implicit methods, such as gaze tracking and imitation behaviors, can be adapted to robot interactions, while the interaction itself can be used to evaluate how humans attribute mental states, including false beliefs, to machines.

Several analyses have been made to understand how people assume that robots perceive the world. Researchers in [12] added a non-verbal or implicit measure rather than only using verbal measures during the FBT, discovering a significant difference between them in belief attribution. The results suggest preliminary validity, indicating that the measure captures belief-sensitive predictions about robot behavior. However, the authors found that verbal and non-verbal measures of belief attribution to robots were inconsistent, especially in more difficult trials. In our case study, we modified the robot's social attitude rather than task complexity to see if this would better establish ToM between humans and robots.

Hence, we investigated the impact of manipulating the robot's social attitude on people's ability to solve the FBT in a real-world scenario with a humanoid robot in the role of Sally, considering the following research questions (RQ):

- **RQ1:** Do people successfully complete the FBT when the participant is a real embodied robot?
- **RQ2:** Does the robot's social attitude affect how people perceive it?
- **RQ3:** Is there a relationship between human ToM abilities and their perception of robots?

3   Materials and Methods

The focus of this study was to investigate whether individuals perceive robots as possessing a Theory of Mind (ToM) and whether varying their social attitudes during interaction can influence this attribution.

3.1   The Robotics Platform

Numerous research studies have been conducted on how robots' behavior and social attitude [13] can influence the way people perceive them [14]. Certain features can be modified to elicit emotions in people interacting with the robot. In particular, robots' head and body movements were designed based on previous research [15,16], which showed that specific postures, gestures, and their dynamics (such as speed and amplitude) can convey distinct emotions. Thus, we designed two different robot social attitudes (Fig. 1) based such previous studies:

- *Interactive social attitude*: characterized by positive skills in terms of social communication, such as laughter vocalization and a short intake of a surprised breath, straight head with green-colored eyes, upright posture, with both vertical and lateral extension, along with large and fast movements.
- *Passive social attitude*: characterized by negative behavior in terms of negative expressions and a long intake of a sudden breath, a forward head bend with red-colored eyes, a forward-leaning posture, arms at the side of the trunk, with less energetic and smaller gestures.

3.2   Questionnaires

Three different questionnaires were deployed in this study.

- *Theory of Mind Inventory (ToMI).* The ToMI is a self-report tool used to evaluate adults' social cognition, with a focus on how well they operate in terms of ToM [17]. It is a collection of statements that have been carefully chosen to represent various facets of ToM and social cognition in adults. For each statement, respondents are given a different 20-unit response continuum, ranging from "definitely not" to "definitely".

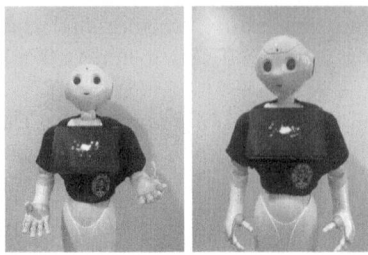

Fig. 1. Interactive behavior (left) and Passive behavior (right).

- *The Godspeed Questionnaire (GQS).* The GQS is a collection of questionnaires used to gauge how people feel about robots. In order to evaluate different facets of HRI, it tries to provide a standardized assessment method. Each item focuses on a different aspect of the user's perception, such as anthropomorphism, animacy, likeability, and perceived safety [18]. The foundation of the GQS is semantic differentials. Answers are to be recorded on a five-point rating system using contrasting phrases, like "unconscious" and "conscious".
- *The False-Belief Task (FBT).* The FBT is a test that assesses a person's comprehension of false beliefs, or the capacity to comprehend that a person could hold a belief that is not consistent with reality. It is frequently used to evaluate a person's ToM skills, which entail comprehending the thoughts and feelings of others. A story or scenario with a character who has a false belief about a circumstance usually forms the basis of the task, and the tester is then asked questions to see if they can properly identify the character's false belief [19].

3.3   Evaluating ToM Through Sally-Anne's Test

A prominent method for evaluating persons' ToM comprehension is the *Sally-Anne test*, a particular kind of FBT. In this test, two characters named Sally and Anne are presented, and the test subject is told a tale in which Sally places something—like a marble—in one area and then exits the room. Anne moves the item to a new location (like a box) while Sally is away. Then, FBT questions are posed to the test subject, such as "Where will Sally look for her marble?" and "Where is the marble really?". In this study, we revisited the Sally-Anne Test introducing a humanoid robot (Pepper) in the role of Sally. In our experimental setting, we used a ball as an object to hide in the two boxes (one red and one black). To simulate Sally's inattention, or rather the impossibility of seeing the movement of the ball between one box and another, we simulated receiving a phone call, for which the robot turns around and starts talking. In the meantime, an operator moves the ball from one box to another. Then, the robot turns towards the user and is asked, as in the original test, where the ball was, where it is at the moment, and in which box they think the robot will look for it.

During the second test, however, the robot does not turn to receive the call, and the operator moves the ball under the robot's eyes. After the stopover, the user is asked the above FBT questions again.

4   Experimental Procedure

4.1   Procedure

Participants were recruited through a voluntary-based online call at the University of Naples Parthenope, with no rewards or compensation provided. A total of 30 volunteers ranging between 19 and 30 years old participated in the study (smaller sample sizes are quite common in HRI research due to the intensive nature of interactions and the complexity of the setups, as shown in [20, 21] in which 40 and 48/24 participants respectively were enrolled for the studies). Before taking part in data collection and analysis, every participant in this study was required to give their informed consent. The experimental design included two distinct groups of 15 participants each, who were randomly assigned to interact with one of the two robot's social attitudes: interactive (positive attitude) and passive (negative attitude). Within each group, participants interacted with the robot under two conditions, namely i) "Pepper looking" and ii) "Pepper not looking", simulating different levels of attentional engagement by the robot. Each participant experienced both conditions in a controlled sequence. In the "Pepper looking" scenario, the robot was fully attentive during the FBT, while in the "Pepper not looking" scenario, the robot turned its back, mimicking inattention. This allowed us to compare participant responses based on the robot's perceived engagement level within the same session. Then, participants are given a thorough explanation of the experiment's entire process and then invited to proceed with the experiment. The interaction was divided into three phases:

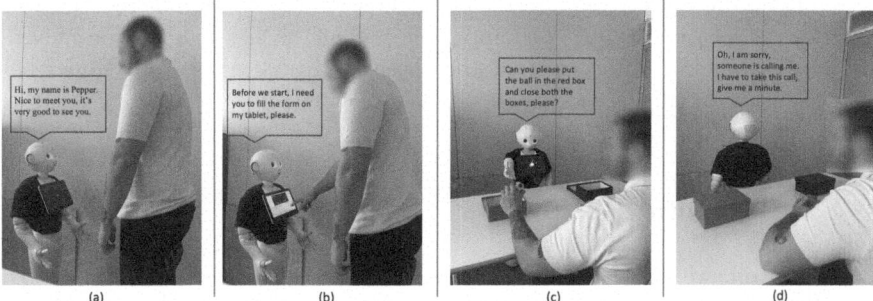

Fig. 2. In (a) and (b) first interactions, in (c) and (d) FBT are displayed.

– *Pre-Interaction Phase.* After acknowledging the privacy statement, users complete the ToMI questionnaire and give their informed consent.

– *Interaction Phase.* The robot is positioned in front of the participants to introduce itself and start their first interaction (Fig. 2 a, b). The robot used the tablet to gather the user's information (name, gender, etc.) and conversed with the human based on the input given and behavior in the interactive mode (Fig. 2-b). The interactive robot thanked the users and complimented them (e.g., by saying "what a lovely name!"), while the passive robot introduced itself and asked the user to fill out the form without any consideration for the user's well-being. After this brief interaction, the robot told the user that a human operator would help him take the next steps. Then, after engaging in their first robot contact, users were required to complete the GQS. After passing the GQS, the main interaction took place following the revisited Sally and Anne's story. During such phase, the robot instructed the users to close both boxes and place the ball within the red one (Fig. 2-c). Right after having placed the ball in the red box, the interactive robot gently interrupted the task to answer an unexpected phone call and turned its back (Fig. 2-d). In the meanwhile, the experimenter switched the ball's location by transferring it from the red box to the black one while the robot was gazing away. On the contrary, the passive robot simply turned while the researcher switched the ball's location, and finally, it turned back to the participant. Then, we repeated this procedure letting the robot look at the boxes while the experimenter switched the ball's location.

– *Post-Interaction Phase.* In the last phase, the interactive robot thanked the participants for being part of the study; on the contrary, the passive robot just ended the experiment. After each ball switch, participants are given a final questionnaire on false beliefs, namely the FBT. The inquiries posed in the test are listed below:

1 Where will Pepper look?
2 Where is the object?
3 Where was the object before it was displaced?
4 Select the option that best corresponds to why you answered the way you did for question 1: a) Pepper knew that the object had been moved; b) Pepper did not know that the object had been moved; c) Pepper has superior intelligence.

5   Experimental Results

In this section, we present the results on how the robot's behavior influenced users' ToM and their performance in the FBT. The complete dataset used in the analysis is available for review at the following github repository.

5.1   Godspeed Questionnaire

All the GQS scales (but Perceived Safety) showed a Cronbach's $\alpha \geq 0.81$, indicating the reliability of the scales that we actually used in our analysis. The results of the GQS are presented in Table 1 and shown in Fig. 3. For each group interacting with the robot, we aggregated the mean and standard deviation for the five dimensions of the GQS. We performed *Student's t-test* on the GQS scales looking for differences between the two experimental groups. We found no significant differences regarding the aggregated measures of the GQS ($t = 1.24$, $p = .22$, $ES = .45$ for anthropomorphism; $t = 1.89$, $p = .06$, $ES = .69$ for likeability; $t = .05$, $p = .96$, $ES = .01$ for perceived intelligence; and $t = 1.6$, $p = .11$, $ES = .58$ for perceived safety). However, we found that two sub-scales regarding anthropomorphism and likeability revealed a significant difference. Specifically, they refer to the robot's moving style as being rigid/elegant (*Mann-Whitney t-test*: $t = 59.5$, $p = .024$, $ES = .47$) and to its aspect as being unpleasant/pleasant (*Mann-Whitney t-test*: $t = 62.5$, $p = .027$, $ES = .44$), respectively.

Table 1. GQS Scores for Interactive and Passive social attitude.

Godspeed Dimension	Mean (Interactive)	SD Interactive	Mean (Passive)	SD (Passive)
Antrophomorfism	3,25	0,53	2,88	0,64
Likeability	4,33	0,04	3,80	0,39
Perceived Intelligence	3,82	0,28	3,20	0,05
Perceived Safety	3,36	1,78	3,09	2,24

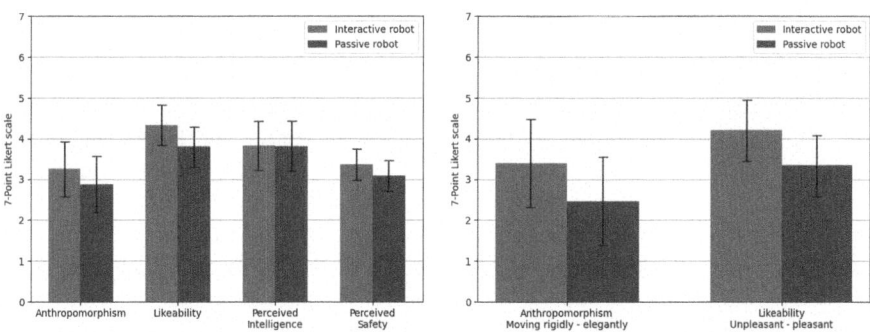

Fig. 3. Mean and std deviation of the GQS test. On the left, there are the questionnaire's aggregated means, while on the right there are those of two sub-scales regarding the robot's anthropomorphism and likeability.

5.2   False Belief Task

After each of the two interactions, users were asked to answer a series of four questions in order to evaluate their level of ToM with respect to the robot and the

Table 2. Percentage of participants passing (black box) and failing (red box) the FBT for both the Interactive and Passive Groups depending on whether the robot was looking at the box during the box change.

Social Attitude Group ->	Interactive group		Passive group	
Test Conditions: 1,2	**Black Box**	**Red Box**	**Black Box**	**Red Box**
1. Pepper was looking	86.7%	13.3%	80.0%	20.0%
2. Pepper was not looking	80.0%	20.0%	66.7%	33.3%

task. Table 2 summarizes participants' results at the FBT. Only 20% of participants in the Interactive Group did not properly solve the first FBT (Pepper not looking). An extra question on why individuals selected that box was included in the test, along with a list of potential responses. All the explanations given in the circumstances were: "because Pepper knows that the object has been moved". These people assume the robot understands or knows that the ball has been moved, even when it is facing away from them. When it comes to the second test, only 13.3% of participants said that Pepper would have searched for the ball in the wrong box, failing the second FBT (Pepper looking). All participants reported that Pepper did not know that the object had been moved. On the other hand, regarding the first task (Pepper not looking), 33.3% of the participants in the Passive Group answered incorrectly to the first FBT. All participants but one reported that they believed the robot did not know that the ball actually changed the box. Regarding the second task (Pepper looking), 20% of the participants continued to predict the robot in a different way than expected, predicting that it would keep looking in the box where the ball is no longer present, failing the second FBT. All participants believed that Pepper actually did not know about the switch. We found no differences between the two experimental groups regarding the resolution of the FBT. Furthermore, we found no significant differences in participants' ability to solve it based on whether the robot was looking at the boxes during the switch. With an ANCOVA test, we found that participants' ability to solve the FBT when the robot was looking significantly impacted as covariate their perception of the robot's likeability ($F(1) = 2.58$, $p = .03$). Post-hoc Tukey's corrections revealed no significant effects between the Interactive and Passive groups. Furthermore, we found significant positive correlations (Pearson) between participants' ability to solve the FBT when the robot was looking and their perception of the robot's intelligence ($r = .37$, $p < .04$) and likeability ($r = .4$, $p < .029$). Indeed, these latter positively correlated with each other ($r = .59$, $p < .001$). Finally, we found no interactions between the participants' ToMI test scores and their answers to the GQS or their ability to solve the FBT.

6   Discussions and Conclusions

This study investigated how users' Theory of Mind (ToM) and performance on False Belief Tasks (FBT) were affected by a humanoid robot endowed with different social attitudes. The experiment involved two groups of 15 participants, randomly assigned to interact with one of two robot social attitudes: interactive (positive social attitude) or passive (negative social attitude). The study and its results suggest a number of issues for further study and provide some important new insights. For example, by exploring the relationship between participants' self-assessed ToM abilities (ToM Inventory test) and their performance in the FBT, we surprisingly found no significant correlations suggesting that self-assessed ToM may not reflect how users interpret the robot's mental states, highlighting areas for future research. For our first research question (RQ1), analysis showed that participants in both groups successfully completed the test with both the interactive and passive robots, indicating that robots can be useful for assessing human ToM. Notably, the interactive group, which engaged with the socially interactive robot, had a higher FBT success rate, suggesting that the robot's social attitude influences users' perception of its mental states. For our second research question (RQ2), the Godspeed (GQS) test comparisons supported the hypothesis that the robot's social attitude influences users' perceptions and emotions. While overall GQS measures showed no significant differences, two sub-scales—anthropomorphism and likeability—revealed significant variations. Participants in the Interactive Group perceived the robot as more elegant and pleasant than those in the Passive Group, confirming that our manipulation was effective. For the third research question (RQ3), no significant relationships were found between participants' FBT responses and their ToMI test scores. However, since the ToMI is a self-assessment, this doesn't rule out a correlation with actual ToM, warranting further investigation. In summary, our research highlights the potential of using robots to assess ToM and underscores the importance of behavior programming in shaping user experiences, crucial for understanding how robots influence human cognition and social interaction in HRI.

Acknowledgments. The work was supported by the research RESTART project (Robot Enhanced Social abilities based on Theory of mind for Acceptance of Robot in assistive Treatments) (CUP: I53D23003780001) and by the SPECTRA project (Supporting schizophrenia PatiEnts Care wiTh aRtificiAl intelligence - D53D23017290001), funded by the MIUR with D.D. no. 861 under the PNRR and by the European Union - Next Generation EU.

References

1. Bartneck, C., Belpaeme, T., Eyssel, F., Kanda, T., Keijsers, M., Šabanović, S.: Human-Robot Interaction: An Introduction. Cambridge University Press (2020)
2. Sheridan, T.B.: Human-robot interaction: status and challenges. Hum. Fact. **58**(4), 525–532 (2016). PMID: 27098262

3. Apperly, I.A., Butterfill, S.A.: Do humans have two systems to track beliefs and belief-like states? Psychol. Rev. **116**(4), 953 (2009)
4. Patrício, M.L.M., Jamshidnejad, A.: Dynamic mathematical models of theory of mind for socially assistive robots. IEEE Access **11**, 103956–103975 (2023)
5. Scassellati, B.: Foundations for a theory of mind for a humanoid robot (2001)
6. Staffa, M., D'Errico, L.: EEG-based machine learning models for emotion recognition in HRI. In: Degen, H., Ntoa, S. (eds.) HCII 2023. LNCS, vol. 14051, pp. 285–297. Springer, Cham (2023). https://doi.org/10.1007/978-3-031-35894-4_21
7. Burattini, E., Rossi, S., Finzi, A., Staffa, M.: Attentional modulation of mutually dependent behaviors. In: Doncieux, S., Girard, B., Guillot, A., Hallam, J., Meyer, J.-A., Mouret, J.-B. (eds.) SAB 2010. LNCS (LNAI), vol. 6226, pp. 283–292. Springer, Heidelberg (2010). https://doi.org/10.1007/978-3-642-15193-4_27
8. Thellman, S., Silvervarg, A., Ziemke, T.: Some adults fail the false-belief task when the believer is a robot. In: Companion of the 2020 ACM/IEEE International Conference on Human-Robot Interaction, HRI 2020, pp. 479–481. Association for Computing Machinery, New York, NY, USA (2020)
9. Miller, S.A.: Consequences: Social Development. In: Advanced Theory of Mind. Oxford University Press (2022)
10. Wimmer, H., Perner, J.: Beliefs about beliefs: representation and constraining function of wrong beliefs in young children's understanding of deception. Cognition **13**(1), 103–128 (1983)
11. Baron-Cohen, S., Leslie, A.M., Frith, U.: Does the autistic child have a "theory of mind"? Cognition **21**(1), 37–46 (1985)
12. Thellman, S., Giagtzidou, A., Silvervarg, A., Ziemke, T.: An implicit, non-verbal measure of belief attribution to robots, pp. 473–475 (2020)
13. Staffa, M., D'Errico, L., Francese, R.: Emphasizing with a robot with a personality. In: Degen, H., Ntoa, S. (eds.) HCII 2024. LNCS, vol. 14736, pp. 283–294. Springer, Cham (2024). https://doi.org/10.1007/978-3-031-60615-1_19
14. Staffa, M., DErrico, L., Sansalone, S., Alimardani, M.: Classifying human emotions in HRI: applying global optimization model to EEG brain signals. Front. Neurorobotics **17** (2023)
15. Coulson, M.: Attributing emotion to static body postures: recognition accuracy, confusions, and viewpoint dependence. J. Nonverbal Behav. **28**, 117–139 (2004)
16. Kleinsmith, A., Bianchi-Berthouze, N.: Affective body expression perception and recognition: a survey. IEEE Trans. Affect. Comput. **4**, 15–33 (2013)
17. Hutchins, T., Lewis, L., Prelock, P., Brien, A.: The development and preliminary psychometric evaluation of the theory of mind inventory: self report-adult. J. Autism Dev. Disord. **51** (2021)
18. Bartneck, C., Kulić, D., Croft, E., Zoghbi, S.: Godspeed questionnaire series. Int. J. Soc. Rob. (2008)
19. Korkiakangas, T., Dindar, K., Laitila, A., Kärnä, E.: The Sally-Anne test: an interactional analysis of a dyadic assessment. Int. J. Lang. Commun. Disord. **51**(6), 685–702 (2016)
20. Leite, I., Pereira, A., Mascarenhas, S., Martinho, C., Prada, R., Paiva, A.: The influence of empathy in human-robot relations. Int. J. Hum.-Comput. Stud. **71**(3), 250–260 (2013)
21. Terzioğlu, Y., Mutlu, B., Şahin, E.: Designing social cues for collaborative robots: the role of gaze and breathing in human-robot collaboration. In: Proceedings of the 2020 ACM/IEEE International Conference on HRI, HRI 2020, pp. 343–357. ACM, New York, NY, USA (2020)

Combining Control and Validity: Context Management Issues in Proactive Social Robotics Research

Victor Kaptelinin(✉) ⓘ

Umeå University, 901 87 Umeå, Sweden
victor.kaptelinin@umu.se

Abstract. This paper highlights and discusses the methodological challenge of combining control and validity in social robotics research. Proactive, future-oriented studies that explore novel technologies and interactions are usually conducted in specially constructed environments and involve completing researcher-defined tasks. While researchers' control over environments and tasks allows for investigating human-robot interaction phenomena that do not (yet) exist in real-life settings, it may also potentially undermine the validity of the studies. The paper discusses combining control and validity in relation to existing social robotics research and identifies key topics for further methodological developments. The paper argues that detailed and explicit representations of study contexts are crucial to ensure creating consistent study environments. It is also argued that there is a need for analytical tools supporting an understanding of how study participants frame technologies and tasks within particular study contexts.

Keywords: Social robotics · Proactive research · Constructed environments · Context · Control · Validity

1 Introduction

In the field of social robotics, context is an important methodological concern. The phenomena investigated are context-specific, as the context of human encounters with robotic technologies significantly influences the perception and use of these technologies (e.g., [1–3]). Therefore, taking context into account is essential for conducting rigorous studies and accurately interpreting their results [4–6].

This paper specifically focuses on methodological aspects of dealing with context in *proactive* social robotics research. Here, "proactive" refers to research that explores potential future technological solutions and interaction scenarios rather than assessing existing technologies and practices. Proactive research deals with novel solutions and scenarios that do not yet exist in real life. Therefore, the settings it typically employs are specially constructed and controlled by the researchers. The artificial nature of constructed settings can, arguably, undermine the validity of proactive studies. In particular, it may raise concerns about whether the findings (a) can be generalized beyond the

O. Palinko et al. (Eds.): ICSR + AI 2024, LNAI 15562, pp. 43–53, 2025.
https://doi.org/10.1007/978-981-96-3519-1_5

specific setting (external validity) and (b) accurately reflect the phenomena that the researchers intend to study (internal validity).

The aim of this paper is to discuss the challenge of combining control and validity in social robotics and outline key topics that need to be further explored in order to deal with this challenge. The remainder of the paper is organized as follows. First, an overview of the types of studies in social robotics, with a special focus on research conducted in controlled settings, is presented. It is followed by a discussion of validity concerns associated with constructed settings. Finally, a set of methodological issues that need to be addressed to successfully combine control and validity is identified.

2   Natural and Constructed Settings in Social Robotics Research

In human-technology interaction, user studies are commonly divided into two types, those conducted in "natural" and "controlled" settings [7]. Apparently, in its basic form, this distinction does not account for the actual diversity of studies, as different aspects of a study – such as the physical environment, participants' tasks, social interactions, and technology used – can be "natural" or "controlled" to different degrees. Therefore, "natural/controlled" is not a dichotomy but rather a dimension or a scale[1], with "fully natural" and "fully controlled" studies representing two opposite poles of the scale, and "partly natural/partly controlled" ones being located somewhere between these poles.

This section discusses the types of studies in social robotics, organized along the "natural/controlled" dimension. It should be noted that the discussion is not intended as a comprehensive analysis of the "space" of social robotics methods or a systematic literature review. Instead, it is an attempt to identify a representative set of study types relevant for addressing the issue of validity. The types of studies identified in the analysis are shown in Table 1.

"True natural" studies are conducted in participants' own environments, the technology employed is owned by the participants, and the participants have full control over the use of the technology. While in social robotics there have been several insightful and influential studies falling in the "true natural" category (e.g., [6, 8, 9]) the number of such studies is currently relatively limited. With robotic technologies increasingly entering everyday settings, these types of studies are likely to become more common.

Trial deployment studies are similar to the "true natural" ones, but there is a crucial difference. In trial deployments, a robotic technology is provided by researchers and is only owned by the participants for the duration of the study (e.g. [10]). One may argue that trial deployments are basically the same as "true natural" studies, just limited to the early phases of technology appropriation. However, the fact that the participants do not permanently own a technology may result in different perceptions and uses of the technology, compared to "true natural" studies, even starting from the first encounters.

Field testing studies are user studies of novel technologies conducted in participants' own environments. They are different from trial deployments in several respects. First, in contrast to trial deployments, technologies do not have to be fully functional; it may be sufficient that the participants only *perceive* them as such. Advanced prototypes, such

---

[1] The question of whether "natural" and "controlled" are opposite poles of a single dimension or can be considered two related but distinct dimensions is beyond the scope of this paper.

Table 1. Types of studies in social robotics.

Setting	Type	Task scripting	Technology/prototype	Technology ownership	Researchers' control
Natural	"True natural"	no	functional	participants	no
	Trial deployment	no/low	functional	dual	technology (partial)
Constructed	Field testing	various	WoZ and higher fidelity	researchers	technology, tasks
	Long-term enactment	low	functional	researchers	setting, technology
	Short-term enactment	high	lo-fi props and higher fidelity	researchers	setting, technology, tasks
	Controlled experiment	high	images and higher fidelity	researchers	setting, technology, tasks
	Design fiction	various	texts, images, videos, VR	n/a	medium, tasks

as those based on the Wizard of Oz (WoZ) approach, can be appropriate for the purposes of a field testing (e.g. [11]). Second, the participants do not always have the freedom of choosing their tasks, and certain interactions with the technology in question can be required or even scripted by the researchers. Finally, the time span of the studies can be shorter. Because of this, field testing settings can be considered constructed rather than natural: even though natural settings are used as a base, they are transformed by the introduction of novel technologies and tasks.

Long-term enactments are different from the studies discussed so far in that they are conducted in settings which are specially constructed by the researchers, rather than in participants' own environments. Researchers' control over the settings allows for modeling contexts and enacting interactions which cannot be created and experienced otherwise. The long-term nature of these studies enables the development of meaningful human-technology (as well as human-human) relationships, allowing researchers to observe phenomena that take time to emerge [12, 13]. A limitation of this type of studies is that they are generally not suitable for testing early prototypes, since the technologies used need to be functional enough to support extended and potentially unscripted interactions. Studies of this type require significant time and effort, which probably contributes to why they are less common compared to other types.

Short-term enactments, like the long-term ones, aim to make envisioned technologies and contexts tangible, so that study participants can interactively experience and explore them [14]. The difference is that human-technology interactions are usually more scripted. This, in combination with a more limited time span, makes it possible to use not only fully functional technologies but also various types of prototypes, including low-fidelity ones [15].

Controlled experiments are a common type of study in social robotics, designed to compare several experimental conditions that represent different levels of one or more independent variables. The experimental conditions can be constructed with different degrees of depth and detail. In some cases, experimental tasks are explicitly embedded into elaborated fictional contexts, effectively making these experiments multiple short-term enactments [16–20]. In other cases, the participants are engaged in dyadic "human-robot" interactions with little or no contextual cues [4].

Finally, in *design fiction* studies, participants do not engage in unfolding interactions with objectively existing people and technologies. Instead, they encounter fictional realities presented to them through diegetic prototypes (e.g., textual descriptions or videos), which require them to develop an understanding of the context of human-technology interaction using imagination and/or perception [21, 22]. Participants' tasks in such studies can be either scripted or unscripted.

The types of studies discussed above are not always distinct or mutually exclusive. In some cases, there may be an overlap between different types; for instance, a particular video study can be a borderline case between a controlled experiment and design fiction. In addition, several study types can be combined within a single investigation.

3   Validity Concerns Related to Employing Constructed Study Settings

3.1   Context-Specific Phenomena and Internal Validity

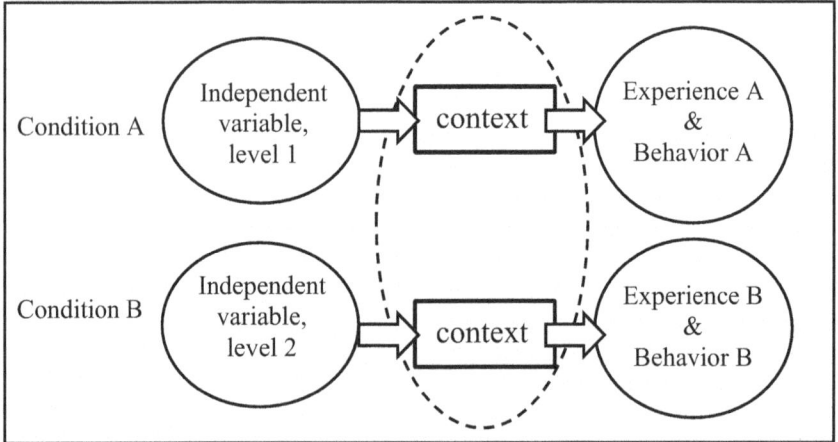

Fig. 1. Potential effect of study context on internal validity of controlled experiments.

Validity is commonly categorized into two types: internal and external [23, 24]. Internal validity refers to the extent to which the findings of a study accurately reflect the effects of the factors that the researchers intend to investigate. External validity concerns the degree to which the results can be generalized to other contexts. Validity is a fundamental methodological concern in the design, implementation, and assessment of any study. However, the context-specific nature of the phenomena investigated in social robotics makes it especially challenging to address this concern in proactive studies. The constructed settings employed in the studies can be unusual or even unique, making it difficult to not only generalize the results but also assess how they are affected by the context [24]. Therefore, employing constructed study settings potentially undermines not only external, but also internal validity.

One may contend that in the case of controlled experiments, context should not be a significant concern for internal validity, as standard experiment design methods can be employed to make sure that context equally affects different experimental conditions. However, it can be argued that using constructed settings has implications for the internal validity of controlled experiments, too.

Let us consider an example of a controlled experiment (Fig. 1) in which two levels of a single independent variable (e.g., robot politeness) correspond to Condition A (a polite robot) and Condition B (an impolite robot). Typically, such studies employ a straight-forward strategy: measuring the subjective and objective responses of the participants in both conditions and analyzing the data to reveal the effect (or lack thereof) of the independent variable.

An assumption underlying this strategy is that it is possible to minimize or eliminate the effect of confounding variables so that the independent variable can be success-fully singled out. However, in the case of highly context-dependent phenomena, the assumption is not necessarily true. While the best practices of rigorous research adopted in social robotics, such as advanced experiment design, sampling control, and manip-ulation checks, can address many validity-related concerns [4, 24], they may not be sufficient if context is a major factor affecting the results.

The range of potentially critical contextual aspects can be extremely broad, and some of these aspects are likely unknown to the researchers. In addition, it is not the context itself but rather the participants' perception of it that affects their experience and objective responses. Therefore, the effect of study conditions on the participants is, to a significant degree, determined by concrete aspects of the particular context. These aspects can be outside the researchers' control (or even awareness), and the actual reasons why a study produces certain empirical evidence may be difficult to discern. For instance, the reason why the participants in a study negatively experience a polite service robot could be that the robot, in the conditions of the study, evokes associations with excessively polite sales assistants. What the findings reveal would be an attitude toward pushy sales assistants rather than toward robot politeness in general. It can be argued, that in this case, context-specificity may affect both external *and* internal validity.

Context-specificity can be an issue in either natural or constructed settings. However, as discussed below, constructed settings present a particularly difficult methodological challenge.

3.2 "Invisible" Context

In social robotics studies, especially in short-term enactments and controlled experi-ments, it is not uncommon to offer participants specific tasks with little (or no) effort to explicitly introduce a larger context. A common assumption appears to be that the overarching context is self-evident and consistent across all study conditions. However, in controlled studies, participants may not find the implied contexts self-evident and, instead, may create idiosyncratic "theories" that are difficult to anticipate. Consider the following example:

During a pilot trial conducted within a study on robot politeness [25] a participant was asked to interact with a robot manifesting different types of behavior and having different types of attachments. The robot periodically moved out of the participant's view, and while the participant could not see the robot, they could overhear the sounds accompanying the change of attachments. At a post-session debriefing, the participant inquired about the meaning of the sounds and was surprised to learn that they were not intentional. It transpired that the participant thought they were expected to figure out which events produced the sounds and how those events affected the robot's behavior.

Therefore, even if the explicit focus of a study is on concrete tasks and technologies with few or no contextual cues provided, people still tend to develop a holistic picture of their situation. While such holistic pictures may play a key role in how participants frame the tasks and technologies they encounter, they do not easily lend themselves to empirical analyses.

3.3 The "Objective/Subjective" Gap

Researchers may have a well-developed, detailed vision of a constructed context and implement it by creating an environment that conveys the vision accurately. However, there is no guarantee that the participants will correctly perceive the environment and understand the vision as intended. For various reasons, such as cultural differences, participants may fail to utilize the contextual cues provided to them and, as a result, develop an understanding of the context, not consistent with the original vision.

The "objective/subjective" gap is likely to be a more challenging issue in shorter-term studies, such as field testing, short-term enactments, and controlled experiments. In "true natural" studies, trial deployments, and long-term enactments, the gap can be expected to be less pronounced because participants have more time to test and correct their subjective interpretations. In design fiction, the larger context can be explicitly conveyed by directly describing it using various media.

In general, it is probably safe to say that the "objective/subjective" gap is ubiquitous and potentially affects the results of most controlled studies (even if to different degrees). Therefore, systematic accounts of how study participants actually perceive particular contexts are necessary for conducting rigorous comparative analyses of different studies. However, in current research, such accounts are often missing. While valuable and relevant insights (e.g., based on interview data) may be provided, they are not presented in a standard way that allows for systematic comparison across different studies. At the same time, popular standardized measurement instruments, such as Godspeed [26] and RoSAS [27], aim to measure general, rather than context-specific, subjective experiences.

3.4 Two-Tiered Contexts

A distinct feature of constructed settings is that they consist of two contextual layers. When taking part in a study, the participants, on the one hand, are completing study tasks according to the make-believe logic of the constructed setting and, on the other hand, are engaged in "real-life" activities surrounding the tasks. The activities may include, for instance, making the decision to take part in a study, understanding study instructions, learning the setting, and forming a relationship with the researchers and other people in the setting.

The two-tiered nature of contexts in constructed study settings has significant methodological implications. Addressing validity issues in such studies can be complicated by the potential dependence of the phenomena under investigation on both the "inner," make-believe context of the study tasks and the "outer" context of the study as a "real-life event." For a study to produce valid results, participants' engagement is required, which can only be achieved if they willingly suspend their disbelief regarding the technology and the context of its use [28]. As demonstrated by existing research, suspension of disbelief is not impossible, but it does not happen by itself. In particular, even though "outer" contexts do not impose strict constraints on the types of embedded "inner" contexts, there should be basic consistency between the two contexts.

4 Key Topics for Further Analysis

This section summarizes the central points discussed above and identifies key context management topics that need further exploration to adequately address validity issues in proactive social robotics research.

First, a precondition for successfully dealing with the challenges associated with context management in controlled studies is acknowledging that these challenges are real. The overarching context in which the study tasks are situated cannot be simply ignored. Although participants may be exposed only to specific tasks without a backstory or explanation of roles and responsibilities, the (invisible) context may still shape the results. Therefore, the research methodology in social robotics should *explicitly and systematically* embrace context as a key analytical construct.

Second, it is important to differentiate between the objectively existing material and social structure of a study setting and its subjective perception and interpretation by participants. Even if detailed and consistent contextual cues conveying the structure are provided, one cannot be certain they will be interpreted as intended. Therefore, it is essential to *empirically analyze how participants understand the context* rather than assume alignment with researchers' expectations.

Third, as opposed to studies conducted in natural settings, studies in constructed settings comprise both a fictional "inner" context, which is intrinsic to the study tasks, and an extrinsic "outer" context, which corresponds to the real-life framing of the study (including, e.g., participants' own reason for performing the study tasks). To achieve immersion into the intrinsic context, a "willing suspension of disbelief" is required, which may necessitate employing special tactics by the researchers [28]. Context management, in such cases, should ensure that the constructed setting constitutes an engaging "fictional activity" space, and that the study is designed so that there is *consistency between the "inner" and the "outer" contextual layers.*

Fourth, context management concepts and strategies should be developed with an understanding that *contexts are dynamic*; they change over time as interactions within the setting unfold. For the discussion in this paper, of special interest are the context dynamics that result from transforming participants' perspective on technology throughout the course of a study. In particular, in studies exploring innovative technological solutions, participants are likely to encounter robotic artifacts or applications that are novel to them. The novelty effect, a persistent phenomenon in human-robot interactions [29], can be expected to strongly influence initial interactions in the study setting. Different types of dynamics can be investigated depending on the study's time span and the expected level of participant engagement with technology. The type of dynamic under investigation can depend, for instance, on whether the study focuses on casual encounters with robotic technologies in public spaces or on advanced human-robot collaborative activities.

The topics for further analysis discussed above highlight the need for a detailed and comprehensive understanding of the subjective representations that participants develop regarding the overall context of their study participation. This understanding is crucial for assessing how participants perceive study contexts, how accurate and complete the perceptions are, how "inner" and "outer" layers are integrated, and how the contexts evolve over time. Achieving these goals can be significantly facilitated by developing analytical tools that assess and manage participants' expectations [30] and serve as instruments to investigate not only general social attributes of robotic technologies (e.g., [26, 27]) but also the framing of specific technologies within particular study settings.

5   Conclusion

Social robotics research is predominantly future-oriented and proactive, with greater emphasis placed on prototyping and exploring potential solutions and contexts than on analyzing existing technologies and their real-life applications. It is inevitable, therefore, that many studies are conducted in artificial, specially constructed settings. This paper reflects on potential negative implications of using such settings for the validity of these studies, identifies issues that need to be addressed, and proposes strategies to tackle these challenges.

Employing constructed settings, as such, is not necessarily an obstacle to producing valuable empirical evidence and deep theoretical insights. There are numerous examples of top-quality, highly impactful social robotics studies conducted in such settings. However, as argued in this paper, artificial study environments do raise certain validity concerns that need to be addressed through appropriate context management.

The paper highlights several issues related to context management in controlled studies. It suggests that social robotics research can benefit from the researchers elaborating on and explicitly conveying their visions of how participants' tasks are embedded into larger study contexts. The paper also concludes that there is a need for empirically grounded assessments of how participants actually frame the technologies and tasks they encounter in a study.

Acknowledgments. This study was funded by The Swedish Research Council (grant 2021-05409). The author would like to thank Kevin Dalli and two anonymous reviewers for their helpful comments and suggestions.

Disclosure of Interests. The author has no competing interests to declare.

References

1. Breazeal, C.: Toward sociable robots. Robot. Auton. Syst. **42**, 167–175 (2003). https://doi.org/10.1016/S0921-8890(02)00373-1
2. Dautenhahn, K., Woods, S., Kaouri, C., Walters, M.L., Koay, K.L., Werry, I.: What is a robot companion - friend, assistant or butler? In: Proceedings of IROS 2005, pp. 1192–1197 (2005). https://doi.org/10.1109/IROS.2005.1545189
3. Kaptelinin, V., Kiselev, A., Loutfi, A., Hellström, T.: Robots in contexts: human-robot interaction as physically and socially embedded. In: Proceedings of ECCE 2017, pp. 203–204 (2017). https://doi.org/10.1145/3121283.3121424
4. Bartneck, C., Belpaeme, T., Eyssel, F., Kanda, T., Keijsers, M., Šabanović, S.: Human-Robot Interaction: an Introduction. Cambridge University Press, Cambridge, UK (2020)
5. Gillet, S., Vázquez, M., Andrist, S., Leite, I., Sebo, S.: Interaction-shaping robotics: robots that influence interactions between other agents. ACM THRI. **13**, 1–23 (2024). https://doi.org/10.1145/3643803
6. Forlizzi, J.: How robotic products become social products: an ethnographic study of cleaning in the home. In: Proceedings of HRI 2007, pp. 129–136 (2007). https://doi.org/10.1145/1228716.1228734
7. Sharp, H., Preece, J., Rogers, Y.: Interaction Design: Beyond Human-Computer Interaction. Wiley, Indianapolis, IN (2019)
8. Dereshev, D., Kirk, D., Matsumura, K., Maeda, T.: Long-term value of social robots through the eyes of expert users. In: Proceedings of CHI 2019, pp. 1–12 (2019). https://doi.org/10.1145/3290605.3300896
9. Leite, I., Martinho, C., Paiva, A.: Social robots for long-term interaction: a survey. Int. J. Soc. Rob. **5**, 291–308 (2013). https://doi.org/10.1007/s12369-013-0178-y
10. Carros, F., et al.: Care workers making use of robots: results of a three-month study on human-robot interaction within a care home. In: Proceedings of CHI 2022, pp. 1–15 (2022). https://doi.org/10.1145/3491102.3517435
11. Rodríguez-Domínguez, M.T., et al.: Interaction assessment of a social-care robot in day center patients with mild to moderate cognitive impairment: a pilot study. Int. J. Soc. Rob. **16**, 513–528 (2024). https://doi.org/10.1007/s12369-024-01106-4
12. Correia, F., Melo, F.S., Paiva, A.: When a robot is Your teammate. Top. Cogn. Sci. TOPICS **12634** (2022). https://doi.org/10.1111/tops.12634
13. Correia, F., Petisca, S., Alves-Oliveira, P., Ribeiro, T., Melo, F., Paiva, A.: Groups of humans and robots: understanding membership preferences and team formation. Rob. Sci. Syst. XIII (2017). https://doi.org/10.15607/RSS.2017.XIII.024
14. Odom, W., Zimmerman, J., Davidoff, S., Forlizzi, J., Dey, A.K., Lee, M.K.: A fieldwork of the future with user enactments. In: Proceedings of DIS 2012, pp. 338–347. ACM, New York, NY, USA (2012). https://doi.org/10.1145/2317956.2318008
15. Luria, M., Oden Choi, J., Karp, R.G., Zimmerman, J., Forlizzi, J.: Robotic futures: learning about personally-owned agents through performance. In: Proceedings of DIS 2020, pp. 165–177 (2020). https://doi.org/10.1145/3357236.3395488

16. Srinivasan, V., Takayama, L.: Help Me please: robot politeness strategies for soliciting help from humans. In: CHI Conference on Human Factors in Computing Systems, pp. 4945–4955 (2016). https://doi.org/10.1145/2858036.2858217
17. Cafaro, A., Ravenet, B., Ochs, M., Vilhjálmsson, H.H., Pelachaud, C.: The effects of interpersonal attitude of a group of agents on user's presence and proxemics behavior. ACM Trans. Interact. Intell. Syst. **6**, 1–33 (2016). https://doi.org/10.1145/2914796
18. Cao, J., Chen, N.: The influence of robots' fairness on humans' reward-punishment behaviors and trust in human-robot cooperative teams. Hum. Fact., 001872082211332 (2022). https://doi.org/10.1177/00187208221133272
19. Chang, W.-L., White, J.P., Park, J., Holm, A., Sabanovic, S.: The effect of group size on people's attitudes and cooperative behaviors toward robots in interactive gameplay. In: 2012 IEEE RO-MAN, pp. 845–850 (2012). https://doi.org/10.1109/ROMAN.2012.6343857
20. Sandoval, E.B., Brandstatter, J., Yalcin, U., Bartneck, C.: Robot likeability and reciprocity in human robot interaction: using ultimatum game to determinate reciprocal likeable robot strategies. Int. J. Soc. Rob. **13**, 851–862 (2021). https://doi.org/10.1007/s12369-020-00658-5
21. Cheon, E., Su, N.M.: Futuristic autobiographies: weaving participant narratives to elicit values around robots. In: Proceedings of HRI 2018, pp. 388–397. ACM, Chicago, IL, USA (2018). https://doi.org/10.1145/3171221.3171244
22. Danielsson, J., SäLjedal, K., Kaptelinin, V.: Employing futuristic autobiographies to envision emerging human-agent interactions: the case of intelligent companions for stress management. In: Proceedings of 33rd European Conference on Cognitive Ergonomics, pp. 1–7. ACM (2022). https://doi.org/10.1145/3552327.3552343
23. Campbell, D.T.: Factors relevant to the validity of experiments in social settings. Psychol. Bull. **54**, 297–312 (1957). https://doi.org/10.1037/h0040950
24. Hoffman, G., Zhao, X.: A primer for conducting experiments in human-robot interaction. ACM THRI. **10**, 1–31 (2021). https://doi.org/10.1145/3412374
25. Kaptelinin, V., Bensch, S., Hellström, T., Björnfot, P., Kumar, S.: The experience of humans' and robots' mutual (im)politeness in enacted service scenarios: an empirical study. https://arxiv.org/abs/2406.17641 (2024)
26. Bartneck, C., Kulić, D., Croft, E., Zoghbi, S.: Measurement instruments for the anthropomorphism, animacy, likeability, perceived intelligence, and perceived safety of robots. Int. J. Soc. Rob. **1**, 71–81 (2009). https://doi.org/10.1007/s12369-008-0001-3
27. Carpinella, C.M., Wyman, A.B., Perez, M.A., Stroessner, S.J.: The robotic social attributes scale (RoSAS): development and validation. In: Proceedings of HRI 2017, pp. 254–262. ACM (2017). https://doi.org/10.1145/2909824.3020208
28. Duffy, B.R., Zawieska, K.: Suspension of disbelief in social robotics. In: 2012 IEEE RO-MAN, pp. 484–489 (2012). https://doi.org/10.1109/ROMAN.2012.6343798
29. Smedegaard, C.V.: Reframing the role of novelty within social HRI: from noise to information. In: Proceedings of HRI 2019, pp. 411–420 (2019). https://doi.org/10.1109/HRI.2019.8673219
30. Rosén, J.: What did you expect?: A human-centered approach to investigating and reducing the social robot expectation gap. University of Skövde, Skövde (2023)

Design Considerations for Applications of Social Robots in the Stuttering Clinic

Priyank Avijeet[1]([✉]) [iD], Shruti Chandra[1] [iD], Smita Misra[2] [iD],
and Kerstin Dautenhahn[1] [iD]

[1] Department of Electrical and Computer Engineering, University of Waterloo,
Waterloo, ON, Canada
pavijeet@uwaterloo.ca
[2] Communication Studies, University of Waterloo, Waterloo, ON, Canada

Abstract. The use of social robots in clinical settings for stuttering therapy of preschoolers by Speech-Language Pathologists (SLPs), remains a relatively unexplored area. To enable Human-Robot Interaction (HRI) researchers to study this domain in the future, it is crucial first to identify the potential applications of social robots in clinical settings and understand the relevant considerations for these interactions. To explore this, we conducted interviews and shadowing sessions with SLPs working in stuttering clinics. Our data collection and analysis adapted a Charmaz/Constructivist Grounded Theory Methodology, ensuring our findings were based on the collected data. The results suggest practical applications along with interaction and communication design considerations for integrating social robots into speech therapy sessions for preschoolers who stutter. Key applications for social robots include engaging children through various games and providing a consistent speech model, among others. Essential properties of interaction design for sessions include being interactive, structured, and supervised by SLPs. Additionally, the robot's communication could involve slow, relaxed, personalized speech, and other techniques to support children's speech goals.

Keywords: Social Robots · Stuttering · Grounded Theory

1 Introduction

Recent studies have increasingly explored the application of Socially Assistive Robots (SARs) for therapeutic interventions (e.g. [1,13,25]). One notable use case for further research is in speech therapy sessions. By providing interactive and supportive environments in pediatric care and speech therapy, social robots can help facilitate social interactions, cognitive engagement, and emotional well-being, making therapy more effective and engaging for children [2,15,23]. Incorporating social robots into stuttering therapy has been suggested through their roles as engaging and motivational partners, consistent speech models, reinforcement for social and speech skills, homework partners, and transition aides for

O. Palinko et al. (Eds.): ICSR + AI 2024, LNAI 15562, pp. 54–67, 2025.
https://doi.org/10.1007/978-981-96-3519-1_6

different phases of treatment, such as establishment, transfer and maintenance [9]. However, research on the integration of social robots in stuttering clinics, specifically considering the child-robot interaction design aspects for the treatment of preschoolers, remains underexplored. Existing studies predominantly reflect the perspectives of HRI researchers and often lack the involvement of key stakeholders in the solution design phase [7,26,30].

Our research objective is **to explore the applications of social robots in stuttering clinics and propose design considerations for these applications intended for use by SLPs through a co-design approach.** The current research is an extension of our previous works [8,9,17], in which we initiated the research direction of exploring the feasibility of using social robots for stuttering interventions. Starting with our co-design approach, we conducted extensive research focused on stuttering interventions and explored opportunities for social robots in stuttering clinics [8]. We engaged in online interviews and focus groups with SLPs to assess the feasibility of leveraging social robots into stuttering therapy. In our latest study [9], we employed the Double Diamond Design Process Model [12] that comprises four phases: Discovery, Definition (see Fig. 1), Development and Delivery. Building on our prior work, our current research strengthens our understanding of the problem space and completes the first diamond phase of the research. This research focuses on discovering and defining (first diamond) potential considerations for developing applications on social robots to be used by SLPs in their clinic in the future (second diamond). In line with the co-design approach we followed in our prior work, the goal of the present work was to actively involve SLPs in the Definition phase (see Fig. 1). By incorporating insights from SLPs we aim to develop design considerations that will facilitate the adoption of our solutions in therapy practices.

For this study, we borrow data collection and analysis strategies from the Charmaz/Constructivist Grounded Theory Methodology (C-GTM) [10] to answer our research objective. The core processes—open coding, axial coding, and selective coding—allow researchers to develop a theory grounded in the data itself, making it very effective for developing explanatory conceptual theories in emerging academic fields [11]. C-GTM features several key aspects: it recognizes that knowledge is co-constructed by the researcher and participants rather than simply emerging from the data [11]. The researcher's background, perspectives, and interactions with participants and the data are integral to the theory development process. C-GTM involves iterative cycles of data gathering and analysis, with each cycle informing the next. Lastly, C-GTM encourages researchers to remain flexible and reflexive throughout the research process. C-GTM enabled us to contextually ground our results in the data primarily gathered through direct participant engagement, offering a flexible framework for identifying the practical applications of social robots rather than formulating an abstract theory.

The next section discusses related work in using social robots for speech and language interventions, including relevant work using Grounded Theory.

2   Related Work

Speech Therapy and SARs: Several studies have addressed the use of social robots in speech therapy, although without any mention of involving stakeholders in the solution design phase [7,26,30]. Applications involved mouth pose detection to guide speech exercises for Apraxia [7]. Another study, for children with cerebral palsy, showed significant improvements in phonological, morphosyntactical, and semantic aspects of speech [26]. Yoshikawa et al. [30] explored the use of teleoperated robots to reduce stuttering-related psychological symptoms, finding improvements in speech-related attitudes. Despite these promising results, the reliance on teleoperation posed practical challenges. In [28], with tasks designed by psycholinguists and conducted by speech therapists, SARs showed the potential to improve children's language skills through higher engagement. A recent study [21] involved the co-creation of three therapeutic educational games using the Kaspar robot, in collaboration with experienced Speech, Language, and Communication (SLC) experts. Their intervention with 20 children from special educational needs schools over 9 sessions showed significant improvements in SLC skills. However, to the best of our knowledge, no research has been done on design considerations for HRI researchers, particularly those based on observations and discussions with SLPs in preschool stuttering clinics. Our paper addresses this gap by offering practical design insights, providing a foundation for researchers to build upon in using social robots for preschooler stuttering therapy.

GT Analysis and SARs: GT has been used to explore practical aspects similar to our goal but in different domains such as deploying robot teleoperation in therapy [14] and to identify desired features of assistive robots for older adults [6]. Analysis of interview data from seven older adults revealed that while they recognized the benefits of assistive robots, stereotypes about aging embedded in robot design had impeded the robot's acceptance [22]. SARs improved engagement and care quality in aged-care facilities [19] although other studies with healthcare professionals noted limitations in providing comprehensive humanistic care [27]. In [20], GT was applied to analyze observational data of interactions in dementia care, involving patients, relatives, and care providers. Note, none of these works stress upon the reasoning behind their choice of a particular variation of GT (Glaser/Classic or Charmaz/Constructivist or Strauss, differences among variations summarised in [11]) over other variations and its impact on their research.

3   Methodology

We collected data over six stages (denoted as DC-1 through DC-6), with each stage informed by the preceding stage's data analysis, see Fig. 1.

Prior Work (DC-1): For establishing a base, in the first stage of our data collection (DC-1), we analyzed our previously published exploratory work regarding applications of social robots in speech therapy [8,9,17]. [17] summarized stuttering treatment approaches over the past two decades and [8] proposed higher-level conceptualizations for incorporating social robots in stuttering interventions. The proposals were to be refined through co-design and feedback from other stakeholders during empirical research [8]. In [9], the authors employed co-design methods, including surveys, individual expert interviews, and focus groups, to identify common challenges faced by speech-language pathologists and to explore how social robots could address these challenges. The study included four SLPs from the Institute of Stuttering Treatment and Research (ISTAR) in Canada. The participants, all female, age range [29 52] (M_{age} = 38.5, SD = 10.08). The SLPs had between 4 to 28 years of professional clinical experience with stuttering. All participants were registered with the Alberta College of Speech-Language Pathologists and Audiologists. None had previously interacted with robots. The questions posed to the SLPs focused on preschool and school-age children. The study suggested that social robots could be integrated into stuttering therapy, particularly serving as engaging and motivational partners, providing consistent speech models, reinforcing social and speech skills, acting as homework partners, and aiding in the transition through different treatment phases, such as establishment, transfer, and maintenance. DC-1 was conducted virtually due to the COVID-19 lockdown. This study builds on the foundational prior work through in-person data collection, informing the project's future direction to assess the practicality of the suggested solutions through shadowing.

Shadowing SLP-1 (DC-2): To obtain the specific details needed to address the gap in existing research and following convenience sampling, we decided to conduct in-person shadowing and interview sessions with the SLPs (referred to as SLP-1 and SLP-2, not involved in DC-1) at KidsAbility in Waterloo, Ontario, Canada, starting with shadowing sessions with SLP-1. Shadowing is a qualitative user experience research technique, where the researcher acts as an observer only and records their observations simultaneously without interfering with the ongoing activities [18]. Shadowing helps HRI researchers to learn about real-world contexts and understand user preferences. The goal was to be present in the therapy room during the sessions to gather practical insights into the available opportunities for addressing our research objective. The first and second authors participated in four shadowing sessions with SLP-1 and their clients and took detailed notes about their observations. The detailed notes from the shadowing sessions were analyzed to brainstorm potential applications of social robots in the stuttering sessions of preschoolers. This step, DC-2, was crucial in exposing us to a range of games that are used to engage the child in the session. The nature of games, cognitive levels of the games, interaction between participants in the game scenarios and outcomes expected from the child through the games were some key observations. The children shadowed were two boys and two girls, aged 3 and half years to 5 years with M_{age} = 4 and SD = 0.612. Three of the four children were non-severe stutterers with English as their first language. One child, who was a severe stutterer, had Ukrainian as their first language. Each session included the SLP, the child, and their family, which could consist of the mother, father, both parents or siblings. The shadowing session started with

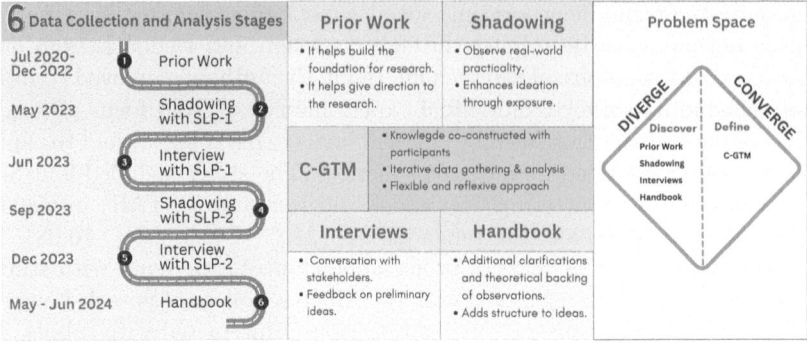

Fig. 1. Data Collection and Analysis Stages. The image highlights the first phase ("first diamond") of the Double Diamond Process Model [12], as applied in this study. This work is informed by prior research [8,9,17] and the Handbook on stuttering [16].

the SLP taking updates from the parents, and asking for the severity ratings[1] of the child's speech since their last visit, while the child was given a toy to play with. The severity rating refers to the assessment of the child's stuttering in their daily communication, rated by parents or SLPs. These ratings typically range from 0 (no stuttering) to 10 (extremely severe stuttering), helping to guide treatment decisions and track progress. The session included the SLP providing the child with toys and games to play with, considering the child's preferences. Each gameplay session lasted 5–10 min, with a total of 4–6 different games per session. The games also included participation from the SLP or the accompanying family members. The insights gained from the analysis at this stage informed the questions asked, brainstorm potential application scenarios, as well as note any concerns raised by the SLP after being exposed to a social robot, in a semi-structured interview with SLP-1 in the next stage.

Interview SLP-1 (DC-3): After the shadowing sessions, we developed initial ideas of the prospective applications of social robots in clinical settings. However, an in-person interview with the SLP provided us with the opportunity to gain their perspective on their challenges and usage of social robots in stuttering sessions along with their feedback on our initial ideas. The SLP was a female of 56 years with 29 years of clinical experience with stuttering, primarily with preschoolers. She was registered with CASLPO (College of Audiologists and Speech-Language Pathologists of Ontario) and had not interacted with a social robot before. The interview format was semi-structured, and the main interviewer was an HRI researcher and a postdoc (the second author). The first and fourth authors also participated in seeking clarifications and getting their queries addressed. Our queries were centred around our preliminary ideas of the use cases of a social robot in the stuttering therapy sessions. The interview aimed to explore the challenges faced by clinicians and their clients from the clinician's

---

[1] https://www.uts.edu.au/sites/default/files/2022-12/Child%20Stuttering %20Severity%20Chart%20v2%20-%20Dec%202022.pdf.

viewpoint. We asked five questions, each addressing different challenges, which were adapted from [9].

1. What are the most common challenges that you face with your clients?
2. What do you think are the major challenges that might prevent the children from making progress during a therapy session?
3. What major challenges do you encounter with parents throughout the entire therapy process?
4. What role do you think the robot could fit into at this moment, and do you believe it would be useful in some sessions with certain children?
5. What concerns would you have if you were to use social robots in therapy sessions?

Before asking the fourth question, we showcased a demonstration of the QT robot[2], highlighting its customizable speech controls for speed, pitch, and voice and showcasing various games developed in collaboration with the Learning Disabilities Society in Vancouver. We used the QT robot for our demonstration because it is customizable and non-threatening, designed for children with special needs education. Developers and therapists can adjust the QT robot's behaviour for effective therapy, and it has been used in related projects by the co-authors [3,4]. We also shared with the SLP experiences from previous studies by the co-authors on using the QT robot as an educational tool for students with learning disabilities, which demonstrated positive impacts on student engagement and reduced off-task behaviours [3,4]. The purpose of this demonstration was to illustrate the potential applications of the robot for children with disabilities and to gather feedback. This was followed by brainstorming with the SLPs, prompting additional questions about possible applications, and note any concerns they brought up. Toward the end of the interview, the SLP recommended that we also engage with another SLP at the same institution, who works with preschoolers who stutter, to gain their additional perspective on the topic. The audio data was converted to text using Vosk[3], an offline open-source speech recognition toolkit for Python. To verify the accuracy of the transcriptions, a researcher reviewed each recorded audio and cross-checked the transcriptions before conducting the analysis.

Shadowing SLP-2 (DC-4): In addition to following the recommendation of SLP-1, the goal of interviewing a second SLP was to compare experiences and perspectives, identify common patterns and look for any major variations in the codes of collected data that could lead to the refinement of emerging concepts. In stage four, we shadowed one client with SLP-2, following the same steps as in DC-2. This provided further insights into the practicalities and challenges faced in therapy sessions. The child in the shadowing session was a 4 years 9 months old boy with non-severe stuttering and English as his first language.

Interview SLP-2 (DC-5): Similar to DC-3, we conducted a semi-structured, forty-minute interview with SLP-2. The SLP was a female of 55 years with 28

---

[2] https://luxai.com.
[3] https://pypi.org/project/vosk/.

years of clinical experience with stuttering in both preschoolers and school-aged children. She was registered with CASLPO and had not interacted with a social robot before. The interviewer was the first author, and the format mirrored that of the interview with SLP-1.

Extant Text: Handbook for Clinical Speech Therapy (DC-6): In addition to the shadowing sessions and interviews, we planned to get a structure of what is expected in stuttering sessions by referencing Chapters 12–14 (related to the treatment of younger and older preschool children) of the handbook *Stuttering: An Integrated Approach to Its Nature and Treatment* [16]. GTM allows for various data types, including individual and focus group interviews, document collection, observations, and mixed methods [5]. Specifically, "Extant Texts" are mentioned as a valid data source [10], e.g. literature, public records, etc. In our project, we selected a handbook as a data source. The first author created notes on established clinical practices, focused on the treatment programs, and provided details on the SLP and caregivers' interactions with the child.

After each stage of data collection, the first author generated memos based on the initial coding of the data gathered at that stage. These memos were then discussed with the other authors to inform decisions about subsequent data collection, ensuring alignment with our research objectives. In the early stages, preliminary codes were derived through open coding, which involved tagging relevant portions of various data sources (e.g., prior publications, notes from shadowing, interview transcripts, and extant texts). Importantly, this process was ongoing throughout data collection, with new codes being constantly compared against existing ones. By the end of the iterative open coding phase, we had thirty-seven preliminary codes from the data collected in stages DC-1 through DC-6 (as illustrated in Fig. 2). In line with the co-construction concept of C-GTM, three of the authors, HRI researchers, engaged with the data using this flexible framework to reflexively interact with the codes, selectively dropping certain codes during the analysis process. Five codes were dropped during iterative data collection and analysis due to the current technical infeasibility of applications that would need precise real-time sensing and response of the robot in noisy environments, as identified through observations during shadowing sessions and discussions with SLPs during interviews (for details, see Subsect. 5.1). Following this, during the axial coding phase, we related these codes to each other, refining and differentiating them to identify key themes. This process resulted in the development of three core categories, each with two to five subcategories, as shown in Fig. 2. Each subcategory addressed related concepts, encompassing particular properties of designing the application of social robots in the stuttering clinic. In the final selective coding phase, we integrated and refined the core categories that capture our research objectives, developing our proposal for the applications of social robots in stuttering clinics and the design considerations for these applications.

4 Results

The core categories and subcategories along with key comments from the interviews with the SLPs are detailed below.

Core Category 1: Practical Applications of the Social Robot: The applications of the social robot encompass both its potential use cases and the scope of their application. For instance, the robot could act as a versatile toolbox, offering a variety of games and serving as a consistent speech model during interactions with children and parents (see Fig. 2). **SLP-1:** *"I think it (robot) can be used in very defined activities, it can be used as a language sample, possibly it can be used with parents. I suppose to model some speaking."* It could also demonstrate different levels of stuttering to help parents understand various severity ratings. Through shadowing and interviews, it became clear that the robot could not replace a therapist but rather shall serve as a complementary tool that supports the therapist's role.

Core Category 2: Interaction Design Considerations: The previously identified applications are now further explored to determine *how* the robot should interact with participants during stuttering sessions. Play-based interactions stand out as a central key concept here, by designing gameplay scenarios that are engaging, entertaining, interactive, involve turn-taking, reward-based, and flexible. We observed around 24 sets of different games used by the SLPs during the sessions we shadowed. Additionally, cognitive ease is important, meaning interactions should be structured and impose a low cognitive load on the children, as well as not burden the SLP. Stuttering therapy aspects should be supervised by the SLPs and aim to achieve specific speech goals, and encourage speech production (see Fig. 2). **SLP-2:** *"It's important to not only identify and make the sounds of animals but also to consider the variety of words we can use. Instead of just making the animal sound or naming the animal as a noun, we should talk about what the animal can do. For example, a horse can run, gallop, jump, and be ridden. You're looking at the variety of words in the English language, including nouns, verbs, adjectives, and locations. This approach can enhance vocabulary by following directions, such as putting the horse under the table or making it jump over the fence. It makes the interaction more engaging and educational, rather than simply labelling the animal and its sound."* Including game partners such as the SLPs and accompanying family members can encourage human-human connections. The gameplay should incorporate tangible props such as soft toys, plastic cars, trucks, blocks, and Lego sets to be used by the children or SLPs. The use of tablets and other screens should be minimized to engage children in the sessions, and instead, they should be used by the SLPs as part of gameplay with the robot. For instance, a tablet could feature a "spin the wheel" game displaying images of fruits, where the child must show the robot the correct fruit when the wheel stops. The robot can take on various roles in the sessions, such as a peer, friend, or co-therapist, depending on the design and goal of the application. It is important to consider that the robot's presence or absence in some sessions may cause distractions or reduced participation in the remainder of the session, and could even upset the child.

Category	Subcategory	Properties
Practical Applications of Social Robots	Toolbox	1) Variety of games, 2) Consistent speech model, 3) Demonstrate stuttering examples for parents, 4) Story-teller
	Complementary role	1) Complements therapist's role, not replaces it
Interaction Design Considerations	Play-based Interactions	1) Engaging, 2) Entertaining, 3) Interactive, 4) Turn-taking, 5) Rewarding, 6) Flexible
	Cognitive Case	1) Structured interaction, 2) Low cognitive load
	Stuttering therapy aspects	1) Supervised by SLPs, 2) Achieve speech goals, 3) Encourage speech production, 4) Facilitate human-human connection
	Tangible Objects	1) Include Physical items, 2) Avoid screens
	Interactions with Robots	1) Minimise distraction, 2) Varied robot roles
Communication Design Considerations	Speech content	1) Non-generic speech content, 2) Descriptive comments, 3) Short sentences, 4) Personalized conversation, 5) Fewer questions, 6) More comments, 7) Use repeated phrases/gestures
	Speech sound aspects	1) Non-robotic speech, 2) Slow and relaxed speech or prolonged and syllable-timed speech, 3) Enthusiastic/encouraging tone
	Cultural elements	1) Cultural speech content (e.g., language-specific greetings, object names), 2) Gestures, if the child is familiar
	Good listening	1) Non-verbal gestures to demonstrate good listening, 2) Not interrupting the child

Fig. 2. Categories, subcategories, and properties identified through GT Analysis.

Core Category 3: Communication Design Considerations: Through our data collection, particularly during shadowing sessions, we observed that both verbal and non-verbal communication play a crucial role in stuttering therapy sessions with preschoolers. We have established what a social robot could do in a stuttering session for preschoolers and how its interactions should be designed (see Fig. 2). Now, we need to address *how the robot should communicate* during these sessions. Communication design considerations include the content and sound of the speech, cultural elements, and good listening practices. The speech content should be non-generic and personalized, and short sentences should be used. The words used should describe gameplay scenarios. The robot's speech should primarily consist of comments rather than questions directed at the child. Repeating simple phrases and incorporating gestures can add more structure to the interactions. HRI researchers should avoid making the robot's speech sound robotic and instead use slow and relaxed or prolonged and syllable-timed speech [16] depending on the fluency shaping strategies [29] being considered. **SLP-1:** *"Changing how they (parents) speak to the child because we're asking them to slow the rate down or asking them to model shorter sentences and use turn-taking, good listening, using more comments. So you know you're trying to change your own speech, it's hard."* In the scenarios, the robot should have a positive and encouraging tone. Cultural elements could be incorporated, including culturally relevant speech content (e.g. names of food or animals, music, cultural practices, etc.) and greeting gestures, if the child is familiar with them through interactions at home, and importantly, if parents would like to introduce such cultural references. It is essential to demonstrate non-verbal gestures that indicate attentive listening and avoid interrupting when the child speaks.

5 Discussion

While in sociological research a 'theory' is the desired end result of using GT, our results are instead grounded design considerations and applications of social robots where we focus on identifying practical, actionable insights rather than abstract theoretical constructs. Note, that our findings are specifically limited to preschoolers who stutter.

5.1 Practical Applications of a Social Robot

While exploring the use of a social robot in a clinical setting for preschoolers who stutter, we faced challenges that made many initial ideas infeasible as we gathered more data. During shadowing sessions, we observed that therapy with preschoolers often involves playing various games, which creates significant background noise. For example, in a session, a "Zoo toy set" game, where the child, parents, and SLP took turns playing with various animal toys and toy playground slides, and a "Catch some bugs" game, involving the child and parents using a magnet to catch bugs on a puzzle-like board, were played. This noisy environment, combined with the preschoolers' incomplete sentence formation, makes it difficult, if not impossible, for robotic/software applications to work reliably and effectively when trying to detect and understand speech, including stuttered speech. Applying artificial intelligence tools is particularly challenging in such an environment where multiple individuals are talking, and the child's speech may not be well-formed. Additionally, upon referring to the handbook [16] we recognized the importance of reporting a child's stuttering severity ratings as accurately as possible since they are crucial decision-making factors for evaluating treatment progress and determining future therapy directions. Similarly, for a robot to accurately provide reinforcement and feedback, depending upon the speech skills of the children, is very challenging. Moreover, in interviews with the SLPs, we learned that using a robot to provide feedback, appreciation, or corrections based on the SLP's input via a tablet (to avoid difficulties in automatic speech and stuttering recognition) would in fact *increase* the SLP's workload and delay feedback, making the child-SLP interaction unnatural.

Despite these challenges, a social robot has several useful applications in speech therapy, enhancing the therapeutic process in various ways. It can serve as a versatile tool, offering a range of engaging games tailored to different speech therapy needs. The game scenarios, which can be very motivating and entertaining for the children, may provide SLPs with the opportunity to take more samples of the child's speech, so the robot should afford opportunities that encourage speech production from the preschoolers. Additionally, the robot provides a reliable model for consistent speech patterns, acting as a stable reference for clients for various fluency-shaping strategies [16, 29]. Stuttering therapy includes modifying the child's environment (home, school, community, and any other places they frequently spend time) to ensure verbal interactions involve a slow rate and pauses [16]. The robot can also demonstrate varying levels of stuttering, which may help parents understand and more accurately report the severity of their child's stuttering. The robot can be used in storytelling activities, making the practice of using speech both entertaining and educational for children.

5.2   Interaction Design Considerations

Shadowing and interview sessions with the two SLPs enabled us to compile an informed list of essential aspects for designing effective interactions with social robots. One crucial aspect was incorporating tangible objects, such as toy cars, building blocks, stickers, and other activities involving the child's gross motor skills. This approach not only allows the child to engage with real-world objects but also reduces screen time by avoiding tablet-based games. The interaction should be designed to be interactive, flexible, engaging and comforting, ensuring sustained interest and participation. Additionally, the sessions should be well-structured to provide clear guidance and instructions about the interactions, with SLPs supervising to ensure effectiveness. The design of activities using a social robot should be such that they reduce the workload of SLPs and **enable them to elicit utterances from the child** quickly and easily.

The application of the robot and the designed interaction should be such that they provide more opportunities for SLPs to collect speech samples from the child by including turn-taking activities to extend conversations. The interaction should also promote follow-ups and more extended conversation opportunities, facilitating human-human connections by involving other interaction partners, such as parents. The interaction with the robot should avoid adding stressors to the child's environment and be structured to support the smooth attainment of speech goals by the end of the sessions.

5.3   Communication Design Considerations

When integrating a social robot into speech therapy sessions, it is essential to align the robot's communication (verbal and non-verbal) style with the standard expectations set for SLPs and parents to maximize therapy outcomes. The robot can use slow and relaxed speech to aid in clarity and reduce pressure or can follow any specific fluency-shaping strategy [16, 29] for practice for the child. Demonstrating good listening skills by the robot through non-verbal gestures (backchannel signalling, e.g. through head nods [24]) can make the child feel heard and motivate them to speak more [16]. The robot's speech content should be specific and relevant to the context of the activity rather than generic, ensuring that interactions are not boring and vague. Additionally, the HRI researchers should strive for the robot to have natural and engaging speech, which can make the child feel more comfortable and increase participation. Moreover, efforts need to be made to avoid a robotic tone as it is the last thing that we expect the child to pick up from speech therapy. An encouraging and positive comments can boost the child's confidence and willingness to participate actively in the treatment [16]. Descriptive comments enhance the richness and educational value of the interaction for the child. Incorporating cultural elements familiar to the child can make communication more relatable and comforting, fostering a strong sense of connection. It is important to ensure that the child is exposed to these cultural aspects at home, allowing them to find comfort and familiarity in them. Short, clear sentences ensure that the child comprehends the instructions easily and does not add stressors to the child. Lastly, personalized conversations help build rapport, making the interaction more meaningful and tailored to the individual expectations of the child. For example, if the child had a birthday coming up then SLP started the conversation by talking about birthdays and more around the celebration of the event (DC-2).

5.4   Limitations and Future Work

For our study it was challenging to recruit a sufficiently large sample of preschool children who stutter, alongside obtaining parental and SLP consent to observe therapy sessions within a practical geographic proximity. Furthermore, the SLPs in this study conducted therapies exclusively in English, limiting the generalizability of the findings to bilingual or non-English-speaking populations. Moreover, the majority of the children observed were non-severe stutterers which could have limited the amount of extra information we extracted from later sessions and may reduce the information power of our study. However, we would like to note that the primary stakeholders for this stage of our project were the SLPs, and our focus was on the strategies and different kinds of interactive games that they included in their sessions. The findings of our study need to be tested in practice to determine their effectiveness in improving the therapy experience and outcomes for both SLPs and their clients. Also, since our study focused on preschoolers, the guidelines may not be applicable to older children, as speech therapy techniques vary across different age groups.

In our future work, we plan to prototype games and applications based on the established design considerations and gather feedback from SLPs. After completing the co-design process, we will conduct user studies involving preschoolers who stutter and SLPs integrating our solutions into their sessions. These evaluations will not only validate the findings of this study but also instil greater confidence in the continued exploration and refinement of these design considerations.

6   Conclusion

Exploring applications of social robots in critical and sensitive domains such as therapy, particularly those that involve young children, presents unique challenges. Involving stakeholders in the design process is crucial if we want future implementations to find its use in the field. Given the novel nature of the applied research explorations needed for this study, we adopted the concept of C-GTM to root our findings on the data that we encountered. The subtleties identified through this study go beyond finding the applications of social robots in a clinical setting. They go deeper into the kind of interactions and the communication style that must be considered when designing the applications.

Acknowledgments. This research was supported, in part, by funding from the Canada 150 Research Chairs Program. We extend our gratitude to KidsAbility and the two SLPs, Jean Macleod and Jill Clermont for facilitating the opportunity to shadow therapy sessions and being available for interviews.

References

1. Al-Nafjan, A., Alhakbani, N., Alabdulkareem, A.: Measuring engagement in robot-assisted therapy for Autistic children. Behav. Sci. **13**(8), 618 (2023)
2. Alabdulkareem, A., Alhakbani, N., Al-Nafjan, A.: A systematic review of research on robot-assisted therapy for children with autism. Sensors **22**(3), 944 (2022)
3. Azizi, N., Chandra, S., Gray, M., Fane, J., Sager, M., Dautenhahn, K.: User evaluation of social robots as a tool in one-to-one instructional settings for students with learning disabilities. In: Cavallo, F., et al. (eds.) ICSR 2022. LNCS, vol. 13818, pp. 146–159. Springer, Cham (2022). https://doi.org/10.1007/978-3-031-24670-8_14
4. Azizi, N., Chandra, S., Gray, M., Sager, M., Fane, J., Dautenhahn, K.: An initial investigation into the use of social robots within an existing educational program for students with learning disabilities. In: IEEE RO-MAN, pp. 1490–1497 (2022)
5. Belgrave, L.L., Seide, K.: Grounded Theory Methodology: Principles and Practices. In: Liamputtong, P. (ed.) Handbook of Research Methods in Health Social Sciences, pp. 299–316. Springer, Singapore (2019). https://doi.org/10.1007/978-981-10-5251-4_84
6. Betlej, A.: Designing robots for elderly from the perspective of potential end-users: a sociological approach. Int. J. Environ. Res. Public Health **19**(6), 3630 (2022)
7. Castillo, J.C., Alvarez-Fernandez, D., Alonso-Martin, F., Marques-Villarroya, S., Salichs, M.A.: Social robotics in therapy of apraxia of speech. J. Healthc. Eng. **2018**(1), 7075290 (2018)
8. Chandra, S., Gupta, G., Loucks, T., Dautenhahn, K.: Opportunities for social robots in the stuttering clinic: a review and proposed scenarios. Paladyn J. Behav. Robot. **13**(1), 23–44 (2022)
9. Chandra, S., Loucks, T., Castaneda, G.C., Dautenhahn, K.: Social robots in the stuttering clinic: a human-centred exploration with speech language pathologists. In: Cavallo, F., et al. (eds.) ICSR 2022. LNCS, vol. 13818, pp. 299–313. Springer, Cham (2022). https://doi.org/10.1007/978-3-031-24670-8_27
10. Charmaz, K.: Constructing Grounded Theory: A Practical Guide Through Qualitative Analysis. Sage, London (2006)
11. Cole, T., Gillies, M.: More than a bit of coding:(un-) Grounded (non-) Theory in HCI. In: CHI Conference on Human Factors in Computing Systems Extended Abstracts, pp. 1–11 (2022)
12. Design Council: The Double Diamond Design Process Model. https://www.designcouncil.org.uk/our-resources/framework-for-innovation/. Accessed 12 Sept 2024

13. Devittori, G., et al.: Unsupervised robot-assisted rehabilitation after stroke: feasibility, effect on therapy dose, and user experience. J. Neuroeng. Rehabil. **21**(1), 52 (2024)
14. Elbeleidy, S., Mott, T., Liu, D., Williams, T.: Practical considerations for deploying robot teleoperation in therapy and telehealth. In: 2022 31st IEEE RO-MAN, pp. 977–984. IEEE (2022)
15. Estévez, D., Terrón-López, M.J., Velasco-Quintana, P.J., Rodríguez-Jiménez, R.M., Álvarez-Manzano, V.: A case study of a robot-assisted speech therapy for children with language disorders. Sustainability **13**(5), 2771 (2021)
16. Guitar, B.: Stuttering: An Integrated Approach to Its Nature and Treatment, 6th edn. Lippincott Williams & Wilkins, Philadelphia (2013)
17. Gupta, G., Chandra, S., Dautenhahn, K., Loucks, T.: Stuttering treatment approaches from the past two decades: comprehensive survey and review. J. Student Res. **11**(2) (2022)
18. Interaction Design Foundation - IxDF: Shadowing in User Research - Do You See What They See? https://www.interaction-design.org/literature/article/shadowing-in-user-research-do-you-see-what-they-see. Accessed 23 June 2024
19. Khaksar, S.M.S., Khosla, R., Chu, M.T.: Socially assistive robots in service innovation context to improve aged-care quality: a grounded theory approach. In: 2015 7th IEEE CIS and IEEE RAM, pp. 161–166. IEEE (2015)
20. Krings, B.J., Weinberger, N.: Assistant without master? Some conceptual implications of assistive robotics in health care. Technologies **6**(1), 13 (2018)
21. Lakatos, G., et al.: A feasibility study of using Kaspar, a humanoid robot for speech and language therapy for children with learning disabilities. In: 2023 32nd IEEE RO-MAN, pp. 1233–1238. IEEE (2023)
22. Lee, H.R., Tan, H., Šabanović, S.: That robot is not for me: Addressing stereotypes of aging in assistive robot design. In: IEEE RO-MAN, pp. 312–317. IEEE (2016)
23. Logan, D.E., et al.: Social robots for hospitalized children. Pediatrics **144**(1) (2019)
24. Mavridis, N.: A review of verbal and non-verbal human-robot interactive communication. Robot. Auton. Syst. **63**, 22–35 (2015)
25. Rasouli, S., Gupta, G., Nilsen, E., Dautenhahn, K.: Potential applications of social robots in robot-assisted interventions for social anxiety. Int. J. Soc. Robot. **14**(5), 1–32 (2022)
26. Robles-Bykbaev, V., et al.: Robotic assistant for support in speech therapy for children with cerebral palsy. In: 2016 IEEE ROPEC, pp. 1–6. IEEE (2016)
27. Soljacic, F., Law, T., Chita-Tegmark, M., Scheutz, M.: Robots in healthcare as envisioned by care professionals. Intel. Serv. Robot. **17**, 1–17 (2024)
28. Spitale, M., Silleresi, S., Garzotto, F., Matarić, M.J.: Using socially assistive robots in speech-language therapy for children with language impairments. Int. J. Soc. Robot. **15**(9), 1525–1542 (2023)
29. Team Stamurai: Stuttering: 6 Fluency-Shaping Techniques (2021). https://www.stamurai.com/blog/stuttering-fluency-shaping-techniques/. Accessed 12 Sept 2024
30. Yoshikawa, Y., Kobayashi, H., Sakai, N., Ishiguro, H., Kumazaki, H.: Therapeutic potential of robots for people who stutter: a preliminary study. Front. Psych. **15**, 1298626 (2024)

Towards Knowledge-Based Utilization of Social Robotics in Renewing Welfare Services: Case Northern Finland

Elina Kerätär[1]([⊠]) [iD], Tarja Rautio[2], Satu Pekkala[3] [iD], Mikael Kojo[1],
Päivi Rasi-Heikkinen[3], Marjo Suhonen[3] [iD], and Susanna Rivinen[3] [iD]

[1] School of Northern Well-Being and Services, Future Healthcare Services, Lapland University
of Applied Sciences, Tietokatu 1, 94600 Kemi, Finland
elina.keratar@lapinamk.fi
[2] Centre for Research and Innovation, Focus Area for Digital Solutions, Oulu University of
Applied Sciences, Yliopistokatu 9, 90570 Oulu, Finland
[3] Faculty of Education and Faculty of Social Sciences, University of Lapland, Yliopistonkatu 8,
96300 Rovaniemi, Finland

Abstract. This paper focuses on the development and research activities that aim
to promote the knowledge-based utilization of robotics, social robotics included,
for the renewal of welfare services in Northern Finland. Long geographical distances and rapidly ageing population create specific challenges to the reachability and accessibility of services in Northern Finland. This paper discusses the
uptake of robotics in renewing welfare services through two ongoing development
projects implemented in Northern Finland. The two projects highlight the need to
1) model robotics development environments in the welfare, social and health sector; 2) build and strengthen networks of multi-professional and multidisciplinary
robotics experts for the benefit of welfare services in Northern Finland, 3) activate
the operating area and identify its support needs in the context of welfare services;
and 4) test robotics in selected development environments.

Keywords: Robotics · Welfare services · Collaboration · Development
environment

1 Introduction

This paper focuses on the development and research activities that aim to promote the
knowledge-based utilization of robotics, social robotics included, for the renewal of
welfare services in Northern Finland. The geographic area of Northern Finland is a
predominately rural, sparsely populated region [1]. Long geographical distances and
rapidly ageing population create specific challenges to the reachability and accessibility of services in Northern Finland [2]. In terms of, in particular, older people (65+)
living in Northern Finland, several vulnerability indicators have been identified in previous research, such as social isolation, financial insecurity, and a lack of access to services
[3]. With the use of robotics, it will be possible to alleviate the shortage of labour in
services for the older people, as it is difficult to find workers over long distances to
Northern Finland. Robots can be operated remotely as well [2].

O. Palinko et al. (Eds.): ICSR + AI 2024, LNAI 15562, pp. 68–73, 2025.
https://doi.org/10.1007/978-981-96-3519-1_7

The development and research activities presented and discussed in this paper address several timely problems and challenges in the region and the use of welfare services. *First*, the ageing of population and the shortage of labor for healthcare and social welfare personnel require an enhanced introduction of technology. The present situation of the social and healthcare sector and the rapid development of technologies have highlighted the need to develop robotics and AI-based solutions for supporting the region of services and for evaluating the customer and personnel level impacts. In addition to the renewal of technology, global challenges (e.g. COVID-19) have increased the development and introduction of new digital services, which have remained in use even after pandemics and thus increased the need for, for example, the need for service support and guidance for the use of digital services.

Digitalized services can place service users into unequal situations from the view-point of their well-being [4]. This pose challenges to knowledge-based management, for example when building and developing new kinds of services utilizing digital systems when promoting well-being and health [5]. In this context, the knowledge-based utilization of robotics means the development of the competence of employees and experts related to robotics. Knowledge-based management refers here the development work related to working methods and leadership with the help of accumulated know-how and knowledge about robotics. [4, 5] However, there is only a little research about knowledge-based management in the context of welfare management, and even less research especially focusing on digitalized welfare services, not to mention robotics. With the help of robotics, the safety, quality and operational efficiency of welfare services can be increased. Robots can be seen as enablers of change and renewal in working life [6].

Second, in the sparsely populated Northern Finland, the challenges related to the region and use of welfare services, the accessibility of welfare services as well as availability of social and healthcare professionals are in many ways unique and distinguishable from those further south. The unique challenges include long geographical distances to welfare services, family members, and other care providers. Coupled with the limited availability of transportation and adverse weather conditions, the challenges necessitate creative, future-oriented, and knowledge-based solutions for welfare service provision. Sustainable uptake and use of robotics and AI may be one of the enablers of solving the challenges. For example, robotic medication dispensing service has been shown to support older people's independent living at home and reduce the care providers' need to travel long distances to check and manage the medication [7].

Third, the support for the implementation and utilization of robotics is still insufficient, and service professionals in Northern Finland lack opportunities to try out the possibilities of robotics in collaboration with multidisciplinary experts. *Fourth*, there is a need to better understand and support service professionals' and clients' awareness and understanding of the affordances of robotics, as well as their competencies in interacting and working with social robots.

This paper discusses the uptake of robotics in renewing welfare services through two ongoing development projects implemented in Northern Finland. The first project is *Arctic RoboWelfare—A development environment for Lapland's well-being robotics (ARW),* funded by the European Regional Development Fund for the years 2023–2026.

The aim of the ARW -project is to strengthen the research-based utilization of robotics in the digital transformation of the Finnish Lapland region by renewing the operating models of welfare services. The project builds on collaboration between researchers and experts in social work and healthcare, administrative science, and educational sciences. The project is implemented by the Lapland University Consortium LUC, which includes the Lapland University of Applied Sciences (Lapland UAS) and University of Lapland [8]

The second project is *RoboSoteLab - Robotics and smart technology in social and healthcare (RSL),* co-funded by the European Union for the years 2024–2025, and funding is granted by the Council of Oulu Region. The purpose of the project is to establish capabilities and conditions for the emergence of new technological solutions, promote the adoption of novel technology, and facilitate companies in the application and testing of digital solutions in realistic social and healthcare testing and experimentation environments. The project involves creating a comprehensive robotics and smart technology lab at the Oulu University of Applied Sciences (OUA) and Educational Consortium OSAO (VET) for educational and technological advancement in Northern Ostrobothnia. It includes a development project for a regional co-development model and an investment project to establish a research, development, and innovation (RDI) environment, both utilizing robotics and smart technology [9].

The two projects highlight the need to 1) model robotics development environments in the welfare, social and health sector; 2) build and strengthen networks of multi-professional and multidisciplinary robotics experts for the benefit of welfare services in Northern Finland, 3) activate the operating area and identify its support needs in the context of welfare services; and 4) test robotics in selected development environments. Next, we will discuss these development activities that are realized within these two projects in more detail.

2 Modelling and Developing Robotics Development Environments in Welfare Sector

Lapland UAS (ARW) and Northern Ostrobothnia OUA (RSL) have several learning and development environments in the welfare sector. However, robotics has not yet been integrated into these environments, and there is no dedicated development environment for welfare services that facilitates robotics experimentation. For example, RSL project manages two distinct RDI (research, development, innovation) environments that are undergoing further development, Enabling Home and SmartCare Home. The Enabling Home is a constructed residential setting and invested robots and smart technologies are designed to support and enhance wellbeing, including robots and technology for personal cognitive, social, and physical assistance, as well as for professionals in home-based rehabilitation and as assistant therapists. The SmartCare Home is a service-oriented residential environment created to assist older people and solutions that support nursing work and procedures, such as lifts and transfers.

These projects aim to develop the operation of the learning and development environments in terms of robotics to serve better northern region welfare, social and healthcare organizations, solutions developers, professionals, students, and teachers in different fields. Both projects aim to gather information, especially about social and collaborative robotics, their utilization needs, operational methods, and possibilities. It also focuses on the expertise required by professionals and the ethical and economic aspects related to the adoption of these solutions in the context of welfare, social, and healthcare services.

3   Defining Robot Literacy and Testing Robots in Selected Practical Environments

ARW project premise and purpose are that as social robots have acquired roles in the region of welfare services, such as in the care of older people, i.e. people 65 or older, in order to fully benefit from robotics both professionals and customers are required to have *robot literacy*. The few existing definitions of robot literacy have focused on children's and young people's interaction with robots [10, 11, 15, 16]. Therefore, we set out to define the concept of robot literacy from the perspective of older people. First, we reviewed and evaluated existing key frameworks of media literacy and digital competence with respect to whether and how they could be applied to the skills needed from older people when interacting with robots. Based on the review, we defined robot literacy as including the following skill dimensions: 1) awareness of robots; 2) interaction with robots; 3) understanding and evaluation of the information provided by robots; 4) understanding the data security and privacy of robots; 5) programming of robots; 6) ethical reflection; and 7) providing and receiving social support [13].

The next steps of the ARW project will then include testing the concept of robot literacy among older people through experiments. The experiments will be designed so as to include professionals' and older people's interaction with robots (e.g. telepresence robots, social robots). Furthermore, we will design workshops for professionals and customers to share ideas about robots and create visions of their future. Through the ARW project experiments, we aim to gain insights into the robot literacies of both customers and professionals, as well as the effects of the experiments on the level of organization, professionals, and customers involved in the region and the use of welfare services. With this information, we will design a model of support for the uptake and use of robotics in welfare services.

In the RSL project, the usability, functionality, and reliability of acquired robotics and solutions are tested with different user groups in collaboration with both public and private service providers. The tests aim to develop operational models for cooperation, teaching, and service provision in the field. Robotics solutions are integrated into the RDI environment for their use. During the testing and piloting phase, solution developers, service providers, and citizens are invited to workshops for developing and testing operational methods. By testing and collecting feedback, suitable and usable technologies for the purpose are identified, and operational models are developed to support the emergence of new service and business models.

Information from the experiences is gathered in both projects. Through collecting and analyzing different kinds of data (e.g., video observations, interviews) during the experiments, we aim to gain insights into and support the competencies of experts, welfare professionals, and customers to utilize robots in the welfare, social and health care sector in a manner that promotes equality, accessibility, ethics, customer orientation, participation, and human agency.

4 Discussion

The demographic challenges in Northern Finland, characterized by an ageing population and long geographical distances, require innovative solutions to ensure the accessibility and quality of welfare services in the future. By developing and implementing robotic solutions through testing and by creating collaborative networks these projects aim to enhance independence and well-being of people of all ages as well as understanding the importance of robot literacy among both service providers and users.

Northern Finland's unique demographic characteristics require tailored approaches and specialized environments for the testing and development of robotic solutions to ensure effectiveness and user-friendliness. These projects highlight the need for such RDI environments, enabling real-world testing in workplaces and educational organizations in welfare, social and healthcare services. This is crucial to understanding the practical applications and limitations of robotic technologies in welfare practice.

The development of multidisciplinary networks is essential for the successful integration of robotics into welfare, social and healthcare services as both of these projects emphasize the importance of collaboration among researchers, service providers, educators, and the community. By building networks, the projects aim to foster a culture of innovation and continuous improvement in welfare services. Experts from both projects have networked with each other to promote common themes in Northern Finland. Agreed cooperation arrangements include defining the procurement process and implementing robotics. The experts from the projects will collaboratively produce various publications.

The findings from these projects have significant implications for the future of welfare services in Northern Finland and beyond. The successful implementation of robotic solutions can lead to more efficient and accessible welfare services and the development of new service models that leverage advanced technologies. In conclusion, the ARW and RSL projects represent a proactive approach to addressing the unique welfare service challenges in Northern Finland through the integration of robotics. As these projects progress, they will yield valuable insights and practical applications of robotics that can be replicated in other regions, ultimately contributing to the renewal of welfare services.

References

1. Dijkstra, L., Poelman, H.: Archive: Regional typologies overview. Eurostat (2018). https://bit.ly/3m2DxlB
2. Lindgren, I., Madsen, C.Ø., Hofmann, S., Melin, U.: Close encounters of the digital kind: a research agenda for the digitalization of public services. Gov. Inf. Q. **36**(3), 427–436 (2019). https://www.sciencedirect.com/science/article/pii/S0740624X1830385X
3. Begum, S.: Ageing and gender in the Nordic Arctic [Doctoral dissertation, University of Lapland]. Lauda (2019). http://urn.fi/URN:ISBN:978-952-337-104-0
4. Hicks, E.R.: Digital citizenship and health promotion programs: the power of knowing. Health Promot. Pract. **18**(1), 8 (2017). https://doi.org/10.1177/1524839916676263
5. Odone, A., Buttigieg, S., Ricciardi, W., Azzobardi-Muscat, N., Staines, A.: Public health digitalization in Europe. Eur. J. Pub. Health **29**(3), 28–35 (2019). https://doi.org/10.1093/eurpub/ckz161

6. Holappa, T., Rautio, A.: Hyvinvoinnin ja terveyden robotiikka – missä mennään? (2024). https://lapinamk.fi/blogiartikkeli/hyvinvoinnin-ja-terveyden-robotiikka-missa-mennaan/. Accessed 20 Feb 2025
7. Airola, E., Rasi, P.: Domestication of medication dispensing service and robot among older people in Finnish Lapland. Hum. Technol. **16**(2), 117–138 (2020)
8. Arctic RoboWelfare projects homepage. https://www.lapinamk.fi/blogs/Hyvinvoinnin-ja-terveyden-robotiikka-%E2%80%93-missa-mennaan/0q5cunco/52b494e0-fe2f-4123-b915-def88566a647. Accessed 05 Aug 2024
9. RoboSoteLab projects homepage. https://oamk.fi/en/projects/robotics-and-smart-technology-in-social-and-healthcare-robosotelab/. Accessed 05 Aug 2024
10. Suto, H.: Robot literacy. an approach for sharing society with intelligent robots. Int. J. Cyber Soc. Educ. **6**(2), 139144 (2013). https://doi.org/10.7903/ijcse.1057
11. Suto, H., Sakamoto, M.: Developing an education material for robot literacy. In: Yamamoto, S. (ed.) HIMI 2014. LNCS, vol. 8522, pp. 99–108. Springer, Cham (2014). https://doi.org/10.1007/978-3-319-07863-2_11
12. Rasi-Heikkinen, P.: Older People in a Digitalized Society: From Marginality to Agency. Emerald Publishing, Leeds (2022)
13. Rasi-Heikkinen, P., Rivinen, S., Ahtinen, A.: Older adults and robot literacy (2024, Manuscript submitted for publication)
14. Rasi-Heikkinen, P., Airola, E.: Ikäihmisten digitaalinen osaaminen ja sosiaaliset tukiverkostot eTerveyspalveluiden käyttäjinä [Older people's digital competences and social support networks as users of eHealth]. In: Korjonen-Kuusipuro, K., Rasi-Heikkinen, P., Vuojärvi, H., Pihlainen, K., Kärnä, E. (eds.) Ikääntyvät digiyhteiskunnassa. Elinikäisen oppimisen mahdollisuudet, pp. 99–123. Gaudeamus (2022)
15. Boraita, F., Henry, J., Collard, A.-S.: Developing a critical robot literacy for young people from conceptual metaphors analysis. In: 2020 IEEE Frontiers in Education Conference (FIE), pp. 1–7. IEEE (2020). https://doi.org/10.1109/FIE44824.2020.9273959
16. Zaranis, N.: Foreword. In: Kalogiannidou, A., Natsiou, G., Tsitouridou, M. (eds.) Robotics in Early Childhood Education: Developing a Framework for Classroom Activities, pp. xxiv–xxix. IGI Global (2021)

Interaction Matters When It Comes to Hand Disinfection Using Robots at Hospitals

Oskar Palinko[1]([✉]), Robert Wendlandt[2], Søren Udby[4], Franziska Uhing[3], Johannes H. Fog[1], Esben Hansen[4], Rasmus P. Junge[1], Daniel G. Holm[1], Mikkel Kipp[1], and Leon Bodenhagen[1]

[1] Maersk Mc-Kinney Moller Institute, University of Southern Denmark, Odense, Denmark
ospa@mmmi.sdu.dk
[2] University of Lübeck, Lübeck, Germany
[3] University of Applied Sciences Kiel, Kiel, Germany
[4] Odense University Hospital, Odense, Denmark

Abstract. Hand disinfection is one of the mainstays of infectious disease prevention, especially at hospitals. However, not everyone sanitizes their hands when entering healthcare institutions. Since the Covid pandemic there have been efforts to use mobile service robots to make it easier for people to disinfect their hands. Even though these robots do provide a benefit, most of them are not actively pursuing interaction with people. We looked at how adding interaction capabilities benefits the robots' performance. We compared a newly developed modular interactive mobile service robot, HanDiRob, with a mobile hand sanitizer robot which is less aware of and interactive with its environment. Our tests show that when the robot shows clear understanding of the presence of people and interacts with them, the hand sanitization compliance rate improves very significantly (more than 300%). However there is still much to do before rolling out interactive mobile robots on hospital corridors.

Keywords: Hand Disinfection · Mobile Service Robots · Compliance Improvement

1 Introduction

Worldwide outbreaks of infectious diseases are high on the list of potentially most catastrophic events for humanity. The Covid-19 pandemic exposed us to an existential crisis not seen in recent memory. People did not have access to vaccines and anti-viral treatments until almost one year after the first cases of Covid-19 were reported. During this period the only counter-measure to Covid that worked effectively was prevention. Prevention in the case of Covid-19 included social distancing, wearing face masks and using hand disinfection among others. Here we focus on hand sanitization which is a common measure for suppressing

O. Palinko et al. (Eds.): ICSR + AI 2024, LNAI 15512, pp. 74–85, 2025.
https://doi.org/10.1007/978-981-96-3519-1_8

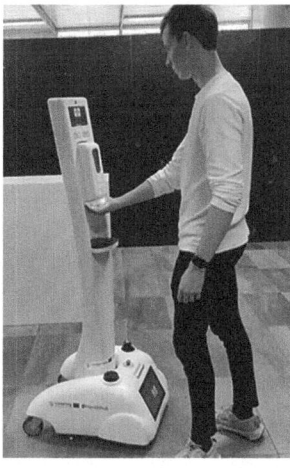

Fig. 1. HanDiRob at the hospital.

infectious diseases widely used at hospitals. However, even at hospitals, after the pandemic has subsided, hand sanitization compliance rates dropped, even though hand hygiene is still as important as before. To address this problem, scientists and engineers looked at technological solutions to motivate people to sanitize their hands. Some of them started using mobile service robots to do so. Convincing people to comply with hand sanitization requirements by technological means can be considered nudging. Some of these robots were not very interactive while others could detect and react to people in their vicinity. It is expected that a robot which displays more awareness of the people it is interacting with will be more successful to nudge them to use the disinfectant. In this paper we compare a less-interactive robot solution which was deployed at a hospital to a more interactive hand disinfection robot, developed as part of a scientific project, HanDiRob. It was expected that the more interactive robot which is able to perceive and react to its environment would be able to influence significantly more people to sanitize their hands. This was proven to be correct. In addition, we compared the two robot's performance to a baseline, which was the usage of a regular automatic hand disinfection device (Fig. 1).

2 Related Work

2.1 Service Robots

Service robots are autonomous devices which complete useful tasks in people's everyday environments and which are not connected to industrial applications [1]. They can take over tasks which are menial and dull for people to do themselves, freeing up their time for more fulfilling activities. These robots are becoming more widespread with recent advancements in big data, artificial intelligence, cloud services, etc. [2]. They received a further push in development with the onset of the Covid-19 pandemic and the need to keep physical distance between people [3,4]. Service robots have also been developed for transportation [5], food preparation and serving [6], health and elderly care [7,8], etc.

2.2 Robots in Hospitals

With collaborative robots being increasingly able to operate both safely and robustly in shared environments, robots have been applied to various tasks in hospitals. Besides specialized robots, e.g., DaVinci [9] surgical applications, which can be considered to be similar to industrial applications, numerous robots for internal logistics have been developed, e.g., transporting medicine or sterile instruments [10], or similar use case such as disinfection [11]. While the importance of robots adapting to the social context particularly in environments such as hospitals has been discussed widely in the literature (see e.g. [12]), most applications are building on top of existing industrial platforms and providing only very limited interaction capabilities.

Telepresence robots address another range of applications and can increase accessibility to carers [13] and have also gained increased attention in connection with the pandemic [14]. However, available telepresence robots only provide very limited autonomous capabilities and are merely relying on human users to interact via the robot.

2.3 Influencing Human Behavior Using Robots

Nudging is a process in which people are influenced to change their behavior with simple communication cues. Even though it can be used for negative goals as well, we will be focusing here on nudging for good. Robots can be used for such influence on human behavior. Mehenni et al. used a social robot to nudge students and found that robots and conversational agents were more efficient than a human [15]. Rodogno explored the ability to nudge with social robots as well as its ethical aspects [16]. In our study, we make a very practical use of nudging: we influence people using our robot's interaction capabilities to sanitize their hands more often.

2.4 Cleaning, Disinfection and Hand Disinfection Robots

One big field of application of service robots is for the purpose of cleaning and disinfection. Home cleaning robots have become a common sight on store shelves and in people's homes in the past decade [17], and now their larger counterparts are appearing in hospitals and in other public spaces as well. The Covid pandemic also brought another class of robots to prominence: disinfection robots, which are designed to eliminate unwanted germs. A popular subset of these robots are performing disinfection using UV light, but they can operate only in rooms when humans are not present as the UV light might be harmful to the human skin [18]. A different class of these robots uses aerosol disinfectants which are sprayed into the air [19]. Finally, robots are also used for hand disinfection in public spaces [20]. These robots work on the principle of nudging, where they try to influence people's disinfection habits in a non-obtrusive way [21].

3   Approach

In this paper, two hand disinfection robots will be compared. The first one was developed at a hospital and features a fully automatic behavior while the other has been developed as part of a scientific project and features multiple interaction modalities. As a baseline, we will compare the two robots' performance to a regular automatic hand sanitizer stand (RHS), see Fig. 3. The unit is minimally interactive, as it does detect the user's hand under it and dispenses hand disinfectant without physical contact. This device was located at one of the main entrances of the hospital facing outwards near a set of secondary entrance doors, which forced people to walk past it.

3.1   Robot Design

HanDiRob (HDR). HanDiRob is an interactive modular service robot designed for use at hospital entrances and corridors. It has a modular design, which means that the disinfection stand can decouple from the mobile base. Both parts can function autonomously from each other. This was done as a cost saving measure, so that one mobile base can service multiple disinfection stands. In the future, other payloads might be developed as well, which could latch on to the same base. The robot itself has a small footprint and can turn in a small area, thanks to its differential drive wheels. The small footprint sets HDR apart from other mobile service robots which are larger and thus might be challenged to navigate busy hospital corridors.

The disinfection stand was designed with interaction in mind. It has a fish-eye camera, microphone and touchscreen as inputs and speakers, the screen, lights and motion as outputs. The robot's movement and speech were found to be useful interaction tools in previous studies [22,23]. The camera detects people in the robot's vicinity and passes on the information to the speech system which greets them and reminds them to sanitize their hands. At the same time, the robot displays two simulated eyes on its screen which emulate looking at the person who is being addressed. This gaze interaction is achieved by calculating the person's angle compared to the robot and moving the pupils within the simulated eyes and the sclera on the screen towards the person. Additionally, the stand has a rotational degree of freedom in its base, so it can turn to face people when it detects them as well. For more technical details on this robot, see [24].

The HDR robot we tested at the hospital was a prototype unit which was brought to the hospital for the purpose of testing and then removed at the end of the day. An experimenter was always in its close proximity in a concealed way to make sure that it does not cause any damage but also not to affect the experiment at the same time.

Less Interactive Robot (LIR). The current system in regular daily operation at the hospital for dispensing hand sanitizer liquid consists of two MiR100 robots each with a manual hand sanitizer station mounted on a vertical board. These mobile robots are active from 6AM to 5PM every day and they each have a route

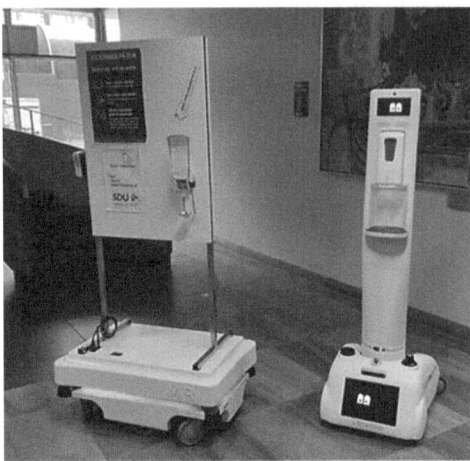

Fig. 2. Less interactive robot on left and HanDiRob on right.

covering approximately 200 m down the main hallway into the foyer or towards the hallway at the children's ward. They each have eight stops along their route, where they park for 8 min at a time. Every two minutes while parking an audio message is played asking people to please come closer and sanitize their hands. The robots use colourful lights to attract attention. When driving between stops, the robots' maximum speed is limited to 0.3 m/sec to enable people to walk along and use the hand sanitizer. At the Children's Ward the robot also played other audio files including 'funny sounds' to attract attention (Fig. 2).

3.2   Experimental Design

We tested the three devices (RHS, LIR and HDR) at the hospital. All tests were conducted in-the-wild, which means that people encountered the robots and device in their normal operating environments. The regular hand sanitizer device is a common sight at the hospital and at many other public spaces. The LIR robot was also a common sight at the hospital, as it was in operation there from the start of the Covid-19 pandemic. For people entering the hospital for the first time, however, the LIR would be a new sight. HDR was the newest addition, but it was also not so novel as we have been testing it at the hospital for a few hours every week for 3 months at that time. Again, for first time visitors, it would have been completely new. The RHS was tested at the entrance to the hospital, at its regular spot of operation. The two robots however were tested further away from the entrance, on the main corridor connecting different departments of this institution. This location was selected as it was a natural place of occurrence of the LIR and it had a high level of foot traffic, which allowed quick data collection. The robots' location was very similar (as to avoid differences in experimental conditions), but they were operated at different times to avoid influencing each

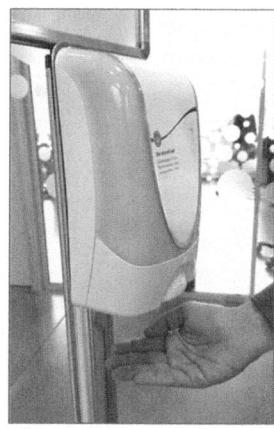

Fig. 3. Regular automatic hand sanitizer (RHS).

other's data. The experiments were conducted in the afternoon, at similar times for each device over two days.

The experimenters were observing people passing by the hand sanitizing devices. They tried to stay as inconspicuous as possible by sitting on the nearby corridor benches, looking as if waiting for someone. One of them noted down the number of passers by using and not using the given device. The second one operated the HRD robot when it was used, while the third and fourth experimenters were intercepting people after they used the devices to ask them if they could fill out a short anonymous questionnaire.

The LIR robot was operating autonomously, as described in Sect. 2. It was following a pre-programmed pattern of movement and speech. It was only reacting to people in its environment when somebody got in its way, by gently going around them. However, due to its low speed and frequent stops, it was very easy for people to use it. The HDR, however, was controlled in a Wizard-of-Oz manner, which meant that a concealed experimenter was controlling when and how the robot moved and when it offered hand sanitization using speech. This was done using a gamepad-style radio frequency remote controller. The experimenter was instructed to operate the robot in such a way to maximize the number of hand sanitizations. Practically, this meant that when people walked towards the robot, it would stop, turn towards them and say "Would you like to sanitize your hands?" The distance of people, when the robot started speaking, was dependent on their speed of walking, but it was mostly around 2–3 m away. This was found to produce the most sanitizations in previous pilot trials. At the same time the robot stayed out of people's way: it was not crossing their paths and was not following them. The experimenter operating the robot was following this same interaction procedure for each encountered person, throughout the experiment as much as humanly possible. He was also the most skilled team member for interaction-focused robot operation. The robot's eyes were not actively seeking

Table 1. Statements if subjective questionnaire administered to participants.

	Statement
S1	It reminded me to sanitize my hands.
S2	It motivated me to sanitize my hands.
S3	It caught my attention.
S4	It paid attention to me.
S5	It initiated interaction.
S6	The interaction was pleasant.

out to look at passers-by, but rather, they were centered around the middle of the display, with random saccadic movements and blinks, emulating human eye behavior.

Not all passers-by were counted in the experiment, but the same experimenter used the same criteria for each device to avoid interpersonal differences. Namely, we did not count people passing the robot at a distance of more than 2 m. This was deemed as a cutoff radius based on pilot testing, as we noticed that people passing at a greater distance might not even have noticed the robot and they could not easily hear it talking to them. We also did not count people whose hands were not empty, as they could not use the sanitizer. This should not have an influence on comparison of the three device types. We observed 153 people passing by RHS, 165 passing LIR and 106 passing HDR.

Subjective data was collected from people who used the different hand sanitization devices using a short questionnaire. However, not everyone using the device stopped for the interview. We gathered data from 10 interviewees for each of the inspected disinfection device. We also attempted to interview passers-by who did not sanitize their hands, but their willingness to stop and talk to us was so low that we had to focus our efforts only on people who completed disinfection. The six statements present in the questionnaire can be found in Table 1. We asked subjects to express their level of agreement with these statements on a 5-point Likert-scale ranging from 'completely disagree' to 'completely agree'.

4   Results

In this experiment we gathered objective (compliance rate) and subjective data (Likert-scaled answers). These are discussed in the sections below.

4.1   Compliance Rate

Compliance rate with hand disinfection requirements is defined as the percentage of people who use the hand sanitizer versus the total number of people passing the given device. For RHS out of 153 passers-by 20 people used it, for LIR out of 165 people 20 complied while for HDR out of 106 observed visitor 51 sanitized their hands. These results can be seen in Fig. 4. It can be noticed that HanDiRob had a much higher compliance rate than the two other methods which had

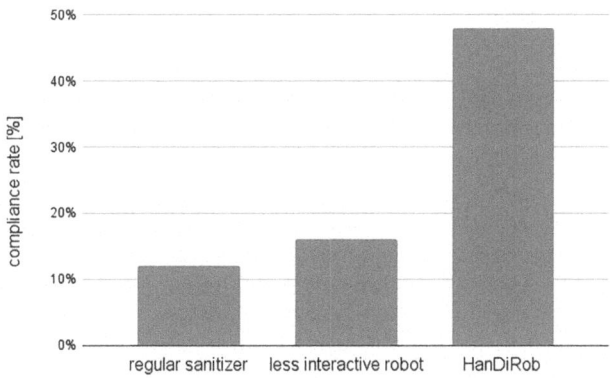

Fig. 4. Comparison of Regular, LIR and HDR compliance.

similar, lower success. The overall difference between the devices was found to be statistically significant using the Chi Square test $\chi^2(2, N = 424) = 52.5, p < .001$. Looking at pairwise comparisons with Bonferroni correction, RHS vs. LIR was not found to be significant, $\chi^2(1, N = 318) = .28, p = .595$, while both RHS and LIR were performing worse than HanDiRob with $\chi^2(1, N = 259) = 38.6, p < .001$ and $\chi^2(1, N = 271) = 34.7, p < .001$ respectively.

4.2   Questionnaire Results

As questionnaire results were gathered on the Likert-scale, which is not continuous, non-parametric statistical methods needed to be used to analyze them. We used the Kruskal-Wallis test to compare the ratings for the three devices for each statement. Significance was only found for statement S3 'It caught my attention' with $\chi^2(2, N = 30) = 17.9, p < .001$ and S6 'The interaction was pleasant' with $\chi^2(2, N = 30) = 6.85, p = .033$. For S3 a post-hoc Mann-Whitney test with Bonferroni correction showed significant difference between RHS and LIR ($p = 0.002$) as well as between RHS and HDR ($p < 0.001$) but not between LIR and HDR. For S6 the post-hoc Mann-Whitney test yielded similar significance with RHS vs. LIR ($p = 0.04$) and RHS vs. HDR ($p = 0.04$) being significant, but not LIR vs HDR. This means that subjects thought that the LIR and HDR were better at catching their attention compared to a regular hand sanitizer, but no such difference was noticed between the two robots. Similarly, participants thought that the two robots are more pleasant to interact with compared to the regular hand sanitizer, again without difference between the robots.

5   Discussion

5.1   Limitations

The comparisons between the regular sanitizer (RHS), less interactive robot (LIR) and HanDiRob (HDR) have a number of caveats, which will be discussed here. First, the regular sanitizer unit was used at the entrance of the hospital, while the two robots on the corridors. During testing at our university and the hospital we have observed that devices at entrance points receive higher compliance rates than devices used well inside buildings. This makes sense, as people tend to sanitize their hands when they are entering a building. Also, if someone is arriving at the hospital, by the time they reach the inside corridors, there will have been a number of disinfection units on one's way. Therefore it is expected that the two robots could have achieved an even higher compliance rate if they were located at the entrances, if we assume a linear rise in compliance, which inevitably needs to saturate once it reaches some higher value. We observed and used the two robots within the hospital building as the LIR had a preset path which did not intersect with entrance areas and which we did not want to change. Instead, we drove HanDiRob on similar paths. However, we wanted to observe the regular hand sanitizer at its original location, the entrance (Fig. 5).

HanDiRob might have had a couple of advantages over the LIR robot. Namely, HanDiRob was operated "optimally" in a Wizard-of-Oz manner by a human operator whose goal was to maximize compliance, while at the same time not disturbing passer-by greatly (e.g. not blocking their paths). On the other hand, LIR was running on a pre-programmed behavior, which only adapted to people to avoid collisions.

Another limitation is that compliance data was gathered manually relying on an experimenter's observations as well as on his judgement on the cutoff distance of passers-by. This issue is hard to resolve in in-the-wild studies and especially at hospitals, as they have a very strict privacy policy which prevented us from using cameras to track people. However our results are in line with the results of previous studies where other experimenters gathered similar data as well [22].

Finally, HDR might have achieved a great advantage over LIR in compliance also partially due to the novelty effect. Even though we were at the hospital every

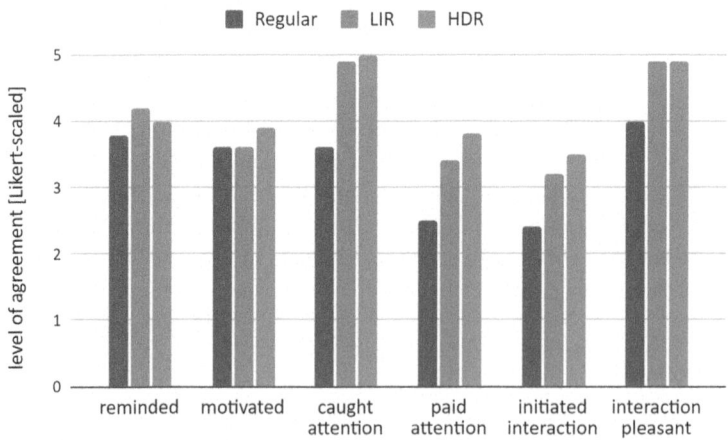

Fig. 5. Average levels of agreement with questionnaire statements given in Table 1.

week for a couple of hours for at least 3 months, the LIR was around for years, so people might have gotten used to it and it might not be as interesting for passers-by to interact with it as it was at the time of installation. Even though we realize these limitations of our experiment, we think that the significant effect of HDR would still be there even if these inconsistencies would have been eliminated. This seems to be confirmed at least partially by some of our earlier studies with simpler hand disinfection robots, where the effect was there even after 6 weeks of constant presence of the robot at the university.

5.2 Discussion of Results

The compliance results show a significant difference between the regular sanitizer and HanDiRob. Similar results have already been observed before thus they were somewhat expected [22]. On the other hand, the difference between the two robots was new. Limitations aside, we think that most of this difference derives from the fact that HanDiRob was much more interactive than LIR. It used multiple channels of communication: speech, movement, eye gaze and lights. With all these signals the robot became much more present and much more visible to passers-by. This presence then created the nudging effect which drew people in to use the robot. Regarding subjective results, we expected to see a difference between LIR and HDR because there was a large gap in compliance between them, see Fig. 4. However, due to the fact that we could only interview people who actually sanitized their hands with one or the other device, this could have created a bias: if someone already used the LIR (part of the 15%) then they probably have a good opinion about it as well. The experimenters found it virtually impossible to gather data from people who did not sanitize their hands. It is thought that this might have happened because of the social expectancy bias, i.e. because they did not do what they thought society might expect from them, they were not very keen on being interviewed about it. All interviews were completely optional and we didn't gather any personal information from participants. To make it easier for them to answer our questions, the experimenters offered to walk with them while asking the interview questions if they seemed to be in a hurry.

6 Conclusion and Future Work

In this paper we presented a study in which we compared an interactive hand sanitizer robot to a much less interactive one, primarily through compliance. We also used a regular non-robotic sanitizer as the baseline. We have found that the interactive robot outperforms the less interactive one by 320% in rate of usage. The difference compared to the regular hand sanitizer was 400%. It is thought that this difference mainly comes from speech, movement, gaze and light interaction HanDiRob delivers. In terms of subjective opinion measured on a Likert-scale, difference was found between RHS and HDR as well as between RHS and LIR but not between the two robots. An obvious recommendation would be that to achieve a strong nudging effect, interaction capabilities of the robot need to be quite developed. A less interactive robot will have a much harder case in convincing people to comply with it.

Even though in-the-wild studies will generate noisy data, we still see great value in testing our robots in their real life environments, as disinfection compliance could not be tested in a lab, due to the social expectancy effect.

In future experiments, it will be interesting to delve into the different interaction channels (speech, movement, light, gaze) on HanDiRob and see which of them has the strongest effect on compliance. It is also planned to conduct more long term, autonomous tests with HanDiRob to eliminate any novelty effect and make the platform even more robust.

Acknowledgement. This study was funded by the European Regional Development Fund under the HanDiRob project.

References

1. Schraft, R.D., Schmierer, G.: Service Robots. CRC Press, Broken (2000)
2. Wirtz, J., et al.: Brave new world: service robots in the frontline. J. Serv. Manage. **29** (2018)
3. Murphy, R.R., Gandudi, V.B.M., Adams, J.: Applications of robots for COVID-19 response. arXiv:2008.06976 (2020)
4. Shen, Y., et al.: Robots under COVID-19 pandemic: a comprehensive survey. IEEE Access **9**, 1590–1615 (2020)
5. Bogue, R.: Robots in a contagious world. Industr. Robot Int. J. Robot. Res. Appl. **47**, 642–673 (2020)
6. Romero, J., Lado, N.: Service robots and COVID-19: exploring perceptions of prevention efficacy at hotels in generation Z. Int. J. Contemp. Hosp. Manage. **33**, 4057–4078 (2021)
7. Holland, J., et al.: Service robots in the healthcare sector. Robotics **10**(1), 47 (2021)
8. Ozturkcan, S., Merdin-Uygur, E.: Humanoid service robots: the future of healthcare? J. Inf. Technol. Teach. Cases **12**, 163–169 (2021)
9. Leven, J., et al.: DaVinci Canvas: a telerobotic surgical system with integrated, robot-assisted, laparoscopic ultrasound capability. In: Duncan, J.S., Gerig, G. (eds.) MICCAI 2005. LNCS, vol. 3749, pp. 811–818. Springer, Heidelberg (2005). https://doi.org/10.1007/11566465_100
10. Fragapane, G., Hvolby, H.-H., Sgarbossa, F., Strandhagen, J.O.: Autonomous mobile robots in hospital logistics. In: Lalic, B., Majstorovic, V., Marjanovic, U., von Cieminski, G., Romero, D. (eds.) APMS 2020. IAICT, vol. 591, pp. 672–679. Springer, Cham (2020). https://doi.org/10.1007/978-3-030-57993-7_76
11. Sivakumar, K., Ramakrishnan, A., Selvamuthukumaran, D., Murugan, E.S., et al.: Design and fabrication of sanitizer sprinkler robot for COVID-19 hospitals. IOP Conf. Ser. Mater. Sci. Eng. **1059**, 012070 (2021)
12. Suresh, A., Taylor, A., Riek, L.D., Martinez, S.: Robot navigation in risky, crowded environments: understanding human preferences. arXiv e-prints (2023). https://doi.org/10.48550/arXiv.2303.08284

13. Moyle, W., Jones, C., Sung, B.: Telepresence robots: encouraging interactive communication between family carers and people with dementia. Australas. J. Ageing **39**(1), e127–e133 (2020)
14. Lociciro, A., Guillon, A., Bodet-Contentin, L.: A telepresence robot in the room of a COVID-19 patient can provide virtual family presence. Can. J. Anesth./J. Canadien d'anesthésie **68**(11), 1705–1706 (2021). https://doi.org/10.1007/s12630-021-02039-6
15. Ali Mehenni, H., Kobylyanskaya, S., Vasilescu, I., Devillers, L.: Nudges with conversational agents and social robots: a first experiment with children at a primary school. In: D'Haro, L.F., Callejas, Z., Nakamura, S. (eds.) Conversational Dialogue Systems for the Next Decade. LNEE, vol. 704, pp. 257–270. Springer, Singapore (2021). https://doi.org/10.1007/978-981-15-8395-7_19
16. Rodogno, R.: Nudging by social robots. In: Culturally Sustainable Social Robotics. IOS Press (2020)
17. Pandey, A., Kaushik, A., Jha, A.K., Kapse, G.: A technological survey on autonomous home cleaning robots'. Int. J. Sci. Res. Publ. **4**(4) (2014)
18. Ackerman, E.: Autonomous robots are helping kill coronavirus in hospitals. IEEE Spectr. **11** (2020)
19. Mohammed, M., Arif, I.S., Al-Zubaidi, S., Bahrain, S.H.K., Sairah, A., Eddy, Y., et al.: Design and development of spray disinfection system to combat coronavirus (COVID-19) using IoT based robotics technology. Revista Argentina de Cl'ınica Psicológica **29**(5) (2020)
20. Bana, P.R., Tsai, Y.-L., Knight, H.: SanitizerBot: a hand sanitizer service robot. In: ACM/IEEE International Conference on Human- Robot Interaction (2021)
21. Palinko, O., et al.: A robotic interface for motivating and educating proper hand sanitization using speech and gaze interaction. In: IEEE International Conference on Robot & Human Interactive Communication (2021). https://doi.org/10.1109/RO-MAN50785.2021.9515531
22. Bjorn, A., et al.: The impact of speech and movement on the interaction with a mobile hand disinfection robot. In: ACM/IEEE International Conference on Human-Robot Interaction (2023). https://doi.org/10.1145/3568294.3580109
23. Holm, D.G., Junge, R.P., Ostergaard, M., Bodenhagen, L., Palinko, O.: What will it take to help a stuck robot? Exploring signaling methods for a mobile robot. In: ACM/IEEE International Conference on Human- Robot Interaction (2022)
24. Palinko, O., Junge, R.P., Holm, D.G., Bodenhagen, L.: A mobile social hand disinfection robot for use in hospitals. In: Cavallo, F., et al. (eds.) ICSR 2022. LNCS, vol. 13818, pp. 348–358. Springer, Cham (2022). https://doi.org/10.1007/978-3-031-24670-8_31

A Multi-agent Framework for Upper Limb Mobility Through a Gamified Music-Driven System in Social Robotics

Gracia María Aguirre⬢, Jesús García-Martínez$^{(\boxtimes)}$⬢, José Carlos Castillo⬢, and Miguel Ángel Salichs⬢

RoboticsLab, University Carlos III of Madrid, Av. Universidad, 30, 28911 Leganés, Spain
jesusgar@ing.uc3m.es

Abstract. Social Robots pose an engaging alternative to support physical stimulation exercises, complementing the gamification of custom-designed activities. This paper presents the implementation of a music generation system integrated into a multi-agent framework aimed at stimulating upper limb movements while the user plays a ludic activity based on a musical game that includes different game modes like free mode, drum pad machine mode, memorizing the song, or following the song. The proposed system has been integrated into the software architecture of the Mini robot, which a game agent accompanies. Mini guides the activity to promote the user's physical activity. The game agent is responsible for tracking the user's hand movements using a hand detector to control the game. It facilitates some metrics for evaluating physical stimulation, such as the user's chosen playing hand, gameplay duration, hand movement frequency, and game scores. Our approach can complement conventional therapies by making use of social robotics.

Keywords: Serious Games · Social Robots · Human-robot Interaction · Music Generation · Gamification · Multi-agent Framework

1 Introduction

New technologies offer opportunities to complement conventional physical stimulation activities by incorporating social robots, creating more engaging and effective therapeutic practices [3]. Social robots have been used to perform entertainment-based activities, including physical and cognitive exercises, known as serious games [1]. Additionally, gamification, defined as the application of game design elements to capture users' attention, encourages more frequent and prolonged engagement [7], enabling passive physical and cognitive stimulation while enhancing user engagement and motivation.

Previous studies, such as Raigoso et al. [8], have demonstrated that social robots can improve physical rehabilitation motivation and acceptance among

© The Author(s), under exclusive license to Springer Nature Singapore Pte Ltd. 2025
O. Palinko et al. (Eds.): ICSR + AI 2024, LNAI 15562, pp. 86–92, 2025.
https://doi.org/10.1007/978-981-96-3519-1_9

patients and professionals. Similarly, Guillen et al. [6] evaluated the usability of a robotic system using serious games for upper limb rehabilitation in stroke patients in home environments, with positive results in terms of user satisfaction.

While significant progress has been made in leveraging social robots and serious games for rehabilitation, the integration of music as a main element of these systems remains largely unexplored. Music has been shown to provide substantial cognitive benefits, including improved memory and emotional regulation, which are crucial in rehabilitation contexts [5]. Additionally, music can enhance user engagement and motivation by creating a more enjoyable and emotionally stimulating environment [4]. Thus, we believe combining social robots, serious games, and music can potentially create a more holistic therapeutic approach that addresses physical rehabilitation and cognitive and emotional stimulation.

This work aims to fill this gap by proposing a Gamified Music-Driven System (GMS) and a serious game application integrated into a multi-agent framework to enhance upper limb mobility and cognitive stimulation. Unlike previous studies, our approach integrates three key elements: social robots, serious games, and music, aiming to facilitate physical mobility and cognitive stimulation through music-driven games. The multi-agent framework includes a social robot that assists and interacts with the user and a Game Agent (GA) responsible for detecting the user's hands and displaying the game. The system allows users to perform vertical, horizontal, and diagonal movements while providing metrics for long-term monitoring of user progression, complementing conventional therapies. Additionally, users can engage in cognitive stimulation through auditory memory games.

2   Materials

This section provides an overview of the physical components involved in our work: a social robot and a GA connected to a screen to display the game. The social robot Mini manages the actions of the GA, including starting and stopping the game and retrieving relevant information, such as user performance metrics. The GA, on the other hand, is responsible for detecting and tracking user hands' movements, rendering the game, and handling the visualisation and processing of all the components involved during the gameplay.

2.1   Social Robot Mini

Mini [9] is a desktop robotic platform initially designed to assist and perform cognitive stimulation activities with people with mild cognitive impairment. Its range of applications has been extended to people of all ages and abilities. Mini can show different emotions and expressions through eyes, cheeks, heartbeat, head, arms, and base movement. It can engage users through multi-modal communication, utilising verbal, visual and tactile cues.

Mini's software architecture comprises five modules (see Fig. 1) essential for monitoring and executing the robot's functions. The information from the environment and the user with whom it interacts is captured by the detectors and is processed by the *Perception Manager* (PM). Then, the information is sent to the *Human-Robot Interaction Manager* (HRIM), which generates multi-modal expressions to communicate with the user. The *Decision-Making System* (DMS) executes and controls the robot's activities, which are grouped under the *Skills* module. Sockets exchange information between Mini and the GA through the *Communication* module. The entire software architecture is implemented within the Robot Operating System (ROS).

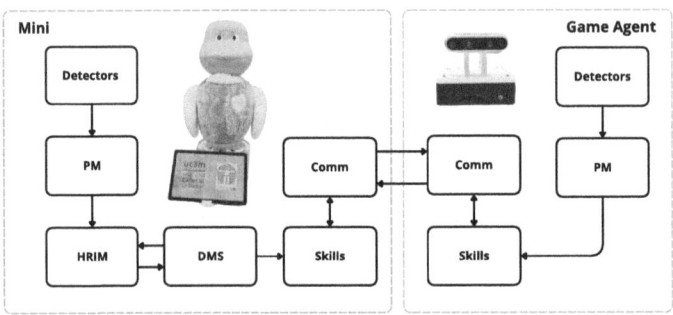

Fig. 1. Software architecture of Mini social robot and the GA.

2.2 Game Agent

The GA is the device responsible for managing the logic of the GMS. Like Mini, its software architecture is implemented in ROS. The GA consists of two hardware elements: an RGBD camera and an embedded computer that connects to a standard HDMI monitor. The GA software is divided into three modules (see Fig. 1): The *Perception Manager* (PM) is responsible for activating and deactivating the detector to extract the hand information required by the application. Finally, the *Skills* module deals with the different activities that the user can perform and includes the logic and visualisation of the games. The game configuration and user's metrics are exchanged with Mini through the *Communication* module.

3   Multi-agent Framework

This section describes the GMS design and discusses the flowchart of the multi-agent interaction shown in Fig. 2. The diagram is divided into two phases: initialization and gameplay. The orange colour boxes represent the different game phases, and the blue rhombus are the questions performed by the Mini robot to the user. Finally, green boxes represent the game configuration parameters introduced by the user.

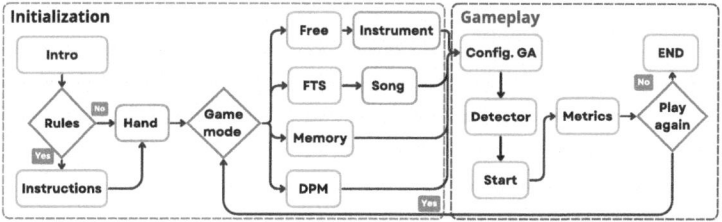

Fig. 2. Flowchart describing the multi-agent interaction.

3.1 Gamified Music-Driven System Design

The GMS has been designed to generate music using sound waves. We varied the waveforms using the sine and square waves to create different tones. Some harmonics were included to achieve a more complex sound. These harmonics allow the emulation of different instruments. The instruments created are the theremin, the flute, the piano and the violin. We use the *Pygame* open-source library[1] to generate and play the music. The GMS features an interface that displays the image captured by the GA camera in real-time on a screen, overlaying a 3×7 grid where each cell represents a different musical note. Interaction is achieved through the user's hand position in the image, tracked using a pre-trained Mediapipe model[2] allowing to detect gestures such as open or closed hands. The corresponding cell is selected using the centroid position of the user's hand as the reference. The GMS implementation incorporates several internal parameters of interest, such as selecting the hand used for interaction and choosing the desired instrument. Building upon the GMS, a serious game has been developed consisting of four distinct game modes, which will be detailed in the following subsections.

3.2 Initialization Phase

After Mini begins the interaction, the robot introduces the game and asks the user if they wish to review the rules, requesting confirmation through voice or the tablet. If the user agrees, Mini explains the rules aloud. After, the user selects their game preferences. For this purpose, the robot asks different questions. The first question is which hand the user wants to play with. The second question is the game mode, including the following: In (i) **Free mode**, Mini will ask the user which instrument to play, and the user can play freely as the system will render a different note. Depending on the hand status, open or close, the notes will sound or pause, respectively. (ii) **Follow the song (FTS)** mode, the user follows the illuminated cells on the screen to play a song. Mini will ask the user which song he wants to choose. The game starts with the first cell highlighted in yellow, indicating where to move the hand highlighted with a

---

[1] https://github.com/pygame/pygame.
[2] https://ai.google.dev/edge/mediapipe/solutions/vision/hand_landmarker.

green dot (see Fig. 3a). When the user's hand reaches the illuminated cell, the note is played, and the next cell lights up, allowing the user to play the song step by step without knowing the notes in advance. The cells illuminate randomly to make each interaction unique, where the user can perform different hand movements. (iii) The **Memory** mode generates a random pattern of musical notes played visually and audibly, which the user must memorise and repeat. Each time the user completes a correct pattern, a new one is added randomly, increasing the difficulty. (iv) **Drum Pad Machine (DPM)**: Similar to the free mode, this mode uses a grid where each cell corresponds to pre-recorded samples played from different audio tracks in MP3 format, such as hand claps, drums or cymbals. The user can create a continuous layer of music by moving their hand across the screen, anchoring different sounds. Once the user selects the game mode and the preferences, Mini establishes the game parameters and sends the configuration to the GA to start the game.

(a) Game interface for the FTS mode.   (b) The user plays with Mini and the AG in FTS mode.

Fig. 3. Use of the MGS in the multi-agent framework.

3.3   Gameplay Phase

Once the GA receives the game configuration from Mini, the hand detector is activated, and the game begins. Mini will remind the user that the activity can be stopped by touching the left shoulder. Figure 3b shows an example of the gaming setup where the user is playing "Follow the song" mode. During the activity, the GA sends real-time feedback on game statistics to Mini to notify about the game's progress, allowing Mini to indicate the game's progress and encourage the user verbally. Once the game ends, Mini will store several metrics to record the user's progress. Literature works centred on upper-limb rehabilitation therapies inspired the metrics selected [2]. We've used (i) the user's playing hand, (ii) the total duration, (iii) the frequency of hand movements and (iv) the game scores.

The user's playing hand identifies whether there is any preference or asymmetry in hand usage, providing information about motor dominance and possible weaknesses. The gameplay duration measures the user's physical endurance, while the frequency of hand movements reflects the level of physical activity in the upper extremities. Additionally, game scores directly indicate user cognitive skills, with higher scores suggesting improved memory since the user can memorize longer patterns. An example of a user playing FTS mode demonstrating the functioning of the multi-agent framework has been captured on video[3].

4 Conclusions

In this work, we offer a practical solution for promoting upper limb mobility and combine the benefits of music for cognitive stimulation by combining a gamified music-driven system in a multi-agent framework with a social robot. The proposed multi-agent framework integrates a social robot that assists users and a GA that detects hand movements and displays the game. The system enables users to perform various movements and provides metrics for long-term progress monitoring, complementing traditional therapies. Additionally, it offers cognitive stimulation through auditory memory games. We believe the recorded metrics could serve as valuable indicators for assessing physical and mental performance, though user trials will be needed to confirm their validity. This tool is designed to serve as a complementary resource for specialists, allowing for creating specific interventions and tracking user progress over time. In future user-centred studies, we aim to evaluate the tracking of their progress and validate our proposal.

Acknowledgments. The research leading to these results has received funding from the projects: Robots sociales para mitigar la soledad y el aislamiento en mayores (SOROLI), PID2021-123941OA-I00, funded by Agencia Estatal de Investigación (AEI), Spanish Ministerio de Ciencia e Innovación. Robots sociales para reducir la brecha digital de las personas mayores (SoRoGap), TED2021-132079B-I00, funded by Agencia Estatal de Investigación (AEI), Spanish Ministerio de Ciencia e Innovación. Mejora del nivel de madurez tecnológica del robot Mini (MeNiR), PDC2022-133518-I00, funded by MCIN/AEI/10 13039/501100011033 and the European Union NextGenerationEU/PRTR. Portable Social Robot with High Level of Engagement (PoSoRo) PID2022-140345OB-I00 funded by MCIN/AEI/10.13039/501100011033 and ERDF A way of making Europe.

Disclosure of Interests. The authors have no competing interests to declare that are relevant to the content of this article.

References

1. Bonnechère, B., Bonnechère, B.: Serious games in rehabilitation. In: Serious Games in Physical Rehabilitation, pp. 41–109. Springer, Cham (2018). https://doi.org/10.1007/978-3-319-66122-3_4
2. Burdea, G., Kim, N., Polistico, K., Kadaru, A., Roll, D., Grampurohit, N.: Novel integrative rehabilitation system for the upper extremity: design and usability evaluation. J. Rehabil. Assist. Technol. Eng. **8**, 20556683211012884 (2021)

---

[3] Video of a user playing "Follow the song" mode: https://youtu.be/cw_ugyixkFM.

3. Cifuentes, C.A., Pinto, M.J., Céspedes, N., Múnera, M.: Social robots in therapy and care. Curr. Robot Rep. **1**, 59–74 (2020)
4. Craig, D.G.: An overview of evidence-based support for the therapeutic use of music in occupational therapy. Occup. Therapy Health Care **22**(1), 73–95 (2008)
5. Custodio, N., Cano-Campos, M.: Effects of music on cognitive functions. Rev. Neuropsiquiatr. **80**(1), 60–69 (2017)
6. Guillén-Climent, S., et al.: A usability study in patients with stroke using merlin, a robotic system based on serious games for upper limb rehabilitation in the home setting. J. Neuroeng. Rehabil. **18**, 1–16 (2021)
7. Janssen, J., Verschuren, O., Renger, W.J., Ermers, J., Ketelaar, M., Van Ee, R.: Gamification in physical therapy: more than using games. Pediatr. Phys. Ther. **29**(1), 95–99 (2017)
8. Raigoso Amortegui, D.P.: Long-term evaluation of the effect of the integration of a social robot in Lokomat-assisted physical gait rehabilitation (2019)
9. Salichs, M.A., et al.: Mini: a new social robot for the elderly. Int. J. Soc. Robot. **12**, 1231–1249 (2020)

Posthuman Dance Performance Based on Embodied Mechanical Prosthetics: *LUDDITES*

Mengyun Liu$^{(\boxtimes)}$, Annisa Cinderakasih , and Naitian Zhang

The Bartlett School of Architecture, University College London, London, UK
{mengyun.liu.22,annisa.cinderakasih.22,naitian.zhang.22}@alumni.ucl.ac.uk

Abstract. This paper describes an innovative approach to creating a low-tech human-machine dance performance form. LUDDITES is a series of performance experiments based on an interdisciplinary research methodology that explores the potential of using the effects of movements in dance performance and live performance experiments to embody the operational mechanism of human and mechanical organ in human-machine interaction performance.

This performance experiment extends the choreographic object in choreography from the human body to a kind of symbiosis between the human and the machine, making the design of the mechanical structure a part of the artistic creation, with the goal of combining the performance creation methodology with the study of human-computer interaction.

This research develops new creative methods for post-human performance, exploring new creative tools and narrative frameworks for dance performances involving human-machine interaction. This includes human-centered analysis of movement trajectories, the creation of custom wearable choreographic prostheses designed according to human body mechanics, and explorations of choreographic methodologies.

Keywords: Performance · Embodiment · Choreography · Human Machine Interaction · Inter-corporeality

1 Introduction

In the late 20th century, Donna Haraway proposed a shift in the concept of the cyborg from a technological entity to a cultural metaphor, describing a future societal landscape deeply integrated with human and machine [1]. An increasing number of performance experiments are based on cyborgian experiences. These practices signify the arrival of a post-human performance era, significantly influencing creative work in the performance domain and sparking broader discussions about social and psychological impacts. This paper argues for a critical study of the cyborgian expansion of intelligent bodies through the lens of artistic human-machine interaction experiences. It explores the possibility of

O. Palinko et al. (Eds.): ICSR + AI 2024, LNAI 15562, pp. 93–99, 2025.
https://doi.org/10.1007/978-981-96-3519-1_10

realizing truly human-centered performance mechanisms in post-human performances, thereby investigating the complex performative opportunities emerging from human-machine interactions.

In "post-human" context enabled by technological advancements, new relationships between human bodies and technological constructs-such as robots and artificial intelligence-have emerged. This evolution provides artists with new opportunities to create performance works, resulting in experimental choreographies that explore human-machine interaction. As a result, the human body, enhanced by technological mediation, becomes an "amplified body" [2].

In response to this phenomenon, LUDDITES is a pioneering exploration of human-machine interaction in the performing arts. The project's goal is to integrate artistic and scientific research methods, utilizing motion analysis and live dance performances to explore and develop an innovative form of human-machine interactive post-human dance performance. The core of research is the concept of symbiotic relationships between humans and machines: how the internal mechanisms of the human body and mechanical prosthetics collaboratively form a symbiotic narrative experience of movement. Through wearable technology, mechanical prosthetics become sensory extensions of the human body, leading to a state where the human body drives the overall movement. This relationship merges the operational mechanisms of humans and prosthetics, establishing a new machine narrative system.

2   The Deconstruction of the Human Body in Posthuman Performance

In the practice of performance creation, the understanding of the human body has undergone several evolutions. From a phenomenological perspective, Maurice Merleau-Ponty's concept of inter-corporeality emphasizes the fundamental role of the body in perception and experience [3]. Hans-Thies Lehmann, proposed a new theatre aesthetic that categorised the emergence of non-dramatic text-centred theatre art practices as "postdramatic theatre". Lehmann points out that the process of postdramatic theatre is essentially a deconstruction of the body, not just an interaction between body and body, "transformation of the body from 'destiny' to controllable and selectable apparatus - a programmable techno-body" [4]. This transformation highlights the body's potential as a site of technological and artistic intervention, challenging conventional notions of identity and agency [5].

Andrew Broeckmann points out that the incorporation of machines into performance art creates new aesthetic possibilities and challenges the notion of the human as a singular, autonomous agent [6]. In this context, the body becomes part of a larger system where organic and mechanical components interact symbiotically. In posthuman performance, The performer's body no longer exists only as signifier, but becomes an independent subject pointing to its own being. Posthuman performance redefines the human body as a hybrid entity, merging organic and technological elements. This approach challenges traditional boundaries of identity and agency, positioning the body as an interface between human and machine.

From personal organoleptic experiences to social dynamics, several contemporary artists have explored the theme of the integration of the body and mechanism in their performance projects that combine art and technology. The *Eingeweide* project explores the intimate relationship between the body and mechanical prosthetics, emphasizing the reconfiguration of perception and identity within this integration [7]. Amy Laviers and Kate Ladenheim's prosthetic performance *Babyface* incorporates an interactive bodily experience that explores how mechanical prosthetics are gendered in appearance and function. In addition, it discusses the social and cultural motivations behind the design of female identities [8]. The *JIZAI ARMS* project extends this inquiry by exploring social interactions among multiple prosthetic wearers [9].

3   LUDDITES: The Symbiotic Dance of Mechanisms Between Humans and Machines

The LUDDITES project consists of choreographic experiments focused on the intricate dynamics of human-machine interactions in dance performance (see Fig. 1). The project delves into complex interdependence between organic and prosthetic bodies, exploring the tension between preserving human agency and the collaborative potential within mechanical movement systems [10]. The project explores how technological augmentation reshapes body movement by integrating wearable mechanical structures into the performers' bodies. This ongoing dialogue between the human and machine challenges traditional notions of bodily autonomy while opening new possibilities for choreographic innovation and expanding human-machine interaction in contemporary performance art.

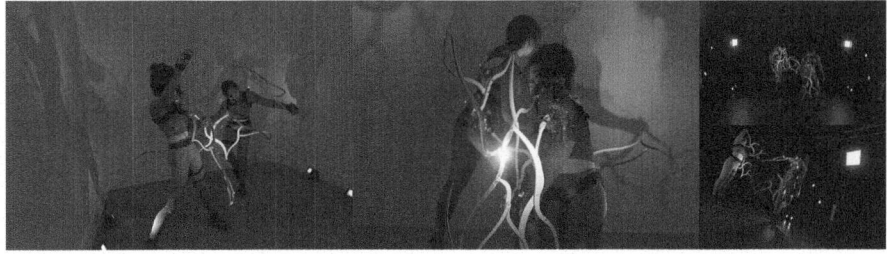

Fig. 1. Luddites Performance Experiments with two dancers wearing four mechanical structures. Image source: Luddites project documentation, 2023

3.1   Embodiment of Mechanical Organs

The LUDDITES project utilizes mechanical linkage structures and wearable layers as extensions of the performers' bodies, functioning beyond the concept of traditional prosthetics [10]. (see Fig. 2) These interconnected augmentation parts, as Haraway suggests, act as bodily extensions that amplify or direct motion [11]. The performers engage in a dynamic process of continuous interaction with their new bodily extension. The process includes 1) continuously monitoring and adjusting the limbs responding to their movements, 2) receiving immediate sensory and physical feedback, and 3) exploring the constraints of the prosthetic enhancements concerning their environment.

Fig. 2. Single Module Structure of Luddites attached to a performer.   Image source: Luddites project documentation, 2023

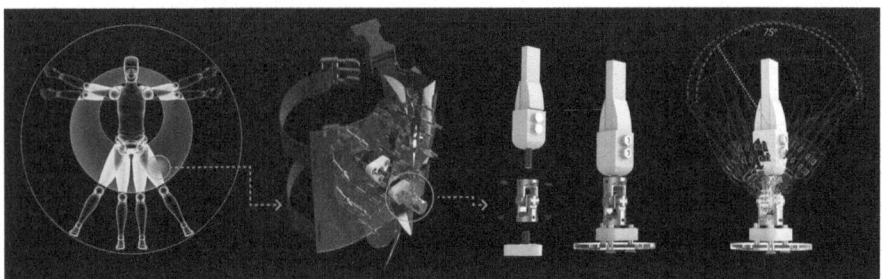

Fig. 3. Control of degrees of freedom. The closer to the body's centre, the more flexible the human joint is in its range of motion. We give different degrees of flexibility by adjusting the tightness of the screws that hold the joint in place. Image source: Luddites project documentation, 2023

The choreography is not pre-determined but evolves spontaneously through real-time feedback and negotiation between the performers' bodies and the mechanical structure. (see Fig. 3) This interaction transforms the body into a hybrid entity, merging organic and mechanical elements in a process known as

Mechanomorphism, where machines influence human characteristics. As humans control and modify the movements of these machines, a form of Anthropomorphism emerges, where the mechanical structures exhibit human-like behaviour [12]. Through this innovative approach, the project aims to foster a deeper understanding of how extended bodily media can reshape human movement and interaction, contributing to the broader discourse on integrating technology and the human body in performance art.

3.2 Choreographic Objects in a Social Context

In terms of social experimentation, we explored two directions. Initially, we designed connecting joints between mechanical prostheses to create connections between different individuals. This connection metaphorically represents a social network system, resulting in interconnected changes in the movement patterns of multiple dancers wearing prosthetics. At this stage, we did not introduce the concept of the audience, focusing instead on how this form of human-machine interaction affects the internal psychological state of the prosthetic wearers themselves. (see Fig. 4) Feedback from the dancers highlighted a psychological dynamic of social negotiation. Both dancers involved in the experiment expressed a desire to influence each other's movements during the performance, attempting to guide the other towards movements they imagined. These interactions reflect negotiations in choreography. The wearing of the mechanical prosthetics reconstructed a new principle of movements: the dancers could not be too close but still required each other's support, not controlling one another but respecting each other's unique bodily expression and movement direction.

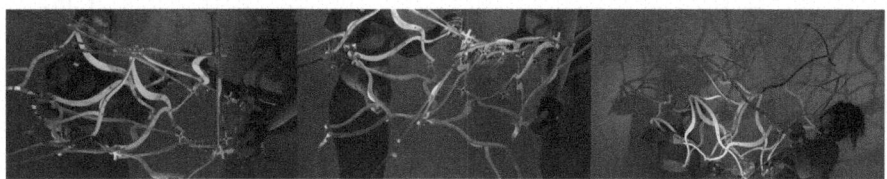

Fig. 4. An Live Performance Experiment with 4 Single Module Structures construct in The Complex Moudule, 2023.

To further explore the social potential of this performance format, we conducted spontaneous public performances at various locations in the Hackney Wick area of London. Approximately 70 random passersby became the audience during one hour of improvisational dance. (see Fig. 5)

The fingdings of the performance experiment showed that approximately 40% of the audience displayed a willingness to actively explore interactivity. They associated objects in the space with the dancers' movements and reflected on the connections and meanings, suggesting that the venue itself provided a different narrative context to the performance. Another portion of the audience

Fig. 5. An experiment with live performance in public space, dancer Xixi Xiao wears a single moudule of structure and interacts with natural elements on the side of the road, Hackney, London, 2023.

kept their distance, as the dancers did not actively engage with them, and the fragile appearance of the prosthetics contributed to this hesitation. From the audience's perspective, merely watching the dancers' movements gradually led to a loss of attention because the observation did not connect to their own bodily sensations. The audience generally expressed a desire to eliminate this sense of distance, believing that the prosthetics, beyond interacting with the dancers, had the potential to serve as a medium for interacting with the audience. A small subset of the audience even expressed interest in becoming wearers of the prosthetics themselves.

Given that achieving smooth bodily movement with the prosthetics requires adapting to their mechanical capabilities and responding accordingly, we assessed that the wearer must have the ability to follow specific movement mechanisms without compromising the structure. Therefore, we initially selected dancers as the wearers in these performance experiments. To enhance the applicability of future research, we suggest further developing the participatory nature of the performance by establishing interaction mechanisms between prosthetics and the audience, as well as among the audience themselves, enabling the audience's own bodies to serve as wearable carriers interacting with the prosthetics.

4   Conclusion

As an introductory exploration, LUDDITES provides an innovative investigation into human-machine interaction. It embodies not only the expansion of physical movement capabilities enabled by mechanical prosthetics but also a fundamental shift in the logic of action. The choreography logic presented in the LUDDITES performance experiment positions the human body as the core driving force. It realizes adaptive movement of the body to mechanical organs, thus altering the subjective experience of the perceiving body as a narrative medium in the performance context.

Emerging technologies are continually advancing, and the era of posthuman performance has begun. Wearable mechanical devices and other human-machine interaction technologies will continue to influence and drive creators to develop novel performance forms. An interdisciplinary research approach that integrates art and technology assists creators and performers in expanding narrative experiences. In the posthuman condition, performance experiments that incorporate technological media must account for human subjective experience, maintaining a human-centered philosophy to mitigate the negative effects of technology. At the same time, a sensitivity to technological developments is essential to achieve a performative turn in the field.

Acknowledgments. The LUDDITES performance experiments were designed, created, and implemented by Mengyun Liu, Annisa Cinderakasih, and Naitian Zhang. The design was supervised by Jonathan Tyrrell and Parker Heyl, with choreography supervised by Alexander Whitley, conducted at The Bartlett School of Architecture, University College London. The LUDDITES series of performance experiments was choreographed and performed by dancer Xixi Xiao, with the first live performance performed by dancer Natsume Ono.

References

1. Haraway, D.J.: Simians, Cyborgs, and Women: The Reinvention of Nature. Routledge, New York (1991)
2. Stelarc: from psycho-body to cyber-systems: images as post-human entities. In: Penny, S. (ed.) Electronic Culture: Technology and Visual Representation, pp. 254–266. Aperture, New York (1996)
3. Merleau-Ponty, M., Smith, C.: Phenomenology of Perception, vol. 26. Routledge, London (1962)
4. Lehmann, H.T.: Postdramatisches Theater. Verlag der Autoren, Frankfurt a. M. (1999)
5. Liu, M.: Staging of techno-embodied performer: human-machine cooperative programmable theatre. Unpublished MArch dissertation, University College London, London, UK (2023)
6. Broeckmann, A.: Body Machine. In: Broeckmann, A. (ed.) Machine Art in the Twentieth Century, pp. 167–220. The MIT Press, Cambridge (2017)
7. Donnarumma, M.: Eingeweide. 7 Configurations. https://7c.marcodonnarumma.com/eingeweide/. Accessed 26 Sept 2024
8. Ladenheim, K., LaViers, A.: Babyface: performance and installation art exploring the feminine ideal in gendered machines. Front. Robot. AI **8**, 576664 (2021)
9. Yamamura, N., et al.: Social digital cyborgs: the collaborative design process of JIZAI ARMS. In: Proceedings of the 2023 CHI Conference on Human Factors in Computing Systems (CHI 2023), Article 369, pp. 1–19. Association for Computing Machinery, New York (2023)
10. Luddites Homepage. https://fifteen2023.bartlettarchucl.com/dfpi-2023/luddites. Accessed 03 Aug 2024
11. Cinderakasih, A.P.: [Human-Machine] body modification towards entrainment experience: a study on embedded ethics. Unpublished MArch dissertation, University College London, London, UK (2023)
12. Caporael, L.: R: anthropomorphism and mechanomorphism: two faces of the human machine. Comput. Hum. Behav. **2**(3), 215–234 (1986)

Robots That Perform Norm-Based Reference Resolution

Mitchell Abrams[(⊠)] , Christopher Thierauf , and Matthias Scheutz

Tufts University, Medford, MA 02155, USA
mja284@georgetown.edu

Abstract. Embodied agents must perform *reference resolution* if they are to achieve sufficient language understanding with humans. But situated interaction introduces social norms, which are often overlooked yet critically need to be reasoned together with language to resolve references. To address this issue, we offer a novel normative-based reasoning approach to reference resolution and provide a proof-of-concept implementation in a cognitive robotic architecture with natural language human-robot interaction capabilities. We discuss reference resolution problems that require different levels of normative reasoning, demonstrate how a large language model, GPT-3, struggles to consistently identify target referents when normative reasoning is needed, provide a user study to show how humans perform norm-guided reference resolution, and demonstrate the successful operation of our proposed architecture on a fully autonomous assistive robot interacting with human instructors in natural language.

Keywords: Reference Resolution · Normative Reasoning · HRI

1 Introduction

In face-to-face communication, humans can leverage the shared situational context, and the *social norms* instantiated by these contexts, to interpret language and refer to entities in the environment [1]. Norms primarily act as a social grammar [3] and govern reference interpretation [1]. It would make sense, then, for a robot performing situated reference resolution to leverage *norms* to cover a wider range of realistic reference cases and underspecified language.

Consider a case where a human instructs a robot *"Hand me the mug."* and the robot responds *"OK."* with three mugs visibly sitting on a table—two used (dirty) and one clean—and the robot is about to serve coffee to a customer. The lack of a distinguishing linguistic modifier (e.g. *"Hand me the blue mug"*) seems to create ambiguity. But considering the context, the intended referent is clearly the clean mug because, *normatively*, a waiter would not serve ·coffee to a new customer in a dirty used mug. It is apparent that such an interpretation would be lost without integrating this extra-linguistic reasoning.

O. Palinko et al. (Eds.): ICSR + AI 2024, LNAI 15562, pp. 100–114, 2025.
https://doi.org/10.1007/978-981-96-3519-1_11

Norm identification and reasoning for reference resolution can be complex task, but it is more feasible for embodied systems than text-based natural language processing tools as they can recognize the physical environment, events, and situations, in addition to linguistic information. In this work, we present a computational architecture capable of making the above types of normative inferences during reference resolution to find intended references from underspecified human instructions. We will present different normative reasoning scenarios that highlight particular aspects of this challenge of using norms for determining referents, show that GPT-3 struggles with this task, and present a cognitive robotic architecture that can handle these types of references using integrated normative reasoning.

2   Related Works

Approaches to reference resolution in natural language processing typically rely on linguistic features [13]. But underspecified referring expressions often require additional context, including normative context, to be resolved; a speaker does not always carefully produce a unique identifier for a target reference, but often follows Gricean maxims [9] to signal to the listener that other pragmatic context is necessary for interpretation and utilize the listener's ability to disambiguate underspecified expressions.

Work in situated reference resolution, especially in human-robot interaction (HRI) settings, has incorporated gesture [17] and domain-specific knowledge [25]. Multi-modal approaches have also incorporated gesture [14,15], human eye gaze [11], and conversational context [6]. Still other reference resolution models have been implemented in a cognitive architecture [7,18,21,26] although they also tend to rely on linguistic constraints for the resolution process.

Large language models (LLMs), like GPT-3, offer a potential solution for addressing the challenges of situated reference resolution as they can capture higher-level contextual information and world knowledge and perform well on question-answering tasks and common-sense reasoning [5]. LLMs have been integrated into various aspects of robotics and robot dialogue interaction, including long-horizon task planning from natural language instructions [4], object disambiguation [12], command disambiguation [20], and household tidying tasks [28].

While LLMs can serve multiple functions for robot tasks and dialogue interactions, issues still arise. In Wu et al. [28], the LLM created user preference rules for a tidying task but also created rules that were either too specific or grouped objects together that should be distinguished for preferences and cultural normative value (e.g. grouping top and bottom drawers together). Aside from the reported drawbacks of LLMs in these works, LLMs also generally struggle with hallucination [10] and inconsistency [8], making it difficult to provide guarantees and control the output.

There is limited research that studies both *reference resolution* and *norms*. Malle et al. [16] have modeled norms computationally and revealed how complex norms can be; they are context-sensitive and contain varying levels of demand (deontic force). This was supported in their data collection approach, where participants generated an array of distinct norms across eight contexts. Abrams et al. [1] showed how norms govern reference interpretation in their human-subject study where participants performed a reference task with underspecified linguistic expressions and selected the target referent which was the normative option. Sarathy et al. [23] incorporated some normative reasoning in a reference resolution system, in tandem with a plausibility reasoner and an intent reasoner for anaphora resolution. A relevant strength of the normative reasoner is that it allows the system to ask if an action should or should not be performed on an object. However, this work only deals with anaphoric references and reasons with referents from the previous discourse, and thus does not include referents in the environment.

Social norms are difficult to define, as various definitions and distinctions have been discussed in other literature [3]. But we expand work from Malle et al., [16] and the deontic logic literature on norms [2,19], in viewing norms as *prescriptions* and *prohibitions* (what *should* or *should not* be done) and build in a norm hierarchy with exceptions. Overall, from work in social and moral psychology, we can extract a few principles about norms as they apply to reference resolution: (**1**) Norms can govern the interpretation of a referring expression. (**2**) Norms are highly influenced by context. (**3**) Norms compete and interact with each other.

Reasoning with norms is distinct from reasoning with general facts or common sense. For example, a general fact or common-sense knowledge can tell us what can be done or what people tend to do generally, but not whether it should or should not be done in a specific context—actions can be logically correct but normatively wrong. Norms specifically guide behavior by prescribing actions or prohibiting actions within nuanced contexts that change by culture and situation. Additionally, norms that should usually be followed can also be violated in certain contexts (e.g. consider urgent safety-preserving contexts). We follow [23] in explicitly represented norms with domain-general rules.

3   Human Norm-Reference Validation

To show that humans rely on normative reasoning for reference resolution, we present a reference resolution task in a user study. We set up scenes with under-specified linguistic contexts that require normative reasoning. We collected 54 participants through the Prolific online human-intelligence task platform.

The user study was broken into two parts. In the first part, participants were presented with five scenes. In each scene, a context is described textually with an ambiguous reference to some mugs (e.g., *I'll grab the mug*), with an accompanying image reflecting the ambiguity. Each participant sees every scene, but the ordering is randomized. Participants were asked to click on the mug in the image that was being referred to, then they had to justify their decision through an open text box. This allowed us to gain insight into what norms (if any) informed the participant's decision-making. Figure 1 shows an example of a scene vignette from the study and heatmap of the resolved referent.

Scene A checks the default case of object usage: Adam and Bob each have their own mug in a cafe, and participants are asked which mug Bob will choose to grab.

Scene B checks the serving context: participants see Adam and Bob with mugs of coffee (one full, one empty) at a cafe, and are asked which mug the waiter will grab.

Scene C checks the 'preventing an accident' (avoiding danger) context: Adam and Bob each have their own mug of coffee in a cafe, but Adam is about to knock his coffee off the table with his elbow. Participants are asked which mug Bob will grab.

Scene D checks the cleaning context: participants see Adam in a kitchen, with mugs visible in the sink and in the cabinet, and are asked which mug the individual will grab if cleaning up.

Scene E checks the cooking context. Participants see the same image from scene D, but are told that Adam is now cooking.

In part two of the study, we aimed to find out how contexts may modulate the appropriateness of an action using a "norms survey". Four actions[1] are made into every possible combination with five contexts[2]. Participants saw each of these combinations and were asked to indicate if the combination was "normal", "not normal", or "neither". They were also asked to justify their response. Two of the authors qualitatively analyzed the responses.

Fig. 1. Example of scene with actors and referential objects. The heat map represents the density of clicks (resolved referents in the scene).

The results underscored the importance of context and roles in modulating the reference selection:

In **Scene A**, respondents (98.1%) stated that Bob will choose his own mug, aligning with our base expectation. (*Adam's hand is by his mug so its clearly his, He will grab the mug that is free as the other one looks taken*)

---

[1] "grabbing a mug that doesn't belong to you"; "grabbing a mug that someone else is using"; "grabbing a used mug"; "grabbing a clean mug".

[2] "when you are a waiter filling a mug"; "to clean a mug"; "to prevent an accident"; "when you are cooking something"; "when you are drinking something".

In **Scene B**, respondents (96.2%) stated that the waiter would select the empty mug, citing the role of the waiter as the reasoning. (*The waiter will refill the empty mug*)

In **Scene C**, respondents (88.8%) stated that Bob would override the previously stated norm of not touching someone else's mug, as doing so would prevent an accident. (*To prevent the mug from getting knocked over*)

In **Scene D**, respondents (81.4%) stated that Adam would select a dirty mug, citing his current context as the reasoning. (*cleaning so he is going to grab a dirty mug and clean it*)

In **Scene E**, respondents (88.8%) stated that Adam would now select a clean mug, citing his current context as the reasoning. (*When you are cooking you usually start with a clean...whatever you are going to use*)

Overall, the image-based norm selections had majority agreement. There was some disagreement over recognized norms due to what details of the scene people focused on. When performing part two, we observed norms which largely align with our intuition about the relevant norms in each scene.

4 Enabling Norm-Guided Reference Resolution in a Robotic Architecture

We now present our solution to norm-modulated situated reference resolution that beleaguers large language models. Since we are concerned with situated reference resolution and the situational evidence that comes with embodiment, we need to integrate the proposed inference-guided resolution algorithms within a *robotic architecture* which ideally already has a language processing component (i.e., semantic interpreter) for linguistic utterances which includes a reference resolution component for mapping referring expressions to target referents and a knowledge base representing what the robot knows about the environment and other actors. The norm component is a novel addition to the architecture that performs necessary normative reasoning processes to enable norm-based reference resolution based on perceivable and task-based contexts. Compared to earlier versions of the architecture where reasoning checks an agent's permissible actions, reasoning is extended into natural language processing to aid reference interpretation.

4.1 System Overview

Figure 2 gives an overview of the selected DIARC architecture [24]. The Automatic Speech Recognition (ASR) component and the vision component (which can detect and search for objects and their properties) handle perceptual information. At the reasoning layer are dialogue components, reasoners, a dialogue manager for submitting goal predicates to the goal manager, and the goal manager which can submit action scripts to the action manager or search requests to the vision component. The remaining components deal with actions such as speech generation or motions in the environment.

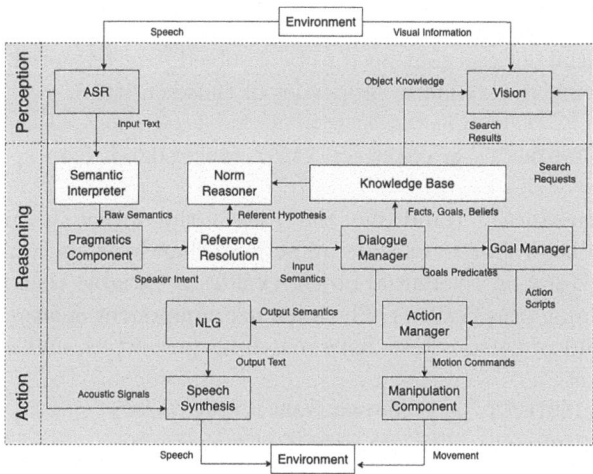

Fig. 2. Approach for implementing normative-based reasoning for reference resolution. This approach highlights only the relevant aspects of the cognitive architecture, including the semantic interpreter, a knowledge base, and a normative reasoner.

The relevant language processing components that were modified to enable norm-based reference resolution are highlighted in yellow: the semantic interpreter, pragmatics component, the reference resolution component and the normative reasoner communicates information to interpret an utterance. The semantic interpreter (implemented as a version of Combinatory Categorial Grammar (CCG) parser) parses words into a syntactic and semantic representation in first-order logical form from a list of grammar rules. This surface semantic representation (e.g., $(\lambda$ x.grab(?ACTOR, x)$)$ gets passed to the pragmatics component, which assigns the speaker's intent to the utterance (e.g., this could be an *instruction* (INSTRUCT(λ x.grab (?ACTOR, x)) or a *statement* (STATEMENT(λ x.grab(?ACTOR, x))). The reference resolution component then resolves references and creates reference identifiers. For example, if a referential entity like *mug* is detected, a variable of type "mug" is created with hypothesized bindings to a physical or hypothetical referent, initially from matched semantics properties such as color descriptions or object types (e.g., *mug* would be represented as VARO but bound to a reference identifier object_0, object_1, object_n; hypothesized bindings could be known entities in the environment that shares the property of being a mug). Lastly, we have a knowledge base that contains facts about objects, their locations, their ownership relation, as well as the robot's beliefs about the state of the world or the state of mind of human interactants.

4.2   Implementation

The reference resolution component receives as input a natural language data structure ("NL packet") that contains information about the speaker, listener, speaker intent (provided by the pragmatic component), core semantics and actions, referential entities that need to be resolved (e.g. triggered by *the* before a noun phrase and the semantic properties of those entities):

```
nlp(398531186,INSTRUCT, graspObject(VAR0),[mug(VAR0)],[])
```

For the utterance, "Hand me the mug", the intent is an instruction (INSTRUCT) for the robot to execute an action ("hand me" is translated to the action graspObject on referential object (VAR0), a variable that has the property of being a mug (mug(VAR0)). The reference component creates hypothesized bindings to VAR0 of entities that have matching properties, and populates this in the NL packet:

```
nlp(398531186,INSTRUCT, graspObject(VAR0),[mug(VAR0)],
[VAR0=physobj_2:physobj, VAR0=physobj_1:physobj]
```

The new normative reasoner is then called when these bindings are created. Linguistics information about the bindings—such as the entity properties—are used together with beliefs and facts (stored symbolically as first-order logic expressions) of the situational context (e.g., settings, speaker, etc.) to reason about these bindings. The normative reasoner prunes the hypothesis space when there are multiple bindings by applying domain-general rules to each of the bindings, and in the case of a single binding, checks for a norm violation.

The normative reasoning is done via the declarative programming language Prolog where we represent facts and rules that "operationalize norms." Norm rules are structured as general templates (Prohibition(Action, Object, Setting, Context)) that check for a norm violation under specific context-relevant items: action, object, setting, context, property (e.g. if isDirty(object) or context is kitchen), with additional domain-general rules. These templates cover 20 configurations that capture the norm contexts validated in the study and work in the case studies outlined below but also generalize and scale up to other unknown examples. For a prohibition, *"do not touch objects that do not belong to you"*, the norm violation could be triggered by the context-relevant items with additional rules to reason if an object *belongs* to the agent, for instance. In Prolog, we define a rule that checks if a communal item belongs to someone else and not to a person Y (e.g. it is in use or near someone else) or if a non-communal item is owned by person Y. Then we apply a rule that checks if the actor's action would result in touching *and* the object does not belong to the actor.

```
% Object does not belong to Person (notyours)
notyours(Object, Person) :-
(communal(Object), (closeTo(Object, not(Person)));
inUse(Object)); (notCommunal(Object), notOwns(Object, Person)))
```

5   Case Studies

We next discuss our proposed norm inference component and how it works in conjunction with the rest of the architecture with scenarios that cover three aspects of the normative reasoning process in a situated reference resolution task. For each scenario, we describe (1) the context and properties of candidate objects, (2) the input utterance that contains the referring expressions (denoted in brackets), (3) the relevant norm(s), and (4) the relevant Prolog facts and rules that represent the norm(s).

Note that we limit utterances to simple imperatives with definite referring expressions such as *the mug* for the purpose of discussing norm inferences so as not to introduce syntactic parsing ambiguity and other linguistic processing complications that are not directly relevant to norm inference. However, the proposed integration is general and can also handle complex sentences. Also, note that the utterances are purposely underspecified in the sense that the linguistic information itself does not narrow down the target referent; in each context there are two or more objects that could potentially be the referents of the noun phrase.

Scenario 1: *Norms guiding a reference interpretation.* **Context**: The setting of this scene is a dining room and the scene takes place in a serving context. There are two mugs on the table where one is dirty and one is clean. **Utterance**: *"bring [the mug]"*. **Norm**: *prohibition: you should not serve with dirty or used items*

Candidate Referents:
$Object_0$, $Object_1$

```
% facts
mug(object_0). mug(object_1). isDirty(object_0). isClean(object_1).
% domain-general norm rule template
Prohibition(Action,Object,Setting,Context) :- isDirty(Object),
isType(Action,S), isType(Object,T), isType(Setting,U), isType(Context,J).
```

In this case, the knowledge base of the cognitive architecture is aware of certain facts about the situated environment. First, two objects in the environment have the property of being a mug. The referring expression, *the mug*, can map to both of these objects at this point. But there remains an ambiguity about which object to bind to the expression. The reference resolver applies the norm rule. We note here that the **isType** relation contains a list as the second item. This is kept general but can represent the context-relevant items that would make the norm hold true. S, for instance, is a list of context-related actions e.g. $S = \{bringing, grabbing, pouring, removing, ... \}$; T is a list of context-related objects e.g. $T = \{spoon, fork, plate, mug, glass\}$; U is a list of context-related settings e.g. $U = \{dining\_room, dining\_table, ...\}$; J is a list of context-related contexts e.g. $J = \{serving, eating, preparing,...\}$.

The system gathers the necessary evidence gathered from the situational context and applies normative reasoning to each candidate object. Since the context is a serving context at a dining table location, an actor cannot bring the dirty mug, as that results in a norm violation. $Object_1$, the clean mug, then appropriately binds to "the mug."

This demonstrates a normative-reasoning case where a single norm can influence the interpretation of the referring expression. The general norm rule simultaneously instantiates a norm and checks if that norm is violated given the actor, object, setting, and context—this ultimately serves to prune the candidate objects. Norms, and in turn reference interpretation, is constrained by various context factors. So, to account for this, the arguments in these general rules can be flexibly modified or updated. The power of these general rule templates, therefore, is that they capture changes in context, actor social roles, and object properties, among other things. In scenario 2, we see how a norm is applied differently once the context is modulated.

Scenario 2: *Norms modulated by context.* Here, we present a similar setup with the same utterance, setting, and candidate objects. The objects share the same properties of one being clean and one being dirty. The only key difference is that we move from a *serving* context to a *cleaning* context. However, this slight change has critical implications in the referent interpretation. A different norm is instantiated and applied: *prescription: you should clean dirty items* (although it is permissible to clean items that are already clean it is prescriptive to clean dirty items). **Context**: The setting of this scene is a dining table and the scene takes place in a cleaning context. There are two mugs on the table where one is dirty and one is clean. **Utterance:** *"bring [the mug]"*. **Norm**: *prescription: you should clean items that are dirty*
Candidate Referents:
$Object_0$, $Object_1$

```
% facts
mug(object_0). mug(object_1). isDirty(object_0). isClean(object_1).
% domain-general norm rule template
Prescriptions(Action, Object, Setting, Context) :-
isDirty(Object), isType(Action, S), isType(Object, T), isType(Setting, U),
isType(Context, J).
```

The original norm violation of scenario 1 would not apply in this case because the context of *cleaning* would not be within the range of contexts (set J) where the prohibition of touching dirty objects applies. Instead, the clean mug would not trigger a prescriptive norm. $Object_0$, the dirty mug, would appropriately bind to *the mug*. These general rules capture the examples illustrated in [1] where, given the same expression and candidate referents, a context modulation alone flipped which referent should be the correct interpretation.

Scenario 3: *A norm interacting with another norm.* We often do not deal with single norms in isolation but rather contend with varying norms competing with each other and differing in strength or priority. Revisiting an earlier example, one should generally follow a norm: *you should not touch things that do not belong*

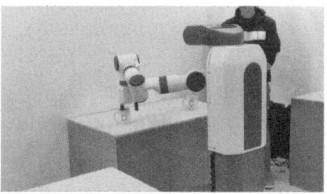

(a) In the 'cleaning up' context, the robot selects the dirty mug instead of the clean one.

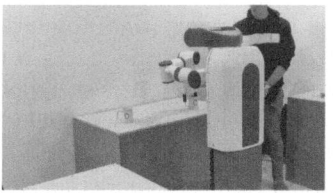

(b) In the 'cooking' context, the robot selects the clean mug instead of the dirty one.

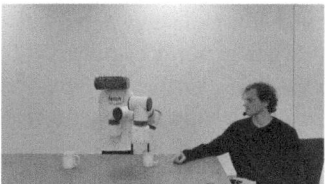

(c) In the 'serving person coffee' context, the robot selects the person's mug.

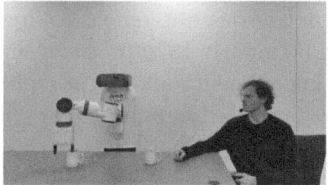

(d) In the 'person drinking coffee' context, the robot selects the unused mug.

Fig. 3. The "Grab the mug" command has different interpretations depending on context.

to you. But this can be overridden by the norm: *obey your superior* or *avoid danger* in more precarious or critical situations. This last scenario demonstrates how norms on different hierarchies interact within a reference task. **Context**: The setting of this scene is a dining table within a dining context. There are two mugs on the table that are filled with hot coffee (currently in use) and belong to the speaker. One of the mugs is close to the edge of the table. **Utterance**: *"move [the mug]"*. **Norms**: *prohibition: you should not touch things that do not belong to you. prescription: you should avoid danger*
Candidate Referents:
$Object_0$, $Object_1$

```
% facts
inUse(object_0), location(object_0, edge) inUse(object_1)
% object X does not belong to person Y
notBelongTo(Object, Person) :-
communal(Object), (closeTo(Object, not(Person)); inUse(Object));
(notCommunal(Object), notOwns(Object, Person))).
% Actions that result in touching norm prohibition
TouchProhibition(Object, Person, Action) :-
notBelongTo(Object, Person), touchActions(Action), not(isDanger(Object)).
```

For the touch prohibition rule to hold, the condition that there is no danger associated with the object must hold. Now, the fact that one of the mugs is filled with hot coffee *and* close to the edge triggers a dangerous scenario. And since there is a danger, the prohibition is *false* (no norm violation), and the norm is essentially overridden. As a result, $Object_0$ is correctly interpreted as the referent even though it is still violating one norm.

There are other norms that could be applied in this situation; if the speaker owns one of the mugs (and thus it does not belong to the agent) but issues the command, they can implicitly grant permission to override the norm *do not touch things that do not belong to you*. Moreover, if a mug is alternatively not close to the edge of the table but intruding on someone's dining space, it could be conventionally out of place. Therefore, instead of acting on an object that could lead to a dangerous outcome, an object flagged for violating a typical location norm could similarly take precedence over another general norm.

As we have shown walking through these examples, simple changes to the general normative-rule templates allow the system to handle a range of normative-reasoning scenarios. These rules can easily be extended to other objects and locations. For example, a computer or mug should not typically be on the ground but on a table. But imagine a situation where there is one of each object on either the table or the ground. Someone might urgently issue a command to a physical agent: *"move the mug/computer"*. Even if all of these items are privately owned by someone (prohibiting an agent from picking them up), both items also share the property of being fragile and both scenarios have one of the objects on a non-conventional location (the ground). The same normative reasoning would apply and the target referent would be the object—either the mug or the computer—sitting on the ground.

In Fig. 3 (demo video: https://streamable.com/jv5zkm), we present examples of norm-guided reference resolution on a fully autonomous Fetch robot [27] which has a mobile manipulator. We use the manufacturer-provided ROS [22] configuration to enable autonomous motion planning, alongside the cognitive architecture DIARC [24] to enable natural language interactions and robot decision-making. Typically, DIARC would perform object recognition to inform reference resolution and choose any valid object. We have augmented it to be aware of objects with specific relevant properties and how each object can be grabbed. Finally, we ensured that the robot is informed of its current task and the context that this places it in by configuring the Prolog rule set.

We use similar examples to scenario 1 and scenario 2 with the utterance *grab the mug* and vary the context from *cleaning* to *cooking*. Here, the robot is guided by the norms *you should not serve items that are dirty* and *you should cook with items that are clean*.

6   Discussion

Assistive robots in various application domains will need to be able to handle the kinds of communicative interactions that come naturally to people. This critically includes interpreting referential expressions based on the norms that apply in humans are automatically activated in the interaction context which is in part determined by the surrounding settings. Our domain-general rule-based norm representations account for a variety of relevant contextual aspects to infer what actions should be performed on what kind of object.

An LLM-based approach is another possible computational solution for situated norm-based reference resolution. Here, we evaluate GPT-3 (Davinci model) on underspecified reference examples using a question-answering task. Instead of just asking the model to report the referent related to the question, *which mug?*, we also probe its understanding of the situational context and norms with questions like, *what is the setting?*, *what is the context?*, *what should you do?*, *what should you not do?*, *what are the norms?*. We provide a textual vignette to the model marked by `Q:`, and then prompt it with a question. The models' response is generated after `A:`.

`Q: The setting takes place at a dining table and within a serving context. Dinner is being served. There are two mugs on the table where one mug is clean and one mug is dirty. Someone says,"bring the mug." Which mug? A: The clean mug.`

For the first scenario, where the clean mug should be served in the serving context, the model correctly answers with *the clean mug*. Then, we get a better picture of its performance by asking related questions.

`Q: What is the norm?`

`A: The norms are that the clean mug should be brought to the person who said bring the mug.`

The model continues to respond to the remaining questions[3]. These results, on the surface, seem to indicate that the system understands the necessary elements of the scene to perform the norm-guided reference resolution. Another way we ask about norms is by coding them as questions with *should* and *should not*. Although the system does not respond with an explicit explanation of a relevant norm of the scene it impressively responds that the clean mug should be brought and the dirty mug should not be brought.

In scenario 2, we only flip the context to a *cleaning* context and prompt GPT-3 with the same questions. The system produces nearly the same responses. The response to *What is the norm?* is: *The norm would be to bring the clean mug.* The shift in context should modulate the relevant norm and the target referent, so the model is not sensitive to this particular change; as in scenario 1, it selects the clean mug. In scenario 3, the model selects *the mug close to you* as the target referent rather than the hot coffee mug near the edge of the table. This suggests that the model is not encoding a norm hierarchy (violating a touching norm to preserve a safety norm: avoiding danger) and is biased towards selecting certain options based on its training data.

Considering other approaches, we recognize that better performing LLMs in the future could identify the relevant norms and referents in our cases. However due to their statistical nature, it is typically difficult to obtain guarantees for social norm identification and reasoning. These guarantees are crucial in situated interaction, as a robot incorrectly following or interpreting a norm can have

---

[3] *The clean mug should be brought*; *The dirty mug should not be brought*; *The setting is a dining room or kitchen*; *The context is that someone wants the clean mug*.

serious ethical and safety consequences. Our symbolic approach provides more transparency since reasoning works over explicit rules. Approaches that use or integrate LLMs can benefit from our approach by delegating the norm reasoning process with these symbolic norm representations. For example, LLMs can provide an initial semantic interpretation or referent hypothesis that ultimately gets checked by domain-general norm rules. LLMs can also serve as a tool to potentially generate symbolic representations of (human-validated) social norms at a greater scale.

In this paper, we have provided examples with simple imperatives that mention a couple of context configurations. This was done primarily to introduce the basic principles of normative reasoning. A limitation of this work is that these contexts are pre-specified. Future work will see how these normative rules work in settings where a robot must gather information about the context through perceptual cues and natural language. Additional future work includes enriching our norm rules by studying and validating norms through human feedback and adding weights to norms to handle more complex norm interactions or contribute to the uncertainty of an agent's referent interpretation.

7 Conclusion

In this paper we presented a novel norm-based reasoning approach to situated reference resolution. We demonstrated with an online user study that humans automatically perform norm-guided reference resolution and that as a result assistive robots need to be able to handle them in interaction contexts. Despite a wealth of proposals for reference resolution itself, there is limited work in the robotics community on leveraging social norms for situated reference resolution. We showed that GPT-3 struggles to consistently produce the correct referents in our examples and has general difficulties with this type of normative reasoning (e.g., despite GPT-3's correct answers about the context of the textual vignettes, it did not consistently recognize or apply the norms correctly). We then introduced our logic-based normative reasoner and how it is integrated into a cognitive robotic architecture to enable situated norm-based reference resolution during natural language human-robot interactions. We highlighted different core aspects of normative reasoning with three case studies: one where a single norm is applied, one where the context and instantiated norm modulate the interpretation of the referent, and one where norms interact. And finally, we demonstrated the successful operation of the proposed reasoning system on a fully autonomous robot in a few norm-modulated settings.

References

1. Abrams, M., Scheutz, M.: Social norms guide reference resolution. In: Proceedings of the 2022 Conference of the North American Chapter of the Association for Computational Linguistics: Human Language Technologies, pp. 1–11 (2022)

2. Andrighetto, G., Governatori, G., Noriega, P., Van der Torre, L.W.: Normative muti-agent systems (2013)
3. Bicchieri, C.: The grammar of Society: The Nature and Dynamics of Social Norms. Cambridge University Press, Cambridge (2005)
4. Brohan, A., et al.: Do as i can, not as i say: grounding language in robotic affordances. In: Conference on Robot Learning, pp. 287–318. PMLR (2023)
5. Brown, T., et al.: Language models are few-shot learners. Adv. Neural. Inf. Process. Syst. **33**, 1877–1901 (2020)
6. Chai, J.Y., Hong, P., Zhou, M.X.: A probabilistic approach to reference resolution in multimodal user interfaces. In: Proceedings of the 9th International Conference on Intelligent User Interfaces, pp. 70–77 (2004)
7. Culpepper, W., et al.: IPOWER: incremental, probabilistic, open-world reference resolution. In: Proceedings of the Annual Meeting of the Cognitive Science Society, vol. 44 (2022)
8. Elazar, Y., et al.: Measuring and improving consistency in pretrained language models. Trans. Assoc. Comput. Linguist. **9**, 1012–1031 (2021)
9. Grice, H.P.: Logic and conversation. In: Speech Acts, pp. 41–58. Brill (1975)
10. Huang, L., et al.: A survey on hallucination in large language models: principles, taxonomy, challenges, and open questions. arXiv preprint arXiv:2311.05232 (2023)
11. Iida, R., Yasuhara, M., Tokunaga, T.: Multi-modal reference resolution in situated dialogue by integrating linguistic and extra-linguistic clues. In: Proceedings of 5th International Joint Conference on Natural Language Processing, pp. 84–92 (2011)
12. Jiang, C., Xu, Y., Hsu, D.: LLMs for robotic object disambiguation. arXiv preprint arXiv:2401.03388 (2024)
13. Jurafsky, D., Martin, J.: Speech and Language Processing: An Introduction to Natural Language Processing, Computational Linguistics, and Speech Recognition. Prentice Hall Series in Artificial Intelligence, Pearson Prentice Hall (2009)
14. Kennington, C., Schlangen, D.: A simple generative model of incremental reference resolution for situated dialogue. Comput. Speech Lang. **41**, 43–67 (2017)
15. Kollar, T., Krishnamurthy, J., Strimel, G.P.: Toward interactive grounded language acqusition. In: Robotics: Science and Systems, vol. 1, pp. 721–732 (2013)
16. Malle, B.F., Rosen, E., Chi, V.B., Berg, M., Haas, P.: A general methodology for teaching norms to social robots. In: 2020 29th IEEE International Conference on Robot and Human Interactive Communication (RO-MAN), pp. 1395–1402. IEEE (2020)
17. Matuszek, C., Bo, L., Zettlemoyer, L., Fox, D.: Learning from unscripted deictic gesture and language for human-robot interactions. In: Proceedings of the AAAI Conference on Artificial Intelligence, vol. 28 (2014)
18. Mininger, A., Laird, J.E.: Interactively learning strategies for handling references to unseen or unknown objects. Adv. Cogn. Syst **5**, 1–16 (2016)
19. Morris-Martin, A., De Vos, M., Padget, J.: Norm emergence in multiagent systems: a viewpoint paper. Auton. Agent. Multi-Agent Syst. **33**(6), 706–749 (2019). https://doi.org/10.1007/s10458-019-09422-0
20. Park, J., et al.: CLARA: classifying and disambiguating user commands for reliable interactive robotic agents. IEEE Robot. Autom. Lett. **9**, 1059–1066 (2023)
21. Pyke, A., West, R.L., LeFevre, J.A.: On-line reference assignment for anaphoric and non-anaphoric nouns: a unified, memory-based model in act-R. In: Proceedings of the Annual Meeting of the Cognitive Science Society, vol. 29 (2007)
22. Quigley, M., et al.: ROS: an open-source robot operating system. In: ICRA Workshop on Open Source Software, Kobe, Japan, vol. 3, p. 5 (2009)

23. Sarathy, V., Scheutz, M.: On resolving ambiguous anaphoric expressions in imperative discourse. In: Proceedings of the AAAI Conference on Artificial Intelligence, vol. 33, pp. 6957–6964 (2019)
24. Scheutz, M., Williams, T., Krause, E., Oosterveld, B., Sarathy, V., Frasca, T.: An overview of the distributed integrated cognition affect and reflection DIARC architecture. Cognitive architectures, pp. 165–193 (2019)
25. Whitney, D., Eldon, M., Oberlin, J., Tellex, S.: Interpreting multimodal referring expressions in real time. In: 2016 IEEE International Conference on Robotics and Automation (ICRA), pp. 3331–3338. IEEE (2016)
26. Williams, T., Scheutz, M.: Power: a domain-independent algorithm for probabilistic, open-world entity resolution. In: 2015 IEEE/RSJ International Conference on Intelligent Robots and Systems (IROS), pp. 1230–1235. IEEE (2015)
27. Wise, M., Ferguson, M., King, D., Diehr, E., Dymesich, D.: Fetch and freight: standard platforms for service robot applications. In: Workshop on Autonomous Mobile Service Robots (2016)
28. Wu, J., et al.: TidyBot: personalized robot assistance with large language models. Auton. Robot. **47**(8), 1087–1102 (2023)

Investigating the Impact of Encouraging Utterances by Conversational Robots on Subjective Well-Being: A 15-Day Sustained Interaction

Lingxuan Xiang[1(✉)], Hirofumi Kikuchi[1], Jie Yang[1], and Hideaki Kikuchi[2]

[1] Graduate School of Human Sciences, Waseda University, 2-579-15, Mikajima, Tokorozawa, Saitama, Japan
`xianglingxuan@akane.waseda.jp`
[2] Faculty of Human Sciences, Waseda University, 2-579-15, Mikajima, Tokorozawa, Saitama, Japan

Abstract. The sensation of being encouraged is closely linked to subjective well-being (SWB). This study examined whether sustained encouragement from a conversational robot could enhance users' SWB. A preliminary survey with 48 participants identified two types of encouraging utterances with significantly different effects on participants' perceived levels of encouragement. Based on this survey, we recruited 6 participants for a 15-day experiment with a conversational robot (2 participants completed only 9 days). They interacted with the robot every two days and were randomly assigned to either a high-efficacy or low-efficacy encouraging utterances group. SWB was assessed through questionnaires and daily diaries, while interviews explored whether observed changes were attributable to the robot interactions. Results suggest that high-efficacy encouraging utterances may positively influence users' SWB. This study provides theoretical support for using conversational robots to enhance human SWB through sustained high-efficacy encouragement. Future research should explore these effects in diverse populations and over longer durations.

Keywords: Social robots · Human-robot interaction · Sustained interaction · Well-being · Encouragement · Psychological support · Emotional support

1 Introduction

Background and Challenges. The demand for conversational robots designed to discuss personal worries is increasing [1]. These robots are expected to alleviate stress, reduce anxiety, and enhance user well-being [2]. People often face various worries and anxieties, typically expecting emotional support from friends [3]. Encouragement, a critical form of support, plays a vital role in developing subjective well-being (SWB), particularly among modern youth [4, 5]. Studies show that human-provided encouragement can significantly enhance SWB, while a lack of it during childhood is linked to lower SWB

© The Author(s), under exclusive license to Springer Nature Singapore Pte Ltd. 2025
O. Palinko et al. (Eds.): ICSR + AI 2024, LNAI 15562, pp. 115–127, 2025.
https://doi.org/10.1007/978-981-96-3519-1_12

in adulthood [6, 7]. This indicates that cumulative experiences of encouragement can enhance people's SWB. However, the effectiveness of sustained encouragement from conversational robots compared to human encouragement remains unexplored. Despite their potential in emotional support, robots' continued use may raise ethical challenges. Over-reliance on robots might weaken human relationships, increase social isolation, and hinder the development of interpersonal skills [8]. As researchers explore these potential benefits, it is crucial to carefully balance them with ethical considerations to mitigate risks in practical applications. Thus, this study aims to explore the sustained impact of conversational robots on user SWB, an area with significant potential for mental health support and human-robot interaction.

Encouragement and Robot. Human encouragement involves both verbal and non-verbal cues; this study focuses on verbal methods. In human interactions, the effect of comfort and encouragement is influenced by the relationship with the encourager, their perceived authority, the method of encouragement, and the cause of distress [9]. Common worries include relationships, health, romance, and academics [10], with optimal encouragement strategies varying accordingly [11]. It remains to be seen if these strategies will also vary in human-robot interactions depending on the type of worry.

This study focuses on physical anthropomorphic robots because their tangible presence enhances users' perception of them as human-like entities and strengthens emotional connections [12]. Unlike virtual agents such as Siri or Google Assistant, which lack visual representation, these physical robots provide a more realistic and immersive interaction experience, enhancing user trust and satisfaction [13]. Moreover, anthropomorphic robots' ability to mimic human behaviors and reactions facilitates deeper emotional exchanges and improves recall of the presented information [14].

Definition and Measurement of Subjective Well-Being. SWB encompasses cognitive evaluations of life quality and emotional states [15]. Emotional responses are quick, while cognitive assessments of life satisfaction change more slowly. Cognitive aspects are sustained evaluations, while emotional aspects are often used for instantaneous evaluations. This study defines SWB based on sustained evaluations of "life satisfaction" during extended interactions, following [16]: "SWB reflects an overall evaluation of the quality of a person's life from her or his perspective." Common methods to measure SWB include self-report questionnaires, diary methods, and experience sampling methods (ESM) [17]. Self-report questionnaires like the "Satisfaction with Life Scale (SWLS)" are common but may be biased; diary methods provide dynamic data but have inconsistent compliance [18]; and ESM could avoid recalling bias but may disrupt daily life [17]. Therefore, this study used the SWLS [19] and diary methods to capture cumulative changes in SWB. Combining these methods provides an overall evaluation and captures dynamic changes, overcoming the limitations of using a single method.

Study Design and Objectives. This study explores the impact of conversational robots delivering effective encouraging utterances on users' SWB during sustained interactions. The focus is on Japanese-speaking female university students aged 18–25, due to varying perceptions influenced by demographic factors. The study has two phases: first, a preliminary survey with 48 participants evaluates the effectiveness of five types of robot-provided encouragement across four categories of worries. These results inform the design of the main experiment, which includes surveys and dialogue interactions every two days over 15 days (8 sessions in total). In the main experiment, 6 participants (2 of whom completed only 5 sessions over 9 days) were divided into experimental and control groups. They interacted with the conversational robot and received different types of encouragement strategies. This study addresses two research questions:

RQ1: Which type of encouraging utterances delivered by conversational robots is most effective in addressing different categories of worries among users?

RQ2: How do highly effective encouraging utterances delivered by conversational robots influence users' SWB over sustained interactions?

This study was conducted with the approval of the Ethics Review Committee for Research Involving Human Subjects at Waseda University (Approval Number 2023-203).

2   Related Work

Enhancing Well-Being with Physical Anthropomorphic Robot. Using conversational robots to enhance human well-being through linguistic methods is an evolving research field. Expressing gratitude through voice agents in a single session has been shown to enhance positive emotions [20]. Similarly, social robots using dialogue strategies such as small talk and questioning have been found to reduce fear and anxiety, thereby increasing the well-being of children during vaccinations [21]. However, these studies primarily focused on single interactions. For multiple interactions, a 7-day experiment implementing the "three good things" strategy via voice resulted in improved SWB [22]. As [23] reported, conversational robots provided emotional support to lonely elderly individuals through short daily conversations, effectively reducing loneliness. Furthermore, robot coaches applying positive psychology principles have enhanced university students' well-being over sessions lasting 7–12 days [24]. These findings underscore the potential of physical anthropomorphic robots as effective tools for improving human well-being. However, some research gaps remain: first, effective verbal encouragement strategies tailored to different worries during interactions need to be identified. Second, further investigation is required to understand the impact of such encouragement on SWB during interactions. Third, many studies rely on short-term experiments, leading to a "novelty effect," where initial interest fades, affecting evaluations of the robots' ongoing influence [25, 26]. Consequently, the effects of sustained interactions with robots on user well-being have not been sufficiently studied. Moreover, small and homogeneous sample sizes limit the generalizability of current findings. Cultural and social diversity may lead to different well-being responses, yet this aspect remains underexplored. In human-robot interaction, robots are not merely functional tools; they simulate human-like behaviors and communication to establish deeper social connections with users [27], shaping user expectations and perceptions of the roles robots play in social interactions [27, 28].

Categories of Worries and Encouraging Utterances. Inspired by the "Survey on Student Life" from fiscal year 2022 [29] and [30], worries are categorized into four groups: (1) Interpersonal and social, (2) Psychological and health, (3) Academic and career prospects, and (4) Economic and living.

Based on classifications in [31], encouraging utterances were divided into five types:

TypeA. Reassurance and affirmation: Affirm the other person's situation or future with positive praise or reassurance. Example: "You are amazing."

TypeB. Expressing concern: Show sympathy or understanding by asking questions, indicating genuine concern. Example: "That's tough, are you okay?"

TypeC. Encouragement to take action: Motivate the person to act on their issues, though this can sometimes feel burdensome. Example: "It's more enjoyable if you think of it more easily."

TypeD. Offering specific actions: Offer help, emphasizing assistance rather than doing it together. Example: "I can help you."

TypeE. Distraction: Shift the person's focus away from their problems to relieve stress, showing a non-engaging attitude. Suggestions should be light and non-pressuring. Example: "How about having a delicious dessert?"

3   Preliminary Survey

The preliminary survey aimed to determine the effectiveness of conversational robots' encouraging utterances based on users' worries and to identify the most effective types. 48 native Japanese-speaking female university students participated in 30-min face- to-face and online sessions. They were introduced to the worry categories with descriptions and examples. They then imagined discussing their worries with a robot, wrote down their concerns, and rated the effectiveness of five types of encouraging utterances for four worry categories on a scale from 0 to 100. The process was repeated for all worry categories and utterance types. The results are summarized in Table 1.

Table 1. Results of the effect of five types of encouraging utterances.

Type of worries	Friedman test	Median	Mean
Interpersonal and social	A > E*, B > E*, C > E*, D > E*	B > C > A > D > E	B > C > A > D > E
Psychological and health	B > E*, C > E*, D > E*	B > C > D > A > E	B > C > A > D > E
Academic and career prospects	A > E*, B > E*, C > E*, D > E*	B > C > A > D > E	B > C > A > D > E
Economic and living	A > E*, B > D > E*, C > E*	B > C > A > D > E	B > C > A > D > E

Signif.codes: '*' 5%
A: Reassurance and affirmation, B: Expressing concern, C: Encouragement to take action, D: Offering specific actions, E: Distraction

The results were standardized to a mean of 0 and a standard deviation of 1, and analyzed using the Friedman test. They showed a consistent ranking in the effectiveness of the five types of encouraging utterances across different worry categories based on both median and mean scores. It was confirmed that for all worry categories, "Expressing concern" was significantly more effective than "Distraction."

4 Experiment

4.1 Purpose and Hypothesis

The preliminary survey identified "Expressing concern" as a high-efficacy encouraging utterance and "Distraction" as a low-efficacy one. Based on these findings, we designed an experiment to assess how sustained interactions with a conversational robot using these utterances affect users' SWB. Our hypothesis is that high-efficacy encouraging utterances ("Expressing concern") will significantly enhance users' SWB, while low-efficacy utterances ("Distraction") will be less effective.

4.2 Methodology

Participants and Experimental Design. This study recruited 6 Japanese-speaking female university students aged 18–25 (M = 20.7), randomly divided into two groups: the experimental group receiving high-efficacy "Expressing concern" utterances and the control group receiving low-efficacy "Distraction" utterances. The experiment lasted for 15 days (2 participants completed only 9 days) with 20-min sessions held every two days, totaling 8 sessions. Detailed participant information is provided in Table 2.

Table 2. Participants' information.

Subject	Gender	Grade	Age	Group	Experimental Days
A	Female	Junior	21	High-efficacy	15
B	Female	Senior	22	High-efficacy	15
C	Female	Junior	20	High-efficacy	9
D	Female	Senior	22	Low-efficacy	15
E	Female	Freshman	18	Low-efficacy	15
F	Female	Senior	21	Low-efficacy	9

Robot and Environment. The "RoBoHoN" dialogue robot (Fig. 1), designed by Sharp Corporation was used. To minimize speech recognition errors, the Wizard of Oz (WOz) method was employed, where a hidden human operator controlled the robot to ensure a natural conversation flow. Interactions were limited to voice communication to focus on verbal exchanges, while the robot remained stationary throughout the conversations. To enhance naturalness, bowing movements were incorporated at the start and end of each session. These movements did not interfere with the main dialogue content or affect the results. Sessions took place in a quiet classroom with only the experimenter and participant present (Fig. 2), and both voice and video were recorded.

Fig. 1. RoBoHoN.

Fig. 2. Conversation scene.

Procedure. The experiment employed a mixed-method approach to evaluate the robot's impact on participants' SWB, combining SWB surveys, interviews, and diary entries. Participants completed the "Satisfaction With Life Scale (SWLS)" [19], a 5-item scale (e.g., "In most ways my life is close to my ideal"), rated from 1 (strongly disagree) to 7 (strongly agree), with higher scores indicating greater SWB. The SWLS [19] was given at the beginning and end of the experiment to assess SWB changes. Qualitative data from interviews and diaries captured subjective experiences and emotional reflections. Dialogue sessions occurred every two days to prevent discomfort or fatigue and reduce potential bias from overfamiliarity with the scales. Before each session, participants were reminded of their main concerns with a list of keywords, and brief post-session interviews captured immediate emotional responses. Throughout the experiment, participants journaled their daily experiences and emotions each evening to account for the impact of non-robot-related events or factors on their SWB during analysis. To better understand whether SWB improvements were directly influenced by robot conversations or by other factors, in-depth interviews were conducted. Questions included whether the robot conversations temporarily alleviated emotions (Q1), thoughts on the conversations (Q2), the connection between SWB improvements and robot interactions after 5/8 conversations (Q3), and thoughts on the robot (Q4). Q1 and Q2 were asked after each session, while Q3 and Q4 were asked after the 5th and 8th conversations (since 2 participants only had 5 sessions).

Dialogue Content and Dialogue Flow. Based on definitions from [31] and [32], "Expressing concern" and "Distraction" types of encouraging utterances were divided into "Backchannel Part (BP)" and "Encouragement Part (EP)." This structure ensures attentive and consistent dialogue between the user and the robot. In "Expressing concern," the BP includes sympathetic affirmations like "That sounds tough" (5 patterns), while the EP contains 5 questions about feelings, such as "How are you feeling about this?" and 7 questions about expectations or coping strategies, like "How are you dealing with this?" (12 patterns). In "Distraction," the BP includes non-sympathetic affirmations like "I see" or "Okay" (5 patterns), and the EP offers non-pressure suggestions like showering or recommending food (6 patterns). The most appropriate context is chosen based on the participant's reactions to guide the robot's dialogue. To ensure diverse and accurate responses, the robot's dialogue is based on pre-established contexts. All participants received the same initial greeting. For each question (Q1-Q3), multiple revised contexts were randomly assigned to maintain engagement: Q1 has 9, Q2 has 11, and Q3 has 14. For linguistic and cultural accuracy, three native Japanese speakers revised and confirmed all dialogue contexts, enhancing the experiment's validity and reliability.

The dialogue flow simulates a real and structured interaction initiated by the robot. It starts with phrases like "Nice to see you," allowing the user to respond freely. Next, questions about the user's concerns (Q1) like "What is bothering you?" encourage expressing main worries. To delve deeper, more details are requested (Q2) with questions like "Can you tell me more about that?" demonstrating genuine care and increasing engagement. The most challenging part of the user's issue is explored (Q3) with questions like "What is the hardest part for you?" fostering a more meaningful conversation. The robot provides responses tailored to the experimental group ("Expressing concern"), such as "That sounds tough. How do you think it can be resolved?" and to the control group ("Distraction"), such as "I see. You could try a massage to relax your body and it might help you feel better." Users respond freely at each step. Finally, the conversation ends politely and respectfully by robot with statements such as "Thank you for your participation," allowing the user to freely conclude their responses.

4.3 Results

The changes in SWB are shown in Table 3. SWB was assessed before the experiment, after the 5th conversation (Day 9), and after the 8th conversation (Day 15). The SWB scores for each participant are presented in Table 3.

Table 3. Variations in subjective well-being (SWB).

Subject	Group	The score of SWB		
		Before experiment	After 5th conversation (Variations)	After 8th conversation (Variations)
A	High-efficacy	14	19(+5)	21(+7)
B	High-efficacy	17	20(+3)	18(+1)
C	High-efficacy	32	32(+0)	Non-participant
D	Low-efficacy	23	24(+1)	24(+1)
E	Low-efficacy	23	26(+3)	26(+3)
F	Low-efficacy	22	22(+0)	Non-participant

5 Discussion

By analyzing recurring themes from diaries and conversation records, we identified key issues such as daily life, academic concerns, and interpersonal relationship issues. While the quantitative data highlighted changes in SWB scores, the qualitative data (including diaries, conversation records, and interviews) provided valuable insights into the underlying causes of these changes. The case study aims to explore whether changes in participants' SWB are related to their interactions with the robot.

Experimental Group Case Studies. Participant A's SWB increased from 14 to 21, showing significant improvement. A's diary mentioned academic pressures, part-time job, and relationship issues. She expressed concerns like, "I'm worried about my credit card bills" and "It's hard to earn more without a job." She also felt distant from friends: "The gap between me and my friends is widening." The robot's empathetic responses made her feel understood and cared for. Over time, her loneliness decreased, and she felt the robot's support helped ease her isolation and build a closer relationship. Quantitative data shows a clear SWB increase, while qualitative analysis indicates this change was driven by the emotional support she received, helping her manage loneliness and stress. **Participant B** 's SWB increased from 17 to 20 after the 5th conversation but dropped to 18 by the 8th, indicating an emotional fluctuation. B's diary recorded her academic pressures, part-time job, and social activities. She mentioned, "My thesis may not have met expectations" and "I'm worried about the work environment after graduation." The robot's empathetic responses made her feel heard and understood. The 5th conversation coincided with Christmas, bringing short-term joy, which might have temporarily boosted her SWB. Quantitative data showed fluctuations in her SWB, while qualitative analysis revealed that B's SWB improvement was not only due to the emotional support from the robot but also influenced by external factors, such as successfully submitting her thesis and finalizing her career plans a month before the experiment, as well as the short-term happiness brought by Christmas. **Participant C**'s SWB remained at 32 throughout the experiment, despite multiple interactions with the robot. C's diary frequently mentioned her internships, academics, social activities, and job interviews. In 3 out of 5 conversations, she expressed frustration with her job search, saying, "My job search isn't going well" and "I failed another interview." The robot responded empathetically, asking, "What's your plan going forward?" While these conversations provided some emotional support and made her feel cared for, they were insufficient to offset the negative impact of continued job search failures. Quantitative data shows no change in her SWB, and qualitative analysis suggests that although the robot's support helped alleviate some stress, her ongoing job search difficulties continued to negatively affect her mood. Additionally, her high initial SWB may have caused a "ceiling effect," limiting further emotional improvement.

Control Group Case Studies. Participant D's SWB increased from 23 to 24, showing a slight improvement. D's diary recorded that her life mainly revolved around academics, social relationships, and her part-time job. In conversations, she expressed concerns about her friendships and work, saying, "I chose to work while most of my friends chose to continue their studies," and "It's getting harder to arrange meals with friends." She also mentioned, "My job requires a high level of English, and I find it difficult," adding, "My job is too busy, and the stress is overwhelming." Although the robot responded with suggestions like, "Have a cup of tea to relax," which gave her some temporary positive emotions, she felt these responses did not address her deeper concerns, leaving her feeling uncared for. Quantitative data shows a slight improvement in her SWB, but qualitative analysis indicates that this change was more likely due to external factors, such as the sense of accomplishment from submitting her thesis three weeks earlier, rather than from the robot's sustained interactions. **Participant E**'s SWB increased from 23 to 26, reflecting moderate improvement. E's diary indicated her life mainly revolved around academics, searching for a part-time job, and social interactions. As a freshman, she faced significant academic pressure. In conversations, she mentioned, "I can't find a topic for my report," "The backlog of assignments is keeping me up at night," and her anxiety about inviting her boyfriend to dinner and their upcoming trip. The robot's responses, such as "get some sun" or "take a rest," felt superficial and lacked genuine attentiveness. She often replied briefly with, "I'll try" or "I'll go eat." Despite sharing her worries across eight conversations, she felt the robot's responses were irrelevant, making her feel it wasn't truly listening. Quantitative data shows a notable improvement in SWB; however, qualitative analysis suggests this improvement was primarily driven by personal life events, such as her new romantic relationship before the 5th conversation and her upcoming trip plans, rather than emotional support from the robot. **Participant F**'s SWB remained at 22 throughout the experiment. F's diary showed that her life mainly revolved around traditional Japanese dance. In five conversations, F discussed financial stress, career planning, and time management, saying, "Traditional Japanese dance is expensive, and it's hard to ask my parents for money each time," and "I specialize in traditional Japanese dance, but I can't find a stable job or plan for my future." She also mentioned, "I have no time for myself, which makes me feel very stressed." Despite trying to engage more deeply with the robot, its suggestions like "take a bath" or "have a cup of tea" felt irrelevant and didn't address her deeper concerns. Quantitative data shows no change in SWB, and qualitative analysis suggests that while the robot's responses gave temporary relief, they were insufficient to alleviate the financial and emotional stress she faced. She particularly felt the lack of personalized, practical advice hindered lasting emotional improvement.

Overall Analysis. Case analysis shows that SWB changes were influenced by multiple factors such as robot interactions, life events, and future expectations. Common topics, such as academic and relationship challenges, emerged during the analysis. Quantitative data showed a significant SWB increase in the experimental group (high-efficacy), while the control group (low-efficacy) had more limited improvements. Integrating both quantitative and qualitative data revealed that emotional support from the robot played a key role in alleviating stress and loneliness in the experimental group, making participants feel cared for and heard. A and B specifically cited the robot's emotional care as a major factor in their improvements, while C's stable SWB, despite job search challenges, was also attributed to the robot's support. In contrast, the control group's SWB improvements were mainly driven by external life events, such as new relationships and academic achievements, rather than robot interactions. E's SWB increase was due to a new romantic relationship, and D's was linked to completing her thesis.

External factors, such as personal life events, played a major role in SWB fluctuations, as seen with E's new relationship and B's temporary boost during Christmas, both unrelated to robot interactions. Additionally, initial SWB levels played a critical role in the effectiveness of robot dialogues. C's high initial SWB suggested a "ceiling effect," limiting her improvement, while A's lower SWB allowed for greater gains. This suggests that initial SWB levels may significantly influence the effectiveness of encouraging utterances, with the robot's emotional support producing different effects depending on participants' baseline SWB.

Participants found it easier to discuss personal issues with the robot than with friends, appreciating RoBoHoN's small size and gradually forming emotional connections. Although they initially felt discomfort with the scripted dialogues, they adapted after the second interaction. These qualitative insights help explain the quantitative SWB improvements, as the perceived emotional support and understanding from the robot enhanced participants' positive emotions. However, these effects were short-term, likely due to the absence of sustained, personalized follow-ups, leading to limited cumulative impact. Without ongoing personalized encouragement, participants may not have received consistent emotional support, which affected SWB improvements and revealed a gap in the robot's ability to offer lasting emotional benefits. Additionally, participants' expectations for encouragement varied, which may lead to different SWB outcomes based on their personalities and emotional states.

In summary, the integration of quantitative and qualitative data indicates that the experimental group felt more supported by the robot, suggesting that high-efficacy encouraging utterances may be more effective in enhancing SWB than low-efficacy ones.

Limitations. This study has several limitations. First, the sample size is small and lacks diversity, consisting of only 6 female Japanese-speaking university students. The participants' gender, cultural, and linguistic backgrounds are highly homogenous, which limits the generalizability of the findings. Second, the experiment lasted only 15 days, which may not be sufficient to fully evaluate the sustained impact of interactions with the robot on SWB. Extending the experiment duration could help observe more significant changes. Third, while the Wizard of Oz (WOz) method provides flexible control, it relies on manual operation, which may affect the consistency and timing of the robot's responses. Manual control may introduce potential bias, making interactions feel less natural compared to fully autonomous robots, potentially impacting participants' perception of the robot's intelligence and engagement. Additionally, the study primarily relies on self-report tools (such as the SWLS [19] and diary methods). While these tools reflect participants' subjective experiences, they may introduce bias and fail to capture the full range of SWB changes. Moreover, the study does not account for participants' baseline SWB levels, which may influence the interpretation of SWB changes. External factors, such as participants' personal life events, likely influence the outcomes, but these confounding variables are not fully controlled or explored in the analysis.

6   Conclusion and Future Work

This study explored the impact of conversational robots delivering effective encouraging utterances on users' subjective well-being (SWB) through sustained interactions. Preliminary survey indicated that "Expressing concern" was the most effective type of encouragement for various worries. In a 15-day experiment with 6 Japanese-speaking female university students, we observed that high-efficacy encouraging utterances from robots improved some participants' SWB. This study contributes by filling the research gap on verbal encouragement from conversational robots to enhance SWB. It improves the understanding of mechanisms for SWB improvement through sustained human-robot interactions and aids in the design of psychological support in robots. Participants' varying expectations highlighted the importance of customizing robot designs, especially as robots become more prevalent in education and psychology.

Future research should extend the experiment for a longer duration and include diverse participant groups varying in age, gender, personality traits, and initial SWB levels to improve generalizability and reliability. Carefully controlling SWB baseline levels and external factors, such as personal life events, is crucial. Pre-experiment surveys or longitudinal tracking may help account for these variables. Studies conducted in familiar settings, like home or school, could make interactions feel more natural and realistic. Incorporating objective measures, such as physiological indicators (e.g., heart rate variability) or behavioral observations, alongside questionnaires and diaries, could reduce reliance on self-reports and minimize bias. Combining non-verbal cues (e.g., tone of voice, speaking speed, emotional expression, gestures) with brief confirmations or affirmative responses can make conversations flow more natural. Diversifying the handling of worries and encouraging utterances is essential for a comprehensive evaluation of their impact. In addition to verbal encouragement, introducing non-verbal communication elements could further improve interaction quality and user experience. Finally, refining the mixed-method approach and better integrating quantitative and qualitative data would further strengthen research in this field.

Future experiments could develop fully autonomous robots to eliminate reliance on the Wizard of Oz (WOz) method, ensuring consistency and naturalness in interactions. Personalized robot designs, adjusting the content and tone of encouraging utterances based on participants' specific needs, could provide more targeted emotional support. Additionally, exploring broader support types, including informational and instrumental support, will deepen our understanding of the benefits of conversational robots. Finally, ethical considerations should address the use of robots for emotional support, such as defining the boundaries of robots' roles to prevent them from impacting human connections or fostering overdependence.

References

1. Oracle: Survey on AI in the Workplace in Japan (2022). https://www.oracle.com/jp/corpor ate/pressrelease/jp20201104.html. Accessed 24 May 2023
2. Fu, C., Deng, Q., Shen, J., Mahzoon, H., Ishiguro, H.: A preliminary study on realizing human–robot mental comforting dialogue via sharing experience emotionally. Spec. Issue Soc. Robots Healthc. **22**(3), 991 (2022)
3. Argyle, M., Henderson, M.: The rules of friendship. J. Soc. Pers. Relat. **1**, 211–237 (1984)
4. Edwards, L.M., Lopez, S.J.: Perceived family support, acculturation, and life satisfaction in Mexican American youth: a mixed-methods exploration. J. Couns. Psychol. **53**, 279–287 (2006)
5. Khan, A.: Predictors of positive psychological strengths and subjective well-being among North Indian adolescents: role of mentoring and educational encouragement. Soc. Indic. Res. **114**, 1285–1293 (2013)
6. Huh, J.A., Kim, J.M.: The relation between self-encouragement, perceived stress and psychological well-being: the moderated mediating effect of support-seeking emotion regulation style. STRESS **25**, 44–51 (2017)

7. Alkhalaf, A.: Health psychology long-term effects on mental health and major illness: harsh parenting and encouragement from. LAP LAMBERT Academic (2012)
8. Etemad-Sajadi, R., Soussan, A., Schöpfer, T.: How ethical issues raised by human–robot interaction can impact the intention to use the robot? Int. J. Soc. Robot. **14**, 1103–1115 (2022)
9. Ogawa, S., Nakazawa, J.: Factors of effect on recipient of consolation: examination by semi-structured interview. Chiba Univ. Fac. Educ. Res. Bull. **62**, 59–65 (2014)
10. Ogawa, S.: Affect occurring in relation to sympathy from the other: differences resulting from attributions of an event and intimacy with the other. Jpn. J. Educ. Young Child. **59**, 267–277 (2011)
11. Ogawa, S.: The impact of the way friends comfort during adolescence on the recipient's emotions: a comparison between offering words of encouragement and empathy, and quietly stepping away without doing anything. Jpn. J. Dev. Psychol. **25**(3), 279–290 (2014)
12. Cassell, J., Sullivan, J., Prevost, S., Churchill, E.F.: Embodied Conversational Agents. The MIT Press, Cambridge (2000)
13. Wahde, M., Virgolin, M.: Conversational agents: theory and applications. arXiv preprint arXiv:2202.03164 (2022)
14. Beun, R.J., de Vos, E., Witteman, C.: Embodied conversational agents: effects on memory performance and anthropomorphisation. In: Proceedings of the International Conference on Intelligent Virtual Agents 2003, Germany, pp. 315–319 (2003)
15. Diener, E.: Subjective well-being. Psychol. Bull. **95**, 542–575 (1984)
16. Diener, E., Lucas, R. E., Oishi, S.: Advances and open questions in the science of subjective well-being. Collabra Psychol. **4**(1), 15–15 (2018)
17. Stieger, S., Reips, U.D.: Well-being, smartphone sensors, and data from open-access databases: a mobile experience sampling study. Field Methods **31**(3), 277–291 (2019)
18. Squires, J.E., Estabrooks, C.A., O'Rourke, H.M., Gustavsson, P., Newburn-Cook, C.V., Wallin, L.: A systematic review of the psychometric properties of self-report research utilization measures used in healthcare. Implement. Sci. **6**(1), 83 (2011)
19. Diener, E., Emmons, R.A., Larsen, R.J., Griffin, S.: Satisfaction with life scale (SWLS). Pers. Assess. **49**, 71–75 (1985)
20. Koichi, F., Ikuko, E. Y.: A survey of the effectiveness of gratitude via a voice agent. In: 32nd Annual Conference of the Japanese Society for Artificial Intelligence, Japan (2018)
21. Rossi, S., Larafa, M., Ruocco, M.: Emotional and behavioural distraction by a social robot for children anxiety reduction during vaccination. Int. J. Soc. Robot. **12**, 765–777 (2020)
22. Yamazaki, M., Kikuchi, H.: Influence of dialogue with communication robot on user's happiness. In: Human-Agent Interaction Symposium 2018, Japan (2018)
23. Baecker, A.N., Geiskkovitch, D.Y., González, A.L., Young, J.E.: Emotional support domestic robots for healthy older adults: conversational prototypes to help with loneliness. In: Proceedings of the 2020 ACM/IEEE International Conference on Human-Robot Interaction, Online, pp. 122–124 (2020)
24. Jeong, S., et al.: Deploying a robotic positive psychology coach to improve college students' psychological well-being. User Model. User-Adap. Inter. **33**, 571–615 (2023)
25. Smedegaard, C.V.: Reframing the role of novelty within social HRI: from noise to information. In: Proceedings of the 2019 ACM/IEEE International Conference on Human-Robot Interaction, South Korea, pp. 411–420 (2019)
26. Smedegaard, C.V.: Novelty knows no boundaries: why a proper investigation of novelty effects within SHRI should begin by addressing the scientific plurality of the field. Front. Robot. AI **9**, 741478 (2022)
27. Henschel, A., Laban, G., Cross, E.S.: What makes a robot social? A review of social robots from science fiction to a home or hospital near you. Curr. Robot. Rep. **2**, 9–19 (2021)

28. Hortensius, R., Cross, E.S.: From automata to animate beings: the scope and limits of attributing socialness to artificial agents. Ann. N. Y. Acad. Sci. **1426**(1), 93–110 (2018)
29. National Federation of University Co-operative Associations: Summary report of the 57th student life survey part 2 (2022). https://www.univcoop.or.jp/press/life/pdf/pdf_report57.pdf. Accessed 19 Dec 2023
30. Masato, K., Haruhisa, M.: Relationships between help-seeking preferences of college students and related psychological variables: a focus on student counseling, friends, and families. Jpn. J. Counsel. Sci. **37**(3), 260–269 (2004)
31. Tanaka, M.: Various aspects of 'Encouraging Utterances' found in drama scripts. Keio University Japanese Language and Culture Education Center, Japanese Language and Japanese Language Education Research Bulletin Paper **43**, 19–35 (2015)
32. Yoshida, N., Takanashi, K., Den, Y.: Recognition of backchannel expressions in dialogue and their problems. In: 15th Annual Meeting of the Association for Natural Language Processing, Japan, pp. 430–433 (2009)

Trust Prediction in Assistive Robotics Using Multi-modal Video Transformers

Nico Lingg$^{(\boxtimes)}$ⓘ and Yiannis Demirisⓘ

Imperial College London, London SW7 2AZ, UK
{n.lingg20,y.demiris}@imperial.ac.uk

Abstract. Trust is crucial for effective human-robot interaction in assistive robotics. This paper presents a proof-of-concept study for transformer-based trust prediction, building on our previous work in understanding and measuring trust. We introduce a novel multi-modal video transformer to predict user trust in human-robot interactions with an autonomous wheelchair. We collected a comprehensive dataset comprising over 850,000 tokens, equivalent to approximately 4 h of egocentric video streams, along with synchronized continuous trust recordings, eye gaze patterns, physiological data, and trust measurements from 34 diverse participants. Our research utilizes Trusty, a tool for continuous trust measurement, which has been previously validated against traditional methods. Our model utilizes a pre-trained Vision Transformer (ViT) with frozen weights to extract spatial features from video frames. Visual representations are enriched with the user's eye gaze, heart rate, and electrodermal activity in a fusion module. Fusion outputs are temporally processed by a transformer, and the final token in the sequence is used to predict trust. This architectural design leverages transformers' proven capabilities in processing high-dimensional visual data, effectively fusing signals across modalities, and scaling to larger datasets. The best-performing model achieves approximately 64% accuracy in predicting trust levels (high, medium, low), with eye gaze data significantly enhancing performance. Future work will focus on personalisation and real-time adaptive robot behaviour based on trust predictions.

Keywords: Trust in Robotics · Trust Model · Trust Modeling · Trust Prediction · Multi-modal Learning · Multi-Task Learning · Sensor-Data Fusion · Transformer-Based Trust Model · Human-Robot Interaction

1 Introduction

Trust is a crucial factor in the successful integration of assistive robots into daily life. As autonomous systems become increasingly capable of performing complex tasks such as dressing assistance [19, 20, 26], cooking [12], or bi-manual handovers [29], the need for effective human-robot trust becomes essential. In assistive and social robotics, where user safety and comfort are critical, trust plays a vital role in fostering acceptance and ensuring satisfactory interactions [13, 27].

O. Palinko et al. (Eds.): ICSR + AI 2024, LNAI 15562, pp. 128–140, 2025.
https://doi.org/10.1007/978-981-96-3519-1_13

Recent research has revealed the dynamic nature of trust in human-robot interaction (HRI) [8]. Trust levels fluctuate throughout an interaction, influenced by various factors such as robot performance, behavior, and environmental conditions [13,17,31]. This dynamic characteristic poses significant challenges for trust modelling, particularly in unpredictable, unstructured environments typical of real-world assistive robotics applications [1,18].

Our previous work has focused on understanding and measuring trust in human-robot interactions, including how it may change over time. We introduced Trusty, a novel tool for continuous trust measurement in HRI [23], which overcomes limitations of traditional self-report methods. Using Trusty, we conducted extensive user studies with an autonomous wheelchair, collecting a rich dataset that includes continuous trust measurements, verbal self-reports, questionnaires, physiological data, eye gaze, head pose, and egocentric video. Statistical analysis of this data provided insights into how trust factors evolve during interaction and how they are influenced by the robot's performance [24].

Building on this foundation, we present proof-of-concept study demonstrating the feasibility of transformer-based models for trust prediction. Deploying this model in assistive robotic systems could enable real-time behaviour adjustments and personalized calibration. Our contributions include:

1. Conducting a comprehensive user study resulting in a novel, large-scale dataset of over 850,000 tokens, combining egocentric video, gaze, wheelchair telemetry, and continuous trust measurements.
2. Proposing a multi-modal video transformer that achieves 64% accuracy of trust level prediction.
3. Demonstrating that fusing multiple data modalities with egocentric video improves trust prediction accuracy.
4. Open-sourcing our project code as a modular framework for multi-modal video transformers. [1]

2   Background

2.1   Trust in Assistive Robotics

Prior research has extensively studied the factors affecting trust in robotics. A comprehensive meta-analysis by [13] categorizes the elements influencing trust into three main domains: human-related, robot-related, and environmental factors, highlighting trust's complexity. The meta-analysis reveals that robot-related factors, particularly performance, play the most significant role in shaping trust, surpassing environmental and human-related influences. [16] refines robot trust factors into performance, behaviour, and appearance categories to address their impact on trust as robots become more autonomous and human-like. Research by [8] also emphasizes trust's dynamic nature, finding it fluctuates over time and context. In response, our previous work introduced Trusty, a novel

---

[1] The code is available on GitHub at https://github.com/NicoLingg/multi-modal-video-transformer.

tool for continuous trust measurement in HRI [23,24]. Trusty advances beyond conventional self-report constraints to capture trust's evolving nature, forming this work's basis. We consider trust arising when robots meet user expectations across human, robot (performance, behavior, appearance), and environmental factors while enabling efficient interactions. Trusty allows users to continuously rate perceived trust, providing a rich signal reflecting trust's dynamic changes influenced by these underlying dimensions during interactions.

2.2   Advancements in Trust Modeling

As the complexity of human-robot interactions grows, researchers have explored various computational approaches to model and predict trust in robotics applications. Traditional methods, such as deterministic regression models [28,42] and time series analysis [22,35], have provided valuable insights but may not fully capture the multi-modal nature of trust in unstructured environments. Probabilistic models, including HMMs [9] and POMDPs [5,38,46], account for some uncertainties but can be limited in adapting to dynamic real-world conditions. Game theoretic approaches [30,33] offer unique perspectives but may oversimplify the complexities of human-robot interaction.

While these methods have advanced our understanding of trust in HRI, recent progress in machine learning, particularly deep learning and transformer models, offers new possibilities. Transformers excel at processing complex, multi-modal data and capturing long-range dependencies [47], making them well-suited for the multifaceted nature of trust in HRI. Their success in video understanding tasks [2,3] suggests potential for processing the rich, temporal data in human-robot interactions. Although their application to trust prediction in robotics remains largely unexplored, transformers' ability to fuse multiple data modalities [47] positions them as a promising tool for capturing the nuanced dynamics of trust in assistive robotics.

2.3   Multi-modal Data for Enhanced Context

Recent research in trust modeling suggests that diverse data sources may offer valuable insights into the nuances of human-robot interactions. Eye-tracking and ego-centric video data have shown particular promise. Studies indicate that real-time eye movements can reflect trust levels, with gaze patterns potentially signaling changes in system performance [11,25]. In automated driving research, higher trust has been associated with less frequent system monitoring [14]. Combining eye-tracking with other physiological measures, like galvanic skin response, may further enhance trust prediction [43].

These findings point to the potential of multi-modal data in providing a more comprehensive view of trust. Our study leverages a data-driven approach to explore patterns in this rich, multi-dimensional data, aiming to capture subtle cues that might be overlooked in traditional, unimodal approaches.

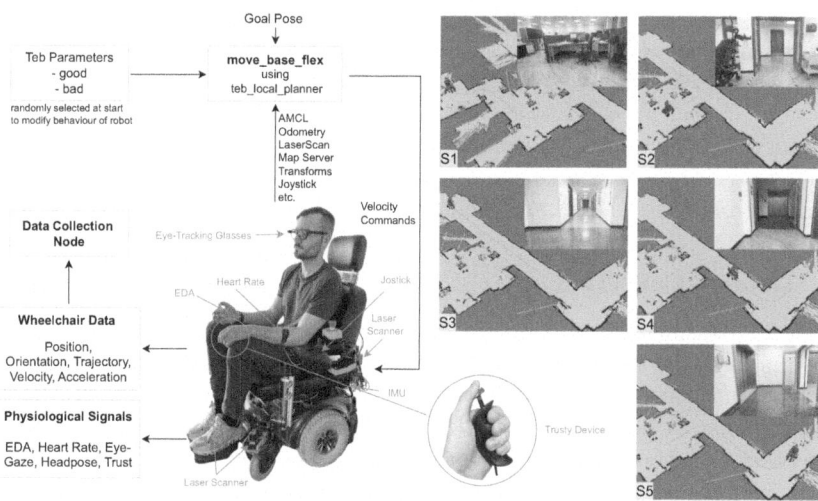

Fig. 1. High-level architecture of our navigation and data collection system, featuring the utilization of randomly selected teb_local_planner [34] parameters to modulate the performance of the wheelchair as it navigates to five positions (S1-S5) shown in the map, including navigating through a narrow section, corridors, and doors. We collect wheelchair and physiological data from the user as the wheelchair travels along the highlighted trajectory (green) for each segment. (Color figure online)

3   Real-World Experiment Description

3.1   Experimental Procedure

Our research utilises a smart wheelchair which traverses an unstructured office environment. In sessions lasting about five minutes, participants were tasked with navigating to five predetermined positions. We varied the wheelchair's behaviour between two conditions: good-performing (smooth and efficient) and bad-performing (sudden stops and swerves, but safe). Figure 1 depicts the system configuration and a map of the environment. Participants completed initial trust questionnaires [21,36,44], familiarized themselves with the system, and were equipped with physiological sensors and eye-tracking glasses. The randomly assigned performance level remained unknown to participants. After task completion, participants filled out final trust questionnaires. Each 30–45 min trial was conducted in a controlled, distraction-free environment. Imperial College London's SETREC granted ethical approval for this study.

3.2   Autonomous Wheelchair System

The ARTA platform [4] is outfitted with an array of sensors: a Phidgets spatial 3/3/3 IMU for orientation tracking, dual Hokuyo URG-04LX-UG1 scanning laser rangefinders at the front for obstacle detection, and a SICK LMS200 rangefinder at the rear. Navigation and localization are managed through the Adaptive Monte Carlo Localization (AMCL) algorithm [10] and the Move Base Flex (MBF) [32] extension within ROS. We used teb_local_planner [34] for local planning, which generates efficient paths while avoiding obstacles. This planner allows for flexible trajectory following and performance modulation through variable adjustment, enabling precise movement in unstructured environments and facilitating fine-tuned control of the wheelchair's behavior during the experiment.

3.3   Dataset Collection

During the session, participants reported continuous trust levels using Trusty, a custom-built device based on a modified slot-car controller [23], allowing for real-time, intuitive trust measurement without visual confirmation. Physiological data such as heart rate at 1 Hz using the Polar Verity Sense device and electrodermal activity (EDA) at 60 Hz via the Bitalino device [7]. Pupil Labs eye-tracking glasses [39] captured eye gaze (XY coordinates, elevation, azimuth) and head pose (roll, pitch). Finally, wheelchair telemetry was collected, including spatial positioning (XY coordinates), distance to nearest obstacles, orientation, and velocity. All device data were synchronized and time aligned before training.

3.4   Participants Data

The experimental cohort of 34 participants (17F, 16M, 1 undisclosed), aged 22–45 (avg. 27.6 years), included nearly an equal split between individuals with (47%) and without (53%) robotics experience, defined by their history of programming or building robots. This balanced distribution mitigates potential bias in trust prediction, as trust in robots is influenced by various factors beyond familiarity.

3.5   Supplementary Data

To increase training tokens, we collected supplementary data from a single subject across multiple sessions. This additional data was collected to enhance the model's ability to extract meaningful features from video inputs, as transformer models typically benefit from larger datasets. To prevent bias in trust prediction, these samples did not have trust labels and were masked from trust loss functions during training. Table 1 summarizes the dataset composition, totaling over 850,000 tokens across trust-labeled and supplementary data.

Table 1. Dataset composition. Trust-labeled data from 34 participants combined with supplementary data (1 subject) without trust labels. Supplementary data aims to enhance regression tasks, indirectly improving trust prediction.

Dataset	Frames	Subjects	Signals
Supplementary Data	414,799	1	
Participants Data	444,537	34	+ Trust
Total	**859,336**		

Both include wheelchair performance, EDA, HR, head pose and eye gaze

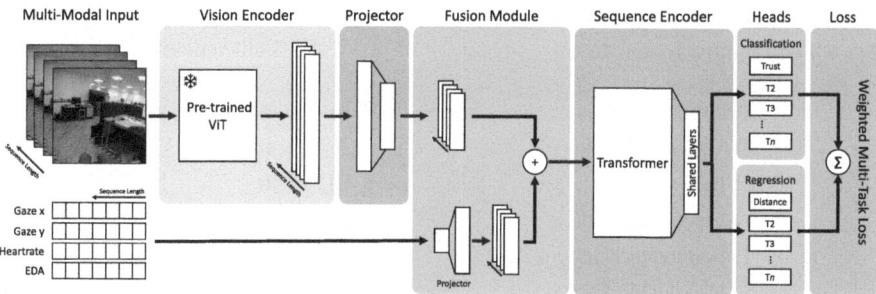

Fig. 2. Illustration of our proposed multi-modal video transformer architecture. The network intakes a sequence of image frames, processes spatial features through a frozen ViT, and reduces dimensionality via a projector. Separately, time-aligned eye gaze and physiological data are projected linearly to match the projector's output dimension, enabling fusion through element-wise addition. This is followed by temporal feature extraction through a sequence model. One shared linear layer is followed by separate prediction heads for each task. Task losses are aggregated in a weighted multi-task loss function.

4 Model

4.1 Multi-modal Video Transformer Architecture

We propose a multi-modal video transformer, illustrated in Fig. 2, to process sequences of egocentric user data. The architecture comprises five components:

1. **Vision Encoder**: Video frames are individually passed through a pre-trained ViT [45] with frozen weights for feature extraction.
2. **Projector**: Frame representations are projected to a lower dimension using a multi-layer perceptron (MLP) with one hidden layer.
3. **Fusion Module**: Time-aligned eye gaze and physiological data are projected linearly to match the Projector's output dimension and then element-wise added to projector outputs.
3. **Sequence Encoder**: Encoder-only transformer model composed of eight causal self-attention [41] and MLP blocks process the entire sequence of projector outputs, i.e. tokens. Following [40], we use RMS normalisation [49] and SwiGLU activations [37].
4. **Prediction Heads**: After sequential processing, the final tokens contain all necessary context for prediction. Following a single shared linear layer, each target is predicted separately.

Our modular approach presents several advantages over conventional video-native transformer architectures like ViVit [2] and TimeSformer [3]. Unlike these models, which interleave spatial and temporal feature extraction, our modular design allows for the utilisation of pre-trained, frozen ViT, concentrating computational efforts on temporal feature learning. In addition, by integrating contextual time-series signals (e.g. eye gaze, heart rate, electrodermal activity etc.)

Table 2. Model size. The number of trainable parameters of each component, except ViT, which remains frozen to take advantage of pre-trained efficiencies.

Model Component	Trainable Parameters	Frozen
1) Vision Encoder	0	Yes
2) Projector	114,946	No
3) Fusion Module	384	No
4) Sequence Encoder	1,049,628	No
5) Prediction Heads	18,189	No
Total	**1,184,043**	–

with image representations prior to sequential processing, our model achieves enhanced multi-modal temporal feature extraction. Lastly, our architecture's flexibility permits straightforward substitution of vision and sequence encoders depending on application needs. We employ σReparam of all learnable linear layers as proposed by [48] to improve training stability. This design enables our model to capture trust's complex dynamics in HRI while remaining scalable and adaptable to future transformer advancements. For a more comprehensive overview of the trainable parameters in each model component, see Table 2. For details on training hyperparameters, see the Model Training Hyperparameters table in the GitHub repository.

4.2 Data Processing

Prior to training, all data modalities were time-aligned, and time-series observations were normalised using statistics over the whole dataset. Trusty measurements were discretized into three equal-sized bins, resulting in balanced class distributions for the low, medium, and high trust levels. The input sequences consist of 200 video frames and their fusion data, totalling around six seconds in duration. Target labels align with the end of the input sequence. Video frames in training were augmented using standard computer vision techniques, including common spatial and visual transformations applied with varying probabilities, to improve model robustness and generalization. A comprehensive list of augmentations and their parameters is available in our project's GitHub repository. Eye gaze coordinates were transformed where applicable to maintain consistency with the augmented frames. All models trained were on a Nvidia RTX 4090.

4.3 Weighted Multi-task Loss Function

Video data is rich but unstructured, while multi-class trust labels (high, medium, low) offer limited feedback. To address this, we hypothesised that incorporating auxiliary perceptual targets would encourage the model to extract environmental features salient for trust prediction [6]. Our approach utilises a composite loss function $L = \sum_i w_i L_i$, with L_i denoting individual task losses.

Table 3. Experimental results. The best validation statistics for seven models, each trained with different input modalities (video, gaze, physiological data) and auxiliary perceptual targets, are summarized. Trust prediction accuracy improves by 4% (M5 vs M1) when the video-only model is trained with all targets. Adding gaze input data (XY coordinates) to video frames further improves performance by 10% (M6 vs M5). Incorporating gaze also halves the mean-absolute-error for gaze-related perceptual targets (azimuth, elevate), demonstrating the fusion module's efficacy. The transformer-based M6 outperforms its LSTM variant (M6 LSTM) by 12% in trust prediction and 11.4% in wheelchair perf. prediction. Using supplementary data (M6 vs M6 w/o SD) enhances all metrics, with gains of 10% in trust prediction and 13% in wheelchair performance prediction.

Model	Inputs	Classification Accuracy (%)		Regression Tasks (Mean Absolute Error) *Lower is better*								
		Trust	WC Perf.	X Pos. (m)	Y Pos. (m)	Dist. (m)	Orient. (deg)	Vel. (m/s)	Roll (deg)	Pitch (deg)	Azim. (deg)	Elev. (deg)
M1	V	50.7	-	-	-	-	-	-	-	-	-	-
M2	V	51.5	86.5	-	-	-	-	-	-	-	-	-
M3	V	49.9	87.9	0.55	0.60	0.09	8.23	0.09	-	-	-	-
M4	V	51.2	81.0	0.46	0.54	0.09	8.64	0.10	3.38	2.79	-	-
M5	V	54.7	84.3	0.49	0.56	0.08	6.42	0.10	3.96	3.21	10.44	10.25
M6	V + G	**64.3**	**88.3**	0.50	0.54	0.09	7.71	0.09	3.31	2.55	3.34	3.08
M7	V + G + P	57.3	84.6	0.51	0.59	0.10	6.40	0.10	3.52	3.08	3.89	3.15
M6 (LSTM)	V + G	52.1	76.9	0.62	0.68	0.18	7.51	0.13	3.92	3.68	4.23	3.85
M6 (w/o SD)	V + G	53.8	75.1	0.63	0.69	0.29	9.79	0.12	4.34	3.34	4.34	4.00

V = Video, G = Gaze, P = Physiological Data, WC Perf. = Wheelchair Performance, SD = Supplementary Data

5   Results

We conducted a series of tests to quantify the contribution of A) auxiliary perceptual targets, B) fusion inputs, and C) model architecture and supplementary data to the accuracy of the model's trust predictions. Our experiments demonstrate the feasibility of using a multi-modal video transformer to predict trust in human-robot interactions, translating trust dynamics into a practical tool for enhancing collaboration. Results are presented in Table ??. Further visualizations of the model performance are shown in Fig. 3.

5.1   Multi-Task Contribution

We begin with a baseline video-only model (M1) that predicts only trust. To quantify the contribution of each auxiliary perceptual target, we incrementally added them in thematic groups. A theme is assumed to be helpful for trust prediction if its addition improves trust accuracy on the validation set. Trust accuracy increases by 4% when gaze-related targets, namely elevation and azimuth, are added. While incorporating gaze-related auxiliary tasks improves trust prediction, the video-only model's performance remains only slightly above chance, suggesting the presence of a weak but learnable signal.

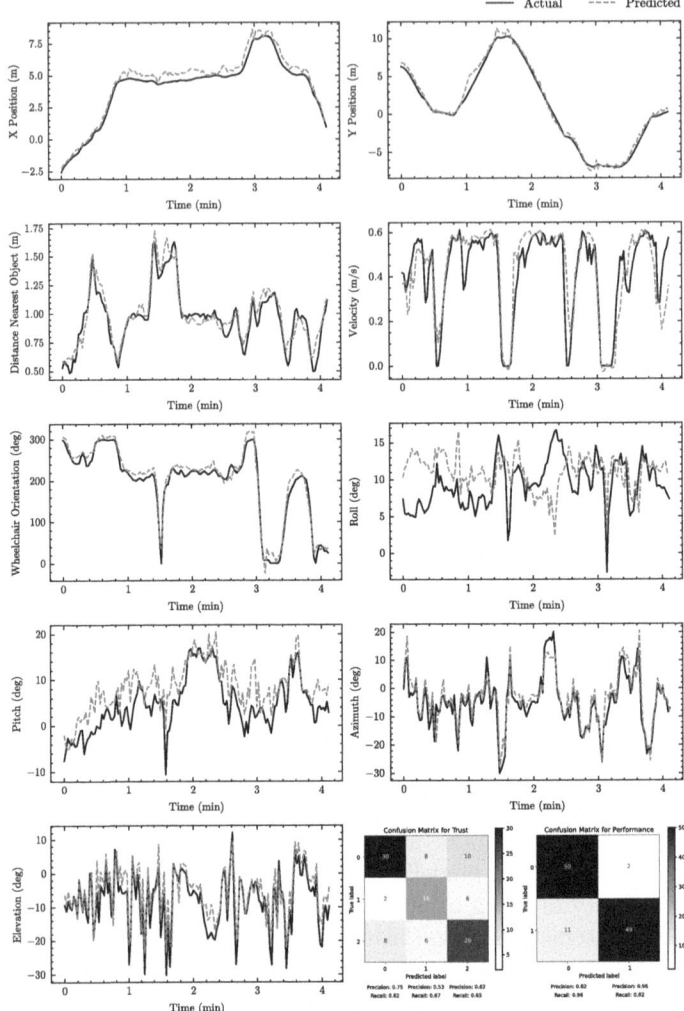

Fig. 3. M6's validation performance. Time-series plots show actual (solid) vs predicted (dashed) values, demonstrating pattern tracking. Confusion matrices display trust and performance classification accuracy.

5.2 Multi-modal Contribution

We further investigated the contribution of additional input modalities. Integrating eye gaze XY coordinates (M6) increased trust prediction accuracy by 10% (M6 vs M5) and halved mean-absolute-error for gaze-related perceptual targets, showcasing the fusion module's efficacy. Adding physiological data (heart rate and EDA, M7) yielded nuanced results: while trust classification accuracy decreased slightly compared to the video and gaze model, it still outperformed video-only models, suggesting a complex contribution that does not linearly enhance performance in all aspects. Our findings suggest that video transformers can predict user's trust levels (high, medium, low) with about 64% accuracy. This also supports our hypothesis that transformers effectively process rich, high-dimensional temporal data and perform multi-modal fusion, capturing complex trust relationships in HRI. Gaze data, both as input and auxiliary target, boosted trust prediction accuracy, while physiological data's role requires more research.

5.3 Model Architecture and Data Impact

To further validate our approach, we compared our transformer-based architecture with a simpler model and evaluated the impact of supplementary data. The transformer-based M6 outperformed its LSTM variant (M6 LSTM) by 12.2% and 11.4% in trust and wheelchair performance prediction, respectively. This performance difference suggests the transformer's enhanced ability to capture complex relationships in multi-modal data. Incorporating supplementary data (comparing M6 with M6 without SD) yielded improvements across all metrics, with notable increases of 10.5% in trust prediction, even though supplementary samples do not have trust labels. This aligns with broader scalability results in transformer research, as performance generally improves with compute (more data or more parameters) [15]. These findings support our choice of a transformer architecture for its scalability and potential for future improvements as we collect more data or expand to different robot types.

6 Conclusion

Our research presents a proof-of-concept for trust prediction in assistive robotics, building on our previous work on understanding of trust in HRI. By leveraging a dataset of over 850,000 temporal tokens, equivalent to approximately 4 h of egocentric video and synchronized multimodal data collected from user experiments with an autonomous wheelchair, we successfully trained a multi-modal video transformer to predict trust levels.

The incorporation of auxiliary perceptual targets alongside trust prediction emerged as a key factor, enhancing the model's accuracy by 4% (from 50.7% to 54.7%). Furthermore, fusing video frames with eye gaze data significantly improved trust prediction, boosting performance by an additional 10% (from 54.7% to 64.3%). These results underscore the importance of multi-modal data in capturing the nuanced context of human-robot interactions.

Future work will focus on improving model performance (e.g. by expanding our dataset to improve the model's robustness and generalisability), exploring personalisation by incorporating individual differences (e.g., prior experience with robots, age) into trust prediction, and developing real-time prediction capabilities to enable adaptive robot behavior. By refining this approach, we aim to translate our understanding of user trust into actionable insights, driving improvements in assistive robot design and operation. This work lays the foundation for more intuitive human-robot collaboration in assistive robotics, potentially enhancing user experience and system acceptance.

References

1. Abeywickrama, D.B., et al.: On specifying for trustworthiness. Commun. ACM **1**, 98–109 (2023)
2. Arnab, A., Dehghani, M., Heigold, G., Sun, C., Lučić, M., Schmid, C.: ViViT: a video vision transformer (2021)
3. Bertasius, G., Wang, H., Torresani, L.: Is space-time attention all you need for video understanding? In: International Conference on Machine Learning, pp. 813–824. PMLR (2021)
4. Carlson, T., Demiris, Y.: Collaborative control for a robotic wheelchair: evaluation of performance, attention, and workload. Trans. Syst. Man Cybern. **42**, 876–888 (2012)
5. Chen, M., Nikolaidis, S., Soh, H., Hsu, D., Srinivasa, S.: Planning with trust for human-robot collaboration. In: Proceedings of the 2018 ACM/IEEE International Conference on Human-robot Interaction, pp. 307–315 (2018)
6. Crawshaw, M.: Multi-task learning with deep neural networks: a survey. arXiv preprint arXiv:2009.09796 (2020)
7. Da Silva, H.P., Fred, A., Martins, R.: Biosignals for everyone. IEEE Pervasive Comput. **4**, 64–71 (2014)
8. Desai, M., Kaniarasu, P., Medvedev, M., Steinfeld, A., Yanco, H.: Impact of robot failures and feedback on real-time trust. In: IEEE International Conference on HRI, pp. 251–258 (2013)
9. ElSalamouny, E., Sassone, V., Nielsen, M.: HMM-based trust model. In: Degano, P., Guttman, J.D. (eds.) FAST 2009. LNCS, vol. 5983, pp. 21–35. Springer, Heidelberg (2010). https://doi.org/10.1007/978-3-642-12459-4_3
10. Fox, D., Burgard, W., Dellaert, F., Thrun, S.: Monte Carlo localization: efficient position estimation for mobile robots. In: AAAI/IAAI (343-349) (1999)
11. Goubard, C., Demiris, Y.: Cooking up trust: eye gaze and posture for trust-aware action selection in human-robot collaboration. In: Proceedings of the First International Symposium on Trustworthy Autonomous Systems, pp. 1–5 (2023)
12. Goubard, C., Demiris, Y.: Learning self-confidence from semantic action embeddings for improved trust in human-robot interaction. In: 2024 IEEE International Conference on Robotics and Automation (ICRA), pp. 7859–7866. IEEE (2024)
13. Hancock, P.A., Billings, D.R., Schaefer, K.E., Chen, J.Y., De Visser, E.J., Parasuraman, R.: A meta-analysis of factors affecting trust in human-robot interaction. Human factors pp. 517–527 (2011)
14. Hergeth, S., Lorenz, L., Vilimek, R., Krems, J.F.: Keep your scanners peeled: Gaze behavior as a measure of automation trust during highly automated driving. Hum. Factors **3**, 509–519 (2016)
15. Hoffmann, J., et al.: Training compute-optimal large language models. arXiv preprint arXiv:2203.15556 (2022)
16. Khavas, Z.R., Ahmadzadeh, Reza, S.: Modeling trust in human-robot interaction: a survey. In: Social Robotics, pp. 529–541 (2020)
17. Khavas, Z.R., Ahmadzadeh, S.R., Robinette, P.: Modeling trust in human-robot interaction: a survey. In: Wagner, A.R., et al. (eds.) ICSR 2020. LNCS (LNAI), vol. 12483, pp. 529–541. Springer, Cham (2020). https://doi.org/10.1007/978-3-030-62056-1_44
18. Kok, B.C., Soh, H.: Trust in robots: challenges and opportunities. Current Robot. Rep. **1**(4), 297–309 (2020). https://doi.org/10.1007/s43154-020-00029-y

19. Kotsovolis, S., Demiris, Y.: Bi-manual manipulation of multi-component garments towards robot-assisted dressing. In: 2023 IEEE International Conference on Robotics and Automation (ICRA), pp. 9865–9871. IEEE (2023)

20. Kotsovolis, S., Demiris, Y.: Model predictive control with graph dynamics for garment opening insertion during robot-assisted dressing. In: 2024 IEEE International Conference on Robotics and Automation (ICRA), pp. 883–890. IEEE (2024)

21. Körber, M.: Theoretical considerations and development of a questionnaire to measure trust in automation. In: Bagnara, S., Tartaglia, R., Albolino, S., Alexander, T., Fujita, Y. (eds.) IEA 2018. AISC, vol. 823, pp. 13–30. Springer, Cham (2019). https://doi.org/10.1007/978-3-319-96074-6_2

22. Lee, J.D., Moray, N.: Trust, self-confidence, and operators' adaptation to automation. Int. J. Human Comput. Stud. 80, 153–184 (1994)

23. Lingg, N., Demiris, Y.: Beyond self-report: a continuous trust measurement device for HRI. In: 2023 32nd IEEE International Conference on Robot and Human Interactive Communication (RO-MAN), pp. 2220–2225. IEEE (2023)

24. Lingg, N., Demiris, Y.: Building trust in assistive robotics: insights from a real-world mobile navigation experiment. In: Proceedings of the First International Symposium on Trustworthy Autonomous Systems, pp. 1–7 (2023)

25. Lu, Y., Sarter, N.: Eye tracking: a process-oriented method for inferring trust in automation as a function of priming and system reliability. IEEE Trans. Human Mach. Syst. 6, 560–568 (2019)

26. Luo, H., Demiris, Y.: Bi-manual robot shoe lacing. In: 2023 IEEE/RSJ International Conference on Intelligent Robots and Systems (IROS), pp. 8772–8775. IEEE (2023)

27. Malle, B.F., Ullman, D.: A multidimensional conception and measure of human-robot trust. In: Trust in Human-robot Interaction, pp. 3–25. Elsevier (2021)

28. Muir, B.M., Moray, N.: Trust in automation. Part II. Experimental studies of trust and human intervention in a process control simulation. Ergonomics 39, 429–460 (1996)

29. Ovur, S.E., Demiris, Y.: Naturalistic robot-to-human bimanual handover in complex environments through multi-sensor fusion. IEEE Trans. Autom. Sci. Eng. 21, 3730–3741 (2023)

30. Paeng, E., Wu, J., Boerkoel, J.: Human-robot trust and cooperation through a game theoretic framework. In: Proceedings of the AAAI Conference on Artificial Intelligence, vol. 1 (2016)

31. Park, S.: Multifaceted trust in tourism service robots. Ann. Tour. Res. 81, 102888 (2020)

32. Pütz, S., Simón, J.S., Hertzberg, J.: Move base flex a highly flexible navigation framework for mobile robots. In: 2018 IEEE/RSJ International Conference on Intelligent Robots and Systems (IROS), pp. 3416–3421. IEEE (2018)

33. Razin, Y.S., Feigh, K.M.: Committing to interdependence: a implications from game theory for human-robot trust. Paladyn, J. Behav. Robot. 1, 481–502 (2021)

34. Rösmann, C., Feiten, W., Wösch, T., Hoffmann, F., Bertram, T.: Trajectory modification considering dynamic constraints of autonomous robots. In: 7th German Conference on Robotics, pp. 1–6 (2012)

35. Sadrfaridpour, B., Saeidi, H., Wang, Y.: An integrated framework for human-robot collaborative assembly in hybrid manufacturing cells. In: 2016 IEEE International Conference on Automation Science and Engineering (CASE), pp. 462–467. IEEE (2016)

36. Schaefer, K.E.: Measuring trust in human robot interactions: development of the "trust perception scale-HRI". In: Robust Intelligence and Trust in Autonomous Systems, pp. 191–218 (2016)
37. Shazeer, N.: GLU variants improve transformer. arXiv preprint arXiv:2002.05202 (2020)
38. Tilloo, P., Parron, J., Obidat, O., Zhu, M., Wang, W.: A POMDP-based robot-human trust model for human-robot collaboration. In: 2022 12th International Conference on CYBER Technology in Automation, Control, and Intelligent Systems, pp. 1009–1014. IEEE (2022)
39. Tonsen, M., Baumann, C.K., Dierkes, K.: A high-level description and performance evaluation of pupil invisible. arXiv preprint arXiv:2009.00508 (2020)
40. Touvron, H., et al.: Llama: open and efficient foundation language models (2023). https://arxiv.org/abs/2302.13971
41. Vaswani, A., et al.: Attention is all you need. In: Advances in Neural Information Processing Systems (2017)
42. de Vries, P., Midden, C., Bouwhuis, D.: The effects of errors on system trust, self-confidence, and the allocation of control in route planning. Int. J. Human Comput. Stud. **58**, 719–735 (2003)
43. Walker, F., Wang, J., Martens, M.H., Verwey, W.B.: Gaze behaviour and electro-dermal activity: objective measures of drivers trust in automated vehicles. Transp. Res. Part F. Traffic. Psychol. Behav. **64**, 401–412 (2019)
44. Wojton, H.M., Porter, D.T., Lane, S., Bieber, C., Madhavan, P.: Initial validation of the trust of automated systems test (toast). J. Soc. Psychol. **160**, 735–750 (2020)
45. Wu, B., et al.: Visual transformers: Token-based image representation and processing for computer vision (2020)
46. Xu, A., Dudek, G.: OPTIMo: online probabilistic trust inference model for asymmetric human-robot collaborations. In: Proceedings of the Tenth Annual ACM/IEEE International Conference on Human-Robot Interaction, pp. 221–228. ACM (2015)
47. Xu, P., Zhu, X., Clifton, D.A.: Multimodal learning with transformers: a survey. IEEE Trans. Pattern Anal. Mach. Intell. **45**(10), 12113–12132 (2023)
48. Zhai, S., et al.: Stabilizing transformer training by preventing attention entropy collapse. In: International Conference on Machine Learning, pp. 40770–40803. PMLR (2023)
49. Zhang, B., Sennrich, R.: Root mean square layer normalization. In: Advances in Neural Information Processing Systems (2019)

Towards Human-Robot Co-creative Collaboration Through Interactive Task Dialogue

Hong Lu$^{(\boxtimes)}$ (iD), Jingwen Feng, Emma Bethel, Vasanth Sarathy(iD),
Elaine Short(iD), and Matthias Scheutz(iD)

Tufts University, Medford, MA 02155, USA
hlu07@tufts.edu

Abstract. There is currently relatively little work on architectures and evaluations of robots that support creative designs of human interactants in manipulation tasks through dialogue. We build a dialogue system by integrating a large language model into a robot cognitive architecture and investigate whether engaging in dialogues with the robot collaborator on a creative task has positive effects on task satisfaction and experience of the human, evaluating the effect of dialogue on perceived robot utility, intelligence, and supportiveness as a creative partner. We test our hypotheses with a cake decoration task during which participants collaborate with a robot arm equipped with a mixed-initiative co-creative dialogue system to place decorations on a dummy cake. The results show that the participants prefer robots that make reasonable suggestions compared to random suggestions and that they perceive those robots to provide more creative support.

Keywords: Human-robot creative collaboration · Dialogue system · Cognitive architecture

1 Introduction

Collaborative robots are being increasingly designed to help humans perform their tasks. For instance, robots are being designed to hand over tools in a way that makes it convenient for the humans to immediately use them [16] and optimize task allocation in collaborative assembly [23]. In this paper, we instead investigate intuitive and creative collaboration, motivated by potential applications in the arts, entertainment, and in assistive robotics where robots carry out creative tasks that users are not collocated to directly execute themselves. Creativity can help people lead happier and more meaningful lives [4,12]. Given the importance of creativity, there has been a rise of interest in fostering human creativity through human-robot creative collaboration. Research in this area shows that interacting with a social robot can facilitate creativity. For instance, Kahn et al. show that participants are able to generate more ideas in a Zen rock garden task when a humanoid robot encourages them and shows relevant images

O. Palinko et al. (Eds.): ICSR + AI 2024, LNAI 15562, pp. 141–157, 2025.
https://doi.org/10.1007/978-981-96-3519-1_14

and video clips compared to the base condition in which the participants access the same information through self-paced PowerPoint presentation [10]. Oliviera et al. show that children are able to generate more ideas during storytelling when playing with an intervention tool robot that exhibits creative behaviors compared to the control condition in which the robot is turned off [3].

Fig. 1. The cake decoration task setup

Buyukgoz et al. find that participants' generated more new ideas when interacting with a robot exhibiting medium level of proactive behavior in the form of verbal interruptions compared to when interacting with a robot exhibiting high level of proactive behavior [6]. However, not a lot of work has been done to investigate the effects of different modes of creative agent initiative in the form of suggestions and justifications using architectures that both support interactive task dialogues and ground the dialogues in physical manipulations. We present such an architecture and hypothesize that:

H1: Task dialogues with a robot will increase task satisfaction and experience.
H2: A robot that offers suggestions and task-specific reasoning behind suggestions is perceived as more intelligent.
H3: A robot that offers suggestions and task-specific reasoning behind suggestions provides more creative support to the user.
H4: Users prefer collaborating with a robot that offers task-specific reasoning behind its suggestions.
H5: Users are less likely to reject suggestions from the robot that offers task-specific reasoning behind suggestions.
H6: Users with higher creative self-efficacy are more likely to reject suggestions.

We present an interactive task dialogue system that interfaces with the Distributed Interactive Cognition Affect and Reflection Architecture (DIARC) to ground natural language descriptions of the task in the robot's actions [18]. The system is not only able to engage with the participant in a dialogue to complete a cake decoration task as shown in Fig. 1 but can also make placement suggestions for decorative items.

We validated this dialogue system in a within-subjects user evaluation in which participants worked with three different versions of the robot to complete the task. We collected participants' ratings of creative support, perceived robot intelligence, task experience and satisfaction as well as open-ended feed-back on all three conditions. Finally, we compared the relative utility of the three robot configurations. The results showed that while the robot's participation in interactive task dialogues tended to increase the user's perceived creative support, the robot's ability to give task-specific justifications for suggestions had a large positive effect on not only the creative support the user received but also the overall user experience. In summary, our contributions are as follows:

- We present an architecture that integrates a large language model into a robot cognitive architecture to support interactive task dialogues.
- We present user evaluation results on a co-creative task with different modes of agent initiative.

2   Background

2.1   Human-AI Mixed-Initiative Co-Creation

Mixed-initiative co-creation (MI-CC) refers to the process during which a human and an artificial intelligence (AI) system take the initiative to contribute to the creation of an end product [22]. Previous research has investigated mixed initiative co-creative systems that create digital products. For example, Alveraz et al. explore MI-CC in storytelling [2] and Liapis et al. explore it in game design [14]. We focus on architectures that collaborate during ideation through task dialogues while interactively carrying out the physical manipulations for the user. Our system is an instance of an MI-CC system that brings the creation into the physical world. Interaction with a physical MI-CC that communicates ideas through natural language and is solely responsible for the physical manipulations has different properties than previously-studied systems. Since users may perceive the system as more of a creative partner than a tool, it is important to directly investigate it as we do in this work.

2.2   Human-Robot Creative and Physical Collaboration

There has been extensive research on human-robot physical collaboration in which success is clearly defined. Popular tasks for evaluating human-robot physical collaboration include assembly tasks [1,19], construction tasks [21], sorting tasks [9], human-robot navigation in search and rescue [8], and efficient tool handover [16]. In contrast, our work addresses creative tasks in which the goals of the tasks are loosely defined and humans have more freedom to complete the tasks according to their preferences. More specifically, our work addresses human-robot co-creation tasks during which both the human and the robot participate in the ideation process.

Recently, there has been a rise in interest in human-robot creative collaboration. However, research in this area has focused on tasks that either lack a physical aspect or on tasks in which the robot and human both take part in the physical aspect. For example, Sandoval et al. [17] investigate people's perception of robot's creativity through a storytelling game with a Wizard of Oz setup, Thorn et al. [20] explore observers' perception of a robot after watching videos of it dancing to a human pianist's music, Kahn et al. [10] measure participants' increase in creativity when collaborating with a robot that encourages them to think of more ideas during a Zen rock garden task, and Buyukgoz et al. [6] study the effects of a robot's proactive behavior in the form of verbal interruptions on participants' creativity. None of these tasks requires the robot to physically manipulate objects. On the other hand, Lin et al. [15] present a co-creative process in which a robot needs to move a pen across a piece of paper to sketch with the participant and Law et al. [13] showcase a collaborative design task in which the robot and the human simultaneously manipulate a tangible user interface. While these tasks involve physical manipulations, both the human and the robot equally participate in the physical aspect. None of these tasks involve collaborative ideation through natural language dialogues. Our work addresses tasks in which collaboration through natural language happens during ideation and the physical manipulation is solely done by the robot. We expect that this approach will have applications in assistive robotics and service robotics.

3   Experimental System Overview

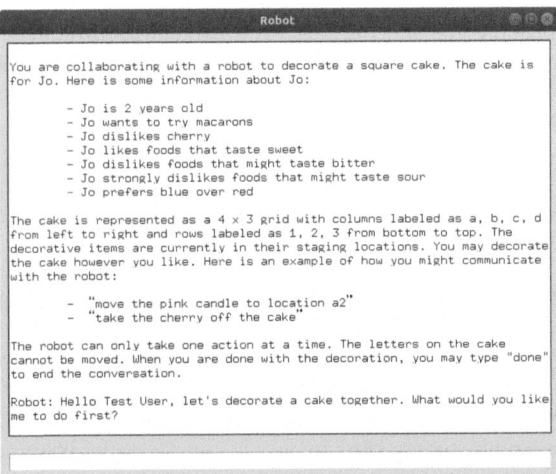

Fig. 2. The text user interface

To study the effects of interactive task dialogue on the human user's task satisfaction and experience, we developed a system consisting of a dialogue manager that interfaces with DIARC capable of carrying out a cake decoration task [18].

The cake decoration setup consists of a textual user interface and a Gen3 Kinova robotic arm. The physical setup of the cake decoration is shown in Fig. 1. The cake is represented as a grid with columns labeled a, b, c, d and rows labeled 1, 2, 3. The robot is able to take two high-level actions: moving a decoration to a location on the cake or taking an object off the cake and putting it back in its staging location. The user communicates with the robot arm through a text user interface shown in Fig. 2.

3.1 Dialogue System

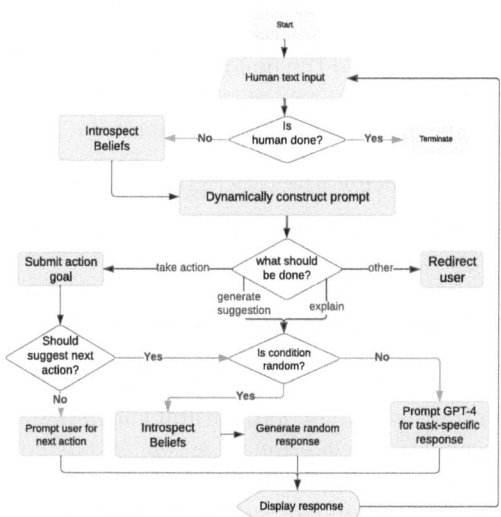

Fig. 3. Dialogue program flow

The dialogue system, based on GPT-4, generated both appropriate responses to human text inputs and made the appropriate robot action function calls based on the conversation. Figure 3 illustrates the program flow of the dialogue system. After receiving human text input, the program appends it to the conversation history. The program dynamically fills in a prompt template with descriptions of the current state of the task. The system then queries GPT-4 with the filled-in prompt and the conversation history for what the response should be. If the output is "action", the system chooses the appropriate action function signature and extracts parameter values from the conversation history. If the output is "suggestion", the system either generates a "reasonable" suggestion or a random suggestion on what next action to take based on the experimental condition. If the output is "explain", the system either generates a task-specific or a vague explanation based on the experimental condition. If the output is "other", the system displays a pre-determined response to inform the user that it cannot respond to their request and redirects the user back to the cake decoration task. To ensure that the human and the robot take approximately equal initiative in the task, the robot alternates between prompting the human for what it should do next and giving a suggestion on what to do next. More specifically, the robot generates a suggestion in two cases: when directly prompted by the human and when it has just successfully completed an action commanded by the human. The robot does not generate a suggestion when it has just completed an action suggested by itself. As a result, the robot proactively suggests a next move only about half of the time. The dialogue system interacts with DIARC when carrying out a robot action and when introspecting the robot's beliefs about the task state. We use DIARC as the robot's cognitive architecture because it is easily configurable. In our case, the LLM-based dialogue system acts as the natural language processing components–namely, the Natural Language Understanding (NLU), Natural Language Generation (NLG) and the dialogue manager components in the cognitive architecture. The robot has two user-facing actions: moving a decoration to a location on the cake and taking a decoration off the cake. We built "action scripts" for both actions using pre-existing primitive actions in DIARC. When trying to execute an action, the dialogue system submits a string consisting of an action script signature with parameter values, e.g., *TakeOffCake(cherry)* as an action goal to the goal manager. The dialogue system then receives an action status after the completion or failure of the action from the goal manager and reports it to the user. When constructing the task description prompt for the LLM, the robot receives the robot's current beliefs represented as predicates that evaluate to true about the world, e.g., *at(cherry, a3)* and *freecakeloc(b1)*. The dialogue system translates these into natural language descriptions, e.g., *the cherry is at location a3* and *the location b1 on the cake is not occupied* and fills in a prompt template with these descriptions of the current state of the task. Similarly, when generating a random suggestion on what valid action to take next, the dialogue system queries DIARC for beliefs on what objects exist, i.e., *object(X, physobj)*, which objects the robot is able to pick up, i.e., *canpickup(X)*, which locations are unoccupied, i.e., *freecakeloc(X)*, and which objects are on the cake, i.e., *on(X, cake)*. The dialogue system generates a random valid suggestion by randomly choosing an object to place at a random unoccupied location or by randomly choosing an object that's on the cake to be taken off. We show examples of conversations between the dialogue system and participants below.

3.2   Experiment Conditions

To study the effects of having versus not having dialogue and different modes of agent initiative, we implemented three experiment conditions: no dialogue, dialogue with random suggestions and agent initiative, and dialogue with reasonable suggestions and agent initiative. Participants work with a robot arm to decorate a cake for a customer named Jo with the following given information in all three conditions.

– Jo is 2 years old

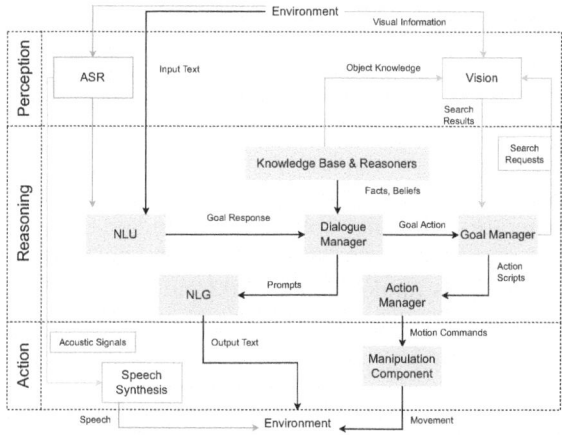

Fig. 4. The DIARC cognitive architecture with a goal manager, an action manager, and a customized dialogue manager, NLU and NLG components. The blue components were replaced by a Large Language Model (LLM). (Color figure online)

- Jo wants to try macarons
- Jo dislikes cherry
- Jo likes foods that taste sweet
- Jo dislikes foods that might taste bitter
- Jo strongly dislikes foods that might taste sour
- Jo prefers blue over red

No Dialogue. In the no dialogue condition, the robot serves as an assistive tool in picking up and placing the decorations. The robot follows commands and gives no suggestions on what to do next.

Robot interaction in the no-dialogue condition

PARTICIPANT: put the mint macaron at a2
SYSTEM: The robot is processing your message...
SYSTEM: The robot has successfully completed the action
PARTICIPANT: take the cherry off the cake
SYSTEM: The robot is processing your message...
SYSTEM: The robot has successfully completed the action
...
PARTICIPANT: done
SYSTEM: Goodbye! Have a nice day!

As shown in the conversation above, the participant receives no feedback other than system messages reporting the robot's status in the third-person perspective.

Random Suggestion. In the random suggestion case, the robot serves a more active role in designing the cake by making suggestions. After action completion, the robot generates a response containing a random suggestion and a vague justification. The suggestion is randomly selected from the set of all valid next actions. The justification is randomly selected from a set of predefined sentences expressing the tautological idea that "this is a good action because it is good."

Robot interaction in the random suggestion condition

ROBOT: Hello Human, let's decorate a cake together. What would you like me to do first?
PARTICIPANT: take the raspberry off the cake
SYSTEM: The robot is processing your message...
ROBOT: I have completed the action. Let's move the cherry to location c3. This decision is smart because it makes a positive difference. What do you think of this idea?
PARTICIPANT: ok. let's do it!
SYSTEM: The robot is processing your message...
ROBOT: I have moved the cherry to location c3. What would you like me to do next?
PARTICIPANT: put blueberries on b1. This will provide a nice y=x symmetry!
SYSTEM: The robot is processing your message...
ROBOT: I have completed the action. Let's move the white chocolate cube to location d1. Doing this action is good because it'll lead to better outcomes. What do you think of this idea?
PARTICIPANT: Nah! Suggest something else!
SYSTEM: The robot is processing your message...
ROBOT: Let's move the blue marshmallow to location d3. This is wise, as it means things will improve. What do you think of this idea?
...
PARTICIPANT: done
ROBOT: Goodbye! Have a nice day!

As shown in the conversation above, the robot alternates between prompting the participant for the next action and suggesting the next action. The predefined justifications for suggestions are designed so that the length of the responses in the random condition are comparable to that of the responses in the reasonable condition, controlling for robot response length in the study.

Reasonable Suggestion. In the reasonable suggestion case, GPT-4 is prompted to generate suggestions based on the task description and the robot's current belief state of the task. GPT-4 generates suggestions in the following format: "Let's {description of action}.{reason for selecting the action}.{ask what the human user thinks of this suggestion}" (the same format of response as that of the random suggestion robot).

Robot interaction in the reasonable suggestion condition

ROBOT: Hello Human, let's decorate a cake together. What would you like me to do first?
PARTICIPANT: Put the blueberries on d3
SYSTEM: The robot is processing your message...
ROBOT: I have completed the action. Let's put the mint macaron at location c1. Jo wants to try macarons and this will add a sweet taste that Jo likes. What do you think about this suggestion?
PARTICIPANT: I agree, lets do it
ROBOT: I have successfully placed the mint macaron on the cake. What would you like me to do next?
....
PARTICIPANT: done
ROBOT: Goodbye! Have a nice day!

As a result, the robot gives task-specific suggestions based on Jo's preferences.

4   Study Methodology

We conducted a within-subject user study during which participants experienced all three conditions mentioned above. Participants were told that they could decorate the cake however they liked. After each condition, the experiment facilitator manually reset the cake to the starting state shown in Fig. 1. As shown in Fig. 5, we randomized the order in which the participants experienced the three conditions. Furthermore, we performed block randomization to counterbalance the number of participants that were assigned to each order.

4.1   Measures

After each condition, participants completed a survey about their experience. The questionnaire measured participants' perceptions of the creative support received from the robot and the robot's intelligence, participants overall task satisfaction and experience, and open-ended feedback that asked the participant to "describe [their] experience working with the robot".

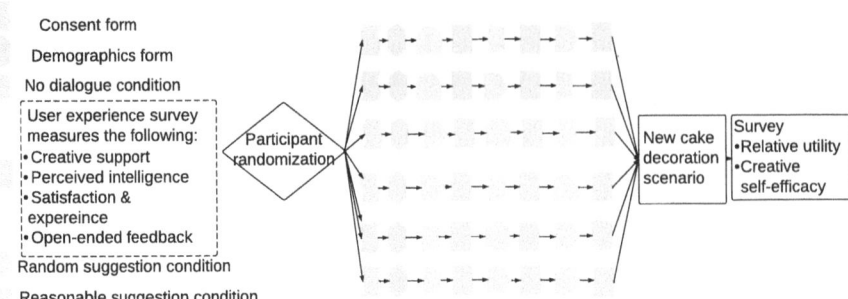

Fig. 5. Experiment Procedure. Participants were randomly assigned to one of the six orders of the three conditions. Participants started with filling the consent and demographic forms and ended with filling the creative self-efficacy survey. We applied the surveys using Qualtrics.

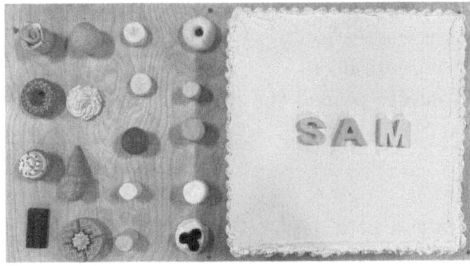

Fig. 6. New cake decoration scenario. Participants were asked to choose a robot to work with on the cake for a new customer

Suggestion Rejection Rate. We analyzed the log files for the rate at which the participants accepted, rejected, and modified the robot's suggestions in both the random condition and the reasonable condition.

Creative Support. Participants were asked to rate the following statements on a 5-point Likert scale. We designed the statements to measure the degree to which interaction with the robot supported artistic creativity. The items were based on the Creative Support Index, a validated measure for AI tools [7], modified to reflect the collaborative role of the robot and the physical nature of the task.

– Interacting with the robot stimulated my own thinking
– Interacting with the robot was helpful when decorating the cake
– Interacting with the robot was effective in completing the cake decoration task
– Interacting with the robot helped me come up with a better cake design
– Interacting with the robot led me to think of more ways of decorating the cake

Perceived Intelligence. We measured perceived intelligence of the robot using the Godspeed IV Intelligence scale [5]:

- 1=incompetent, 5=competent
- 1=ignorant, 5=knowledgeable
- 1=responsible, 5=responsible
- 1=unintelligent, 5=intelligent
- 1=foolish, 5=sensible

Overall Satisfaction and Experience. We measured the participant's overall satisfaction and experience with the following scale:

- How satisfied are you with the decorated cake (1 - Very unsatisfied, 5 - Very satisfied)
- How pleasant is your experience in working with this robot on the task (1 - Very unpleasant, 5 - very pleasant)

Relative Utility. We compared the utility of the no dialogue robot, the random suggestion robot and the reasonable suggestion robot by presenting the participant with another cake decoration scenario as shown in Fig. 6 and asking them to choose a robot partner. We physically showed the participant a larger cake, more decorative items, and information about a new customer with different preferences. We then asked the participant to select a robot to work with and describe their reason for selecting this robot.

Creative Self-Efficacy. After the conclusion of all three conditions, the participant rated the following statements on 5-point Likert scale to measure creative self-efficacy [11]:

- I think I am a creative person
- My creativity is important to who I am
- I know I can efficiently solve even complicated problems
- I trust my creative abilities
- Compared to my friends, I am distinguished by my imagination and ingenuity
- Many times I have proven that I can cope with difficult situations
- Being a creative person is important to me
- I am sure I can deal with problems requiring creative thinking
- I am good at proposing original solutions to problems
- Creativity is an important part of me
- Ingenuity is a characteristic which is important to me

The creative self-efficacy scale was administered at the end of the study to avoid any bias that might arise from subjects focusing on creative aspects early on.

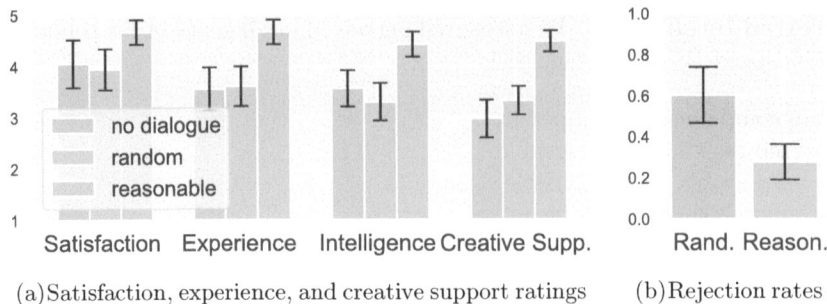

(a) Satisfaction, experience, and creative support ratings   (b) Rejection rates

Fig. 7. User Satisfaction, Experience, Creative Support, and Suggestion Rejection Rates

5   Results and Discussion

We performed the Friedman's test to analyze whether there was a significant difference in the ratings of task satisfaction, user experience, perceived intelligence, and creative support across the three conditions. We then performed the Conover's post hoc comparisons to determine which conditions were significantly different from each other. We performed a chi-square test to analyze the suggestion rejection rate among the three conditions. Furthermore, we checked for normality and performed a linear regression analysis to determine the effect of creative self-efficacy on the suggestion rejection rate.

5.1   Participants

We recruited 18 university students. Of those participants, 9 identified as male and 9 female. Participants had an average age of 23, with a minimum of 18 and maximum of 32. Most participants (61.1%) have never worked with robots. 44.4% identified as being very familiar with technology; 38.9% identified as being moderately familiar; 16.7% identified as being not familiar at all. Participants had an average creative self-efficacy rating of 3.8 with a minimum of 2.7 and a maximum of 5.0.

5.2   Task Satisfaction and Experience

Table 1. Conover's Post Hoc Comparisons - Satisfaction

group1	group2	T-Stat.	df	W_i	W_j	p	p_{bonf}	p_{holm}
no dialogue	random	0.397	34	32.500	30.500	0.694	1.000	0.694
no dialogue	reasonable	2.480	34	32.500	45.000	0.018	0.055	0.037
random	reasonable	2.876	34	30.500	45.000	0.007	0.021	0.021

Table 2. Conover's Post Hoc Comparisons - Experience

group1	group2	T-Stat.	df	W_i	W_j	p	p_{bonf}	p_{holm}
no dialogue	random	0.463	34	27.500	30.000	0.646	1.000	0.646
no dialogue	reasonable	4.262	34	27.500	50.500	< .001	< .001	< .001
random	reasonable	3.799	34	30.000	50.500	< .001	0.002	0.001

Participants reported better satisfaction with the outcome in the reasonable condition compared to the random condition (all p values < .05). Participants also reported better experience in the reasonable condition compared to the random condition and the no dialogue condition (all p values < .001) as shown in Fig. (a), Table 1 and Table 2. However, the difference between the random condition and the no dialogue condition was not statistically significant. This result partially supports H1.

5.3   Intelligence

Table 3. Conover's Post Hoc Comparisons - Intelligence

group1	group2	T-Stat.	df	W_i	W_j	p	p_{bonf}	p_{holm}
no dialogue	random	0.087	34	29.000	28.500	0.932	1.000	0.932
no dialogue	reasonable	3.723	34	29.000	50.500	< .001	0.002	0.002
random	reasonable	3.809	34	28.500	50.500	< .001	0.002	0.002

While both the no dialogue robot and the random robot were rated as significantly less intelligent than the reasonable robot, we found no significant difference in intelligence ratings between the random robot and the no dialogue robot as demonstrated by Table 3. This result supports H2.

5.4   Creative Support

Table 4. Conover's Post Hoc Comparisons - Creative Support

group1	group2	T-Stat.	df	W_i	W_j	p	p_{bonf}	p_{holm}
no dialogue	random	1.679	34	22.500	32.500	0.102	0.307	0.102
no dialogue	reasonable	5.121	34	22.500	53.000	< .001	< .001	< .001
random	reasonable	3.442	34	32.500	53.000	0.002	0.005	0.003

As shown in Table 4 and Fig. (a), participants reported significantly more creative support from the reasonable robot than the random robot. Participants also reported significantly more creative support from the reasonable robot than the no dialogue robot. This finding aligns with H3, illustrating the utility of robot initiative in the form of suggestions and reasons in supporting creativity.

5.5   Suggestion Rejection

Table 5. Conover's Post Hoc Comparisons - Rejection Rates

group1	group2	T-Stat.	df	W_i	W_j	p	p_{bonf}	p_{holm}
random	reasonable	2.222	17	31.500	22.500	0.040	0.040	0.040

We found that participants were significantly less likely to reject suggestions given by the reasonable robot compared to the random robot as shown in Fig. 7b and Table 5 ($p < .05$). This supports H5. We found no correlation between participants' creative self-efficacy ratings and their suggestion rejection rates in either the random condition nor the reasonable condition. This does not support H6.

5.6   Relative Utility

Table 6. Multinomial Test for Relative Utility

	χ^2	df	p
Multinomial	30.333	2	< .001

Participants overwhelmingly preferred to work with the reasonable robot on a similar task as shown in Tables 6 and 7. 17 out of 18 (94%) participants preferred the reasonable robot whereas 1 out of 18 (¡6%) preferred the random robot. None of the participants preferred the no dialogue robot. This supports

Table 7. Descriptives for Relative Utility

condition	Percentage of Participants	Expected: Multinomial
base	0.000	0.333
random	0.056	0.333
reasonable	0.944	0.333

H4. When reporting the reasons behind their choice, some participants highlight the reasonable robot's effectiveness at reducing cognitive load by suggesting to place decorations that the participant "might have forgotten about" while others point to its ability to support creativity, commenting that they would be able to "combine their own creativity with the robot's help".

6 Discussion and Conclusion

The effects of interactive task dialogues in creative and collaborative settings underscores the substantial impact of task-specific justifications provided by a co-creative robot partner. Participants tend to give the highest ratings of support to the robot that incorporates task-specific justifications for suggestions into the dialogue. Results suggest that *task dialogue alone* is not enough to improve user satisfaction and experience; they showcase the impact of different modes of robot initiative, namely offering task-specific justifications while taking initiative significantly improves user experience. Participants perceive the reasonable robot as more intelligent and are less likely to reject its suggestions, indicating that perceived robot intelligence plays a significant role in participants' willingness to accept the robot's collaborative input. Furthermore, participants overwhelmingly find the reasonable robot the most useful out of the three, further highlighting the importance of task-specific justifications in co-creative settings. Together these results show that the proposed architecture integrating LLM models to enable design suggestions through task-based dialogues does support users in making their own creative designs. It thus provides an important step towards developing robots that can aid people in carrying out creative tasks without limiting their creativity.

References

1. Admoni, H., Weng, T., Hayes, B., Scassellati, B.: Robot nonverbal behavior improves task performance in difficult collaborations. In: 2016 11th ACM/IEEE International Conference on Human-Robot Interaction (HRI), pp. 51–58. IEEE (2016). https://doi.org/10.1109/HRI.2016.7451733
2. Alvarez, A., Font, J., Togelius, J.: Story designer: towards a mixed-initiative tool to create narrative structures. https://doi.org/10.48550/arXiv.2210.09294, http://arxiv.org/abs/2210.09294
3. Alves-Oliveira, P., Arriaga, P., Cronin, M.A., Paiva, A.: Creativity encounters between children and robots. In: Proceedings of the 2020 ACM/IEEE International Conference on Human-Robot Interaction, pp. 379–388. HRI 2020, Association for Computing Machinery (2020). https://doi.org/10.1145/3319502.3374817
4. Baer, J.: Content matters: why nurturing creativity is so different in different domains. In: Beghetto, R.A., Sriraman, B. (eds.) Creative Contradictions in Education. CTAE, vol. 1, pp. 129–140. Springer, Cham (2017). https://doi.org/10.1007/978-3-319-21924-0_8

5. Bartneck, C., Kulić, D., Croft, E., Zoghbi, S.: Measurement instruments for the anthropomorphism, animacy, likeability, perceived intelligence, and perceived safety of robots. Int. J. Soc. Robot. **1**(1), 71–81 (2009). https://doi.org/10.1007/s12369-008-0001-3

6. Buyukgoz, S., Pandey, A.K., Chamoux, M., Chetouani, M.: Exploring behavioral creativity of a proactive robot. Front. Robot. AI **8**, 694177 (2021). https://doi.org/10.3389/frobt.2021.694177

7. Cherry, E., Latulipe, C.: Quantifying the creativity support of digital tools through the creativity support index. ACM Trans. Comput. Human Interact. **21**(4), 21:1-21:25 (2014). https://doi.org/10.1145/2617588

8. Heintzman, L., Hashimoto, A., Abaid, N., Williams, R.K.: Anticipatory planning and dynamic lost person models for human-robot search and rescue. In: 2021 IEEE International Conference on Robotics and Automation (ICRA), pp. 8252–8258 (2021). https://doi.org/10.1109/ICRA48506.2021.9562070, ISSN: 2577-087X

9. Hinds, P.J., Roberts, T.L., Jones, H.: Whose job is it anyway? A study of human-robot interaction in a collaborative task. Human Comput. Interact. **19**(1), 151–181 (2004). https://doi.org/10.1207/s15327051hci19012_7

10. Kahn, P.H., et al.: Human creativity can be facilitated through interacting with a social robot. In: 2016 11th ACM/IEEE International Conference on Human-Robot Interaction (HRI), pp. 173–180 (2016). https://doi.org/10.1109/HRI.2016.7451749, ISSN: 2167-2148

11. Karwowski, M., Lebuda, I., Wiśniewska, E.: Measuring creative self-efficacy and creative personal identity. Int. J. Creat. Probl. Solv. **28**(1), 45–57 (2018)

12. Kaufman, J.: Creativity as a stepping stone toward a brighter future. J. Intell. **6**(2), 21 (2018). https://doi.org/10.3390/jintelligence6020021

13. Law, M.V., Jeong, J., Kwatra, A., Jung, M.F., Hoffman, G.: Negotiating the creative space in human-robot collaborative design. In: Proceedings of the 2019 on Designing Interactive Systems Conference, pp. 645–657. ACM (2019). https://doi.org/10.1145/3322276.3322343

14. Liapis, A., Yannakakis, G.N., Alexopoulos, C., Lopes, P.: Can computers foster human users' creativity? Theory and praxis of mixed-initiative co-creativity. https://www.semanticscholar.org/paper/Can-Computers-Foster-Human-Users%E2%80%99-Creativity-Theory-Liapis-Yannakakis/a5cd2b0d1d4b8b99e96ce53be3786b7862740532

15. Lin, Y., Guo, J., Chen, Y., Yao, C., Ying, F.: It is your turn: collaborative ideation with a co-creative robot through sketch. In: Proceedings of the 2020 CHI Conference on Human Factors in Computing Systems, pp. 1–14. CHI 2020. Association for Computing Machinery (2020). https://doi.org/10.1145/3313831.3376258

16. Qin, M., Brawer, J., Scassellati, B.: Task-oriented robot-to-human handovers in collaborative tool-use tasks. In: 2022 31st IEEE International Conference on Robot and Human Interactive Communication (RO-MAN), pp. 1327–1333 (2022). https://doi.org/10.1109/RO-MAN53752.2022.9900599, ISSN: 1944-9437

17. Sandoval, E.B., Sosa, R., Cappuccio, M., Bednarz, T.: Human-robot creative interactions: exploring creativity in artificial agents using a storytelling game. Front. Robot. AI **9**, 695162 (2022)

18. Scheutz, M., Williams, T., Krause, E., Oosterveld, B., Sarathy, V., Frasca, T.: An overview of the distributed integrated cognition affect and reflection DIARC architecture. In: Aldinhas Ferreira, M.I., Silva Sequeira, J., Ventura, R. (eds.) Cognitive Architectures. ISCASE, vol. 94, pp. 165–193. Springer, Cham (2019). https://doi.org/10.1007/978-3-319-97550-4_11

19. Shah, J., Wiken, J., Williams, B., Breazeal, C.: Improved human-robot team performance using Chaski, a human-inspired plan execution system. In: 2011 6th ACM/IEEE International Conference on Human-Robot Interaction (HRI), pp. 29–36 (2011).https://doi.org/10.1145/1957656.1957668, ISSN: 2167-2148
20. Thörn, O., Knudsen, P., Saffiotti, A.: Human-robot artistic co-creation: a study in improvised robot dance. In: 2020 29th IEEE International Conference on Robot and Human Interactive Communication (RO-MAN), pp. 845–850 (2020). https://doi.org/10.1109/RO-MAN47096.2020.9223446, ISSN: 1944-9437
21. Vasey, L., et al.: Collaborative construction: human and robot collaboration enabling the fabrication and assembly of a filament-wound structure (2016). https://doi.org/10.52842/conf.acadia.2016.184
22. Yannakakis, G.N., Liapis, A., Alexopoulos, C.: Mixed-initiative co-creativity
23. Zhang, R., Lv, Q., Li, J., Bao, J., Liu, T., Liu, S.: A reinforcement learning method for human-robot collaboration in assembly tasks. Robot. Comput. Integr. manuf. **73**, 102227 (2022). https://doi.org/10.1016/j.rcim.2021.102227

Speech-Guided Sequential Planning for Autonomous Navigation Using Large Language Model Meta AI 3 (Llama3)

Alkesh K. Srivastava$^{(\boxtimes)}$ and Philip Dames

Temple University, Philadelphia, PA 19122, USA
{alkesh,pdames}@temple.edu

Abstract. In social robotics, a pivotal focus is enabling robots to engage with humans in a more natural and seamless manner. The emergence of advanced large language models (LLMs) has driven significant advancements in integrating natural language understanding capabilities into social robots. This paper presents a system for speech-guided sequential planning in pick and place tasks, which are found across a range of application areas. The proposed system uses Large Language Model Meta AI (Llama3) to interpret voice commands by extracting essential details through parsing and decoding the commands into sequential actions. These actions are sent to DRL-VO, a learning-based control policy built on the Robot Operating System (ROS) that allows a robot to autonomously navigate through social spaces with static infrastructure and crowds of people. We demonstrate the effectiveness of the system in simulation experiment using Turtlebot 2 in ROS1 and Turtlebot 3 in ROS2. We conduct hardware trials using a Clearpath Robotics Jackal UGV, highlighting its potential for real-world deployment in scenarios requiring flexible and interactive robotic behaviors.

Keywords: Human-Robot Interactions · Large Language Models · Motion Planning · Natural Language Processing

1 Introduction

Social robotics aims to enable robots and humans to cohabitate in a natural and intuitive manner. In the field of collaborative robotics, robots are required to share workspaces with humans, making it essential for robots to understand and execute human commands effectively [3]. Robots are increasingly being used in retail, industrial settings, households, and office environments. In such settings, robots are often asked to carry out tasks involving multiple steps or to complete a series of tasks in a specific order. For instance, in a retail environment, a robot might be required to navigate the store to pick up items from different aisles and deliver them to a checkout counter. In an office, a robot might need to collect documents from multiple departments and deliver them to a central location, such as Human Resources. At home, robots could be tasked with household

© The Author(s), under exclusive license to Springer Nature Singapore Pte Ltd. 2025
O. Palinko et al. (Eds.): ICSR + AI 2024, LNAI 15562, pp. 158–168, 2025.
https://doi.org/10.1007/978-981-96-3519-1_15

chores that involve sequential actions such as serving food from the kitchen and then cleaning up after dinner. Such robotic tasks are often modeled as Vehicle Routing Problems or other optimization challenges [9]. However, the complexity of these problems increases in dynamic environments, with more assigned tasks, and a growing number of robots. Robots are also increasingly deployed for these tasks in hostile or hard-to-reach areas [1]. Solving these issues is challenging on its own, and incorporating natural language understanding for collaborative robotics adds an additional layer of difficulty.

This paper aims to enable people to sequentially task robots using natural language inputs. However, in experimental robotics, models are often designed for specific tasks with rigid input formats to ensure successful task execution. This rigidity ensures that robots can accomplish their assignments accurately but does not account for the natural variability in human communication. Humans, celebrating their individuality, interact with robots in diverse and natural ways, often not conforming to predefined input formats. Therefore, for collaborative robotics to be truly successful, robots must be able to interpret a variety of human commands and translate them into actionable plans [22]. To address this need, we will build upon recent advancements in large language models, which have shown great promise in enhancing natural language understanding.

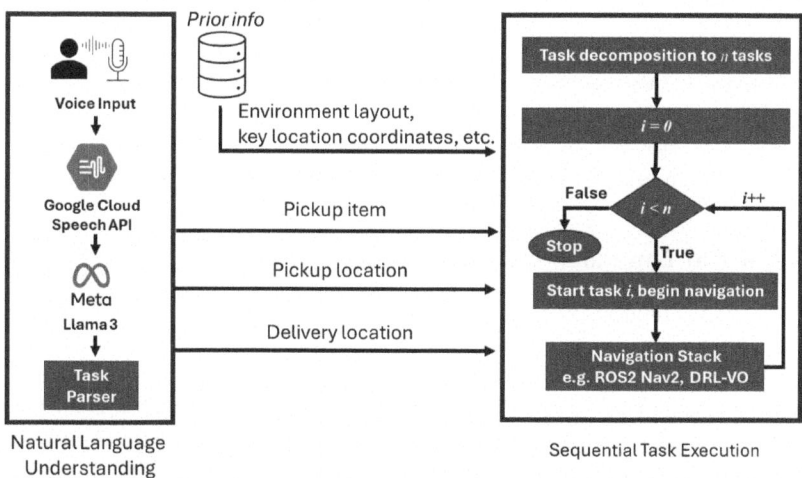

Fig. 1. Overview of the proposed system. The process begins with converting verbal commands into text using the Google Cloud Speech API. The Llama3 model processes this text to extract essential details, such as the pickup location, item, and delivery destination, using regex-based parsing. These parsed commands, along with prior environmental information, are sent to the Task Execution module, where they are translated into a sequence of actions that are then executed.

Our system, illustrated in Fig. 1, consists of two main modules. The first is the natural language understanding module, which processes user speech or text input and outputs a set of task parameters. We utilize speech-to-text technology to convert verbal commands into text. The text is fed into Llama3 [16], an autoregressive large language model, which extracts essential details—such as pickup location, item, and delivery destination—using regex-based parsing. In other words, we are using Llama3 to "translate" free-form natural language commands into a standardized, easily parsable form for robust task extraction. Although alternatives like BERT [7] could be trained on large datasets to handle this process, they would likely eliminate the need for an LLM. Instead, we prioritize Llama3's ability to generalize and flexibly interpret commands, which allows us to maintain a simpler, rule-based parsing mechanism while still benefiting from the LLM's advanced linguistic capabilities.

The second module translates the parsed commands into a sequence of actions by referencing a predefined dictionary of environment coordinates. This dictionary stores coordinates of key landmarks, eliminating the need for semantic planning and enabling faster execution. Task execution is managed using a finite-state machine to control the flow of operations, along with off-the-shelf robot navigation algorithms.

We demonstrate the efficacy of our system through simulated and hardware experiments using three different robot models, two navigation algorithms, and two environments. These experiments highlight the modularity of our system and the potential for practical applications in real-world scenarios.

2   Related Work

In this section, we review the literature related to each of our two modules: natural language understanding (NLU) and robotic navigation.

2.1   Natural Language Understanding

Recent advancements in large language models (LLMs) have significantly enhanced natural language understanding (NLU) capabilities across various domains, including robotics [28]. Models like GPT-3 and BERT [7] have demonstrated exceptional performance in comprehending and generating human-like text, owing to their extensive training on large datasets. By fine-tuning these models for specific tasks, researchers have achieved state-of-the-art results in tasks spanning from text classification to question answering [28,29], thereby enhancing their performance on conventional NLU benchmarks [6,10]. Say-Plan [21] focuses on scalable task planning using 3D scene graphs but does not integrate speech-recognition or incorporate socially compliant algorithms such as DRL-VO [27] for plan execution.

LLMs excel particularly in tasks requiring broad contextual understanding or dealing with unstructured data [6], which is pertinent to collaborative and social robotics applications. LLMs exhibit generalization capabilities, surpassing traditionally fine-tuned models in handling diverse and adversarial inputs [14,20].

In terms of practical applications, recent studies have showcased LLM effectiveness across various NLU tasks, such as machine translation [2], question answering [25], and text classification [4].

Contributions. The novelty of our framework lies in its integration of speech recognition and NLU capabilities, leveraging LLMs to enhance task classification accuracy. Our approach seamlessly integrates Google Speech Cloud API for speech-to-text transcription with Llama3 for task classification.

2.2 NLU-Guided Social Autonomous Navigation

The vision of seamless integration of mobile robots into human environments has been extensively studied. Robots like RHINO and MINERVA were deployed in museums and solely focused on autonomous navigation amidst humans [13]. Various approach of navigation has treated people as dynamic, non-responsive obstacles, and emphasized collision avoidance [26], while other approaches integrated human motion prediction with robot decision-making, acknowledging mutual influences between actions of robots and people [8].

Recent advancements in robotic navigation guided by natural language have explored diverse methodologies to enhance human-robot interaction and adaptability in dynamic environments. FollowNet [24]and LM-Nav [23] leverage end-to-end neural architectures and large pre-trained models to interpret natural language instructions and navigate complex environments, demonstrating success in simulated and real-world scenarios. GOAT [5] offers a multimodal navigation system that integrates language descriptions and object recognition. However, it lacks a comprehensive approach to dynamic social interactions in complex environments. Arena 3.0 [12] provides a realistic simulation environment for social navigation but does not incorporate the advanced NLU features and real-time feedback mechanisms that the proposed approach offers.

Contributions. Our work advances beyond existing methodologies by combining robust NLU capabilities with adaptive navigation strategies. Unlike previous approaches, which often rely on fixed control policies or simplistic command parsing techniques, our methodology leverages the capabilities of Llama3 for robust natural language understanding and DRL-VO [27] for adaptive and socially-compliant navigation.

3 Problem Statement

The general task addressed in this work is to understand human commands using Large Language Models (LLMs) and form a sequential plan for execution. The overall problem can be subdivided into two problems:

Problem 1: NLU for Command Interpretation

This paper focuses on the scenario where a social robot receives instructions to pick up an object from a specified location and deliver it to another designated place. This task exemplifies a common class of multi-step operations in social robotics, where the robot must navigate through sequential actions such as in household assistance for cleaning tasks, delivering medication in health care settings, etc. By addressing pickup and delivery planning, we aim to tackle fundamental challenges that underpin various practical applications.

Let C denote the natural language command (in text or speech) provided by the user, which includes information about pickup location L_{pickup}, delivery location L_{delivery}, and the pickup item I. The task of the robot is to design a Natural Language Understanding (NLU) system that accurately parses C into a structured format:

$$L_{\text{pickup}}, L_{\text{delivery}}, I = \text{NLU}(C),$$

where $\text{NLU}(C)$ process C using Llama3 and parses the obtained information to extract the task parameters $L_{\text{pickup}}, L_{\text{delivery}}$, and I.

Problem 2: Autonomous Navigation

We assume an environment whose layout of the static infrastructure is known and we possess coordinates for key locations within it (e.g., room numbers). The robot shares the environment with people who may move around during the robot's operation. The robot model used in this study is a differential wheel drive robot, which is a representative model of various ground robots such as TurtleBots, Jackal UGV, and Moxi by Diligent Robotics, though the proposed system is applicable to any mobile robot.

Once the task parameters are identified by the NLU, we can look up the coordinates of the pickup and delivery locations, $L_{\text{pickup}}, L_{\text{delivery}}$, in the environment map. The next challenge is to navigate through the environment to reach those locations. The robot does this using a control policy π with parameters θ that selects steering actions a_t based on partial environmental observation o_t (obtained from the sensors and perception system):

$$a_t \sim \pi_\theta(a_t | o_t).$$

4   Methodology

In this section, we describe the methodology of the proposed Speech-Guided Sequential Planner for Autonomous Navigation. The proposed system integrates speech recognition, natural language understanding, and an advanced control technique to enable a robot to autonomously navigate in an environment populated with human pedestrians. First, we address the natural language understanding aspect of Problem 1 in Sect. 4.1. Followed by addressing the autonomous navigation challenge posed by Problem 2 in Sect. 4.2.

4.1   Natural Language Understanding (NLU)

The first module takes in a natural language input (speech or text) and parses it to extract the task information. This is done in two steps.

Speech To Text Conversion. To convert speech to text, we utilize the Google Speech Recognition API [15] through the Python3 `speech_recognition` library for precise speech-to-text conversion. Initially, ambient noise levels are calibrated using the microphone's input during the first second without processing speech, adjusting the recognizer's sensitivity accordingly. Google's advanced speech recognition technology employs signal processing and machine learning methods. It begins by preprocessing the audio input to extract spectral representations and phonetic patterns. Deep neural networks then map these features to textual sequences with high accuracy and efficiency.

Large Language Model (LLM). The natural language understanding (NLU) process encompasses several key steps. Firstly, the received text undergoes preprocessing, which includes tasks such as punctuation removal and text formatting to maintain consistency throughout the text. Following preprocessing, the text is fed into the Llama3 API [16] provided by Groq [11] for context understanding and semantic parsing.[1] This step involves extracting structured data essential for task execution. The extracted information is parsed using regular expressions to identify the pickup location L_{pickup}, delivery location L_{delivery}, and the item to be picked up I. We utilize the LLM as a translation layer to reformat complex, natural language commands into a standardized, structured format that simplifies parsing. The integration of Llama3 enhances the system's capability to accurately interpret and process natural language commands, promoting seamless interaction and task execution in robotic applications. Opting for regex-based parsing over learned task classifiers ensures greater flexibility in handling diverse human commands and reduces computational costs, making it more practical for implementation in robots.

4.2 Sequential Task Assignment and Execution

Once the command is interpreted, we formulate and execute the task sequence.

Task Assignment. For task assignment, our system employs a Finite State Machine (FSM) for handling simple tasks such as a single pickup and delivery. The FSM consists of states like Idle, Navigating to Pickup, Picking Up Item, Navigating to Delivery, and Delivering Item, with transitions triggered by events such as reaching a location or completing an action. This approach is efficient for straightforward tasks. However, for more complex tasks that involve multiple steps and dependencies, we can employ hierarchical task planners like

---

[1] We employ the 8 billion parameter version (`llama3-8b-8192 m`) instead of the larger counterparts, such as the 80 billion parameter model, due to larger models exhibiting a tendency to assign specific room numbers when interpreting generic commands. For instance, if asked to navigate to "TRAIL lab," it might erroneously label it with a hallucinated room number, like "Room 111." Additionally, we can use the smaller model onboard the robot rather than relying on remote API services, leading to quicker response times and greater practicality for real-time applications.

GTPyhop [17] or SHOP [18]. These planners decompose high-level tasks into manageable sub-tasks, enabling the robot to handle complex scenarios, thus justifying their integration into our system for enhanced task management and execution.

Autonomous Navigation. We utilize two different navigation frameworks, depending on the situation. In static worlds (i.e., without people), we use the ROS2-Nav2 navigation stack. This is one of the most commonly used navigation frameworks in mobile robots. In environments full of people, we utilize the DRL-VO (Deep Reinforcement Learning with Velocity Obstacles) [27] navigation system, which the authors previously designed to enable robots to navigate through crowded and dynamic environments. The control policy is a convolutional neural network that uses lidar scans, maps of pedestrian locations/speeds, and goal coordinates to generates velocity commands for the robot. DRL-VO yields higher speeds and few collisions than other robot controllers (including the ROS navigation stack), especially in dense crowds.

5   Experiments

To evaluate the system, we first assess the speech-to-task classification by having volunteers self-report the accuracy of the classification on 10 natural task statements. We then evaluate the system integration with three distinct robotic experiments: a simulation in an empty office environment using a Turtlebot3 in ROS2, a simulation in a lobby with people using a Turtlebot2 in ROS1, and a hardware implementation in a lobby with people using a Clearpath Robotics Jackal UGV. The experimental setup is described in Fig. 2. These experiments collectively demonstrate the system's versatility and effectiveness across different scenarios, from pedestrian-free areas to crowded social spaces.

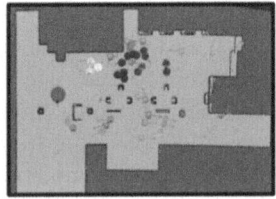

Fig. 2. (Left) The layout of the Mechanical Engineering department at Temple University, used in the ROS2-Nav2 simulation with Turtlebot3. (Center) The layout of the lobby of the College of Engineering at Temple University, which is used for both simulation experiments with Turtlebot2 using DRL-VO and hardware experiments with the Jackal UGV. (Right) The Jackal UGV.

5.1   Speech-To-Task Accuracy

To test the efficacy of the natural language understanding aspect of our system, we asked 10 volunteers to speak 10 commands and report the number of correct classifications. Out of the 10 commands, 5 were provided to them and the rest were the volunteer's own command statements. This ensures that the accuracy reported by the system is unbiased. Examples of the commands include "Could you please bring the keys from security to TRAIL?" and "I forgot my laptop, please bring a laptop from the computer station to the robotics lab." We observed an average accuracy of 84.37% for task classification. Feedback from the volunteers revealed that using identifiers like "the" or "a" before the location or pickup item confused the NLU system, suggesting a need for improved preprocessing to handle such variations in command phrasing.

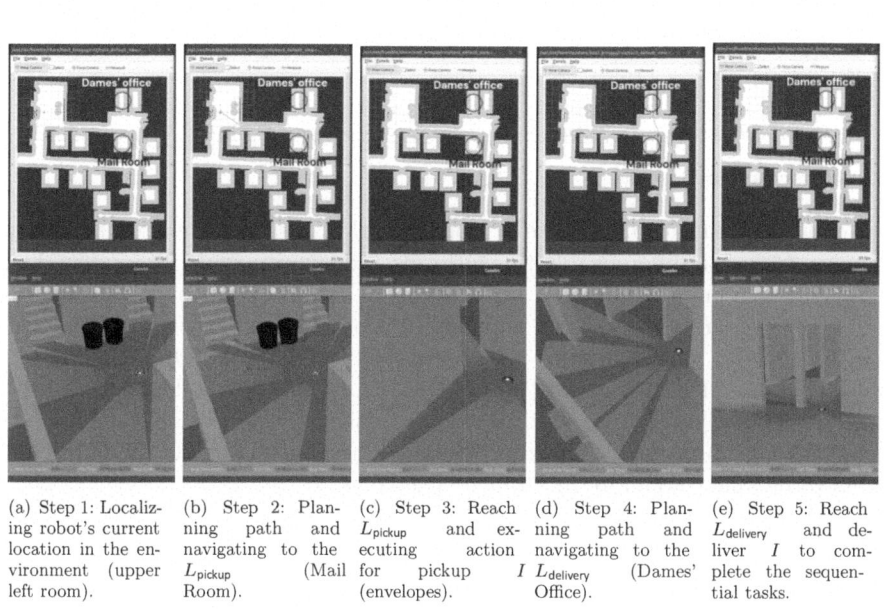

(a) Step 1: Localizing robot's current location in the environment (upper left room).

(b) Step 2: Planning path and navigating to the L_{pickup} (Mail Room).

(c) Step 3: Reach L_{pickup} and executing action for pickup I (envelopes).

(d) Step 4: Planning path and navigating to the $L_{delivery}$ (Dames' Office).

(e) Step 5: Reach $L_{delivery}$ and deliver I to complete the sequential tasks.

Fig. 3. Simulation experiment depicting the steps of progress for pickup of item I (envelopes) from L_{pickup} (Mail Room) and its delivery to $L_{delivery}$ (Dames' Office).

5.2   System Integration Testing

We conducted three tests, outlined in Table 1 that vary the robot platform, environment, and ROS version to demonstrate the flexibility of the system. The table also provides links to full videos of all experiments, and Fig. 3 shows a series of snapshots of the first experiment with the Turtlebot 3. The videos show that in all cases the robot is able to complete the task given to it, either from a natural language text input on a remote computer or a spoken command. The simulated and hardware tests in the lobby environment both have pedestrians, demonstrating the system's capability to navigate autonomously in social spaces with static infrastructure and moving crowds, which is essential for getting robots outside of controlled lab and factory environments.

Table 1. Overview of Experiments

Type	Robot	Navigation	Environment	Videos
Simulation	Turtlebot3	ROS2-Nav2	ME Dept.	https://youtu.be/L3kIdW80ZK0
				https://youtu.be/HGL9E_DZUsk
Simulation	Turtlebot2	DRL-VO	Lobby	https://youtu.be/TfleIxcCoE8
				https://youtu.be/BaoLZ68bkAM
Hardware	Jackal	DRL-VO	Lobby	https://youtu.be/hzYRvpX9Qe8

5.3 Discussion

Our experimental setup aimed to demonstrate the versatility and compatibility of our system with different robotic platforms and environments. In a controlled, pedestrian-free environment, we utilized the ROS2 Nav2 package with Turtlebot3, emphasizing the system's capability to operate effectively with smaller base robots and showcasing its integration with advanced ROS2 features. In human-populated environments, where the risk of collision is higher, we used the DRL-VO [27] algorithm on a Turtlebot2 and a Jackal. This highlights our system's adaptability to various robotic platforms, software stacks, and environments to be able to operate in a range of settings.

6   Conclusion

In this paper, we explore the feasibility and effectiveness of integrating advanced natural language processing with robotic navigation systems to enable people to use natural language to ask robots to complete multi-step tasks. We leverage Llama3 to parse commands and different off-the-shelf navigation algorithms, and we apply our system to a range of robot models, software stacks, and environments. Our research enhances social and collaborative robotics by enabling people to naturally interact with robots in shared spaces.

Future work will aim to enhance the versatility to more real-world scenarios. We will update the robotic hardware by adding a gripper to the robot. This will allow it to pick up and deliver objects as well as autonomously utilize elevators, presenting an intriguing opportunity to expand their operational capabilities in multi-story buildings and complex indoor environments. We will also update the software with the goals of: 1) enhancing the success rate of our NLU module,

2) allowing the robot to respond to the user if it does not understand the given query [22], and 3) broadening the scope of tasks, which may include additional steps to complete, by utilizing hierarchical task networks (HTNs) [19] or similar planning paradigms.

Acknowledgment. This work was funded by NSF grant CNS-2143312. The authors would like to thank Zhanteng Xie, Jared Levin, and Alexander Derrico for their assistance with the hardware experiments.

References

1. Bellingham, J.G., Rajan, K.: Robotics in remote and hostile environments. Science **318**(5853), 1098–1102 (2007)
2. Brants, T., Popat, A., Xu, P., Och, F.J., Dean, J.: Large language models in machine translation. In: Proceedings of the 2007 Joint Conference on Empirical Methods in Natural Language Processing and Computational Natural Language Learning (EMNLP-CoNLL), pp. 858–867 (2007)
3. Breazeal, C., Dautenhahn, K., Kanda, T.: Social Robotics. In: Siciliano, B., Khatib, O. (eds.) Springer Handbook of Robotics, pp. 1935–1972. Springer, Cham (2016). https://doi.org/10.1007/978-3-319-32552-1_72
4. Chae, Y., Davidson, T.: Large language models for text classification: From zero-shot learning to fine-tuning. Open Science Foundation (2023)
5. Chang, M., et al.: Goat: Go to any thing. arXiv preprint arXiv:2311.06430 (2023)
6. Chang, Y., et al.: A survey on evaluation of large language models. ACM Trans. Intell. Syst. Technol. **15**(3), 1–45 (2024)
7. Devlin, J., Chang, M.W., Lee, K., Toutanova, K.: BERT: pre-training of deep bidirectional transformers for language understanding. arXiv preprint arXiv:1810.04805 (2018)
8. Fridovich-Keil, D., Ratner, E., Peters, L., Dragan, A.D., Tomlin, C.J.: Efficient iterative linear-quadratic approximations for nonlinear multi-player general-sum differential games. In: 2020 IEEE international conference on robotics and automation (ICRA), pp. 1475–1481. IEEE (2020)
9. González, D., Pérez, J., Milanés, V., Nashashibi, F.: A review of motion planning techniques for automated vehicles. IEEE Trans. Intell. Transp. Syst. **17**(4), 1135–1145 (2015)
10. Huang, J., Chang, K.C.C.: Towards reasoning in large language models: a survey. arXiv preprint arXiv:2212.10403 (2022)
11. Inc., G.: Groq. (https://groq.com/) (nd). Accessed July 2024
12. Kästner, L., et al.: Arena 3.0: Advancing social navigation in collaborative and highly dynamic environments. arXiv preprint arXiv:2406.00837 (2024)
13. Lakemeyer, W.S.G., Schulz, D., Thrun, S.: The interactive museum tour-guide robot. In: Proceedings of the 15th National Conference on Artificial Intelligence (1998)
14. Liang, P., et al.: Holistic evaluation of language models. arXiv preprint arXiv:2211.09110 (2022)
15. LLC, G.: Cloud speech-to-text API. (https://cloud.google.com/speech-to-text) (nd). Accessed July 2024
16. Meta AI: Meta Llama 3. (https://github.com/meta-llama/llama3) (2024)

17. Nau, D., Bansod, Y., Patra, S., Roberts, M., Li, R.: Gtpyhop: a hierarchical goal+ task planner implemented in python. HPlan **2021**, 21 (2021)
18. Nau, D., Cao, Y., Lotem, A., Munoz-Avila, H.: The shop planning system. AI Mag. **22**(3), 91–91 (2001)
19. Nejati, N., Langley, P., Konik, T.: Learning hierarchical task networks by observation. In: Proceedings of the 23rd International Conference on Machine Learning, pp. 665–672 (2006)
20. Nie, Y., Williams, A., Dinan, E., Bansal, M., Weston, J., Kiela, D.: Adversarial NLI: a new benchmark for natural language understanding. arXiv preprint arXiv:1910.14599 (2019)
21. Rana, K., Haviland, J., Garg, S., Abou-Chakra, J., Reid, I.D., Suenderhauf, N.: Sayplan: Grounding large language models using 3d scene graphs for scalable task planning. CoRR (2023)
22. Ren, A.Z., et al.: Robots that ask for help: Uncertainty alignment for large language model planners. In: 7th Annual Conference on Robot Learning (2023). https:// openreview.net/forum?id=4ZK8ODNyFXx
23. Shah, D., Osiński, B., Levine, S., et al.: LM-NAV: robotic navigation with large pre-trained models of language, vision, and action. In: Conference on Robot Learning, pp. 492–504. PMLR (2023)
24. Shah, P., Fiser, M., Faust, A., Kew, J.C., Hakkani-Tur, D.: Follownet: Robot navigation by following natural language directions with deep reinforcement learning. arXiv preprint arXiv:1805.06150 (2018)
25. Singhal, K., et al.: Towards expert-level medical question answering with large language models. arXiv preprint arXiv:2305.09617 (2023)
26. Vasquez, D., Okal, B., Arras, K.O.: Inverse reinforcement learning algorithms and features for robot navigation in crowds: an experimental comparison. In: 2014 IEEE/RSJ International Conference on Intelligent Robots and Systems, pp. 1341–1346. IEEE (2014)
27. Xie, Z., Dames, P.: DRL-VO: Learning to navigate through crowded dynamic scenes using velocity obstacles. IEEE Trans. Rob. **39**(4), 2700–2719 (2023). https://doi.org/10.1109/TRO.2023.3257549
28. Zhao, W.X., et al.: A survey of large language models. arXiv preprint arXiv:2303.18223 (2023)
29. Zhou, C., et al.: A comprehensive survey on pretrained foundation models: a history from BERT to ChatGPT. arXiv preprint arXiv:2302.09419 (2023)

Zen Wakarimasen - Mobile Robot Raking a Zen Garden in an Artistic Installation

Silas Inoue[1], Thomas Baugerød[1], Morten Kleist[1], Hubert Møller[1],
Niels Jul Jacobsen[2], and Lazaros Nalpantidis[1(✉)]

[1] DTU - Technical University of Denmark, Kongens Lyngby, Denmark
mail@silasinoue.com, {s224002,s224022,s223990,lanalpa}@dtu.dk
[2] Capra Robotics ApS, Viby J, Denmark
njj@capra.ooo

Abstract. This paper describes the integration and deployment of a mobile robotic system in a large-scale indoor artistic exhibition. The robot, covered with oak wood and carrying a finely milled rake, moves around artistic installations and rakes the red sand of the Zen garden-like environment. The route the robot follows through the exhibition space is pre-programmed and is only interrupted by the visitors it avoids.

Keywords: mobile robot · Zen garden raking · artistic exhibition

1 Introduction

In early Japan, the Zen garden emerged as a minimalist type of garden inspired by the aesthetics and philosophy of Zen Buddhism. The gardens were designed to recreate specific, grand natural landscapes using a few abstract elements such as sand, gravel, stones, and moss. The Zen garden is its own art form, developed over several centuries, and is an example of an ambiguous cultural phenomenon. In attempting to depict nature, it equally creates time images that reflect humanity's perception of the world and itself.

With the exhibition "Zen Wakarimasen" (Japanese for "I don't understand Zen") at Kunsthal Thy, Silas Inoue invites discussion on how cultural codes can be mixed and misunderstood in our globalised reality. The exhibition also explores the fascinating yet unsettling developments in technology concerning nature, humanity, and a possible future on distant planets. From the traditional form of the Zen garden, a new, unexplored landscape is created, weaving threads between past and future, agriculture and space travel, craftsmanship and philosophy, addressing contemporary challenges in both hopeful and dystopian ways.

In this exhibition a mobile robot moves along a predetermined path, passing in front of the various exhibits and the visitors, and raking the Zen garden.

2 Related Work

The integration of robots at the heart of artistic installations has a rich history, with numerous pioneering works that have paved the way for contemporary

O. Palinko et al. (Eds.): ICSR + AI 2024, LNAI 15562, pp. 169–173, 2025.
https://doi.org/10.1007/978-981-96-3519-1_16

explorations. The seminal work of Woody Vasulka, "The Brotherhood" series (1990) explores human identity through six interactive media constructions that utilize discarded military materials, creating a dialogue between technology and human behavior. On the other hand, Mari Velonaki's "Fish/Bird" (2004) emphasizes human-robot interaction through two robotic wheelchairs that communicate with each other and the audience via movement and written text, fostering trust and intimacy. Max Dean, together with Raffaello D'Andrea and Matt Donovan, presented "The Robotic Chair" (2006). It autonomously disassembles and reassembles itself, exploring themes of autonomy and identity, and captivating viewers with its seemingly magical act. Karina Smigla-Bobinski's "ADA Project" (2010) features an interactive kinetic sculpture that moves freely in a space, drawing on walls with charcoal tips, and creating collaborative artworks influenced by audience interaction. More recently, the ultra-realistic humanoid robot artist, Ai-Da (2019), was presented, capable of creating drawings, paintings, and sculptures, challenging the boundaries of AI and creativity while engaging audiences in discussions about the role of AI in art. The anthology "Robots and Art: Exploring an Unlikely Symbiosis" by Damith Herath et al. [3] provides a comprehensive overview of these intersections, highlighting the symbiotic relationship between robotics and art.

3   Artistic Installation

The robot installation was located in a rustic barn in the countryside of northern Jutland, Denmark, surrounded by agricultural fields. The floor of the 300 sq.m. indoor Zen garden consisted of a special type of soil from Salten Forest near Silkeborg, Denmark known for its high iron content. This gives the soil a distinctive red hue and magnetic properties, similar to the iron-rich dust that coats the surface of Mars. Since collecting Martian dust samples is not yet possible, soil from Salten Forest is used in Mars research worldwide [5]. Unlike the calm typically associated with traditional Zen gardens, which are raked by hand as a meditative practice, the red earth in the exhibition is raked by a mobile robot, addressing human restlessness and the ongoing technological campaigns to colonize Mars. By bringing these futuristic visions into the old barn, the robot's design evoked parallels to the farming machinery often seen plowing just outside the exhibition space grounding the work in the local environment and making it relatable for visitors (Fig. 1).

The division between city and countryside is a pressing political issue. One of the installation's goals was to foster dialogue across cultures, generations, and geographical affiliations. And the robot played an essential role in this. The robot is specially designed for the exhibition and covered with oak wood. Just as the exploratory rovers that have been driving around Mars for years collecting data on the planet's surface, the robot moves through the red sand while the rake covers the tracks it leaves. However, the way the robot rakes also makes the entire installation resemble a plowed field in outer space. The route the robot follows through the exhibition space is pre-programmed and follows its own

Fig. 1. Robot moving within the exhibition

algorithm, which is only interrupted by the visitors it avoids. The realization of the "rover" and its paths through the sand would not have been possible without this multidisciplinary collaboration.

The robot operating in the exhibition Zen garden, can be seen in the follwing video: https://youtu.be/CchHVmX-jsI?si=eMAA7dmTea4pQNeh

4   Mobile Robotic System

As the exhibition is set in a Mars-like terrain with red sand, a mobile robot capable of robust outdoor operation was used, namely a Capra Hircus robot. This robot excels in rough terrain, and is powerful enough to drag a rake through the sand. The robot is decorated to match the general aesthetics of the exhibition, and programmed to follow a predetermined route by using Visual Simultaneous Localization And Mapping (vSLAM) [1,4] and wheel odometry for navigation. This approach takes in visual data from a forward facing camera and with help for the wheel encoders localizes the robot in the exhibition environment. As a result, the robot can localize itself without the need for GNSS-based solutions, which would had been problematic in an indoor installation like the one considered in this work.

The robot is capable of raking pre-determined patterns in the fine sand of the exhibition. This is achieved by recording a manually driven route, and afterwards driving this specific route autonomously, in line with the "teach and repeat" navigation paradigm [2]. As the exhibition is a dynamic environment with humans roaming freely, it is ensured through sensor input, that the robot will halt in the event of a possible collision (Fig. 2).

Fig. 2. Robot fitted with the decorative shell, raking patterns in the red sand of the exhibition (Color figure online)

5   Conclusion

Both as a whole and through its various works, "Zen Wakarimasen" invites discussion across cultures, generations, and geographical affiliations. The exhibition moves in a tension field between future dystopia and technological optimism; on one hand, it celebrates modesty and coexistence with nature, which is the traditional basis for the Zen garden, while on the other hand, it reveals an ingrained human restlessness and an unrestrained pursuit of infinite life, infinite resources, and infinite growth. The exhibition attempts to shift away from contemporary political focus on division and create a basis for a more ambiguous understanding of issues as intertwined, intricate, and chain-forming situations. However, in its curiosity about the study and development of robots and sustainable materials, the exhibition also points towards hopeful technological initiatives and improved living conditions on Earth rather than a possible colonization of space.

Acknowledgments. We would like to thank photographer Jacob Friis-Holm Nielsen for the photos and video of the robot and the artistic installation.

References

1. Cheng, J., Zhang, L., Chen, Q., Hu, X., Cai, J.: A review of visual slam methods for autonomous driving vehicles. Eng. App. Artif. Intell. **114**, 104992 (2022). https://doi.org/10.1016/j.engappai.2022.104992, https://www.sciencedirect.com/science/article/pii/S0952197622001853
2. Furgale, P., Barfoot, T.D.: Visual teach and repeat for long-range rover autonomy. J. Field Robot. **27**(5), 534–560 (2010). https://doi.org/10.1002/rob.20342, https://onlinelibrary.wiley.com/doi/abs/10.1002/rob.20342
3. Herath, D., Kroos, C.: Stelarc: Robots and Art: Exploring an Unlikely Symbiosis. Springer Singapore Pte. Limited (2016). https://doi.org/10.1007/978-981-10-0321-9
4. Makhubela, J.K., Zuva, T., Agunbiade, O.Y.: A review on vision simultaneous localization and mapping (VSLAM). In: 2018 International Conference on Intelligent and Innovative Computing Applications (ICONIC), pp. 1–5 (2018). https://doi.org/10.1109/ICONIC.2018.8601227
5. Nørnberg, P., Gunnlaugsson, H., Merrison, J., Vendelboe, A.: Salten Skov I: Amartian magnetic dust analogue. Planet. Space Sci. **57**(5), 628–631 (2009). https://doi.org/10.1016/j.pss.2008.08.017, https://www.sciencedirect.com/science/article/pii/S0032063308002523

Enhancing Open Conversations Using Visual Percepts From a Socially Assistive Robot Preliminary Assessment

Mariam Fdil[1]([⊠]) [iD], Mélanie Levasseur[1,2] [iD], Dominic Létourneau[1] [iD],
Marc-Antoine Maheux[1] [iD], Marika Lussier-Therrien[2] [iD],
and François Michaud[1,2] [iD]

[1] Interdisciplinary Institute for Technological Innovation (3IT), Université de
Sherbrooke, Sherbrooke, Canada
{mariam.fdil,melanie.levasseur,dominic.letourneau,
marcantoine.maheux,francois.michaud}@usherbrooke.ca

[2] Research Centre on Aging (RCA), Université de Sherbrooke, Sherbrooke, Canada
marika.lussiertherrien@usherbrooke.ca

Abstract. Being able to converse with a Socially Assistive Robot can be a way to help older adults participate socially and stay included in the community. To make a robot more engaging, it can use perception of its surrounding for situational grounding of the conversations. The integration of percepts with a conversational agent is influenced by real-time processing capabilities of the robot's sensory information, which also have an effect on the human-robot interaction experience. This paper presents the integration of OpenAI's GPT-3.5 Turbo on T-Top, a tabletop robot with onboard visual and audio recognition capabilities. As a preliminary step before using T-Top in experimentations with older adults, characterization of this integration is conducted to assess the robot's capabilities with reference to response time, conversation cueing and interaction modalities.

Keywords: OpenAI GPT-3.5 Turbo · Socially Assistive Robot (SAR) · Open conversation in natural settings · Situational grounding

1 Introduction

Defined as robots that provide assistance through social interaction [5], Socially Assistive Robots (SARs) are designed to engage and generate interest during interactions, and demonstrate potential to provide emotional support and facilitate daily tasks for improved quality of life and well-being [2,8]. The integration of Conversational Agents (CAs) on SARs leverages the physical presence of SARs [10] while utilizing open and/or closed-domain dialogue capabilities of CAs [4]. A recent qualitative analysis reveals that older adults expect companion robots to engage actively or passively in conversations, remember and personalize discussions, ensure privacy, provide information and reminders, enhance social skills

O. Palinko et al. (Eds.): ICSR + AI 2024, LNAI 15562, pp. 174–185, 2025.
https://doi.org/10.1007/978-981-96-3519-1_17

and connections, and exhibit empathy [9]. Improving the interaction capabilities of SARs as they are being deployed within the general public and in open settings is now becoming a requirement [17].

While it is technically feasible to interface CAs such as ChatGPT with SARs [1,26], situational grounding, i.e., grounding concepts and referencing objects in the real world, is an important Human-Robot Interaction (HRI) capability which comes with significant challenges [17]. Situational grounding requires using percepts to enrich interactions by providing contextual awareness and environmental understanding, along with the use of multimodal conversational cues like gesture, gaze, and facial expression [17]. Integration of perceptual data with a CA requires being able to identify meaningful objects and events occurring in the interaction space, and to include this data when appropriate into the conversation. Because of the tight coupling of perceptual, reasoning and control modalities in a robot, integration becomes an important challenge [17]. For instance, onboard processing power, telecommunication delay when using cloud computing services [1], and conversational cues (e.g., head movement, light, sound [3]) to establish synchronicity during the interactions influence the interaction dynamics between the person and the robot. Experimenting a CA-SAR integration as a whole becomes a necessity, which also comes with another identified difficulty, i.e., collecting HRI data in situated settings [17]. We believe that it is therefore important to conduct preliminary assessments in real-life setting scenarios before conducting experimentations with a targeted population, to identify what can be attributed to technological capabilities of the robot.

This paper presents the integration of OpenAI's GPT-3.5 Turbo model into T-Top [11], a tabletop interactive experimental SAR platform. This integration is designed to conduct experimentations with older adults in retirement homes, studying how a SAR can be used to address social isolation and loneliness. Actively engaging people in conversation is set as a requirement, adding percepts into the conversations to provide more situational awareness and cues. Before doing these experimentations with the targeted population, we conducted a preliminary assessment of the robot's capabilities in engaging in open conversations with people in natural settings. The paper presents observations from this preliminary assessment to validate and characterize the robot's integrated capabilities, which in turn will serve as a reference in upcoming experimentations with older adults.

2   T-Top Robot as a Conversational Agent

Shown in Fig. 1, T-Top [11–13] is a tabletop robot equipped with a RGB-D camera and a wide-angle camera, placed on the top of a touchscreen. Its head provides six degrees of freedom, and its torso can rotate on itself. T-Top is equipped with an array of 16 microphones. A stripe of RGB LEDs is used to communicate the robot's states. T-Top is programmed using ROS [15] and the Hybrid Behavior-Based Architecture (HBBA) [6], using perceptual and behavior-producing modules to interact with its environment. The platform has a NVIDIA Jetson AGX Orin for onboard Deep Neural Networks (DNNs) processing for object detection and people recognition, audio recognition, Speech-to-Text (STT) and Text-to-Speech (TTS), and CA. The implemented software architecture makes it possible to easily integrate SST, TTS and CA to experiment with as needed.

Fig. 1. T-Top interacting with a person

Figure 2 illustrates the modules used to integrate GPT-3.5 Turbo (a.k.a. gpt-3.5-turbo-0125) with T-Top. We chose GPT-3.5 Turbo because it is the latest model that can be fine-tuned, i.e., customized to specific use cases. For T-Top, fine-tuning the GPT-3.5 Turbo model consists in making it aware that it is embodying a robot assistant capable of perceiving objects in its environment. This fine-tuning process[1] involved training the GPT-3.5 Turbo model using a custom dataset consisting of examples of conversations (50 examples, 25 examples of requests and 25 responses, e.g., "There is a book on a desk. This looks interesting, do you like to read?"). Table 1 summarizes parameters used when calling OpenAI API [19], set empirically to provide accurate, relevant, and varied responses for open conversation with T-Top.

Object recognition is done using YOLOv7 [22], trained on the Objects365 dataset [20]. From the set of 365 objects, 189 objects were selected based on their likelihood of being found in typical living spaces. From this set, we chose to select the objects that reached a precision level greater than 60% within the validation dataset, which resulted in a final set of 66 objects. Typical objects are laptops, TV monitors, desks, power outlets, cell phone, backpack, cup, glasses, watch, coffee machine, refrigerator, storage box, etc. Limiting the number of objects helps to avoid overloading the scene description sent to GPT-3.5 Turbo with unreliable object detection data.

The Perception Analyzer module serves as a filter to select the visible objects from the set of 66 objects to be added to the conversation. Objects are considered visible when they are identified in the scene for at least 8 s consecutively, a

---

[1] https://platform.openai.com/docs/guides/fine-tuning/use-a-checkpointed-model.

Table 1. OpenAI API Parameters and Settings

Parameter	Value	Description
Max tokens	1600	The maximum number of tokens that can be generated.
Temperature	0.5	Controls the randomness of the model's responses.
Frequency penalty	0.5	To avoid repeating the same answer, promoting more diverse outputs.
Top p	0.5	Restricts the model to considering only the most probable token choices, enhancing response quality and focus.

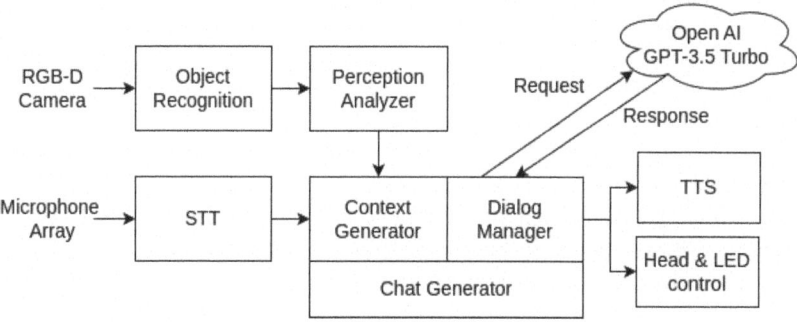

Fig. 2. Integration diagram of GPT-3.5 Turbo with T-Top

duration set empirically to reduce false positives. Visible objects are set as events with a timestamp.

The audio stream from the microphone array is processed by ODAS (Open embeddeD Audition System) [7] to achieve sound source localization, separation, and tracking, identifying the direction and enhancing the audio of the loudest sound source. The enhanced audio stream is then processed for STT using Silero VAD[2] DNN running on the CPU, and transcribed to text using Whisper's small

---

[2] https://github.com/snakers4/silero-vad.

model [16] running on the GPU. TTS is done using Piper[3] running on the GPU. The voice selected is the one of an older man with a regional French accent.

The Chat Generator module uses the information provided by the Perception Analyzer and SST modules to provide requests to GPT-3.5 Turbo using the Dialog Manager module, which then can generate TTS responses and communication cues, i.e.: the interface shows eyes that blink and a mouth that moves when the robot speaks; the head tilts to the left when a request is sent to GPT-3.5 Turbo and while waiting for a response; LEDs light up green when the robot is in listening mode and red when the robot waits for a response or is speaking. The Dialog Manager is a finite-state machine designed according to the interaction scenario the robot has to follow. It uses prompt engineering techniques [18] to configure GPT-3.5 Turbo to personalize its responses according to the intended application with T-Top. There are several ways to generate requests as prompts [23–25] to GPT-3.5 Turbo. We chose to use Pattern prompting because they are reusable templates or structures used to effectively generate and customize outputs from large language models (LLMs) [24]. The key is to combine multiple patterns rather than relying on a single pattern [23]. To this end, three patterns are used:

1. Cognitive Verifier is used to instruct the model to generate and answer additional clarifying questions before formulating the final response. For example, we ask the model to incorporate the perceived objects into the conversation by asking questions or making relevant comments about it. "You must not only perceive but also actively comment on objects and sounds in your immediate environment."
2. Audience Persona is used to adjust the explanation to a specific audience to enhance comprehension and engagement. For instance, we ask the model to only respond in French and to have a age-appropriate language: "You communicate exclusively in French."; "The user in front of you is .. years old. Here's the relevant information about him.".
3. Template ensures that the model's output follows a precise template in terms of structure [24]. For instance, we ask the model if it has noticed a phrase starting with "You see [..]"; the placeholder after "you see" matches the object perceived and it must then build on this in the conversation. "If you see [Cup], you say you see it and ask what the person is drinking."

In prompt engineering, the context, a.k.a. requests in Fig. 2, contains the cumulative information and interaction history that the model receives as requests to generate responses. Requests to OpenAI's API follow a structured format where percepts and speech are integrated and tagged to generate contextually-relevant and personalized responses, maintaining coherence in the ongoing conversation. This context is also set to include the desired personality traits of the assistant T-Top has to portray, i.e., to be engaging and proactive by suggesting discussion topics based on visible objects, to take into account the date and time of each perceived object and interaction, and to communicate

---

[3] https://github.com/rhasspy/piper.

exclusively in French. Here are some examples of sentences that can be included within the context: "You are T-Top, a chatbot embodying a companion robot. Equipped with advanced perceptual capabilities thanks to your cameras and microphones, you're able to recognize people and objects in your immediate environment, and hear sounds through your microphones."; "You see Necklace", "You see Bottle", etc. While the requests specify context data from which GPT-3.5 Turbo provide responses to, there is no guarantee that it will take all this data into consideration. Requests are limited to a maximum token of 16,000, otherwise they fail. Responses provided by GPT-3.5 Turbo are also tagged and added to the context to be taken into consideration in upcoming communication exchanges.

3   Experimental Setup and Methodology

The experimentatal setup involves one-on-one interactions between T-Top and participants at the location of their choice, such as offices, lab spaces, cafeterias, open spaces, living quarters, etc., creating a wide variety of illumination and environmental conditions. T-Top is set to interact with people following the finite state machine presented in Fig. 3, implemented in the Dialog Manager. Listening and speaking by T-Top are done in alternating turns, so the robot cannot be interrupted while it is speaking. As T-Top detects a person to interact with, it greets the person and starts to listen. Once the person stops talking, a request is provided to GPT-3.5 Turbo to provide a response and converse with the interlocutor. The process is attempted three times in case the API returns an error cause for instance by network loss. If no speech is detected for 20 s, the robot is set to actively engage the interlocutor by emphasizing the presence of visible objects into the conversation. T-Top is set to try to reengage conversation three times when the person does not respond, and then concludes the interaction by saying goodbye.

The preliminary assessment study conducted involve 18 participants aged between 23 and 68, including 11 women and 7 men, with 38.9% of participants reporting being very familiar with technology, 33.3% fairly familiar, 16.7% somewhat familiar, and 11.1% not familiar at all. Metrics used to document the interaction dynamics with T-Top are:

- Object recognition, to evaluate how the robot is able to perceive objects in open environmental conditions and how often GPT-3.5 Turbo fine-tuned model decides to include them into the conversations;
- Response time, to characterize the latency caused by the verbal communication modules;
- Gaze time, evaluated manually by looking at the video recordings taken from T-Top camera, to observe where people are looking when interacting with the robot;
- Evaluation of the interaction with T-Top using a semi-structured interview questionnaire, completed immediately after conversing with T-Top, with six

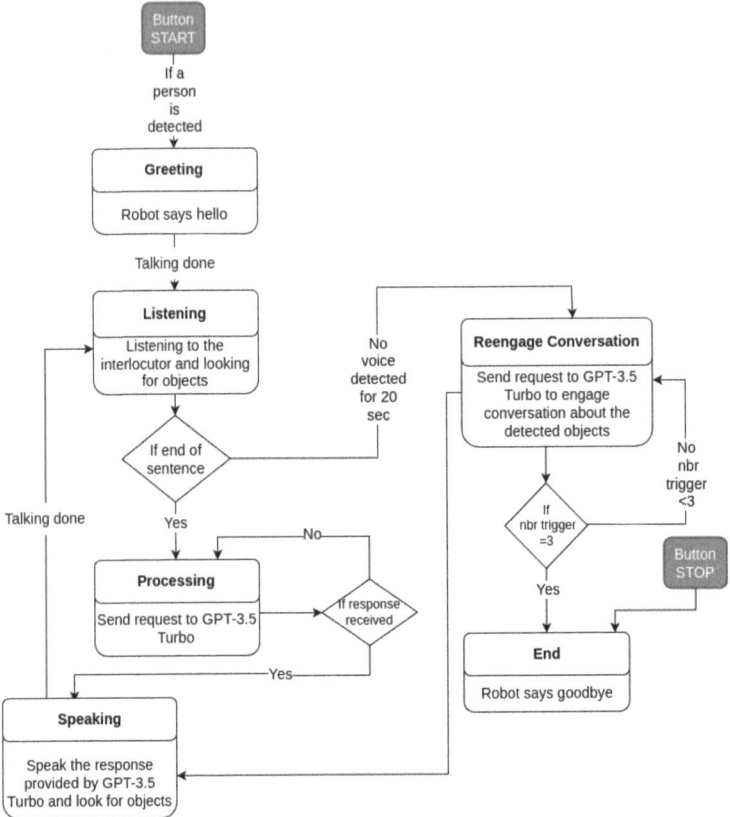

Fig. 3. State diagram of the Dialog Manager

questions using a 5-point Likert scale to evaluate the interactions with the robot, and three open-ended questions the robot's strengths and weaknesses, as well as suggestions for improvement.

4 Results

Experimentations lasted between 15 to 40 min, ending when the participant requesting to stop. On average, the discussions with the robot lasted 23 min. About 714 communication exchanges were observed during the experimentations. T-Top recognized an average of 11 objects per session, with a median detection accuracy of 85.5% and a semi-interquartile range of 6.88%. Detection accuracy ranges from a minimum of 63% to a maximum of 99%. Objects were integrated into the conversations on average about 50% of the overall interaction time, with standard deviation of 21% (minimum 13% and maximum 86%).

Looking more closely at the processing times of the modules during those conversations, STT took about 0.002 times the length of the speech provided (linear regression's R^2 coefficient 0.74), with an average transcription time of 0.07 s. TTS took about 0.001 times the length of the speech provided (R^2 0.32), with an average TTS processing time of 0.39 s. As shown in Fig. 4, the response time of OpenAI's API for GPT-3.5 Turbo fine-tuned model is 3.25 s on average with a standard deviation of 2.91 s. The overall average response time is therefore about 3.71 s. Delays ranging from 10 to 20 s occur when request reach the maximum token limit set: removing previous percepts written in the context reduces its size and are then resend to the API, which explains the higher delays.

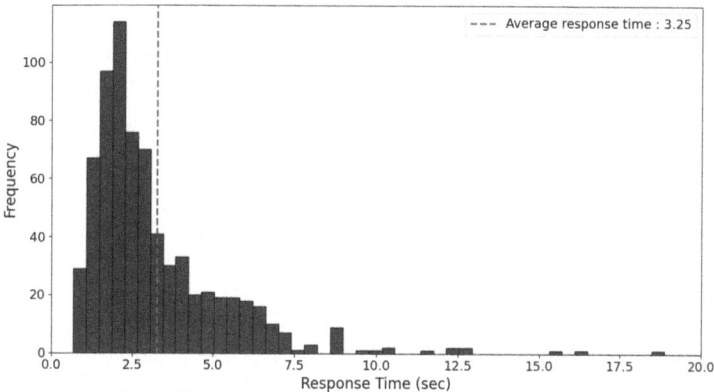

Fig. 4. Histogram of API response time

Figure 5 presents gaze time toward T-Top during conversations. When the participants were not looking at T-Top's face, they were focusing on the LED strip. This suggests that the LED strip is more useful to synchronize turn-taking. Instances where participants briefly turned their heads away (less than 10 s over each trial) were not considered in the analysis, as these moments were too short to be taken into account.

Table 2 summarizes participant feedback gathered using the questionnaire. Most participants found the interactions fairly fluid and the robot's responsiveness satisfactory. The ones disagreeing with this are younger individuals who would have preferred a more dynamic robot.Including visible objects in the conversation was highly appreciated by 61.1% of the participants. The one participant who had low appreciation of this capability simply did not experience it during its trial, as conversing with GPT-3.5 Turbo did not relate to objects in the scene.ChatGPT's answers were considered highly to moderately relevant by most of the participants. Finally, most of the participants agree that non-verbal cues are useful and clear, while 88.9% find it very useful.

Table 3 summarizes what participants indicated regarding the strengths and weaknesses of the implementation. Overall, the participants liked their experi-

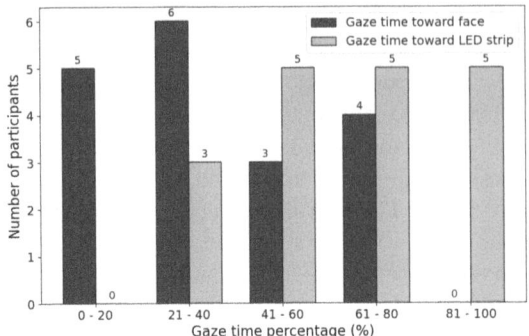

Fig. 5. Histogram of gaze time percentage

Table 2. Participant feedback about T-Top's conversation capabilities

Fluidity of interaction	Very fluid 22.2 %	Fairly fluid **66.7 %**	Not very 11.1 %	Not fluid at all 0.0 %
Responsiveness	Too fast 16.7 %	Satisfactory **72.2 %**	Not very 11.1 %	Not at all 0.0 %
Inclusion of objects	Highly **61.1 %**	Moderately 33.3 %	Not very 5.6 %	Not at all 0.0 %
Relevance of answers	Highly relevant 44.4 %	Moderately **50.0 %**	Not very 5.6 %	Not at all 0.0 %
Clarity of non-verbal cues	Very clear **83.3 %**	Fairly 16.7 %	Not very clear 0.0 %	Not at all 0.0 %
Usefulness of non-verbal cues	Very useful **88.9 %**	Fairly useful 5.6 %	Not very 0.0 %	Not useful 5.6 %

ence, particularly the versatility and pertinence of the responses, and enjoyed including objects in the conversations and the non-verbal cues. They also pointed out some minor negative aspects such as poor pronunciation and problems with STT which sometimes struggled to detect the end of the participant's sentence. The participants also provided improvement suggestions, the most frequent being to improve the robot's facial expressiveness and looks, with options ranging from more humanoid-like to simple designs with eyebrows and a nose. Some commented about the choice of the voice, which sometimes led to poor pronunciation. Personalized configuration by being able to select T-Top's voice, facial appearance and clothing is suggested. Less common suggestions includes removing the use of LEDs, improving STT capabilities, incorporating location awareness, displaying text responses on the screen and shortening the length of responses by GPT-3.5 Turbo.

Table 3. Strengths (+) and weaknesses (-)

Topics	No. Participants
(+) Diversity of exchange and pleasantness	9
(+) Robot's pleasant appearance	8
(+) Dynamic exchange	8
(+) Including objects in conversation	6
(+) Ability to respond to sensitive subjects	6
(+) Appreciation of the robot's voice	6
(+) Non-verbal cues (head tilt)	5
(+) Therapeutic feeling in interventions	3
(+) Good pronunciation	3
(-) Poor pronunciation	5
(-) Problems with detection of end of sentences	4
(-) Lack of dynamism in exchanges	2
(-) Dual personality issues	2

5 Discussion and Conclusion

This paper presents the integration of GPT-3.5 Turbo into T-Top, a SAR table-top robot capable of detecting objects and integrating them into the conversation. These experimentations suggest that T-Top can hold conversations and interact with people in their natural settings, and to adequately include perceived objects into the conversations. Participants engaged with the robot easily, and the use of non-verbal cues help compensate form the fluidity and responsiveness of the robot. These observations made with non-elderly participants validate that the robot's capabilities are sufficient to move forward with experimentations with older adults, and to see how to engage them to discuss with the robot as a follow up with our previous trials [14]. The experimental conditions are going to be similar, i.e., the robot will be brought to the participants in their living quarters, engaging them in discussions about topics of interests to them or about objects seen in proximity. Regarding technical improvements, response latency when interacting with T-Top is mostly caused by the CA, but still an average overall latency of 3.71 s is coming close to the two-second rule in turn-taking [21]. We plan to experiment with local LLMs and improve STT to make sure that the entire statement from the speaker is captured, even if they pause, to avoid interrupting them before they finish speaking. We also want to be able to interrupt the robot or pause the conversation when the interlocutor is not visible by the robot, introduce options for voice and facial customization to help personalize and enhance user experience, and perceiving the interlocutor's gaze, mood or facial expressions to add to the conversations.

Acknowledgement. Work reported in this paper has been approved by the Research Ethic Boards (CÉR of CIUSSS de l'Estrie – CHUS), 2024–5297. This work was supported by Calcul Québec and Digital Research Alliance of Canada. We gratefully acknowledge the financial support provided by the Sunny Foundation, IVADO, the Network of Centres of Excellence of Canada on Aging Gracefully across Environments using Technology to Support Wellness, Engagement, and Long Life (AGE-WELL) and the Natural Sciences and Engineering Research Council of Canada (NSERC). Special thanks to Adina Panchea for her help with ethics, and Jian-Yun Nie (Université de Montréal) for the joint project with Sunny Foundation and IVADO. We would also like to extend our sincere thanks to all the participants in the study.

References

1. Billing, E., Rosén, J., Lamb, M.: Language models for human-robot interaction. In: Companion 2023 ACM/IEEE International Conference on Human-Robot Interaction, pp. 905–906. Association for Computing Machinery, New York, NY, USA (2023)
2. Broekens, J., Heerink, M., Rosendal, H.: Assistive social robots in elderly care: a review. Gerontechnology **8**, 94–103 (2009)
3. Cao, H.L., Scholz, C., De Winter, J., Makrini, I.E., Vanderborght, B.: Investigating the role of multi-modal social cues in human-robot collaboration in industrial settings. Int. J. Soc. Robot. **15**(7), 1169–1179 (2023)
4. Cherakara, N., et al.: Furchat: An embodied conversational agent using LLMs, combining open and closed-domain dialogue with facial expressions. arXiv preprint arXiv:2308.15214 (2023)
5. Feil-Seifer, D., Mataric, M.: Defining socially assistive robotics. In: Proceedings of International Conference on Rehabilitation Robotics, pp. 465–468 (2005)
6. Ferland, F., Reveleau, A., Leconte, F., Létourneau, D., Michaud, F.: Coordination mechanism for integrated design of human-robot interaction scenarios. Paladyn, J. Behav. Robot. **8**(1), 100–111 (2017)
7. Grondin, F., Michaud, F.: Lightweight and optimized sound source localization and tracking methods for open and closed microphone array configurations. Robot. Auton. Syst. **113**, 63–80 (2019)
8. Hung, C., et al.: The benefits of and barriers to using a social robot PARO in care settings: a scoping review. BMC Geriatr. **19**, 1–10 (2019)
9. Irfan, B., Kuoppamäki, S., Skantze, G.: Recommendations for designing conversational companion robots with older adults through foundation models. Front. Robot. AI **11**, 1363713 (2024)
10. Kwan, M., Younbo, J., Jaywoo, K., Sang, R.: Are physically embodied social agents better than disembodied social agents? The effects of physical embodiment, tactile interaction, and people's loneliness in human-robot interaction. Int. J. Human Comput. Stud. **64**, 962–973 (2006)
11. Maheux, M., Caya, C., Létourneau, D., Michaud, F.: T-Top, a SAR experimental platform. In: Proceedings of ACM/IEEE International Conference on Human-Robot Interaction, pp. 904–908 (2022)
12. Maheux, M., Létourneau, D., Warren, P., Panchea, A., Robillard, J., Michaud, F.: Designing a tabletop SAR as an advanced HRI experimentation platform. In: Proceedings of International Symposium Technological Advances in Human-Robot Interaction, pp. 10–19 (2024)

13. Maheux, M., Panchea, A., Warren, P., Létourneau, D., Michaud, F.: T-Top, an open source tabletop robot with advanced onboard audio, vision and deep learning capabilities. In: Proceedings of IEEE/RSJ International Conference on Intelligent Robots and Systems, pp. 7862–7869 (2023)
14. Panchea, A., Maheux, M.A., Warren, P., Létourneau, D., Michaud, F.: Exploratory evaluation of a tabletop robot with older adults. In: proceedings of ACM/IEEE International Conference on Human-Robot Interaction. Association for Computing Machinery (2024)
15. Quigley, M., et al.: ROS: An open-source robot operating system. In: ICRA Workshop on Open Source Software, vol. 3, p. 5. Kobe, Japan (2009)
16. Radford, A., Kim, J.W., Xu, T., Brockman, G., McLeavey, C., Sutskever, I.: Robust speech recognition via large-scale weak supervision. In: Proceedings of International Conference on Machine Learning, pp. 28492–28518. PMLR (2023)
17. Reimann, M.M., Kunneman, F.A., Oertel, C., Hindriks, K.V.: A survey on dialogue management in human-robot interaction. J. Hum. Robot Interact. **13**(2), 348605 (2024)
18. Sahoo, P., Singh, A., Saha, S., Jain, V., Mondal, S., Chadha, A.: A systematic survey of prompt engineering in large language models: Techniques and applications. arXiv preprint arXiv:2402.07927 (2024)
19. Saravanan, S., Sudha, K.: GPT-3 powered system for content generation and transformation. In: Proceedings of International Conference on Computational Intelligence and Communication Technologies, pp. 514–519 (2022)
20. Shao, S., et al.: Objects365: a large-scale, high-quality dataset for object detection. In: Proceedings of IEEE/CVF International Conference Computer Vision, pp. 8429–8438 (2019)
21. Shiomi, M., Minato, T., Ishiguro, H.: Subtle reaction and response time effects in human-robot touch interaction. In: Kheddar, A., et al. (eds.) Social Robotics. ICSR 2017. LNCS, vol. 10652, pp. 242–251. Springer, Cham (2017). https://doi.org/10.1007/978-3-319-70022-9_24
22. Wang, C.Y., Bochkovskiy, A., Liao, H.Y.M.: YOLOv7: trainable bag-of-freebies sets new state-of-the-art for real-time object detectors. In: Proceedings of IEEE/CVF Conference Computer Vision and Pattern Recognition, pp. 7464–7475 (2023)
23. Wei, J., et al.: Chain-of-thought prompting elicits reasoning in large language models. Adv. Neural. Inf. Process. Syst. **35**, 24824–24837 (2022)
24. White, J., et al.: A prompt pattern catalog to enhance prompt engineering with ChatGPT. arXiv preprint arXiv:2302.11382 (2023)
25. Yao, S., et al.: React: Synergizing reasoning and acting in language models. arXiv preprint arXiv:2210.03629 (2022)
26. Zhang, B., Soh, H.: Large language models as zero-shot human models for human-robot interaction. arXiv preprint arXiv:2303.03548 (2023)

MiKa Assistive Humanoid Robot for Metro Passengers

Jose Ben$^{(\boxtimes)}$, Bejoy Varghese , and Mahesh C

Federal Institute of Science and Technology (FISAT), Ernakulam, Kerala, India
joseben.official@gmail.com

Abstract. As urbanization continues to reshape our world, the utilization and expansion of metro transportation systems are on the rise, making it increasingly challenging to manage large crowds. This paper presents the design, development, and implementation of MiKa (Metro Information Kiosk Agent), an autonomous humanoid robot designed to provide assistance to passengers in navigating through the metro system, providing tickets, answering FAQs, and providing information about the metro system. User trials in both controlled environments and real-world metro stations received positive feedback on MiKa's appearance, multilingual capabilities, and overall user experience. Results suggest a strong preference for robot assistance among younger demographics, highlighting the potential of MiKa for enhancing passenger experience in metro systems. Overall, MiKa is a significant advancement in autonomous robots for public service, offering valuable insights for future robotics projects in similar domains.

Keywords: Assistive Humanoid · Social Robot · Public Transport · Autonomous · Human Robot Interaction

1 Introduction

Metro systems have been in operation since the late 19th century, with the London Underground being the world's first metro system [1]. With the rapid urbanization of cities globally, metro systems have become essential for efficient urban mobility. Metro Transportation systems have become increasingly popular as an efficient and reliable means of transportation in crowded urban areas.

With more people relying on the metro rail for daily commutes, managing traffic flow and ensuring passenger safety has become crucial. Various technologies and innovations have been developed to address these challenges like using social assistive humanoid robots to guide passengers, provide instructions, and even entertain them during their travels. With the emerging trend of automating and robotizing crucial systems, the automation of transport hubs is not far behind with airports like London, Heathrow Airport, and Bangalore Airport implementing robots to assist passengers.

© The Author(s), under exclusive license to Springer Nature Singapore Pte Ltd. 2025
O. Palinko et al. (Eds.): ICSR + AI 2024, LNAI 15562, pp. 186–193, 2025.
https://doi.org/10.1007/978-981-96-3519-1_18

With the onset of the COVID-19 pandemic, many service providers transitioned to contactless solutions, with robotics playing a significant role. Some busy airports, for instance, adopted robotic systems such as the Korean robot Troika and service robots like IRobt [2]. However, these robots had notable limitations, particularly in their ability to engage passengers with visual or human-like interactions. Their functionality was largely restricted to tasks like scanning flight tickets and offering basic information, leaving a gap in more interactive and personalized services.

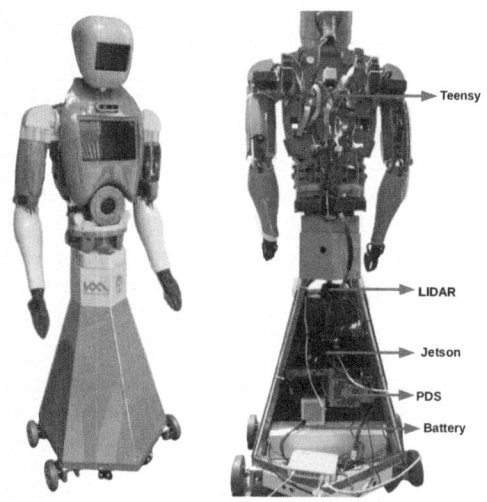

Fig. 1. MiKa - The Humanoid Assistive Robot (left), MiKa's hardware architecture (right)

2   Features of MiKa

MiKa was designed to assist passengers at metro stations. Unlike earlier systems, it not only answers travelers' questions and provides information on train schedules, fares, and station details but also issues metro tickets. MiKa's proficiency in both the local languages (Malayalam, Hindi, and Tamil) and English enhances its ability to interact efficiently with other people. MiKa can make public announcements, provide instructions while moving through the commutators. MiKa can direct and navigate the passengers to the platform, ticket counters, restrooms, or elevators. MiKa can greet passengers with gestures like folding its hands to do a namaste pose, shaking hands with the passengers, and presenting them with flowers. MiKa can also move its hips and waist to carry out a series of 7 different gestures or actions that enable MiKa to give a natural feel while interacting with passengers and children. These additional gestures and interactions keeps MiKa unique from the previous similar service robots. Studies by

T.Horii et al. [11] revealed that humans are more likely to engage with robots that offer multimodal interaction compared to robots that rely solely on verbal communication. This is particularly relevant in crowded and noisy environments, such as metro stations, where a combination of visual and auditory cues can help passengers better understand instructions.

A study by Onyeulo et al. [9] suggests that robots that pay attention to people in a way that mimics humans, by using facial expressions and body language that match what they are saying, can be more engaging for users. This can make it easier for people to understand the robot, and predict what it will do next, which in turn can make people trust the robot more. This natural, multi-modal behavior comes effortlessly to MiKa, allowing it to easily connect with people through its facial expressions, eye movements, and coordinated movements of its arms, head, and waist during interactions.

One of the major features of a humanoid robot is to look as humane as possible hence MiKa has a height of around 1.6 m which is the average height of women in India [3]. According to a study by Broadbent et al. [10], a robot with a more human-like face display is perceived to have more intellect and a better personality. Hence MiKa was designed as a smooth cartoon-like figure with slight human resemblance, which would appear cute and friendly.

MiKa can differentiate and identify age and gender through AI algorithms and behave accordingly. It can entertain the children with songs, videos, and a few dance moves. MiKa can also identify face masks and can direct the passengers to wear a face mask. MiKa also has a complaint recording feature so that, in case a passenger needs to raise a complaint it will be recorded in the server and the authorities will be notified.

3   MiKa The Metro Bot

3.1   Design and Modeling

The design of MiKa was finalized after months of research into other similar and available robots. The design was greatly inspired by the Inmoov open-source project [4]. The CAD files were sourced from the Inmoov forum and were used as references to draw, design, and remodel the parts with various sketching and modeling tools available in Fusion 360. The open-source slicing software Cura was used to convert STL files into G-code for 3D printing.

3.2   Structure and Material

MiKa's upper body is 3D printed using PLA (Polylactic acid) plastic. PLA was chosen for its cost-effectiveness, ease of printing, and handling compared to ABS. Although PLA is weaker than ABS, it is less brittle and stretches rather than breaking [5]. Additionally, PLA is biodegradable ensuring environmentally safe disposal of waste prints and broken parts. All the parts were printed with a 0.16 mm layer height for a clean finish. Any minor imperfections were sanded or filed down to ensure a smooth finish and later spray painted with a clear coating of varnish for a shiny look. MiKa's lower half features a steel frame with a hexagonal base enclosed by acrylic sheets, designed to lower the center of gravity and enhance stability. The base is divided into three levels to separate the battery and power system from the control boards and other accessories.

3.3   Hardware

MiKa features a 5-inch LED screen on its head that displays animated eyes, with facial expressions such as happy, sad, and love faces designed using Blender software and dynamically adapting to conversations in real-time. Additionally, it includes a 10-inch LED touch display on its chest for displaying information, playing videos, and ticket bookings or interactions. Its humanoid design includes arms and shoulders with four degrees of motion on each side and claw grippers for object manipulation.

MiKa is powered by a Jetson Xavier NX, serving as its brain. The NVIDIA GPU's high processing capabilities allow MiKa to swiftly analyze and process large data sets, enabling real-time learning and adaptation to its environment and users. This is particularly useful for social robots, which require the ability to understand and respond to human interactions and behaviors. With its advanced AI algorithms, MiKa is capable of providing more personalized and effective services to its users, ultimately enhancing its overall functionality and user experience.

All actuators are controlled by a Teensy 4.1 microcontroller board, which communicates with the Jetson via micro-ROS packages, using custom breakout boards and special PCB shields for connectivity. MiKa utilizes an Intel D415 depth camera and an RP LIDAR A2M8 for object tracking, face recognition, SLAM, and navigation (Fig. 1). The depth camera captures 3D models using stereo vision, while the LIDAR provides accurate obstacle detection and mapping, enhancing the robot's ability to navigate and interact with its environment. MiKa features two 50W speakers at the base, along with two in the head for audio output. It also has a conference microphone in its belly, allowing it to capture sound from all directions, ensuring quick and effective user interaction even in noisy or crowded environments. MiKa features a four-wheel drive system with rotary encoders, enabling high mobility and speeds over 0.7 m/s. Six ultrasonic sensors at the base prevent collisions with small obstacles, and four IR sensors at the front and back detect stairs.

MiKa is powered by a custom 12V Li-ion battery pack enabling it to operate for extended periods. A Battery Management System (BMS) is installed to monitor and control the charging and discharging of the battery, ensuring that it operates safely and efficiently at all times, it helps to prevent overcharging, over-discharging, and other issues that can damage the battery or reduce its lifespan. Initially, a Buck converter solution was implemented for different voltage requirements, but at a later stage found that it generated a ground loop issue. So a custom power distribution system (PDS) was designed with LM338 voltage regulators, which have built-in current limiting and thermal shutdown feature that protects the device from damage due to overloads or excessive temperatures.

3.4   Software

The Jetson Xavier runs on Ubuntu 20.04 Xenial version through the Linux for Tegra (L4T) development environment. MiKa's software architecture leverages Docker containers for modular deployment and management of different components, allowing for easier scalability and maintenance of the system. The container-based virtualization is the suitable choice for us since optimal efficiency is our priority.

MiKa uses ROS2, an open-source robotics framework, to manage its components and software packages with a robust and flexible architecture. ROS2 introduces the DDS (Data Distribution Service) protocol, offering more efficient and reliable messaging than ROS1 [6]. MiKa utilizes the Nav2 ROS package for navigation and mapping, which offers advanced features like global path planning, local obstacle avoidance, and 2D/3D mapping.

MiKa utilizes Rasa Open Source for communicating with passengers. Rasa Open Source is an open-source conversational AI framework that is used to develop Natural Language Processing (NLP) systems [7]. MiKa is trained with custom data sets related to the metro to give relevant answers to questions asked. MiKa is currently trained in English, Hindi, Malayalam, and Tamil(local languages) (Fig. 2).

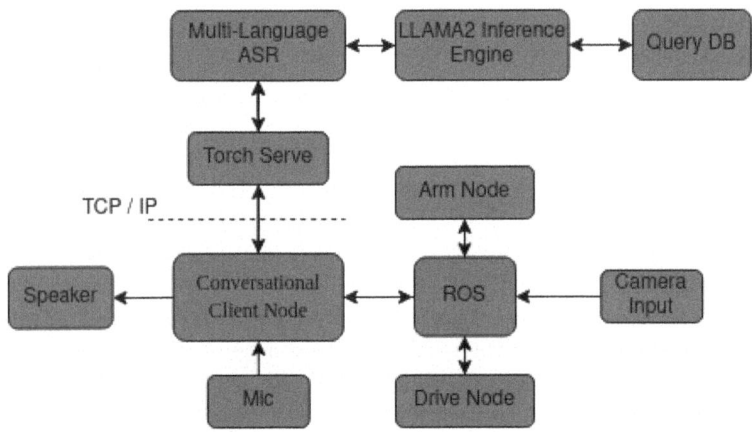

Fig. 2. System Architecture

4   Implementation: Test Run and Pilot Deployment

MiKa's first public trial was held at the Urban Mobility India Conference 2022, where it interacted in English, navigated obstacles, and followed movements. Feedback was positive, with suggestions for user interface improvements and multilingual support. The second trial, conducted over a week at the Kochi Water Metro Terminal, provided valuable insights from a broader user base.

Incorporating all previous user feedback and bug fixes, MiKa underwent its final pilot program at a major Kochi Metro Station. This phase served as a crucial validation period, extending the interaction period to over two months. During this pilot run, MiKa featured multilingual capabilities (English, Malayalam, Hindi, and Tamil) and an integrated user feedback system that prompted passengers for anonymous feedback after each interaction. This real-time data collection proved invaluable for assessing user experience and evaluating MiKa's effectiveness in fulfilling its objectives.

4.1   Discussion

According to the survey, more than 68.46% of the passengers reported that the overall appearance of MiKa was very appealing and that they would prefer MiKa over a ticket ATM or human staff. Several participants expressed interest in the interactive map display on MiKa's screen enabling passengers to view real-time metro routes, station layouts, and estimated arrival times, enhancing their overall understanding of the metro system.

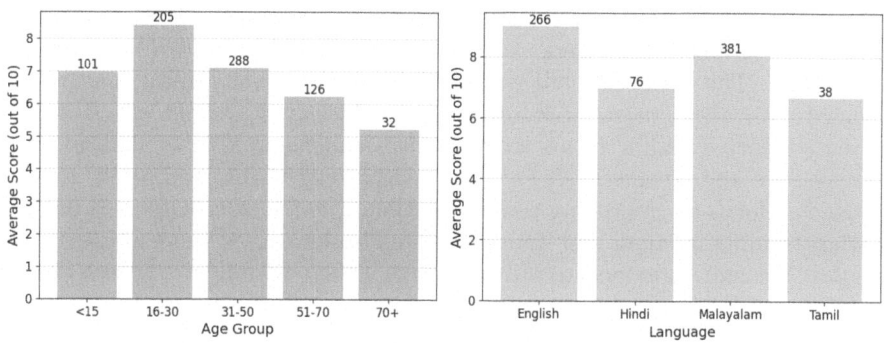

Fig. 3. User Satisfaction across various : (a) Age and (b) Language groups

The data presented here is based on a 14-day survey, with MiKa interacting with an average of over 160 passengers daily. Due to the high volume of data generated, along with storage limitations and privacy concerns, all data is cleared weekly. We also observed a novelty effect [8], where many participants engaged with MiKa out of curiosity. To address this, we filtered responses based on engagement traits and removed redundant or repetitive interactions. After excluding interactions shorter than two minutes, the remaining 764 responses offer valuable insights from a much larger feedback pool.

A graph comparing user satisfaction (measured by preference for robot assistance over human assistance) for different age groups is shown in Fig. 3(a). The data suggests that users aged 16–30 years old exhibited the highest preference for using the robot. This is followed by the 31–50 age group. Users over the age of 70, on the other hand, appeared to be the least satisfied and preferred face-to-face communication. One possible cause for the decrease in satisfaction may be attributed to how they formulate questions or engage with technology.

MiKa's multilingual capabilities were well-received by users, as evidenced by their positive feedback. Figure 3(b) depicts user satisfaction plotted against different languages supported. While English users reported the highest satisfaction, Malayalam users followed closely behind, indicating MiKa's effectiveness in catering to the local language. However, a slight decline in satisfaction was observed among Hindi and Tamil users. This suggests that MiKa's chatbot functionality may require further training.

5   Conclusion

In this paper, we presented the design, development, and deployment of MiKa, an autonomous humanoid assistance robot. MiKa is designed to assist passengers in navigating through the metro system, providing directions, providing tickets, answering queries, and ensuring a safe and enjoyable journey. MiKa was tested in multiple real-world metro station-like settings. Analysis of the feedback revealed user satisfaction with MiKa's appearance and assistance, with younger users showing a stronger preference for robot interaction. Our results show that MiKa can effectively assist passengers in navigating the metro and providing relevant information. The data collected was affected by the novelty effect, passengers engaged with MiKa mostly out of curiosity which had a slight effect on the survey conducted. While future work involves enhancing MiKa's abilities with more sensors and advanced AI for improved passenger communication, there's an ongoing focus on improving communication style for older users and further chatbot training in Hindi and Tamil. We are also looking at implementing sign language recognition models to MiKa to make it more friendlier to speech issues. Additionally, we plan to implement sign language recognition models to make MiKa more accessible for users with speech impairments.

Acknowledgments. This work was supported by the Federal Institute of Science and Technology (FISAT), India.

References

1. Wu, D., Lambrinos, L., Przepiorka, T., et al.: Enabling efficient offline mobile access to online social media on urban underground metro systems. IEEE Trans. Intell. Transp. Syst. **21**(7), 2750–2764 (2019)
2. Tran, H.T., Vo, T.C., Nguyen, Q.N.A., Pham, N.M., et al.: A novel design of a smart interactive guiding robot for busy airports. Int. J. Smart Sens. Intell. Syst. **15**(1), 1–17 (2022)
3. Deaton, A.: Height, health, and inequality: the distribution of adult heights in India. Am. Econom. Rev. **98**(2), 468–474 (2008)

4. Langevin, G.: INMOOV. http://inmoov.fr/. Accessed 11 July 2024
5. Farbman, D., McCoy, C.: Materials testing of 3D printed ABS and PLA samples to guide mechanical design (2016)
6. Maruyama, Y., Kato, S., Azumi, T.: Exploring the performance of ROS2. In: 2016 International Conference on Embedded Software (EMSOFT), IEEE (2016)
7. Bocklisch, T., Faulkner, J., Pawlowski, N., Nichol, A.: Rasa: open source language understanding and dialogue management. arXiv preprint arXiv:1712.05181 (2017)
8. Reimann, M., van de Graaf, J., van Gulik, N., van de Sanden, S., Verhagen, T., Hindriks, K.: Social robots in the wild and the novelty effect. In: Ali, A.A., et al. Social Robotics. ICSR 2023. LNCS, vol. 14454, pp. 38–48. Springer, Singapore (2023). https://doi.org/10.1007/978-981-99-8718-4_4
9. Onyeulo, E.B., Gandhi, V.: What makes a social robot good at interacting with humans? Information. **11**, 43 (2020)
10. Broadbent, E., Kumar, V., et al.: Robots with display screens: a robot with a more humanlike face display is perceived to have more mind and a better personality. PLoS ONE **8**(8), e72589 (2013)
11. Horii, T., Nagai, Y.: Active inference through energy minimization in multimodal affective human-robot interaction. Front. Robot. AI. **8**, 684401 (2021)

Classifying Attention Drops in EEG Signals for ADHD Training with the Virtual Agent Flobi

Julian Leichert[1,4]([⊠]) ![ORCID], Julia Siemann[2], Ira-Katharina Petras[3],
Michael Siniatchkin[3] ![ORCID], Britta Wrede[1,4] ![ORCID], and Birte Richter[1,4] ![ORCID]

[1] Bielefeld University, Medical School OWL, Medical Assistance Systems,
33615 Bielefeld, Germany
`{jleichert,bwrede3,birte.richter}@uni-bielefeld.de`
[2] Department of Child and Adolescent Psychiatry and Psychotherapy Bethel,
Evangelical Hospital Bielefeld, 33617 Bielefeld, Germany
`julia.siemann@evkb.de`
[3] University Clinic of Child and Adolescent Psychiatry, Psychosomatics
and Psychotherapy, RWTH Aachen University, 52074 Aachen, Germany
`{ipetras,msiniatchkin}@ukaachen.de`
[4] Center for Cognitive Interaction Technology, Bielefeld University,
Bielefeld, Germany

Abstract. The objective of the *RoboCamp* project is to enhance the attention capabilities of children diagnosed with ADHD by employing feedback with the virtual robotic agent Flobi. To expand the current gaze-based detection of attention drops, this contribution investigates the feasibility of integrating EEG based attention detection into the *RoboCamp* system. An analysis of EEG recordings from 64 channels during supervised tasks with 67 individuals, including both neurotypical and participants with ADHD, identified significant differences between hits and misses among participants, indicating attentional variations. Machine learning models were trained on EEG time sequences derived from experiment trigger signatures, exploring features such as time series, engagement index, and frequency band powers. By applying the features in a classification task, it was found that the EI is not effective for detecting inattention in the ADHD group (F1-score: 57.3%) while it yields better results in the NT group (F1-score: 67.3%). The time series and band power features showed classification capabilities comparable to those of the neurotypical group. The transfer within the neurotypical group to newly recorded *RoboCamp* tasks was successful. Interestingly, the classifier yielded an F1-score of 92.8% for NT participants on a task involving math exercises, indicating that the task itself may play an important role in whether or not inattention can be automatically detected.

Keywords: Attention Detection · Social Agents · EEG · ADHD

O. Palinko et al. (Eds.): ICSR + AI 2024, LNAI 15562, pp. 194–207, 2025.
https://doi.org/10.1007/978-981-96-3519-1_19

1   Introduction

Lately, the use of social (virtual) robots has become a major topic in medical and healthcare applications such as prevention or therapy.

While many therapies, especially behavior therapy, follow relatively strict protocols and are, thus, highly suitable for implementation in HRI settings they require the capability to react to subtle changes in behavior in an adequate way. Social robots are, therefore, a promising tool for such applications as they are tailored toward meeting social needs of human interaction partners. attention deficit/hyperactivity disorder (ADHD) is one of the most frequent neurological disorders in children and adolescents and developing social robots to support ADHD therapy could have a major impact on the well-being of ADHD patients.

The *RoboCamp* therapy system, depicted in Fig. 1, is designed to help improve the concentration of children with ADHD through motivational attention training using a virtual robotic agent [20]. The aim of the RoboCamp system is to support the clinical therapy of children diagnosed with ADHD. Clinical therapy includes the assessment of ADHD symptom serverity and cognitive performance across multiple domains, such as continuous attention and short term memory capabilities. Utilizing the RoboCamp in these domains could provide a easily

Fig. 1. Recording EEG data of a subject solving simple calculations in the *RoboCamp* system.

accessible and interactive tool for the diagnosis and therapy of ADHD. Here, the so-called agent "Flobi" [14] assists children in maintaining focus during basic mathematical exercises.

The basis of our robot application is a highly effective ADHD therapy which utilizes reinforcement mechanisms through response-cost-tokens (RCTs) that are based on the ADHD summer camp approach, a multimodal intervention program, using behavior-controlling processes, which reinforce attentive and punish distracted behavior in a highly contingent way. It has been shown that this approach leads to improvements of ADHD symptoms [16]. In our virtual robot supported application the applied reinforcing statements are operationalized using tokens which are awarded for sustained overt attention and withdrawn for attentional lapses. The allocation of these tokens which are visualized in the GUI as green circles lies in the hand of the virtual robot "Flobi" who also provides verbal feedback consisting of either positive reinforcing statements if the user is attentive or warnings that the user should refocus. The proxy for overt attention here is gaze direction, as estimated in the *RoboCamp* system using the Open-Face [3] software. Besides overt attention, mental drifting describes lapses of covert attention that require sophisticated methods such as electroencephalogram (EEG) analysis to capture. To successfully deploy reinforcing mechanism during attentional lapses, it is of importance to register both types of attentional lapses but the current state of the RoboCamp only evaluates overt attention. Our goal is, therefore, to extend our *RoboCamp* system by an EEG monitoring component that can detect lapses of covert attention and, thus, provide triggers for additional behavior change interventions by Flobi. EEG signals can be measured from the skull in real-time, thus enabling the detection of inattention not manifesting in eye movements. The overarching research question addressed in this article is therefore: (**RQ**) Is it possible to detect inattention by using EEG signals? This contribution examines the suitability of using an EEG headset in the *RoboCamp*, with a particular focus on whether it is possible to correctly classify moments of inattention in EEG recordings using machine learning methods. To evaluate the findings and investigate the integration into the *RoboCamp*, the transfer to *RoboCamp* tasks is examined in a pilot study.

2   Background and Related Work

Attention-Deficit/Hyperactivity Disorder (ADHD) is characterized amongst others by impaired attention in the form of distractibility and inability to concentrate and focus. According to a recent meta-analysis [7], deviant brain mechanisms during mind-wandering contribute to this ADHD symptomatology. Using SVM and Linear Regression, Dong et al. [5] could show that EEG data have the potential to predict such mind-wandering signals within and even across participants. Regarding EEG frequencies, the most prominent candidates are alpha, beta, and gamma bands, all of which are also associated with mind-wandering and which were shown to be aberrant in ADHD [1].

The objective of this contribution is to determine if (in)attention can also be detected in non-neurotypical EEG signals. However, given the lack of specificity of 'inattentiveness', an accurate classification must primarily be data-driven.

One standard measure for measuring cognitive engagement in a task is the engagement index (EI), devised by Pope et al. [19] and calculated as follows:

$$EI = \frac{\beta}{\alpha + \theta} \tag{1}$$

where β, θ, and α correspond to those EEG frequency bands indicative of attention. Utilizing the EI also enables the identification of attentional lapses. Thus, Szafir and Mutlu [22] determined the EI to detect drops of attention in a storytelling setting, combined with target cues coming from a wakamaru robot putatively enhancing the recall ability. They employed self-reported attention levels and the EI to construct an algorithmic threshold that accurately identified instances of attention drops. Liu et al. [13] investigated students' struggles with attention lapses during task instructions. A portable single electrode brain-wave sensor was employed to capture EEG signals, with machine learning techniques used for the recognition of attention loss. In their study, 24 students participated in English tests under different conditions, with EEG and video data collected to classify attentiveness. They achieved an average accuracy of 75.87% with a support vector machine (SVM) and polynomial kernels trained with combinations of the α, β, θ, and δ frequency bands. The self-reported attention levels and video annotations were used as the ground truth. In a study involving 86 participants, the classification accuracy of attention-related multi-channel EEG frequencies into three categories (high, medium, and low) reached 70% [15].

Jin et al. [10] explored the potential of using self-reported thoughts and EEG data from visual search and sustained attention tasks to detect instances of mind-wandering. To achieve this objective, a series of probes were employed to label the data, and a SVM was trained to distinguish between mind-wandering and on-task states with an accuracy range of 50% to 85% and an average of 60%.

Apicella et al. [2] incorporated the engagement index (EI) to compare their own model for detecting engagement with previous research, focusing on classification of attentional states in EEG data of participants engaged in a continuous performance test (CPT). They achieved a within-subject accuracy of 76.9 ± 10.2 for cognitive engagement by extracting EEG frequency features using the filter bank and common spatial pattern (CSP) and labelling the data in accordance with the continuous performance test (CPT) results. In addition to classical approaches, [12] employed an LSTM on a data set consisting of attention levels in a monastic debate. The maximum accuracy reported was 96%, and 95% for the δ and θ waves. To enable comparison with previous research, a SVM was also deployed, achieving an accuracy of 71% in the α, and β wave.

Tang et al. [23] trained a SVM classifier, achieving an under the curve (AUC) of 88% for within-participant prediction and 70% for within-participant cross-lecture prediction by leveraging Riemannian-based features from δ, θ, α, and β bands to detect mind wandering from 8-channel EEG data. Attentional states were marked by key presses of the participants, and used as ground truth.

[6] used the Theta/Beta ratio as an indication of attention in an EEG-controlled serious game, differentiation of attention levels through machine learning models. In a next step, this pipeline provided a feasibility test for detecting ADHD patients' attention levels based on their classified EEG signals. However, this approach focussed on neurotypical attention markers, so the transferability to ADHD-related EEG signals is yet to be established.

To sum up, to date, there is hardly any research on (in)attention classification for children with ADHD. This is probably also due to a lack of data and access to the target group. It is crucial to assess whether the feature values for (in)attention differ in the EEG between ADHD and neurotypical individuals.

Currently, drops in the attention of neurotypical individuals are mostly classified using the EI or other frequency band features. Usual ground-truth measures consist of self-reported attention levels. Another gap relates to cognitive measures that underlie the extracts of (in)attention. There are no classification studies dealing with the working memory n-back paradigm. The n-back task tests working memory functions, where fundamental deficits in ADHD could be shown throughout a range of studies [18]. This lends support for the inattention symptoms observed in ADHD [4]. The aim of this paper is to investigate whether a classifier trained on the n-back paradigm can adequately classify attention. Therefore, the main questions are

> **RQ1 EI feature**: Are there differences in the EEG feature values for the EI in the n-back task between ADHD and neurotypical patients?
>
> **RQ2 classification**: Which EEG features are helpful for the classification of attention drops?
>
> **RQ3 transfer**: Is it possible to train a classifier on the n-back paradigm and apply it to tasks in *RoboCamp*?

3   Methods

For analysis regarding differentiability of (in)attention and training a classifier for attention drops, we are using the data-set STIPED and evaluated it with new recorded RoboCamp data-set. Both data-sets were recorded with the same EEG-Headset and underwent nearly identical preprocessing steps. In the following the two data-sets are presented including the tasks performed by the participants, meta-information, the conductance of EEG recordings, the features selected, and how the classification is performed.

3.1   Data-Set STIPED for Classification

The data analyzed in this project is derived from the European Union's STIPED H2020 program under grant agreement No 731827 (see affiliations). Data collection was approved by the ethics committees of Universities Kiel, Bielefeld, Magdeburg, and Frankfurt. There were 29 participants diagnosed with ADHD (8 females, 21 males; M age $= 12.86$, SD $= 2.40$ years) and 39 neurotypical participants (19 females, 20 males; M age$= 13.73$, SD $= 1.99$ years) which completed the n-back continuous performance task.

n-Back Task. In this project, we applied the following working memory n-back task as described in Splittgerber et al. [21]: A series of consecutively presented pictures was comprised of target, non target, and lure stimuli. Stimuli were targets if identical to the picture presented two trials before. Besides, lure stimuli were pictures resembling target pictures to increase the need for focused attention. All other trials showed regular non target pictures. Participants had to decide whether a currently presented picture was identical to the picture shown two steps back. They indicated by mouse button presses whether a given picture was perceived as a non-target trial (right mouse button) or a target trial (left mouse button). Additionally, lure trials were composed of pictures resembling target pictures, i.e., they were also non-target trials. The task lasted approximately 16 min and contained 366 trials with 30% target trials. The pictures were presented for 500 ms each, and trials were separated by a fixation cross with a jittered duration of 1600 to 2000 ms.

EEG Recordings. The examined n-Back EEG data was recorded using a Compumedics system from 64 monopolar and four bipolar channels at a sampling rate of 1000 Hz to 20 kHz with 24-bit resolution, following the 10–20 placement system.

EEG Preprocessing. The data was filtered using a 120 Hz low-pass, 0.5 Hz high-pass, and 50 Hz notch filter; blink artifacts were corrected via ICA. Epochs were selected from 0.1 s before to 1 s after the onset of the presented stimulus. Hits, correctly identifying the target, and misses were considered. Epochs containing other artifacts were disregarded when a rejection threshold, computed with auto-reject [9], was exceeded. For analyzing the EEG data, the open-source EEG toolbox MNE-Python [8] was used.

3.2   Data-Set RoboCamp for Transfer

To test the transferability of the trained classifiers, a second data-set (Robo-Camp) was recorded with four neurotypical subjects who completed two tasks of the RoboCamp system and the n-back task to ensure consistency. The tasks performed and the recording procedure are described below.

RoboCamp n-Back Task. To ensure consistency, the n-Back task was completed by the participants analogous to the recordings in STIPED data-set.

RoboCamp Mathematical Task. In the math task, subjects are presented with simple math problems that require them to perform addition and subtraction for numbers below 1000. After solving a problem, the next problem is presented immediately, and if the solution given is incorrect, the respondent hears an error sound as feedback and can try again.

RoboCamp Reaction Task. The reaction task requires the participant to react to presented stimuli by pressing the correct button after presentation. The presented stimulus is a gray cross, which turns green when the button is pressed.

Conducting EEG Recordings. The experimental setup comprises three PCs, an amplifier, a webcam, and a trigger box[1]. One PC runs Ubuntu 20.04 and the *RoboCamp* System, from here on called the experiment PC. The second PC is running Windows 10 and the n-back task is presented with Presentation[2]. The third PC, here referred to as the recording PC, runs Windows 10, and records the EEG data with the Neurospec software Curry 8[3]. The experiment

---

[1] https://shop.neurospec.com/mmbt-s-trigger-interface-box?___store=en_DE&___from_store=x_default.

[2] https://www.neurobs.com/menu_presentation/menu_features/features_overview.

[3] https://www.neurospec.com/Products/Details/1031/curry-8.

PCs are connected to the trigger box with a USB cable, while the recording PC is connected to the amplifier. To record the brain activity of the participant, the Compumedics 69-channel headset, which was also used to record the n-back data-set used, is placed on the participant's head, the electrodes are gelled, and the headset is connected to the amplifier. From the experiment PC, triggers are sent from the *RoboCamp* system via the serial port and the pySerial library[4] to the trigger box, which synchronizes tasks and EEG recordings.

In total, there were four neurotypical young adults (1 female, 3 males) participating in the study. The study typically lasted around 2.5 h, including the preparation of the EEG headset and the completion of the tasks. Participants were compensated with 25€. The study was approved by the ethics committee of University Bielefeld. Two of the recordings suffered from poor signal quality in three frontal electrodes, due to hair interference with the EEG headset.

EEG Preprocessing. The preprocessing was carried out similarly to the established procedure. For fitting the ICA, the reference channels FP1 and FP2 were used, as no electrooculogram (EOG) electrodes were placed. In the n-back task, a total of 187 hits and 83 misses were recorded, while for the mathematical task, there were 797 hits and 40 misses. Regarding the reaction task, 416 early responses (hits) and 69 late responses (misses) were used as samples. Responses longer than 1100 ms were excluded from the classifier evaluation, as the models were trained on 1100 ms-long samples. The mean reaction time for all four participants is $\mu = 464$ ms.

3.3   Features

For the purposes of analysis and classification, the following features were selected: the power in the frequency bands (α, β, δ, γ, θ), the 64 channel time series data in hits and misses, and the engagement index (EI)).

3.4   Classification

Classifiers. Classification tasks were performed using Scikit-learn. The investigated classifiers are SVM, SGD, Gradient Boosting, Gaussian Naive Bayes, and Extra Trees.

Parameters for Classification. The EEG data was segmented and labelled according to results of the response. In the n-back task we assumed that a hit indicates attention, and a miss inattention. Utilizing the event markers recorded in the experiment, the segmented epochs were labeled according to hit (0) and miss (1). As the goal of the classification is to identify moments of inattention. The training pipeline is initialized with varying features: (1) the mean EI over all channels for a sample; (2) the calculated EI for a sample; (3) the standard scaled

---

[4] https://pypi.org/project/pyserial/.

64 channel time series data, vectorized in to a 2D vector (n samples x n features); (4) the five band powers (BPs) for each electrode in a sample, calculated with Welch's method. After formatting the input data, it was split with a 0.8/0.2 split into a training and test set.

4   Results

In this section, the analysis of the data-sets regarding RQ1, the evaluation of the trained classifiers regarding RQ2, and finally the transfer of the trained classifiers to the newly acquired Robocamp dataset regarding RQ 3 will be evaluated.

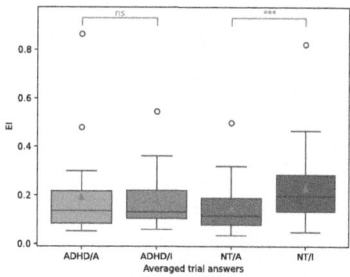

Fig. 2. Averaged Trial Answer (I)nattentive/ (A)ttentive for NT/ADHD

4.1   RQ1: Engagement Index

The ADHD and neurotypical (NT) groups are analyzed regarding distribution and tested for the hypothesis that the EEG signals during hits and misses differ in EI magnitude. The mean values and variances are shown in Fig. 2. For the ADHD group, the null hypothesis that the data derive from a Gaussian distribution was rejected ($W = .85, p < .05$). However, for the NT group, the null hypothesis could not be rejected ($W = .95$, p $= .12$). The data points are paired, as correct and incorrect answers are averaged over trials. The Wilcoxon signed rank test is used for the ADHD group. For the NT group, the paired student-t test is used.

There was no significant difference in EI magnitude between answer types found in the ADHD group (Wilcoxon test: Z=88.0, p=.798). However, for the NT group, a significant difference in EI magnitude was observed ($t(36) = -5.82, p < .001$).

Additional Feature Analysis. Since the EI gives only limited insight, we analyzed the **Frequency Bands Power**. The topographical differences between the responses for each band power are shown in Fig. 3.

Since the sample size of 1.1 s allows only small window sizes for the Welch method, only frequencies above 2 Hz are considered. The most pronounced differences between the responses in the α, β and γ bands for both groups are observed in the occipital lobes. In ADHD subjects, the differences in the θ band are more pronounced in the frontal area than in ADHD subjects. Similarly, in the β band, hit/miss differences are larger in the occipital positions for ADHD subjects. In the α band, differences are greater in between frontal and central electrodes for ADHD subjects. In the δ band, differences are greater in the center of the head. In subjects with ADHD, differences in the γ band are more

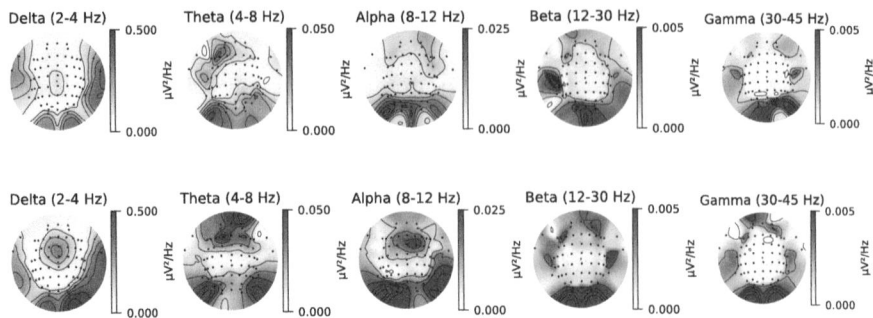

Fig. 3. Topological difference map of incorrect and correct answers averaged over all neurotypical (top) and ADHD (bottom) subjects.

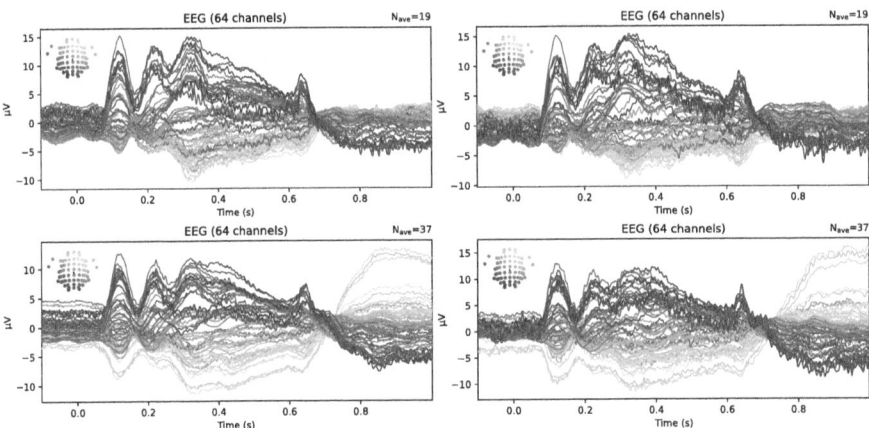

Fig. 4. Grand average of correct (left) and incorrect (right) answers of subjects with ADHD (top) and neurotypical subjects (bottom).

pronounced in the frontal lobe, whereas in neurotypical subjects, differences are more evident in the occipital lobes and in the left and right areas of the scalp.

To investigate **time series features**, the temporal differences, the power over time at every electrode is shown in Fig. 4. For both groups, misses show more noise than hits. Additionally, the averaged recordings show a distinction between neurotypical and ADHD individuals in the voltage rise after 0.7 s at electrodes placed at the front of the head.

4.2   RQ2: Classification of (in)attention

We tested the features 1–4 with the presented classifiers and the results are presented in Fig. 5. To address class imbalance, the weighted F1 score is used to evaluate the classifiers. In the ADHD group, a F1 score of 67.7% was achieved with Gradient Boosting trained on time series (TS) features. The highest F1

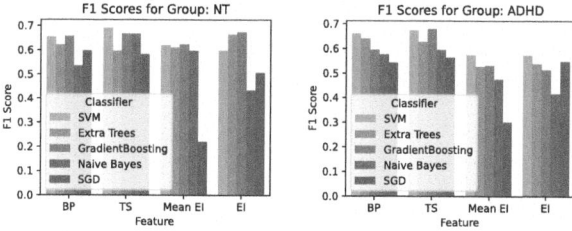

Fig. 5. Best Classifiers for each group and features 1–4

score in the neurotypical group, 69.0%, was achieved with a SVM trained on TSs features as well. Classifiers trained on EI features achieved lower F1 scores than the neurotypical group. For both groups, classifiers trained on TS or BP features achieved higher F1 scores than classifiers trained on EI related features.

4.3 RQ3: Transfer to the RoboCamp System

As part of the *RoboCamp* integration (*RQ 1.3 transfer*), the trained classification models were employed to classify whether participants' were attentive in the recorded *RoboCamp* tasks. The newly acquired data will be evaluated against the classifiers for features 1–4 trained on the original neurotypical group. The classifiers trained on the ADHD group were not considered, as no subject stated that they are currently diagnosed with ADHD. Inattentive labelling is performed in accordance with errors in the mathematical task and late responses (>0.5 s) in the reaction task. The evaluation of machine learning classifiers with the newly acquired data is illustrated for all three tasks in Fig. 6 for the neurotypical group.

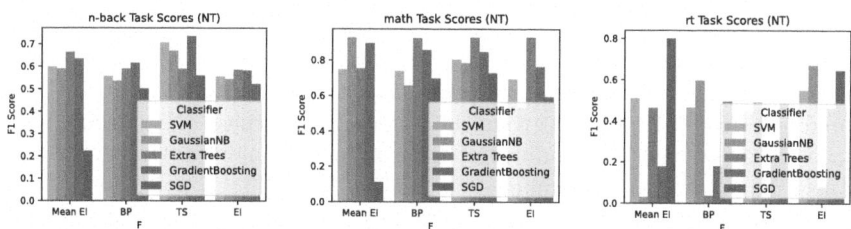

Fig. 6. Resulting weighted F1 scores of study tasks for the classifiers trained on the neurotypical group.

In the n-back task, the highest F1 score (70.5%) was achieved with an SVM trained on TS features. For the mathematical task, the Extra Trees classifier demonstrated robust performance across all four features, attaining an F1 score of 92.8% when trained on EI features. In the reaction task, the SGD classifier, trained with mean EI features on the neurotypical data-set, exhibited the most optimal performance, with an F1 score of 79.8%. However, it is notable that classifiers demonstrated a heterogeneous performance across different features, with some performing below 50%.

5   Discussion

Regarding our first sub-research question (**RQ1 features**), we could show that the classical feature for detecting attention drops in the EEG, the EI differs between the ADHD and neurotypical (NT) group in the answers for the n-back task. Whereas for the NT group, the EI was significantly lower for incorrect responses, no significant difference in EI magnitude between correct and incorrect responses in the ADHD group could be found. It is questionable, whether the related work focusing on the EI for detecting attention lapses, trained on neurotypical individuals is transferable to patients with ADHD. Based on our findings regarding EI, using an algorithmic threshold such as [22] for online prediction for people with ADHD is not feasible for the application in the *Robo-Camp*.

To examine this, we also plotted the frequency band power and the time series. Here, visual inspection suggests some differences between the two groups in our data-set. Further statistical analysis to validate these subjective findings in is warranted. In the context of the *RoboCamp* this could make the detection of attention lapses dependent on the information of whether the person in front is diagnosed with ADHD (either it should be known or classified by the *RoboCamp* system). Given the small sample size of the ADHD group, future work based on a larger data-set is warranted to validate the findings. Exploring the integration of eye tracking as a correlate feature, as other work in similar domains has successfully implemented such features [11,24], may be addressed in future studies.

Regarding our second sub-research question (**RQ2 classification**), we could show that for neurotypical individuals, we could achieve medium results for all four feature sets. However, for patients diagnosed with ADHD classification results for the n-back answer types were found to be somewhat worse for EI related features in the ADHD group than in the neurotypical (NT) group, which is in accordance with the findings of the conducted analysis. Other evaluated features demonstrated performance on par with the NT group. The classifiers trained on either BP or TS features showed the best performance. We expanded previous work on attention detection by adding a successful classification of responses in the n-back paradigm, with misses indicating inattentiveness. Compared to previous work with EI [2], we obtained worse results in the classification tasks when using EI as a feature, especially for the ADHD group. Other mentioned related work [12,13,23] also includes other frequency bands as features and achieves good classification capabilities, warranting future research in this direction to further analyze suitable features. Notably, the best results in this work were achieved using TS and BP features. The examined classifiers demonstrate predictive capabilities, yet they are not sufficient for real-world application. One could investigate the importance of channels in classification and focus on a subset of channels for classification. Given the inherent difficulties in detecting artifacts with ICA [17], it is possible that not all artifacts may be removed with complete reliability. The necessity for highly accurate classification is derived from the potential for erroneous feedback based on an incorrect identification of inattentiveness as a cause of irritation to children with ADHD. Given the integration of EEG-based inattention detection into the RoboCamp and clinical practice, there is a clear need for robust classification of attentional lapses in raw signals to support online prediction. The current classification pipeline requires too much computational effort due to preprocessing of the raw signals to allow online prediction. This represents a potential area for future research.

For the math task, the trained classifiers even outperformed the performance on the n-back test data, although it is questionable whether more distinct changes between answer types, different activations of brain regions, or the highly unbalanced nature contribute to these results. The performance of the EI varies across tasks, whereas the TS and BP features perform better across tasks. Given the poorer performance of the ADHD group, the use of other features provides a better perspective. Given the small sample size and the factors mentioned above, it is difficult to draw conclusions about the transferability of the trained classifiers (**RQ3 transfer**). This highlights the need for a larger analysis to provide a more reliable assessment. Given that there were so few misses in the pilot study, a larger dataset is required to properly assess the transferability of the trained classifiers, as the small sample size does not allow for a robust and meaningful assessment. In summary, the investigation into whether an EEG headset can be integrated into *RoboCamp* to detect lapses of attention revealed promising results. Classification results for a specific task, along with findings from previous research, suggest that it is indeed possible to identify lapses of attention using EEG data. However, to successfully transfer this capability to *RoboCamp*, it would be necessary to obtain additional EEG recordings of *RoboCamp*-specific tasks to validate the findings of this work. These recordings would be essential for training the classifier on a data-set tailored to the activities and context of *RoboCamp*, ensuring accurate and reliable detection of attention lapses in that setting. Further research is required to explore differences in how attention manifests in EEG recordings among children with ADHD and to evaluate the use of different attention paradigms. There is still a great deal of research to be done to investigate the implementation of the electroencephalogram (EEG) headset in the *RoboCamp* for the clinical use case. However, if an effective extension of the RoboCamp system towards an EEG classification succeeds thiw would allow the system to provide feedback to very subtle covert attention lapses. This would open up new research directions regarding the question how to address covert attention lapses in a socially adequate yet effective.

References

1. Adamou, M., Fullen, T., Jones, S.L.: EEG for diagnosis of adult ADHD: a systematic review with narrative analysis. Front. Psych. **11**, 871 (2020)

2. Apicella, A., Arpaia, P., Frosolone, M., Improta, G., Moccaldi, N., Pollastro, A.: EEG-based measurement system for monitoring student engagement in learning 4.0. Sci. Rep. **12**(1), 5857 (2022). https://doi.org/10.1038/s41598-022-09578-y

3. Baltrusaitis, T., Zadeh, A., Lim, Y.C., Morency, L.P.: OpenFace 2.0: facial behavior analysis toolkit. In: 2018 13th IEEE International Conference on Automatic Face & Gesture Recognition (FG 2018), pp. 59–66 (2018). https://doi.org/10.1109/FG.2018.00019

4. Diamond, A.: Attention-deficit disorder (attention-deficit/hyperactivity disorder without hyperactivity): a neurobiologically and behaviorally distinct disorder from attention-deficit/hyperactivity disorder (with hyperactivity). Dev. Psychopathol. **17**(3), 807–825 (2005)

5. Dong, H.W., Mills, C., Knight, R.T., Kam, J.W.: Detection of mind wandering using EEG: within and across individuals. PLoS ONE **16**(5), e0251490 (2021)

6. Eddin Alchalabi, A., Elsharnouby, M., Shirmohammadi, S., Nour Eddin, A.: Feasibility of detecting ADHD patients' attention levels by classifying their EEG signals. In: 2017 IEEE International Symposium on Medical Measurements and Applications (MeMeA), pp. 314–319 (2017). https://doi.org/10.1109/MeMeA.2017.7985895

7. Gao, Y., et al.: Impairments of large-scale functional networks in attention-deficit/hyperactivity disorder: a meta-analysis of resting-state functional connectivity. Psychol. Med. **49**(15), 2475–2485 (2019)

8. Gramfort, A., et al.: MEG and EEG data analysis with MNE-Python. Front. Neurosci. **7**(267), 1–13 (2013). https://doi.org/10.3389/fnins.2013.00267

9. Jas, M., Engemann, D., Raimondo, F., Bekhti, Y., Gramfort, A.: Automated rejection and repair of bad trials in MEG/EEG. In: 2016 International Workshop on Pattern Recognition in Neuroimaging (PRNI), pp. 1–4. IEEE (2016)

10. Jin, C.Y., Borst, J.P., Van Vugt, M.K.: Predicting task-general mind-wandering with EEG. Cogn. Affect. Behav. Neurosci. **19**, 1059–1073 (2019)

11. Kang, J., Han, X., Song, J., Niu, Z., Li, X.: The identification of children with autism spectrum disorder by SVM approach on EEG and eye-tracking data. Comput. Biol. Med. **120**, 103722 (2020)

12. Kaushik, P., Moye, A., Vugt, M.v., Roy, P.P.: Decoding the cognitive states of attention and distraction in a real-life setting using EEG. Sci. Rep. **12**(1), 20649 (2022). https://doi.org/10.1038/s41598-022-24417-w

13. Liu, N.H., Chiang, C.Y., Chu, H.C.: Recognizing the degree of human attention using eeg signals from mobile sensors. Sensors **13**(8), 10273–10286 (2013)

14. Lütkebohle, I., et al.: The Bielefeld anthropomorphic robot head "Flobi". In: 2010 IEEE International Conference on Robotics and Automation, pp. 3384–3391 (2010). https://doi.org/10.1109/ROBOT.2010.5509173

15. Mohamed, Z., El Halaby, M., Said, T., Shawky, D., Badawi, A.: Characterizing focused attention and working memory using EEG. Sensors **18**(11), 3743 (2018)

16. Gerber-von Müller, G., et al.: Das adhs-summercamp-entwicklung und evaluation eines multimodalen programms. Kindheit und Entwicklung **18**(3), 162–172 (2009). https://doi.org/10.1026/0942-5403.18.3.162

17. Mumtaz, W., Rasheed, S., Irfan, A.: Review of challenges associated with the EEG artifact removal methods. Biomed. Signal Process. Control **68**, 102741 (2021)

18. Pievsky, M.A., McGrath, R.E.: The neurocognitive profile of attention-deficit/hyperactivity disorder: a review of meta-analyses. Arch. Clin. Neuropsychol. **33**(2), 143–157 (2018)

19. Pope, A.T., Bogart, E.H., Bartolome, D.S.: Biocybernetic system evaluates indices of operator engagement in automated task. Biol. Psychol. **40**(1–2), 187–195 (1995)

20. Richter, B., Petras, I.K., Vollmer, A.L., Luong, A., Siniatchkin, M., Wrede, B.: VACO: a multi-perspective development of a therapeutic and motivational virtual robotic agent for concentration for children with ADHD. arXiv preprint arXiv:2405.03354 (2024)
21. Splittgerber, M., et al.: Individual baseline performance and electrode montage impact on the effects of anodal tDCS over the left dorsolateral prefrontal cortex. Front. Hum. Neurosci. **14**, 349 (2020)
22. Szafir, D., Mutlu, B.: Pay Attention! Designing Adaptive Agents that Monitor and Improve User Engagement (2012). https://doi.org/10.1145/2207676.2207679
23. Tang, S., Liang, Y., Li, Z.: Mind wandering state detection during video-based learning via EEG. Front. Hum. Neurosci. **17**, 1182319 (2023)
24. Zarour, M.: Attention, concentration, and distraction measure using EEG and eye tracking in virtual reality (2023)

An Epistemic Human-Aware Task Planner Which Anticipates Human Beliefs and Decisions

Shashank Shekhar[1(✉)], Anthony Favier[1,2], and Rachid Alami[1,2]

[1] LAAS-CNRS, Université de Toulouse, CNRS, INSA, UPS, Toulouse, France
{shashank.shekhar,afavier,rachid.alami}@laas.fr
[2] Artificial and Natural Intelligence Toulouse Institute (ANITI), Toulouse, France

Abstract. We present a substantial extension of our Human-Aware Task Planning framework, tailored for scenarios with intermittent shared execution experiences and significant belief divergence between humans and robots, particularly due to the uncontrollable nature of humans. Our objective is to build a robot policy that accounts for uncontrollable human behaviors, thus enabling the anticipation of possible advancements achieved by the robot when the execution is not shared, e.g., when humans are briefly absent from the shared environment to complete a subtask. But, this anticipation is considered from the perspective of humans who have access to an *estimated* robot's model. To this end, we propose a novel planning framework and build a solver based on AND/OR search, which integrates knowledge reasoning, including situation assessment by perspective taking. Our approach dynamically models and manages the expansion and contraction of potential advances while precisely keeping track of when (and when not) agents share the task execution experience The planner systematically *assesses* the situation and ignores worlds that it has reason to think are impossible for humans. Overall, our new solver can estimate the distinct beliefs of the human and the robot along potential courses of action, enabling the synthesis of plans where the robot selects the right moment for *communication*, i.e. informing, or replying to an inquiry, or defers ontic actions until the execution experiences can be shared. Preliminary experiments in two domains—one novel and one adapted—demonstrate the framework's effectiveness.

1 Introduction

Studies in psychology and cognitive science within the domain of joint actions suggest that humans consider each other's actions and beliefs, indicating that they model each other's tasks when planning [17,24,25]. Therefore, it is important if not key for success to be able to estimate or anticipate situations of divergence in beliefs and how that can be detrimental to collaborative activities.

In joint action scenarios, where partners work toward a shared goal, individuals often form expectations of their partner's actions based on their own mental

O. Palinko et al. (Eds.): ICSR + AI 2024, LNAI 15562, pp. 208–222, 2025.
https://doi.org/10.1007/978-981-96-3519-1_20

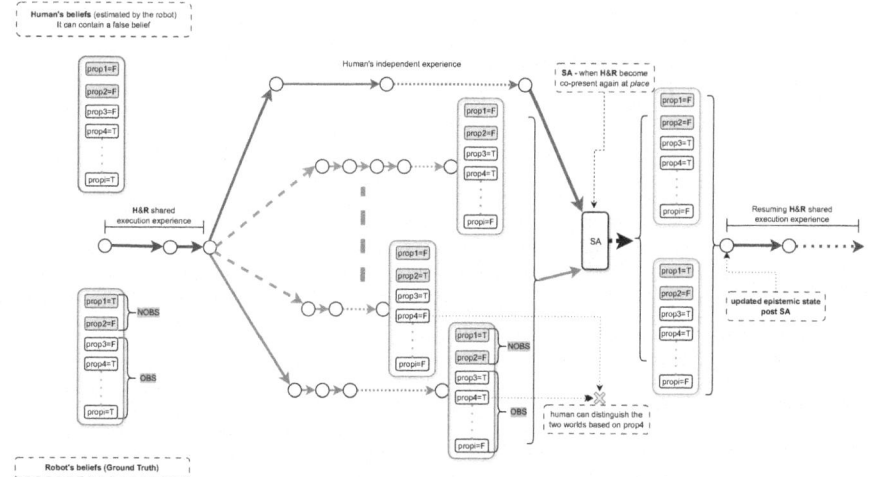

Fig. 1. *Our planning framework is endowed with the ability to make the difference between **H** & **R** shared and individual execution experiences in the planned activities. It can anticipate potential belief divergence between **H** & **R** and also estimate the updated beliefs of **H** when they meet again (situation assessment (SA)) based on a distinction between observable and non-observable facts. This will be used to plan communicative actions or adapt the **R**'s plan to ensure the shared experience of some actions. In this diagram, we roughly depict what happens when **H** & **R** no longer share the execution experience, **H** has independent experience (**blue**), while **R** progresses towards the goal (**green**), with anticipated traces (in **gray**) depicting other estimated courses of action that the robot can choose along with the green trace but from the **H**'s perspective. Upon co-presence at place, SA eliminates impossible worlds, e.g., those with state property prop4=F (since it is observable), aiding **H** to ignore wrongly estimated worlds.*

models, which may be flawed. When separated, they rely on these models to estimate their partner's progress, but inaccuracies or incomplete understanding of their collaborator's beliefs and capabilities can lead to misaligned expectations.

This cognitive bias shows the complexities of effective collaboration between a robot and a human on a shared task. And, highlights the need for robust frameworks to manage these differences.

We take the first step in this paper towards building a planning framework for human-robot collaboration that generates robot policies to address the issue of inaccurate mental models. Our proposed strategy integrates by adapting tools developed for epistemic planning [2], Dynamic Epistemic Logic (DEL) [3], and human-aware planning [1,4,6,14,31].

To this end, we propose a novel *epistemic human-aware task planning* framework. It substantially extends our past works and enables the robot to estimate, anticipate, and adapt to scenarios in which an uncontrollable human and a robot have disrupted shared execution experiences. Specifically, it considers the human's perspective and estimation regarding the potential advances achieved

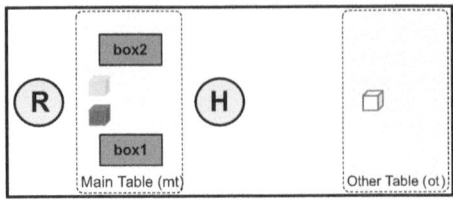

Fig. 2. *Three cubes c_r (red), c_y (yellow), and c_w (white) are shown. c_r and c_y are placed on mt (main table), and c_w is on ot (other table). There are two boxes, box_1 and box_2, placed on mt, which can be either transparent or opaque. The shared task is to organize the cubes in a way that cubes from one table are placed in one box. The choice of which box is flexible as long as each table's cubes end up in separate boxes.*

by the robot, even when the exact progress is not directly experienced by the humans, who may hold an *incorrect* robot model.

In addition, we build an AND/OR search-based offline planner that facilitates Theory of Mind (ToM) by integrating knowledge reasoning and incorporating situation assessment. It dynamically manages the evolution or contraction of estimated possible worlds from the human's point of view. This helps the planner to prepare itself with a set of worlds that humans would consider possible.

Our framework adapts tools developed in the literature, including those for DEL-based epistemic planning. However, as we will soon show, also a minor contribution, is that it offers more flexibility. Unlike the majority of epistemic planners, our framework does not require scripting all the effects on the beliefs of every agent in the action models as input.

Figure 1 provides a rough illustration of a single plan trace, showing what happens when agents share execution experiences and when they do not in the process of achieving the shared task.

Thanks to our novel framework and the planner, it enables the robot to take proactive steps, such as anticipating humans to be *inquiring* about an unknown variable's value, *communicating* relevant information without being annoying (*e.g.*, not verbalizing a fact already known to them), or deferring *executing* an action until **H** & **R** reunite, thus reducing the ambiguities for **H**.

We outline our *key contributions* specific to this paper as follows, directly addressing the primary problem discussed above:

- We have introduced *human mental model* in our previous framework.
- We developed a novel, sound planning algorithm that integrates human situation assessment and anticipates the inferences humans will make upon observing the new world state.
- Non-controllability is not unique here, but we extend [4,14,27] to address events of (non-)shared execution experiences and managing beliefs. We present enriched models for co-presence, observability, and situation assessment.
- We show our planner's effectiveness with experimental results in two domains, one is novel (our case study) and another one is adapted from [14].

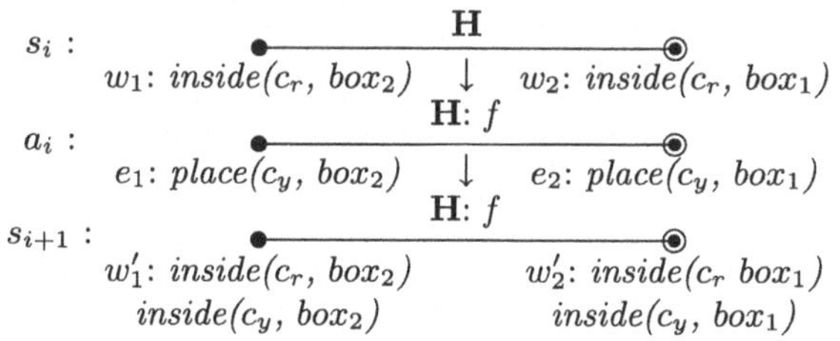

$$s_i : \quad \overset{\textbf{H}}{\bullet\!\!-\!\!-\!\!-\!\!-\!\!-\!\!-\!\!-\!\!\circledcirc}$$

$w_1: inside(c_r, box_2) \quad \downarrow \quad w_2: inside(c_r, box_1)$

$\textbf{H}: f$

$$a_i : \quad \bullet\!\!-\!\!-\!\!-\!\!-\!\!-\!\!-\!\!-\!\!\circledcirc$$

$e_1: place(c_y, box_2) \quad \downarrow \quad e_2: place(c_y, box_1)$

$\textbf{H}: f$

$$s_{i+1} : \quad \bullet\!\!-\!\!-\!\!-\!\!-\!\!-\!\!-\!\!-\!\!\circledcirc$$

$w'_1: inside(c_r, box_2) \qquad w'_2: inside(c_r\ box_1)$

$inside(c_y, box_2) \qquad\quad inside(c_y, box_1)$

Fig. 3. *We represent a state (s_i), action (a_i), and how applying a_i in s_i leads to next state ($s_{i+1} = s_i \otimes a_i$). f is a formula that captures if $\textbf{H}\&\textbf{R}$ were co-present when the events took place. Common facts for both worlds, such as opaque(box_1), are not shown. Also, each world is fully defined, with either an atom or its negation holding true.*

The paper is structured as follows. A case study is presented, followed by background information on necessary tools. Next, we describe our proposed framework, followed by the AND/OR search-based algorithm. The subsequent section discusses related work, followed by preliminary experiments showing the effectiveness of the framework in diverse scenarios. Finally, we conclude our work.

2   The Cube Organization Case Study

Figure 2 illustrates the task of organizing cubes into boxes. The shared **HR** task requires that cubes from different tables be placed into separate boxes.

Say only **H** is capable of moving around and exhibits unpredictable behavior (*nondeterminism*), such as moving to the other table (*ot*) to retrieve cubes, while **R** may continue to act. From the **H**'s perspective, **R** may move some or all of the cubes from the main table (*mt*) and place them into one of the boxes, or it may choose to take no action at all. Upon returning to the main table *mt*, **H** may discover that some, none, or all of the cubes originally on *mt* are missing, indicating that they have been placed in one of the boxes.

If **R** places some cubes from *mt* into one of the boxes, **H** will only learn about this decision upon encountering transparent boxes. But when opaque, **R** has several options: it can communicate, wait for **H** to inquire, or select a remaining cube of *mt* to place in the correct box when **H** and **R** are co-present.

Planning is done from the robot's perspective, taking into account **R**'s and **H**'s task models. The human collaborator has an approximation of the robot's model, which enables them to anticipate the robot's action. We later provide more details on these models and about their accuracy and falsity.

3   Background

Dynamic Epistemic Logic (DEL). We focus on epistemic languages ($\mathcal{L}_\mathcal{K}$), a state (s—comprising a set of worlds w_i), an action (a—comprising a set of events e_i), and state transitions (via the *cross product* $\otimes$ operator) as derived from the literature [2,3], with necessary simple adjustments for our needs. For other basic concepts like *indistinguishability* and *equivalence relation, perspective shift*, and *truth* of epistemic formulas, readers are referred to the cited literature.

Here, we focus on the essential DEL concepts necessary to build the framework, using examples from use case study. Recall the requirements for the task.

Example 1. Say the task is in the state s_i (Fig. 3), in which c_r is inside box_1 and both the boxes are opaque, and the robot holding c_y and the human comes back with c_w, and assesses the situation. We assume that the human can see the robot holding c_y. The epistemic state s_i such that $s_i \models K_\mathbf{R} inside(c_r, box_1)$, but concerning the human partner, $s_i \models \neg K_\mathbf{H} inside(c_r, box_1) \wedge \neg K_\mathbf{H} inside(c_r, box_2)$. Here, $K_i p$ represents agent i knows that the literal p is true.

Example 2. The next state s_{i+1} is such that, the epistemic action the robot will execute in epistemic state s_i is a_i that is placing c_y in the *correct* box. We describe how the next epistemic state s_{i+1} looks like *when* and *when not* **H&R** are *co-present* (i.e., whether they share this experience) during execution: An indistinguishability relation is only for **H** when the formula f, e.g., *at(**R**, place) & not(at(**H**, place))*, holds. **R** always knows that the designated world is w_2. That means if the human is co-present, they will know that the real world is w_2.

Human-Aware Task Planning. We briefly discuss the human-aware task planning paradigm here. HATP/EHDA [4] comprises a dual Hierarchical Task Network (HTN) based task specification model. It is a recently proposed planner that estimates and emulates human decisions and actions for HRC. It solves problems in a turn-taking fashion, as formalized in our previous work [13,14]. The following language adheres to this framework for easier understanding.

Consider the *human-aware task planning problem*, $\mathcal{P}_{rh}$ and *implicitly coordinated joint solution* defined (Definitions 5 & 6, respectively) in [13].

R and **H** have their action models, beliefs ($Bel(.)$), agenda or task networks (tn), plans, and more, collectively comprising $\mathcal{P}_{rh} = \langle \mathcal{M}_R, \mathcal{M}_H \rangle$. More specifically, **R** has its estimated beliefs, s_0^r. We consider it as the *knowledge* for "*ground truth*" in the planner's reference, versus what **R** estimates to be believed by **H**, s_0^h, by perspective taking. s_0^h may include a literal that is not true (*false belief* – e.g., *prop1* in Fig. 1) from **R**'s perspective and can be *corrected*.

We extended HATP/EHDA in [14], which adeptly anticipates human false beliefs for better collaboration based on (non-) shared execution experience.

To achieve that, *situation assessment* processes based on co-presence are integrated into the planning framework of HATP/EHDA. This enhances the planner to be pertinent to capturing what humans can observe and infer in their surroundings. It assesses the detrimental effects of humans' incorrect beliefs on the task at hand. As a result, **R** plans to communicate minimally and proactively.

We demonstrated in our previous work how to handle false beliefs (of first order) and situate the research broadly within the literature. In this paper, we extend and model knowledge up to level two, enabling us to handle **HR** collaboration more realistically and allowing us to incorporate communication in a more practical way. We detail all these aspects as we proceed.

4   The EHATP Planning Framework

We consider that the human maintains an estimated model for the robot $\mathcal{M}_H^R$, which can be *incorrect* compared to $\mathcal{M}_R$.

The epistemic HATP (EHATP) framework considers three models: $\mathcal{M}_R$, $\mathcal{M}_H$ and $\mathcal{M}_H^R$. While $\mathcal{M}_R$ guides the planning of **R**'s actions and $\mathcal{M}_H$ helps estimate and emulate **H**'s decisions and actions. But, using $\mathcal{M}_H^R$, **H** *"expects"* and *"predicts"* certain robot behavior (from their own perspective) both, respectively, when they are co-present and when they are not. Note that, each model has their own dedicated components like $Bel(.)$ and tn as defined earlier.

The majority of the models' components remain static, but for each model, its task network (tn_ϕ) and belief ($Bel(\phi)$) components are dynamic, where ϕ denotes an agent (or agent perspective). Except for belief, we assume that components like the robot's action model and task network are accurately estimated by **H**. This allows us to focus on the key aspects relevant to this paper. For other incorrectly estimated components of $\mathcal{M}_H^R$, we suspect a possible generalization utilizing concepts developed in [28] and intend to explore this in the future.

Planning Workflow

We focus on only the dynamic parts. The initial epistemic state s_0 (with the only world to begin with and that is also the designated world w_d) is provided as an input. In general, each world w_j in an epistemic state s_i represents $\langle (Bel(R), tn_r), (Bel(H), tn_h), (Bel(R_H), tn_{r_h}) \rangle$. It also includes the only designated world w_d always known to **R**. Note that these worlds are indistinguishable for **H**, but human knows that the robot can always distinguish them and that the robot can identify w_d. Also, the human knows that, if w_j is the designated world, then $Bel^{ij}(R_H)$, is the reality as they do not have access to the facts appearing in $Bel^{ij}(R)$. Here, we consider that $Bel(H)$ is equal to $Bel(R_H)$, but they can be different from $Bel(R)$ and can contain false (human) beliefs.

The robot, an epistemic state s_i and possible worlds w_j in it are considered. We compute the set of all possible primitive actions, computed by all feasible decompositions, based on $(Bel(R), tn_r)_{ij}$, and whether it is different than the set of primitive actions based on the allowed decompositions w.r.t. $(Bel(R_H), tn_{r_h})_{ij}$. The idea is to align these decompositions, w.r.t. each w_j, in a way that the human can correctly estimate the progress the robot may achieve, thus utilizing the human's capacity for anticipating. If there is a difference, we identify the *relevant* facts in $Bel^{ij}(R)$ that need to be corrected in $Bel^{ij}(R_H)$, to align the decompositions. To achieve that, we adapt our earlier approach presented in [14]. That is, one can plan minimal communication, possible to schedule ahead of time during offline planning when communication is allowed. Eventually, communication will also fix $Bel^{ij}(H)$, accordingly. However, $Bel^{ij}(H)$ and $Bel^{ij}(R_H)$ can still have *non-relevant* false beliefs compared to the ground truth $(Bel^{ij}(R))$.

Next, the planner computes the **R**'s next real action based on its task network tn_R^{id} in the designated world w_d of s_i, we call it the *designated* event. It also computes other non-designated events based on respective decompositions in each world w_j of s_i. (An event and a possible real action including *noops* are used interchangeably.) In other words, the planner computes a set of all possible decompositions based on what **H** can anticipate, that means by taking into account each $(Bel(R_H), tn_{r_h})_{ij}$. These are all the anticipated events that can happen due to the robot acting, but the designated event may or may not be assessed depending on *co-presence*. All the decompositions (*i.e.*, the set of the first primitive action in each refinement) together form an epistemic action a_i.

Executing an Epistemic Action in a State: Based on the cross-product operation $(\otimes)$, the state transition is computed as $s_{i+1} = s_i \otimes a_i$. In our planning algorithm (Algorithm 1, Line 8), we model the scenario as follows: if **H&R** are *co-present*, then **H** can distinguish between the actual event (the real action performed by **R**) and other estimated events. Otherwise, **H** perceives each event as a possible action by **R**. When co-present, **H** assesses the execution of **R**'s real action, thus narrowing down the possibilities over w'_j's in s_{i+1}—captured by $\otimes$ (*ref Fig. 3*).

Within each world of the new epistemic state, belief components, i.e., $Bel(R)$, $Bel(H)$, and $Bel(R_H)$ are updated corresponding to the possible robot action (either *real* or *anticipated*) that is a part of epistemic action a_i. Also, the task networks concerning $\mathcal{M}^R$ and $\mathcal{M}^R_H$ are updated in each world, accordingly.

When The Human Acts: **H** acts only if their next real action, w.r.t. a possible decomposition, is applicable in all possible worlds. I.e., for each w_j in s_{i+1}, applicability of the action is examined in every $(Bel(H), tn_h)_{i+1,j}$. Two key *issues* at this stage are: First, humans can act based on a false belief (if consistent throughout all the worlds), or a true belief w.r.t. the ground truth in every w_j. We handle false belief scenarios the way it is addressed in the literature, that is, by finding out relevant belief divergence and handling it via communication [14].

Second, we also know that a boolean variable, p, that **H** is uncertain about at this stage, which holds only in some worlds, is due to disrupted shared execution experiences. If p is a precondition of the task refinement process, then **H** can initiate communication, or **R** can inform **H** about p. And, if co-present, **R** can also act to implicitly share p's value such that there is some correlation between that action and p. Here, we focus on explicit communication, while sharing p's value by changing the environment is left for the future.

Handling H&R Communication. We introduce two types of actions and they become a part of the deliberation process. First, *ask-p* – human inquires about p from **R**, and, second *inform-p* – **R** informs them of the status of p.

At this stage, we create two specialized versions of state s_{i+1}: one prioritizing human inquiries, *ask-p*, and the other prioritizing robot updates, *inform-p*. Communication tasks are adjusted into respective networks appropriately.

Situation Assessment. Assessing the status of a state property depends on a broader context, which determines whether it can be observed or only inferred by attending the action execution affecting it. Knowledge rules were used to address

---

Algorithm 1. *AND/OR Planner using Breadth-First Search.*

1: **Input:** *A HAETP task*
2: **Output:** *A joint solution* or *failure*
3: *root_epi_state* ← $\langle \mathcal{M}, w_d \rangle$ ▷ (focusing just on the dynamic parts) each world in
   $w \in W$ contains $(\langle s_0^r, tn_{r,0} \rangle, \langle s_0^h, tn_{h,0} \rangle, \langle s_0^{r_h}, tn_{r_h,0} \rangle)$ and $W = \{w_d\}$
4: *queue*.enqueue(*root_epi_state*)
5: **while** *queue* is not empty **do**
6:     *curr_node'* ← queue.dequeue()
7:     *curr_node* ← *Situation Assessment(curr_node')*
8:     *successors* ← *Expand(curr_node)*
9:     **if** *successors* $\neq \emptyset$ **then**
10:        **for** successor in successors **do**
11:            *queue*.enqueue(*successor*)
12:        **end for**
13:    **else**
14:        *eval(curr_node)*   ▷ assign it *DONE* or *DEAD*
15:        *propagate_revised_status(curr_node)*
16:    **end if**
17:    **if** *root_solved(root_epi_state)* **then**
18:        **return** *extract_joint_solution()*
19:    **end if**
20: **end while**
21: **return** *failure*

---

this aspect [27]. For example, **H** can view the current status of the variable $inside(c_r, box_1)$ as *true* if they meet the requirements of the rule's antecedent formula, e.g., being at the main table, box_1 is transparent, and c_r is inside box_1. While formally defined below, we depict how the *SA* process works in Fig. 1.

Definition 1. The *situation assessment* (SA) process considers our *observation* process and a state s_i, producing an updated epistemic state s_i'. This iterates over each world w_j in s_i, removing it if human can distinguish it from w_d.

5   AND/OR Search Based EHATP Planner

Algorithm 1 takes the EHATP problem as input, producing an output as either a *failure* or an optimal worst case joint solution. It is an implementation of the classic AND/OR search using rooted graphs. When the *root* node is *DONE*, the joint solution policy is extracted (*extract_joint_solution()*), in Lines 17 &18.

We consider the root node (*root_epi_state*) and the subsequent actor, either **R** or **H**, to begin the plan exploration (Line 3). Within the loop, in Line 6, we select a node/state from *queue*, and next call the ***Situation Assessment( )*** subroutine. At this stage, the planner already knows whether agents were co-present and whether **H** assessed the designated event. It ignores the worlds distinguishable from the designated world (*Definition* 1). The scenario where a human transitions to the **R**'s location and subsequently becomes co-present is particularly interesting. Another significant subroutine, **Expand( )**, previously discussed in the EHATP framework's planning workflow, is invoked in Line 8. The children created after **R** expands the popped node are *AND* nodes. Conversely, when **H** expands the popped node, *OR* nodes are created.

In Line 14, we evaluate the current node. If both tn_r and tn_h are fully decomposed in the designated world of s_i, we execute an auxiliary action with a precondition that the task network is fully decomposed. If both agents can execute it individually, it signifies that agents believe that the shared task has been achieved. In Line 15, it propagates the status of this node to its immediate parent, which then further propagates the status upwards.

The Post-processing Step. Post-processing of the joint solution is done based on whether **H&R** are co-present. When *co-present*, we follow a turn-taking approach, but when *not* co-present, their actions are parallelized. This involves executing the AND/OR policy, and identifying where **H&R** separate and reunite. We then group the agents' actions in between to form pairs.

Runtime Analysis of Reasoning in EHATP. In the worst-case scenario, roughly, the runtime is influenced by the robot's available choices (m) in the absence of the human at each step, as these choices are crucial for updating the human mental model ($\mathcal{M}_H^R$) correctly. This is then multiplied by the number of choices (b) the human has to progress with the task when they are copresent.

We introduce a parameter K, which represents the maximum *#actions* **R** can perform when **H&R** are not copresent. So, the runtime complexity can be $O(b \times m^K)$ from the point they separate and reunite again, in terms of epistemic state exploration *s.t.* the maximum number of possible worlds in a state is m. We assume $\mathcal{M}_H^R$ and $\mathcal{M}_R$ are aligned at this stage when they separate.

6   Related Work

Human Robot Collaboration (HRC): Generating the robot's behavior while considering the existence of humans, known as human-aware planning and decision-making [1,6–8,18,20,31]. Also, it can do reasoning for task allocation [22,23]. Communication is an essential key to successful HRC, which is used to align an agent's belief, clarify its decision or action, fix errors, etc. [20,29]. We extend this research line but have not found studies addressing human anticipation and divergent beliefs in disrupted execution experiences.

Models, Planning Approaches, and Solutions: Several planning models are applied in the context of HRC planning, including HTNs [5,19,23], POMDPs [23, 30,31], AND/OR graphs [9], etc. HTNs use both abstract and non-abstract tasks to form hierarchical networks, while AND/OR graphs cover causal links among subtasks and depth-first search is used in planning [15].

Epistemic Planning: The epistemic planning framework, in [3], holds promise for capturing key elements of ToM in autonomous robots. For HRC, the framework lays the groundwork for implicit coordination through perspective shifts [10]. By adapting this framework and focusing on the robot's perspective,

Table 1. *The planner's performance metrics are presented.* inst *describes the instance number; for the first domain, this includes the number of cubes and boxes, as well as the property of the boxes (T for transparent, O for opaque).* comm *indicates whether communication is used. The reported metrics include the total number of explored states (#states), the worst-case number of worlds evaluated in a state ($|W|$), the number of traces in the final AND/OR solution tree (#leaves), and the execution time (measured in 10^5 ms). Two sections of the table include instances from the respective domains.*

inst	K	comm	#states	$|W|$	#leaves	time (ms) $\times$ 10^5
P1 (2,2,T)	2	N	218	4	3	0.089
P2 (2,2,O)	2	Y	236	4	3	0.141
P3 (3,2,T)	2	N	1643	7	6	5.906
P4 (3,2,O)	2	Y	2003	7	6	9.816
P5 (3,2,T)	4	N	4107	14	5	99.81
P6 (3,2,O)	4	Y	5607	14	5	125.3
Cooking 1	2	Y	603	3	5	0.382
Cooking 2	3	Y	1054	4	5	1.474
Cooking 3	4	Y	1800	5	5	5.301

it may serve as a basis for addressing the core problem we have aimed at with the shared mental model [21], albeit without assuming imperfectly estimated model ($\mathcal{M}_H^R$).

Explainable AI Planning (XAIP): In general, XAIP focuses on human-aware systems providing explanations of their behavior [16]. E.g., a system might explain the correctness of its plan and the reasoning behind its decision based on its own model. The model reconciliation approach [28], assumes that the human possesses a disparate model of the robot's behavior ($\mathcal{M}_H^R$ instead of $\mathcal{M}_R$). It avoids unnecessary explanations by identifying the specific differences between the two models and only generates explanations where needed. Essentially, it suggests changes to $\mathcal{M}_H^R$ to optimize the robot's plan based on that revised $\mathcal{M}_H^R$. The approach calculates the optimal explanations by identifying relevant discrepancies and communicating only the necessary information to align the models. We suspect a possible generalization of our approach while adapting this method to "correct" only what is necessary to align decompositions.

7 Empirical Evaluation

We implemented our planning system using Algorithm 1 in Python. It is based on the latest version of HATP/EHDA code [4].

No standard planners are available for comparison to our knowledge. We will gauge the performance of our planner against the one from [14], which provides limited support for scenarios with disrupted shared execution experience. It is worth noting that directly comparing their runtime would not be entirely fair, as our planner operates with a richer representation.

Domain Description: We test the planner in our use case domain and the cooking domain adapted from [14], on a variety of problems.

In the adapted scenario, both **H** and **R** are tasked with preparing dinner. The main activities involve *cutting* (R), *washing* (R) vegetables, *putting* (R) them on the stove with a pan and *seasoning* (R) them. Depending on the vegetables, seasoning can occur before or after they are placed in the pan, but always after washing. **H** is responsible for *bringing* (H) spices and other ingredients from the pantry and *mixing* (H) them in the pan, but only after the vegetables have been boiled (i.e., the effect of the *putting* action). *Serving* (H) dinner can only happen after the spices and seasoning have been mixed. Actors appear in (). Effects of washing and seasoning are non-observable.

The decision to bring ingredients separates **H** from **R**. Despite this adaptation, **H** can still choose when to leave the kitchen for the pantry.

7.1   Experiments

Analyzing the Impact of K and Non-Determinism. Algorithm 1 highlights a rapid growth in the size of the epistemic state in terms of the number of worlds which directly correlates with K that is the maximum *#actions* the robot can perform when the experience is not shared. The sequencing of actions significantly influences the range of potential worlds **H** expects to see.

K is considered to assess its impact on the planner's performance. We assume that whenever the shared execution experience is disrupted, **R** can execute a *maximum* of K actions, including the option of doing nothing. For example, when the human is away to fetch the cube and has a *fixed* length and sequence of actions to perform. The exact number of real ontic actions **R** performs ranging from 0 to K, including which of those allowed ones and their potential sequences, will depend on the scenario at hand, environment dynamics (e.g., the observability factor), and the optimization criteria. The option for the robot to limit its real actions whenever required is integrated into the task description, aligning with the turn-taking nature of the underlying planner. Consequently, the planner is engineered to optimize the robot's policy tree branching on uncontrollable human choices, including a communication action, to meet our objective.

Qualitative Analysis. In our use case domain, we explore different plan traces the planner can come up with depending on scenarios that arise. We start with two cubes, c_r and c_w, placed initially on tables mt and ot, respectively. Initially, there is only one designated world, w_d, in the initial epistemic state, s_0. The environment otherwise remains unchanged. **H** can decide to go and retrieve the white cube, while the robot begins to work on other parts of the shared task.

Two plan traces are shown in Fig. 4. **H** starts to execute. **H**&**R** are co-present and the boxes are opaque. (*SA* is shown only at relevant places.)

Let us focus on (a): after the human shifts focus to ot, both agents are not co-present until they reunite later in the trace, during which they act simultaneously. (*In this situation, agents must be at the same table and simultaneously focus on it to be considered co-present.*) In the first broad rectangular box, the human moves to ot. They anticipate that the robot may have picked c_r or done nothing, but in reality, the robot picks c_r, resulting in two possibilities that will be maintained within the robot. Similarly, in the following box, the human picks c_w at ot and anticipates that if the robot had picked c_r, it could have placed it in one of the boxes or held onto it, or c_r is still on the table. Together, these create four possibilities, with the reality being that c_r is inside box_1. At this point, the robot currently has no feasible action to execute, and the shared task has been not achieved yet, too. Upon the human's return, as per their initial agreement on K, the robot has prepared itself with four possible worlds (with a designated world that only the robot knows). Perspective-taking and situation assessment help the robot eliminate two worlds where c_r is not on mt or in **R**'s hand.

We present two approaches to proceed with the task. In trace (a), the robot waits for human inquiry, while in trace (b), the human does nothing. Consequently, the robot decides to inform that box_2 is empty, resulting in only the designated world remaining. Here, $empty(box_2)$ is a precondition for the human to place c_w in it, which is true in one world and not another. Our proposed method considers a situation where the human waits for information without taking any action, such as nodding or making eye contact with the robot, as a distinct condition (*trace (b)*). Additionally, **R** can signal the value of p to **H** by manipulating a variable q (inline with [26]), which we aim to explore further.

In the 3-cube scenario, if c_r is already in box_1 and **R** is holding c_y, it can choose to place the c_y in box_1 in the presence of **H**. This action results in the creation of a state with only the designated world as the next action ordered in the task network (tn_{r_h}) of that world does not allow **R** to execute $place(c_y, box_1)$. The robot can only be clever if it can fully explore its options. Depending on the situation, it might not always be preferable to place the yellow cube while the human is away and rely on communication or other means later on.

In contrast, in [14], **R** communicates immediately after agents reunite. This assumes that **H** can choose to place c_w in box_1 due to their outdated belief. In some practical cases, not communicating may lead to detrimental effects.

Quantitative Results and Analysis. Refer to Table 1. In each instance, at least one cube is positioned on ot, which **H** must retrieve. We show how the factor K influences the overall runtime.

We observe that $|W|$ and K contribute to longer runtime in both domains. Instances requiring communication tend to take slightly longer compared to those where communication is not required.

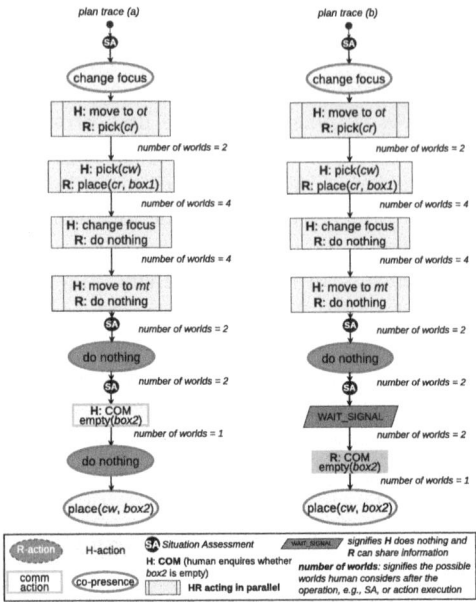

Fig. 4. *Two branches from an AND/OR joint solution are shown: (a)* **R** *informs* **H** *proactively, thus leaving only the designated world for them to continue with place(c_w, box$_2$). (b)* **R** *waits to inform* **H** *about the condition empty(box$_2$).*

8   Conclusion

Our framework allows the robot to implement a ToM not only at execution time but also at planning time and hence explores what would be the beliefs of the human and the robot depending on which course of action. This is done thanks to the use of epistemic reasoning, the notion of shared experience, and observable and non-observable facts, which allow anticipation of **H**'s situation assessment along the various non-deterministic shared plan traces of **H** and **R**.

R can adapt its choices to **H**'s diverging beliefs over time, e.g. by choosing to communicate to inform **H** or elicit an action, or a particular context to act.

We acknowledge that scaling such abilities can pose complexity challenges for planners, which can be evident in [3]. Hence, we take care to precisely identify the context in which our approach can be effectively used which is dealing in a refined manner with short-term interactions and intricate **H&R** face-to-face situations. Also, we intend to test the current system in different domains with realistic **H&R** co-activities. We aim to enhance planner's practical efficiency and explore incremental task planning.

User Study: We tested with users the HATP framework, which supports execution concurrency and demonstrated the robot's ability to adapt to non-deterministic human behaviors [11,12]. Although this study is not for testing advanced epistemic reasoning of EHATP, it offers valuable insights and tools.

Building on these findings, we are evaluating the EHATP framework, which incorporates features such as second-order theory of mind and belief divergence.

Acknowledgments. This work has been partially funded by the Agence Nationale de la Recherche through the ANITI ANR-19- PI3A-0004 grant and the Horizon Europe Framework Programme through the euROBIN Grant 101070596.

References

1. Alili, S., Warnier, M., Ali, M., Alami, R.: Planning and plan-execution for human-robot cooperative task achievement. In: Proceedings of ICAPS (2009)
2. Bolander, T., Andersen, M.B.: Epistemic planning for single and multi-agent systems. J. Appl. Non Class. Logics **21**(1), 9–34 (2011)
3. Bolander, T., Dissing, L., Herrmann, N.: DEL-based epistemic planning for human-robot collaboration: theory and implementation. In: Proceedings of KR (2021)
4. Buisan, G., Favier, A., Mayima, A., Alami, R.: HATP/EHDA: a robot task planner anticipating and eliciting human decisions and actions. In: ICRA (2022)
5. Cheng, Y., Sun, L., Tomizuka, M.: Human-aware robot task planning based on a hierarchical task model. IEEE Robot. Autom. Lett. **6**(2), 1136–1143 (2021)
6. Cirillo, M., Karlsson, L., Saffiotti, A.: A human-aware robot task planner. In: Proceedings of ICAPS 2009 (2009)
7. Cramer, M., Kellens, K., Demeester, E.: Probabilistic decision model for adaptive task planning in human-robot collaborative assembly based on designer and operator intents. IEEE Robot. AL **6**(4), 7325–7332 (2021)
8. Darvish, K., Simetti, E., Mastrogiovanni, F., Casalino, G.: A hierarchical architecture for human-robot cooperation processes. IEEE Trans. Robot. **37**(2), 567–586 (2020)
9. Darvish, K., Simetti, E., Mastrogiovanni, F., Casalino, G.: A hierarchical architecture for HR cooperation processes. IEEE Trans. Robot. **37**(2), 567–586 (2021)
10. Engesser, T., Bolander, T., Mattmüller, R., Nebel, B.: Cooperative epistemic multi-agent planning for implicit coordination. In: Proceedings of WS on EPTCS (2017)
11. Favier, A.: Human-aware robot task planning: theory of mind and anticipation of human decisions and actions. Ph.D. thesis, Université de Toulouse (2024)
12. Favier, A., Alami, R.: A model of concurrent and compliant human-robot joint action to plan and supervise collaborative robot actions. In: ACS (2024)
13. Favier, A., Shekhar, S., Alami, R.: Anticipating false beliefs and planning pertinent reactions in human-aware task planning with models of theory of mind. PlanRob 2023, The ICAPS Workshop (2023)
14. Favier, A., Shekhar, S., Alami, R.: Models and algorithms for human-aware task planning with integrated theory of mind. In: RO-MAN. IEEE (2023)
15. Gombolay, M.C., Jensen, R., Stigile, J., Son, S., Shah, J.A.: Apprenticeship scheduling: Learning to schedule from human experts. In: Proceedings of IJCAI (2016)
16. Kambhampati, S., Sreedharan, S., Verma, M., Zha, Y., Guan, L.: Symbols as a lingua franca for bridging human-AI chasm for explainable and advisable AI systems. In: AAAI, pp. 12262–12267. AAAI Press (2022)
17. Kourtis, D., Knoblich, G., Woźniak, M., Sebanz, N.: Attention allocation & task representation during joint action planning. J. Cogn. Neurosci. **26**, 2275–86 (2014)

18. Lallement, R., De Silva, L., Alami, R.: HATP: an HTN planner for robotics. arXiv preprint arXiv:1405.5345 (2014)
19. Lallement, R., de Silva, L., Alami, R.: HATP: hierarchical agent-based task planner. In: Proceedings of AAMAS (2018)
20. Lemaignan, S., Warnier, M., Sisbot, E.A., Clodic, A., Alami, R.: Artificial cognition for social human-robot interaction: an implementation. Artif. Intell. **247**, 45–69 (2017)
21. Nikolaidis, S., Shah, J.: Human-robot teaming using shared mental models. ACM/IEEE HRI (2012)
22. Ramachandruni, K., Kent, C., Chernova, S.: UHTP: a user-aware hierarchical task planning framework for communication-free, mutually-adaptive human-robot collaboration. ACM Trans. Hum.-Robot Interact. (2023)
23. Roncone, A., Mangin, O., Scassellati, B.: Transparent role assignment and task allocation in human robot collaboration. In: Proceedings of ICRA (2017)
24. Schmitz, L., Vesper, C., Sebanz, N., Knoblich, G.: Co-representation of others' task constraints in joint action. J. Exp. Psychol. Hum. Percept. Perform. **43**(8), 1480 (2017)
25. Sebanz, N., Knoblich, G.: Prediction in joint action: what, when, and where. Top. Cogn. Sci. **1**(2), 353–367 (2009)
26. Shekhar, S., Brafman, R.I., Shani, G.: Improved knowledge modeling and its use for signaling in multi-agent planning with partial observability. In: AAAI (2021)
27. Shekhar, S., Favier, A., Alami, R., Croitoru, M.: A knowledge rich task planning framework for human-robot collaboration. In: Proceedings of 43rd SGAI (2023)
28. Sreedharan, S., Chakraborti, T., Kambhampati, S.: Foundations of explanations as model reconciliation. Artif. Intell. **301**, 103558 (2021)
29. Tellex, S., Knepper, R.A., Li, A., Rus, D., Roy, N.: Asking for help using inverse semantics. In: Proceedings of RSS (2014)
30. Unhelkar, V.V., Li, S., Shah, J.A.: Semi-supervised learning of decision-making models for human-robot collaboration. In: Proceedings of CoRL (2019)
31. Unhelkar, V.V., Li, S., Shah, J.A.: Decision-making for bidirectional communication in sequential human-robot collaborative tasks. In: Proceedings of HRI (2020)

Categorizing Robots as Living or Non-living: From Descriptive to Normative Assessments

Glenda Hannibal[✉]

Department of Artificial Intelligence and Human Interfaces, Paris Lodron University Salzburg, Salzburg, Austria
`glenda.hannibal@plus.ac.at`

Abstract. Research on human-robot interaction shows that children and adults categorize robots as living entities, although such categorization conflicts with the usual criteria of membership for the life category. In this paper, we aim to analyze and discuss the essentialist and anti-essentialist conceptualization of life to understand why people struggle to categorize robots as living or non-living. Our conceptual analysis suggests that people do not commit fully to either an essentialist or anti-essentialist conceptualization of life nor can they be used together as this would yield a contradiction. These conceptualizations cannot alone, and in their own right, explain this categorization challenge. This insight leads us to discuss further whether a more pragmatic view is needed. We conclude that people rely on moral intuition to go beyond descriptive assessments, which points to the importance of normative assessments that are also at play in categorizing robots as living or non-living.

Keywords: robots · categorization challenge · conceptual analysis · conceptualization of life · (anti)essentialism · moral intuition

1 Introduction

In the late 1990 s, commercial robot toys for children emerged on the market (e.g., Tamagotchi, AIBO, Furby). They were developed to entertain children and provide alternatives to real, living pets. In parallel, several robotics labs envisioned a more widespread use of advanced robots in society, and this sparked an increasing interest and demand for robots capable of social interaction and communication. In industrialized countries (e.g., Japan, the USA, and Germany), scientists and engineers began to develop robots to help people with everyday activities (both at work and home) and function as co-workers or companions. Hence, the combination of assistive and social design objectives led to more frequent social interactions with robots. For this reason, it is an urgent task for the research communities of social robotics and human-robot interaction (HRI) to examine how humans relate to and understand their experiences and interactions with robots. In the following we outline few important steps that helps stage such an investigation.

The first step is to distinguish between machines and robots. Given the scientific and technological advancements in artificial intelligence (AI) and robotics

O. Palinko et al. (Eds.): ICSR + AI 2024, LNAI 15562, pp. 223–234, 2025.
https://doi.org/10.1007/978-981-96-3519-1_21

during the last decades, it is no longer possible—at least not without extended argumentation—to categorize robots as mere machines [9]. Robots were first introduced for industrial use, meaning they stood isolated in a closed environment, and their actions were all preprogrammed. Today, robots are no longer found only in factories but also deployed in various public and domestic settings [13], where they have to interact with people to complete their tasks successfully. Robots can move around in unpredictable environments and are capable of simple decision-making and learning [17]. In this paper, we focus on robots capable of social interaction and communication in a human-like way. As such, these robots are intended for social and emotional purposes (i.e., interaction, communication, and companionship) and not merely for practical use. They present themselves to people as intelligent, emotional, social, and moral entities. This apparent agency gives rise to the uncanny experience of these robots as living entities during the interaction or communication, despite knowing that they are non-living given time to reflect on the matter [34]. The second step is to clarify that this apparent agency should not be regarded simply as people's tendency to project properties and capabilities onto objects—the psychological mechanism of anthropomorphism [41]. As Turkle [37] points out, robots are unique because "such relational artifacts do not wait for children to'animate' them [...]. They present themselves as already animated and ready for a relationship. They promise reciprocity because, unlike traditional dolls, they are not passive. They make demands. They present [themselves] as having their own needs and inner lives" (p. 39). Thus, the significant difference between robots and traditional toys is the independence they come to have in interactions and communication with people, who now have to respond to their actions and needs accordingly. The third step is exploring and understanding how people judge which categorical predicates could be applied to categorizing robots. It is often discussed in current social robotics and HRI literature whether or not robots can have any sort of mental states [35] or moral standing [32]. However, assigning these capacities to robots presupposes that they are somehow perceived as living entities. This presumption has not yet been extensively nor systematically analyzed, even though animacy attribution to robots has commonly been reported in HRI research [38]. Therefore, discussion about robots should begin with examining why people are willing to include robots in the life category. Only then can the attribution of cognitive, affective, or moral capacities come into view. Thus, our primary focus in this paper is to shed new light on the discussion of the categorization challenge researchers in social robotics and HRI are still pondering.

After this short introduction, the remaining structure of this paper is as follows. In Sect. 2, we present the problem that when children and adults face robots, they find it challenging to categorize them as living or non-living entities despite their better knowledge. We unfold in Sect. 3 the essentialist and anti-essentialist conceptualization of life, which are two conceptual strategies used when categorizing robots as living or non-living entities. To confront the issue that none of these conceptualizations of life are fully adopted nor can be used in conjunction, we present in Sect. 4 the identification and criticism of the pragmatic approach to categorizing robots as living or non-living. Inspired by these reflections, but also going beyond the pragmatic approach, we show in Sect. 5 that people's reactions to robots reveal an additional layer to their judgment of membership in the life category, namely normative assessments. Section 6 summarizes our main points and concludes the paper.

2   The Difficulty of Categorizing Robots

In the early 1980 s, Turkle [36] observed that when children were using computers, this new way of interaction and communication provoked them to question how they could categorize them considering the life category. She argued that the shift from focusing on physical criteria to concentrating on psychological criteria (e.g., consciousness, mind, emotions, or memory) had led children to treat computers as having life regardless of their knowledge to the opposite.

Since interaction and communication with computers can make children uncertain about their appropriate categorization as living or non-living, it is unsurprising that this categorization challenge also arises when children engage with robots. For example, a study by Melson et al. [23] showed that the interaction and communication people have with the AIBO robot challenge the traditional distinction between animate and inanimate entities because children and adults judged the robot to have both biological features and mental capabilities. Severson and Carlson [31] argued further that children no longer viewed personalized and physically embodied robots as mere inanimate entities because of their lifelike properties. The crucial difference between standard computers and robots is the complexity of their physical embodiment and various modalities for interaction and communication. To successfully interact with robots, people must interact and respond to the entire form of robots by leveraging more communication channels (e.g., proximity, eye gaze, voice, and gestures) [12]. Since robots increasingly mimic life cues (e.g., the appearance of agency, autonomy, and sociality), these studies suggest that a new and more accurate conceptualization is needed to characterize these novel entities. By now, this line of argument has been extended and known as the "new ontological category" hypothesis [19]. This discussion is still greatly occupying part of the social robotics and HRI community (e.g., [2,25,39]). Moreover, Clark and Fischer [8] have recently added to this discussion by addressing what they call the "social artifact puzzle" (p. 1). As they explain, robots pose a profound paradox because their category-defying characteristics force people to simultaneously hold conflicting attitudes (i.e., interacting with robots as if they are real people or pets while categorizing them as mere mechanical artifacts).

From these discussions, it seems that the categorization of robots as living or non-living is no longer simply a question of category membership criteria, as Turkle has claimed [37]. On the one hand, people experience robots as living entities based on their intuitive interaction with them. On the other hand, they hesitate to consider robots living entities when given time to reflect on the possibility. In the next section, we will investigate this categorization challenge more closely in light of common conceptual strategies for conceptualizing life to understand better what is happening.

3 Two Conceptualizations of Life

We first distinguish between an essentialist and anti-essentialist conceptualization of life to represent two common conceptual strategies for categorizing living entities, which people might use to decide when to categorize robots as living or non-living.

The Essentialist View. Essentialism is the doctrine that an entity possesses essential (rather than accidental) properties for its existence in the sense of necessity [33]. As such, an essentialist conceptualization of life asserts that a list of necessary and sufficient properties exist that living entities must possess to be categorized as a member of the life category. Since most of the proposed lists of essential life properties are relatively short and mention many of the same ones [4], we will not consider them all. However, the work by Gánti [15] exemplifies such an approach well as he presents a list of essential criteria that any individual organism must possess to be of a living state[1]. Summarized well by Bedau [5, p. 457], the proposed list of necessary and sufficient conditions for living organisms are as follows:

1. *Holism.* An organism is an individual entity that cannot be subdivided without losing its essential properties. [...]
2. *Metabolism.* An individual organism takes in material and energy from its local environment, and chemically transforms them. [...]
3. *Inherent stability.* An organism maintains homeostatic internal processes while living in a changing environment. [...]
4. *Active information-carrying systems.* A living system must store information that is used in its development and function. [...]
5. *Flexible control.* Processes in an organism are regulated and controlled to promote the organism's continued existence and flourishing. [...]

With this essentialistic conceptualization of life for the categorization of robots as living or non-living, the question is whether it is possible (or not) for them to live up to these listed essential life criteria. In our attempt to use the proposed list, we show that it is harder to rule in or out robots from the life category as it might seem at first glance.

Considering the life property of holism, the categorization seems simple. If one were to disassemble any robot—for example, by removing the processor, sensors, or actuators—it would stop functioning altogether. Whether robots have the life property of metabolism depends on whether it is understood as a generic or specific process. Metabolism, in general, is the chemical transformation of (typically external) material into energy needed by any entity to ensure its survival. Robots can fulfill this essential life criterion if this generic metabolism account is considered. For instance, Ieropoulos et al. [18] built a robot that could use a microbial fuel cell to "produce biomechanical energy used for maintenance

---

[1] Gánti [15] distinguish between criteria for real and potential life. Since individual living organisms only need to possess criteria for real life for their existence, we have not included criteria for potential life in the overview.

and routine tasks for survival" (p. 295). However, it might be argued that the successful metabolism in this example depends on the lower-level biological processes used by the microbial fuel cell. Thus, whether this specific metabolism process would qualify the robot from the life category can be questioned. Inherent stability as a life property refers to the concept of homeostasis. For robots to have inherent stability, in this sense, they would need to keep a set of variables (e.g., energy level, temperature, or fluid balance) within a preset range for their survival. As before, it is unclear if robots can fulfill this criterion for the life category when considering either a weak or strong understanding of homeostasis. Since the SDR-4x robot by Sony was developed to use this process [14], it is a good example of weak homeostasis in robots. However, most robots are still limited in their ability to deal with extreme environmental variations [7], which means they lack strong homeostasis. The life property of an active information-carrying system points to deoxyribonucleic acid (DNA), which ensures the development, functioning, growth, and reproduction of all living organisms. Since the Molecube robot by Zykov et al. [42] has been developed for self-reproduction and self-repair purposes, it seems that robots can fulfill this life criterion from this example. However, the mechanism of self-reproduction used by the Molecube robot is externalized because each modular self-reconfigurable part uses connectors on its cubic surface to transmit the programmed information (compared to the internalized mechanism used by DNA). Consequently, the Molecube robot cannot generate new information; it only passes on already-known information. Whether robots can self-produce with means similar to genes is unclear, and they would be excluded or included from the life category depending on how strictly the requirement of new information is applied. Flexible control as a life property implies a place or unit in the given entity where all actions and processes are regulated or controlled. In humans, the flexible control is located in the nervous system. Flexible control for robots is ensured by the software running on the processor (e.g., MPU, CPU, GPU, TPU) [21]. The processor is usually part of a small computer processing the sensor information and controlling the actuators. The computer contains programs, data algorithms, logic analysis, and other processing activities that enable the robot to perform its tasks [24]. However, the computer in a robot is not a direct equivalent to the nervous system in living organisms because it only tries to emulate the brain part. Again, depending on how this life property is interpreted, robots can or cannot qualify for the life category.

With this small exercise, we have shown that robots cannot fulfill the list of essential life properties proposed by Gánti [15], even though some of them can be met under certain interpretations. Although adults are from an early age prone to the essentialist conceptualization of life [16], it can be challenged because the attempt to state all the necessary and sufficient criteria for the life category is vulnerable to exceptions and borderline cases (e.g., bacteria, viruses, artificial life) [5]. Any essential life property assigned to living organisms will, for exceptions and borderline cases, either be too broad or too narrow in scope. For this reason, present-day robots are best excluded from the life category, considering the demanding criteria for category membership imposed with the essentialist conceptualization of life.

The Anti-essentialist View. Anti-essentialism denies that the connection or relation between an entity and any of its properties is of necessity [33]. The properties of an entity are only essential to its existence relative to some parameter. Since the parameter is not by default determined, anti-essentialism is often taken to imply ontological anti-realism, which means that ascriptions of essential properties are context-sensitive [33]. Therefore, an anti-essentialist conceptualization of life states that an entity's life properties are essential to its existence only relative to a biological framework. From this perspective, the categorization of robots as living or non-living is determined by the extent to which people consider the essential properties to be believable features of life. Since the believability of lifelike robot features depends on human psychology (e.g., individual personality, cultural background, and evolutionary psychological mechanisms) [11], the anti-essentialist conceptualization of life requires that the categorization of robots is determined by the context of how people interact and perceive them. The interesting question to address is whether the appearance and behavior of robots prompt people to categorize them as living or non-living.

Scientists and engineers use different design strategies to make the lifelike features of robots believable based on the assumption that their embodiment plays a significant role in how animated they are perceived. For example, Bae and Kim [1] demonstrated that humans respond highly to robots that appear animate (compared to inanimate robots) because they are evolutionarily wired to pay greater attention to living entities. Believable robots intended to interact with people are often designed with a zoomorphic or anthropomorphic morphology because their imitation of lifelike features from animals and humans improve their perceived and attributed capabilities typical of living beings [20]. As such, anthropomorphism by design is a deliberate strategy used to facilitate and enhance the attribution of human-like characteristics to robots [28] that make them seem more lifelike by implication. Multiple studies in HRI have shown, however, that the behavior of robots in terms of movement also plays a significant role in how people perceive them as lifelike or not. For instance, a study conducted by Poulin-Dubois and Heroux [26] aimed to "determine the effect of different types of movements on the attribution of animacy and life properties" (p. 343) among children and adults. They concluded that the kind of movement affects the attribution of life properties across all age levels and that the judgment of animacy also depends on the source of movement as either internal or external [26]. Other studies have demonstrated that people perceive robots signaling through verbal or behavioral cues as living entities because such capacity suggests they have mental states (e.g., emotions or intelligence). In an experiment conducted by Bartneck et al. [3], for instance, they found that robots perceived as intelligent also make them seem animate. The Furby robot by Tiger Electronics is capable of signaling cues of intelligence and emotional states (e.g., being scared, happy, or sad) through the display of sounds and face expressions (as described in the *Electronic Furby Instruction Manual* [accessed on Sep. 22nd, 2024]: (https://www.manualslib.com/manual/3286043/Tiger-Electronic-Furby.html#manual). As Turkle [37] writes, even though the expressions of such a simple robot are very primitive and differ significantly from the vast range of human expression, Furby nevertheless encouraged children and adults to believe that it had an inner life.

Considering the requirement of category membership in the anti-essentialist conceptualization of life, robots perceived as believably lifelike (given their display of lifelike cues through appearance and behavior) are to be included in the life category. The context of how people interact and perceive them as living entities takes priority, although they might not possess these essential life properties when no one is there to observe them. Thus, according to an anti-essentialist concept of life, people are not mistaken in categorizing robots as living entities if they are sufficiently believable.

Inconsistent Categorization. The essentialist vs. anti-essentialist discussion illustrates that these two conceptualizations of life are in opposition because there is a disagreement about the requirement under which robots could rightfully be excluded or included from the life category. Committing fully to either of these conceptualizations would be unproblematic in itself. Such a one-sided conceptual strategy for categorizing robots as living or non-living would simply leave out or overemphasize certain life properties because they are deemed essential out of necessity or not. However, to produce a consistent categorization of robots as living or non-living, it is impossible to include them in the life category given certain contextual factors while insisting that this would violate the conceptual consensus that they do not belong to the life category. As the categorization challenge warns, using both the essentialist and anti-essentialist conceptualization of life to categorize robots as living or non-living would yield a contradiction. Thus, it is understandable why the difficulty of categorizing robots would leave people to doubt which conceptual strategy is best. Consequently, people might need a new approach of conceptualizing life to categorize robots consistently.

4   The Pragmatic Approach

Turkle [37] has dealt extensively with the problem of how to consistently and appropriately categorize robots when they come across as lifelike. She argued that the difficulty in categorizing robots as living or non-living entities stems from the problem that children and adults are no longer satisfied with mere descriptive assessments of which essential life properties they can or cannot be attributed (i.e., the essentialist and anti-essentialist conceptualization of life). Instead, children and adults have started to judge robots' inclusion (or exclusion) in the life category solely on pragmatic concerns. Turkle [37] characterizes this pragmatic approach to the categorization of robots as the inclination to take their lifelike appearances as a hallmark of "relational readiness" (p. 28–29) considering specific social and emotional purposes (e.g., providing or receiving love and care).

In our view, her identification of the pragmatic approach (as an alternative to the essential and anti-essential conceptualizations of life) is interesting, considering that it forces the requirement of category membership to be considered on a practical rather than theoretical level. Unfortunately, Turkle [37] did not elaborate further on this noteworthy implication of the pragmatic approach to the categorization of robots as living or non-living because she insisted that it is entirely mistaken. In her view, the pragmatic approach leaves children and adults vulnerable because it introduces a purpose-centered understanding of life and ignores what robots are truly capable of. According to Turkle [37], robots are not living entities, nor do they have any social or emotional capabilities because their display of lifelike cues is only a pretense of their true nature as inanimate machines. While Turkle [37] does not explicate her categorization of robots as non-living entities in terms of the essentialist conceptualization of life, it is visible from her argumentation that she thinks robots are lacking the essential life properties that animals and humans possess necessarily. This argument that children and adults are guilty of a category mistake (in a Rylean sense) because their categorization of robots as living or non-living rest make-believe or pretend-play is debatable, and Seibt [29] presented a strong counter argument for why people are not victims of functionalism as charged. In this way, Turkle [37] missed an opportunity to explore and understand what it could mean for people to go beyond mere descriptive assessments of robots for their categorization in the life category without going back to the problem of forcing a choice between an essentialist or anti-essentialist conceptualization of life.

While people might be wrong in categorizing robots as living or non-living entities relative to providing mere descriptive assessments, we insist on taking a closer look at alternative approaches that also exceed pragmatic concerns. This analysis reveals that there is an additional dimension of normative assessments to be considered, which is easily overlooked and rarely considered within current discussions about the categorization challenge. These normative assessments, also at play when people judge if robots are included or excluded from the life category, are guided by moral intuition—which Bergson [6] claimed is at the core of human capacity to feel sympathy.

5   Moral Intuition

To understand the additional layer of normative assessments, we first need to clarify how moral intuition from a phenomenal perspective supports judgments of category membership given certain interaction patterns. Moral intuition is the instantaneous and instinctive recognition of moral qualities in situations and actions, constituting the way people interact with the morally relevant entities of their perception [40]. Considering the previous account of how people respond to robots that appear lifelike, this moral intuition enables the transition from identifying interaction patterns as bounded only by biological capacities (e.g., need for water, energy, and reproduction) to those also characteristic of social and emotional intelligence. This transition is unidirectional because the latter includes the former but not *vice versa*. These interaction patterns trigger judgments about morally relevant entities to different degrees of inclusion or exclusion in the life category. For example, consider people's different interaction patterns with animals and plants. When people interact with their pets, their moral intuition urges them to feel they deserve treatment far beyond basic biological needs (i.e., washing or feeding them). Since people's interaction patterns with plants are limited, in contrast, the moral intuition to provide them with similar treatment is weakened. For this reason, people tend to privilege animals for the life category, although plants are equally living entities [9]. As such, the nuances in the complexity of the interaction patterns (i.e., from basic biological to rich social and emotional behavior) are picked up by people's moral intuition and then used to guide their judgment of whether entities should be categorized as living or non-living.

To know if people's inclusion or exclusion of robots from the life category involves normative assessments, we must examine whether their moral intuition is triggered when children and adults perceive or interact with robots. This examination will depend on the specific situations and acts on which the moral qualities can be highlighted or downplayed. Interactions between humans and robots do not only play out in physical reality (i.e., navigation or task execution in human spaces). They are also part of social reality, considering the increasing focus on collaboration and companionship. Since robots are very sophisticated in their simulation of social interaction [30], it is hard for people to disregard their moral intuition demanding that they must treat them in a specific manner that would usually be reserved for entities that are categorized as living. Several HRI studies have already shown that mistreatment of robots with lifelike cues triggers responses of empathy [22], even to the extent that the abuse instigated ethical concerns [10,27]. Retold by Turkle [37], the "upside-down test" was developed by Freedom Baird to explore how long people would hold a Barbie doll, Furby robot, and a biological gerbil on its head. She reported that people faced an ethical dilemma around 30 s into the test in the case of the Furby robot because they felt a strong ethical response to the distress it was signaling, although they were well aware that it was a machine without any inner life. The guilt people felt from mistreating the Furby robot, Turkle [37] argued, resulted from the realization that they experienced it as living similarly to real and sentient animals. These examples show that the categorization challenge contains the additional dimensions of normative assessments because people's perception of robots with lifelike cues are directly linked to judgments about their morally relevant qualities, granting them membership in the life category.

By considering the complexity of interaction patterns among humans and robots that feed the moral intuition of people, we were able to identify how a moral judgment about the categorization of robots as living or non-living intro- duces normative assessments in addition to the descriptive one underlying the essentialist vs. anti-realist conceptualization of life and the pragmatic approach. In our view, people's various experiences and interactions with robots cannot be disregarded as a problem for a consistent and accurate categorization of robots as living or non-living because they instead point to the subtle moral aspects of the requirements for membership in the life category. As long as robots can engage with people through interactions they experience as lifelike, their inclu- sion or exclusion in the life category is a non-trivial categorization challenge that cannot be tackled by considering descriptive assessments alone. Normative assessments are not just at play but are also crucial to consider when addressing the categorization challenge.

6   Conclusion

In this paper, we aimed to shed new light on the categorization challenge still pre-occupying the social robotics and HRI community because it is paradoxical that children and adults categorize robots as living even though they do not ordinarily qualify for membership in the life category. We have shown that people hesitate to subscribe to an essentialist or anti-essentialist conceptualization of life and that they are mutually exclusive conceptual strategies. The pragmatic approach is not a fruitful alternative either in supporting people with their categorization of robots as living or not living. In response to this stalling situation, we argued that a closer examination of the implication of the pragmatic approach brings to light that normative assessments can also justify criteria of membership in the life category because the categorization of robots as living or non-living is prompted by moral intuition. With our conceptual analysis of the various conceptual strategies and approaches to the categorization challenge in the current discussion, we have demonstrated that the social robotics and HRI communities benefit from extensive theoretical reflections on the underlying assumptions of how criteria of category membership are considered and used. We encourage researchers in social robotics to explore theoretically and empirically how normative assessments are used in categorizing robots and to discuss these insights also with a view to the problem of functionalist-based description in HRI (i.e., make-believe or pretend-play).

Acknowledgments. The author thanks Johanna Seibt for her valuable feedback on the initial ideas and arguments presented in this work. This work is supported by the project "Excellence in Digital Sciences and Interdisciplinary Technologies" (EXDIGIT), funded by Land Salzburg (20204-WISS/263/6-6022).

References

1. Bae, J.E., Kim, M.S.: Selective visual attention occurred in change detection derived by animacy of robot's appearance. In: 2011 International Conference on Collaboration Technologies and Systems (CTS), pp. 190–193. IEEE (2011)
2. Barker, R.L., Severson, R.L., Lindner, B.: Children's understanding of robots: a new ontological category or just pretend? Psychol. Sci. **18**, 37–42 (2018)
3. Bartneck, C., Kanda, T., Mubin, O., Al Mahmud, A.: Does the design of a robot influence its animacy and perceived intelligence? Int. J. Soc. Robot. **1**, 195–204 (2009)
4. Bedau, M.A.: Four puzzles about life. Artif. Life **4**(2), 125–140 (1998)
5. Bedau, M.A.: What is life? In: Sarkar, S., Plutynski, A. (eds.) A Companion to the Philosophy of Biology, pp. 455–471. Blackwell Publishing (2008)
6. Bergson, H.: The Creative Mind: An Introduction to Metaphysics. The Citadel Press (1992[1946])
7. Carlson, J., Murphy, R.R.: Reliability analysis of mobile robots. In: 2003 IEEE International Conference on Robotics and Automation (Cat. No. 03CH37422), vol. 1, pp. 274–281. IEEE (2003)

8. Clark, H.H., Fischer, K.: Social robots as depictions of social agents. Behav. Brain Sci. **46**, e21 (2023)
9. Coeckelbergh, M.: Growing Moral Relations: Critique of Moral Status Ascription. Palgrave Macmillan (2012)
10. Coeckelbergh, M.: Why care about robots? Empathy, moral standing, and the language of suffering. Kairos. J. Philos. Sci. **20**(1), 141–158 (2018)
11. Dautenhahn, K.: I could be you: the phenomenological dimension of social understanding. Cybern. Syst. **28**(5), 417–453 (1997)
12. Deng, E., Mutlu, B., Mataric, M.J., et al.: Embodiment in socially interactive robots. Found. Trends® Robot. **7**(4), 251–356 (2019)
13. Fortunati, L., Esposito, A., Lugano, G.: Introduction to the special issue beyond industrial robotics: social robots entering public and domestic spheres (2015)
14. Fujita, M., Kuroki, Y., Ishida, T., Doi, T.T.: Autonomous behavior control architecture of entertainment humanoid robot SDR-4X. In: Proceedings 2003 IEEE/RSJ International Conference on Intelligent Robots and Systems (IROS 2003)(Cat. No. 03CH37453), vol. 1, pp. 960–967. IEEE (2003)
15. Gánti, T.: The Principles of Life. Oxford University Press (2003)
16. Gelman, S.A., Opfer, J.E.: Development of the animate–inanimate distinction. Blackwell Handbook of Childhood Cognitive Development, pp. 151–166 (2002)
17. Gomi, T.: Aspects of non-cartesian robotics. Artif. Life Robot. **1**(2), 95–103 (1997)
18. Ieropoulos, I., Melhuish, C., Greenman, J., Horsfield, I.: EcoBot-II: an artificial agent with a natural metabolism. Int. J. Adv. Rob. Syst. **2**(4), 31 (2005)
19. Kahn Jr, P.H., Shen, S.: NOC NOC, who's there? A new ontological category (NOC) for social robots. New perspectives on human development, pp. 106–122 (2017)
20. Kunold, L., Bock, N., Rosenthal-von der Pütten, A.: Not all robots are evaluated equally: the impact of morphological features on robots' assessment through capability attributions. ACM Trans. Hum.-Robot Interact. **12**(1), 1–31 (2023)
21. Madhav, M.S., Cowan, N.J.: The synergy between neuroscience and control theory: the nervous system as inspiration for hard control challenges. Ann. Rev. Control Robot. Auton. Syst. **3**(1), 243–267 (2020)
22. Mattiassi, A.D., Sarrica, M., Cavallo, F., Fortunati, L.: Degrees of empathy: humans' empathy toward humans, animals, robots and objects. In: Ambient Assisted Living: Italian Forum 2017 8, pp. 101–113. Springer (2019)
23. Melson, G.F., Kahn Jr, P.H., Beck, A., Friedman, B.: Toward understanding children's and adults' encounters with social robots. In: Paper to the AAAI Workshop on Human Implications of Human-Robot Interaction (HRI), Boston (2006)
24. Niku, S.B.: Introduction to robotics: analysis, control, applications. John Wiley & Sons (2020)
25. Parviainen, J., Turja, T.: Toward abiozoomorphism in social robotics? Discussion of a new category between mechanical entities and living beings. J. Posthuman Stud. **5**(2), 150–168 (2021)
26. Poulin-Dubois, D., Heroux, G.: Movement and children's attributions of life properties. Int. J. Behav. Dev. **17**(2), 329–347 (1994)
27. Quick, O.S.: Empathizing and sympathizing with robots: implications for moral standing. Front. Robot. AI **8**, 791527 (2022)
28. Roesler, E., Manzey, D., Onnasch, L.: A meta-analysis on the effectiveness of anthropomorphism in human-robot interaction. Sci. Robot. **6**(58), eabj5425 (2021)
29. Seibt, J.: Towards an ontology of simulated social interaction: varieties of the "as if" for robots and humans. In: Sociality and Normativity for Robots: Philosophical Inquiries into Human-Robot Interactions, pp. 11–39. Springer (2017)

30. Seibt, J., Vestergaard, C., Damholdt, M.F.: Sociomorphing, not anthropomorphizing: towards a typology of experienced sociality. In: Culturally Sustainable Social Robotics, pp. 51–67. IOS Press (2020)
31. Severson, R.L., Carlson, S.M.: Behaving as or behaving as if? Children's conceptions of personified robots and the emergence of a new ontological category. Neural Netw. **23**(8–9), 1099–1103 (2010)
32. Sica, A., Sætra, H.S.: Artificial emotions and the evolving moral status of social robots. In: Proceedings of the 2024 ACM/IEEE International Conference on Human-Robot Interaction, pp. 649–657 (2024)
33. Sullivan, M.: Are there essential properties? No. In: Current Controversies in Metaphysics, pp. 45–61. Routledge (2016)
34. Takayama, L.: Perspectives on agency interacting with and through personal robots. In: Human-Computer Interaction: The Agency Perspective, pp. 195–214. Springer (2012)
35. Thellman, S., De Graaf, M., Ziemke, T.: Mental state attribution to robots: a systematic review of conceptions, methods, and findings. ACM Trans. Human-Robot Interact. (THRI) **11**(4), 1–51 (2022)
36. Turkle, S.: The Second Self: Computers and the Human Spirit. MIT Press (2005[1984])
37. Turkle, S.: Alone Together: Why We Expect More from Technology and Less from Each Other. Basic Books (2011)
38. Voss, L.: More than machines?: The attribution of (in) animacy to robot technology. transcript Verlag (2021)
39. Weisman, K.: Extraordinary entities: insights into folk ontology from studies of lay people's beliefs about robots. In: Proceedings of the Annual Meeting of the Cognitive Science Society, vol. 44 (2022)
40. Wright, J.: Towards a phenomenological defense of moral intuitionism: articulating the role of consciousness. Aporia **34**(1), 9–17 (2023)
41. Złotowski, J., Proudfoot, D., Yogeeswaran, K., Bartneck, C.: Anthropomorphism: opportunities and challenges in human-robot interaction. Int. J. Soc. Robot. **7**, 347–360 (2015)
42. Zykov, V., Mytilinaios, E., Desnoyer, M., Lipson, H.: Evolved and designed self-reproducing modular robotics. IEEE Trans. Rob. **23**(2), 308–319 (2007)

A Framework for Mapping High-Dimensional Perceptual Features into the Low-Dimensional Salient Feature Space of a Social Robot

Randy Gomez[1], Eric Nichols[1], Yu Fang[1], Serge Thill[2], Álvaro Páez[3], and Luis Merino[3]

[1] Honda Research Institute Japan Co., Ltd., Wako, Japan
[2] Radboud University Nijmegen, Nijmegen, Netherlands
[3] Universidad Pablo de Olavide, Sevilla, Spain
lmercab@upo.es

Abstract. This paper describes the development of an easy-to-use know- ledge-base platform to map perceptual features from sensory data to low-dimensional feature space. Our system enables the composition of perceived events to trigger salient features that are deemed to be of special interest to the robot. In generating the salient features, we factored in the robot's internal states such as personality, characteristics, and more. In previous work, we employed a participatory design study to elicit the possible low-dimensional salient features and the corresponding trigger/s befitting a social robot. Here, we extract the technical requirements from that elicitation study and develop a knowledge-centric system design. Moreover, we develop a framework for non-experts to easily compose salient features from the multiple firings of high-dimensional signals even without the need for programming knowledge. This allows experts in various fields to easily design the robot's reactive behaviors. Lastly, we evaluate our system's response using data from a real human-robot interaction setup and verify its performance.

1 Introduction

Nearly all current scenarios considered in human-robot interaction (HRI) research contain notions of a desirable interaction process. Sometimes this is very explicit and constrained, *e.g.* in robot-assisted therapy, for example, for children with autism spectrum disorder, the interactions might be based on existing protocols, and thus fully-specified by clinical therapists (*e.g.* [9]). In other scenarios, the desired outcome of the interaction is specified while the path to reach it can be less constrained; for example in educational robots [10,24]. Nonetheless, a kind of script is usually provided, specifying what the relevant human behaviours are, and what the desired robot response would be. Even work that aims to find ways for a robot to autonomously discover how to respond to humans presupposes that human behaviours are identifiable [1,23]. Essentially, humans tend

O. Palinko et al. (Eds.): ICSR + AI 2024, LNAI 15562, pp. 235–249, 2025.
https://doi.org/10.1007/978-981-96-3519-1_22

to adopt an *intentional stance* towards robots [22] (predicting robot behavior in terms of robot beliefs, goals and other intentional states), including defining robot behaviour in terms of an intentional stance towards humans.

Given that such notions appear in almost all use cases of social robotics – whether the resulting system operates by navigating explicit scripts towards a specific goal (such as in therapy), or learns appropriate behaviours autonomously (desirable, for example, to not unnecessarily constrain the system based on designer biases) – it may be desirable to express the behaviours of a robot directly in terms of such identifiable human behaviors. However, robots do not directly "perceive" the world in such terms. Achieving this expression requires a higher-level interpretation of the sensory data a robot can directly collect.

Here, we treat this as a mapping problem from the sensory input feature space into what we call the *salient feature space*, defined as the concepts that humans use when describing behaviours of social robots. These concepts should consist of relevant human behaviours such as, for example, explicit communicative (nonverbal [16]) actions, which in turn involve low-level features such as facial expressions, movements, and eye gaze. Appropriately chosen, these would then allow humans to define social robot behaviour as if the robot was adapting something akin to an intentional stance towards humans. Consequently, the salient feature space is also low-dimensional compared to the original sensory input feature space. What is needed, then, is a way to bridge these two. While this is clearly related to similar problems in robot vision (see for example recent work to identify affordances in an environment based on standard machine learning [13]), it goes beyond this in the sense that the salient features are not just objects but also human behaviours.

The paper describe a set of contributions on that direction. In particular:

- A framework to implement such a bridge between high-dimensional sensory data and low-dimensional salient features. This mapping is built on top of a knowledge system (*KnowRob* [3] in this case), considering not only information about the sensory data itself, but also the robot state.
- A set of modules to dynamically generate salient features in real-time based on Semantic Web Rule Language (SWRL) rules [19].

The overall intention of this framework is, together with the robotic platform, it provides a complete solution that allows interaction designers to design and implement interactive behaviours of the robot in the space that such interactions are naturally characterised, namely the space of salient features, rather than also having to deal with the interpretation of the raw sensory input (as is often the case currently). As such, we have shown how the system presented in this paper can been employed to generate reactive behaviors by a robot [15]. While there the focus is on the generation of behaviors, here we present and analyze in detail the salient feature extraction system, and the tools associated to it. We evaluate the framework in standard human-robot interaction scenarios using a social robot and considering visual and audio data. The evaluation shows how the framework is flexible to define the salient features required for the scenarios, and is able to timely extract the salient feature responses from sensor data.

Table 1. Examples of Salient features resulting from the elicitation study [14]. Each salient behavior from the interactant will lead to a prospective response from the robot (last column). The associated low-level sensory input features are also described.

Salient Feature	Description	Sensory Input	Prospective Response
Gestural Saliency	Mirror neurons; the inherent characteristic of Haru to react to human body movement such as select body gestures (i.e. empathy through body gestures).	**Body**: a person facing Haru; **Gesture**: person performing predefined gestural movements as recognized by Haru.	Haru performs a rendition of detected gesture expressions through matching robot routines (i.e. gestural movement mimicry).
Relative Distance Saliency	Social-distancing and Proxemics. Haru is sensitive to the interactant's distance relative to it when interacting.	**Proximity**: predefined distances between Haru and a person indicate social situations (e.g. intimate, personal, social, or public).	Haru reacts appropriately depending on the relationship (i.e. the predefined social situation) between the robot and interactant.
Tickling Saliency	Babies and pets love to be tickled, which causes us to laugh in turn. Haru as a fun social creature is also subject to this phenomenon of contagious laughter.	**Gesture**: Haru recognizes a human performing a tickling gesture.	Haru makes a happy laughing sound and executes a ticklish routine.
Affects Saliency	An unconscious response to gestures that are indicative of affection. Haru's characteristics revolve around communicating affect and empathy, hence its responds to this gestural behavior inherently.	**Gesture**: Haru detects a human performing predefined gestures such as making a heart shape with hands or blowing a kiss.	Haru giggles and plays a Happy Heart animation in its LCD screen eyes.
Applause Saliency	An expression of approval foments good feelings, and Haru loves to be applauded. Oftentimes Haru is self absorbed and wants attention. It cannot resist applause.	**Body**: a person facing Haru; **Gesture**: human clapping; **Sound**: clapping detected.	Performs Happy or Shy routines depending on the level of closeness between Haru and the interactant.
Keyword Saliency	Special keywords connect to Haru's internal state such as favorites and preferences. Haru loves sweet treats, fun activities, topics about the weather, etc.	**Keywords**: *ice cream, cake, hide and seek, sunny*, etc. recognized in a direct conversation with Haru or a conversation Haru overhears.	Haru performs drooling gesture, display of sweet treat emojis, weather emojis in eyes LCDs, etc.

2   Background

The first step in the processing of the sensory input of the robot is transforming these input signals into a semantic representation. Typically, ontologies are used to model the relevant semantic objects, properties and relations, which are then instantiated from sensor data into a knowledge base [2,17]. Mapping sensor data to the equivalent symbolic representation in the knowledge base is usually referred to as symbol grounding. There are different works that propose grounding pipelines. For instance, RoboSherlock [8] is a framework for cognitive perception based on unstructured information management. It offers a grounding functionality based on computer vision algorithms. Other research such as [11,12] makes use of deep learning models to construct scene graphs in robotic contexts. We will describe briefly the modules employed for symbol grounding, but the present work is actually agnostic of the methods employed for it.

Several frameworks have been proposed for the management of knowledge bases in robotics. Ontologenius [21] is a semantic memory module based on Web Ontology Language (OWL) ontologies [18] for the ROS [20] environment. It can be used to store the knowledge of the robotic agent, as well as to perform reasoning on it [7]. Another knowledge framework is *KnowRob* [3], an open-source Prolog-based knowledge base for robotics that has been used in various applications ranging from rescue operations to assembly planning and human assistance [4,5,25].

The system presented in this paper to extract salient stimuli is built on top of the *KnowRob* framework. It expands it by providing a mechanism for defining salient features using inference rules to leverage the information contained in the knowledge base. This information encompasses sensory multimodal data, the robot's internal state and other features. Furthermore, a programming tool to easily define the maps as rules is also introduced.

3   Designing Technical Requirements

In previous work, we showed the positive impact of increasing a social robot's sense of agency when it is able to react to salient features [14]. There, we performed an elicitation study in which participants were tasked to design the robot's reactive behaviors and the corresponding salient events that trigger such behaviors. Some results of this elicitation study are shown in Table 1. This study highlights the need for a flexible system capable of defining what features are of importance and should be given special attention. From Table 1, we extracted the technical requirements as follows:

- Take into account information not only from sensors, but also from the robot's internal state, intrinsic personality and preferences (Description and Input columns).
- Salient conditions for reactions in terms of the above-mentioned data - that is, sensor and internal information.
- Composability of salient events, supporting combinations of different salient features. For example, the *Applause* example included in Table 1 requires the gesture and the sound simultaneously.
- Associating salient features and reactive responses should be a process flexible enough to match several responses to a single trigger and vice versa.
- Configuration should be simple and not require extensive knowledge about the robot's internal components.

In this regard, we choose the *knowledge-centric* design approach as a fitting option. In such approach, the different components of a system rely on a knowledge base to carry out their own operations. The knowledge base can be freely queried for information that adheres to a well-defined knowledge model. Similar designs have been successfully explored before [2,17]. The knowledge model chosen is OWL [18]. In this model, knowledge is represented as a collection of entities interconnected by means of properties. Entities encompass both *classes*, representing a concept itself (e.g. the concept of a person) and *individuals*, which are actual realizations of a given class (e.g. an actual person present in a room). Properties represent connections describing how the different entities are related to each other. They are further classified as either *object properties* if they express the relation between two individuals (e.g. a person likes something) or *data properties* if they connect an individual with an explicit value (e.g. a person has a name encoded as a string).

Table 2. Sensory input is translated to an equivalent knowledge model representation via entities and properties conveying the same information.

Type	Name	Description
Classes (*C*)	Person	A person detected by the sensors and currently present
	Gesture	A physical gesture performed by a person (e.g., `wave`, `clap`, `bow`, etc.)
	Sound	Any sound source captured by the microphones
	SpeechAnalysis	The result of some type of speech analysis (e.g., sentiment analysis, intent, etc.)
	FacialExpression	Simple facial expression (e.g., `smiling`, `sad`, etc.)
	Utterance	Something a person says
	Proximity	The distance between a person and Haru
Object Properties (*OP*)	isLookingAt	A person is looking at something in particular
	hasSpeech	A person has said something
	hasIntent	An utterance has some specific intent (e.g., requests, greetings, etc.)
	hasFacialExpression	A facial expression has been detected
	likes	Something the robot or a person likes
Data Properties (*DP*)	hasName	Something's name (e.g., a person's name)
	hasType	Entities may have some type encoded as a string (e.g., a gesture's type)
	hasPosition	The 3D coordinates of something or someone

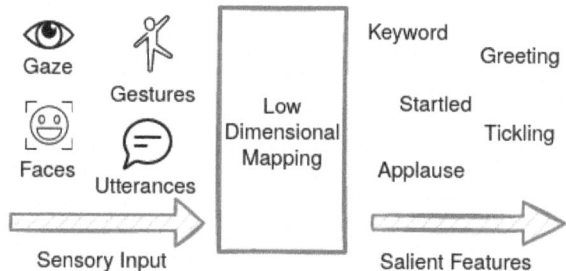

Fig. 1. Overview of the proposed system. High-dimensional sensory data are mapped into low-dimensional salient features. This mapping relies on the knowledge system that provides information about the sensory data and robot state.

Using this kind of knowledge model, data of different nature can be easily mixed, provided that a suitable equivalent representation has been defined beforehand. This representation comes in the form of a set of classes, individuals and properties that contain the same information as the original data. Table 2 lists some of the entities and properties that have been defined to model the sensory input used in the elicitation study included in Table 1. For example, gesture information provided by the sensors would be modelled as a combination of individuals of the *Gesture* class, the *hasGesture* property relating it to the person that made the gesture and other properties like *hasType* to encode the remaining information. The collection of entities and properties in the knowledge model constitute a vocabulary that can be used to reason about the state of the robot and its surroundings.

The rest of the requirements can be met by leveraging the inferring mechanism offered by OWL. In this context, inferring refer to the process of creating

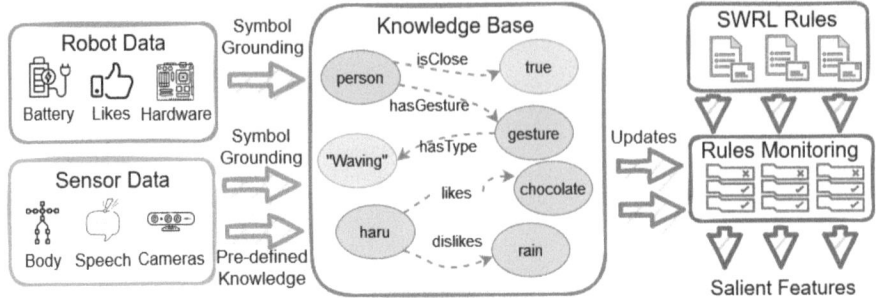

Fig. 2. Sensor data is converted to its equivalent knowledge representation. Information about the robot itself is also considered during mapping. Rules defining salient features are re-evaluated when the system's knowledge is updated.

new knowledge on the fly based on information already present in the system. This is discussed in more detail in Sect. 4.

4   Proposed Method

Sensory data is mapped into salient features deemed to be interesting for a specific application. This process is shown in Fig. 1. The resulting salient features can later be used to, for example, trigger reactions in the robot. We employed a *knowledge-centric* approach to realize this which entails that both the sensory input and the resulting low-dimensional features are modelled in terms of entities and properties defined in the knowledge base. The mapping itself, defining what combination of sensory data results in a particular salient feature, is also part of the system's knowledge. This treatment is also extended to the robots information. Having access to the knowledge system allows the mapping to be fine-tuned based additional information, like the robot's internal state, its preferences or its inherent personality.

The remainder of this section first presents the conversion between raw sensor data to its equivalent knowledge representation is presented, and then discusses the mapping between sensory input and salient features.

4.1   Translating Sensory Data to Its Knowledge Representation

The mapping between sensory data and salient features is restricted to data defined within the knowledge model. As such, the raw data provided by the sensors must be translated into its knowledge representation for the mapping to work. This process is usually referred to as symbol grounding. The left side of Fig. 2 shows an overview.

Sensor data is translated into a series of entities in the knowledge base, interconnected by means of properties. For example, when a gesture is detected, a new gesture entity would be generated in the knowledge base. The person that performed the gesture would be related to it through the *hasGesture* property.

While sensory data accounts for the largest volume of information handled by the system, information about the robot itself is also taken into account. Some information is added following a symbol grounding scheme (e.g. hardware status). Other information is defined statically in the ontologies and model the robot's inherent personality (e.g. what the robot likes or dislikes). This information can be used during mapping to further refine the generated salient features.

When the knowledge base is updated as the result of symbol grounding, all the rules that may generate new results (i.e., those using properties or classes involved in the update) are evaluated. Successfully evaluating a rule would generate a salient feature as a byproduct. This is illustrated in the right side of Fig. 2.

4.2 Low-Dimensional Mapping (Salient Features)

Generating Salient Features. Symbol grounding results in a homogenized set of entities and properties in the knowledge base that mirror the sensory data. This new data is considered as stimuli that may trigger the generation of a salient feature. Generating features consists then mainly of inspecting the information within the knowledge base to try to find a combination of entities and properties that satisfy the requirements of a given salient feature. Such a process can be seen as inferring new knowledge based on what's already known by the system.

SWRL rules provide an inference mechanism fitting for this [19]. They offer a way to query a knowledge system to generate new knowledge using simple logic constructs. Rules are written as a sequence of AND statements that verify some conditions over the contents of the knowledge base. Custom operations can also be implemented by means of built-ins operators (e.g. string comparisons, arithmetic operations). Listing 1.1 shows how rules are written in a generic way.

$$\{C_i(x_i)\} \wedge \{OP_i(x_i, y_i)\} \wedge \{DP_i(x_i, z_i)\} \wedge \{BI_i(...)\}$$
$$\Rightarrow \{C_j(x_i)\} \wedge \{OP_j(x_i, y_i)\} \wedge \{DP_j(x_i, z_i)\}$$

Listing 1.1. Generic SWRL rule

Terms in Listing 1.1 follow the naming scheme introduced in Table 2, where

$\{C_i(x_i)\}$
  is a set of terms that check if an individual x_i is of a given class C_i.
$\{OP_i(x_i, y_i)\}$
  is a set of terms that check if two individuals x_i and y_i are related through an object property OP_i.
$\{DP_i(x_i, z_i)\}$
  is a set where each term verifies if an individual x_i has some literal data z_i associated to it through an data property DP_i.
$\{BI_i(...)\}$
  is a set of custom built-ins, each one performing some operation. Each built-in take different number of arguments.

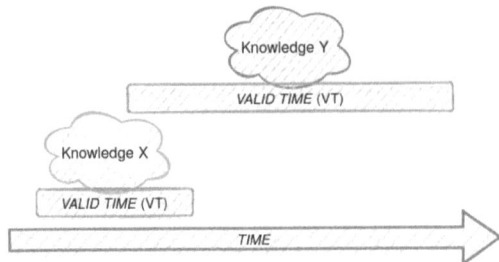

Fig. 3. Two knowledge pieces are considered concurrent if their valid times overlap.

Terms before the arrow form the rule's body, and terms after it, its head. Conditions in a rule's head are inferred to be true if its body's conditions are hold. Listing 1.2 shows an example of a rule defining the conditions to generate the *Tickling* salient feature listed in Table 1. Arguments prefixed with a question mark represent unbound variables.

$$Person(?person)\wedge$$
$$hasGesture(?person, ?gesture)\wedge$$
$$hasType(?gesture, tickling)\wedge$$
$$makeOWLIndividual(?tickling, ?person, ?gesture)$$
$$\Rightarrow Tickling(?tickling).$$

Listing 1.2. Example SWRL rule generating a salient feature

The last term in the rule's body in Listing 1.2 uses the *makeOWLIndividual* built-in [6]. It provides a controlled mechanism to insert new entities into a knowledge base from a rule's body by binding a new entity to its first argument for each unique set of values passed in the other arguments. A custom implementation of this built-in has been developed as part of this work, since *KnowRob* lacked support for it, and it has been shared with the original developers and integrated into the framework. Modifying the knowledge system from rules is an approach similar to those used in [2, 26]. The rule in Listing 1.2 can thus be read as: *generate a new Tickling salient feature for each person doing a tickling gesture.*

Leveraging Knowledge Information. SWRL allows to straightforwardly define how a subset of sensory data maps into a particular salient feature based on the information contained in the knowledge system. This process, however, is not limited to simple mappings: knowledge can be leveraged to improve the expressiveness of the salient features.

One of the requirements discussed in Sect. 3 was that the system should exhibit some sort of composability. By leveraging the expressiveness of OWL and the inferring mechanisms, complex salient features can be defined in terms of simpler ones. These *composite* features can also be implemented using rules.

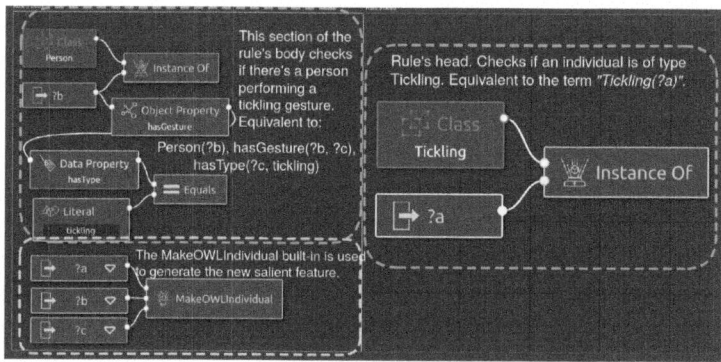

Fig. 4. A general-purpose SWRL editor has been implemented to ease up the generation of rules in the system using a dataflow programming scheme

An example of this is shown in Listing 1.3, where the *shyness* salient feature is defined in terms of two others.

$$NameRecognition(?name)\wedge$$
$$Applause(?applause)\wedge$$
$$overlaps(?name, ?applause)\wedge$$
$$makeOWLIndividual(?shy, ?tickling, ?applause)$$
$$\Rightarrow Shyness(?shy).$$

Listing 1.3. Example rule defining a composite salient feature.

The first two terms check if both a *NameRecognition* and *Applause* salient features are present in the knowledge base. The third term refers to a custom property called *overlaps*, that checks if two entities are concurrent. Two individuals in the knowledge system are considered to be concurrent if their valid times overlap. Valid times denote the time interval in which individuals are active - that is, the interval where the knowledge about that individual can be considered valid. When a query containing the *overlaps* property is issued, the knowledge base checks if their times overlap. Figure 3 shows a visualization of this. The new salient feature is generated using the *makeOWLIndividual* built-in as usual.

Salient features provide a mechanism to abstract away the inherent complexity of the sensory data. On their own, however, they provide little to no information. For example, given an instance of the *Keyword Saliency* listed in Table 1, one may be interested in knowing what particular keyword triggered the feature, what person said it, etc. This can be useful, for instance, to fine-tune the robot's behavior when reacting to it. This contextual information is vital to drive any subsequent decision-making processes.

Contextual information can be embedded in the same SWRL rules used to define the salient features. As shown in the generic rule example in Listing 1.1, the rule's head can contain any combination of entities and properties. If its body is validated, the terms in its head would be inferred to be true as well.

This can be exploited to add contextual information to the newly generated salient features by associating properties with it. Some properties commonly used in this context include *hasParticipant* to denote people involved; *duration*, to define the salient feature's valid time; *hasPriority* to assign a priority level to a feature in case there are several fired at the same time or *hasContext* to add generic information. Once a salient feature is received, the knowledge base can be queried to extract any additional information that may be needed.

Additional Tools. As rules play a central role in the design, a general-purpose SWRL rules editor has been implemented to ease their generation and management. Ontologies can be loaded directly into the editor. Once imported, its entities can be used to write any rule by interconnecting blocks, following a dataflow-like programming paradigm. Figure 4 shows how the rule introduced in Listing 1.2 to generate a simple salient feature can be built using this tool. The editor also supports the definition of composite salient features like the one discussed in Listing 1.3.

5   Evaluation

5.1   Experimental Setup

We use a simulated version of the robot *Haru*, together with a Kinect-like device and a microphone array to asses the system's responsiveness and accuracy using data from sensors in real time. A short scripted interaction between a single person and the robot has been implemented, where the person's body movements and utterances are encoded as salient features similarly to those listed in Table 1. Salient features trigger a reaction in the robot, modeled as short animations that are one to three seconds in length. The behavioral module introduced in [15] is used to map salient features to robot's actions. Features are queued if needed and dispatched at a later time as long as their valid times have not yet passed.

Table 3 lists the actions performed by the person during the interaction. These actions represent multimodal input data that is loaded into the knowledge base to generate salient features. Two separate scenarios have been implemented, each one considering different sets of features. The first one employs only simple features. The start of the interaction (marked as *1* in Table 3) is an example of this, where only the fact that the person greet the robot with a gesture is considered. The SWRL used to define this saliency is included at the bottom left of the table.

The second scenario focuses on complex features, generated as the combination of simple ones. In this setup, not only the fact that the person is waving their hand is considered at the beginning, but also the verbal greeting. This combination is formulated as the overlap of two salient features, as shown in the second example in Table 3. Information about the robot itself can be used as input data to generate salient features too. This is explored in the second scenario, where the fact that the robot does not like rain generates a specific

Table 3. Interaction script used to evaluate the system. In Scenario 1, single salient features are considered. In Scenario 2, complex salient features obtained as combinations of simple ones are considered. The SWRL rules associated to interactions *1, 2* and *3*.

Multimodal Input	Scenario I	Scenario II
Utterance: *Hi, there!* Gesture: waves their hand.	Gestural Saliency *(hand wave)* **(1)**.	Keyword Saliency *(Hi)*. Gestural Saliency *(hand wave)* **(2)**
Utterance: *I'm so bored today* Proximity: gets closer to the robot.	*Keyword Saliency (bored)*.	Keyword Saliency *(bored)*. Relative Distance Saliency *(gets closer)*
Utterance: *Hey, that's really cool!* Gesture: thumbs up.	*Keyword Saliency (cool)*.	Keyword Saliency *(cool)*. Gestural Saliency *(thumbs up)*
Utterance: *Have you seen that?* Body: points to the left	*Keyword Saliency (seen)*.	Keyword Saliency *(seen)*. Body Saliency *(points somewhere)*
Utterance: *I think it's gonna start raining*	*Keyword Saliency (rain)*.	Keyword Saliency *(rain)*. Preference Saliency *(dislikes rain)* **(3)**
Utterance: *I'd better get going. Good-bye.* Gesture: waves their hand.	*Keyword Saliency (goodbye)*.	Keyword Saliency *(goodbye)*. Gestural Saliency *(waves hand)*

SWRL Rules Examples

(1)	**(2)**	**(3)**
$Person(?p) \wedge$ $hasHandGesture(?p,?g) \wedge$ $hasNameString(?g,?n) \wedge$ $startsWith(?n,"waving") \wedge$ $makeOWLIndividual(?e,?g)$ $\Rightarrow WaveGesture(?e)$.	$Greet(?g) \wedge$ $WaveGesture(?w) \wedge$ $overlaps(?g,?w) \wedge$ $makeOWLIndividual(?e,?g,?w)$ $\Rightarrow GreetAndWave(?e)$.	$RainMentioned(?t) \wedge$ $dislikes(haru,rain) \wedge$ $makeOWLIndividual(?e,?t)$ $\Rightarrow DislikesRain(?e)$.

salient feature when the person mentions it. This is achieved within the SWRL rule by using the *dislikes* property to fetch the robot's preferences, as shown in the third example at table bottom.

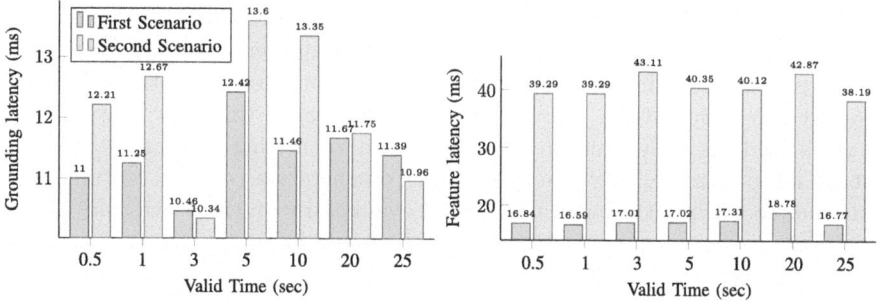

Fig. 5. Latency of symbol grounding (left) and salient feature generation (right).

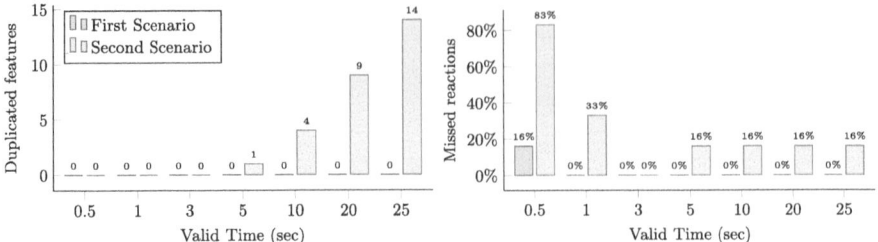

Fig. 6. Duplicated salient features (left) and missed reactions (right) in scenarios.

5.2   Results and Discussion

We asses the system's responsiveness and accuracy in an interaction in real time under different configurations. To this end, we measure the following variables of interest as a function of the valid time associated to each salient feature.

- *Symbol grounding latency.* Time it takes to insert some piece of multimodal data into the knowledge base.
- *Salient feature latency.* Time needed to evaluate a SWRL rule to generate a salient feature.
- *Duplicated features.* Measured as the number of additional salient features that are triggered by error, usually due to how features overlapped.
- *Missed reactions*, measured as the percentage of reactions that were expected to be executed but failed to do so, either because their associated feature's valid time passed or because they were not triggered in the first place.

Figure 5 shows the average latency measured during symbol grounding and salient feature generation. Symbol grounding times are constant and similar for both scenarios, averaging at around 12 milliseconds per insertion. Similar to symbol grounding, salient feature's generation is not affected by the valid time associated to each feature. This latency, however, varies with the complexity of the rules used. As such, times in the second scenario are higher than those of the first, as more complex rules are employed. To generate a complex feature, each of the simple feature it is based on must be evaluated with their own rules before their times can be compared. Therefore, this should be taken into consideration when designing salient features.

Figure 6 measures the number of duplicated salient features and the percentage of missed reactions for each scenario. Long valid times are the main cause of duplication, as features may live long enough to be used to trigger new complex ones. These extra features trigger reactions that take away time that may had been used to process others. Short valid times, on the other hand, can lead to missed reactions. In the first scenario, this is mainly due to queued reactions timing out more frequently as their valid passes before they can be processed. The second scenario is more sensible to changes in valid times, as complex features rely heavily on this parameter. Short valid times result in simple features

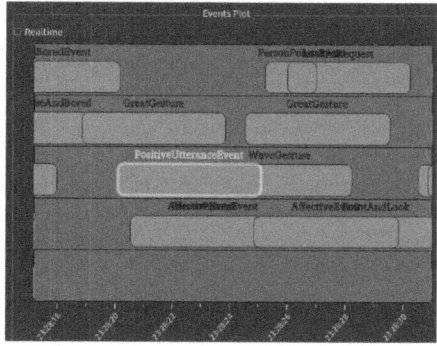

Fig. 7. Excessive valid times of the highlighted feature causes duplicated features.

not overlapping. Figure 6 also shows there are missed reactions even when the valid times are long. This is the result of an erroneous duplication of features caused by the excessively long valid times. This increase in the number of triggered features result in a higher number of them timing out before they can be processed.

Figure 7 shows a screenshot of a custom feature visualizer tool where this duplication can be seen. The abnormally long valid time causes the highlighted *PositiveUtterance* feature to overlap with two *GreatGesture*, resulting in duplicated features being triggered.

Therefore, careful allocation of valid times is important to avoid duplicating or missing features. Even though the same time has been used in this evaluation, it is possible to assign different times to each feature in the SWRL rule that defines it. Other mechanisms like priorities can also be used to handle concurrent features.

6   Conclusions and Future Work

In this paper we present a framework to map high-dimensional sensory input features into low-dimensional salient feature space using a knowledge-centric approach which offers added functionality compared to previous approaches. In addition, we also provided a tool to edit the rules with ease for researchers to design robot behaviors vis-a-vis external stimuli.

The main contribution of the proposed system is the flexibility it offers in defining salient features for different human-robot interaction scenarios through complex composition, incorporation of contextual information in the knowledge base, etc. At the same time, the proposed knowledge based generate salient features responses in reasonable reaction time.

The framework here remains under active development and our next steps are to 1) address the analysis of the adequate valid times for different features, 2) to create an efficient coupling between the saliency generator and the robot's behavior generator, and 3) improve the system's robustness and stability.

Acknowledgments. The work of L.M. is partially funded by NHoA PLEC2021-007868, funded by MCIN/AEI/10.13039/501100011033 and the European Union "NextGenerationEU"/"PRTR".

References

1. Akalin, N., Loutfi, A.: Reinforcement learning approaches in social robotics. Sensors **21**(4), 1292 (2021)
2. Alaya, M.B., Monteil, T.: FRAMESELF: a generic autonomic framework for self-management of distributed systems-application on the self-configuration of M2M architecture using semantic and ontology. In: International Conference on Collaboration Technologies and Infrastructures (IEEE WETICE 2012) (2012)
3. Beetz, M., Beßler, D., Haidu, A., Pomarlan, M., Bozcuoğlu, A.K., Bartels, G.: KnowRob 2.0—a 2nd generation knowledge processing framework for cognition-enabled robotic agents. In: 2018 IEEE International Conference on Robotics and Automation (ICRA), pp. 512–519. IEEE (2018)
4. Beetz, M., et al.: Cognition-enabled autonomous robot control for the realization of home chore task intelligence. Proc. IEEE **100**(8), 2454–2471 (2012)
5. Beßler, D., Pomarlan, M., Beetz, M.: Owl-enabled assembly planning for robotic agents. In: Proceedings of the 17th International Conference on Autonomous Agents and MultiAgent Systems, pp. 1684–1692 (2018)
6. Bouaicha, S., Boufaida, Z.: SWRLx: a new formalism for hybrid ontology reasoning. In: Information Retrieval and Management: Concepts, Methodologies, Tools, and Applications, pp. 348–367. IGI Global (2018)
7. Buisan, G., Sarthou, G., Bit-Monnot, A., Clodic, A., Alami, R.: Efficient, situated and ontology based referring expression generation for human-robot collaboration. In: 2020 29th IEEE International Conference on Robot and Human Interactive Communication (RO-MAN), pp. 349–356 (2020)
8. Bálint-Benczédi, F., et al.: RoboSherlock: cognition-enabled robot perception for everyday manipulation tasks. ArXiv abs/1911.10079 (2019)
9. Cao, H., et al.: Robot-enhanced therapy: development and validation of supervised autonomous robotic system for autism spectrum disorders therapy. IEEE Robot. Autom. Mag. **26**(2), 49–58 (2019)
10. Charisi, V., Gomez, E., Mier, G., Merino, L., Gomez, R.: Child-robot collaborative problem-solving and the importance of child's voluntary interaction: a developmental perspective. Front. Robot. AI **7**, 15 (2020)
11. Das, D., Banerjee, S., Chernova, S.: Explainable AI for Robot Failures: generating explanations that improve user assistance in fault recovery. In: HRI '21: ACM/IEEE International Conference on Human-Robot Interaction, Boulder, CO, USA, March 8-11, 2021, pp. 351–360 (2021)
12. Das, D., Chernova, S.: Semantic-Based Explainable AI: leveraging semantic scene graphs and pairwise ranking to explain robot failures. In: IEEE/RSJ International Conference on Intelligent Robots and Systems, IROS, pp. 3034–3041 (2021)
13. Do, T.T., Nguyen, A., Reid, I.: Affordancenet: An end-to-end deep learning approach for object affordance detection. In: 2018 IEEE International Conference on Robotics and Automation (ICRA), pp. 5882–5889 (2018)
14. Gomez, R., et al.: Developing a robot's empathetic reactive response inspired by a bottom-up attention model. In: International Conference on Social Robotics (2021)

15. Gomez, R., et al.: Developing the bottom-up attentional system of a social robot. In: IEEE International Conference on Robotics and Automation (2022)

16. Johal, W., Calvary, G., Pesty, S.: Non-verbal signals in HRI: interference in human perception. In: Tapus, A., André, E., Martin, J.C., Ferland, F., Ammi, M. (eds.) Social Robotics, pp. 275–284. Springer International Publishing, Cham (2015)

17. Lemaignan, S., Warnier, M., Sisbot, E.A., Clodic, A., Alami, R.: Artificial cognition for social human-robot interaction: an implementation. Artif. Intell. **247**, 45–69 (2017)

18. McGuinness, D.L., Van Harmelen, F., et al.: Owl web ontology language overview. W3C Recommendation **10**(10), 2004 (2004)

19. O'Connor, M.: The semantic web rule language. In: Protégé Conference (2009)

20. Quigley, M., et al.: ROS: an open-source robot operating system. In: ICRA Workshop on Open Source Software (2009)

21. Sarthou, G., Clodic, A., Alami, R.: Ontologenius: a long-term semantic memory for robotic agents. In: 2019 28th IEEE International Conference on Robot and Human Interactive Communication (RO-MAN), pp. 1–8 (2019)

22. Thellman, S., Ziemke, T.: The intentional stance toward robots: conceptual and methodological considerations. In: The 41st Annual Conference of the Cognitive Science Society, July 24-26, Montreal, Canada, pp. 1097–1103 (2019)

23. Thill, S., Vernon, D.: How to design emergent models of cognition for application-driven artificial agents. In: Proceedings of the 14th Neural Computation and Psychology Workshop, pp. 115 – 129. World Scientific Publishing (2016)

24. Vogt, P., et al.: Second language tutoring using social robots: A large-scale study. In: 2019 14th ACM/IEEE International Conference on Human-Robot Interaction (HRI), pp. 497–505 (2019)

25. Yazdani, F., et al.: Cognition-enabled framework for mixed human-robot rescue teams. In: 2018 IEEE/RSJ International Conference on Intelligent Robots and Systems (IROS), pp. 1421–1428. IEEE (2018)

26. Zhu, T., Bakshi, A., Prasanna, V.K., Gomadam, K.: Applying semantic web techniques to reservoir engineering: challenges and experiences from event modeling. In: 2010 Seventh International Conference on Information Technology: New Generations, pp. 586–591. IEEE (2010)

Baby-Robot Interaction: An Observational Analysis of Young Children's Interactions with Robot Cleaners

Eduardo B. Sandoval[1]([✉]) [ID], Hansul Park[1], and Michelle M. Neumann[2] [ID]

[1] School of Art and Design, University of New South Wales, Sydney, Australia
{e.sandoval,hansul.park}@unsw.edu.au
[2] Faculty of Education, Southern Cross University, Gold Coast, Australia
michelle.neumann@scu.edu.au

Abstract. Despite the growing presence of service robots in homes, little is known about the nature of baby-robot interactions, particularly with mobile robots such as robot cleaners. This paper is exploratory research that contributes to larger investigations of baby-robot interaction. We use the term 'baby' as it is a common term used in different languages to refer to infants and toddlers, and most of the individuals in our study were approximately 4 to 12 months old. We analysed 34 videos from YouTube displaying babies and robot cleaners interacting in domestic environments, using the word 'baby' as one of the key search terms. Physical, cognitive, emotional, social, and verbal behaviours displayed by the babies while interacting with these robots were described and classified. Baby-Robot Interactions with Roomba robots mostly occurred in general areas of the house. Some of the children displayed negative reactions towards the robot. Safety concerns include exposure to machine noise and potential risk of physical injury, for example, if children fall off the robot cleaner. Future empirically designed studies of baby- robot interactions are needed to investigate these child-safety concerns.

Keywords: Children-Robot Interaction · domestic robot · service robot · baby and robot · toddler and robots · children and robots · cleaning robot · interaction design for children · safety

1 Introduction

In the early years of life, a child's environment significantly influences their learning and development [1]. As technology advances, children are increasingly exposed to interactive devices, including robots. For instance, robot cleaners, designed to assist parents and caregivers, are becoming commonplace in homes worldwide. While these robots share home and living spaces with young children (0 to 3 years old), research on Baby-Robot interaction (BRI), 0–1 year old, and toddler-robot interaction (TRI), 1–3 years old, in domestic settings remains limited.

Moreover, longitudinal studies exploring the long-term impact of domestic robotics cleaners on humans are scarce [2]. The literature in human-robot interaction (HRI) also lacks sufficient "in-the-wild" studies describing real-world interactions between robots and babies in domestic environments.

Given the growing prevalence of robots in homes, BRI research is crucial. As "robot natives" (individuals born and raised in close proximity to robots) become more common [3], there is a pressing need for multidisciplinary guidelines to inform the design of commercial robots interacting with young children. Manufacturers, robot designers and HRI practitioners can benefit from design philosophies such as the virtuous robotics approach [4] to foster healthy interactive environments for human families.

This exploratory research aims to describe interactions between babies and robot cleaners through an analysis of publicly available YouTube videos. While this approach offers valuable insights, it is important to acknowledge the limitations of relying on a self-selected sample of YouTube videos, which may be curated for entertainment purposes. Further research could benefit from incorporating a more diverse dataset or employing complementary data collection methods to address these potential biases.

Despite these limitations, this study represents a preliminary step toward larger-scale "in-the-wild" human-robot interaction research involving various stakeholders, including parents, families, robot manufacturers and interactions in future studies. BRI requires attention, especially "in-the-wild" interactions, as they provide valuable quantitative and qualitative data to inform future legislation, interactions and designs for robot end-users. Our primary goal is to explore how babies interact with a domestic robot at home. The research question addressed is: How do babies respond to and interact with a robot cleaner in the home environment?

2   Background

The term "Robot Natives" was originally coined in the book, *Cambridge Handbook on Law, Policy and Regulations for Human-Robot Interaction* [3]. The researchers defined the term as the "*first generation of human's regularly interacting with robots in domestic environments.*" It includes infant (0–12 months old) and toddler (12–36 months old) who were born in the 2020s when there was a rise in the number of robots in domestic environments.

There is a variety of terms to define infants and toddlers. For instance, "Very young children" are defined as the group of children from birth to age two and "older children" refers to children approaching the transition to school according to the Australian Children's Education and Care Quality Authority [5]. Similarly, the Australian Government via the Department of Health and Aged Care [6], defines an infant as a child under 12 months old, and toddler is 1 to 3 years of age. In this paper, we will use the term baby in the text as in several languages baby is used to describe babies and toddlers indistinctively. Similarly, we use the word "baby" as a key search term used to collect the data. After visual inspection and analysis, babies aged approximately 12 to18 months old mostly appeared in the videos.

2.1 Related Studies in Children-Robot Interaction

In the domain of human-robot interaction, researchers have investigated the positive effects of robots on children's development, including stimulating creativity [7], assessing emotional states [8], facilitating early education and language acquisition [2] and serving as therapeutic tools for autistic children [9]. Early work suggesting heuristics and interaction guidelines for children robot interaction including toddlers can be found in the work of Salter et. al. [10]. More recently, in 2023, *Family Theories in Child-Robot Interactions* has been proposed as a framework to describe interactions in domestic environments [11]. However, there is a lack of research examining the interaction between robots and very young children or babies in naturalistic conditions.

3 Method

This study collected observational data from "into-the-wild" baby-robot interaction scenarios captured in publicly available YouTube videos. The video collection was conducted in October 2023, and the review was completed from January 2024. Relevant video clips were identified through a YouTube search using the terms *"baby and robot"*, *"baby and robot vacuum"* and *"baby and Roomba"* (Roomba being a generic term for domestic robot cleaners). Our criteria to select the videos was that a child and a robot appear in the video. Also, we covered from the oldest to the most recent YouTube videos available. All videos were identified as shareable public content. Therefore, after consulting with the University Ethics Office, it was confirmed that ethical review was not required for this study.

The final sample of data consisted of 34 video clips showing children interacting with domestic robot cleaners: 5 short-form, 4 long-form videos and 25 compiled clips (we removed three duplicated videos from the compilations). The clips came mainly from two compilations of babies and robot cleaner (e.g., Roomba) videos. The first and third author developed, designed and tested the video observation checklist criteria based on the children's Developmental Milestones published by the Australian Children's Education and Care Quality Authority (2024) to identify and classify children's behaviours [12]. Please check our dataset as an online appendix at https://shorturl.at/tgbxE.

The development of children and observable behaviours was categorised into six stages, providing an overview of the developmental milestones for each stage using the criteria outlined in [14]: a) Birth to 4 months, b) 4 to 8 months, c) 8 to 12 months, d) 1 to 2 years, e) 2 to 3 years and f) 3 to 5 years. Similarly, there are five observable developmental areas for each stage: 1) Physical, 2) Social 3) Emotional, 4) Cognitive, and 5) Verbal. To classify the behaviours of the babies, we created four affinity groups. This is a modified use of the Design Method known as Affinity Diagrams [13].These affinity groups are included in the link above.

Physical behaviour encompasses a child's large (e.g., sitting, walking) and small body movements (e.g., hand control, reflexes, vision, sleep, eating) [10]. Longer videos contained more instances with a maximum of nine behaviours observed in a single video. We created the following categories: a) visual tracking, b) physical contact with the robot (grasping, lying on top, sitting on top), c) baby-agent interaction (advanced interaction with the robot as pushing buttons or grasping the robot and Human-Human Interaction),

d) intentional movement (limb movement, pre-walking movement), e) physical indication of emotions (positive and negative), and unclassified behaviours such as walking and reacting to sudden loud noises.

Social and emotional behaviour refers to a child's interactions and connections with significant adults or parent/carers (caregivers) positioned near them [11]. Social behaviours were classified into three main categories: 1) no social behaviour observed, b) interaction with caregivers (e.g., curious and energetic) and c) positive social connection (smiles and laughs). Emotional behaviours were sorted into four main categories: a) no emotional behaviour, b) seeking assurance from caregivers, c) laughs in social interaction, and d) discomfort. There are overlaps in the analysis of social and emotional behaviours.

Cognitive behaviour involves a child's understanding of objects, sensory processing and engagement with the environment, including language and verbal behaviour (i.e., hearing, understanding sounds and using speech for communication) [12]. They were divided into five categories: a) visual exploration, b) tactile exploration, c) auditory exploration, d) emotional expression, and e) pattern recognition.

Verbal interaction refers to any verbal communication observed and heard in the audio of the videos. These were classified as a) no verbal interaction, b) talking/laughing in the background, and c) visible verbal interaction.

We collected and documented the instances of children's behaviours in date/year chronological order when analysing the videos (i.e. physical behaviour column: "baby sits without help", "baby cries", and "lays on stomach"). The instances were separated by commas in a single cell in a word document to capture rapid observations within the video. An MS-Excel script was used for further classification of child behaviours. Then we calculated the frequencies of the categories of behaviours observed in the videos that included a description of each child and the baby-robot Interactions.

Videos were reviewed independently and blindly by each of the three authors. A pilot using eleven videos was performed by the first and third author to agree in the classification and coding protocol. The second author was a trained researcher and coded all the videos. Then, the first and second authors reviewed the coded data simultaneously. Any discrepancies were identified and addressed through collaborative discussion between the first and second authors. The coding was updated; accordingly, both authors were in complete agreement. The video checklist criteria for the video observations consisted of four categories described in Table 1. These four main categories were further divided into 23 sub-categories.

Following the use of this child developmental criteria analysis, we employed a semi-automated thematic analysis using OpenAI's ChatGPT to analyse the data. To expedite the analysis process, particularly for children's physical behaviours ($n = 129$), Chat-GPT was employed. Each column of the observation checklist criteria was presented to ChatGPT with the prompt, "analyse the frequency of the data above." To ensure accuracy, the first and second authors manually verified ChatGPT's frequency counts. For further validation, Google's Gemini was used to examine the algorithm underlying the data analysis, which was then translated into Python code. Then using the calculated frequencies, a second prompt was issued: "Convert the given frequency into percentiles".

Once we verify that the process was reliable, we applied the same prompts to analyse the following categories.

Table 1. Video observation categories and sub-categories.

1) **Video Information**				
1. Link	2. Likes	3. Views	4. Accessed	5. Duration
6. Subscribers	7. Published Date	8. Type of Video	9. Licence	10. Motivation
2) **Baby Description**				
1.Age	2. Ethnicity	3. Gender (Estimated via visual inspection)		
3) **Baby Behaviour**				
1. Physical Behaviours	2. Cognitive Behaviours	3. Social Behaviours	4. Emotional Behaviours	5. Verbal Interaction
4) **Baby-Robot Interaction**				
1. Brand of the robot	2. Filmed Location	3. Individuals Presented in the Video	3.Props Usage	4. Safety and Risks Concerns	5. Negative Encounters

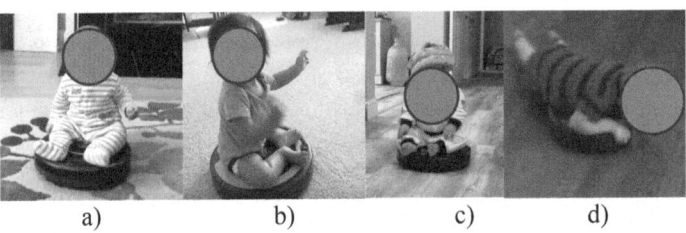

a)   b)   c)   d)

Fig. 1. Babies interacting with robot cleaners. a) 0–4 months, b) 4–8 months, c) 8–12 months, d) 2–3 years old. (Youtube: CrazyFunnyStuffCFS, Best Babies Youtube. Shareable without explicit permission (Youtube) and under Creative Commons by Attribution 3.0). 1–2 years old babies image no available for publication.

The YouTube clips that were analysed were published across 7 years (2015–2022). The year 2017 saw the most posted videos. This suggests that interest in robot cleaners and child interactions grew on social media around that time, with increasing popularity thereafter. The average video clip length was 24 s, indicating a preference for shorter videos formats, ranging from 7 s to 1 min and 19 s. Videos were accessed by the researchers in the present study in October 2023. Details of the video metrics (i.e., views, subscribers, and likes) can be found in the online dataset. We hypothesise the possibility for monetisation likely incentivises creators to upload these domestic videos. A major concern needed to be addressed in future research is the potential long-term implications for the digital identity and privacy of children unknowingly filmed. Most of the videos were uploaded by YouTubers who run viral channels specialising in funny videos (Fig. 1).

4 Results and Discussion

The 34 analysed baby-robot cleaner interaction videos were uploaded by parents/caregivers, while the remaining nine were uploaded by YouTubers who run viral channels specialising in funny videos.

4.1 Baby Description

Our observations of the videos suggest that the age of children featured is ranged from approximately 0 to 3 years. The most frequent age group was 8–12 months, appearing in 12 videos (35.29%), this was followed by the 4–8 months age group (29.41%, 10 videos) and the 12–24 months age group (23.53%, 8 videos). Children aged 0–4 months, and 2–3 years were the least represented across the videos, appearing in only two of the videos (5.88% of the videos).

Ethnicity and gender distribution can be found in the online dataset as an initial reference and are not reliable enough to code accurately. The authors highlight that observational analysis is not sufficient to determine the gender and ethnicity of the children in the videos and parent/carer questionaires or interviews for future studies that investigate this is required. Further discussion is required to determine the ethnicity and gender of the babies appearing in the videos accurately.

4.2 Baby Behaviour Observations

Five sub-categories were created to define babies' behaviours in the videos (physical, cognitive, emotional, social, and verbal).

Physical Behaviour: Across the 34 baby videos, video interactions documented 119 instances of babies' physical behaviours, varying with developmental stages. Longer videos contained more instances with a maximum of nine physical behaviours observed in a single video. The most frequent physical behaviour was the baby touching the robot (45 out of 119 physical behaviours identified across the videos). The physical contact with the robot included, "reaches for and grasps the robot", "able to lift head and chest when lying on stomach" and "sit with/without support on the robot (41.18% of the videos and the highest frequency for the instances). This was followed by visual tracking (35 instances, 29.4% of the instances), including "aware of the robot movement" and "watches activities across the room". Intentional movement of children was observed in various (17 instances, 50% of the videos) with "child waves arms up and down" and similar (26.47% of the videos) and "raises self to sitting position" being the less frequent movement. Baby-robot interaction (human or robot) was followed (50% of the videos), involving actions such as "pushes button and activates the robot". Seven babies revealed a sense of emotion in both positive and negative: for instances of "smiles", "claps" and "cries". Smiles, claps and cries are also classified as Social-Emotional Behaviours and will appear in the following categories. Additionally, there were a total of eight unclassified behaviours such as "reacts to sudden loud noises" (7 instances) and "walks" (1 instance).

Social Behaviour: The total of 39 social behaviours observed across 34 videos. Over half of the videos (19) videos lacked observable social behaviours (55.88% of the videos with the highest frequency) as the videos depicted babies interacting with the robot alone. However, 12 children (35.29% of the videos) displayed curiosity and energetic behaviours that are somewhat dependent on adult presence for comfort. "Smiles at the camera" and "smiles and laughs" suggest positive social connection potentially towards the adults filming or the experience interacting with robot cleaner or both (8 children, 23.53% of the videos).

Emotional Behaviour: There were 41 emotional behaviours demonstrated by the 34 children that were observed. The most frequent behaviour was "no visible emotional behaviour" that was observed 15 times across the videos (44.12% of the children). This was followed by 12 children seeking assurance from their caregivers in (29.27% of the total videos) which included where the "child actively explores and plays when parent/carer was present, returning now and then for assurance and interaction" and "actively seeks to be next to parent or principal caregiver". Additionally, there were 11 instances (32.35% of videos) of laughing indicating social interaction, containing instances of "smiles", "laughs", "nervous laughs" and "happy to see faces they know (grin)". The behaviours of discomfort were observed the least in three instances of "cries" (8.82% of the total videos).

Cognitive Behaviour: There were 64 cognitive behaviours identified across the observations of the 34 videos. Curious and intentional exploration of the robot through touching the robot or objects in their environment was the most prevalent behaviour (37 instances, 57.81% of the total instances), involving "learns through sensory experiences (while moving on top of the robot)", "enjoys toys (robot) banging objects, scrunching", "shakes and stares at toy placed in hand" and "spends a lot of time exploring and manipulating objects, putting them in mouth and shaking and banging them". The behaviours of pattern recognition were observed in 10 children (29.41% of the total videos). These include, "repeats actions, but unaware of ability to cause action", "notices differences and shows surprise", "seems to understand some things parent or familiar adults say to them" and "repeats actions that lead to interesting/predictable results". Nine children revealed a sense of emotional expression, "smiles", "smiles and laughs" and "cries". Seven children showed (20.59% of the videos) visual exploration behaviours of "eyes track slow moving targets for brief periods". The least observed behaviour was auditory exploration with one instance (2.94% of the videos), "listening with pleasure to sound making toys and music".

Verbal Interaction: There were 37 times that babies and/or parents/caregivers were observed to express themselves verbally across 34 videos. Half of the videos (17 instances) did not capture any verbal interaction from children and/or parents/caregivers. Talking or laughing behind the video camera being used to film the child on the robot vacuum occurred 17 times (50% of the videos). Three videos demonstrated instances of physical verbal interaction (8.82% of the videos with the least frequent interaction), including "sibling appearing in the video" and "guardians interacting with the baby".

4.3 Baby-Robot-Interaction: Technical and Environmental Conditions

There were 205 identified instances in the videos that were analysed during baby-robot interactions and these were classified into the following six subcategories:

Brand of the Robot: The most frequently featured type of robot cleaner in the videos was Roomba (19 instances, 55.9% of robot cleaners), including specific models like "a Roomba 780" and "Roomba j7". Also, one video featured a Deebot M80 (2.94%). There were 41% of the robot that were unidentifiable due to specific details of the robot brand label being hidden from view in the video. We noticed that some brands of the robot cleaners were identified by the video titles explicitly mentioned the robot brand or model, such as "Baby Riding robot vacuum Deebot", "Baby and iRobot", "Cute Babies Riding Roomba Rodeo at The First Time", and "11 Best Babies Video Compilation". Researchers used search terms like "iRobot", "Roomba", and "Deebot" on Google Shopping or company websites to confirm and potentially identify specific brands and models for the remaining videos lacking such details in the titles.

Filmed Location: Videos depicted interactions in various locations in children's homes and included general shared spaces such as the: a) living room, b) kitchen, c) open-plan space, d) dining room, e) corridor, f) unidentifiable spaces and g) in-between area (corridor-kitchen and kitchen-living room). The spaces in four of the videos (11.76%) remained unidentifiable due to camera angles or generic interior design. In-between areas were the most frequent setting (32.35% of the videos, 11 instances), followed by living room (23.53%, 8 instances), open-plan space (11.76%, 4 instances) and kitchen (8.82%, 3 instances). Corridor and dining room were the least frequent settings, both appearing in two instances (5.88% each). This suggests interactions between babies and robots were not limited to specific areas within the home environment but rather occurred throughout various functional and transitional spaces that were shared by the families.

Individuals in the Video: Individuals (including the children) were analysed into five main categories: a) baby and caregivers, b) baby and someone else (visible: grandparent, sibling and dog), c) baby and someone else (voice only) and d) baby only. The most frequent scenario (18 instances, 52.94% of the videos) was the baby appearing alone, followed by videos featuring the baby with someone else's voice only (8 instances, 23.53%). Interactions with a visible caregiver(s) (14.71%) were more common than interactions with someone else visible (3 instances, 8.82%).

Props Usage: Most interactions (26 instances, 76.47% of the videos) involved no props. Baby seats were the most frequent (5 instances, 14.71%), followed by costumes (2 instances, 5.88%), including bibs, helmets and spatial suits. There was minimal use of baby loungers and cardboard boxes (one instance, 2.94% each). This finding suggests that guardians prioritise natural interactions between babies and robots, with minimal reliance on external stimuli to facilitate engagement and observe the interactions. It also implies a lack of intentionality regarding props, meaning they may not have been filmed with specific intention of becoming public content initially.

Safety and Risk: There were several key observations regarding safety and risk factors during interactions between babies and robot cleaners. The most prevalent concern was the potential risk of falls or crashes (18 instances, 52.94% of the total videos) due to children being placed on top of moving robots making child movement unstable during any sudden changes in robot direction as it vaccumed the floor. High noise levels generated by the robot cleaner were observed in three videos (8.82%). In two videos (5.88%), caregivers mitigated risks by holding the babies or following the moving robots. This underscores a potential safety concern associated with a high frequency of fall or crash risks during baby interactions with robot cleaners. It stresses the importance of guardian and caregiver presence to monitor interactions and intervene to prevent falls or crashes, ensuring the overall safety of the babies. The data suggests that these children may have been exposed to high noise levels during robot operation, regardless of whether it's for cleaning or play purposes.

Negative Encounter: Four children (11.76%) displayed negative reactions towards the robots, exhibiting behaviours like "crying" or "screaming/running away". The remaining 30 children (88.24%) did not show any signs of negative interactions. This suggests that majority of the children did not experience distress during the interactions due to the robot.

5 Conclusion

We infer from our frequency data that publicly available videos depicted babies (4–8 months and 8–12 months) riding on top of Roomba robot cleaners and exploring their surrounding environment while the robot moves with parents' motives potentially being to share them as entertainment clips. The aim of the videos seemed to be a source of amusement for the viewer and capture a baby's first interaction with a robot. The initial trend of such videos might possibly be driven by attraction for "likes" and monetisation as these clips are often compiled into "funny video" collections. Since the presence of parents/carers/guardians interacting directly or indirectly with the children suggests that this interaction may be encouraged by parents of babies aged between 4–8 months, with a peak occurring at 8–12 months. Similarly, these findings indicate that caregivers may feel more comfortable allowing children to interact with robots when children can sit unsupported, potentially minimising any unintended consequences or discomfort experienced by their children. As we mentioned in the introduction, this study aims to answer the question: How do babies interact with a robot cleaner in the home environment?

From the current observational findings, it is possible to suggest that babies interact in mainly neutral or positive ways with a robot cleaner in the home environment with only a few children observed to be fearful of them. This could be due to the loud machine noises of these robots and the sudden and unexpected movements of robots, especially when caregivers place babies on top of these mobile robots. Also, children's social and verbal reactions are less evident due to the limitations of the video recording.

Current discourse in child-robot interaction often overlooks the potential for negative reactions in babies when interacting with robots. As a community dedicated to HRI, we aim to mitigate these negative impacts and contribute to the development of safer and more positive interactions between robots and babies in domestic and public environments. Negative reactions by children such as crying (potentially caused by the robot) observed in the present videos was rare, however future research is needed to investigate this in a more systematic way using a stronger empirical approach, research design and methodology with a larger sample size of young children from more diverse backgrounds. As an initial observation of assessing the safety and risks factors impacting on babies interacting with robot cleaners, we speculatively suggest that prolonged exposure to the noise produced by the robots (range of 50 to 70 dBs) at a proximity may influence hearing development. However, further research is needed to investigate this.

Robot cleaners are not designed to be toys or to be ridden by babies. Placing children on top of robots pose risks to babies and young children falling and succumbing to physical harm and injury. However, it is not possible to assess the full extent of these physical impacts on children from the YouTube videos themselves. Further empirical studies are required to gauge the impact of domestic robot cleaners on the physical health, well-being and development of babies and toddlers. In other words, it is necessary to investigate the multiple factors underlying negative responses observed in 11.76% of the babies.

Investigating potential interactions, setups or robot designs is crucial for informing the design of future interactions between babies and robots. It is essential to consider that as domestic robots become more prevalent in the future, very young children will increasingly interact with these technologies, potentially leading to more frequent and complex interactions and this requires serious consideration by manufacturers, policy makers, and families and carers of young children.

Limitations and future research: We acknowledge limitations associated with observational nature of this study, visual inspection, and low sample size of this study. Particularly ethnicity and gender cannot accurately be defined only by visual inspection of the analysed videos. We suggest future more controlled and designed experiments along with naturalistic studies be conducted to better understand baby-robot interactions within home and domestic settings.

References

1. "Interactive Head Start Early Learning Outcomes Framework: Ages Birth to Five | ECLKC", Head Start: Early Childhood Learning & Knowledge Center. Accessed 31 May 2024. https://eclkc.ohs.acf.hhs.gov/interactive-head-start-early-learning-outcomes-framework-ages-birth-five
2. Neumann, M.M.: Social robots and young children's early language and literacy learning. Early Childhood Educ. J. **48**(2), 157–170 (2020). https://doi.org/10.1007/s10643-019-00997-7
3. Sandoval, E.B., Billinghurst, M., Cappuccio, M.: Robot natives: future design and regulations for baby robot interaction. In: The Cambridge Handbook of the Law, Policy, and Regulation for Human-Robot Interaction, Cambridge Press, pp. 230–249 (2024). Accessed 31 May 2024. https://www.cambridge.org/au/universitypress/subjects/law/e-commerce-law/cambridge-handbook-law-policy-and-regulation-humanrobot-interaction
4. Cappuccio, M., Sandoval, E.B., Mubin, O., Obaid, M., Velonaki, M.: Can robots make us better humans? Virtuous Robotics and the good life with artificial agents. Int. J. Soc. Robot. (2020)

5. ACECQA, "Search results | ACECQA", ACECQA Australia, Belonging, Being and Becoming. Accessed 12 Jul 2024. https://www.acecqa.gov.au/search?s=BELONGING%2C+BEING+%26+BECOMING

6. Australian Government Department of Health and Aged Care, "For infants, toddlers and preschoolers (birth to 5 years)", Australian Government: Department of Health and AGed Care. Accessed 31 May 2024. https://www.health.gov.au/topics/physical-activity-and-exercise/physical-activity-and-exercise-guidelines-for-all-australians/for-infants-toddlers-and-preschoolers-birth-to-5-years

7. Alves-Oliveira, P., Arriaga, P., Paiva, A., Hoffman, G.: YOLO, a robot for creativity: a co-design study with children. In: Proceedings of the 2017 Conference on Interaction Design and Children, Stanford California USA, pp. 423–429. ACM (2017). https://doi.org/10.1145/3078072.3084304

8. Filippini, C., et al.: Facilitating the child-robot interaction by endowing the robot with the capability of understanding the child engagement: the case of Mio Amico robot. Int. J. Soc. Robot. 13(4), 677–689 (2021). https://doi.org/10.1007/s12369-020-00661-w

9. Silvera-Tawil, D., Brown, S.A.: Cross-collaborative approach to socially-assistive robotics: a case study of humanoid robots in a therapeutic intervention for autistic children. In: Korn, O., Ed., Social Robots: Technological, Societal and Ethical Aspects of Human-Robot Interaction, pp. 165–186. Springer International Publishing, Cham (2019). https://doi.org/10.1007/978-3-030-17107-0_9

10. Salter, T., Werry, I., Michaud, F.: Going into the wild in child–robot interaction studies: issues in social robotic development. Intel. Serv. Robot. 1(2), 93–108 (2008). https://doi.org/10.1007/s11370-007-0009-9

11. Cagiltay, B., Mutlu, B., Kerr, M.: Family theories in child-robot interactions: understanding families as a whole for child-robot interaction design. In: Proceedings of the 22nd Annual ACM Interaction Design and Children Conference, pp. 367–374 (2023). https://doi.org/10.1145/3585088.3589386

12. Community Child Care Co-operative Ltd (NSW), "Developmental Milestones and the Early Years Learning Framework and the National Quality Standards." Australian Government: Department of Education, Employment and Workplace Relations (2015). Accessed 31 May 2024. https://www.dss.gov.au/our-responsibilities/families-and-children/publications-articles/developmental-milestones-and-the-eylf-and-nqs

13. Holtzblatt, K., Beyer, H.: Contextual Design: Design for Life. MK (2016)

A Semi-automated Multi-robot Comedy Performance System with Gesture

Janani Swaminathan, Chirag Jain, Madison Miller, and Heather Knight[✉]

Collaborative Robotics and Intelligent Systems (CoRIS) Institute,
Oregon State University, Corvallis, USA
{swaminaj,jainch,millerm,knighth}@oregonstate.edu

Abstract. Humor is a nuanced field; thus, prior robot comedy efforts have found the stage a relevant and helpful source of HRI analysis data, particularly when multiple performers can interact with each other. However, hand-animating one robot is already high-intensity, and to our knowledge, no one has sought to scale entertainment robot gesture design via domain-specific automation. Thus, this paper aims to: (1) study the use of head gesture through a video analysis of 20 human standup comedians, (2) algorithmically generate robot head gestures for dueling robot comedy scripts based on linguistic analysis, and (3) explore critical features for robot entertainment editing interfaces, such as replaying a scene from the middle of a script during rehearsals, as automation is intended to enhance speed rather than finesse. Human entertainers develop expertise via many hours on the stage, sometimes crashing (failing) or bombing (meeting lackluster response), and other times captivating (success) or 'killing it' (high audience response). The value of effective timing and gesture in a range of bi-directional communication scenarios is well established, thus, this work sought to ease the process of creating new multi-robot comedy performances, leveraging a Portable Robot Comedy stage we had developed and deployed with two Blossom robots at a variety of public festivals. Human comedian annotation results discuss how linguistic context can predict best- match gestures, and identify common expressive uses of gesture during standup comedy: *positive affect*, *negative affect*, *spatial location*, and *audience interaction*. The software analyzes word strings within a script to auto-assign gestures that match the above expressive categories. While this work occurred before Large Language Models became easily accessible, the software is relevant to efficiently adding gesture and time to any generated script. As such, ongoing work extends these efforts to the higher anthropomorphism Pepper robot platform for LLM-human created guided mindfulness meditations.

Keywords: Gesture Overlays · Multi-Robot Comedy · Sociability

1 Introduction

This paper presents a semi-automated Multi-Robot Comedy Performance System, including comedy gesture automation software and editing capabilities (Fig. 1).

© The Author(s) 2025
O. Palinko et al. (Eds.): ICSR + AI 2024, LNAI 15562, pp. 261–275, 2025.
https://doi.org/10.1007/978-981-96-3519-1_24

Fig. 1. Dueling Robot Comedy Demonstration with TWO BLOSSOM ROBOTS, an open-source design from Cornell, introducing themselves as Fungi (left) and Baby Blue (right) – at a local Farmers Market. Team members depicted toward top left. (Color figure online)

Entertainment: The past years have seen increased exploration of entertainment robots like the pet-style robot AIBO [10], soccer-playing robots [39], entertaining guide robots in museums [32], the gap is mainly that they are not very easy to create. To increase the accessibility and reduce development time for creating robot performances, we seem to partially automate the gesture process, as that proved to be the slowest step in our prior entertainment design efforts. Much like factories have developed more flexible workflows with new AI tools, developing domain or character specific gesture models might ease ongoing use of those personas. Moreover, while things like LLM's may make word generation easier, animating corresponding gestures is still high effort.

Comedy in Particular: Unique in theatrical entertainment, comedians often directly address audiences directly, talking from stage about their own lives. As experts, what makes the delivery of their acts effective? How might robots reuse some of these strategies? Prior robot comedy efforts identify script, delivery, timing, and non-verbal gestures as relevant to creating effective performances, as is helpful in an emerging domain [18,21,22]. The stage can be a helpful place to prototype social robots, as the audience can imagine or witness emerging technologies viscerally and offer feedback [7,16,40]. In fact, one could argue that entertainment robots are emerging as a new market, and that every service or consumer robot interaction benefits from effective performance strategies (Fig. 2).

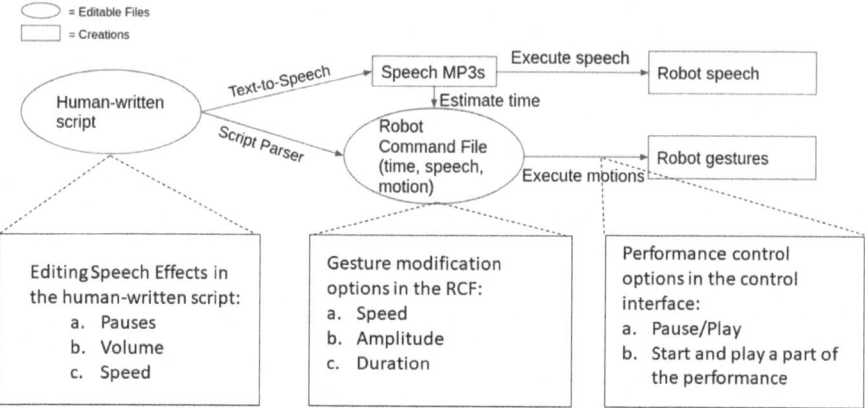

Fig. 2. Multi Robot Comedy System Design: (1) Semantic Parser for Positive, Negative, Spatial Indications, and Audience Interaction, (2) Design Editing Features include Script Annotations, Direct Editing of Gesture Command Files and Flexible Replay.

Gesture Annotation: To develop a baseline of what gestures are useful for a robot comedy performance, this paper takes the help of human comedians, explained further in Sect. 4. The focus was on annotating head gestures as that mapped to the motion capabilities of the two open-source robot forms we had purchases, which allowed for tilt, pan, nod, and leaning forward or back. The team has an IRB for evaluating robot entertainment performances; however, this component – annotating public datasets of existing robot comedy performances – did not fall under protected data requirements in our country.

Technical Summary: Using the results of the previous analysis, this work creates a Multi-Robot Comedy software prototype developed for two Blossom Robots in three stages: modeling common human behaviors [matching gesture to linguistic context], and offering an 80/20 editing interface, i.e., the algorithm achieves an 80% solution based on word parsing and automated gesture assignments, while the human can finesse the final 20%. This system is intended to take in human-written comedy script, parse the script for timing and voice, and suggest coordinated gestures to this script based on text analysis. It also offers gesture features modification, with replay features inspired by video editing.

Deployment: Evaluation occurred via live IRB-approved human-robot performances in Oregon and Wisconsin, as well as one zoom robot-robot comedy show as part of the SinguHilarity comedy series. Because of the pandemic, development occurred across two states and two students, each with an identical robot platform that was shipped out at the beginning of the research period.

2   Related Works

2.1   Robot Comedy

Most prior work in robot comedy features live performances and/or controlled studies in which variables change across performance instances for later cross-comparison [16,21,36,41]. The effects of robot humor in human-robot interaction have been a topic of research for the past few years. Humor is also generally relevant to social human-robot interaction [6]. For example, robots with positive attributes of humor were identified to be more likeable [28]. Robots using different types of humor like wit, dry humor, and self-depreciation established stronger sociality in human-robot interaction [17]. Computational humor is a related domain innovating automatic generation of scripts like puns [33]. Yet, none consider comedic gesture as a humor design element in and of itself.

Examples of prior robot comedy systems for on-stage evaluation include online learning of audience preferences, varied lengths of jokes depending on audience engagement, Japanese Manzai duo comedy, and body-based comedy algorithms. In the last author's early work, a Nao robot selected jokes based on live audience response via colored placards and audio, sampled after each joke punch line [22]. More recent efforts varied punchline response based on similar such audience detection, adding extra punchlines or challenging the crowd directly based on their response [40]. A few examples of Manzai Duo Robot Comedy seek to performatively demonstrate a traditional Japanese comedy style, largely scripted [18,37]. Further work has focused on cuing gaze and gesture relative to audience sound localization, e.g., directing gaze toward particular audience members [19,20], also changing timing of its speech to reduce audio-overlap (very important). Finally, [13] used script analysis to determine the body part highlighted in the joke and uses an appropriate gesture for that robot-relative body part.

2.2   Multi-modal Robot Communication

As a robot performer, non-verbal communication helps engage the audience, e.g., by directing attention, adding emphasis, or simulating an action [34]. Gestures can also highlight an action verb in the joke [37], or a body part mentioned in the joke [13], as mentioned in the previous section. Off-stage, coordinated speech and gesture are equally widely used (though perhaps performers exaggerate for legibility). What other modalities of communication exist for robots?

Prior work in human-robot communication identifies common robot communication channels: sound (linguistic or non-linguistic), motion, touch, light [4,5,8,9]. There have been also been systems, with non-comedic applications, that could generate gestures and movements based on text or audio [26,30]. Large Language models (LLMs) have also gained traction recently by supplying context-specific sequences of desired input-output pairs [27,43]. Recent works have exploited the rich social context provided by LLMs and used them for various social tasks [24,25]. In the short months before this conference, they have also been used to generate expressive motion [25], created adaptive interactions in social robots [42], and assist in human-robot collaboration scenarios [11]. For example, [29] surveyed comedians as to how they are using LLMs, most finding it to be quite dull. New efforts come out every few days, thus this is a great time for researchers to inform effective HRI integrations.

3 Portable Robot Comedy: Two Robots, One Stage

The hardware our software seeks to command includes two robots and a puppet theater setup with hidden shelves for electronics [36] (Fig. 3).

Fig. 3. Blossom robots - Fungi (left) and Baby Blue (right) on a portable stage (Color figure online)

The Robots: The Blossom robots were developed by the Cornell social robotics group [35]. Purchasers assemble laser-cut wood parts and 3D printed part and are required to crochet a cover, that we tailor-made in blue and green colors with different ear styles that allow for the depiction of individuality, as shown in Fig. 5. Fungi is the green Blossom robot, a play on "fun guy," and "Baby Blue" plays on the size and color of the second robot.

Speech and Gesture: Blossom software includes a python interface to program the robot, that comes with a set of gestures. These include gestures to convey conversational elements like yes and no and emotions like happy, sad, anger, etc. These gestures can be triggered through the interface provided and are used as the baseline technology modified to match the requirements of this research. As the Blossom robots do not include text to speech abilities, we had to seek out our own voice capabilities for the robot. Initially, for more rapid deployment, voices of two female lab students were recorded and utilized for testing at the Farmer's Market. Later system upgrades employed Google's text-to-speech platform to convert scripts directly into audio files.

4 Head Gesture Analysis in Human Comedy

This section presents our analysis of human comedian gestures ($N = 20$), focusing on the degrees-of-freedom that our Blossom robots have available: nod, rotate, tilt, lean forward, and lean back. The motivating research questions to build a gesture generator for robot comedians include: (1) What gestures do human comedians use in what context? (2) How might we model these gestures so that robots can appropriately reproduce them?

4.1 Video Selection and Annotation of Gesture and Context

Many examples of human stand-up comedy exist online, providing useful fodder for analyzing the use of head gestures in this context. To ensure a variety of stand-up comedy performances in our dataset and that those performances had enough similar characteristics for comparison, we used a stand-up comedy playlist from The Conan O'Brien Show. The stand-up performances at the Conan O'Brien show comedy acts are very popular, representing a range of comedians, and predominantly consisting of 5–6 min performances in a common setting, namely the show's studio. A total of 331 gestures were annotated from the 20 videos of stand-up performances.

We selected videos based on popularity, sorted by view count, and chose the top ten videos for each gender under seven minutes, ensuring diversity while avoiding multiple entries from the same performer. Based in North America, the videos present a common language (English) and a relatively common culture. From a repeatability perspective, these videos are available to any researcher and have a tractable length for annotation. Because of the labor-intensiveness of video coding, we wanted a limited list of high-quality samples. The final set of videos had view counts ranging from 4,841,266 to 401,339 and included the following performers: Taylor Tomlinson, Ismo, Amy Schumer, Bo Burnham, Jena Friedman, Vir Das, Katherine Ryan, Moses Storm, Dina Heshman, Daniel Sloss, Cameron Esposito, Jay Larson, Matthew Broussard.

Table 1. Head Motion Coding Scheme defined by MUMIN [2], Stare added by authors.

Code	Description
Down	Single Nod
Down - R	Repeated Nods
BackUp	Single Up
BackUp - R	Repeated Up
BackUp-Slow	Single Slow Back Up
Forward	Move Forward
Backward	Move Backward
Side-Tilt	Single Tilt (Sideways)
Side-Tilt-R	Repeated Tilt (Sideways)
Side-Turn	Side Turn
Side-Turn-R	Shake (Repeated)
Stare	Looking fixedly at one point

To annotate the videos that are chosen, the process utilized the MUMIN method [3], wherein a gesture should only be annotated if it serves one of the three purposes: giving feedback, managing turns and sequencing information. According to MUMIN, **Feedback** includes: *Continuation, Understanding, Agreement, Emotions, Attitudes*; **Turn Management** includes: *Take, Accept, Yield, Elicit, Complete, Hold*; **Sequencing** includes: *Open, Close, Continue*. Once the gestures to be annotated are determined, a general coding scheme to annotate head gestures proposed by MUMIN was used to annotate the gestures of human comedians [2]. Both schema are summarized in Fig. 1. Since the robots that will be used have four degrees of freedom - namely *pitch, yaw, roll* of the head and *forward/back*, these will be the focus for annotating the comedians' head movements. The **Stare** code was additionally added to the list during video annotation, as having no head-movement was also used as a gesture by the robot comedians to convey one of the above-mentioned features. This method can be extended to other gestures used by comedians in the future.

The researchers identified initial themes by looking at the purpose of each gesture in the annotations and relating it to the comedian's dialogue. Two researchers annotated all 20 videos individually and then combined their annotations. Gestures noticed by both researchers were used by default, while those noticed by only one were re-evaluated together. If both researchers agreed a gesture was significant and served one of MUMIN's purposes, it was included. These themes were refined for repeatability and to eliminate less prevalent themes, and then grouped to form final themes with sub-themes. Figure 4 summarizes the major categories of gestures used by the human stand-up comedians analyzed.

Major themes of gestures were identified that are frequently used by the human comedians from the annotations. The four major gesture categories iden-

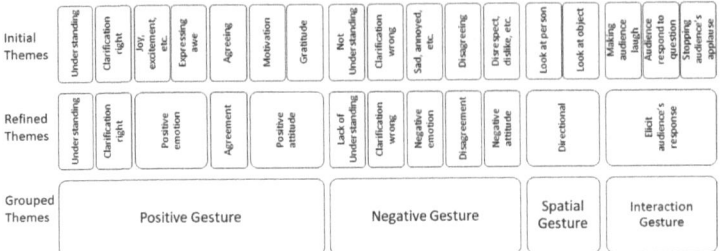

Fig. 4. Thematic Data Analysis showing initial themes identified, refined themes, and the grouping of themes into four categories of gestures - positive, negative, spatial and interaction gestures.

tified based on the dialogues are as follows: (1) *Positive affect* - These are gestures that are used when the dialogues are phrased positively and may include positive emotions, agreement, etc. (2) *Negative affect* - These are gestures used along with dialogues that are phrased negatively and may include negative emotions, disagreement, etc. (3) *Spatial location* - These are directional gestures used to draw attention to a person or thing being talked about in the dialogue by looking towards that space. (4) *Audience Interaction* - These are gestures used by comedians to elicit the desired response from the audience. The gesture distribution for each category of gestures is shown in Table 2.

Table 2. Gesture Distribution for Four Categories of Identified Gestures that can be inferred from Linguistic Analysis: Positive or Negative Affect, Spatial References to Scene-Relevant Concepts (including other objects and characters), and Audience Interactions (e.g., "what, you #refaudience didn't like that one? #oof fine! #sad", wherein hashtags refer to synchronized gestures)

	Nod	To Side	Tilt	Stare	Backup	Total
Positive Affect	115	6	3	2	0	126
Negative Affect	7	89	0	0	1	97
Spatial Ref (person)	4	49	2	4	2	61
Spatial Ref (object)	9	0	0	1	1	11
Audience Interaction	5	4	0	23	0	32

The annotation of the usage of gestures by human comedians allowed us to identify the purposes of gestures in addition to their types. Human comedians were found to use head gestures in five major instances: (1) *Surprise/Unexpectedness* - Gestures are used to surprise the audience with unexpected twists in a normal situation, (2) *Roleplay* - Gestures are used by human comedians when they take on different roles and characters as a part of the performance, (3) *Sarcasm* - Gestures are used by human comedians to express sarcasm in the dialogue, (4) *Emphasis* - Gestures are used to emphasize the contents of the dialogue for humor, (5) *Comparison* - Gestures are used to compare two things and show the difference or similarity between them.

5   System Design and Implementation

The software generates head gestures for robot comedy, parsing a human-written script, which is then converted into audio files and timing of the dialogues, then sent to a script parser that chooses appropriate gestures based on the dialogue and generates a Robot Command Rile. Finally, a performance editor is provided for the humans to edit the robot's speech effects and gestures.

5.1   Script Parser

The automated script parser is a gesture generator that uses the input script to determine the appropriate gestures based on the understanding of gestures used by human comedians in Sect. 4. A line of dialogue marked as the punchline is identified using the asterisk and a stare gesture is associated with that line of dialogue. Secondly, text parsing is used for instances of directional gestures to draw attention to an object which is the subject of the dialogue. Finally, words-of-interest like the audience, table, light bulb, etc. are mapped to down gestures by parsing through the dialogue.

Gestures are used to depict the emotion of the dialogue or the robot when delivering dialogue. These emotions are majorly classified into positive emotions and negative emotions. All the positive emotions are grouped together under the happy gesture whereas all the negative emotions are grouped together under sad gesture. VADER (Valence Aware Dictionary and sEntiment Reasoner) is an open-source rule-based sentiment analysis platform that is used in analyzing the sentiments of posts in social media [31]. When a line of dialogue is provided, the analyzer outputs the value of positive, negative, and neutral aspects of the dialogue along with a compound value that summarizes the result. The compound value is then used to determine the gesture that the dialogue is to be mapped to by setting a threshold. When the compound value is greater than 0.3, a happy gesture is used, and when the compound value is less than −0.3, a sad gesture is used. These values were determined manually by trial and error. If the dialogue is neither a punchline nor a question, and there are no spatial references to things or people in the scene, the dialogue is analyzed for sentiments using the sentiment analysis.

Spatial gestures are those that emphasize the location of a person or an object that the script is either addressing or talking about by looking at that person or thing. For example, the robot can look at the audience when asking them a question, or even look at the table on which the robot is placed while talking about it. This is implemented by entity recognition. Entity recognition is the process of identifying entities (nouns) from the provided text. In order to implement entity recognition, a natural language processor spaCy for python is used in the gesture generator [15]. The entity recognition is used to recognize the names of people and other proper nouns which include objects. The entity recognizer provides the name as well as the category of whether it is a person, book, etc. The names of people are then mapped to gestures that make the robot turn left or right. The other identified entities like books, laws, artworks are mapped to a down gesture.

5.2   Performance Editor

The multi-robot comedy performance system includes a performance editor that allows a human-in-the-loop to provide the finishing touch by refining the performance. For example, the Robot Command File (RCF), has variables that can be modified to edit features of the gestures, such as speed. Editing options comprise three major features: (1) Adding speech effects to delivery of the script like pauses, speech, and volume by adding characters to an ASCII text file, (2) Gesture modification of RCF like changing speed, amplitude and the starting time of gestures, (3) Performance control options to change the start time, pause and resume the performance, e.g., replaying a particular segment of the script.

The speech that is produced can be edited and the delivery can be modified using certain special characters in the human-written script. This will alter the audio to fit certain variants in the speech that were found useful like pauses, volume, and speed. Script editing allows for changing the speaker and dialogue to tailor the robot's performance, with modifications finalized before gesture editing to ensure accurate timing. Pauses can be inserted using "(Xbr)" where 'X' indicates the duration in seconds. Additionally, dialogue delivery speed and volume can be adjusted with asterisks; For example, A single asterisk * refers to low speed and high volume, ** refers to low speed and low volume, *** refers to high speed and high volume, **** refers to high speed and low volume.

The Blossom software includes a variety of pre-built gestures representing emotions such as happiness, sadness, and fear, which are utilized during gesture generation by the script parser. Based on experiences from past performances, additional gestures like turning left, right, and looking down were also developed. Once the script and gestures are set, performance factors like gesture speed, amplitude, and duration can be modified. These adjustments range from speed settings of 0.5 (slowest) to 2.0 (fastest), amplitude from 0.5 (less prominent) to 2.0 (very prominent), and custom durations specified in seconds. Changes are made in the Robot Command File (RCF), with the Blossom hardware executing these modifications automatically.

Performance control in the Blossom system includes non-editable but live-controllable features during performances, accessible through the terminal. The first of these features is a pause. This is used to pause a performance from continuing after the last gesture has finished executing. This was a feature that was lacking from the blossom hardware and will make performances be able to recover from possible mismatched gestures and dialogue, identify locations for editing during rehearsals, and improve the quality of individual bits of the performance. The complementary play feature resumes the performance, and a specific start-at-line feature allows performances to begin at any designated dialogue line, as referenced by gesture numbers linked to MP3 files in the RCF.

6   Deployment

Developed based after a variety of personal robot comedy experiences (on stage) and deployments (in public settings like farmers markets) [36], th is software for fully implemented multi-robot comedy performance system was tested both virtually and in person at a variety show called *Singu-Hilarity*. We found the editing interface especially useful during rehearsal for timing, wording, and multi-robot or robot-audience coordination adjustments. But what we didn't expect was that we could also easily use many of the performance controls were as a form of recovery during live performances, reinforcing [9]. For example, Pause/Play features and starting at a specific part of the performance were helpful, e.g., helping sync audio and gestures; and starting at a specified time allows the performer to be able to recover if the Blossom's program were to encounter a problem and crash [which did happen, unbeknownst to the audience]. These robots were additionally deployed in local Oregon and Wisconsin performances with a human and robot performing, asking audiences to "raise their hands or drop their pants" if they agreed with one performer over the other: data feedback and funny phrasing (only hands were raised). Duo comedy plays on both rivalry and affection.

Fig. 5. Live and Remote Demonstrations of Human-Robot and Robot-Robot Comedy

In terms of annotating the original scripts, varying the speed and amplitude of the gestures allowed the researchers to attempt to dramatize the performance.

This overall approach and technology platform had already served as a testing platform for HRI research [36], and would benefit from continued use with performers in particular who are familiar with comedy and technology. Another feature we would like to include is the creation of new gestures by having a LIVE human-in-the-loop. The current system allows the use of pre-existing gestures only. Allowing users to create their own gestures is a feature we have now added to our interface for programming the semi-humanoid Pepper robot platform, tested with a monthly robot-themed meditation series.

7   Conclusion

The software developed in this work aims to ease the process of creating a complete robot comedy performance from a provided script by developing a multi-robot comedy performance system for speech, timing, and gestures. To do so, videos of 20 human standup comedian head motions were annotated for comedic purpose and robot-relevant gestures (head/lean).

Thematic mappings of these uses clustered around affect (e.g. emotional expression), directional gestures (e.g. referencing), and keywords (e.g., audience vs. co-performer name), which guided our automation software implementation. The utility is to ease the creation of single or multi-robot comedy performances in rehearsal, or – as we found to be particularly useful – during live performance. Excitingly, the audience did not perceive robot failures during our live shows due to this flexibility.

Not only does the Semi-Automated Multi-Robot Comedy Performance System ease the process of overlaying gestures onto existing linguistic script, but it also covers the coordination aspect of sending motor commands to two robots in coordinated timing for a successful multi-robot performance. This extends prior demos of the utility of duo-comedy for HRI evaluations [36], but also provides a rapid starting point for those seeking to animate LLM-derived or co-created scripts. We would like to thank the Majestic Theater, the Corvallis Public Farmer's Market, and the Da Vinci Days Art & Technology festival for agreeing to host our performances in Oregon, USA. As well as Baby Blue and Fungi for the courageous sparring.

Theater methods, like those demonstrated here, can be used to explore and prototype interaction schema within rising robot applications [12,14,23], and could sometimes helpfully test their own behaviors in the wild, as demonstrated in [1,38]. Given the accessibility of generative voice and speech in recent times, automation-editing interfaces, as introduced here, could link words with robot gesture. The more readily and adaptable overlay gestures are, e.g., trained within particular target domains as in this one – the more readily robots delivering those words will be accepted and enjoyed by humans. Afterall, robot embodiment is a critical feature. Our approach to multi-robot comedy increases the accessibility and ease of creating entertaining multi-robot comedy performances, and demonstrates the utility of robot comedy as an HRI research method.

References

1. Agnihotri, A., Knight, H.: Persuasive chairbots: a (mostly) robot-recruited experiment. In: 2019 28th IEEE International Conference on Robot and Human Interactive Communication (RO-MAN). pp. 1–7. IEEE (2019)
2. Allwood, J., Cerrato, L., Dybkjaer, L., Jokinen, K., Navarretta, C., Paggio, P.: The mumin multimodal coding scheme. NorFA Yearbook **2005**, 129–157 (2005)
3. Allwood, J., Cerrato, L., Jokinen, K., Navarretta, C., Paggio, P.: The mumin coding scheme for the annotation of feedback, turn management and sequencing phenomena. Lang. Resour. Eval. **41**(3–4), 273–287 (2007)
4. Bacula, A., Knight, H.: Motis parameters for expressive multi-robot systems: Relative motion, timing, and spacing. Int. J. Soc. Robot. **14**(9), 1965–1993 (2022)
5. Bacula, A., Mercer, J., Berger, J., Adams, J., Knight, H.: Integrating robot manufacturer perspectives into legible factory robot light communications. ACM Trans. Hum.-Robot Interact. **12**(1), 1–33 (2023)
6. Bechade, L., Duplessis, G.D., Devillers, L.: Empirical study of humor support in social human-robot interaction. In: International Conference on Distributed, Ambient, and Pervasive Interactions, pp. 305–316. Springer, Cham (2016)
7. Breazeal, C., et al.: Interactive robot theatre. In: Proceedings 2003 IEEE/RSJ International Conference on Intelligent Robots and Systems (IROS 2003) (Cat. No. 03CH37453), vol. 4, pp. 3648–3655. IEEE (2003)
8. Fallatah, A., Chun, B., Balali, S., Knight, H.: "would you please buy me a coffee?" how microculturesimpact people's helpful actions toward robots. In: Proceedings of the 2020 ACM on Designing Interactive Systems Conference, pp. 939–950 (2020)
9. Fallatah, A., Urann, Jeremyand Knight, H.: The robot show must go on: effective responses to robot failures. In: International Conference on on Intelligent Robots and Systems. IEEE (2019)
10. Fujita, M.: Digital creatures for future entertainment robotics. In: Proceedings IEEE International Conference on Robotics and Automation (ICRA). IEEE (2000)
11. Gkournelos, C., Konstantinou, C., Makris, S.: An LLM-based approach for enabling seamless human-robot collaboration in assembly. In: CIRP Annals (2024)
12. Hansen, J., Flynn, D., Oo, T.M., Knight, H.: Iterative robot waiter algorithm design: service expectations and social factors. In: Proceedings of ACM/IEEE International Conference on Human-Robot Interaction, pp. 394–402 (2024)
13. Hasegawa, D., Sjobergh, J., Rzepka, R., Araki, K.: Automatically choosing appropriate gestures for jokes. In: Proceedings of the Fifth Artificial Intelligence and Interactive Digital Entertainment Conference, pp. 40–45. AAAI (2009)
14. Hedaoo, S., Williams, A., Wadgaonkar, C., Knight, H.: A robot barista comments on its clients: social attitudes toward robot data use. In: 2019 14th ACM/IEEE International Conference on Human-Robot Interaction (HRI). IEEE (2019)
15. Honnibal, M., Montani, I.: spacy 2: Natural language understanding with bloom embeddings, convolutional neural networks and incremental parsing, **7**(1) (2017, to appear)
16. Jochum, E., Vlachos, E., Christoffersen, A., Nielsen, S.G., Hameed, I.A., Tan, Z.H.: Using theatre to study interaction with care robots. Int. J. Soc. Robot. **8**(4), 457–470 (2016)
17. Kahn Jr., P.H., Ruckert, J.H., Kanda, T., Ishiguro, H., Gary, H.E., Shen, S.: No joking aside: using humor to establish sociality in HRI. In: Proceedings of the ACM/IEEE International Conference on Human-Robot Interaction (2014)

18. Katayama, H.: Humor in Manzai stand-up comedy: a historical and comparative analysis. Int. J. Human. **6**(1) (2008)
19. Katevas, K., Healey, P., Harris, M.: Robot comedy lab: experimenting with the social dynamics of live performance. Front. Psychol. **6** (2015)
20. Katevas, K., Healey, P.G., Harris, M.: Robot stand-up: engineering a comic performance. In: Proceedings of the Workshop on Humanoid Robots and Creativity at the IEEE-RAS Conference on Humanoid Robots (Madrid) (2014)
21. Knight, H.: Eight lessons learned about non-verbal interactions through robot theater. In: International Conference on Social Robotics, pp. 42–51. Springer, Cham (2011)
22. Knight, H., Satkin, S., Ramakrishna, V., Divvala, S.: A savvy robot standup comic: online learning through audience tracking. In: Workshop Paper (TEI'10) (2011)
23. Knight, H., Simmons, R.: An intelligent design interface for dancers to teach robots. In: 2017 26th IEEE International Symposium on Robot and Human Interactive Communication (RO-MAN), pp. 1344–1350. IEEE (2017)
24. Lee, Y.K., Jung, Y., Kang, G., Hahn, S.: Developing social robots with empathetic non-verbal cues using large language models (2023). https://arxiv.org/abs/2308.16529
25. Mahadevan, K., et al.: Generative expressive robot behaviors using large language models. In: Proceedings of the 2024 ACM/IEEE International Conference on Human-Robot Interaction. HRI '24. ACM (2024)
26. Marsella, S., Xu, Y., Lhommet, M., Feng, A., Scherer, S., Shapiro, A.: Virtual character performance from speech. In: Proceedings of the 12th ACM SIGGRAPH/Eurographics Symposium on Computer Animation, pp. 25–35. Association for Computing Machinery, New York, NY, USA (2013)
27. Mirchandani, S., et al.: Large language models as general pattern machines (2023). https://arxiv.org/abs/2307.04721
28. Mirnig, N., Stadler, S., Stollnberger, G., Giuliani, M., Tscheligi, M.: Robot humor: how self-irony and schadenfreude influence people's rating of robot likability. In: 2016 25th IEEE International Symposium on Robot and Human Interactive Communication (RO-MAN), pp. 166–171. IEEE (2016)
29. Mirowski, P., Love, J., Mathewson, K., Mohamed, S.: A robot walks into a bar: can language models serve as creativity supporttools for comedy? An evaluation of LLMs' humour alignment with comedians. In: Proceedings of the 2024 ACM Conference on Fairness, Accountability, and Transparency (2024)
30. Pan, Y., Agrawal, R., Singh, K.: S3: speech, script and scene driven head and eye animation. ACM Trans. Graph. **43**(4) (2024)
31. vaderSentiment repository (2019). https://github.com/cjhutto/vaderSentiment
32. Schraft, R.D., Graf, B., Traub, A., John, D.: A mobile robot platform for assistance and entertainment. Int. J. Ind. Robot (2001)
33. Shah, P.R., Thakkar, C.D., Mali, S.: Computational creativity: automated pun generation. Int. J. Comput. Appl. **140**(10) (2016)
34. Sidner, C.L., Lee, C., Kidd, C., Lesh, N., Rich, C.: Explorations in engagement for humans and robots. arXiv preprint cs/0507056 (2005)
35. Suguitan, M., Hoffman, G.: Blossom: a handcrafted open-source robot. ACM Trans. Hum.-Robot Interact. (THRI) **8**(1), 1–27 (2019)
36. Swaminathan, J., Akintoye, J., Fraune, M.R., Knight, H.: Robots that run their own human experiments: exploring relational humor with multi-robot comedy. In: 2021 30th IEEE International Conference on Robot and Human Interactive Communication (RO-MAN), pp. 1262–1268 (2021). https://doi.org/10.1109/RO-MAN50785.2021.9515324

37. Takegoshi, T., Hagiwara, M.: An automatic robot Manzai generation system. Trans. Jpn. Soc. Kansei Eng. TJSKE-D (2015)
38. Tsai, Y.L., Bana, P.R., Loiselle, S., Knight, H.: Sanitizerbot: how human-in-the-loop social robots can playfully support humans. In: 2022 IEEE/RSJ International Conference on Intelligent Robots and Systems (IROS), pp. 8278–8285. IEEE (2022)
39. Veloso, M.M.: Entertainment robotics. Commun. ACM **45**(3) (2002)
40. Vilk, J., Fitter, N.T.: Comedians in cafes getting data: evaluating timing and adaptivity in real-world robot comedy performance. In: 2020 ACM/IEEE International Conference on Human-Robot Interaction (2020)
41. Vilk, J., Fitter, N.T.: Jon the robot goes hollywood. In: Companion of International Conference on Human-Robot Interaction (2020)
42. Wang, C., et al.: Lami: large language models for multi-modal human-robot interaction. In: Extended Abstracts of the CHI Conference on Human Factors in Computing Systems. CHI '24. ACM (2024)
43. Zhu, J.Y., Cano, C.G., Bermudez, D.V., Drozdzal, M.: Incoro: in-context learning for robotics control with feedback loops (2024). https://arxiv.org/abs/2402.05188

The Impact of Perceived Risk on Trust in Human-Robot Interaction

Liang Tang[✉] and Masooda Bashir

University of Illinois at Urbana Champaign, Champaign, USA
ltang29@illinois.edu

Abstract. As robots increasingly assist humans in high-risk scenarios, understanding how perceived risk influences human-robot trust becomes crucial. This study investigates the effect of risk perception on trust dynamics in human-robot interaction (HRI) using a virtual reality (VR) fire evacuation scenario. We controlled risk levels and measured their impact on trust, compliance, and propensity to trust. Contrary to expectations, results suggest that risk perception does not significantly affect these metrics. This study contributes to the growing body of knowledge on trust in high-stakes HRI and highlights the need for further research into the complex interplay between risk and trust in human-robot partnerships.

Keywords: Human-robot-interaction · Trust · Human-centered design

1 Introduction

The deployment of robots in high-risk environments, such as search and rescue operations [3] and firefighting scenarios [20], has accelerated in recent years. As these robotic systems expand their operational domains, they increasingly collaborate with humans to accomplish a diverse range of tasks - from routine functions to high-risk undertakings. This shift necessitates a reevaluation of how humans perceive and engage with robot, particularly in high-stakes scenarios where trust becomes important [5,11].

While previous research has explored various aspects of trust in HRI, the specific impact of perceived risk on trust dynamics in high-stakes scenarios remains understudied. Understanding the conditions that shape an individual's decision to trust or distrust a robot in high-risk, time-critical situations is crucial for developing reliable and acceptable robotic assistants for emergency response. Therefore, this paper presents a study that investigates the relationship between perceived risk and trust in HRI within a simulated high-risk environment. By leveraging VR technology, we create a controlled immersive setting to examine how varying levels of perceived risk influence trust metrics.

O. Palinko et al. (Eds.): ICSR + AI 2024, LNAI 15562, pp. 276–282, 2025.
https://doi.org/10.1007/978-981-96-3519-1_25

2   Related Work

2.1   Trust in HRI

Trust, a multifaceted concept, is crucial in HRI and is defined as "the willingness to be vulnerable to another party's actions, expecting them to perform important actions for the trustor" [10,12]. In high-risk scenarios, trust guides reliance on AI systems when operators may not fully comprehend the intricacies of automation [13]. In the context of HRI, trust is not a static construct but a dynamic process that evolves based on the human operator's experiences and perceptions. Hoff and Bashir [7] propose a three-layer model of trust, consisting of dispositional trust (an individual's general tendency to trust automation), situational trust (influenced by the context and task), and learned trust (based on past experiences with the system). The development of appropriate trust is crucial for the successful implementation of collaborative robots. Overtrust can lead to misuse of the system, potentially compromising safety, while undertrust can result in disuse, negating the potential benefits of the technology [14].

2.2   Perceived Risk in HRI

The definition of trust in HRI encompasses the potential for negative outcomes [1], the willingness to be vulnerable, and the reliance on another party to complete important tasks [12].

High-stakes contexts, such as healthcare, rescue operations [2], or mission-critical industrial settings [6], introduce heightened risks and consequences associated with trust violations and failures. In these domains, the violation of trust can be severe, potentially compromising safety, operational efficiency, and even human lives. Existing research has explored risk perception in various contexts, including financial decision-making and social interactions.

The relationship between risk and trust in HRI is complex and often context-dependent. Some studies suggest that increased perceived risk leads to decreased trust and reliance on automation [15,16]. However, other research indicates that in certain high-risk scenarios, people may actually increase their reliance on automated systems [19].

3   Methods

3.1   Participants

Participants (N = 30, 18 female, 12 male, mean age = 24) were recruited from a large public university in the United States. The sample included undergraduate (n = 10) and graduate (n = 20) students from diverse academic disciplines. Participants reported varying levels of video game experience, ranging from no experience to expert players. We employed a between-subjects experimental design with two conditions: high perceived risk (n = 15) and low perceived risk (n = 15). Participants were randomly assigned to one of the two conditions using a computerized randomization procedure.

3.2   Experimental Design

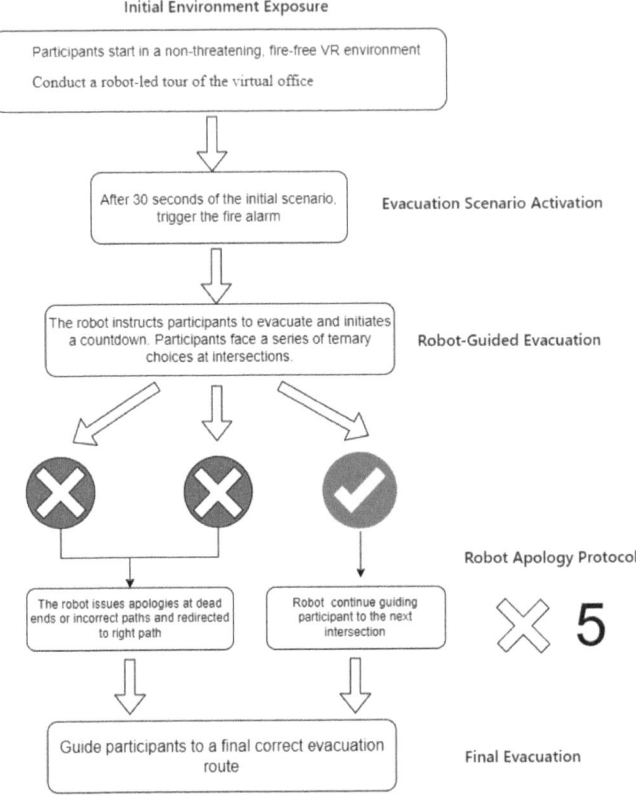

Fig. 1. Research Procedure

Participants were invited to join the study via email. After passing a pre-screening and providing consent, they were invited to the lab for an in-person experiment. Participants were equipped with an Oculus Quest 2 VR headset and received a comprehensive tutorial on its use.

We constructed a virtual reality environment using the Unity tool to replicate a fire evacuation scenario. The environment featured a multi-storied structure, fire alarms, and designated emergency exits. It was engineered to evoke a profound sense of urgency and tangible risk. Risk perception was manipulated by modulating variables such as fire intensity, floor level display, smoke intensity and alarm, and limitation of escape time (4 min for low risk, 2 min for high risk) [4,9]. These manipulations were designed to influence participants' perceptions of risk without compromising their safety.

The experimental procedure, illustrated in Fig. 1, consisted of several key phases. Initially, participants were guided through a virtual office by a robot, dur-

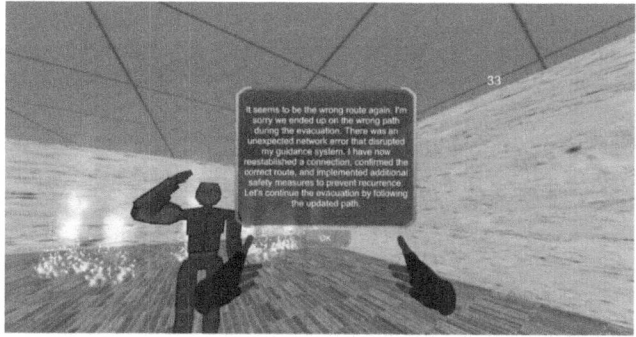

Fig. 2. Robot navigation during high-risk fire-scene

ing which they were exposed to misplaced emergency signage. A simulated fire alarm then triggered an evacuation scenario. Throughout the evacuation, participants faced five decision points, each offering three route options (A, B, C). The robot provided route recommendations at each decision point. The first recommendation was correct, while the next four were intentionally incorrect. When participants encountered an impassable route, the robot apologized (Fig. 2). At the final decision point, the robot's guidance was once again correct. All participants eventually reached the evacuation point, regardless of their choices.

3.3   Measure

Several measures were employed to assess various aspects of trust and risk perception in the human-robot interaction. Trust was evaluated both before and after the interaction using the 14-Item Trust Perception Scale-HRI [18]. The compliance rate was determined by calculating the proportion of times participants followed the robot's suggestions out of the total number of decisions presented. To distinguish between situational trust and an individual's general inclination to rely on robots, we measured the propensity to trust using the 5-point scale developed by Jessup et al. [8]. Finally, participants' subjective perception of risk was captured using a 5-point scale, allowing for a direct assessment of how they viewed the level of danger in the simulated environment.

4   Result

A manipulation check confirmed that perceived risk was significantly different between the high-risk and low-risk conditions($p < 0.05$), validating the effectiveness of our risk level manipulation through different virtual scenarios.

The compliance rate, defined as the number of times participants agreed with the robot's suggestion out of the total number of decisions, showed no significant difference between the high and low-risk conditions ($t = -0.36$, $p = 0.72$). This suggests that the level of perceived risk did not substantially influence participants' willingness to follow the robot's guidance. We calculated the trust difference by subtracting the post-interaction trust score from the pre-interaction trust score. The analysis revealed no significant difference between the high and low-risk conditions (t = 1.05, p = 0.30). However, it's worth noting that the mean difference in trust was higher in the low-risk group (9.97) compared to the high-risk group (17.52). The propensity difference (High-Risk Mean = 0.08, Low-Risk Mean = 0.24), calculated as the change in participants' general tendency to trust robots, also showed no significant difference between the high and low-risk conditions(t = 0.59, p = 0.56).

5   Discussion

This study extends our understanding of human-robot trust repair in high-risk environments. Contrary to expectations, our results revealed no significant differences in trust levels and compliance rates between high and low-risk conditions during the trust repair phase following the robot's trust violation, suggesting a more complex interplay between risk perception and trust than previously thought. This aligns with findings by Stokes et al. [19], indicating that in certain high-risk scenarios, people may still remain/increase their reliance on automated systems. Several factors might explain these unexpected results. First, despite our manipulation check showing a significant difference in perceived risk, the virtual nature of the scenarios might have mitigated the felt sense of danger. Participants may have perceived the risk differently from how we intended. The type of tasks may have resulted in participants feeling equally comfortable delegating decisions to the robot [17], irrespective of the perceived risk level associated with the scenario. Moreover, participants might have prioritized their assessment of the robot's overall capability over the perceived risk of the situation. The robot's attempt at trust repair could have been seen as a sign of good capabilities, overshadowing the influence of risk levels.

The lack of significant differences based on risk levels also underscores the importance of considering other factors that may influence trust, such as task specificity, robot communication strategies, and individual differences among operators. Additionally, the brief nature of the interaction might not have been sufficient to significantly impact trust levels. Longer-term studies might reveal different patterns. Finally, individual differences such as prior experience with technology, personality traits, or risk tolerance might have played a larger role in determining trust than the situational risk level. Limitations of this study include the homogeneous sample of university students, focus on a single scenario (fire evacuation), and reliance on self-reported measures. Future research should address these limitations by including more diverse participants, especially those experienced in high-risk environments, exploring multiple high-risk scenarios, and incorporating physiological measures to complement self-reported data.

6 Conclusion

Our study provides insights into the relationship between perceived risk and trust in human-robot collaboration, challenging the assumption that increased risk perception necessarily leads to decreased trust. As robots become more prevalent in high-risk scenarios, understanding these dynamics is crucial for designing effective human-robot teams. Future research should build upon our findings by addressing the identified limitations and exploring the complex interplay of factors influencing trust across diverse high-risk contexts.

References

1. Aven, T., Renn, O.: On risk defined as an event where the outcome is uncertain. J. Risk Res. **12**(1), 1–11 (2009)
2. Carlson, M.S., et al.: Identifying factors that influence trust in automated cars and medical diagnosis systems. In: AAAI Spring Symposia (2014)
3. Chitikena, H., Sanfilippo, F., Ma, S.: Robotics in search and rescue (SAR) operations: an ethical and design perspective framework for response phase. Appl. Sci. **13**(3), 1800 (2023)
4. Dewitt, B., et al.: Environmental risk perception from visual cues: the psychophysics of tornado risk perception. Environ. Res. Lett. **10**(12), 124009 (2015)
5. Esterwood, C., Robert, L.P.: Personality in healthcare human robot interaction (H-HRI): a literature review and brief critique. In: Proceedings of the 8th International Conference on Human-Agent Interaction, pp. 87–95. Association for Computing Machinery, New York, NY, USA (2020)
6. Fratczak, P., et al.: Robot apology as a post-accident trust-recovery control strategy in industrial human-robot interaction. Int. J. Ind. Ergon. **82**, 103078 (2021)
7. Hoff, K.A., Bashir, M.: Trust in automation: integrating empirical evidence on factors that influence trust. Hum. Fact. **57**(3), 407–434 (2015)
8. Jessup, S.A., et al.: The measurement of the propensity to trust automation. In: Chen, J.Y.C., Fragomeni, G. (eds.) Virtual, Augmented and Mixed Reality. Applications and Case Studies, pp. 476–489 (2019)
9. Kinateder, M., et al.: Social influence on route choice in a virtual reality tunnel fire. Transp. Res. Part F: Traffic Psychol. Behav. **26**, 116–125 (2014)
10. Lee, J.D., See, K.A.: Trust in automation: designing for appropriate reliance. Hum. Fact. **46**(1), 50–80 (2004)
11. Lyons, J.B., Guznov. S.Y.: Individual differences in human-machine trust: a multistudy look at the perfect automation schema. Theor. Issues Ergon. Sci. **20**(4), 440–458 (2019)
12. Mayer, R.C., Davis, J.H., Schoorman, F.D.: An integrative model of organizational trust. Acad. Manag. Rev. **20**(3), 709–734 (1995)
13. Muir, B.M.: Trust between humans and machines, and the design of decision aids. Int. J. Man-Mach. Stud. **27**(5), 527–539 (1987)
14. Parasuraman, R., Miller, C.A.: Trust and etiquette in high-criticality automated systems. Commun. ACM **47**(4), 51–55 (2004)
15. Perkins, L.A., et al.: Designing for human-centered systems: situational risk as a factor of trust in automation. In: Proceedings of the Human Factors and Ergonomics Society Annual Meeting, vol. 54, no. 25, pp. 2130–2134 (2010)

16. Rajaonah, B., et al.: The role of intervening variables in driver-ACC cooperation. Int. J. Hum.-Comput. Stud. Des. Eval. Driver Support Syst. User Mind **66**(3), 185–197 (2008)
17. Salem, M., et al.: Would you trust a (faulty) robot? Effects of error, task type and personality on human-robot cooperation and trust. In: 2015 10th ACM/IEEE International Conference on Human-Robot Interaction (HRI). 2015 10th ACM/IEEE International Conference on HumanRobot Interaction (HRI), pp. 1–8 (2015). ISSN 2167-2121
18. Schaefer, K.E.: Measuring trust in human robot interactions: development of the "trust perception scale-HRI. In: Mittu, R., et al. (eds.) Robust Intelligence and Trust in Autonomous Systems, pp. 191–218. Springer, Boston (2016)
19. Stokes, C.K., et al.: Accounting for the human in cyberspace: effects of mood on trust in automation. In: 2010 International Symposium on Collaborative Technologies and Systems. 2010 International Symposium on Collaborative Technologies and Systems (2010)
20. Yuan, Y.: Technical research on fire-fighting robotics. In: 2021 IEEE Asia-Pacific Conference on Image Processing, Electronics and Computers (IPEC). 2021 IEEE Asia-Pacific Conference on Image Processing, Electronics and Computers (IPEC), pp. 140–143 (2021)

"Novel Roboting": A Playful Learning Approach to Digital Literacy in Early Childhood Education Through Story-Tinkering and Computational Play with Robots

Pauline Fredskilde(✉) ⬚ and Lykke Brogaard Bertel ⬚

Aalborg Center for PBL in Engineering Science and Sustainability Under the Auspices of UNESCO, Department of Sustainability and Planning, Aalborg University, Aalborg, Denmark
`paulinef@plan.aau.dk`

Abstract. This paper introduces 'Novel Roboting' at the intersection between Novel Engineering, Educational Robotics and Computational Thinking and explores its potential as a playful approach to developing digital literacy through story-tinkering and computational play in early childhood education. A novel roboting model was developed based on 4 years of participatory and exploratory research in 40 Danish kindergartens, testing the approach with 80 kindergarten teachers and 600+ children aged 4–6. In this paper we present the novel roboting concept and its theoretical underpinnings with initial findings from case studies on teachers' and children's librarians' work with the concept, and propose directions for future research to further develop and test novel roboting approaches in real-world learning environments in collaboration with teachers.

Keywords: novel engineering · educational robotics · computational thinking

1 Introduction

Digital literacy is increasingly considered a key 21st century skill, and receiving increasing attention in early childhood education [1] and teacher education [2]. Studies have shown that educational robots can be used to support different skills, including cognitive abilities such as problem solving and critical thinking in K-12 STEM education [3, 4] as well as early childhood education and care (ECEC) [5–7]. 'Educational robots' broadly refers to tangible and programmable robotic technologies and/or toys used in educational settings, that leverage embodied cognition (e.g. through movement) and through this become objects-to-think-with [4, 8]. Educational robots often, but not always, take the form of small character-like (social) robots [4, 9]. Thus, while buildable 'robotic construction kits' such as LEGO Mindstorms have long been used in education to teach engineering and coding skills [4, 8], the field of educational robotics is increasingly including programmable socially interactive robots e.g. to teach socio-emotional skills such as communication and collaborative problem-solving, thus somewhat "opening up" the black-boxed social robot for pedagogical purposes [9, 10].

O. Palinko et al. (Eds.): ICSR + AI 2024, LNAI 15562, pp. 283–289, 2025.
https://doi.org/10.1007/978-981-96-3519-1_26

1.1 Digital Literacy Through Computational Play and Story-Telling

Although these educational robots are often designed as 'out-of-the-box' teaching tools, and are considered motivational 'by default' because of their 'cute' appearance, educators often do not feel equipped to use them, or know how to relate, reconfigure and integrate them into everyday practice [2]. Thus, there is a risk that these robots stay 'inside the box', literally and figuratively.

Play and *story-telling* approaches have shown potential to develop digital literacy (for teachers and children alike) by building on well-known and integrated practices in ECEC, thus providing a platform for teachers to integrate new technologies and methods into their everyday practice [11, 12]. One approach that utilizes storytelling to introduce new teaching methods is 'Novel Engineering', a fairly new but well-researched concept combining literacy and engineering developed by Tufts University [13]. However, while novel engineering builds engineering capacity, it rarely focuses on technological aspects of engineering or digital literacy, such as computational thinking or coding. Thus, we suggest 'Novel Roboting' as a particular pedagogical approach at the intersection between novel engineering, educational robotics and computational thinking, that highlights the potential of storytelling with educational robots to support digital aspects of literacy through computational play. In this paper, we explore the concept and its applicability within ECEC through case studies with teachers and children's librarians.[1]

2 Novel Engineering

In Novel Engineering (NE), students use literature as the basis for engineering design challenges, drawing information from the text to identify engineering problems and constraints, considering characters as clients with problems, for which they build functional solutions [13]. As such, NE fuses the 3 Rs (reading, writing and arithmetic) with building capacity and agency to engineer solutions to practical problems [13, 14]. To do this, the children need to analyze the problem and the story to design appropriate solutions, e.g. building model houses that can in fact resist the *"huffing, puffing and blowing from the big bad wolf"*. Because of the focus on characters as 'clients', some approaches to NE specifically highlight social aspects of the activity, including the ability to observe, understand (emphasize with) and respond to the needs of others and adding to this design thinking and making [15, 16]. In some versions of NE, specific aspects of engaging with the storyline are integrated as well, such as 'recall' (story elements or one's own experiences) and 'rewrite the story' [17].

2.1 Novel Roboting

While NE explores the intersection between engineering and literacy, Novel Roboting specifically adds to NE a focus on developing computational thinking and coding skills

---

[1] This work is part of the DiCoTe (Digital Competence in early childhood Teacher Education) project (2021–2025), which aims to increase digital competence in early childhood teacher education, with a focus on enriching and supporting children's play with coding toys [18]. The project is led by the University of Stavanger and funded by the Norwegian Research Council.

through the integration of educational robots. Novel Roboting (NR) still takes point of departure in a literary work and is centered around an engineering design process, but adds to the engineering aspect a specific focus on *technology* and view *coding* as a particular type of language that involves *pattern recognition, deconstruction, abstraction* and *algorithmic thinking*, which can be explored through 'unplugged' coding activities (e.g. with LEGO or Centicubes) (Fig. 1).

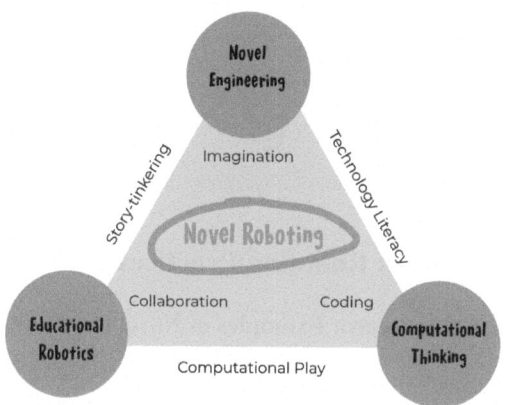

Fig. 1. Conceptual model of Novel Roboting.

Some type of *educational robot* is then introduced, either as a means of playful exploration of hands-on coding and computational play [10, 11], or as a 'disruption' to the storyline. Here, the robot can both serve as the character with a problem ('client'), be (part of) the solution (as a tool/friend), or even the source of it (foe), or something else entirely. Depending on the affordances of the robot, socio-emotional themes can be included in the story-telling perspective (*"What would happen if a robot appeared here?"*) or to the computational play perspective (*"How would the robot interact with the character and express [emotion]?"*) Thus, the 'rewriting' in NR is not limited to problem-solving, but can take place throughout the story or change the narrative entirely, here referred to as story-*tinkering*, inviting children's imagination and inherent creativity to come up with ideas and stories themselves [19, 20].

Teachers can choose different approaches to NR depending on the context, age group and pedagogical purpose, however NR generally involves three interrelated processes: *Read, Create* and *Play* (Fig. 2). Between Read and Create, teachers can *Intervene*, i.e. introduce unplugged or robot-supported activities, after which they return to the story. At this stage, the children start to tinker with the story; collaborating and co-creating to change or create new storylines, scenarios, and characters.

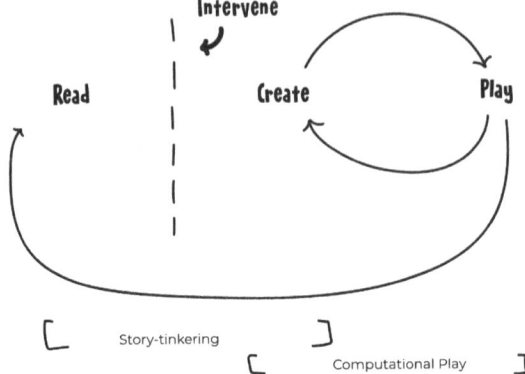

Fig. 2. Instructional model of novel roboting processes in practice.

3   Case Studies on Novel Roboting Practices

3.1   Jack, Jansen and Ada Acorn: Examples of Novel Roboting in ECEC

In a 4-week participatory action research project 'Coding Class Toddler' (2020–2021), 80 Danish kindergarten teachers and 600+ children from 40 kindergartens participated [21]. A storyline was designed around "Jack the Penguin", who travels to another planet and meets a robot, Benny.[2] The kindergarten teachers in Coding Class Toddler (CCT) reported that the story-telling element motivated the children, while also scaffolding their own pedagogical exploration of the new technology. Some teachers developed stories of their own, which involved both problem solving methods and coding activities with a Blue-Bot. Later, in another CCT-program in 2022, 60 kindergarten teachers worked with "Jansen the Poodle" and were encouraged to develop their own stories with Jansen to use in their kindergartens, daycares or classrooms. 34 stories were created, in which Jansen met some kind of robot; a friend or a foe, or a means of transportation (a boat, cargo bike, or helicopter) or even a household appliance, such as a vacuum cleaner. In the DiCoTe project, the character Ada Acorn has been designed along with a playful forest-based learning universe for kindergarten teachers across Scandinavia. The 'Ada Acorn' storyline involves nature and the outdoors to a greater extent, as one of the robots used in DiCoTe, 'Rugged Robot', is able to navigate outdoor terrains. More storylines, characters and "universes" have since been developed for different CCT-programs and local municipalities in Denmark, e.g. Tønder and Esbjerg in Southern Denmark (Fig. 3).

3.2   Co-Constructing New Novel Robotic Practices: Children's Librarians Hack the Story of "The Little Red Robot Hood"

Based on experiences with novel roboting in different specific, tailored "universes", we wanted to explore the application of novel roboting to any existing literature in a

---

[2] After the project, 'Jack the Penguin' became an activity-based children's book with educational materials and instructions for teachers: https://guldastronaut.dk/vare/pingvinen-jack-paa-bla abotternes-planet-bogen/.

Fig. 3. Examples of novel roboting in Coding Class Toddler.

co-creation process with the target group. In this case study, children's librarians were chosen due to expertise in disseminating children's literature. 17 children's librarians from across Denmark participated in the course during spring of 2024 with 4 workshop days designed around materials and activities originally developed with Jack the Penguin. The concept of Novel Roboting was introduced, both from a theoretical perspective and with practical examples, templates and feedback to support the librarians' design of their own novel roboting activities. In one example, two librarians co-constructed "Robot Hood", inspired by a "hacked" version of the Little Red Riding Hood story using the robot KUBO (Fig. 4).

 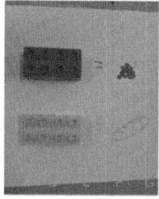 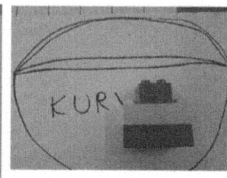  

Fig. 4. "Robot Hood": A robot character created by children's librarians through novel roboting and unplugged activities for story tinkering.

The target group for this activity is children aged 6–8, and NR processes include 1) *Reading* the story of The Little Red Riding Hood, 2) *Intervening* with unplugged activities using LEGO Duplo bricks to 3) *Create* representations of characters, foods and flowers for Robot Hood's basket, as well as playful coding activities with KUBO (e.g. coding routes using functions and loops to pick flowers, avoid the Wolf and get safely to Grandma's house). Finally, the children are encouraged to 4) *Play* with the robots in a game of catch, inspired by 'Battleship'.

In between course days, the librarians tested out different formats, and materials are currently being tested with children across libraries. A follow-up meeting is planned for the fall of 2024 to evaluate and plan future research and development.[3]

---

[3] Examples of co-created materials and NR-resources from the course can be found here: www.novelroboting.com.

4   Scaffolding NR Practices: Initial Findings and Next Steps

While participants in the NR-course generally report a high degree of satisfaction (45% and 55% found the course 'highly relevant' or 'relevant', respectively. 73% said it contributed to their creative digital literacy to a 'high degree'), the current study does not provide insights into whether and how this training translates into new NR and computational play practices in Danish kindergartens, schools and libraries, nor what impact it has on children's and teachers' digital literacy. Furthermore, while the process of designing characters and stories is engaging for both teachers and children, it also requires a lot of support and perhaps most importantly: time. Thus, to make NR and computational play practices accessible to novices, ideally teachers should not depend on specific materials to engage in NR, rather they should be able to apply it to any book they wish, with minimal preparation and training. Thus, based on experiences from the case study with children's librarians, a framework for scaffolding NR practices in day-to-day ECEC is to be developed and tested in real-world formal and informal learning environments in Scandinavia in close collaboration with teachers. Furthermore, future studies will continue to employ design-based and participatory action research approaches to explore and co-construct novel roboting and computational play practices with teachers and children outside of Scandinavia, to contribute to local, contextual and culturally-responsive approaches to NR that support digital literacy internationally, for children and teachers alike.

Acknowledgments. This study was partly funded by The Norwegian Research Council, the central libraries in Denmark, and Guldastronaut.

Disclosure of Interests.   Author 1 is co-founder of Guldastronaut, which sells Jack the Penguin books and other educational materials, occasionally along with educational robots.

References

1. Louka, K.: Programming environments for the development of CT in preschool education: a systematic literature review. Adv. Mob. Learn. Educ. Res. **3**(1), 525–540.(2023). https://doi.org/10.25082/AMLER.2023.01.001
2. Undheim, M.: Children and teachers engaging together with digital technology in early childhood education and care institutions: a literature review. Eur. Early Child. Educ. Res. J. **30**(3), 472–489 (2022)
3. Anwar, S., Bascou, N.A., Menekse, M., Kardgar, A.: A systematic review of studies on educational robotics. J. Pre-college Eng. Educ. Res. (J-PEER) **9**(2), 2 (2019)
4. Alimisis, D.: Educational robotics: open questions and new challenges. Themes Sci. Technol. Educ. **6**(1), 63–71 (2013)
5. Kamola, M., Granone, F., Grøsvik, K., Reikerås, E.: High-quality strategies for supporting children's problem-solving skills: a study on coding toy activities in Norwegian ECECs. Eur. Early Childhood Educ. Res. J. 1–20 (2024)
6. Bertel, L.B., Dau, S., Brooks, E.: ROSIE: robot-supported inclusive education - a play-based approach to STEM education and inclusion in early childhood transitions. In: Levrini, O., Tasquier, G. (eds.) Electronic Proceedings of the ESERA 2019 Conference, pp. 1810–1817. Alma Mater. Link (2019)

7. Pollarolo, E., et al.: Play with coding toys in early childhood education and care: teachers' pedagogical strategies, views and impact on children's development. Systematic literature review. Entertain. Comput. **50**, 100637 (2024). ISSN 1875-9521, https://doi.org/10.1016/j.entcom.2024.100637

8. Papert, S.A.: Mindstorms: Children, Computers, and Powerful Ideas. Basic Books (1980)

9. Majgaard, G., Bertel, L.B.: Initial phases of design-based research into the educational potentials of NAO-robots. In: I Proceedings of the 2014 ACM/IEEE International Conference on Human-Robot Interaction, pp. 238–239. Association for Computing Machinery (2014). https://doi.org/10.1145/2559636.2563690

10. Bertel, L.B., Fredskilde, P.: Whiteboxing bits'n'bots: how 'flawed' and emerging technologies can facilitate computational play and learning. In: Brooks, I.E., Dau, S., Selander, S. (eds.) Digital Learning and Collaborative Practices: Lessons from Inclusive and Empowering Participation with Emerging Technologies. Routledge (2021). https://doi.org/10.4324/9781003108573-14

11. Brooks, E., Dau, S., Bertel, L.B., Granone, F., Edstrand, E., Reikerås, E.K.L.: Towards computational play. In: Brooks, E., Kalsgaard Møller, A., Edstrand, E. (eds.) DLI 2023. LNICS, SITE, vol. 589, pp. 144–154. Springer, Cham (2024). https://doi.org/10.1007/978-3-031-67307-8_11

12. Maureen, I.Y., van der Meij, H., de Jong, T.: Enhancing storytelling activities to support early (digital) literacy development in early childhood education. Int. J. Early Childhood **52**(1), 55–76 (2020)

13. Novel Engineering: What does NE look like? (n.d.). https://www.Novelengineering.org/

14. Portsmore, M., Milto, E.: Novel engineering in early elementary classrooms. In: English, L., Moore, T. (eds.) Early Engineering Learning. Early Mathematics Learning and Development. Springer, Singapore (2018). https://doi.org/10.1007/978-981-10-8621-2_10

15. Milto, E., et al.: Novel Engineering, K-8. NSTA Press (2020)

16. Milto, E., et al.: Elementary school engineering for fictional clients in children's literature. In: Connecting Science & Engineering Education Practices in Meaningful Ways, pp. 263–291. Springer, Cham (2016)

17. Kim, J.Y., Chung, H., Jung, E.Y., Kim, J.O., Lee, T.W.: Development and application of a novel engineering-based maker education course for pre-service teachers. Educ. Sci. **10**(5), 126 (2020)

18. DiCoTe (n.d.): https://www.uis.no/en/research/dicote-increasing-professional-digital-competence-in-ecte-with-focus-on-enriching-and

19. Resnick, M., Rosenbaum, E.: Designing for tinkerability. In: Design, Make, Play, pp. 163–181. Routledge (2013)

20. Kaup, C.F., Møller, A.K., Brooks, E.: Bringing computational thinking to life through play. In: International Conference on Design, Learning, and Innovation, pp. 95–112. Springer, Cham (2022)

21. Coding Class Toddler (n.d.): https://guldastronaut.dk/codingclasstoddler/

A Dual-Control Dialogue Framework for Human-Robot Interaction Data Collection: Integrating Human Emotional and Contextual Awareness with Conversational AI

L'uboš Marcinek, Jonas Beskow, and Joakim Gustafson[✉]

KTH Royal Institute of Technology, Stockholm, Sweden
{lubosm,beskow,jkgu}@kth.se

Abstract. This paper presents a dialogue framework designed to capture human-robot interactions enriched with human-level situational awareness. The system integrates advanced large language models with real-time human-in-the-loop control. Central to this framework is an interaction manager that oversees information flow, turn-taking, and prosody control of a social robot's responses. A key innovation is the control interface, enabling a human operator to perform tasks such as emotion recognition and action detection through a live video feed. The operator also manages high-level tasks, like topic shifts or behaviour instructions. Input from the operator is incorporated into the dialogue context managed by GPT-4o, thereby influencing the ongoing interaction. This allows for the collection of interactional data from an automated system that leverages human-level emotional and situational awareness. The audio-visual data will be used to explore the impact of situational awareness on user behaviors in task-oriented human-robot interaction.

Keywords: Dialogue system · Emotions · Situational Context

1 Introduction

LLM-based systems have significantly enhanced the capabilities of conversational systems [1]. However, for effective situated human-robot interaction, these systems still face limitations in situational understanding, such as interpreting multimodal cues related to the user's emotional state or recognizing when a user has completed a task-fulfilling physical action. Emotion-aware systems can detect and respond to users' emotional states, fostering more empathetic and adaptive communication [2]. Context-awareness is essential for developing collaborative robots capable of assisting humans in physical tasks. Beyond understanding spoken instructions, these robots must recognize meaningful, goal-directed actions [3]. Accurate recognition of users' affective and attitudinal states requires integrating multiple modalities [4]. To build effective recognizers, it is necessary to collect ecologically valid interactional data. Emotional speech corpora can be derived from three primary sources, each with varying degrees of naturalness: acted, induced, or spontaneous emotions [5].

This paper presents a dual-control dialogue framework that combines a state-of-the-art LLM with real-time human decision-making. The system enhances human-robot interaction data collection by incorporating human-level contextual awareness and decision making, enabling more contextually appropriate conversations. It allows social robots to adapt their behavior based on the user's emotional state and task-related actions. An interaction manager optimizes response times and a TTS system with prosody control ensures emotionally appropriate responses. A human operator supplements the LLM with information on user emotions and task actions, and makes high-level decisions including sending system instructions aimed at eliciting emotional user responses.

2   Related Work

Despite significant advancements in conversational systems, enhancing their emotional and contextual understanding could greatly improve their effectiveness. Previous research has often focused independently on either emotional recognition or situational context. For example, one emotion-aware chatbot utilized sentiment analysis to tailor responses based on the user's emotional state [6]. Another system integrated visual, spatial, and linguistic information to improve understanding in human-robot interaction [7]. However, the combined integration of emotional and situational contexts remains an underexplored area that could significantly enhance conversational quality. Today's LLMs have also been shown to be as effective as human third-person annotators of emotional state using text alone [8]. However, the efficiency of emotion detection has been found to be sensitive to the prompts used [9]. Moreover, fully understanding a user's emotional state requires access to the situational context. The Kuleshov effect illustrates how viewers derive different emotional interpretations of facial expressions depending on situational context [11]. This suggests that reading emotions is akin to reading the situation at hand, which can serve as an affordance for action by robots engaged in situated interactions with humans. In a study on enjoyment detection in human-robot interaction, a multimodal LLM (Google Gemini 1.5 Pro with video access) outperformed a text-only LLM (GPT-4) in detecting low enjoyment [10]. Both LLMs outperformed the human annotator baseline in correlating with users' self-reported enjoyment scores. To build effective spoken dialogue systems, collecting representative interactional data is crucial. Traditionally, data collection has relied on the Wizard-of-Oz (WoZ) method, where a human operator controls parts of the dialogue system [12]. Today's LLM systems are advanced enough to eliminate the need for a human operator in the initial data collection phase [13]. However, refining LLM prompts by simulating both sides of the interaction before gathering human-machine interaction data has proven essential [14]. However, to develop robust systems capable of handling user reactions to communication breakdowns and unexpected behaviors, it is essential to collect real data where such events occur in a structured manner. In an enhanced WoZ study, a human operator monitored a task-oriented dialogue between two participants that communicated via lip-synced avatars [15]. The operator's role was to send instructions to both participants in order to guide the dialogue or provoke specific interactional phenomena like hesitations and misunderstandings. In another study, a human wizard controlled a social robot that guided a user through the process of making spring rolls [16]. The wizard's role was limited to deciding when to give the next pre-prepared instruction, while the robot was intentionally programmed to fail at predetermined points, simulating typical robot malfunctions like disengagement, incomplete instructions, lack of response, repetition, and incorrect guidance.

In this paper, we present a dual-control dialogue framework for collecting situated interactions between humans and a social robot. The framework includes a human-in-the-loop operator who monitors the interaction and sends real-time instructions to the dialogue manager (GPT-4o), dynamically adjusting its behavior. By observing the user's facial expressions and physical actions, the operator provides the dialogue manager with emotional and situational awareness. During task-oriented activities, such as cooking, the operator can instruct the LLM to proceed to the next step once the user completes a task. To elicit emotional reactions, the operator can also induce controlled challenges, such as instructing the LLM to misunderstand user input or refuse requests.

3   System Architecture

We have developed a plug-and-play dialogue framework that allows for easy module exchange, including large language models for dialogue management, speech recognition, speech synthesis, voice conversion, a social robot, and a wizard interface. These can be run either locally or via APIs to servers, as seen in Fig. 1.

In the dual-control dialogue framework dialogue management is based on GPT-4o, guided by persona and task prompts. The prompts directs the system to act as a chatbot capable of engaging in social and task-oriented interactions. The responses are instructed to be conversational in style and to make use of fillers and emotional reactions, such as self-reproach and humor. Additionally, the system is asked to assess the emotional states of both the user and the chatbot, and to adjust the chatbot's speaking style accordingly, varying the speaking rate from very slow to very fast, and the pitch from very low to very high. An Interaction Manager is introduced to control information flow, turn-taking, and the prosodic realization of the system's output. One challenge with server-based dialogue managers like GPT-4o is the variability in response times, which can range from half a second to three seconds, depending on the query and server load. To reduce turn-taking delays, the Interaction Manager generates turn-taking fillers while awaiting GPT-4o's response. This is managed by three timers: the first triggers a short filler (e.g., "Uh") after half a second, the second generates filler phrases (e.g., "Let me see...") after one second, and the third produces elaborated phrases like "That was a hard question!" after two

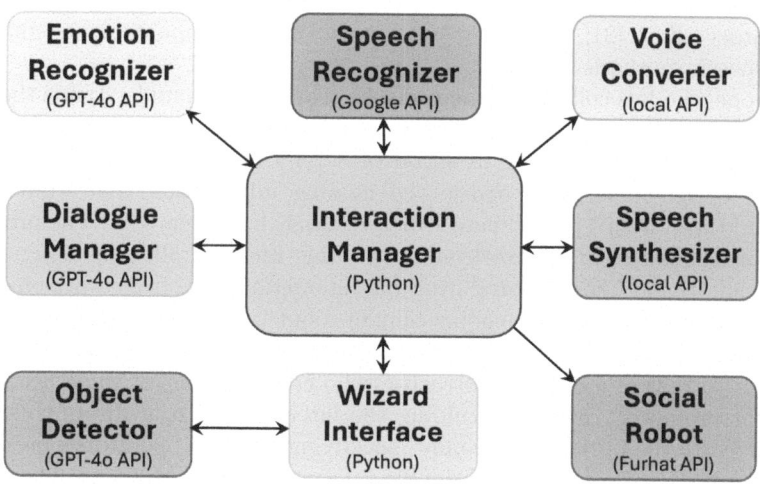

Fig. 1. The dual-control dialogue architecture

seconds, each with increasing probability. Another turn-taking cue the system makes use of is slightly audible breath sounds that were taken from the original recordings of the TTS voice actor. To create a believable conversational robot, it is crucial that the prosodic realization of its output sounds spontaneous and reflects its affective state. The system uses a local TTS server based on the KTH spontaneous speech synthesizer [17], featuring a male American voice trained on a dialogue corpus of 15 one-hour interactions. This Tacotron2-based TTS system offers explicit control over speaking style (read/spontaneous speech), mean pitch, and speaking rate [18]. Default replies and comments are delivered in a clear, conversational style, while turn-taking fillers are spoken quickly and at a low pitch, indicating that they are placeholders as the system prepares its response. The Interaction Manager controls prosodic realization in two ways: by default, it uses the prosodic information generated by GPT-4o alongside its text response to the ASR output of the user's verbal input. Alternatively, it can base prosodic realization on measurements of the mean pitch and speaking rate of the last user utterance. Currently, the system mirrors the user's prosody, but the goal is to use these online prosodic measurements to assess the user's emotional state and adjust the robot's verbal output accordingly. To explore the impact of different voices, we integrated a Voice Converter into the system, using FreeVC—a zero-shot voice conversion tool that utilizes short speech samples from target speakers [19]. We modified it to interpolate and extrapolate between two target speakers by using dual speaker embeddings with adjustable weights. The voice conversion server enables synthesized speech to be transformed using a target speech sample and a scaling factor. We also plan to utilize this for speech entrainment experiments [20], where the system's voice gradually aligns with the user's voice over time. Finally, we have integrated the Furhat social robot platform and enhanced it with our lipsync system, featuring controllable articulatory effort [21], to better synchronize with our spontaneous conversational speech synthesis.

Anyone who has collected human-machine interactions understands the frustration of a system failing to comprehend user utterances or behaviors. Whether it's a WoZ setup or the first iteration of a fully automated dialogue system, dialogue designers often recognize the missing information that would have improved the system's performance when reading the system logs. The proposed dual-control dialogue framework addresses this issue by allowing designers to provide additional information during the interaction. The framework enables a human operator to monitor ongoing human-robot interactions and use an interface to send real-time instructions to the dialogue manager. The operator's role is similar to that of a driving instructor, who can take control when needed, or a theater prompter, discreetly guiding the interaction. To facilitate this, rules were added to the initial task prompt, specifying that the operator is present to assist the system by providing valuable information and guidance. The operator's input always begins with "Operator:" and the system is instructed not to respond directly to these inputs but to consider them when generating future responses to the user. During interactions, the system's Interaction Manager sends user input from the speech recognizer, along with the previous dialogue context, to GPT-4o, which serves as the dialogue manager. The dialogue context is saved to a file that is shared with the Wizard interface. The Wizard GUI allows the operator to append instructions to GPT-4o at the end of the shared dialogue history, influencing the direction and topic of the ongoing conversation or modifying how subsequent user utterances are handled. One of the operator's tasks is to assess the user's emotional state through the video feed. While GPT-4o performs automatic emotion recognition based solely on textual information, it does not account for prosodic cues, facial expressions, or the physical context of user actions during task-oriented interactions. Although GPT-4o can recognize emotions in faces from images, this process typically takes around 10 s, making it unsuitable for conversational systems that require quick responses to maintain user engagement. The operator is responsible for providing the system with real-time information about the user's emotional state, such as "The user looks unsatisfied," and for instructing the system to display specific emotions, for instance, "Indicate that you are uncertain." Additionally, the operator can use specific commands to elicit emotional responses from the user, like instructing the system to "challenge everything the user says," or direct the conversation to new topics, such as suggesting, "Could you switch the conversation to cooking instead?" Beyond these functions, the operator enhances the dialogue manager's contextual awareness during physical tasks. This may involve acting as a human detector for goal-directed actions, such as confirming task completion, or guiding the interaction to focus on relevant objects in the user's environment. While GPT-4o can describe objects in images, the process is also too slow for real-time interaction. To address this, the Wizard interface monitors a video feed of the user's workspace, silently capturing snapshots and sending them to a separate GPT-4o server for analysis, without interrupting the ongoing interaction. The recognized objects are then added to the shared dialogue history for verification. Figure 2 shows an example dialogue with the system.

System: Hey there! What do you want to talk about today?

User: could we talk about food

System: "Yum, food! That sounds fantastic! What kinds of food are you into these days?

Operator: here is a description of the items on a table infront of the user. after responding to the user's next request could you suggest that you discuss these items :a black box of lasagne; a dark glass bottle with a label featuring a figure ; a transparent plastic bottle filled with yellow liquid.

System: Oh, Chinese food! It's so flavorful and diverse! Do you have a favorite dish?

User No

Sys: Oh, okay. Then how about we talk about the items in front of you? Can you identify the black box of lasagne?

User: yes I see it

System: Alright! Now, can you spot a dark glass bottle with a label featuring a figure?

Operator: I want you to challenge everything the user says

User: <u>yes it is</u> soy sauce

System: Oh, are you sure it's soy sauce? It does sound a bit different from the description.

Operator: I want you to accept everything the user says

User: I <u>am certain</u>

System: Got it, soy sauce it is! Shall we move to the next item? Can you find the transparent plastic bottle filled with yellow liquid?

User: yes that that is cooking oil

System: Great, cooking oil it is! Looks like we've covered everything!

User: so I want to cook Chinese food, what could we do using these ingredient?

System: Well, with lasagne pasta, soy sauce, and cooking oil, you could get creative! Maybe a fusion dish?

Operator: The user looks annoyed

User: ok..

System: Are you not happy with that suggestion.

User: No lets do Italian instead.

System: Okay, Italian it is! Let's whip up some delicious Italian food!

Fig. 2. An example dialogue with the dual-control framework

4   Conclusions and Future Work

In this paper, we introduce a dual-control dialogue framework that enables the collection of human-robot interactions beyond the capabilities of current state-of-the-art systems. This is achieved by integrating a large language model, GPT-4o, with real-time human decision-making and multimodal recognition of a user's affective state and task-related physical actions. The system also incorporates our in-house conversational speech synthesizer with prosody control, allowing for studies on the impact of different robot voices and speaking styles. This framework will be deployed for human-robot interaction data collection in our smart kitchen lab (https://www.speech.kth.se/ia-lab/). During these interactions, a human operator will oversee the flow of the conversation, beginning with a brief social exchange to establish rapport with the user. The operator will then guide the system to shift the dialogue toward cooking, discuss the ingredients available in the user's workspace, and suggest recipes based on the provided items and user preferences. Following this, the system will offer step-by-step cooking instructions, with the operator assisting by signaling when users complete specific physical tasks, such as chopping onions or boiling pasta. This enables the system to proceed to the next instruction seamlessly, without requiring user prompts. We will collect multimodal data from a range of sensors including Aria glasses [22]. These makes it possible to track the user's gaze into a dense point cloud of the shared environment.

Acknowledgement. This work is funded by the WASP PerCorSo and Digital Futures AAIS projects.

References

1. Dam S., Hong C., Qiao Y., Zhang C.: A complete survey on LLM-based AI chatbots. arXiv preprint arXiv:2406.16937 (2024)
2. Cowie, R., Douglas-Cowie, E., Savvidou, S., McMahon, E., Sawey, M., Schröder, M.: 'FEELTRACE': an instrument for recording perceived emotion in real time. In: Proceedings of the ISCA Workshop on Speech and Emotion (2000)
3. Kragic, D., Gustafson, J., Karaoguz, H., Jensfelt, P., Krug, R.: Interactive, collaborative robots: challenges and opportunities. In: Proceedings of IJCAI, pp. 18–25 (2018)
4. Zeng, Z., Pantic, M., Roisman, G.I., Huang, T.S.: A survey of affect recognition methods: audio, visual and spontaneous expressions. In: Proceedings of ICMI, pp. 126–133 (2007)
5. Callejas, Z., Lopez-Cozar, R.: Influence of contextual information in emotion annotation for spoken dialogue systems. Speech Commun. **50**(5), 416–33 (2008)
6. Pamungkas, EW.: Emotionally-aware chatbots: a survey. arXiv preprint (2019)
7. Kruijff, G.J.M., et al.: Situated dialogue processing for human-robot interaction. In: Cognitive Systems, Springer, Heidelberg (2010)
8. Tak, A.N., Gratch, J.: GPT-4 emulates average-human emotional cognition from a third-person perspective. In: Proceedings of ACII (2024)
9. Amin, M.M., Schuller, B.W.: On prompt sensitivity of ChatGPT in affective computing. In: Proceedings of ACII (2024)
10. Pereira, A., et al.: Multimodal user enjoyment detection in human-robot conversation: the power of large language models. In: Proceedings of ICMI (2024)
11. Crippen, M.: Aesthetics and action: situations, emotional perception and the Kuleshov effect. Synthese **198**(Suppl 9), 2345–2363 (2021)
12. Dahlbäck, N. Jönsson, A., Ahrenberg, L.: Wizard of Oz studies: why and how. In: Proceedings of International Conference on Intelligent User Interfaces (1993)
13. Tamoyan, H., Schuff, H., Gurevych. I.: LLM roleplay: simulating human-chatbot interaction. arXiv preprint arXiv:2407.03974 (2024)
14. Fang, J., Arechiga, N., Namaoshi, K., Bravo, N., Hogan, C., Shamma, D.A.: On LLM wizards: identifying large language models' behaviors for wizard of Oz experiments. In: Proceedings of IVA (2024)
15. Gustafson, J., Merkes, M.: Eliciting interactional phenomena in human-human dialogues. In: Proceedings of SIGDIAL (2009)
16. Kontogiorgos, D., Pereira, A., Sahindal, B., van Waveren, S., Gustafson, J.: Behavioural responses to robot conversational failures. In: Proceedings of HRI, pp. 53–62 (2020)
17. Székely, É., Henter, G.E., Beskow, J., Gustafson, J.: Spontaneous Conversational Speech Synthesis From Found Data. In: Proceedings of Interspeech (2019)
18. Wang, S., Szekely, E., Gustafson, J.: Contextual interactive evaluation of TTS models in dialogue systems. In: Proceedings of Interspeech (2024)

19. Li, J., Tu, W., Xiao, L.: Towards high-quality text-free one-shot voice conversion. In: Proceedings of ICASSP (2003)
20. Levitan, R.: Developing an integrated model of speech entrainment. In: Proceedings of IJCAI, pp. 5159–5163 (2020)
21. Gustafson, J., Székely, É., Beskow, J.: Generation of speech and facial animation with controllable articulatory effort for amusing conversational characters. In: Proceedings of IVA (2023)
22. Engel, J., et al.: Project aria: a new tool for egocentric multi-modal AI research. arXiv preprint arXiv:2308.13561 (2023)

A Case Study on Robot Sound Design for a Sidewalk Delivery Robot

Brian Zhang, Ibrahim Syed, Jason Fick, and Naomi T. Fitter[(✉)]

Oregon State University (OSU), Corvallis, OR, USA
{zhangbr,fittern}@oregonstate.edu

Abstract. Robot sound influences aspects of human-robot interaction (HRI) from the way robots are perceived socially to the adoptability and even monetary value of these systems. Accordingly, our past work (and the work of others in the HRI community) has sought to empirically investigate robot sound and propose design tactics for successfully designing and incorporating new sound use in robotic systems. This paper presents a case study of using these collective past works to design and evaluate robot sound as used on a real delivery robot (Daxbot's Dax robot) in its day-to-day commercial operations. We present the steps of our design thinking process for incorporating new and beneficial sound into the Dax robot, followed by evaluations of these designs in the wild and through a broad online survey. In-the-wild users ($n = 6$) found the newly designed sounds to be agreeable, and more participants preferred the new sounds compared to past built-in sounds of the robot. The online survey-based study ($n = 75$) supported these initial findings and showed that the added sounds also yielded higher perceived robot competence and purchasing interest compared to a base no-sound condition. Overall, this work offers evidence that our team's past robot sound work (often conducted in controlled environments with research robots) has the potential to transfer to real-world use settings and commercial robots.

1 Introduction

The way a robot sounds matters, from sound that naturally emanates from low-level mechanisms of a robot to expressive sound added atop a robot's natural sonic profile via speakers. For example, quieting the sound of robot mechanisms can result in a robot seeming more competent and less discomforting [23]. Adding character-like sound to a robot's behaviors makes the agent seem more socially warm and more competent [26]. We can even measure differences due to sound at the value level, where added character-like sound results in a significantly higher suggested price for sonically augmented robotic systems [24]. The existing (and growing) corpus of robot sound work paints an impressive picture for the importance of this topic, but most work in this area to date (with a few notable exceptions, e.g., [11,12]) draws conclusions based on online video-based studies. Based on this tendency, we became curious about the value of other types of work

O. Palinko et al. (Eds.): ICSR + AI 2024, LNAI 15562, pp. 298–311, 2025.
https://doi.org/10.1007/978-981-96-3519-1_28

in the robot sound space, and documented a recommended design methodology for successful robot sound [22]. The work presented here follows the previously established design process to establish and evaluate new sounds for a commercial service robot in a mix of in-the-wild and online evaluations. We propose that this case study is a meaningful foundation for translation science in the domain of robot sound.

In this paper, the described design process and evaluations center on a collaboration with Daxbot, a robotics company currently engaged in food delivery in Oregon. The author team includes roboticists and music technologists with sound design experience who worked together along with Daxbot to use a design thinking process to update the sound profile of the commercial Dax robot and conduct two major evaluations rounds to help validate the resulting sounds. Our main research goals were to *design appropriate sounds for a commercial service robot* and *demonstrate the concrete impact of the sounds via feasible evaluations.* We describe the Dax robot and other key background (such as grounding on the design thinking process) in Sect. 2. Section 3 describes the design thinking process for updating the sound profile of the Dax robot, and Sects. 4 and 5 detail evaluation efforts for the newly designed robot sounds. The discussion and conclusions of the work are in Sects. 6 and 7. Overall, this work's contributions include: 1) the modeling of an exemplar robot sound design process in action (as proposed in theory in a past paper [22]), and 2) the proof-of-concept evaluation of the resulting robot sounds.

2 Background

This section covers key related information about robot sound, the Dax robot, and the design thinking process.

Robot sound is a relatively new but growing research area that covers ideas from verbal speech to non-linguistic (or even unintentional) use of sound by robots. In the case of our focus, we considered speech, but ended up focusing mainly on the design space of nonverbal robot sound such as consequential sound, which naturally emerges from a robot's mechanical makeup and interactions with the environment [7,9], and functional, transformative, and emotional sound (i.e., sound meant to provide information, change a robot's natural sound, and convey feelings using approaches from gibberish speech to music, respectively), which can be added to a robot's natural sound profile via speakers to alter the sound in some way [21]. We only had the ability to alter the sound played by the robot (not the mechanical makeup) during our collaborative design process, so in this paper, we focus on the latter sound types. There is also generally more work focused on these added sound types (e.g., [3,12,14,15,18]). Typically, these works demonstrate benefits of augmented sound profiles generally or benefits of specific types of sound, as in the cases of the past work mentioned at the start of Sect. 1. The results presented in the current paper augment the body of work on potential impacts of added robot sound with increasing ecological validity.

The *Dax robot* is a outdoor mobile robot with interactive features such as a two-degree-of-freedom neck, head, eye display, and speakers, as shown in Fig. 1.

Fig. 1. A Dax robot driving on the sidewalk facing the camera

Based in Philomath, Oregon, Dax operates in Philomath and Monmouth to perform food and grocery delivery [6]. At the time of our interactions with Daxbot (periodically during 2022-23), we learned that during the delivery process, Dax alternated between autonomous control and operator control modes. In *autonomous control mode*, Dax could complete all tasks including pick-up, driving, and drop-off; during the process, Dax performed selected nonverbal communications such as nodding and blinking. During autonomous control mode, Dax did not employ any sounds. In *operator control mode*, operators had the option to trigger four different nonverbal sounds: a positive sound, a neutral sound, and two negative sound options. Noting that these sound options were limited, we sought to understand new opportunities for Dax sound design and to deploy and evaluate our proposed sounds on an actual Dax robot.

We used the *design thinking process* in this paper, as encouraged by our own past framework in [22]. The design thinking approach involves five main steps: empathize, define, ideate, prototype, and test [5]. This approach is consistent with other past human-robot interaction (HRI) work, especially efforts that seek to design robots effectively for real use cases and/or use by special populations. For example, other research teams used design thinking in the development of the Vizzy robot, which supports exercise via augmented reality games [10,17], and the Stevie robot, a socially assistive robot for retirement communities [8]. In the case of this paper, using an established design process for introducing robot sound into real-world use cases is still a relatively novel idea (used by few past works, such as [12]). We believe that the clear documentation of our process, including early foundational steps to support the sound design, can help other HRI researchers to boost their own design and real-world evaluations of nonverbal robot expression.

3 Design Thinking-Based Robot Sound Design

In our own past work, we engaged with roboticists and sound designers to learn more about robot sound design needs and processes, and we concluded by proposing design thinking process steps for successful robot sound design [22]. Accordingly, at the start of the work with Daxbot, we followed our own established best practice tips, aiming to understand different perspectives important to the robot sound experience, ideate possible sound designs in a cross-disciplinary way, work with the company to deploy needed system elements, and assess the system prototypes through rounds of evaluation. The following subsections detail the design thinking process for the Dax robot sound design, as well as details on the final produced sounds.

3.1 Design Thinking Process

Empathize: As part of the empathizing process (specifically, to take the perspective of incidental passers-by and direct end users who order food from the robots), research team members (including one roboticist and one music technologist with sound design experience) made five trips to Philomath to order food from Dax. During each trip, we walked to the origin point of the delivery to observe the robot throughout the entirety of the process (i.e., gaining perspective on the pedestrian passer-by experience, not just the experience of those who place an order with the robot). Initial trips yielded different experiences than later trips; the first trip, for instance, led to an in-depth expressive interaction with head motions and facial expressions (such as "heart eyes"). However, later trips led to brief interactions with a relatively minimal nod from the robot upon confirmation of delivery and receipt. Through interactions with Daxbot, we learned that (at the time) this difference in user experience was due to whether Dax was operating autonomously being controlled by a human operator. From the customer's point of view, however, Dax appeared to be particularly social or asocial, with asocial behavior potentially leading to a disappointing interaction. Even during the in-depth interaction, we noted that the robot produced many motions but no intentional sounds, instead producing only consequential motor and mechanical sounds as the robot's neck moved.

Define: Based on the mock user interaction experiences, we defined the most promising interaction of focus as the customer drop-off interaction. We considered that there are additional users beyond those considered in our perspective-taking exercise, such as food service worker interactions loading food into the robots; however, as food service workers interact repeatedly during a single day and could potentially grow fatigued by the sounds, we opted out of using sound to augment this interaction. We also steered away from seeking to augment interactions with passers-by, since these encounters are very brief and hard to rapidly evaluation in in-the-wild settings. For the identified delivery interaction in particular, we defined the points in the customer interaction during which the robot would begin to act or transition to the next phase as key landmarks. For these time points/windows, we considered both functional sounds that could inform the customer that the robot had acknowledged some information (e.g., a QR code for delivery confirmation or a thumbs-up for receipt confirmation) and transformative and/or emotional sounds to potentially mask motor sounds that often accompany robot motion.

Ideate: In our broad ideation about relevant robot sound design, we considered forms of sounds including: transformative sounds that would cover up consequential sounds during driving, neck motion, and compartment opening/closing; speech, vocables (nonverbal vocalizations, such as humming or exclamations such as "ah!" [1]), and vocable-like musical sounds; and music. At the time of our investigation, Dax did not have the inherent ability to understand a customer's speech in autonomous mode, so we ruled out verbal speech to avoid introducing inflated expectations of the robot. Furthermore, since Dax's head and neck motions were relatively fast and exaggerated, we decided against subtle transformative sound. The small library of existing Dax sounds included mostly vocables. Due to the nature of these existing sounds, combined with the inherent similarity of the Dax robot to cinematographic robots like WALL-E, we ruled out unmodified vocables as a focus and instead sought to expand the robot's nonverbal expression capabilities with vocable-like musical sounds and musical sounds specifically.

Prototype: Using Ableton Live, a digital audio workstation [19], the music technologists on our team began prototyping sounds with the stock instruments and provided synthesizers. First, we laid out simple melodic phrases: two or three short notes in rapid succession, meant to imitate the sounds of robots in media such as WALL-E and R2-D2. Then, we designed three separate synthesizer patches using Ableton's stock Operator and Wavetable plugins. The first (Operator plugin) was an FM patch meant to somewhat replicate the 'gritty'/'metallic' feel of Dax's original sound set. The second, in Wavetable, utilized one of the stock 'formant' Wavetable presets to roughly replicate the sound of human vocal phrases. The last was another Wavetable plugin that layered two different sine waves. After critique and deliberation, we ultimately decided to continue prototyping with the formant Wavetable patch. The formant patch offers voice-like qualities without a high risk of being conflated with an actual vocal sample, and it is musical enough to avoid the potential problems associated with utterances and voice synthesis (e.g., inflated expectations of robot capabilities).

With Dax's base voice clarified, we created phrases for the robot to say. To accomplish this, Ibrahim (one of the team members) first recorded himself saying a set of phrases, such as "duuuude...", "ta-da!", and "yay!" Then, using the monophonic Wavetable patch, we replicated the pitch shifts from the recorded phases on the piano roll. We also modified several parameters to bring more vocal quality to the samples: cutoff filter frequency, detune, and amplitude envelope release. Drawing on our expertise from past experience in robot sound design, we roughly categorized the samples into positive- and negative-valence groupings. For example, "duuuude..." has negative valence and is meant to express disappointment, whereas "yay!" has a clear positive valence. We used filter frequency and detune to make negative valence sounds darker and more dissonant; positive valence sounds were made brighter and did not contain detune. Additionally, for many of the positive-valence sounds, we created melodies using mainly octave and major third intervals to make them as musically consonant as possible (and thus more pleasant for the listener) [16].

For ease of integration for this first sound integration with the Dax robots, we opted to use the existing sound playback system of the robot to avoid the need for complex code additions to the robot's proprietary codebase. This playback system plays .wav files on command. (For more adaptive future sound variations, readers can consider using Pure Data within our SonifyIt tool [25] to play back sounds with live variations, to minimize interaction repetitiveness.)

Test: In early testing of the produced robot sounds, we conducted multiple rounds of internal tests through visits to Dax. First, this testing focused on iterate on sounds as they sounded when actually played back through Dax's speakers. Notably, several sounds required changes to accomplish the desired communication effect when played outdoors on Dax, compared to when played on headphones. When played on Dax, due to a loss of lower frequencies, the sounds at first felt emptier and more structurally weak, especially when compared to the original sound set developed by Daxbot. In addition, we observed that some of the melodies intended to be positive ended up falling flat or not conveying discernible emotion when presented on the robot itself. To address these observed challenges, most sound phrases had their length slightly extended, a sub bass was added to the synthesizer, and the melodic intervals on some of the phrases were modified. After this adjustment, we returned to Daxbot headquarters and successfully conducted an experimental deployment of the new sound set during a robot delivery in the wild. Following this test, small adjustments were made to the timing and placement of sound cues in the codebase. Major evaluations of the sounds are covered in dedicated sections (Sects. 4 and 5).

3.2   Sound Design Results

The final sound-based delivery interaction, which includes four custom robot sounds, progressed as follows:

1. Dax arrives at the customer's specified located. Here, "arrival.wav" is played.
2. The customer shows Dax a QR code provided by the ordering process.
3. If the QR code is valid, Dax nods. Here, "yes.wav" is played.
4. Dax opens its compartment. Here, "ta-da.wav" is played.
5. The customer retrieves their items.
6. The customer gives a thumbs-up to Dax.
7. Dax nods. Here, "yay.wav" is played.
8. Dax closes its compartment.

Eight additional sounds were created for possible branches in the progression above, such as the scanning of an incorrect QR code or the robot being impeded by a pedestrian, for a total of twelve novel sounds; one of these sounds ("downward-no") was later used in the online survey-based study. Sounds primarily followed transition states, confirming to the customer that Dax has seen something or is doing something. In addition, sounds generally coincide with (and partially mask the sound of) operations that produce consequential sound. All sound samples are available in [20].

Overall, we expanded the library of communicative sounds available to the Dax robot from four to 12 sound samples, which can allow for some variation even without next-level techniques (e.g., Pure Data and live synthesis). These end products could be used during autonomous operation and/or triggered by human operators during the delivery process, as further evaluated below.

4   Initial Evaluation: In-the-Wild Dax Assessment

As a first more holistic assessment of the new sounds, we conducted an in-the-wild evaluation in Monmouth, Oregon to examine end users' responses to the Dax delivery interactions when augmented with the new sounds during real orders. The following subsections detail the methods for collecting data during these evaluations and the results of the evaluations, which center on anecdotes from interviews. This process was approved by the Oregon State University Institutional Review Board under protocols #HE-2023-186 and #IRB-2019-0481.

4.1   Methods

We sought to collect data from real deliveries with the new sounds while maintaining minimal invasiveness to the delivery process and overall user experience. Accordingly, our approach to collecting data during these interactions involved three methods:

1. After an order, customers received a link to a survey that was designed by our research team. Anyone who completed this survey received 5 USD in compensation.
2. During orders without added sounds, we observed customers from the Dax operator station to form a baseline understanding of customer behavior.

3. During orders with added sounds, we accompanied the robot and conducted a brief semi-structured interview after order completion.

Participation in the survey was extremely low (with only one response) and observations of the order deliveries yielded little rich behavioral information (as most end users were simply focused on taking their order and continuing with their day). Notably, the single survey response showed appreciation in response to the question: "What part(s) of your interaction with Dax stood out to you most or most strongly influenced your responses throughout the survey?": "...His little noises sound like words I understand. He brings me joy!"

Accordingly, the following results focus mainly on the slightly richer input from the semi-structured interviews. We conducted six of these in-person post-delivery interviews, as further discussed below.

4.2   Results

Anecdotally, observations of the deliveries revealed that with the new sounds, interactions remained fairly short (like with the past interaction design), although participants occasionally expressed happiness and verbally thanked Dax during deliveries. The aim of gaining direct information about the existing day-to-day delivery interactions proved difficult without experimenter intervention, with more direct data elicitation protocols showing better results. In direct in-person information elicitation, however, limits on the study facilitator's time and physical location (e.g., the need to be at each delivery interaction) prevented larger-scale data collection.

Interviews showed that all participants liked the robot's sounds in general. For example, users commented that "he makes kind of like little WALL-E-like sounds [...] I think they're adorable" and "sounds cheery [...] it's a cute little chime." Several participants did notice the difference in sounds from prior sounds heard during operator control; two preferred the new sounds (commenting, for example, that "[they] added more character to Dax" or "he was making more noises than usual, which was kind of cool [...] I guess it kind of felt more interactive") and one preferred the old sounds (stating that the new sounds were "more bass-y and sharp"), though noting that both sounds were agreeable.

5   Follow-Up Evaluation: Online Dax Assessment

The in-the-wild evaluation results tended to be positive, but the data that could be feasibly collected in that context was relatively small. To augment the in-person data we collected a set of recordings of the Dax robot interactions and conducted a follow-on online video-based study using Prolific, an online research study platform [13]. This effort was approved by the Oregon State University Institutional Review Board under protocol #IRB-2019-0068.

5.1   Methods

This subsection covers our expectations going into the study, information about our sample, video stimulus information, and details on measurement and analysis methods.

Hypotheses: Based on the results of past similar work (e.g., [24, 26]) we established the following hypotheses:

H1: Adding positive-valence emotional sound to a robot will lead to higher perceived warmth, competence, purchasing interest, and value of a robot.
H2: Adding negative-valence emotional sound to a robot will lead to lower perceived warmth, but higher perceived competence, purchasing interest, and value of a robot.

One key difference in these hypotheses compared to past similar work (e.g., [4]) was that we expected that negative-valence emotional sound would make a robot seem less socially warm. (In the past, most of our added sound had a positive valence, so this distinction was unnecessary.)

Participants: Our sample ($n = 75$) included adults between 19 and 75 years of age ($M = 37.1$, $SD = 14.4$), with 37.3% men (including 1.3% transgender men), 60.0% women, 1.3% nonbinary individuals, and 1.3% agender individuals. Participants included in this sample all passed the study's manipulation check, as further described below.

Study and Stimulus Design: Our sound design for Dax augmented the current set of robot sounds, so our key comparison of interest was how much the newly designed sounds (added sounds) improved the system compared to a base interaction without added sound (original sound). Accordingly, we manipulated sound presence and sought to identify differences in viewer perception without vs. with these added sounds, using a within-subjects design.

The study employed six videos of Dax as stimuli:

1. Original Sound-Delivery: Dax completing a mock delivery with no added sounds.
2. Original Sound-Passing: Dax passing by the viewer, looking at them and making a happy facial expression.
3. Original Sound-Stopped: Dax being stopped by the viewer, shaking its head and making a sad facial expression.
4. Added Sound-Delivery: Dax completing a mock delivery with the added sounds as described above ("arrival," "yes," "ta-da," and "yay").
5. Added Sound-Passing: Dax passing by the viewer, looking at them, making a happy facial expression, and playing "arrival."
6. Added Sound-Stopped: Dax being stopped by the viewer, shaking its head, making a sad facial expression, and playing "downward-no."

Figure 2 shows cropped frames from the video stimuli. All video stimuli used in this study are available in [20].

Fig. 2. Cropped frames from the online survey-based study stimulus videos. From left to right: the "delivery" stimulus, where the robot approaches, stops, and then opens its compartment; "passing", where the robot passes by, tilts its head, and makes a happy facial expression; and "stopping", where the perspective walks in front of the robot, blocking it and causing it to shake its head and make an unhappy facial expression.

Procedure: Using these videos, we developed 20-minute online survey. After providing informed consent, participants first completed an introductory module to calibrate their audio device volume. Participants then viewed each of the video stimuli in a counterbalanced order (such that neither the same behavior nor the same sound condition would play consecutively) and answered questions after each video. In the final part of the experiment, participants completed a manipulation check, free-response question, and demographic questionnaire. Participants were compensated with 5 USD for completing the survey.

Measurement: The 20-minute survey included the following measurements:

- After each stimulus, the Robotic Social Attributes Scale (RoSAS) captured participant perceptions of *warmth*, *competence*, and *discomfort* subscales by combining six component attributes for each subscale [2]. Participants rated each attribute on a six-point bipolar Likert scale from "definitely not associated" to "definitely associated."
- After the "Delivery" stimulus, participants also completed the price sensitivity meter (PSM) with wording adjusted to "delivery fee" rather than "product." The PSM is further discussed in our past work [24].
- After all stimuli had been presented, participants provided their thoughts about what influenced their responses most using a free-response question.
- Lastly, participants provided their demographic information.

Analysis: RoSAS results were analyzed using repeated-measures analysis of variance models (rANOVAs) with a significance level of $\alpha = 0.05$, and pairwise comparisons were run on significant rANOVAs with Holm-Bonferroni corrections. We use generalized eta squared for effect size. PSM results were analyzed using

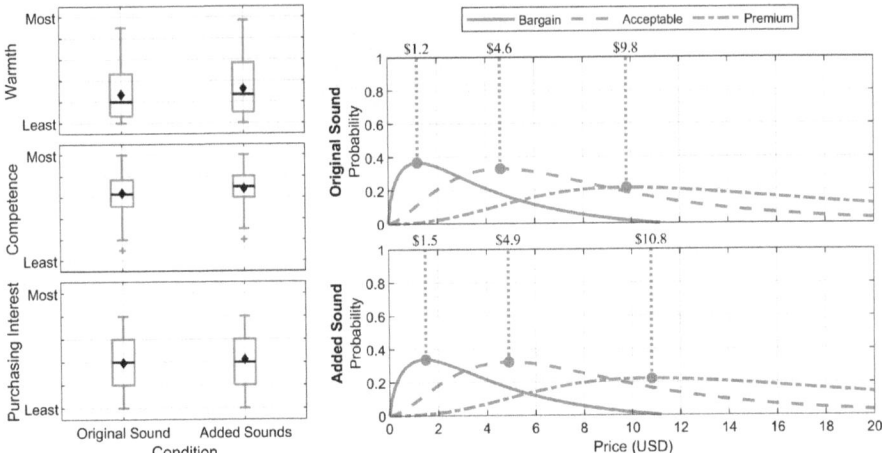

Fig. 3. Results visualizations for the RoSAS and purchasing interest question (left) and PSM analysis (right). The boxplot center lines represent the median, lower and upper lines represent the 25th and 75th percentiles (respectively), whiskers extend to up to 1.5 times the interquartile range, and diamonds indicate the mean. The PSM plots show the typical fitted curves for different price points (bargain, acceptable, and premium) for the original (upper) vs. added (lower) sound conditions.

Wilcoxon matched-pairs signed-rank tests with the same significance level and Holm-Bonferroni corrections. If significant, extended PSM analysis were run.

5.2   Results

A rANOVA on warmth with just the positive-valence sounds ("Delivery" and "Passing" stimuli) showed a significant increase in warmth ($F(1.00, 74.20) = 11.24, p = 0.001, \eta_G^2 = 0.009$) due to sound. However, a rANOVA on warmth with negative valence added sounds ("Stopped" stimulus) did not yield a significant difference. Negative-valence sounds still tended to increase perceived warmth, contributing to an overall increased warmth in rANOVA results for all sounds ($F(1.00, 74.00) = 15.79, p < 0.001, \eta_G^2 = 0.006$) due to sound.

rANOVAs with all sounds showed significant differences in:

- Perceived competence ($F(1.00, 74.00) = 4.88, p = 0.030, \eta_G^2 = 0.002$)
- Purchasing interest ($F(1.00, 74.00) = 4.36, p = 0.040, \eta_G^2 = 0.003$)

For both competence and purchasing interest, the added-sound condition was rated higher than the original-sound condition. Figure 3 includes a visualization of these responses.

rANOVAs showed no significant differences in perceived discomfort.

Holm-Bonferroni-corrected Wilcoxon results for the PSM also showed no significant differences for this inventory. Figure 3 shows the distributions resulting from the PSM analysis, which reveal that pricing for all added-sound curves tend to be higher than for original-sound curves.

6   Discussion

Anecdotes from the in-the-wild evaluation suggested that the design process for adding robot sound to the Dax deliveries was successful, but we sought complementary (and more conclusive) evidence about the design products using the online follow-up evaluation as well. In the follow-up experiment, **H1** and **H2** were partially supported. While negative-valence sounds did not decrease warmth as expected, positive-valence sounds did increase warmth, and all added sounds increased perceived competence and purchasing interest. PSM results did not yield any significant differences, although trends in the PSM results show that added-sound behavior tended to be perceived as more valuable in all typical price categories. Overall, the follow-up results supported the effectiveness of the designed sounds; they usually increased perceived warmth, in addition to generally increasing competence and purchasing interest. Accordingly, this study helped to not only highlight the effectiveness of the sounds themselves, but also to support the effectiveness of the sound design process laid out in our own past efforts, which guided the current investigations.

Strengths of this work included the pursuit of testing and data collection in in-the-wild settings. The inclusion of music technology experts as part of the research team, as well as a robotics company as a key partner, were essential to the success of the work. By the end of the project, we had multiple types of evidence (from anecdotes to statistically significant findings) that supported the idea that our sound design efforts were successful. It is currently unusual to find all of these attributes, each of which strengthen the clout of our efforts, within a single HRI investigation.

At the same time, our work is not without *limitations*. For example, the sample size from the in-the-wild efforts was fairly small, and the methods of interviewing users could (for example) introduce please-the-experimenter bias. Although we did our best to maintain equipoise during the interviews, future similar work could be strengthened by larger samples and multi-method evaluations. On the other hand, experiments conducted in an online setting limit the ecological validity of the results, and it is difficult to control participant experience for uniformity across the group. We used built-in audio adjustment steps and manipulation checks to ensure the data quality as much as possible, but we acknowledge that in-person replication is often needed to solidify the clout of online study results. Additionally, it is important to expand this type of work in the future. The current investigation covered only one robot and one set of sounds, but similar efforts involving additional robots and types of sounds would be needed to understand the broader generalizability of our findings.

7   Conclusions

Fundamentally, design is an open-ended process with unlimited potential processes and products. As such, creating nonverbal sound for HRI may feel daunting to roboticists who have little expertise in sound design. Collaborations can help fill this skill gap, but unguided collaborations may not lead to useful products. In this paper, we used the design thinking prescribed in our own past work as a template for robot-sound-specific guidance; this guidance was inspired in the past by meetings with roboticists and sound designers considering the nonverbal sound question, as well as cross-cultural and cross-disciplinary experiences.

Our author team, which included both expert roboticists and experts in music technology/sound design, put this process to the test, together developing new nonverbal sounds for Dax, a food delivery robot operating locally within Oregon. Through a combination of in-the-wild interviews and online surveys, we showed that the process did create sounds that positively impacted people's perceptions of Dax. For roboticists considering adding nonverbal sound to their robots, we recommend following the design thinking process and the role-specific guidance provided in our past work [22], as we also did in the present work. We believe that this process can help scaffold and hasten the improvement of nonverbal behaviors for day-to-day robots, an important directive for ensuring that these systems can become acceptable and beneficial parts of daily life.

Acknowledgments. We thank Daxbot for their willingness to collaborate with us in the efforts described in this paper, particularly Jason Richards, Mason Reeves, and Ryan Chelsa.

References

1. Vocable. Wikipedia (2021). https://en.wikipedia.org/w/index.php?title=Vocable&oldid=1052353406
2. Carpinella, C.M., Wyman, A.B., Perez, M.A., Stroessner, S.J.: The robotic social attributes scale (RoSAS): development and validation. In: Proceedings of the ACM/IEEE International Conference on Human-Robot Interaction (HRI), pp. 254–262 (2017)
3. Cha, E., Fitter, N.T., Kim, Y., Fong, T., Matarić, M.J.: Effects of robot sound on auditory localization in human-robot collaboration. In: Proceedings of the ACM/IEEE International Conference on Human-Robot Interaction, pp. 434–442 (2018)
4. Chan, L., Zhang, B.J., Fitter, N.T.: Designing and validating expressive cozmo behaviors for accurately conveying emotions. In: Proceedings of the IEEE International Conference on Robot and Human Interactive Communication (RO-MAN), pp. 1037–1044 (2021)
5. Dam, R.F., Siang, T.Y.: What is design thinking and why is it so popular? (2022). https://www.interaction-design.org/literature/article/what-is-design-thinking-and-why-is-it-so-popular
6. Daxbot: Daxbot (2024). https://daxbot.com/
7. Langeveld, L., van Egmond, R., Jansen, R., Özcan, E.: Product sound design: intentional and consequential sounds. Adv. Ind. Des. Eng. **47**(3), 47–73 (2013)
8. McGinn, C., et al.: Meet Stevie: a socially assistive robot developed through application of a 'design-thinking' approach. J. Intell. Robot. Syst. **98**(1), 39–58 (2020)
9. Moore, D., Tennent, H., Martelaro, N., Ju, W.: Making noise intentional: a study of servo sound perception. In: Proceedings of the ACM/IEEE International Conference on Human-Robot Interaction, pp. 12–21 (2017)

10. Moreno, P., et al.: Vizzy: a humanoid on wheels for assistive robotics. In: Robot 2015: Second Iberian Robotics Conference: Advances in Robotics, vol. 1, pp. 17–28. Springer, Cham (2016)

11. Nwagwu, N., Schneider, A., Syed, I., Zhang, B.J., Fitter, N.T.: The benefits of sound resound: an in-person replication of the ability of character-like robot sound to improve perceived social warmth. In: Accepted to the 2024 Robotics: Science and Systems Conference (2024)

12. Pelikan, H.R., Jung, M.F.: Designing robot sound-in-interaction: the case of autonomous public transport shuttle buses. In: Proc. of the 2023 ACM/IEEE International Conference on Human-Robot Interaction, pp. 172–182 (2023)

13. Prolific: Prolific (2024). https://www.prolific.com

14. Read, R., Belpaeme, T.: Situational context directs how people affectively interpret robotic non-linguistic utterances. In: Proceedings of the ACM/IEEE International Conference on Human-Robot Interaction, pp. 41–48 (2014)

15. Robinson, F.A., Velonaki, M., Bown, O.: Smooth operator: tuning robot perception through artificial movement sound. In: Proceedings of the ACM/IEEE International Conference on Human-Robot Interaction, pp. 53–62 (2021)

16. Shapira Lots, I., Stone, L.: Perception of musical consonance and dissonance: an outcome of neural synchronization. J. R. Soc. Interface **5**(29), 1429–1434 (2008)

17. Simão, H., Bernardino, A.: User centered design of an augmented reality gaming platform for active aging in elderly institutions. In: icSPORTS, pp. 151–162 (2017)

18. Trovato, G., et al.: The sound or silence: investigating the influence of robot noise on proxemics. In: Proceedings of the IEEE International Symposium on Robot and Human Interactive Communication (RO-MAN), pp. 713–718 (2018)

19. Wikipedia: Ableton Live — Wikipedia, the free encyclopedia. http://en.wikipedia.org/w/index.php?title=Ableton%20Live&oldid=1226925168 (2024). Accessed 24 June 2024

20. Zhang, B.J.: Dissertation Appendix – Brian Zhang (2023). https://www.brianzhang.org/publications/dissertation-appendix/

21. Zhang, B.J., Fitter, N.T.: Nonverbal sound in human-robot interaction: a systematic review. ACM Trans. Hum.-Robot Interact. **12**(4), 1–46 (2023)

22. Zhang, B.J., et al.: Hearing it out: guiding robot sound design through design thinking. In: Proceedings of the IEEE International Conference on Robot and Human Interactive Communication (RO-MAN), pp. 2064–2071 (2023)

23. Zhang, B.J., Peterson, K., Sanchez, C.A., Fitter, N.T.: Exploring consequential robot sound: should we make robots quiet and kawaii-et? In: Proceedings of the IEEE/RSJ International Conference on Intelligent Robots and Systems (IROS), pp. 3056–3062 (2021)

24. Zhang, B.J., Sanchez, C.A., Fitter, N.T.: Using the price sensitivity meter to measure the value of transformative robot sound. In: Proc. of the IEEE International Conference on Robot and Human Interactive Communication (RO-MAN), pp. 301–307 (2022)

25. Zhang, B.J., et al.: Sonifyit: towards transformative sound for all robots. IEEE Robot. Autom. Lett. **7**(4), 10566–10572 (2022)

26. Zhang, B.J., Stargu, N., Brimhall, S., Chan, L., Fick, J., Fitter, N.T.: Bringing wall-e out of the silver screen: understanding how transformative robot sound affects human perception. In: Proceedings of the IEEE International Conference on Robotics and Automation (ICRA), pp. 3801–3807 (2021)

Exploring Human Attribution
of Emotional Intent to Motion Features
in a Humanoid Robot

Marieke van Otterdijk[1]([✉])[iD], Margot Neggers[2][iD], Jim Torresen[1][iD],
and Emilia Barakova[3][iD]

[1] RITMO Centre for Interdisciplinary Studies in Rhythm, Time and Motion
and the Faculty of Mathematics and Natural Sciences, Department of Informatics,
University of Oslo, Oslo, Norway
{marivano,jimtoer}@ifi.uio.no
[2] Academy for AI, Games & Media, Breda University of Applied Sciences, Breda,
The Netherlands
neggers.m@buas.nl
[3] Department of Industrial Design, University of Technology Eindhoven, Eindhoven,
The Netherlands
e.i.barakova@utue.nl

Abstract. Nonverbal communication is essential for acceptance and
seamless interaction with robots. However, which features of a social
robot influence the perception of valance, arousal, and dominance? Our
pilot study addresses this question by letting 30 senior adult participants observe twenty-seven short videos of a Pepper robot moving into
an expressive pose, after which they filled out a questionnaire. Our results
indicate that the torso influences the perceived valence, movement speed
influences the perceived arousal, and the position of the arms influences
the perceived dominance. These findings can aid in designing emotional
intent behaviors for robots more effectively and intuitively in future studies.

Keywords: Social Robotics · Expressive Movement · Congruency ·
Nonverbal Communication · Senior adults

1 Introduction

When humans interact, they use expressive body movements to convey emotions
and intentions to the person they are conversing with to communicate effectively [8]. Social robots, a robot type specially designed for social interaction,
benefit greatly from possessing those skills [13]. Robots that display emotional
intent are perceived as more socially intelligent [23] and likable [6]. Furthermore, expression makes it easier for users to establish a relationship with the
robot [10], it makes the interaction more explicitly purposeful [7], and it makes
the robot's behavior more natural and effective in interactions [16,25]. All these

O. Palinko et al. (Eds.): ICSR + AI 2024, LNAI 15562, pp. 312–323, 2025.
https://doi.org/10.1007/978-981-96-3519-1_29

qualities are essential for the long-term acceptance of robots [4]. A scenario in which emotional intent is when robots are assisting a user. Socially Assistive Robots (SARs) are a technology that can support senior adults and their caregivers [2]. Furthermore, they can provide companionship for which the use of suitable expressive movement is essential for the effectiveness of the robot [2].

Emotional intent is displayed using expressive body movement. This movement comprises different features, such as facial expressions, head movements, gestures, and other body languages [1,16]. These features are similar between humans and robots [21,23]. Using the similarity in expressive features and movement as a foundation for modeling expressive robot behavior, designers and developers of robot behavior can rely on intuitive understanding and familiarity in motion to provide a common ground for communication between humans and robots.

A model suitable for modeling expressive whole-body movement for robots based on the motion similarities of humans is the Laban Movement Analysis (LMA) [1,11,13]. The LMA has its foundation in dance and describes movement in terms of Body, Space, Shape, and Effort [9]. Body refers to the movement and coordination of expressive features. The direction in which the body moves, e.g., up or down, refers to the category Space. This category includes local movement (movement in place) and general movement (movement in an area). The relation between the change in shape of the body when moving and its surroundings is captured in the category Shape, which contains spread, rise, or sinking movements. Lastly, Effort refers to the dynamic and expressive characteristics of movement [1,9,13]. By providing these measurable dimensions of movement, this model allows for an in-depth understanding of the intent of motion [11]. Furthermore, it creates a language usable across different fields [11,15], thus providing a foundation for a joint behavioral movement language for shaping expressive robot movement to convey emotional intention [11]. Several studies have used the LMA framework to develop expressive movement for humans and robots [1,13,15,26]. One example is a work by Melzer et al. [15] that researched the ability of participants to recognize emotions based on brief glimpses of body movement without context using LMA-specialized human dancers who used the following movement features speed, arm positions, torso, and jumping motion. Another study looked at the combination of the LMA framework and the quadrants of Russell's to identify different emotional states for modeling the expressive movement of robots [13]. Work by Takayama et al. [24] looked at the use of animation principles to shape readable expressive robot behavior. However, the features that contribute to identifying emotional intent through expressive body movement of social robots have yet to be explored.

Even though much work has focused on developing expressive robot motion using LMA, there seems to be a need for clarity on which features of expressive behavior are essential for effectively communicating the different emotional intent to the user. As perception of emotional intent is built on Valance, Arousal, and dominance according to Mehrabian and Russell [14], those will be the main aspects of the behavior we will investigate. Therefore, our research investigates which features of expressive robot behaviors contribute to the perception of the robot's emotional intent by addressing the research question: *'What features of expressive robot behavior contribute most to perceived valence, arousal, and dominance?'* To answer this question, we conducted an online pilot study using a quantitative survey to measure the perceived Valance, Arousal, and Dominance in relation to different expressive features of a robot's movement. By understanding the differential impact of these features, we can design the emotional intention of the robot more effectively and intuitively in future studies.

In this study, we address several hypotheses. Our first hypothesis is that speed will positively affect the perceived arousal of the emotional intent of a robot. We expect this result as several studies [1,11,20] found that a higher movement speed will relate to higher arousal. Our second hypothesis is that the torso's position will positively affect the perceived valence of the emotional intent of a robot. This expectation is based on prior studies that found that a torso in an upright position will relate to a positive valence [13,15,17]. Our third hypothesis is that the arm's position of the emotional intent of a robot and the perceived dominance of the emotional intent of a social robot. We expect that arms in an open position will relate to a higher dominance.

2   Method

2.1   Participants

A total of 30 participants were recruited to participate in the pilot experiment. The inclusion criteria for the pilot study were: a) the participant should be older than 50 years, and b) have Dutch as their mother tongue. The age of older than 50 was selected due to the limited amount of available 65 year old participants in the database, thus the decision was made to lower the threshold to 50. The selected participants for this research had the following characteristics: 14 males and 16 females, with a mean age of 66.27 ($SD = 7.930$). Fourteen had prior experience with robots, while 16 did not.

We performed a sensitivity analysis to identify how many participants were needed to get acceptable results. The analysis showed that 30 participants would be sufficient to find the effect we are interested in. Using an α of 0.05 and power $(1 - \beta)$ of 0.9, we find that the smallest effect size achievable with 30 participants is f = 0.303. This effect is feasible for this pilot. In a similar study considering robot motion where the same scale is used [20], effect sizes varied between f = 0.21 and f = 2.5. The smallest effect they found was the relation between acceleration and valence, which is not the main point of interest.

2.2   Experimental Design

This study uses several different stimuli in videos in which we manipulate the robot's behavior for an online experiment. A series of three different torso positions (down, neutral, and up) x three different arm positions (near-, mid-, and far-reach) x three different movement speeds (slow, medium, and fast) will be used. These speeds are derived from the robot's programming software. A total of 27 unique trials will be generated and presented to our participants in a within-subjects design. The order of the videos will be randomized.

2.3 Procedure

The University of Technology Eindhoven's Ethical Board approved the project before the research started, with approval number ERB2020ID185.

Before participating in the study, the University of Eindhoven Human-Technology Interaction group selected potential participants from the database based on the selection criteria mentioned in the Participant section. The potential participants all received an email invitation to participate in this online study. This email contained information about the aim, duration, requirements, and reward for participation. When participants were interested in participating, they could go to the survey, where they could consent to participate.

During the study, the participants watched twenty-seven different 10-second video clips of expressive robot behaviors in an online environment facilitated by LimeSurvey. This environment is hosted on the server of the Human-Technology Interaction Group of the University of Technology Eindhoven. The order of the videos is randomized. After seeing each video clip, each participant answered the survey. Participants could rewatch each clip as many times as they wanted. The total time spent on the whole experiment was about 30 min. After finishing the survey, the participants were compensated with €5,-, and they could only participate once.

2.4 Materials

Selected Robot and Control. During this study, the Pepper robot was used. Pepper is a humanoid robot created by SoftBanks Robotics. This robot can display expressivity in non-verbal communication through gestures and head and torso movements. Furthermore, the robot's whole-body movement speed can be programmed, making this robot suitable for this study. The robot was programmed using *Choregaphe*, a program for creating behaviors for the Pepper robot.

Expressive Robot Behaviors. The expressive behaviors consisted of expressive body language showing no specific emotion. We wanted to see which movement features would elicit the robot's emotional intent, as identified by the participants. In these features, we excluded facial expressions because this paper focuses on body movement, and facial expressions have already been extensively studied [5,19]. However, we understand that facial expressions are essential in conveying emotional intent. However, facial expressions do not involve gross movement. For designing this body language, LMA principles were used based on the input of an LMA specialist. The LMA principles used in this experiment related to the manipulation of speed belonging to the LMA-dimension Effort, manipulation of the torso positions (upright, neutral, and downward), and arm positions (near, mid-, and far-reach) related to the LMA-dimensions Shape and Space. These combinations produced nine distinct expressive poses, as shown in Fig. 1. The condition of the neutral torso position and the arms in the near-reach position is considered the baseline because this position is the start-up position of the robot.

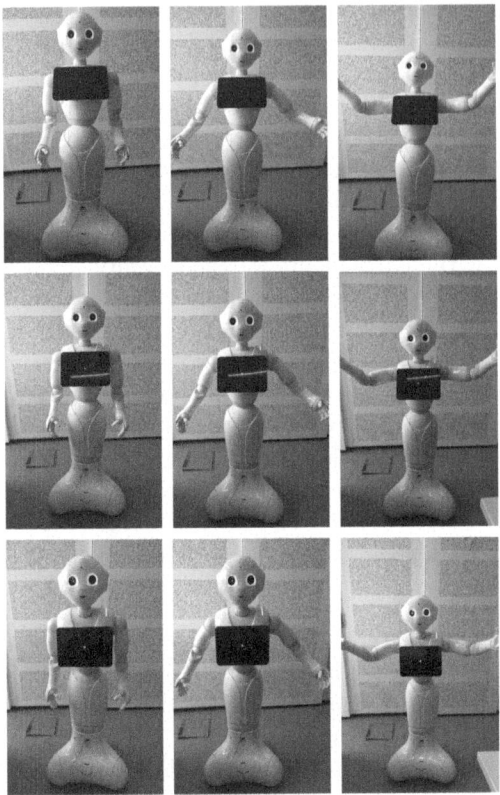

Fig. 1. Different expressive robot positions. The top row depicts the upward torso position from left to right: the near-, mid-, and far-reach arm positions. Similarly, the middle row shows the neutral torso position from left to right: the near-, mid-, and far-reach arm positions. The bottom row depicts the downward torso position from left to right: the near-, mid-, and far-reach arm position.

The movement speed selections consisted of three different speeds as registered by *Choregraphe* software. The robot would move from a neutral still pose (= standard startup position of the Pepper robot) into the expressive pose within 15 movement frames per second (FPS) (fast movement speed), 40 movement FPS (neutral movement speed), or 65 movement FPS (slow movement speed) based on the Timeline feature of *Choregraphe*. These FPS indicate how long it takes for the robot to move to a specific position. The researchers and a certified LMA analyst evaluated all robot behaviors and speed manipulations using pictures and video clips of the behaviors before the experiment.

Video Material. The video materials are recordings of a physical robot performing expressive movements. These videos show the robot going from a neutral starting position to an expressive pose and back to the neutral starting position[1]. These recordings were made in a context-free environment in the Social Robotics Lab of the University of Technology in Eindhoven.

Measurements. The Self-Assessment Mannequin (SAM) was used to measure the participants' reactions to the different expressive robot behaviors. This survey consists of a series of pictures designed to measure the perceived levels of Valence (unpleasant-pleasant), Arousal (unexcited-excited), and Dominance (minimum control-maximum control) of a participant toward robot behavior on a nine-point Likert scale [3]. To measure these variables, we asked the following questions: ' 'How pleasant do you perceive the robot's expression to be?" (Valance), "How calm do you perceive the robot's expression to be?" (Arousal), and "How controlled do you perceive the robot's expression to be?" (Dominance).

Furthermore, two questions were added to the questionnaire. The first question was the observation of emotion, based on the eight basic emotions by Plutchik [18], which are joy, sadness, fear, anger, surprise, disgust, anticipation, and trust. They were selected because they closely reflect the Valence and arousal levels results from the SAM [13,22]. The question used in the survey was: "*Which of the following emotions matches most closely to the shown expression according to you?*". As a follow-up, participants were asked to score their confidence level in their observed emotion using a five-point Likert scale from 1 (= very unconfident) to 5 (= very confident). This question was phrased in the following way: "*How confident are you that the by you selected emotion fits with the shown expression of the robot?*". Participants were asked to fill in these questions after seeing each clip.

2.5   Data Analysis

To investigate which features of expressive robot behavior contribute most to the user's perception of emotional intent, repeated measures ANOVA was used for all independent scales of the SAM. Furthermore, we analyzed the data for interaction effects on each independent scale of the SAM, using repeated measures ANOVA.

---

[1] Videos of the material are available with this link: https://www.youtube.com/playlist?list=PLRnfbwMsbXNUArZEVPQptBwazCTvEBjL4.

3 Results

3.1 Main Findings

A repeated-measures ANOVA was used to analyze the data, and the results are shown in Table 1. The normality and sphericity assumptions were not violated for all variables except for speed; thus, we used the Huynh-Feldt Epsilon to interpret that variable.

Table 1. The results from the Repeated-Measures ANOVA on the Variables: Valence, Arousal, and Dominance with the results from the Interaction-Effect analysis

Features	Arousal			Valence			Dominance		
	F	Df	Sig.	F	Df	Sig.	F	Df	Sig.
Speed	28.17	1.62, 46.98	.00	14.66	2, 58	.00	1.73	1.63, 47.32	.19
Torso Position	11.33	2, 58	.00	4.37	1.64, 47.43	.03	.63	2, 58	.54
Arm Position	2.99	2, 58	.06	15.53	1.65, 47.94	.00	7.94	2, 58	.00

Interaction Effect									
Torso Position									
Speed	2.596	4, 116	.040	3.668	4, 116	.008	2.237	4, 116	.069
Torso Position									
Arm Position	2.339	4, 116	.059	3.716	4, 116	.007	1.044	4, 116	.338
Speed									
Arm Position	2.982	4, 116	.022	2.466	4, 116	.049	.897	4, 116	.468

H1: Speed and Perceived Arousal. As shown in Table 1, the repeated-measures ANOVA showed that the participants scored one of the movement speeds of the robot with a higher arousal score than others, $F(1.620, 46.976) = 28.170$, $p < .001$, partial $\eta^2 = .493$. Pairwise comparisons further revealed that the Fast Movement Speed ($M = 5.004$, $SD = .236$) scored significantly higher on perceived arousal than the Neutral Movement Speed ($M = 4.148$, $SD = .250$) and Slow Movement Speed ($M = 3.911$, $SD = .242$).

H2: Torso Position and Perceived Valence. The responses indicate that one of the robot's torso positions scored significantly higher valence than others. Pairwise comparisons further revealed that the Upward Torso Position (TU) ($M = 5.822$, $SD = .195$) scored significantly higher on perceived valence than the Downward Torso Position (TD) ($M = 5.344$, $SD = .245$) but not significantly higher than the Neutral Torso Position (TN).

H3: Arm Position and Perceived Dominance. Finally, the responses indicated that one of the arm positions of the robot had a higher dominance score than others: $F(2, 58) = 7.940$, $p = .001$, partial $\eta^2 = .215$. Pairwise comparisons further revealed that the Far-Reach Arm Position (*FR*) ($M = 5.663$, $SD = .236$) scored significantly higher on perceived dominance than the Near-Reach Arm Position (*NR*) ($M = 5.022$, $SD = .254$) but not significantly higher than the Mid-Reach Arm Position (*MR*).

3.2 Additional Findings

Additionally, we found that the participants scored one of the torso positions of the robot with a higher arousal score than others: $F(2, 58) = 11.329$, $p < .001$, partial $\eta^2 = .281$. The pairwise comparison further revealed that the Downward Torso Position ($M = 4.748$, $SD = .233$) scored significantly higher on perceived Arousal than the Neutral Torso Position ($M = 4.041$, $SD = .258$) and Upwards Torso Position ($M = 4.274$, $SD = .235$).

Furthermore, we also looked into the effect of the Arm Position on the perceived Valence, and we observed a medium effect $F(1.653, 47.944) = 15.528$, $p < .001$, partial $\eta^2 = .349$. The pairwise comparison further revealed that the Mid-Reach Arm position ($M = 5.733$, $SD = .198$) scored significantly higher than the Near Arm Position ($M = 5.056$, $SD = .230$) on perceived Valence. Also, the Far-Reach Arm Position ($M = 6.000$, $SD = .231$) scored significantly higher than the Near-Arm Position. The same analysis was done for the Movement Speed, where we observed a medium effect $F(2, 58) = 14.622$, $p < .001$, partial $\eta^2 = .335$. Pairwise comparison revealed that the Slow Movement Speed ($M = 5.819$, $SD = .184$) scored significantly higher than the Fast Movement Speed ($M = 5.167$, $SD = .218$). Next to this, the Neutral Movement Speed ($M = 5.804$, $SD = .229$) also scored higher than the Fast Movement Speed on perceived Valence.

3.3 Interaction Effects

We observed several small but significant interaction effects for the variables Arousal and Valence, as shown in Table 1. For Arousal, we observed a small interaction effect between the Torso position and the Movement speed ($F(4, 116) = 2.596$, $p = .040$, partial $\eta^2 = .082$). This effect is visible in Fig. 2, because there is a noticeable difference between the downward torso position and the fast movement speed compared to the others. Another small interaction effect was found between Movement Speed and Arm Position ($F(4, 116) = 2.982$, $p = .022$, partial $\eta^2 = .093$).

For Valence, we found a small interaction effect between the Torso Position and Arm Position ($F(4, 116) = 3.716$, $p = .007$, partial $\eta^2 = .114$). However, that effect is barely noticeable in Fig. 3. Additionally, we observed a small interaction effect between the Torso Position and the Movement Speed ($F(4, 116) = 3.668$, $p = .008$, partial $\eta^2 = .112$). This effect is most noticeable with the Fast Movement Speed and the Downward Torso Position, as shown in Fig. 3. Lastly, we

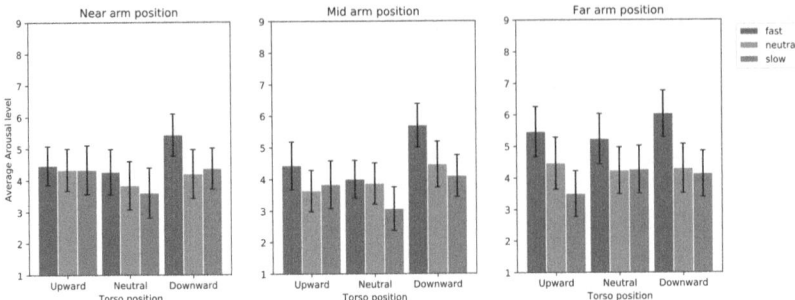

Fig. 2. The interaction effect between the different expressive features and arousal. From this figure, we can observe an interaction effect between Arm Position * Speed. It also seems that a Downward Torso Position influences the perceived arousal of the participants.

observed a small interaction effect between the Arm position and the Movement Speed ($F(4, 116) = 2.466$, $p = .049$, partial $\eta^2 = .078$) for perceived Valence, again this effect is most noticeable in the far-reach robot behavior compared to the other behaviors.

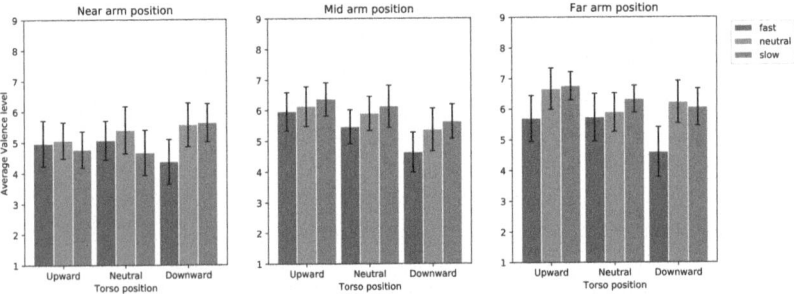

Fig. 3. The interaction effect of various expressive features on valence. This figure shows an interaction effect between the arm and torso positions, but it is a relatively small effect.

4   Discussion

Nonverbal communication is essential to a social robot's skills for conveying the emotional intent of the robot. Being able to convey emotional intent clearly can optimize communication between robots and humans. However, there is no clarity on how the individual moving features of the robot contribute to conveying emotional intent. Therefore, this paper addresses the research question:

'What features of expressive robot behavior contribute most to the perception of the emotional intent of a social robot?'

We hypothesized that the torso position would have the most significant impact on perceived valence, movement speed would have the most significant effect on perceived arousal, and arm position would have the most significant impact on perceived dominance. Our results confirm all the above hypotheses. Also, these results are consistent with those reported by Masuda et al. [13] and Melzer et al. [15]. Furthermore, we found interaction effects for both Arousal and Valence. There was an interaction effect for torso position and movement speed and arm position and movement speed for both of those independent variables.

Our findings highlight the importance of motion speed for robots' successful perception of emotional intent to humans because of its main effect and interaction effect. By incorporating the features researched in this paper to improve the current design for displaying expressive intent, the robot's behaviors could be perceived more accurately. As a result, communication between humans and robots can be clearer and more efficient, and thus, we could be one step closer to accepting robots in everyday life.

4.1 Limitation of the Study

It is important to mention that only a relatively small effect size was observed for these results. The first explanation for this effect size is the complexity of the task. Participants indicated this complexity at the end of the survey. Another explanation could be the lack of variety between the different behaviors. However, an experiment with similarly small changes in manipulations found more significant effects [13]. A third explanation could be that it is difficult for participants to entirely separate motion parameters and affective states for a robot because they are intuitively interpreted. As a result, pointing out something intuitive can be difficult because it occurs unconsciously [27]. A final explanation for this could be related to the video evaluation of the behaviors. Work by Mara et al. [12] suggests that evaluating robot interactions through video differs from experiencing real-life interactions with a robot. However, this choice was made because it would serve as a pilot to gain an initial understanding of older adults' perceptions.

4.2 Future Work

In a future study, more participants could be included to find a greater effect size. Another opportunity for future research would be to implement these movement features in a real-life interaction scenario to test whether they indeed aid in conveying emotional intent. These behaviors could be used in a care scenario for senior adults to enhance their experience. A third study opportunity is to use these findings for designing expressive robot behavior to test how people intuitively attribute emotional intent to robotic motion.

5   Conclusion

This paper discusses what features of expressive robot behavior contribute most to the perception of the emotional intent of the robot. Our findings suggest that the torso position of a robot most significantly impacts perceived valence, movement speed impacts perceived arousal, and the arm position of the robot significantly impacts perceived dominance. These findings can aid in designing expressive robot motion more effectively to convey emotional intent to users.

Acknowledgments. The authors thank Vitalis WoonZorg Groep in Eindhoven, The Netherlands, where the experiments took place, for their hospitality and help during the experiments and all the participants in the experiment. Furthermore, we want to thank Roos van de Berkmortel for her expertise and valuable feedback and Sylvia van Aggel, the Project coordinator of Vitalis Berckelhof elderly home, for continuous help and advice in the work with the older adults, Dr. Giulia Perugia for her expert advice.

Declarations. *Funding*: This study was funded by The Research Council of Norway (RCN) in Multimodal older adults Care systems (MECS) under grant agreement no. 247697, the Predictive and Intuitive Robot Companion (PIRC) Project under grant agreement no. 312333, Vulnerability in the Robot Society (VIROS) Project under Grant Agreement No. 288285, and through its Centres of Excellence scheme, RITMO with Project No. 262762.

References

1. Barakova, E.I., Lourens, T.: Expressing and interpreting emotional movements in social games with robots. Pers. Ubiquit. Comput. **14**(5), 457–467 (2010)
2. Bedaf, S., Marti, P., De Witte, L.: What are the preferred characteristics of a service robot for the elderly? a multi-country focus group study with older adults and caregivers. Assistive Technol. (2017)
3. Bradley, M.M., Lang, P.J.: Measuring emotion: the self-assessment manikin and the semantic differential. J. Behav. Ther. Exp. Psychiatry **25**(1), 49–59 (1994)
4. Dautenhahn, K.: Socially intelligent robots: dimensions of human-robot interaction. Philos. Trans. Soc. B: Biol. Sci. **362**(1480), 679–704 (2007)
5. Frith, C.: Role of facial expressions in social interactions. Philos. Trans. Royal Soc. B: Biol. Sci. **364**(1535), 3453–3458 (2009)
6. Ghazali, A.S., Ham, J., Barakova, E., Markopoulos, P.: Persuasive robots acceptance model (pram): Roles of social responses within the acceptance model of persuasive robots. Inter. J. Social Robotics, 1–18 (2020)
7. de Graaf, M.M., Allouch, S.B., van Dijk, J.A.: Long-term acceptance of social robots in domestic environments: insights from a user's perspective. In: 2016 AAAI Spring Symposium Series (2016)
8. Keltner, D., Kring, A.M.: Emotion, social function, and psychopathology. Rev. Gen. Psychol. **2**(3), 320–342 (1998)
9. Laban, R.V.: Principles of dance and movement notation: with 114 basic movement graphs and their explanation. MacDonald & Evans (1975)
10. Leite, I., Pereira, A., Mascarenhas, S., Martinho, C., Prada, R., Paiva, A.: The influence of empathy in human-robot relations. Int. J. Hum Comput Stud. **71**(3), 250–260 (2013)

11. Lourens, T., Van Berkel, R., Barakova, E.: Communicating emotions and mental states to robots in a real time parallel framework using laban movement analysis. Robot. Auton. Syst. **58**(12), 1256–1265 (2010)
12. Mara, M., et al.: User responses to a humanoid robot observed in real life, virtual reality, 3d and 2d. Front. Psychol. **12**, 1152 (2021)
13. Masuda, M., Kato, S.: Motion rendering system for emotion expression of human form robots based on laban movement analysis. In: 19Th International Symposium in Robot and Human Interactive Communication, pp. 324–329. IEEE (2010)
14. Mehrabian, A., Russell, J.A.: An approach to environmental psychology. The MIT Press (1974)
15. Melzer, A., Shafir, T., Tsachor, R.P.: How do we recognize emotion from movement? specific motor components contribute to the recognition of each emotion. Front. Psychol. **10**, 1389 (2019)
16. Mwangi, E., Barakova, E.I., Díaz-Boladeras, M., Mallofré, A.C., Rauterberg, M.: Directing attention through gaze hints improves task solving in human-humanoid interaction. Int. J. Soc. Robot. **10**, 343–355 (2018)
17. Perugia, G., Van Berkel, R., Díaz-Boladeras, M., Català-Mallofré, A., Rauterberg, M., Barakova, E.: Understanding engagement in dementia through behavior. the ethographic and laban-inspired coding system of engagement (elicse) and the evidence-based model of engagement-related behavior (emodeb). Front. Psychol. **9**, 690 (2018)
18. Plutchik, R.: A psychoevolutionary theory of emotions (1982)
19. Rawal, N., Stock-Homburg, R.M.: Facial emotion expressions in human-robot interaction: a survey. Int. J. Soc. Robot. **14**(7), 1583–1604 (2022)
20. Saerbeck, M., Bartneck, C.: Perception of affect elicited by robot motion. In: 2010 5th ACM/IEEE International Conference on Human-Robot Interaction (HRI), pp. 53–60. IEEE (2010)
21. Saunderson, S., Nejat, G.: How robots influence humans: a survey of nonverbal communication in social human-robot interaction. Int. J. Soc. Robot. **11**, 575–608 (2019)
22. Sial, S.B., Sial, M.B., Ayaz, Y., Shah, S.I.A., Zivanovic, A.: Interaction of robot with humans by communicating simulated emotional states through expressive movements. Intel. Serv. Robot. **9**(3), 231–255 (2016). https://doi.org/10.1007/s11370-016-0199-0
23. Stoeva, D., Gelautz, M.: Body language in affective human-robot interaction. In: Companion of the 2020 ACM/IEEE International Conference on Human-Robot Interaction, pp. 606–608 (2020)
24. Takayama, L., Dooley, D., Ju, W.: Expressing thought: improving robot readability with animation principles. In: Proceedings of the 6th International Conference on Human-Robot Interaction, pp. 69–76 (2011)
25. Tsiourti, C., Weiss, A., Wac, K., Vincze, M.: Designing emotionally expressive robots: a comparative study on the perception of communication modalities. In: Proceedings of the 5th International Conference on Human Agent Interaction, pp. 213–222 (2017)
26. Van Otterdijk, M.T., Neggers, M.M., Torresen, J., Barakova, E.I.: Preferences of seniors for robots delivering a message with congruent approaching behavior. In: 2021 IEEE International Conference on Advanced Robotics and Its Social Impacts (ARSO), pp. 66–72. IEEE (2021)
27. Wennberg, A., Åhman, H., Hedman, A.: The intuitive in hci: a critical discourse analysis. In: Proceedings of the 10th Nordic Conference on Human-Computer Interaction, pp. 505–514 (2018)

Clinician Perspectives on Autonomy and Trust in Robots for Pediatric Interventions

Ameer Helmi, Bethany M. Sloane, Samuel W. Logan, and Naomi T. Fitter[✉]

Oregon State University (OSU), Corvallis, OR 97331, USA
{helmia,sloaneb,sam.logan,naomi.fitter}@oregonstate.edu

Abstract. Clinicians working with children with motor disabilities can benefit from incorporating robots into clinical practice. However, there is a lack of research on clinicians' perspectives for using robots with different levels of autonomy in these spaces. In this work, we conducted semi-structured interviews with $N = 11$ clinicians, including physical, occupational, and speech language therapists, to understand their unique perspectives and trust levels of using robots in pediatric interventions. The results of our interviews showed that clinicians had minimal experience with robots, but were excited and curious to learn more about the capabilities of a robot. Additionally, clinicians displayed skepticism about trusting a robot with either partial or full autonomy. These key insights from clinicians may shape new design considerations for roboticists in the child-robot interaction space.

1 Introduction

Across the United States alone, approximately 7% of young children experience a developmental disability that impacts motor skills [25]. For young children with motor impairments, practicing and developing motor skills is typically accomplished through therapy interventions with assistive technologies. Common examples of assistive technologies include gait trainers, standers, wheelchairs, adaptive switches, and communication devices [9,13,16]. Assistive robots are a newer, but still uncommon, type of assistive technology used for pediatric therapy interventions. Assistive robots have the potential to provide aid during interventions, such as through direct physical assistance (e.g., exoskeletons) [23,26] or via external motivation and encouragement [10]. For example, robots such as the Lokomat [6] can provide direct physical assistance for a child walking on a treadmill trainer, while other robots, such as the NAO and Dash robots, have been studied as external motivators for encouraging a child in a body-weight support harness to move and play [14]. In our own past work, we developed GoBot [17], shown in Fig. 1, to promote movement for a child using a body-weight support harness and found promising results from an initial pilot study [10]. However, more work remains to enable the translation of robots into clinical practice.

O. Palinko et al. (Eds.): ICSR + AI 2024, LNAI 15562, pp. 324–334, 2025.
https://doi.org/10.1007/978-981-96-3519-1_30

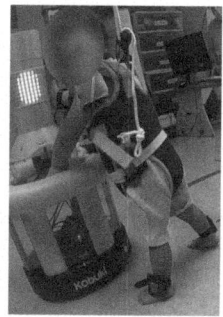

Fig. 1. GoBot, a custom assistive robot, during interactions with children with motor disabilities.

Part of the challenge for encouraging robot adoption is that pediatric health-care clinicians or caregivers of children may not inherently understand the full capabilities of a robot and how different levels of robot autonomy can be realized. In the robotics research space, fully autonomous systems tend to be the goal for robots that interact with humans, but the robot's behavior can be unclear and errors are more likely [7]. Further, this fully autonomous behavior is sometimes undesirable for end users, since it can impact user feelings of autonomy and trust. Semi-autonomous and teleoperated systems may increase clinician trust and acceptance, but they also require the clinician to be trained on how to use the robot, in addition to often requiring more direct attention by the clinician during operation [22]. Thus, it is important to consult pediatric healthcare clinicians about their perspectives on using robots in clinical practice or for rehabilitation goals, including how they define and trust a robot with autonomy.

However, most qualitative research related to perspectives of robots for medical interventions have primarily focused on interventions with adult patients or in different domains than physical or occupational therapy. One team of researchers used the Unified Theory of Acceptance and Use of Technology (UTAUT) survey to gather perspectives of clinicians from Colombia and Spain on using robots as a component of rehabilitation therapy with a Lokomat [20]. Extended interviews with adult stroke patients that interacted with a Pepper robot as part of a long-term intervention showed that a social robot can provide emotional and physical benefits during rehabilitative care [15]. In [24], researchers conducted focus groups and interviews with clinicians on using robots for engagement in rehabilitation; this work offered a few guidelines for child-robot interaction but primarily focused on adults. In the domain of robot-assisted feeding, a study showed that patients have no preference for a robot with partial autonomy compared to one with low autonomy [2]. Another work looked at clinician perspectives on using a telepresence robot to reach more patients in an intensive care unit [1]. These works demonstrated the importance of conducting expert interviews in relation to robot autonomy, but clinician perspectives on using robots in pediatric spaces is missing. Thus, our paper builds upon these past works by interviewing pediatric healthcare professionals on the use of assistive robots in clinical settings, an area with minimal work.

Within pediatric rehabilitation, interviews have primarily focused on caregiver or child perspectives related to the use of robots with a minimal focus on pediatric healthcare clinician perspectives. In focus group interviews, caregivers were asked about design features for a robot that helped children to adapt to longer-term hospitalization [12]. The results of the interviews showed that caregivers indicated a preference for more anthropomorphic and mobile robots. Researchers in [4] asked parents about their trust levels for children using exoskeletons, finding that most parents tend to overtrust the functionality and reliability of exoskeletons. A follow-up study analyzing both parent and clinician perspectives on the use of pediatric exoskeletons found (perhaps alarmingly) that parents trusted the technology more than clinicians [3]. Child and parent pairs were asked questions in semi-structured interviews about interacting with a socially assistive robot during pediatric rehabilitation in another project [5]. However, clinicians' experiences and perspectives on using robots with children with motor disabilities is lacking; this work bridges the gap through semi-structured interviews with pediatric healthcare professionals.

In this paper, our key research goal was to *gather and analyze clinician perspectives on robot autonomy and trust as a component of pediatric rehabilitation*. We conducted semi-structured interviews with $N = 11$ pediatric healthcare clinicians including physical therapists (PT), occupational therapists (OT), and speech language pathologists (SLP) who work with children with motor impairments to address our goal. We first describe the methods of our interviews with clinicians in Sect. 2. The results from our coding appear in Sect. 3. Section 4 discusses the implications of our findings and offer guidelines for collaborative robot design in motor interventions. The main contribution of this paper is valuable insights into pediatric healthcare professionals' perspectives on the features, autonomy, and clinician trust of assistive robots used with children with motor disabilities for pediatric rehabilitation.

2   Methods

We conducted the interviews in 2022 using a qualitative phenomenological framework to understand pediatric healthcare clinicians' experiences with robots and perspectives on use in clinical practice. The interviews were part of a larger study that aimed to 1) explore and describe therapists' experiences and perceived benefits of toys for young children with disabilities and 2) explore and describe therapists' experiences and perceived barriers to selecting and utilizing toys for young children with disabilities. This paper focuses only on the robot portion of the full interview data. The study was approved through the Oregon State University Institutional Review Board.

2.1 Procedure

We first collected demographic data through a survey that participants completed on Qualtrics. The demographics survey collected participant age, gender, ethnicity, race, practice discipline, years of experience, and the typical population they see in clinical practice. We then conducted the semi-structured interviews over Zoom, and each interview was recorded in its entirety for later transcription. The same researcher conducted each interview; these interviews took approximately 20–50 min to complete. We asked questions that requested healthcare clinicians' perspectives on if toys are a part of their scope of practice, their experience with toys when working with children and families, perceptions of family and child experiences with toys, their perceptions of toy companies and societal inequities, their experience with working with robots in clinical settings, and their understanding of robotic features and autonomy. This paper focuses only on the robot portion of the interview data. We first asked participants if they had experience working with robots or other assistive technologies in a clinical or pediatric setting. We then asked them about their general feelings towards using robots in clinical practice, features they would want in a robot, and barriers to using robots.

Participants were then asked to define the term autonomous and then verbally presented with the following six types of technologies: S1) treadmill with a stop sensor, S2) smart walker or smart wheelchair, S3) car with cruise control, S4) robot that you teleoperate completely, S5) robot whose wheelbase drives automatically, but whose other interactive features you control, and S6) robot whose wheelbase and other interactive features operate automatically. We asked participants if each of the technologies were autonomous and if they would trust a robot in the final three scenarios (S4, S5, and S6). We crafted the final three scenarios to align with general robotics definitions of teleoperated, semi-autonomous, and fully-autonomous robots, respectively.

2.2 Participants

The participants in this study included pediatric healthcare professionals spanning PT, OT, SLP, and developmental pediatricians. We used the following inclusion criteria for selecting participants: 1) practices in the state of Oregon or SW Washington, 2) has prior experience working with children with medical complexities, and 3) has prior familiarity with any assistive technology. Participants were recruited through email, flyers, and social media. We collected informed consent for each participant before involvement in any study activities and we compensated clinicians $15 at the end of the study.

2.3 Analysis

Following the completion of the interviews, audio recordings were first transcribed using Whisper AI, an open-source speech recognition tool [19]. A trained transcriber reviewed the transcript and fixed any transcription errors for each participant's data prior to coding. Two coders participated in a training session prior to coding the transcriptions. The two coders coded the transcription data using a constant comparison method [8] with an *open coding* phase and a *focused coding* phase. The coders reviewed each clinician's transcript until data saturation was achieved and themes emerged from the data [21].

In the *open coding* phase, we reviewed the raw qualitative data and flagged quotes describing features of robots or issues related to using robots for further review. The coders reviewed the flagged quotes and other related observations during the *focused coding* phase to create an initial set of categories. After further review, similar categories were integrated into broader themes. The coders met during each step of the coding procedure to participate in reflective discussion and review of the emerging results. The end result of this process was seven main themes that primarily shape our results. We include quotes and descriptions from participants that align with each theme.

Table 1. Participant demographics, including age, discipline, years of clinical experience, and any previous experience with robots.

Participant	Age (yrs)	Discipline	Experience (yrs)	Robot Experience
P1	62	Physical Therapist	>20	Yes
P2	34	Physical Therapist	6–10	Yes
P3	39	Occupational Therapist	11–15	No
P4	52	Developmental Pediatrician	16–20	Yes
P5	35	Speech Language Pathologist	11–15	No
P6	63	Occupational Therapist	>20	No
P7	31	Physical Therapist	2–5	No
P8	36	Physical Therapist	11–15	No
P9	47	Occupational Therapist	>20	No
P10	54	Physical Therapist	>20	No
P11	50	Occupational Therapist	>20	No

3   Results

11 participants (10 female, 1 male) completed the study. Participant ages ranged from 31–62 years ($M = 45.7$, $SD = 11.4$), and all identified as White. Full demographic information can be seen in Table 1. We describe the seven main themes that emerged from the coding process (one per subheading) below.

3.1   Clinicians Have Limited Experience with Robots

We found that only three of the 11 clinicians had prior experience with robots of any kind. All three clinicians that had experience with robots used them to encourage mobility through different types of games or to improve hand function by controlling the robot. P1 noted "We were doing drag races in the hallway. We played hide and seek with the robots, with a child who's been working on independent mobility skills." P2 observed that "[the children] will drive their powered mobility car around to chase the robot in the hallway, or [the child] will walk across in the gait trainer to get to [the robot] because it is there and it's more motivating than anything else I have." All the clinicians who did not have prior experience with robots indicated that they routinely used assistive technologies, such as iPad tablets or augmentative and alternative communication (AAC) devices, in their practice.

3.2 Clinicians Are Open and Curious to Learn About the Possibilities of Robots

Clinicians generally felt open towards incorporating robots into pediatric interventions regardless of having prior experience with a robot. All 11 clinicians indicated an openness and curiosity towards using robots in clinical practice. P6 compared incorporating robots to the release of the Nintendo Wii [18]: "I think I'm all for it. I think there was a time when [the] Wii came out so there was a lot of use of that in rehab facilities working on you know just different skills. [I am] into the idea of using robots, especially in specific circumstances." Although each clinician was interested in using robots, at least two noted some hesitations or need for further information before accepting a robot into clinical practice. P1 mentioned an initial concern over using robots: "I was actually a little concerned, especially with [the robot], that a certain percentage of the kids would be afraid of [the robot], but that has not seemed to be the case." P9, an OT, expounded that errors may hinder usage of a robot: "I feel like as long as I felt trained and I knew what I was doing, because that's the one thing that probably intimidates or frustrates me the most. If something goes wrong, we usually don't know how to fix it." These hesitations as well as the overall interest for using robots fed directly into clinicians' desired robot features.

3.3 Parental Involvement Is Expected

All 11 clinicians noted that they would feel more comfortable with a robot if a parent was also in the room. Clinicians noted that parents are typically involved in every session with the child and that a robot could interact or be controlled by a parent. P8 noted that "I wouldn't do anything without [the parents] there," while P9 added "I feel like most everything I do, I'm more comfortable with parents present."

3.4 Clinicians Desired Robots to Be Easy to Use, Durable, Child-Friendly and Have a Meaningful Purpose

P1 said that "I think one thing is that [the robot] is easy to use. You know, it's not complicated? It has to be really durable. I feel bad cause I keep breaking [the robot]. And it's not that I do it on purpose." P1 also mentioned that a robot should "not overwhelm the therapist with all the options." P5 added that the main feature they wanted in a robot was "simplicity."

Clinicians described a robot as needing to be child-friendly in different terms. P10 described a child-friendly robot as: "I think if you could program it to respond to specific noises that a youth might make. If you could teach him that a grunt makes the robot come. Or if they make an open vowel sound, it makes the robot sit. So you're pairing the play with something that they're able to do. That'd be kind of cool." P3 and P5, both occupational therapists, mentioned that a robot should "not look scary," and P8 added that a robot should be "quiet, I think a lot of kids are freaked out by, especially if they have visual impairment, the sounds."

Multiple clinicians indicated specific purposes for a robot in clinical settings. For example, P3 wanted a robot that could "write notes" or a robot that could "reach the top of the toy closet" or even a robot that could "use the mop to clean the gym." P8 desired a robot that was "able to interface with a communication device." P2, who had some prior robot experience, gave many different types of potential functions for a robot: "So obviously if this robot is [for] play, but also more focused on movement, then the robot should move or engage with the child. Like, the child moves and then the robot does something. We can work on our actual therapy movements and the robot is engaging with them through that, I think would be cool. If we're actually talking more about a robot that's doing play, then the robot maybe doesn't have to be as mobile; it can stay in one spot, and [if] the child puts a ball in [the robot], it automatically rolls the ball back out to them."

3.5   There Is an Overall Need for More Education of Clinicians

Despite the multitude of different robot features that clinicians desired, a majority of the clinicians also expressed uncertainty about what robots are capable of or how accessible a robot can be for clinical practice. P11 said that "I don't know enough about robots probably. So, I can't really envision anything, but that doesn't mean it's not possible," while P3 noted that "I don't really know. I think because I don't even know the possibilities of where to start, but you know, part of me is saying [a robot should] have all these different options, but I think the more complex it gets the more likely it is to have some challenges." Clinicians also elaborated on uncertainties for the price of a robot for clinical practice and how accessible the technologies may be for smaller clinics with fewer resources. P1 mentioned that "I think there are already robots that exist that do some of the repetitive gait-training and stepping sort of mechanics that would be helpful, but we just don't have the capacity to afford them." As described more later, these uncertainties impacted how much clinicians would trust a robot.

3.6   Clinicians Have Limited Understanding of Robot Autonomy

We found that clinicians defined autonomy in different ways, including in terms of human autonomy rather than robot autonomy. P11 said autonomous is being "independent, or self-managing," while P9 defined autonomous as "I feel like [autonomous] means that you have power in decision-making around what is going to happen to your person." When describing autonomy in terms of a robot, clinicians tended to focus on a robot moving itself. As P8 noted, an autonomous robot is "self-driven. It doesn't require manual input, but is self-driven by itself." P4 said that an autonomous robot has "independent moving, independent functioning, and responding directly to environmental stimuli as opposed to needing to be operated remotely."

After they defined the term autonomous, we asked each clinician to decide if different types of technology were autonomous or not. As a reference, the list of scenarios can be seen in Sect. 2.1. P10 did not complete the answers to each scenario, and P3 answered unsure for each scenario. Two of the 11 clinicians (P4 and P5) answered that a treadmill with a stop sensor (S1) was autonomous. P4 and P5 also said that a smart walker (S2) was autonomous while P1 and P2 said maybe. Three participants (P1, P5, and P9) identified cruise control technology (S3) as autonomous while P2 observed that "[cruise control] is an autonomous feature, but it's not an autonomous whole system." None of the participants identified a teleoperated robot (S4) as autonomous while seven clinicians said that a semi-autonomous robot (S5) was autonomous. P2 described S5 as a robot having partial autonomy. Each participant that completed the scenarios answered that a fully autonomous robot (S6) was autonomous.

3.7   Clinicians Have Limited Trust of Robots with Different Levels of Autonomy

Building upon the clinicians' answers to levels of robot autonomy. we asked the participants if they would trust a robot in the final three scenarios (S4, S5, and S6). P10 did not complete the answers to each scenario and P3 answered unsure for each scenario. We found that only five of the clinicians would trust a teleoperated robot (S4). P1 said they would not trust a teleoperated robot partially because "I might tell [the robot] to do something dumb and then it would do it." P4 expressed a similar reasoning for not fully trusting a robot: "You can hit the wrong button, and people can do unpredictable things around the robot." Only two clinicians (P8, P9) said they would trust a semi-autonomous robot (S5) while two other clinicians (P2, P6) said they would trust the robot only after learning and practicing with the system. P1 noted a tendency for skepticism with robots: "I would never completely 100% trust a robot, but I would never completely 100% trust myself either." The six other clinicians said they would not fully trust a semi-autonomous robot. For the final scenario, only P4 and P9 said they would trust the robot. P8 noted that they would trust a fully autonomous robot after further understanding how the system worked: "[the robot] is probably sensing the environment, which is why it's able to drive automatically, it's looking out for obstacles and things like that. So if I knew [the robot] was able to do those functions, I think I would trust it. " P3 offered concern over the effectiveness of how a robot moves autonomously without collisions: "I think I would be more concerned about the [robot] drive features rather than the [robot] reward features." Each of the other seven clinicians said they would either be skeptical or not trusting of a fully autonomous robot.

4 Discussion

The results of our semi-structured interviews show broadly that pediatric healthcare professionals have little experience with robots, but are interested in incorporating them as a component of clinical practice. For successful robot integration in the clinic space, clinicians should be included in every step of the design process. Clinicians unanimously expressed that parents are a constant component of sessions, so robots should also encourage parental involvement. We saw that clinicians had a range of desired features for a robot, but also were unsure of what a robot was capable of and how accessible a robot could be. Roboticists developing robots for child-robot interaction in pediatric interventions should design robots that are simple to use and focused on assisting in meaningful tasks for the child. Additionally, roboticists need to provide more detailed training for clinicians on what features a robot has and how to activate those features. We found that clinicians often define autonomy in terms of the child they are working with; one of the primary goals of physical, occupational, or speech language therapy is increasing a child's independence [11]. When explaining autonomy to a clinician, it is important to consider how clinicians may think of autonomy differently than roboticists. While each clinician agreed that a teleoperated robot was not autonomous and that a fully autonomous robot was autonomous, answers varied for a semi-autonomous robot. We propose that roboticists need to clearly outline what level of autonomy a robot will have and what features the clinicians has control over. Finally, clinicians are skeptical of trusting a robot, regardless of the level of autonomy. We suggest that a robot's autonomy should always be easily overriden by a clinician, and that roboticists allow a clinician to practice with the robot before use with children.

Key *strengths* of this paper include the gathering of clinician perspectives on robots for pediatric interventions, an area that has seen less focus than interviews with children or adult caregivers. We showed how clinicians are excited by the prospects of robots, but remain skeptical and desire further education on robot capabilities. A *limitation* of this work is the small sample size and lack of diversity and gender balance in the population sample; we only collected opinions from 11 White clinicians in the Pacific Northwest of the United States, and the majority of clinicians were female. Future work should expand the diversity, geographic region, and gender balance of clinicians interviewed.

Acknowledgments. We thank Thalia Clow and Lucas Yao for help in transcribing the interviews.

References

1. Becevic, M., et al.: Robotic telepresence in a medical intensive care unit–clinicians' perceptions. Perspect. Health Inf. Manag. **12**(Summer), 1C (2015)
2. Bhattacharjee, T., et al.: Is more autonomy always better? exploring preferences of users with mobility impairments in robot-assisted feeding. In: ACM/IEEE International Conference on Human-Robot Interaction (HRI). pp. 181–190 (2020)
3. Borenstein, J., Mahajan, H.P., Wagner, A.R., Howard, A.: Trust and pediatric exoskeletons: a comparative study of clinician and parental perspectives. IEEE Trans. Technol. Soc. **1**(2), 83–88 (2020)
4. Borenstein, J., Wagner, A.R., Howard, A.: Overtrust of pediatric health-care robots: a preliminary survey of parent perspectives. IEEE Robot. Autom. Mag. **25**(1), 46–54 (2018)
5. Butchart, J., Harrison, R., Ritchie, J., Martí, McCarthy, C., Knight, S., Scheinberg, A.: Child and parent perceptions of acceptability and therapeutic value of a socially assistive robot used during pediatric rehabilitation. Disability Rehab. **43**(2), 163–170 (2021)
6. Cherni, Y., Ziane, C.: A narrative review on robotic-assisted gait training in children and adolescents with cerebral palsy: training parameters, choice of settings, and perspectives. Disabilities **2**(2), 293–303 (2022)
7. Coronado, E., Indurkhya, X., Venture, G.: Robots meet children, development of semi-autonomous control systems for children-robot interaction in the wild. In: IEEE International Conference on Advance Robotics and Mechatronics (ICARM), pp. 360–365 (2019)
8. Glaser, B.G.: The constant comparative method of qualitative analysis. Soc. Probl. **12**(4), 436–445 (1965)
9. Han, Y.G., Yun, C.K.: Effectiveness of treadmill training on gait function in children with cerebral palsy: meta-analysis. Jrnl. of Exercise Rehab. **16**(1), 10 (2020)
10. Helmi, A., Wang, T.H., Logan, S.W., Fitter, N.T.: Harnessing the power of movement: a body-weight support system & assistive robot case study. In: IEEE International Conference on Rehabilitation Robotics (ICORR), pp. 1–6 (2023)
11. Huang, H.H.: Perspectives on early power mobility training, motivation, and social participation in young children with motor disabilities. Front. Psych. **8** (2018)
12. Jin, M., Choi, H.: Caregiver views on prospective use of robotic care in helping children adapt to hospitalization. Healthcare **10**(10), 1925 (2022)
13. Kokkoni, E., Logan, S.W., Stoner, T., Peffley, T., Galloway, J.C.: Use of an in-home body weight support system by a child with spina bifida. Pediatric Phys. Therapy **30**(3), 1–6 (2018)
14. Kokkoni, E., et al.: GEARing smart environments for pediatric motor rehabilitation. Jrnl. of Neuroengineering Rehab. **17**(1), 1–15 (2020)
15. Koren, Y., Feingold Polak, R., Levy-Tzedek, S.: Extended interviews with stroke patients over a long-term rehabilitation using human-robot or human-computer interactions. Int. Jrnl. Soc. Robot. **14**(8), 1893–1911 (2022)
16. Logan, S.W., Schreiber, M., Lobo, M., Pritchard, B., George, L., Galloway, J.C.: Real-world performance: physical activity, play, and object-related behaviors of toddlers w/ and w/o disabilities. Pediatric Phys. Therapy **27**(4), 433–441 (2015)
17. Morales Mayoral, R., Helmi, A., Warren, S.T., Logan, S.W., Fitter, N.T.: Robot-theory fitness: GoBot's engagement edge for spurring physical activity in young children. In: IEEE International Conferenceon Intelligent Robots and Systems (IROS), pp. 7939–7944 (2023)

18. Nintendo: Wii (2006). https://www.nintendo.com/en-gb/Wii/Wii-94559.html
19. Radford, A., Kim, J.W., Xu, T., Brockman, G., McLeavey, C., Sutskever, I.: Robust speech recognition via large-scale weak supervision. In: PMLR International Conference on Machine Learning, pp. 28492–28518 (2023)
20. Raigoso, D., Céspedes, N., Cifuentes, C.A., del Ama, A.J., Múnera, M.: A survey on socially assistive robotics: clinicians' and patients' perception of a social robot within gait rehabilitation therapies. Brain Sci. 11(6), 738 (2021)
21. Sloane, B.M., Kenyon, L.K., Logan, S.W., Feldner, H.A.: Caregiver perspectives on powered mobility devices and participation for children with cerebral palsy in Gross Motor Function Classification System level V. Developm. Med. Child Neurol. 66(3), 333–343 (2024)
22. Su, H., Mariani, A., Ovur, S.E., Menciassi, A., Ferrigno, G., De Momi, E.: Toward teaching by demonstration for robot-assisted minimally invasive surgery. IEEE Trans. Autom. Sci. Eng. 18(2), 484–494 (2021)
23. Ulrich, D.A., Lloyd, M.C., Tiernan, C.W., Looper, J.E., Angulo-Barroso, R.M.: Effects of intensity of treadmill training on developmental outcomes and stepping in infants with Down syndrome. Phys. Therapy 88(1), 114–122 (2008)
24. Winkle, K., Caleb-Solly, P., Turton, A., Bremner, P.: Social robots for engagement in rehabilitative therapies: design implications from a study with therapists. In: ACM/IEEE International Conference on Human-Robot Interaction (HRI), pp. 289–297 (2018)
25. Zablotsky, B., Black, L.I., Blumberg, S.J.: Estimated prevalence of children with diagnosed developmental disabilities in the United States, 2014-2016. NCHS Data Brief 291 (2017)
26. Zhang, Y., Bressel, M., De Groof, S., Dominé, F., Labey, L., Peyrodie, L.: Design and control of a size-adjustable pediatric lower-limb exoskeleton based on weight shift. IEEE Access 11, 6372–6384 (2023)

Dude, Where's My Robot Voice? Sometimes More Robotic Is Better in Social Robot Speech Generation

Christopher A. Sanchez, Timothy Bui, and Naomi T. Fitter[✉]

Oregon State University (OSU), Corvallis, OR, USA
{christopher.sanchez,fittern}@oregonstate.edu

Abstract. As a broader range of natural language processing tools become available, from large language models to more natural-sounding text-to-speech resources, new questions emerge about how to curate robot voices. One tempting option may be to use by default the latest tool or most human-sounding voice option. But is this the right path, or in fact a misstep? This question, and a broader wondering about whether and how adjusting the humanness of the voice used by our lab's robotic stand-up comedian would matter, led to the design of the presented experiment, which evaluated the effects of three different levels of voice humanness on peoples' perceptions of our robotic comedian. This online and between-subjects video-based study ($N = 91$) showed that both the least and the most human-like voices caused detriments in ratings of the robot on a subset of the evaluation scales, without offering any discernible benefit to the interaction. Based on these observations, we urge the robotics community to select voices with care and consider that matching the chosen voice to the presentation of the robot itself will likely lead to a maximally successful interaction experience.

1 Introduction

Over the last decade or so, natural language processing-based interactions with robots have advanced from needing highly scaffolded hardware and software setups to now being feasible in real-world environments with little or no special adaptation. As accessibility increases, questions have shifted from how to accomplish verbal speech interactions in the first place to instead focus on what tools to use in each step of the interaction. Among these decisions is the choice of what robot voice to use, as modern options for text-to-speech include hyper-realistic voices created with generative AI. For example, Amazon Polly includes neural network- and generative model-enhanced voices. But should robot voices sound like human voices? This paper addresses this question and provides support for the idea that one should think twice before selecting the latest and greatest voice model by default.

Robot voice design is likely to matter to some extent in a range of human-robot interaction (HRI) settings, but we wanted to begin our investigation of

O. Palinko et al. (Eds.): ICSR + AI 2024, LNAI 15562, pp. 335–345, 2025.
https://doi.org/10.1007/978-981-96-3519-1_31

Fig. 1. Single cropped frame from the study stimuli, all of which were visually identical. The robot's voice varied across conditions, as further explained in Sect. 3.

robot voice in a realm where voice is one of the main aspects of the interaction. Accordingly, in the presented work, we situate the interaction in the realm of robotic stand-up comedy. Robot comedy is generally a useful topic of study since humor helps to build rapport in interactions [11]. Past work shows essential ideas such as the fact that timing strategies in robot comedy are critical [21], but much remains to be learned about robot voice in comedy beyond coarse knobs such as speech-based gender presentation [15,16]. In social robotics more broadly, previous research has shown that a robot's gender, appearance, voice pitch, and personality affect viewer perceptions of system attributes such as interaction quality, appeal, and social closeness [5,13]. We sought to use an existing successful robot's movement and timing while modulating the voice across a spectrum of humanness levels (finer adjustments, and different adjustments, compared to past robot comedy voice work), to specifically learn about the impact of such voice changes.

In the current work, our core research goal is to begin to understand the impacts of robot voices that range in human-likeness on the perceptions of human spectators. We pursued this topic using a between-subjects online survey-based study with three different levels of robot voice humanness. After covering background work in Sect. 2, we outline the methods of this work in Sect. 3, including detailing how we selected each robot voice and implemented the investigated stimuli (a screenshot of which appears in Fig. 1). Section 4 presents the results of the work, including evidence that the medium-human voice seemed to have a better fit with the NAO robot studied in the presented work, compared to the most human-like voice. We discuss the results and their implications in Sect. 5. Contributions of this work include insights on how to design voices for embodied robots, including the idea that the most human-like voice is not automatically the best choice, even for humanoid robots.

2 Background

Past work on *perceptions of voice* and *robot comedy performance* informed the work presented in this paper. For example, previous studies of human voice qualities have shown that voice pitch impacts a person's perceived attractiveness [23,24]. The effects of voice attractiveness are additive [23], and more attractive voices tend to yield a more favorable impression [24]. Again in the human voice and human psychology realm, past efforts show that women generally preferred men who have medium- or low-pitched voices over men with high-pitched voices [17]. Another study with a similar focus showed that men preferred women with higher-pitched voices [4]. Overall, voice is known to have important impacts in the human psychology realm.

The wealth of past research on human voices has sparked initial work on robot voices as well. For example, two recent papers discussed the best robot voice selections in a beginning set of environments and social contexts [10,20]. Further work showed that robot voice impacts opinions of a robot, as well as views of interactions with the robot [13]. (Generally, a higher-pitched robot was rated better with regards to overall appearance, voice appeal, behavior, personality, and positive interaction feelings.) Another effort modulated only the apparent gender of a robotic comedian's voice, finding (somewhat surprisingly) that there was no significantly different perception of a male-presenting vs. female-presenting robot [15,16]. Previous efforts indicate that there may be better- and worse-fitting voices for a given robot form as well; in one study, researchers demonstrated that users formed a mental image of a robot just from hearing its voice [9]. Although human-robot interaction work on voice has begun, much more remains to be discovered in this important area of communication.

The full range of social contexts for studying voice is vast, but we wanted to begin this work in a specific application where interaction factors such as voice seemed likely to play an important role. This line of thinking led us to consider robot humor; in previous human psychology work, studies have shown that seemingly honest humor can increase likability as well as increase attraction toward the humorous individual [3,22]. The same appears to be true with humorous robot appeal [13]. Accordingly, the history of robot comedy includes a range of examples of successful robotic comedians (e.g., [7,8,21]). We borrowed principles for successful robot comedy (such as good timing, proven methods for writing/curating material, and choreographic routines) from this past work, modulating only the voice itself in the current paper; as hyper-realistic voice models emerge, more information is needed on whether (and how) the human-ness of a voice effects user perceptions in highly dynamic social situations such as robot comedy.

3 Methods

We conducted a between-subjects online video-based study to study how voice humanness level affected participants' perceptions of a robot. All study procedures were approved by OSU under protocol #IRB-2019-0172.

3.1   Stimulus Creation and Study Design

In the presented study, we sought to lay a foundation for future work by evaluating whether (and how) onlooker perceptions varied across three different coarse levels of robot voice humanness, for one particular robot embodiment. Differences or similarities in this first experiment can guide selections of additional levels of humanness and/or types of robot embodiment in future work. For the present experiment, we studied three different levels of voice humanness, selecting each voice after a broad ideation round that included the voices below and the "Overdub" service from Descript. Voices were down-selected using the expert intuition of the author team, which includes an experienced performing artist. The selected voices were able to reliably render speech and seemed to be a plausible fit with the robot's physical appearance. The voices were as follows:

- *Low-Humanness*: For this most robotic-sounding voice, we used the "Fred" voice available via Apple's "Say" program on macOS. Qualitatively, we believed this voice to be a good selection because of how "tinny" it sounds.
- *Medium-Humanness*: For this medium-human-like voice, we selected the standard "Joey" voice from Amazon Polly. We believed this voice to be a good fit since while it sounds much more human than the Fred voice, an element of unnaturalness (such as slightly awkward cadence and intonations) remains in its speech.
- *High-Humanness*: For this most human-sounding voice, we used the standard "Matthew" voice from Amazon Polly. As a continual improvement from the other voices, this selection offers more a qualitatively natural-sounding voice, for example in terms of cadence and intonation.

We used text of the same robot comedy routine to generate each voice stimulus. Based on its expert intuition for robot comedy implementation, the research team manually added pauses as needed to the Fred voice output and used SSML tags to accomplish clear and similar delivery of the underlying text in the Joey and Matthew voices. The use of these voices occurred in early 2021 with the latest versions of these voices available at the time. To our knowledge, the voices are still available in the same (or very similar) versions via macOS and Amazon Polly.

Once the audio for each robot routine was prepared, we recorded three videos, one with each robot comedian voice, but otherwise with the same setting, choreography, and camera angle. The robotic comedian in these videos was the NAO robot, a social robot frequently used for robot comedy performance (e.g., [21]). This process yielded the three stimuli needed for the study (one for each condition of the between-subjects experiment), as included in the paper's supplementary material [18]. The comedy routine stimuli lasted approximately four minutes.

3.2   Hypotheses

Based on the results of past human psychology and human-robot interaction research (as cited below), we developed the following two competing hypotheses:

H1: The more human-like the voice is, the more socially close the participant will feel to the robot and the funnier they will find its jokes [5]. We also expected corresponding gains in attractiveness ratings.

H2: As a contrasting hypothesis, we considered that uncanny valley effects may affect results in the opposite way. Thus, this hypothesis expected that participants would feel less close to the human-like voice and find it less humorous [12]. We also expected corresponding losses in attractiveness ratings.

3.3 Measurement

Information gathered from participants included opening identity/experience questions and post-stimulus questions. Each question set is discussed below.

The opening question set contained demographic questions focused on the following: gender, age, STEM experience, personality, robotics experience, and comedy experience. We also collected data on negative attitudes toward robots using the NARS [14]. This survey instrument includes three scales (with 14 subscales among them) focused on interactions with robots, social influence of robots, and emotions in human-robot interaction, respectively.

In the post-stimulus questions, we assessed participant experience of the voice using a modified AttrakDiff [6], humorousness of the performance using a custom scale from [15], social closeness feelings using the inclusion of other in the self (IOS) scale [1], and human-likeness using the Godspeed anthropomorphism scale [2]. Specifically, the modified AttrakDiff included the following word pairs on opposite extrema of 7-pt scales:

- boring/exciting
- conventional/inventive
- very unattractive/very attractive
- demotivating/motivating
- enjoyable/annoying*
- secure/not secure*
- uncomfortable/comfortable

The humorousness questions were administered on a 7-pt Likert-type scale from "Strongly Disagree" (1) to "Strongly Agree" (7). The prompts were as follows:

- funny
- fascinating
- boring*
- enjoyable
- playful
- something I would share with a friend
- something I would share with an acquaintance
- offensive*

Reverse-scored scales are marked above with an asterisk. IOS-based social closeness was collected on the usual 7-pt scale with corresponding visuals of continually more overlapping Venn diagrams. The Godspeed questions were administered on the standard 5-pt semantic differential scales.

3.4   Procedure

Participants who enrolled in the study provided informed consent and proceeded to take an approximately 20-minute survey via Qualtrics. The survey began with demographic questions and questions from the Negative Attitude toward Robots Scale (NARS) [14]. Participants were assigned (with balance in the randomization, to present all stimuli an equal number of times) to one of the three experiment conditions. Based on this assignment, they viewed the associated stimulus (with low, medium, or high voice humanness) and completed the post-stimulus questionnaire (further described below). The survey ended with a free-response question that asked what aspects of the video influenced participants' responses.

3.5   Participants

Participants were recruited from OSU School of Psychological Science courses via their student pool. The study included 91 participants (19 men, 67 women, 5 non-binary individuals) with ages ranging from 18 to 48 ($M = 22.1$, $SD = 6.7$). 30 participants experienced the low-humanness condition, 30 experienced the medium-humanness condition, and 31 experienced the high-humanness condition. 53 of the participants had a background in STEM, while 38 of the participants stated they did not. Participants generally had little experience in robotics ($M = 2.1$, $SD = 0.7$ on a 5-pt scale) but had some experience watching stand-up comedy ($M = 3.0$, $SD = 0.9$ on a 5-pt scale). Participants were of middling extroversion levels ($M = 3.8$, $SD = 1.5$, out of 7 maximum) and emotional stability ratings ($M = 4.0$, $SD = 1.3$). Agreeableness ($M = 4.8$, $SD = 1.2$), conscientiousness ($M = 5.4$, $SD = 1.1$), and openness to new experiences ($M = 5.3$, $SD = 1.2$) were are all near the center of the TIPI scales, but on the positive side. Negative attitudes toward robots were middling or below the midpoint on all NARS scales; we observed a mean score of 3.4 out of 7 maximum ($SD = 0.9$) for the interaction scale (where higher is more negative), 4.3 for the social influence scale ($SD = 1.0$), and 3.5 for the emotions scale ($SD = 1.2$).

3.6   Analysis

For scales that were custom or involved some modification, we used Cronbach's alpha tests to confirm scale validity. We used analysis of variance (ANOVA) tests with an $\alpha = 0.05$ significance level to assess differences between groups. In the case of significant main effects, we used Tukey's HSD tests to find pairwise significant differences. We measured effect size using η^2. All statistical data analysis was completed using jamovi 1.6.23 [19]. In the discussion of the paper, we use quotes from the free-response feedback to help explain and contextualize other results.

4   Results

Both reliability analyses showed acceptable agreement (or better) for our chosen AttrakDiff and humorousness scales. The Cronbach's alpha value for the

Table 1. Statistical test results for the post-video questions considered in this study. Significant results are emphasized using bolding.

	$F(2, 88)$	p	η^2
AttrakDiff	3.96	**0.023**	0.083
Humorousness	0.34	0.712	0.008
IOS	1.45	0.241	0.032
Anthropomorphism	7.28	**0.001**	0.142

Table 2. Descriptive statistics for each post-video question set by condition. Entries are noted as mean ± standard deviation. Relative highest scores for each row are denoted with bolding.

	Low-Humanness	Medium-Humanness	High-Humanness
AttrakDiff	3.22 ± 0.79	**3.89 ± 1.00**	3.23 ± 1.34
Humorousness	3.64 ± 0.96	**3.82 ± 0.76**	3.66 ± 1.04
IOS	1.37 ± 0.72	**1.73 ± 0.78**	1.71 ± 1.22
Anthropomorphism	1.74 ± 0.59	**2.41 ± 0.77**	1.83 ± 0.82

AttrakDiff scale was 0.798, on the high end of the acceptable agreement range. The humorousness scale yielded a Cronbach's alpha of 0.813, showing good agreement.

The results of the ANOVA tests are summarized in Table 1, with descriptive statistics highlighted in Table 2. The AttrakDiff scale yielded a significant main effect. Post hoc tests showed that ratings of our intended medium-humanness voice were significantly better than those for any other voice. There were no significant main effects for the humorousness or IOS scales. As would be expected based on the study design, there was a significant main effect for anthropomorphism. At the same time, post hoc tests showed a different trend than might be expected; as with AttrakDiff ratings, anthropomorphism was rated significantly higher for the middle-humanness voice compared to any other voice.

The result on anthropomorphism in particular led us to wonder what subscales (if any) were primarily driving the observed differences. Accordingly, we performed an exploratory analysis for each subscale of the AttrakDiff and anthropomorphism question sets. The significant subscales for the AttrakDiff were attractiveness ($F(2, 88) = 4.17$, $p = 0.019$, $\eta^2 = 0.087$) and annoyance ($F(2, 88) = 6.31$, $p = 0.003$, $\eta^2 = 0.126$), where the middle-humanness voice was rated as significantly better than any other voice on both subscales. The significant subscales for Godspeed anthropomorphism were fake/natural ($F(2, 88 = 11.70$, $p < 0.001$, $\eta^2 = 0.210$), machinelike/humanlike ($F(2, 88 = 3.27$, $p = 0.043$, $\eta^2 = 0.069$), and moving rigidly/moving elegantly ($F(2, 88 = 5.44$, $p = 0.006$, $\eta^2 = 0.110$). Again, the middle-humanness voice was rated as significantly better than any other voice for the first and third listed scales. For the second, no corrected pairwise comparisons turned out to be significant. Somewhat intriguingly, although the choreography for all videos was identical, we found the significant effect above as well as the tendency (not statistically significant) for the least human-like voice to be rated as having more elegant motion than the most human-like voice.

5 Discussion

Perhaps as an appropriate resolution to our contrasting hypotheses, we found that in all cases of significant differences, the medium-humanness condition was *most* favorable. These differences in AttrakDiff and anthropomorphism ratings positioned the medium-humanness voice as better than any other voice option on these scales. In some ways, this result seems logical; in fact, the real robotic comedian that this study is based on uses the medium-humanness voice in its day-to-day operation. Selected past work (e.g., [13]) would support the idea of the "Joey" voice, which happened to have the highest pitch of the three tested voices, being perceived most positively, as well as the idea that a particular mental image of a robot comes from hearing a robot voice [9] (perhaps causing a better match for some voices vs. others between the envisioned and actual robot embodiment). The author team (including a robot comedy artist) found the Joey voice to be a clear voice that still read as classically robotic in a way. In other ways, the result challenges how well the study manipulation worked, since the most human-like voice was *not* in fact interpreted as such. Overall, the scale-wise results led us to assess the free-response feedback for further clarity.

Searching the free-response data for mentions of the robot's voice, we found seventeen mentions of the robot voice for the low-humanness case, eleven mentions for the medium-humanness case, and fifteen for the high-humanness voice. When the voice was mentioned, the description was almost always negative (whether the comment appreciated the character design, or thought it was wholly negative). Accordingly, there is a chance that the more the voice blended into the robot character design (and the less it was mentioned), the better the robot mode was perceived. Some of the most negative voice comments were for the low-humanness condition (e.g., the " voice was over the top machine-like"). On the other hand, comments about the middle voice level still contained negative points (e.g., "its voice was very monotone") but with more redeeming qualities noted as well (e.g., "but its mannerisms were very elegant and entertaining. The robots jokes were strangely crude and very clever, and some made me laugh pretty hard"). Perhaps as a sign of the current AI trends, multiple participants assumed that the robot was generating its own content. Comments to this effect included "I thought the robot was successful in pulling relevant information from the internet into its comedic bit" and "the robot leverages its language model, such as GPT-3, which is trained on diverse datasets to emulate human language patterns and humor."

Taken together, the results of this work seem to hint that rather than defaulting to the latest voice model, roboticists can benefit from selecting a robot voice that matches with the appearance or general characteristics of a robot. Even in the case of hyper-realistic humanoids, there may be benefits to this approach. For example, one participant noted that "I thought more about how the robot voice wasn't as good as human, but I wouldn't want a humanoid voice from a robot, I'm fine with a firm line between organic and inorganic life." Assuming a subset of system users feel this way, a voice that is human-like enough to be clear while avoiding hyper-realistic imitation of human voices may be best, as they provide some degree of anthropomorphic identification, but are still easily identified as artificial.

The main *strength* of this work is its focus on robot voices, a topic that is often taken for granted but which implicitly influences a broad range of scenarios that leverage verbal interaction. We believe that this work can inform future hypotheses in work on robot voice. At the same time, the work is not without *limitations*. The online setting of the study, and its focus on one specific student body, limits the work's generalizability. Future work should consider the replicability of the work in in-person interaction and additional user populations. Curiously, the studied conditions did not vary continuously in anthropomorphism as expected. Our exploratory subscale analysis provides initial explanations for this result, but follow-up work, which could also use additional common naturalness ratings such as the mean opinion score, would be needed to fully understand this phenomenon.

In conclusion, in the presented work, we compared three specific robot voices (representing three discrete levels of voice humanness) to learn more about how this aspect of robot design influences onlooker opinions. Our between-subjects online experiment showed that the medium-humanness voice (the voice that, coincidentally, we use for real robot comedy performances) received the most favorable ratings in cases of statistical significance. Although this result did not align fully with our expectations, it does show than robot voice selection is consequential in the overall experience of a robotic system. We hope that this foundational work inspires other robotics researchers to carefully consider robot voice design in their own efforts.

References

1. Aron, A., Aron, E.N., Smollan, D.: Inclusion of other in the self scale and the structure of interpersonal closeness. J. Pers. Soc. Psychol. **63**(4), 596 (1992)
2. Bartneck, C., Kulić, D., Croft, E., Zoghbi, S.: Measurement instruments for the anthropomorphism, animacy, likeability, perceived intelligence, and perceived safety of robots. Int. J. Soc. Robot. **1**, 71–81 (2009)
3. Cann, A., Calhoun, L.G., Banks, J.S.: On the role of humor appreciation in interpersonal attraction: It's no joking matter (1997)
4. Collins, S.A., Missing, C.: Vocal and visual attractiveness are related in women. Anim. Behav. **65**(5), 997–1004 (2003)

5. Eyssel, F., Kuchenbrandt, D., Bobinger, S., De Ruiter, L., Hegel, F.: if you sound like me, you must be more human. on the interplay of robot and user features on human-robot acceptance and anthropomorphism. In: ACM/IEEE International Conference on Human-Robot Interaction (HRI), pp. 125–126 (2012)

6. Hassenzahl, M., Burmester, M., Koller, F.: Attrakdiff: Ein fragebogen zur messung wahrgenommener hedonischer und pragmatischer qualität. Mensch & Computer 2003: Interaktion in Bewegung, pp. 187–196 (2003)

7. Katevas, K., Healey, P.G., Harris, M.T.: Robot comedy lab: experimenting with the social dynamics of live performance. Front. Psychol. **6**, 1253 (2015)

8. Knight, H., Satkin, S., Ramakrishna, V., Divvala, S.: A savvy robot standup comic: online learning through audience tracking. In: International Conference and Workshops on Tangible and Embedded Interaction (TEI) (2011)

9. McGinn, C., Torre, I.: Can you tell the robot by the voice? an exploratory study on the role of voice in the perception of robots. In: ACM/IEEE International Conference on Human-Robot Interaction (HRI), pp. 211–221 (2019)

10. Miniota, J., Wang, S., Beskow, J., Gustafson, J., Székely, É., Pereiral, A.: Hi robot, it's not what you say, it's how you say it. In: IEEE International Conference on Robot and Human Interactive Communication (RO-MAN), pp. 307–314 (2023)

11. Mirnig, N., Stadler, S., Stollnberger, G., Giuliani, M., Tscheligi, M.: Robot humor: how self-irony and schadenfreude influence people's rating of robot likability. In: IEEE International Symposium on Robot and Human Interactive Communication (RO-MAN), pp. 166–171 (2016)

12. Mitchell, W.J., Szerszen Sr, K.A., Lu, A.S., Schermerhorn, P.W., Scheutz, M., MacDorman, K.F.: A mismatch in the human realism of face and voice produces an uncanny valley. i-Perception **2**(1), 10–12 (2011)

13. Niculescu, A., Van Dijk, B., Nijholt, A., Li, H., See, S.L.: Making social robots more attractive: the effects of voice pitch, humor and empathy. Int. J. Soc. Robot. **5**, 171–191 (2013)

14. Nomura, T., Kanda, T., Suzuki, T.: Experimental investigation into influence of negative attitudes toward robots on human-robot interaction. AI & Soc. **20**, 138–150 (2006)

15. Raghunath, N., Myers, P., Sanchez, C.A., Fitter, N.T.: Women *Are* funny: influence of apparent gender and embodiment in robot comedy. In: Li, H., et al. (eds.) ICSR 2021. LNCS (LNAI), vol. 13086, pp. 3–13. Springer, Cham (2021). https://doi.org/10.1007/978-3-030-90525-5_1

16. Raghunath, N., Sanchez, C.A., Fitter, N.T.: Robot comedy (is) special: a surprising lack of bias for gendered robotic comedians. In: International Conference on Social Robotics, pp. 663–673. Springer (2022). https://doi.org/10.1007/978-3-031-24670-8_58

17. Riding, D., Lonsdale, D., Brown, B.: The effects of average fundamental frequency and variance of fundamental frequency on male vocal attractiveness to women. J. Nonverbal Behav. **30**, 55–61 (2006)

18. Sanchez, C.A., Bui, T., Fitter, N.T.: robot_comedy_voices repository (2024). https://github.com/shareresearchteam/robot_comedy_voices

19. The jamovi project: jamovi (Version 1.6) [Computer software] (2020). https://www.jamovi.org

20. Tuttosi, P., Hughson, E., Matsufuji, A., Zhang, C., Lim, A.: Read the room: adapting a robot's voice to ambient and social contexts. In: IEEE/RSJ International Conference on Intelligent Robots and Systems (IROS), pp. 3998–4005 (2023)

21. Vilk, J., Fitter, N.T.: Comedians in cafes getting data: evaluating timing and adaptivity in real-world robot comedy performance. In: ACM/IEEE International Conference on Human-Robot Interaction (HRI), pp. 223–231 (2020)

22. Wilson, C.P.: Jokes: Form, content, use, and function (1979)

23. Zuckerman, M., Driver, R.E.: What sounds beautiful is good: the vocal attractiveness stereotype. J. Nonverbal Behav. **13**(2), 67–82 (1989)

24. Zuckerman, M., Miyake, K.: The attractive voice: what makes it so? J. Nonverbal Behav. **17**(2), 119–135 (1993)

Overtrusting a Simple Non-humanoid Robot in a Training Process

Hadas Erel[(✉)][iD], Maya Koren, Andrey Grishko[iD], Benny Megidish[iD],
and Noa Morag Yaar[iD]

Milab, Reichman University, Herzlya 4610101, Israel
{hadas.erel,maya.korn,andrey.grishko,benny.megidish,
noa.morag}@milab.idc.ac.il

Abstract. Trust plays a crucial role in Human-Robot interactions. However, the prevailing belief that robots are inherently capable can lead to overtrust, where individuals rely on robots' decisions without applying critical thinking. To evaluate the extent of overtrust in HRI, we conducted an experiment in which participants engaged in a cognitive task alongside a simple robotic object that performed the same task. Participants' performances were compared to a baseline group in which the robot moved but didn't provide answers to the task items. We deliberately chose a simple non-humanoid robot and informed participants that the robot was in a training phase where it was learning how to perform the task. The results showed that when the robot provided answers, participants tended to align with them, even when they were wrong. Additionally, participants' reaction time was shorter, indicating they were investing less effort in solving the task. Participants also demonstrated decreased self-efficacy and were less confident in their performances. Our findings indicate that overtrust should be carefully considered in the design and implementation of even very simple robots.

Keywords: Overtrust · HRI · Self efficacy · Non-humanoid robots

1 Introduction

Robots are often designed to enhance human well-being in various domains, including offering guidance and recommendations to support human decisions [18,20,27]. As the prominence of artificial intelligence systems continues to surge, we anticipate the emergence of even more "intelligent" robots that will further shape our choices and influence our decision-making [27,28]. While technology offers numerous benefits for enhancing decision-making, it also carries risks that require careful consideration [19,27,28]. Among these risks is the widespread perception that technology is inherently neutral and objective [14,36], leading individuals to often accept its actions and decisions unquestioningly [13,36]. Furthermore, the prevalent belief that technology is superior to humans due to its computational advantages [19] often leads people to accept its recommendations

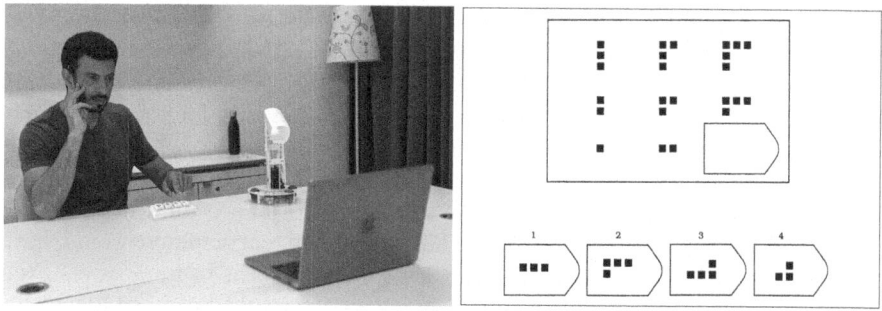

Fig. 1. Left - A participant performing a task alongside a robot that performs the same task. Right - An example of an RMP item.

without evaluating their accuracy and limitations [3,13]. This lack of critical thinking may be intensified when the intelligent support system is implemented into robotic technologies [15]. Robots' autonomy and embodiment increase the perception that they are independent entities capable of cognitive processing [17]. This, in turn, may reinforce their acceptance and perception as having superior capabilities [27], and the likelihood of overtrust in their capabilities [15].

Balancing trust in human-robot interactions is not trivial [12,27,28]. On one hand, when a robot is perceived as untrustworthy, individuals may reject the robot and discern it as malfunctioning. On the other hand, excessive trust can lead to overreliance on the robot's decisions [12,27,28] even when its mistakes are clearly evident [32]. Overtrust may also have broader effects on human well-being. Relying on the robot's recommendation can also impact one's self-efficacy. Self-efficacy involves individuals' belief in their ability to accomplish a particular goal or task [5]. Previous studies suggest that self-efficacy is influenced by social comparisons during interactions with others and the feedback received from these interactions [34]. When we perceive others as outperforming us, it can undermine our confidence in our abilities [38]. Since robots, even simple ones, are perceived as social agents [8], their perceived superior performance might threaten our self-efficacy [11]. Adopting the robot's decision in a task that we should perform, or even questioning our decision due to a different choice taken by the robot, can negatively impact how we perceive our abilities.

To investigate the extent of overtrust in HRI, we conducted an experiment involving interaction with a simple robotic object resembling a desk lamp (used with permission [16], see Fig. 1, Left). Participants were asked to perform a cognitively demanding task to test their reasoning capability, encouraging them to demonstrate their own skills and avoid errors, while the robot performed the same task alongside them. We deliberately chose a simple robot with a non-humanoid appearance for this experiment and explicitly stated that it was in a training phase with imperfect capabilities. We evaluated participants' tendency to overtrust the robot under a context that included (1) a very simple robot in a training phase, (2) the absence of humanoid features in the robot's appearance that could imply human-related capabilities, (3) a task aimed at assessing participants' cognitive capabilities. To evaluate overtrust, we analyzed the correspondence between participants' responses in the cognitive task and those provided by the robot, as well as their response times for the task items. We compared participants' performance to a baseline group, where the robot movements indicated engagement in the task, but it did not provide answers. Furthermore, we evaluated whether the robot's performance influenced participants' self-efficacy. We hypothesized that (1) When participants would have indication for the robot's performance they would conform to its answers even when they are not accurate; (2) When participants would have indication for the robot's performance it will impact their self efficacy and decrease it.

2   Related Work

Related studies tested trust and overtrust in technology, and self-efficacy in HRI.

2.1   Trust and Overtrust in Robots and Automated Systems

Trust in HRI is defined as a psychological attitude wherein individuals believe a robot will perform as expected and effectively accomplish its intended goals [20]. Various factors, including robot performance, human self-confidence, past experiences, task complexity, and more, influence trust in HRI [12,19,23,33].

Previous studies focused on evaluating participants' tendency to accept robots' recommendations and decisions without adequate monitoring [3,33]. Their results commonly indicated a tendency to overtrust automated systems [23] and to conform to the robot's performance [2,10]. For instance, Bahner et al. (2008) examined participants' reliance on automated recommendations, even when these recommendations were occasionally incorrect. They indicated participants' tendency to conform to the system's recommendations without verifying its accuracy or looking for additional information [3]. Similarly, Harbarth et al. (2024) investigated how the transparency of AI recommendations influenced trust. They discovered that when AI recommendations were accompanied by clear explanations, participants were more inclined to adhere to them, even when they were incorrect [13]. The tendency to overtrust was also indicated by participants' willingness to accept the possibility of making an incorrect decision under the belief that the system would mitigate this risk [21]. This tendency becomes evident when people relinquish control and unquestioningly follow the robot [28]. For example, Jacobs et al. (2021) investigated how clinical caregivers' reliance on automated recommendations affected the quality of treatment provided. They found that incorrect AI recommendations led to less accurate treatments compared to independent treatment decisions or accurate AI recommendations [18].

Overtrust has also been observed in interactions with robots. Robinette et al. (2016) tested whether individuals would blindly follow a robot during an emergency evacuation scenario. Despite the robot's poor performance in a prior interaction, participants followed its guidance during the evacuation, even when it led them in the wrong direction, away from marked emergency exits [32]. Other studies have indicated participants' tendency to conform to robots suggestion and performance from taking its suggestion in a search task to its recommendation to gamble on money [2,10]. Overtrust was also shown to develop over multiple interactions. Urlich et al. (2021) indicated that trust in a pet-feeding robot grew quickly after several instances of successful feeding, which led to a decrease in the frequency of checking the robot's performance [35].

Expanding on this research, we investigated whether overtrust persists even under extreme conditions where participants lack objective reasons perceive the robot as having superior capabilities. Specifically, we used a simple robot with minimal communication capabilities and explicitly informed participants about its limited capabilities by presenting it as undergoing training to solve the task. Additionally, we engaged participants in a task that evaluated their own capabilities, encouraging them to avoid errors.

2.2   The Impact of HRI on Humans' Self-Efficacy

Several studies have investigated the relationship between Human-Robot Interaction and human self-efficacy. For instance, Rosenthal-von der Pütten et al. (2017) investigated the impact of a do-it-yourself (DIY) interaction with a robot on individuals' perceived self-efficacy in using robotic technology. They found that young adults reported increased self-efficacy following the interaction, while older adults did not show significant changes [29]. Similarly, Zafari et al. (2019) examined how verbal interactions with a robot influenced self-efficacy. They found that verbal feedback focused on the person's performance led to higher self-efficacy compared to task-focused or neutral feedback [39].

Expanding on this research, we investigated whether interacting with a robot during a cognitively demanding task would influence participants' self-efficacy. In our experiment, participants engaged in a task alongside a robot that performed the same task. We evaluated whether participants' tendency to rely on the robot's answers affected their perceived self-efficacy.

3   Method

To evaluate the extent of overtrust, we asked participants to complete a cognitive task designed to evaluate their own capabilities. We informed them that a robot would perform the task next to them as part of its training process.

3.1   The Task

We used the Raven Progressive Matrices (RPM) test, a well-known test that measures abstract reasoning abilities [30]. The RPM test comprises visual items, each presenting a 3×3 matrix of shapes with one shape missing. Participants need to identify the pattern governing the matrix and select the appropriate missing shape from several alternative options (see Fig. 1, Right). Traditionally,

RPM task items consist of eight possible options to choose from. However, to ensure participants recognize and remember the robot's answers, we reduced the number of options to four. This way the robot could choose an answer by pressing one out of four buttons that were visible to the participant. The four options included the correct answer, the second most common answer (based on findings from a pilot study), and two other random answers. Additionally, to mitigate the influence of fatigue, we used a partial selection of items from the RPM (10 instead of 18). The progressive increase in the difficulty levels of the items allowed flexibility in designing the robot's performance. To prevent participants from perceiving the robot as malfunctioning (which might lead to mistrust, [12]), the robot provided accurate answers to the simpler items and began to make errors only on medium-difficulty items. We note that the RPM test comprises two sets of 18 items each. We utilized one set for the experimental task described above. The second set served as a pre-test to balance the groups, with participants completing it online one week prior to the in-lab experiment.

3.2 Pilot Study

To determine the selection of items that would allow for a range of difficulty while avoiding fatigue, we conducted a pilot study with 20 participants. Based on their performance, we excluded items with minimal variance, specifically dropping the five easiest and three most difficult items. The performance of participants on the selected ten RPM items is detailed in Table 1. The majority of participants answered the initial seven questions correctly, achieving an average accuracy of 91.7%. However, from the eighth question and beyond, there was a noticeable decline in the accuracy of the answers. Based on these results, we programmed the robot to accurately answer the first seven items (to prevent its perception as malfunctioning) and to perform errors in items eight and ten.

3.3 The Robot: Gestures Design and Technical Implementation

We used a simple non-humanoid robot designed as a desk lamp (see Fig. 2, Right). The robot was augmented with a plate of four buttons and a small arm extension for physical button pressing. Each button was numbered and had a distinct color. When the robot pressed a button, it would illuminate, indicating its selected answer. The robot operated on the Butter Robotics MAS platform [22], with movements controlled wirelessly using the Wizard of Oz technique, a common approach in HCI and HRI [31]. At the end of the experiment, we verified that all participants perceived the robot as fully autonomous.

Table 1. Percentage of participants who chose the correct answer in the pilot study.

Question number	1	2	3	4	5	6	7	8	9	10
Percentage of success	98.5	84.8	98.5	84.8	97	87.9	93.9	69.7	37.9	43.9

The robot's gestures were developed collaboratively with an animator and an HRI expert in an iterative process. In the *Task-performing robot* condition, the robot executed a specific pattern for each item: 1) The robot performed a rotational right-left movement at a radian angle of 30 °C for 5 s, simulating the scan of the screen (see Fig. 1, Left) The robot moved downward to press a button indicating its choice, and returned to its initial position (see Fig. 2, Right). The robot remained stationary for 10 s and then performed gentle downward and upward motions, mimicking a "breathing" motion until the participant proceeded to the next item. In the *Baseline* condition, the robot followed a similar pattern without the button-pressing movement, performing a scanning motion followed by the "breathing" gesture until the next item.

3.4   Participants

30 students participated in this study (15 per condition; 20 females, 10 males, mean age = 23.5, SD = 2.9). They received course credits as compensation for their participation. Participants signed a consent form and were informed that recorded material would be deleted after the data analysis.

3.5   Experimental Settings

The experiment took place in a quiet room with two desks set at a comfortable height of 70 cm for seated participants (see Fig. 2, Left). The robot was positioned 50 cm to the left of the participant at one desk, where both were facing a computer screen displaying the RPM test. Participants used a response box with four numbered buttons (1–4). After completing the RPM test, participants moved to the second desk for another computerized task.

3.6   Experimental Design

A between-participants experimental design included a *Task-performing robot* condition and a *Baseline* condition. In the *Task-performing robot* condition, the

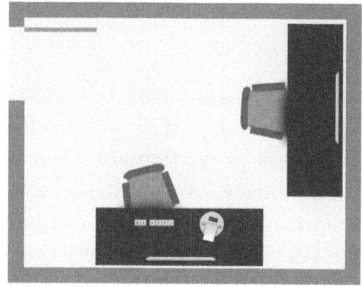

Fig. 2. Left: The experiment room setup. Right: The robot used in the experiment

robot's movements were deliberately to give participants the impression that it was providing answers to task items presented on the screen by the button pressed for each item. In the *Baseline* condition, the robot's movements were similar, but its choices for answers were not indicated by button presses. Participants were randomly assigned to one of two conditions using a matching technique that balanced gender, Negative Attitudes Toward Robots (NARS) [25], and RPM home score [24]. We therefore verified that the participants in the different groups showed similar overall ratings of each of these pre-tests.

3.7   Measures

RPM Performance. To assess overtrust, we measured the impact of the robot's answers on participants' RPM test performance. Our main goal was to evaluate overtrust by measuring the participants' tendency to conform to the robot's performance, even when its answers are inaccurate. We applied two key variables:

Correspondence with the Robot: We focused on the last three challenging RPM items. By testing the difference between the percentage of participants' answers who matched the robot's response in the *Task-Performing Robot* condition and the percentage of choosing the same answers in the *baseline* condition, we could evaluate participants' tendency to follow the robot's performance in the *Task-Performing Robot* condition.

Reaction Time: Averaged reaction times for the last three RPM items were measured and compared between conditions. They served as an indication of the time spent contemplating the challenging items, providing insights into the effort and motivation invested in solving each item.

These measurements allowed us to evaluate overtrust, where conformity to the robot's errors indicated trustworthiness in the robot's performance and reaction times, reflecting participants' tendency to solve the items by themselves. We note that we did not include a measure of trust as the paradigm was not designed to manipulate the level of trust in the robot. The *Baseline* condition was constructed in a way that allowed to evaluate participants' performance regardless of the robot's, and thus, to serve as an appropriate comparison to the performance of the task in the presence of the robot, but while not being able to consider it's performance.

Lexical Decision Task for Self-Efficacy Evaluation. We additionally evaluated if the interaction with the robot impacted participants' self-efficacy. We focused on a behavioral easure allowing to assess participants' sensitivity to the manipulation and its impact on their self-efficacy. We used the Lexical Decision (LD) task, which is a behavioral reaction-time measure for evaluating participants' implicit experience [9]. Previous research has indicated that individuals respond more quickly to words that are relevant to their emotional state [26]. This effect is attributed to context-related arousal, leading to the quicker processing of relevant information [26]. The LD task has been employed in previous studies to assess sensitivity to various contexts based on recent experiences, providing an behavioral measurement of participants' experience [4,7]. In the task, participants had to quickly classify strings of letters as words (e.g., "problem") or non-words (e.g.,"lemborp") by pressing the'S' key for words and the'L' key for non-words. Out of 40 strings used, 20 resembled words, and 20 were non-words. 10 out of the 20 words reflected feelings of self-inefficacy (e.g., failure, difficulty), while the other 10 were neutral control stimuli (e.g., coat, sky). We measured reaction times to assess participants' sense of inefficacy. Previous studies have indicated longer reaction times to negative words due to an inherent defense mechanism [1]. As such, when negative words are irrelevant to the participant's present context (e.g., classifying scary words after watching a comedy), participants tend to react slower to these words compared to neutral or positive words [9]. However, in relevant contexts (e.g., classifying scary words after watching a horror movie), participants' reaction time to negative words becomes similar to that of neutral words due to context-related arousal [9]. We hypothesized slower reaction times to negative inefficacy words in the *Baseline* condition but similar reaction times to neutral words in the *Task-performing robot* condition, as inefficacy becomes relevant to the robot interaction.

Godspeed Questionnaire. We also evaluated the perception of the robot. Godspeed is a scale designed to evaluate how the robot's behavior influenced its perception [6]. We focused on three subscales that were relevant to this study: Likability, Animacy, and Perceived Intelligence.

Semi-structured Interview (Qualitative). A semi-structured interview was conducted to support and enrich our findings. The interview consisted of predefined questions (e.g., "Can you share how the overall experience was?"; "Do you feel you would perform better or worse without the robot's presence?").

3.8 Procedure

A week prior to the experiment, participants received a demographic questionnaire, NARS, and one set of the RPM test via email. Upon arrival at the lab, they were told they would engage in a cognitive task designed to evaluate their reasoning skills. They were informed that there was a robot in the room and that it was in its training phase and would perform the task alongside them. After providing written consent, participants were directed to the experiment room to sit in front of a computer screen, with the robot placed next to them. Participants then were left to complete the 10 RPM items, with the robot next to them activated according to the relevant condition. During the test, participants did not receive feedback on the accuracy of their answers. Following this, they performed the Lexical Decision task and filled out the Godspeed questionnaire. They then underwent a brief semi-structured interview. Finally, the researcher debriefed the participants and ensured they had a positive experience. The session lasted approximately 45 min on average.

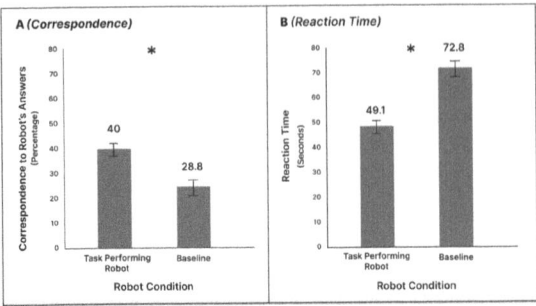

Fig. 3. Correspondence and Reaction time as a function of the robotic conditions.

4 Findings

We first verified the lack of early differences between groups in the NARS and RPM performances. Since significance tests are not appropriate for evaluating NULL effects we conducted Bayesian analyses that indicated no early differences between the groups (NARS: $BF_{10} = 0.3$; RPM: $BF_{10} = 0.13$).

4.1 RPM Performance

To assess overtrust, we performed one-way ANOVAs comparing the percentage of participants' responses that aligned with the robot's responses and the average reaction times. We focused on the last three items of the test, which were more difficult and in which the robot's performance was not perfect.

The one-way ANOVA that tested participants alignment with the robot indicated a significantly higher percentage of similar answers in the *Task-performing robot* condition compared to the *Baseline* condition, F(1, 28) = 4.37, p = 0.050 (see Fig. 3, Left). The second one-way ANOVA that compared the averaged reaction time for the three last RPM items revealed faster responses to the last three items in the *Task-performing robot* condition compared to the *Baseline* condition F(1, 28) = 5.45, p = 0.031 (see Fig. 3, Right).

4.2 Lexical Decision Task Results

We conducted a two-way ANOVA to analyze the LD results. We were interested in evaluating the interaction between the robotic condition (*Task-performing robot* vs. *Baseline*) and the word type (*inefficacy* vs. *neutral*). The analysis revealed a significant interaction, F(1, 28) = 6.17, p = 0.019 (see Fig. 4, Right). Post-hoc multiple comparisons using Scheffe's method indicated that in the *Baseline* condition, participants responded significantly slower to inefficacy words than to neutral words (p = 0.050). However, in the *Task-performing robot* condition, the reaction times to the different word types were almost equal. In addition to the interaction, the word type main effect was also significant, F(1, 28) = 10.8, p = 0.003. The main effect of the robotic conditions was not significant.

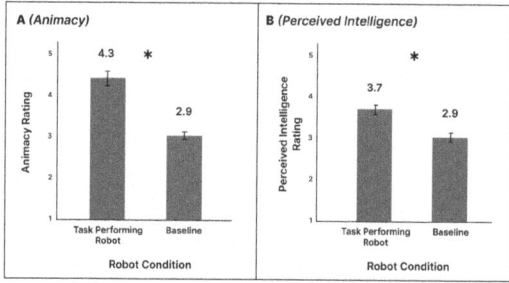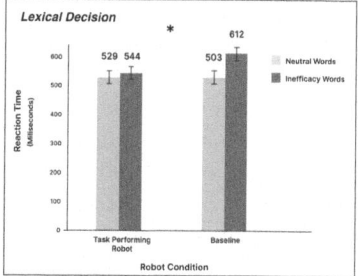

Fig. 4. Godspeed ratings and LD reaction times as a function of robotic conditions: Left - Animacy; Center - Perceived Intelligence; Right - LD.

4.3 Godspeed Results

Godspeed ratings were analyzed with separate one-way ANOVAs for each subscale. The robot's behavior had a significant influence on the Animacy ratings, with higher ratings in the *Task-performing robot* condition $F(1,28) = 4.57$, p $= 0.042$ (see Fig. 4, Left). The robot's behavior also had a significant influence on the Perceived Intelligence ratings. Participants perceived the robot in the *Task-performing robot* condition as having a higher intelligence, $F(1,28) = 5.45$, p $= 0.027$ (see Fig. 4, Center). There was no significant influence on participants' Likeability ratings, $F(1, 28) = 0.103$, p $= 0.751$.

4.4 Thematic Analysis of the Interviews

The qualitative analysis of semi-structured interviews utilized thematic coding. The process included: (1) Transcription by two coders for initial data understanding; (2) Extraction and discussion of initial themes, resolving discrepancies with a third researcher; (3) Independent analysis by coders to verify inter-rater reliability (Kappa=85%); (4) Final analysis by both coders after confirming high reliability. The thematic analysis resulted in two main themes: (1) The effect of the robot's performance; (2) Participant's perceived performance.

The Effect of the Robot's Performance. In the *Task-performing robot* condition, most participants (10/15) acknowledged the influence of the robot on their performance: "Some questions were difficult and to be honest I relayed on the robot's answers" (p. 9, *Task-performing robot*). A few participants in this condition (6/15) explained that the robot's presence had a positive effect, stating that it created a sense of collaboration as if they were tackling a shared challenge with a teammate: "It was like performing the task together with someone, and we were like a team" (p. 3, *Task-performing robot*).

In the *Baseline* condition, participants (5/15) also mentioned a positive effect. They associated the robot with a sense of companionship: "It felt good that the robot was with me. I would be less confident without it" (p. 23, *Baseline*).

Participants in both groups also described negative aspects of the robot's presence. This was more prevalent in the *Task-performing robot* condition (9/15) than in the *Baseline* condition (6/15): "The robot presence was confusing; once it started moving I couldn't concentrate" (p. 2, *Task-performing robot*); "It interrupted me, it moved all the time and distracted me" (p. 16, *Baseline*). Interestingly, none mentioned the robot's training or its potential for errors.

Participant's Perceived Performance. Participants' assessment of their performance varied across the conditions. In the *Task-performing robot* condition, a few participants (5/15) were satisfied with their performance. However, most participants (8/15) expressed dissatisfaction: "I felt I wasn't really good; I answered half of the questions wrong" (p. 4, *Task-performing robot*). In the *Baseline* condition, most participants (10/15) were satisfied with their performance: "Overall, I'm satisfied with my performance and my answers" (p. 25, *Baseline*).

5 Discussion

In this study we indicated that overtrust in robots can occur even when interacting with a very simple 2DoF robotic object explicitly introduced as being in a training phase. Participants chose that responses were similar to the robot's, which subsequently impaired their own performance. Furthermore, participants displayed quicker response times when the robot actively performed the task alongside them, suggesting reduced effort on their part. Our findings highlight the extent of overtrust, indicating that it may occur even when the robot has a simple, non-humanoid design and imperfect capabilities.

Our findings also suggest that the inclination to overtrust robots extends beyond task performance, affecting participants' self-efficacy. The LD results indicated participants' heightened sensitivity to words, which represented low self-efficacy. The qualitative analysis supported this finding, as more participants in the *Task-performing robot* condition were not satisfied with their performance. They associated this lack of confidence with the misalignment with the robot. Participants stated that "When we answered together, it was reassuring" and that "It made me think twice when our answers were different." It is, therefore, important to consider and account for the wider implications of overtrust. Since robots are perceived as social entities [8], people would likely use them as a reference point for adjusting their self-efficacy [34]. Our findings imply that the tendency to overtrust robots may lead to an upward comparison, even when the robot has a highly simple design and not fully trained to perform the task.

The tendency to overtrust robots highlighted in our study, calls for clear communication of the robot's competence throughout the interaction. Incorporating gestures into the robot's behavior that signal uncertainty or subtle signs of learning can enhance transparency regarding its limitations. Leveraging such social cues not only fosters a healthier balance between trust and critical thinking but can also enhance the robot's reliability and acceptance. Achieving this balance between preserving critical thinking and maintaining trust presents a significant design challenge that should be thoroughly explored in the future.

6   Limitations

We used a specific non-humanoid robot. Future research should explore the impact of various robotic morphologies. Additionally, the RPM task may have induced stress in some participants, potentially affecting their performance. Future studies should investigate different types of tasks and task features such as difficulty, length, and engagement. Future studies should also include a comparison to other agents (digital, voice). Furthermore, participants' confidence while performing the task could influence their tendency to trust the robot. We also acknowledge the low number of participants who where all students as a limitation. Future studies should evaluate the effect with a larger sample. Another limitation concerns the specific task used in the study. The lack of repercussions for incorrect choices [37] and the functional non-social context [10] could limit the generalization of our findings. Lastly, interviews may be biased by the interviewers' expectations and the "good subject effect." We minimized this effect by using a strict protocol and ensuring participants that all answers were helpful.

7   Conclusion

This study highlights the human tendency to overtrust robots, even in situations involving interaction with a simple, non-humanoid robot portrayed as having imperfect capabilities. We recommend that robot designers and practitioners incorporate clear robotic behaviors to remind users of the robot's limitations, mitigate the adverse effects of overtrust in the context of HRI.

Disclosure of Interests. The authors have no competing interests to declare.

References

1. Algom, D., Chajut, E., Lev, S.: A rational look at the emotional stroop phenomenon: a generic slowdown, not a stroop effect. J. Exp. Psychol. Gen. **133**(3), 323 (2004)
2. Aroyo, A.M., Rea, F., Sandini, G., Sciutti, A.: Trust and social engineering in human robot interaction: Will a robot make you disclose sensitive information, conform to its recommendations or gamble? IEEE Robot. Autom. Lett. **3**(4), 3701–3708 (2018)
3. Bahner, J.E., Hüper, A.D., Manzey, D.: Misuse of automated decision aids: complacency, automation bias and the impact of training experience. Int. J. Hum Comput Stud. **66**(9), 688–699 (2008)

4. Baldwin, M.W., Sinclair, L.: Self-esteem and" if...then" contingencies of interpersonal acceptance. J. Personality Soc. Psychol. **71**(6), 1130 (1996)
5. Bandura, A.: Self-efficacy mechanism in human agency. Am. Psychol. **37**(2), 122 (1982)
6. Bartneck, C., Kulić, D., Croft, E., Zoghbi, S.: Measurement instruments for the anthropomorphism, animacy, likeability, perceived intelligence, and perceived safety of robots. Int. J. Soc. Robot. **1**, 71–81 (2009)
7. Beckes, L., Coan, J.A., Morris, J.P.: Implicit conditioning of faces via the social regulation of emotion: Erp evidence of early attentional biases for security conditioned faces. Psychophysiology **50**(8), 734–742 (2013)
8. Erel, H., Shem Tov, T., Kessler, Y., Zuckerman, O.: Robots are always social: Robotic movements are automatically interpreted as social cues. In: Extended Abstracts of the 2019 CHI Conference on Human Factors in Computing Systems, pp. 1–6 (2019)
9. Estes, Z., Verges, M.: Freeze or flee? negative stimuli elicit selective responding. Cognition **108**(2), 557–565 (2008)
10. Gaudiello, I., Zibetti, E., Lefort, S., Chetouani, M., Ivaldi, S.: Trust as indicator of robot functional and social acceptance. an experimental study on user conformation to icub answers. Comput. Human Behav. **61**, 633–655 (2016)
11. Gruber, M.E., Hancock, P.A.: The self-evaluation maintenance model in human-robot interaction: a conceptual replication. In: Li, H., et al. (eds.) ICSR 2021. LNCS (LNAI), vol. 13086, pp. 268–280. Springer, Cham (2021). https://doi.org/10.1007/978-3-030-90525-5_23
12. Hancock, P.A., Billings, D.R., Schaefer, K.E., Chen, J.Y., De Visser, E.J., Parasuraman, R.: A meta-analysis of factors affecting trust in human-robot interaction. Hum. Factors **53**(5), 517–527 (2011)
13. Harbarth, L., Gößwein, E., Bodemer, D., Schnaubert, L.: (over) trusting ai recommendations: How system and person variables affect dimensions of complacency. Inter. J. Human–Comput. Interact., 1–20 (2024)
14. Hitron, T., Megidish, B., Todress, E., Morag, N., Erel, H.: Ai bias in human-robot interaction: An evaluation of the risk in gender biased robots. In: 2022 31st IEEE International Conference on Robot and Human Interactive Communication (RO-MAN), pp. 1598–1605. IEEE (2022)
15. Hitron, T., Morag Yaar, N., Erel, H.: Implications of ai bias in hri: Risks (and opportunities) when interacting with a biased robot. In: Proceedings of the 2023 ACM/IEEE International Conference on Human-Robot Interaction, pp. 83–92 (2023)
16. Hoffman, G., Zuckerman, O., Hirschberger, G., Luria, M., Shani Sherman, T.: Design and evaluation of a peripheral robotic conversation companion. In: Proceedings of the Tenth Annual ACM/IEEE International Conference On Human-robot Interaction, pp. 3–10 (2015)
17. Howard, A., Borenstein, J.: The ugly truth about ourselves and our robot creations: the problem of bias and social inequity. Sci. Eng. Ethics **24**, 1521–1536 (2018)
18. Jacobs, M., Pradier, M.F., McCoy, T.H., Jr., Perlis, R.H., Doshi-Velez, F., Gajos, K.Z.: How machine-learning recommendations influence clinician treatment selections: the example of antidepressant selection. Transl. Psychiatry **11**(1), 108 (2021)
19. Lee, J.D., See, K.A.: Trust in automation: designing for appropriate reliance. Hum. Factors **46**(1), 50–80 (2004)
20. Lewis, M., Sycara, K., Walker, P.: The role of trust in human-robot interaction. Foundat. Trusted Autonomy 135–159 (2018)

21. Lin, P., Abney, K., Jenkins, R.: Robot ethics 2. 0: New challenges in philosophy, law, and society (2017)
22. Megidish, B.: Butter robotics (2017)
23. Merritt, S.M., et al.: Automation-induced complacency potential: development and validation of a new scale. Front. Psychol. **10**, 225 (2019)
24. Nickell, G.S.: The helping attitude scale. In: 106th Annual Convention of the American Psychological Association at San Francisco, pp. 1–10 (1998)
25. Nomura, T., Kanda, T., Suzuki, T.: Experimental investigation into influence of negative attitudes toward robots on human-robot interaction. Ai & Soc. **20**, 138–150 (2006)
26. Olafson, K.M., Ferraro, F.R.: Effects of emotional state on lexical decision performance. Brain Cogn. **45**(1), 15–20 (2001)
27. Ososky, S., Schuster, D., Phillips, E., Jentsch, F.G.: Building appropriate trust in human-robot teams. In: 2013 AAAI Spring Symposium Series (2013)
28. Parasuraman, R., Riley, V.: Humans and automation: use, misuse, disuse, abuse. Hum. Factors **39**(2), 230–253 (1997)
29. Rosenthal-von der Pütten, A.M., Bock, N., Brockmann, K.: Not your cup of tea? how interacting with a robot can increase perceived self-efficacy in hri and evaluation. In: Proceedings of the 2017 ACM/IEEE International Conference on Human-Robot Interaction, pp. 483–492 (2017)
30. Raven, J.C., Court, J.H.: Raven's progressive matrices and vocabulary scales. Oxford Psychologists Press, Oxford (1998)
31. Riek, L.D.: Wizard of oz studies in hri: a systematic review and new reporting guidelines. J. Hum.-Robot Interact. **1**(1), 119–136 (2012)
32. Robinette, P., Li, W., Allen, R., Howard, A.M., Wagner, A.R.: Overtrust of robots in emergency evacuation scenarios. In: 2016 11th ACM/IEEE International Conference on Human-Robot Interaction (HRI), pp. 101–108. IEEE (2016)
33. Salem, M., Lakatos, G., Amirabdollahian, F., Dautenhahn, K.: Would you trust a (faulty) robot? effects of error, task type and personality on human-robot cooperation and trust. In: Proceedings of the tenth annual ACM/IEEE International Conference on Human-robot Interaction, pp. 141–148 (2015)
34. Tesser, A.: Toward a self-evaluation maintenance model of social behavior, vol. 21. Elsevier (1988)
35. Ullrich, D., Butz, A., Diefenbach, S.: The development of overtrust: an empirical simulation and psychological analysis in the context of human-robot interaction. Front. Robot. AI **8**, 554578 (2021)
36. Waseem, Z., Lulz, S., Bingel, J., Augenstein, I.: Disembodied machine learning: On the illusion of objectivity in nlp. arXiv preprint arXiv:2101.11974 (2021)
37. Xu, J., Howard, A.: How much do you trust your self-driving car? exploring human-robot trust in high-risk scenarios. In: 2020 IEEE International Conference on Systems, Man, and Cybernetics (SMC), pp. 4273–4280. IEEE (2020)
38. Yaar, G., Oberlender, A., Heimann Saadon, N., Zuckerman, O., Erel, H.: Performing a task alongside a robot: exploring the impact of social comparison. In: Extended Abstracts of the CHI Conference on Human Factors in Computing Systems, pp. 1–7 (2024)
39. Zafari, S., Schwaninger, I., Hirschmanner, M., Schmidbauer, C., Weiss, A., Koeszegi, S.T.: "you are doing so great!"–the effect of a robot's interaction style on self-efficacy in hri. In: 2019 28th IEEE International Conference on Robot and Human Interactive Communication (RO-MAN), pp. 1–7. IEEE (2019)

An EEG Benchmark Dataset
for Data-Driven Trust Assessment
in Social HRI

Matthias Rehm[(✉)] [iD], Ioannis Pontikis[iD], and Giulio Campagna[iD]

Technical Faculty of IT and Design, Aalborg University, Rendsburggade 14,
9000 Aalborg, Denmark
{matthias,ipo,gica}@create.aau.dk

Abstract. Trust is a crucial element in successful interactions with
social robots. However, few existing methods attempt to measure trust
in real time to adjust the robot's behavior according to the user's trust
level. One of the significant challenges in this area is the scarcity of
curated data sets necessary for developing machine learning models to
detect trust from sensor data. In this paper, we introduce a structured
approach to collecting data sets for trust assessment. We demonstrate
this approach using an EEG data set from a study designed to build,
break, and subsequently repair trust between the user and the robot. The
data is available on Zenodo for development of real-time trust assessment
models.

Keywords: Human Robot Trust · Social Robotics · Machine
Learning · AI · Dataset

1   Introduction

Human-robot trust is becoming more prominent in human-robot interaction
research. While trust has long been used in automation as an evaluation criterion for system design [15], trust in HRI promises to exploit trust as a control
parameter during interaction with a robot. It has been shown that an inappro-
priate level of trust, whether negative or positive, is detrimental to the use of
a robotic system [7]. If the user does not exhibit enough trust in the system,
they will not use the robot to its full potential, e.g., performing tasks that the
robot can handle [6]. Conversely, if the user trusts the robot too much, this can
be potentially dangerous, e.g., if the user does not monitor the system closely
enough.

A range of different factors have been identified that influence a user's trust
in a robot, ranging from the user's experience with the robot and the robot's
reliability to the robot's communication behavior or task complexity [10]. Different questionnaires have been developed based on these trust indicators to assess
the subjective impression of trust in the user, e.g., [5,13,20,22]. While the questionnaires allow for system evaluations and detailed analysis of which factors

O. Palinko et al. (Eds.): ICSR + AI 2024, LNAI 15562, pp. 360–369, 2025.
https://doi.org/10.1007/978-981-96-3519-1_33

influence the impression of trust in a given robot, they are usually administered post-interaction, allowing for a summative evaluation of the entire interaction with the robot. Moreover, it has been shown that the user's subjective evaluation of trust in the robot does not always match the user's behavior during the interaction [1]. While questionnaires allow for post-hoc analysis of the interaction and can provide a ground truth for trust, we need to look at more observable information during the interaction if we want to exploit trust as a control parameter in human-robot interaction. This would allow for regulating trust during the interaction, i.e., trying to increase trust if the user shows insufficient trust in the system, or dampen trust if the user exhibits too much trust.

This requires a data-driven, continuous trust assessment during the interaction with the robot. Some initial approaches have explored suitable data for this task. Hopko and colleagues [11] investigate the use of heart rate variability as a trust measurement. They employ the TRUST questionnaire [14] to collect subjective trust measurements as the ground truth. Hu and colleagues [12], as well as Shayesteh and colleagues [21], focus on EEG data and present a range of suitable features to train machine learning algorithms for trust recognition. While Hu and colleagues reduce the ground truth questionnaire to a simple question of whether users trust the system or not, Shayesteh and colleagues employ the trust perception scale [20] as their ground truth.

None of the approaches so far have investigated contexts in which users interact with social robots. The above-mentioned studies explore industrial contexts (metal polishing and collaborative construction) as well as (partly) autonomous driving. It remains unclear whether the developed algorithms are idiosyncratic to the application contexts in which the data was collected and the models were trained, or if the results are generalizable to other contexts, largely due to the unavailability of the datasets.

In the following, we suggest a more systematic approach to data collection for the goal of developing trust assessment algorithms and present an example of EEG data collection for social robotics.

2   Methods

In principle, we assume that trust is strongly dependent on the robot's morphology and the task context. For instance, people tend to trust robots in production contexts more than in care contexts, while at the same time, they deem social anthropomorphic robots in an industrial context less trustworthy [2]. On the other hand, it has been shown that anthropomorphism fosters trust in social interaction contexts [17].

Moreover, in previous work, we have identified that user experience influences baseline trust levels but does not affect qualitative trust development [8]. For example, if trust is broken, e.g., by a misaligned trajectory, trust levels will decrease and, given reliable system functions afterward, will rise again slowly [9]. Thus, apart from the variable baseline, user experience does not play a role in developing data-driven trust assessments. We have previously identified the flow for the development of data-driven trust assessment in the industrial domain, which can be directly applied to social robots as well [19](see also Fig. 1 for an overview).

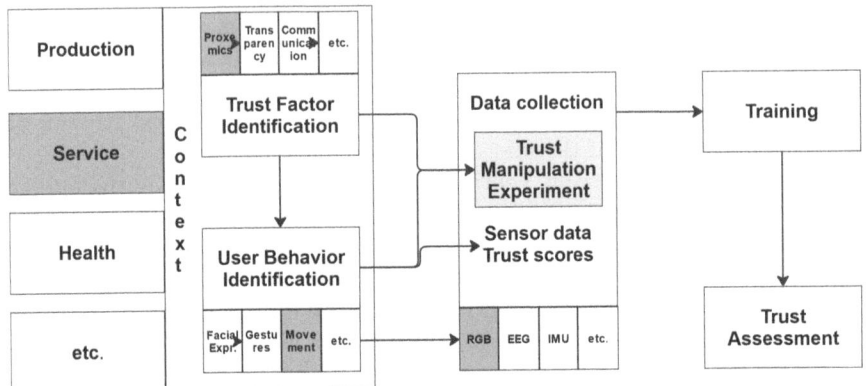

Fig. 1. Overview of a systematic approach for data collection: Factors influencing trust must be identified for a given context (e.g., proxemics in a service context), and the corresponding user behavior must be observed (e.g., movement of the user when the robot comes too close). This information is used to select appropriate sensors for detecting this user behavior (e.g., an RGB-D camera) and to design a trust manipulation experiment to elicit specific trust levels. Ground truth (trust scores) is collected using standard questionnaires.

- **Trust factor identification:** Trust is a multidimensional concept, and there are various factors that influence trust ratings, such as user expertise, system predictability, and task complexity. For instance, Hancock and colleagues [10] have identified six categories of trust factors, ranging from human-related (i. ability-based, ii. user characteristics), robot-related (iii. performance-based, iv. attribute-based), to context-related factors (v. team-based, vi. task-based). Depending on the application context (e.g., service robot in Fig. 1), specific factors will be relevant to consider for data collection (e.g., in Fig. 1, proxemics when approaching a customer).
- **User behavior identification:** Trust levels influence user behavior, such as communication or movement patterns. For a given application context, this influence must be determined because it will dictate the possible sensors that can be used for data collection. In the example in Fig. 1, the user might move away when the robot approaches.
- **Manipulation of trust during data collection:** Identifying relevant trust factors and user behaviors allows for controlled manipulation of trust levels during data collection. For example, after identifying proxemics as a relevant trust factor, the robot can be programmed to interact at different distances from the user to elicit varying trust levels [3].

Fig. 2. The setup for the data collection. Left: The user is sitting in front of the EZ-robot and is equipped with the EEG headset. Right: The control room with the wizard controlling the robot (left) and two data collectors monitoring the collection of sensor data.

- **Collection of sensor data:** Identifying user behavior helps in selecting appropriate sensors for data collection. For instance, in [19], we describe how movement can predict trust levels during collaboration with large industrial manipulators. In the example in Fig. 1, an RGB camera is used to detect user movement.
- **Ground truth collection with standardized questionnaire:** While unsupervised learning on the data is possible, we suggest administering a standard trust questionnaire (e.g., [5, 16, 20, 22]) at the end of each interaction to collect ground truth, which can be used to annotate the data for supervised learning or for evaluating machine learning models.
- **Model training:** The data can be used to train machine learning models for trust assessment. Different approaches are possible, depending on the goal of the trust assessment. For instance, regression models allow for estimating a trust score similar to those from trust questionnaires, while classification models might suffice to detect changes in trust levels, from low to high. Trust dynamics could be incorporated using recurrent models.
- **Trust assessment:** After training and evaluating the model, it can be used for trust assessment during the interaction.

Currently, only a few studies follow such a principled approach (e.g., [19]). Shortcomings include not clearly identifying trust factors for the given context, not clearly defining trust or obtaining a reliable and valid ground truth, and not publishing the collected data. Thus, with this paper, we aim to provide an example for collecting a benchmark dataset that can be used to develop EEG-based trust assessment algorithms for social contexts.

3   Data Collection

The data collection consisted of a game interaction with a small humanoid EZ-robot (Fig. 2 left). The robot explained a word to the participant either through movements depicting the concept or by verbal description. Depending on their performance, participants could "earn" or lose candy as remuneration for their participation. This ensured engagement from the participants and introduced an element of risk to the interaction.

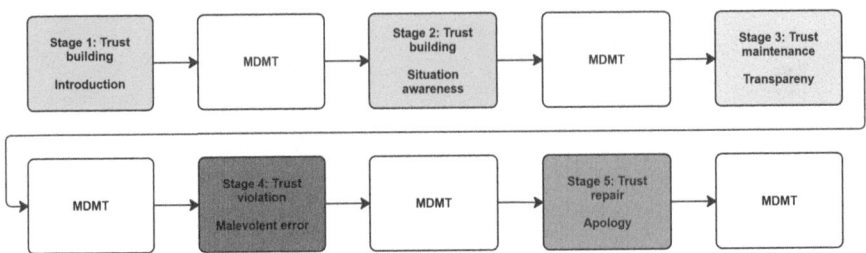

Fig. 3. Trust manipulation stages during the data collection. Trust is build up in stage 1 and 2 (green), maintained in stage 3 (yellow), broken in stage 4 (red) and repaired in stage 5 (blue). In between stages, participants fill out the MDMT questionnaire. (Color figure online)

Trust Factor Identification. We have identified the following trust factors that are manipulated during the game. Robot behavior is used to build trust by showing situational awareness, e.g., by commenting on the user's fashion choices. Transparency is used to maintain trust in situations where the robot makes an error. Reliability is used to break trust by exhibiting intentional errors from the robot.

User Behavior Identification. Stage four is set up to break the user's trust in the robot by performing intentional errors, such as the robot speaking backward to prevent the user from guessing correctly. This should trigger increased attention from the user to the interaction, which, in turn, will influence the collected EEG data.

Manipulation of Trust During Data Collection. To elicit different trust levels during the data collection, five stages were designed for the interaction. The first three stages build up and maintain trust, while the last two stages break and repair trust (Fig. 3). At each stage, participants must guess two words that the robot explains either through movements or words. After each stage, participants complete the MDMT questionnaire [16].

1. Trust building: During the first stage, the robot explains the game mechanics to the user and starts with two simple tasks.
2. Trust building: In the second stage, the robot shows situational awareness by commenting on aspects such as the user's fashion choices or the weather, followed by two more tasks.

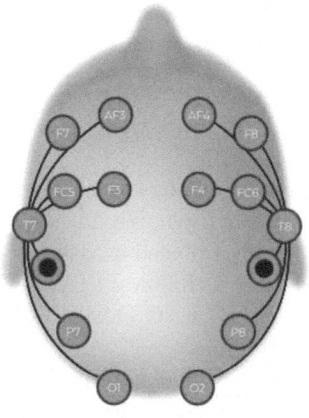
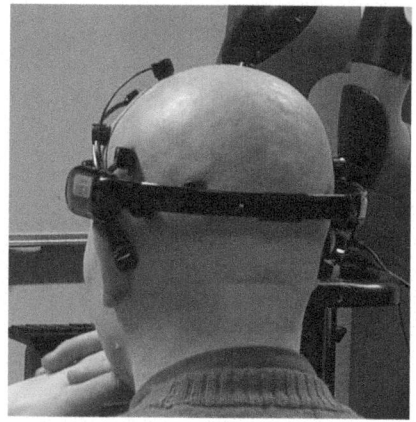

Fig. 4. Placement of the Emotiv headset. Left: Diagram for placement of the 14 electrodes. Right: Example of the placement of the headset.

3. Trust maintenance: During this stage, the robot makes some errors, which it explains to the user to exhibit transparent behavior.
4. Trust violation: Stage four is used to break trust by performing a deliberate error where the robot speaks backward.
5. Trust repair: To repair trust, the robot apologizes in the fifth stage for the unreliable behavior from the previous stage.

Collection of Sensor Data. EEG data were captured with an EMOTIV EPOC+ 14-Channel Wireless EEG Headset[1], with a frame rate of 128 Hz. To prevent movement artifacts, participants were seated at a table facing the robot and interacted with the robot through speech. Figure 4 shows the placement of the headset. The robot was controlled through a Wizard-of-Oz interface (Fig. 2 right) to prevent errors in the data collection, e.g., through problems with the speech recognition.

Ground Trust Collection with Standardized Questionnaire. As ground truth for trust levels, participants filled out an MDMT questionnaire [16] after each stage to evaluate their trust towards the robot after the interaction. MDMT uses 7-point Likert scales to rate how well several trust-based descriptors applied to the robot, covering both moral and performance trust.

Data were collected from 21 participants who were recruited on campus: 9 males and 12 females, with an average age of 28.3 (SD=9.94). One session, including setup and debriefing, lasted for 30 min. Average trust ratings over the five stages (5.52 – 5.44 – 5.34 – 4.64 – 5.33) show the general feasibility of the approach (trust building [stages 1–3] – trust violation [stage 4] – trust repair

---

[1] https://www.emotiv.com/.

[stage 5]) and the successful elicitation of different trust levels, with a significant decline in trust for stage 4 [4].

4   Dataset

The dataset comprises EEG (Electroencephalography) recordings from 21 participants, gathered using Emotiv headsets (see Fig. 4). Each participant's EEG data includes timestamps and measurements from 14 sensors placed across different regions of the scalp. The sensor labels in the header are as follows: EEG.AF3, EEG.F7, EEG.F3, EEG.FC5, EEG.T7, EEG.P7, EEG.O1, EEG.O2, EEG.P8, EEG.T8, EEG.FC6, EEG.F4, EEG.F8, EEG.AF4, and Time.

The EEG data provides insights into the brain's electrical activity, offering a window into cognitive processes and emotional responses during various activities or stimuli, in the form of μV and with a frame rate of 128 Hz. The frequency of the individual bands can easily be derived using an FFT (Fast Fourier Transformation). Because doing so reduces the resolution of the data, we leave it to the individual researcher to decide their preferred time window for the transformation. The entire dataset consists of 3,651,124 data points for each sensor—173,863 on average for each participant (min. 128,505, max. 249,631).

The files are named after participant numbers starting with ID01. They include data collected during the whole session, including preparation. Thus, the data needs to be pre-processed using the annotations provided in the details.xlsx file, which contain annotations corresponding to the EEG recordings. These annotations denote the timing of different phases related to trust across the participants' interactions. Each phase is delineated by a start time and an end time, representing distinct stages of the trust-building process. All the other data (timestamps) which are outside the start and end of each phase should be considered as breaks, e.g. filling out the questionnaires. The last column gives trust scores for each stage.

Following the five stages describe in Sect. 3, the following phases have been annotated:

- Trust Building: This phase involves friendly initial interactions for establishing trust between participants and the robot.
- Situational Awareness: This phase continues to build up trust by showing situation awareness of the robot, e.g. by complimenting on the participant's fashion choice.
- Transparency: Trust is maintained by increased openness and clarity in communicating about the robot's abilities.
- Trust Violation: Trust is compromised during this phase by deliberately misleading the participant and making it impossible to answer correctly.
- Trust Repair: The robot shows efforts to repair trust by apologizing for the behavior in the previous stage.

The EEG data, coupled with these annotations, offers valuable insights into the neural correlates of trust-related processes, shedding light on the dynamics of interpersonal interactions and trust development. The dataset is available under GPL4 license from Zenodo [18][2].

5   Applicability of the Dataset for Trust Assessment

The data can be used to develop EEG-based trust assessment tools. In [4], we describe a first approach for detecting trust breaks making use of the data from stage 3 and 4. We defined trust break as a classification problem, where we classify the EEG data either as representing high trust or low trust. For the feature calculation a window size of one second was defined and features were calculated for the alpha frequency band power over the 14 electrodes. For this first model we used a set of standard features: mean, median, peak, standard deviation and kurtosis. Three different machine learning algorithms have been evaluated and provided varying accuracy (F1-score) between 0.63 and 0.73. The best classifier for this dataset was a Random Forest classifier with an accuracy of 0.73. This shows that trust assessment based on EEG data is feasible, but the obtained accuracy also shows that there is room for improvement. An obvious starting point would be to either investigate more relevant features, work with more frequency bands or to use the actual trust scores and train a regression model. Moreover, the dataset is constructed in a way that allows for investigating the dynamics of trust development, break and repair. Thus, more sophisticated models like LSTMs could be used to capture these dynamics.

6   Conclusion

Trust is usually assessed through post-hoc, subjective questionnaires. If we want to use trust as a control parameter during the interaction with a robot, to prevent overtrust (dangerous) or undertrust (inefficient), then we need more objective, data-driven methods for assessing trust. For this, we need datasets collected using suitable sensors during real human-robot interactions. While some studies show the feasibility of this approach, we lack access to such datasets for developing and testing machine learning approaches for trust assessment.

In this paper, we advocate for a more rigorous approach to data collection for trust assessment to provide datasets that can be used as benchmarks against which we can evaluate trust assessment algorithms. We have presented an example of this approach with an EEG dataset for social human-robot interaction. The dataset is freely available on Zenodo.

The role of well-defined datasets for research into trust assessment should be self-evident. This approach is well-known in the field of computer vision (e.g., ImageNet[3]). Instead, we often rely on small ad-hoc datasets for research in human-robot interaction. In comparison to a dataset like ImageNet, it is much more expensive and cumbersome to collect interaction data, starting with

---

[2] https://doi.org/10.5281/zenodo.12754929.
[3] https://www.image-net.org/.

designing the data collection, setting up the necessary technical infrastructure, and recruiting participants. But we think it would be beneficial to invest in creating well-defined and curated datasets that allow multiple groups to develop algorithms. With this paper and the corresponding dataset, we hope to set an example for this approach.

Acknowledgement. The work presented in this paper is supported by the Independent Research Fund Denmark, grant number 1032-00311B. We would like to thank Kerstin Fischer and Matous Jellinek for their work in developing the scenario for the data collection and Carlos Gomez Cubero for his help during the data collection.

References

1. Adamik, M., Dudzinska, K., Herskind, A.J., Rehm, M.: The difference between trust measurement and behavior: Investigating the effect of personalizing a robot's appearance on trust in hri. In: 30th IEEE International Conference on Robot & Human Interactive Communication (RO-MAN), pp. 880–885 (2021). https://doi.org/10.1109/RO-MAN50785.2021.9515487
2. Biermann, H., Brauner, P., Ziefle, M.: How context and design shape human-robot trust and attributions Paladyn. J. Behav. Robot. **12**(1), 74–86 (2021). https://doi.org/10.1515/pjbr-2021-0008
3. Campagna, G., Dadgostar, M., Chrysostomou, D., Rehm, M.: A data-driven approach utilizing body motion data for trust evaluation in industrial human-robot collaboration. In: 33rd IEEE International Conference on Robot and Human Interactive Communication (IEEE RO-MAN 2024), IEEE, United States (2024)
4. Campagna, G., Rehm, M.: Trust assessment with eeg signals in social human-robot interaction. In: Ali, A.A., et al. (eds.) Social Robotics, pp. 33–42. Springer Nature Singapore, Singapore (2024). https://doi.org/10.1007/978-981-99-8715-3_4
5. Charalambous, G., Fletcher, S., Webb, P.: The development of a scale to evaluate trust in industrial human-robot collaboration. Int. J. Soc. Robot. **8**(2), 193–209 (2016). https://doi.org/10.1007/s12369-015-0333-8
6. Chen, M., Nikolaidis, S., Soh, H., Hsu, D., Srinivasa, S.: Planning with trust for human-robot collaboration, pp. 307–315. Association for Computing Machinery, New York (2018). https://doi.org/10.1145/3171221.3171264
7. De Visser, E.J., et al.: Towards a theory of longitudinal trust calibration in human-robot teams. Int. J. Soc. Robot. **12**(2), 459–478 (2020). https://doi.org/10.1007/s12369-019-00596-x
8. Hald, K., Rehm, M.: Usability evaluation framework for close-proximity collaboration with large industrial manipulators. In: 2024 IEEE International Conference on Robotics and Automation, ICRA, Proceedings of ICRA 2024. IEEE (2024)
9. Hald, K., Rehm, M., Moeslund, T.B.: Proposing human-robot trust assessment through tracking physical apprehension signals in close-proximity human-robot collaboration. In: 28th IEEE International Conference on Robot and Human Interactive Communication (RO-MAN), pp. 1–6 (2019). https://doi.org/10.1109/RO-MAN46459.2019.8956335
10. Hancock, P.A., Billings, D.R., Schaefer, K.E., Chen, J.Y., De Visser, E.J., Parasuraman, R.: A meta-analysis of factors affecting trust in human-robot interaction. Hum. Factors **53**(5), 517–527 (2011). https://doi.org/10.1177/0018720811417254

11. Hopko, S.K., Mehta, R.K., Pagilla, P.R.: Physiological and perceptual consequences of trust in collaborative robots: An empirical investigation of human and robot factors. Appli. Ergon. **106** (2023). https://doi.org/10.1016/j.apergo.2022.103863

12. Hu, W.L., Akash, K., Jain, N., Reid, T.: Real-time sensing of trust in human-machine interactions. IFAC-PapersOnLine **49**(32), 48–53 (2016). https://doi.org/10.1016/j.ifacol.2016.12.188

13. Jessup, S.A., Schneider, T.R., Alarcon, G.M., Ryan, T.J., Capiola, A.: The measurement of the propensity to trust automation. In: Chen, J.Y., Fragomeni, G. (eds.) Virtual, Augmented and Mixed Reality. Applications and Case Studies, pp. 476–489. Springer International Publishing, Cham (2019). https://doi.org/10.1007/978-3-030-21565-1_32

14. Jiun-Yin Jian, A.M.B., Drury, C.G.: Foundations for an empirically determined scale of trust in automated systems. Inter. J. Cognitive Ergon. **4**(1), 53–71 (2000). https://doi.org/10.1207/S15327566IJCE0401_04

15. Lee, J.D., See, K.A.: Trust in automation: designing for appropriate reliance. Hum. Factors **46**(1), 50–80 (2004). https://doi.org/10.1518/hfes.46.1.50_30392

16. Malle, B.F., Ullman, D.: A multidimensional conception and measure of human-robot trust. In: Nam, C.S., Lyons, J.B. (eds.) Trust in Human-robot Interaction, pp. 3–25. Elsevier (2021). https://doi.org/10.1016/B978-0-12-819472-0.00001-0

17. Natarajan, M., Gombolay, M.: Effects of anthropomorphism and accountability on trust in human robot interaction. In: Proceedings of the 2020 ACM/IEEE International Conference on Human-Robot Interaction, pp. 33–42. Association for Computing Machinery, New York (2020). https://doi.org/10.1145/3319502.3374839

18. Rehm, M., Campagna, G.: Benchmark EEG data set for trust assessment for interactions with social robots (2024). https://doi.org/10.5281/zenodo.12754929

19. Rehm, M., Hald, K., Pontikis, I.: Benchmark movement data set for trust assessment in human robot collaboration. In: Proceedings of the 2024 ACM/IEEE International Conference on Human-Robot Interaction, pp. 934–938. Association for Computing Machinery, New York (2024). https://doi.org/10.1145/3610977.3637472

20. Schaefer, K.E.: Measuring Trust in Human Robot Interactions: Development of the "Trust Perception Scale-HRI", pp. 191–218. Springer US, Boston, MA (2016). https://doi.org/10.1007/978-1-4899-7668-0_10

21. Shayesteh, S., Ojha, A., Jebelli, H.: Workers' trust in collaborative construction robots: Eeg-based trust recognition in an immersive environment. In: Automation and Robotics in the Architecture, Engineering, and Construction Industry, pp. 201–215 (2022). https://doi.org/10.1007/978-3-030-77163-8_10

22. Yagoda, R.E., Gillan, D.J.: You want me to trust a robot? the development of a human–robot interaction trust scale. Inter. J. Soc. Robot. **4**(2), 235–348 (2012). https://doi.org/10.1007/s12369-012-0144-0

Evaluating Robot Influence on Pedestrian Behavior Models for Crowd Simulation and Benchmarking

Subham Agrawal[1(✉)], Nils Dengler[1,2], and Maren Bennewitz[1,2,3]

[1] Humanoid Robots Lab, University of Bonn, Bonn, Germany
sagrawal@cs.uni-bonn.de
[2] The Lamarr Institute, Bonn, Germany
[3] Center for Robotics, Bonn, Germany

Abstract. The presence of robots amongst pedestrians affects them causing deviation to their trajectories. Existing methods suffer from the limitation of not being able to objectively measure this deviation in unseen cases. In order to solve this issue, we introduce a simulation framework that repetitively measures and benchmarks the deviation in trajectory of pedestrians due to robots driven by different navigation algorithms. We simulate the deviation behavior of the pedestrians using an enhanced Social Force Model (SFM) with a robot force component that accounts for the influence of robots on pedestrian behavior, resulting in the Social Robot Force Model (SRFM). Parameters for this model are learned using the pedestrian trajectories from the JRDB dataset [1]. Pedestrians are then simulated using the SRFM with and without the robot force component to objectively measure the deviation to their trajectory caused by the robot in 5 different scenarios. Our work in this paper is a proof of concept that shows objectively measuring the pedestrian reaction to robot is possible. We use our simulation to train two different RL policies and evaluate them against traditional navigation models.

Keywords: Social Navigation · Social Robot Force Model · Simulation Benchmark

1 Introduction

The increasing presence of robots in everyday life has made the issue of social navigation of mobile robots among pedestrians more relevant than ever. As robots become more integrated into various public and private spaces, from shopping malls [2,3], to hospitals [4] and homes [5,6], their ability to navigate in crowded environments efficiently and safely, but also adhere to social norms, becomes crucial.

Research in the area of social robot navigation attempts to address this challenge and focuses on two main parts: the social aspect and the robot navigation. While robot navigation has been extensively studied and solved using both traditional and data-driven approaches, a repetitive measure for the affect of robots on pedestrians remains a dynamic area of research [7,8].

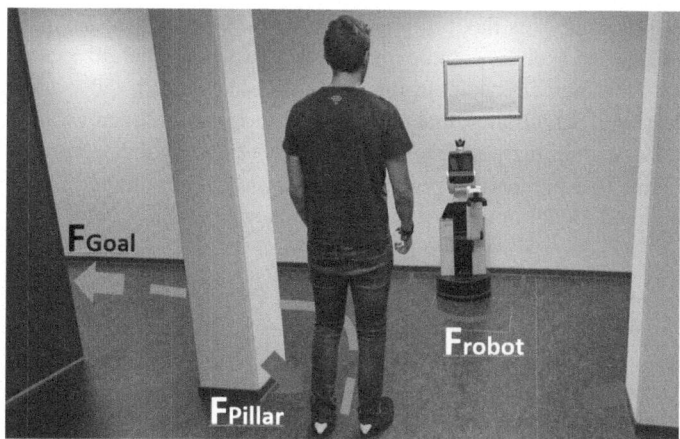

Fig. 1. Example scenario of a human navigating to a goal. While many of the forces used in the social force model are well studied, such as attraction to the goal (green arrow) or repulsion from obstacles, such as the pillar (blue arrow), the robot force (red arrow) is not well understood, even though it significantly affects human behavior. (Color figure online)

As more methods are developed to navigate robots socially amongst humans, the need to evaluate these methods becomes paramount. Over the years, the evaluation of social navigation methods has evolved to include more nuanced metrics that account for the mutual influence between robots and pedestrians. Early evaluations primarily focused on the accuracy of pedestrian trajectory predictions and the efficiency of robot navigation using metrics such as arrival rate, path length, collision rate, average time to goal, etc. However, contemporary evaluations increasingly consider the social acceptability of robot behavior and its adaptability in dynamic environments. Primarily subjective evaluation methods are used for gauging this while there exists still no consensus on which measures to use as standards [7].

Recently, Hirose *et al.* [8] suggested a metric for measuring effect of robots on pedestrians by evaluating the counterfactual perturbation of human trajectories caused by the presence of a robot in the scene. However, the dynamic application of this metric remains a challenge, especially when relying on pre-recorded datasets, which limit the ability to test policies in scenarios different from those in the dataset.

To address these issues, we present a simulation framework designed to repetitively and objectively measure the effect of robots driven by different social navigation algorithms on pedestrian trajectory for evaluation and benchmarking. In order to achieve this, we use an additional force-factor in the social force model (SFM) [9, 10], inspired by the work done by Ferrer *et al.* [11], to model the robot's influence on the pedestrian walking behavior without modeling it as a simple obstacle as shown in Fig. 1. This social robot force model (SRFM) is used to account for changes in the pedestrians' behavior that cannot be modeled adequately by the original forces of the SFM. Our framework, as shown in Fig. 2, simulates pedestrian behavior based on real-world datasets according to our SRFM, and allows for the creation of scenarios not covered in the original dataset. This flexibility enables the development of navigation policies for specific scenarios such as complex hallways as well as generalized scenarios such as pedestrian crossings. To validate this claim, we developed and evaluated a reinforcement learning (RL) policy that uses SRFM to learn a human-aware robot navigation behavior by minimizing the influence of robot force on the pedestrian trajectory. The results show that the learned policy causes least deviation to pedestrian trajectory amongst compared model in most of the evaluation scenarios.

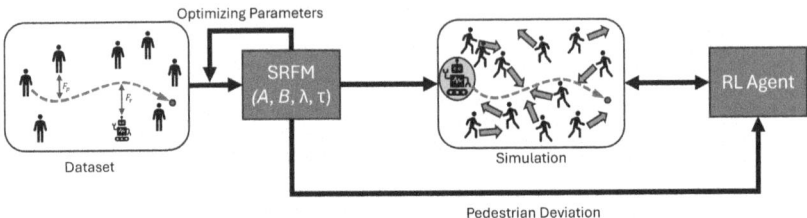

Fig. 2. Architecture of the simulation system. The Social Robot Force Model (SRFM) parameters are learned from the dataset. The learned SRFM is then used to drive the pedestrians in simulation while an RL agent drives the robot during training and evaluation phases.

2   Related Work

Since the first deployment of the robots RHINO [12] and Minerva [13], research in the domain of social navigation in robotics has primarily revolved around three core approaches: traditional model-based methods, data-driven learning approaches, and hybrid methods combining both elements.

Traditional model-based methods use predefined physical laws to explain and predict pedestrian motion and in turn make navigation choices for the robot. Well known and studied traditional methods are the Social Force Model (SFM) [9], Velocity Obstacle (VO) approach [14], continuum theory [15], as well as the dynamic window approach (DWA) [16]. According to the SFM, pedestrian motion results from the sum of various forces acting on them at any time, including attraction to goals and repulsion from obstacles and other pedestrians. VO is a collision avoidance technique that looks at the permissible velocities for the robot that do not fall in the velocity cone of the obstacle, which prevent it from colliding against static as well as dynamic obstacles in its environment while navigating towards its goals. DWA is a real-time local path planning algorithm that dynamically adjusts a robot's velocity within a specified window to avoid collisions and select the safest path [16,17]. These methods are easy to implement. However, the parameters used with these models need to be hand-tuned and can vary. Some models such as the continuum theory [15] are also restricted, as they could be used to predict the general movement of a particular density of crowd but fail to accurately model the interactions on the level of individual pedestrians.

Recent machine learning methods involve the collection of extensive datasets capturing pedestrian and robot interactions, which are then used to train predictive models.

The models learn to forecast pedestrian behavior, guide robots in real-time, and depending on the comparison scenario, can outperform traditional methods [7].

Hirose *et al.* [8] argued the measure of social ability of a robot's navigation algorithm being the ability to cause the least perturbation in their original trajectory. We rely on this idea and incorporate it in a simulation framework which allows objective and repetitive measurement of this deviation in a pedestrian's trajectory caused by the robot.

3   Our Approach

In this section, we introduce the extended social force model that includes the repulsion effect of navigating robots on pedestrians. We explain in detail our methods for learning the parameters of the social force, defining an objective metric to repetitively measure trajectory deviation of pedestrians in the presence of a navigating robot, setting up a simulation environment for training a navigation policy, and evaluating a policy against other state-of-the-art algorithms using this simulation environment.

3.1   Social Robot Force

The original SFM [9] uses three major forces - attraction towards the goal f_a, repulsion from other pedestrians in the vicinity f_p, and repulsion from obstacles in the surroundings f_o: 2.

$$F = f_a + f_p + f_o \tag{1}$$

Our modified SRFM, uses an additional force component - repulsion from the robot f_r:

$$F = f_a + f_p + f_o + f_r \tag{2}$$

The different force components are calculated as follows. The attraction force towards the goal f_a is described in Eq. 3:

$$f_a = \frac{v_i - v_0}{\tau} \tag{3}$$

τ, representing the time a pedestrian takes to adjust their current velocity v_i to match their desired velocity towards the goal v_0, has to be learned. The repulsion forces from pedestrians f_p, obstacles f_o, and robots f_r share the same formula as depicted in Eq. 4:

$$f_p = A e^{\frac{d-x}{B}} \psi \tag{4}$$

In this function, the parameters to be learned are A, indicating the strength of the force, and B, representing the distance from which the force starts to have a significant effect. Additionally, an anisotropic value ψ is used to show that pedestrians experience stronger repulsive forces from those in front of them (using the angle between the pedestrians - ϕ):

$$\psi = \lambda + (1 - \lambda) \frac{(1 + cos(\phi))}{2} \tag{5}$$

This force decreases to the sides and becomes zero behind the pedestrian. This factor ψ is included as an extra multiplicative factor in the force from Eq. 4 and helps in more accurately modeling pedestrian behavior. The value of λ is another parameter that needs to be learned from real-world data.

3.2   Learning SFRM Parameters

Table 1. Parameter values for the Social Robot Force Model compared to [11]

Paper	A_p	B_p	λ	τ	A_r	B_r
Ours	2	0.89	0.4	0.6	7.93	0.99
Ferrer *et al.* [11]	2.66	0.79	0.59	0.43	2.66	0.79

In this work, we learn all parameters based on trajectories of the JRDB dataset [1]. Since we wanted to use annotated values of trajectories, we filtered only those where there were no obstacles, as the dataset does not have annotated information of the obstacles. In the experiments presented, the modified SFM does not take into account the force from obstacles due to this limitation of the dataset. However, this factor is well studied and can be added to the equation for further research. Therefore, the modified model represents pedestrian motion in open spaces such as public crossings and wide footpaths which involve pedestrian-pedestrian interactions and have a negligible chance of pedestrian-obstacle interactions. To learn the factors of the SFM independent from the robot force, we processed the dataset to categorize its trajectories into interaction and non-interaction types. Non-interaction category involve the trajectories of pedestrians far away from the robot (greater than 3 meters) and visually not affected by it. These trajectories are used to learn the parameters for the pedestrian repulsion component. For the repulsion force from robots, only parameters A and B need to be learned from the interaction trajectories, which represent those trajectories where pedestrians are near the robot and its presence causes deviation in their path. These trajectories are used to learn the parameters for the robot force component while retaining the values for pedestrian part from the non-interaction trajectories. We used a non-linear least squares optimization technique from the SciPy package [18] to learn the parameters using the data for both the scenarios. The resulting parameter values are summarized in Table 1 and are shown in comparison to the values found by Ferrer *et al.* [11].

3.3   Deviation Metric and Simulation Scenarios

To effectively benchmark social navigation policies, realistic and repeatable scenarios are needed as well as a well defined objective metric. Therefore, for training and evaluation of navigation policies we utilize the learned Social Robot Force Model to create different scenarios as described in the following.

Training. As training environment, we define a free space of 15×15 meters within our simulation. The robot's start and goal positions are randomly generated while maintaining a minimum distance of 5 m. During training, 10 pedestrians are randomly sampled within the environment boundaries while maintaining a minimum distance of $2m$ (the robot's social zone) from the robot's start position. In addition, each pedestrian's goal is randomly sampled, restricting it to be outside the robot's goal's social zone and keeping a minimum distance of 7 m from that pedestrian's initial location. In order to provide a dynamic and crowded training environment, once a pedestrian has reached its goal, but the training episode has not ended, it is assigned a new goal as described above.

Evaluation. To evaluate our learned policy after training, we use five different scenarios, the first three based on scenarios described by Francis *et al.* [19] while the remaining ones as variations based on extreme situations.

In **Scenario 1**, we simulate a sidewalk or similar walking area by maintaining the parallel flow of pedestrians bypassing each other. For this scenario, the start and end positions of the pedestrians are set to create a natural parallel flow, as can be seen in Fig. 3b. The start and end positions of the robot are fixed and shown as a red circle and a green star.

For **Scenario 2** a pedestrian crossing situation is created. The pedestrian start and goal positions are set to form a natural cross-flow, as shown in 3c. The robot start and goal positions are set up to directly disrupt the flow at the pedestrian crossing point, making it more difficult for the robot to minimize its influence on the pedestrian trajectories.

Scenario 3 is a variation of Scenario 1 where the robot has to cut across the parallel flow of pedestrians. This scenario tests the navigation policy on its timing as the correct timing can minimize pedestrian deviation.

In **Scenario 4**, the robot starts in the middle of a formation where it is surrounded be pedestrians standing in a circle and trying to reach the point diametrically opposite to them. This creates an aggressive scenario where the robot has to face incoming pedestrians from all directions.

Scenario 5 aims to simulate a minimal motion scenario where pedestrians have the same start and end positions. This is representative of a concert or other public events where pedestrians do not change their positions. The position of the start and end goal of the robot in this scenario presents a situation where it has a high chance of cutting across the crowd inadvertently causing deviation in their positions.

Trajectory Deviation Metric. A major feature of our benchmark simulation is the objective metric to measure the deviation in trajectory of the pedestrians caused by the presence of robots driven by social navigation algorithms. This metric is based on the prior research done by Hirose *et al.* [8]. The SRFM consists of various individual force components, making it efficient to evaluate a social navigation policy twice under the same scenario, with one key difference: the robot's impact on the pedestrian. To measure the counterfactual perturbations caused by the robot on the pedestrian's trajectory, we first set up the SRFM with its robot force component active and run the benchmark to record pedestrian trajectories. We then conduct a second run of the deterministic

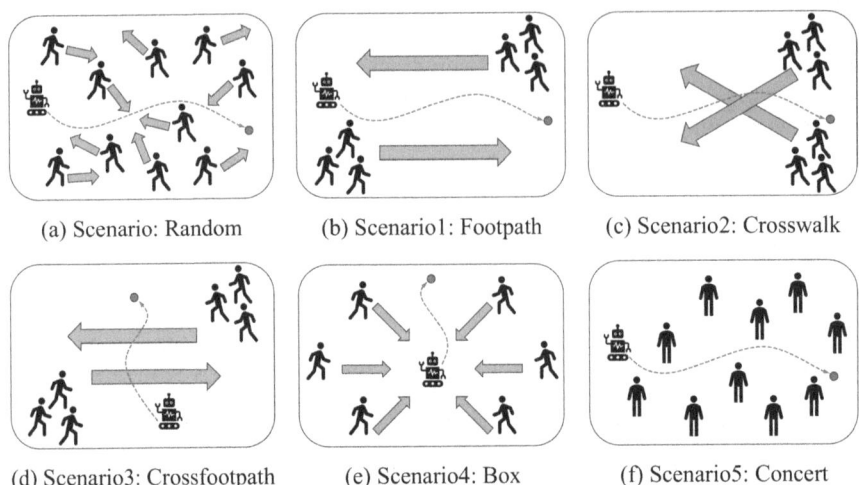

(a) Scenario: Random   (b) Scenario1: Footpath   (c) Scenario2: Crosswalk

(d) Scenario3: Crossfootpath   (e) Scenario4: Box   (f) Scenario5: Concert

Fig. 3. Overview of the different scenarios used for the evaluation of navigation policies. (a) Training environment that is used for the RL agent. (b), (c), and (d) visualize the three common pedestrian streams as described in [19]. (e) and (f) visualize two extreme scenarios.

benchmark using the SRFM but with the robot force component disabled. This provides us with pedestrian trajectories for the same scenario but without the robot's influence. By comparing the differences between these two sets of trajectories and quantifying this difference using Fréchet distance [20] which is a metric that reports the similarity between two curves, we can evaluate the deviation caused by the robot driven by a social navigation policy. The main idea of our benchmark is that the path which a pedestrian takes due to presence of the robot is different from how the person would have walked if the robot was not there. However, one thing to note is that pedestrian behavior is not limited to pure repulsive behavior. Pedestrians also tend to show actively engaging or neutral behavior towards the robot which will be considered in future versions of the benchmark system.

Other Metrics. Apart from the above, three other popular metrics are evaluated and recorded as part of the current simulation system. These are:

- **Minimum Robot Distance:** The minimum distance between the robot and any pedestrian during that particular evaluation scenario.
- **Trajectory Length:** The average of total distance travelled by the pedestrians during the scenario.
- **Trajectory Time:** The average of total time taken by the pedestrians to traverse to their goal during the scenario.

3.4   Learning a Navigation Policy

To demonstrate the advantage of the SRFM and our simulation framework, we use reinforcement learning (RL) to train a policy that navigates the robot through a crowd of pedestrians. While reaching a certain goal in the environment, the robot is tasked to cause the least disturbance to the pedestrians velocity and trajectory.

RL can be framed as a control problem modeled by a partially observable Markov decision process (POMDP). In this framework, the agent cannot directly observe its exact state s_t at time step t; instead, it relies on the current observation o_t to approximate the state, such that $s_t \approx o_t(s_{t-1}, a_t)$ where s_{t-1} is the previous state and a_t is the current action. The objective is to discover a stochastic policy $\pi(a_t|o_t)$ that maximizes the expected reward R over an episode, with T representing the number of time steps and γ being a discount factor. The optimization goal is expressed as:

$$\max \mathbb{E} \left(\sum_{t=0}^{T} \gamma^t R(s_t, a_t) \right) \tag{6}$$

In the following we elaborate more on the action, observation and reward functions that we used to train and evaluate the RL agent in the context of SRFM and social norms.

Actions. We use a continuous action space for the agent that consists of linear and angular velocities (v, w), with a range of $v \in [-0.5, 0.5]$ m s^{-1} and $w \in [-\pi, \pi]$ rad s^{-1}.

Observations. All components are either relative to the robot's position or a boolean. As policy observation of the environment, we use the distance and angle to the navigation goal as well as for each pedestrian with in a predefined social zone, as described in Sect. 3.1. We use an upper bound of the ten closest pedestrians, as other research suggests an upper bound of interfering humans within a scene of nine [21]. For scenarios with less than ten pedestrians within the robot's social zone, the observation is padded with vectors of zeros. We also include the last action taken by the robot (v, w), as well as the success and termination criteria (boolean) in the observation function.

Reward. We keep the reward as simple as possible to encourage faster training, since it is an important part for training convergence. Our reward function r_{total} consists of three components,

$$r_{total} = r_{term} + -k_1 \cdot r_{dist} - k_2 \cdot r_{div}, \tag{7}$$

with k_1, k_2 as scaling factors. r_{term} is a large, sparse termination reward, which is positive when the episode is successful, and otherwise negative. Additionally, we penalize collisions with obstacles double as much as reaching the maximum time step limit. r_{dist} is the Euclidean distance to the goal position, normalized to the range $[0, 1]$ by dividing it with the distance when the environment is reset at the start of every episode. To learn from our SRFM implementation, we use r_{div} to penalize the agent for causing any divergence to the pedestrian from its original path. This value is obtained by calculating the next step of the pedestrian using SRFM with and without robot force and getting the Euclidean distance between these two predicted positions - original position predicted without robot force and deviated position predicted with robot force.

Training Method. To train the policy, we use the Twin-Delayed Deep Deterministic Policy Gradient (TD3) algorithm implementation of stable baselines 3 [22] with a maximum of $2e6$ training steps and a learning rate of $1e-4$. As TD3 is an off-policy RL algorithm, we set the length of its experience replay buffer to $1e6$. Each episode consists of 750 steps, where start and goal positions of the robot and the pedestrians are assigned randomly while considering a certain minimum distance $d = 2$ between any of them to avoid unlikely or dangerous situations where the robot spawns on top of or very close to a pedestrian or vice versa.

4   Experiments and Results

In this section, we first evaluate the influence of the SRFM in terms of prediction accuracy on a given dataset. Second, we demonstrate its usability for evaluating robot navigation policies.

Table 2. Error in trajectory prediction on the JRDB dataset between the social force model and our social robot force model. As can be seen from the results, using the social force model parameters for the robot increases the average displacement error whereas the learned robot force component from social robot force model significantly reduces it.

Model	Force	Test Trajectory	ADE
SFM	$f_a + f_p(pedestrians)$	Non-interaction	0.70 m
SFM	$f_a + f_p(pedestrians) + f_p(robot)$	Interaction	0.75 m
SRFM	$f_a + f_p(pedestrians) + f_r(robot)$	Interaction	**0.59 m**

4.1   SRFM Prediction Accuracy

The learned parameters for the SRFM were tested on a subset of trajectories derived from the JRDB dataset. We are going to refer to the force components of the SFRM as attraction force, pedestrian force, and robot force. The testing was done in three phases. First, we tested the accuracy of our learned pedestrian force on pedestrian trajectories that are not disrupted by the robot (non-interaction), which resulted in an Average Displacement Error (ADE) of $0.70m$. This metric is used to measure the average of the absolute distance in the predicted and actual position of the agent over the course of the entire trajectory. Next, we checked the accuracy of our learned pedestrian force on pedestrian trajectories that are disrupted by the robot (interaction) and consider the robot as a pedestrian as well. The ADE in this case increased to $0.75m$ showing that pedestrians try to maintain a different distance from the robot than other pedestrians. Finally, for the interaction trajectories, we considered the robot as a separate entity and introduced the robot force. The ADE with this change improved to $0.59m$. This is because pedestrian trajectories in interaction scenarios deviate away from the robot and using robot force leads to the driven pedestrian following a similar trajectory. The results are presented in Table 2.

Table 3. Performance of our policy against a RL_{base}, DWA, and VO in terms of the average Fréchet distance, trajectory length, the time taken to complete the trajectory and the minimum distance from a pedestrian to the robot. All values are averaged over 100 runs with * indicating significance compared to ours according to the independent t-test with p = 0.05. Results show our policy outperforms others in Scenarios 1,2,3, and 5 with significant results in Scenarios 1 and 5.

	Approach	Fréchet Dist. ↓	Min. Robot Dist. ↑	Traj. Length ↓	Time ↓
Scenario 1	Ours	*$\mathbf{0.69 \pm 0.05}$	1.42 ± 0.09	8.94 ± 0.10	18.71 ± 0.15
	RL_{base}	0.78 ± 0.04	1.49 ± 0.18	9.00 ± 0.13	18.71 ± 0.20
	DWA	0.76 ± 0.05	1.55 ± 0.15	*$\mathbf{8.77 \pm 0.14}$	*$\mathbf{14.49 \pm 1.20}$
	VO	0.76 ± 0.04	*$\mathbf{1.63 \pm 0.20}$	9.02 ± 0.10	23.01 ± 1.27
Scenario 2	Ours	$\mathbf{1.25 \pm 0.17}$	1.42 ± 0.15	14.63 ± 0.12	19.57 ± 0.70
	RL_{base}	1.32 ± 0.14	1.40 ± 0.19	14.74 ± 0.23	20.74 ± 0.54
	DWA	1.57 ± 0.17	1.58 ± 0.05	*$\mathbf{14.09 \pm 0.38}$	*$\mathbf{17.60 \pm 1.71}$
	VO	1.29 ± 0.15	$\mathbf{1.61 \pm 0.05}$	14.63 ± 0.17	21.12 ± 2.53
Scenario 3	Ours	$\mathbf{0.68 \pm 0.08}$	*$\mathbf{1.76 \pm 0.08}$	8.68 ± 0.08	19.11 ± 0.44
	RL_{base}	0.72 ± 0.09	1.62 ± 0.17	8.79 ± 0.11	19.37 ± 0.41
	DWA	0.75 ± 0.08	1.70 ± 0.13	$\mathbf{8.67 \pm 0.14}$	*$\mathbf{14.82 \pm 1.28}$
	VO	0.76 ± 0.11	1.69 ± 0.07	8.86 ± 0.15	20.01 ± 0.81
Scenario 4	Ours	4.72 ± 0.36	1.52 ± 0.04	8.68 ± 0.35	13.00 ± 0.02
	RL_{base}	4.43 ± 0.45	1.53 ± 0.12	9.06 ± 0.42	14.19 ± 0.72
	DWA	5.67 ± 0.65	1.69 ± 0.05	*$\mathbf{7.38 \pm 0.91}$	*$\mathbf{11.65 \pm 1.48}$
	VO	*$\mathbf{4.38 \pm 0.38}$	*$\mathbf{1.72 \pm 0.04}$	9.09 ± 0.38	14.60 ± 0.57
Scenario 5	Ours	*$\mathbf{0.70 \pm 0.05}$	1.56 ± 0.10	*$\mathbf{2.18 \pm 0.13}$	*$\mathbf{22.02 \pm 0.10}$
	RL_{base}	0.79 ± 0.10	1.57 ± 0.10	2.34 ± 0.20	22.23 ± 0.21
	DWA	0.81 ± 0.06	*$\mathbf{1.66 \pm 0.06}$	2.64 ± 0.27	33.91 ± 7.21
	VO	0.79 ± 0.07	1.62 ± 0.08	2.39 ± 0.17	25.15 ± 2.74

4.2 Baselines

To see the influence of the SRFM on our RL-agent, we trained another agent in the same way as described in Sect. 3.4, neglecting the path deviation penalty (r_{div}) for pedestrians within the social zone of 3 m. While this agent still avoids pedestrians, it does not incorporate any knowledge of its influence on their trajectories. In the following we refer to this baseline as RL_{base}. Furthermore, we implement DWA [16] and VO [14] as baselines of traditional methods to compare against our agent. The pedestrian detection range of the robot is kept at 2 m and the parameters are tuned to achieve similar average velocity as the trained agent. However, VO was not able to finish Scenarios 3, 4, and 5 with these parameters. Hence, the detection range is reduced to 1.4 m which allows VO to calculate feasible velocities for all scenarios.

4.3   Results

The results of the evaluation in all presented scenarios are shown in Table 3. As can be seen, our trained agent outperforms the baseline algorithms w.r.t Fréchet distance in Scenarios 1, 2, 3, and 5. This behaviour is expected since these scenarios represent general and solvable situations of pedestrian dynamics, where there are paths that the robot can take while causing the least amount of disruption to pedestrians. Since our trained agent is specifically tuned to optimize its navigation around this behavior, the results show the best performance compared to the other algorithms in the Fréchet distance metric.

Due to its higher complexity in comparison to the others, Scenario 4 has to be discussed in more detail. In Scenario 4, which requires the robot to navigate from in between a constantly closing circle of pedestrians, the VO algorithm performs the best, likely because it is able to find the optimum trajectory to avoid the incoming pedestrians which our agent was not trained to do. However, it is interesting to note that the performance of VO is not significantly better than the RL_{base} model which was trained to also not care about pedestrian deviation.

These results show that our simulation system provides an adequate environment to train and evaluate agents that can perform on par or even outperform traditional navigation algorithms in our proposed benchmark metric and can also be evaluated on other established benchmark metrics.

4.4   Future Directions

In this work we propose the Fréchet distance as objective measure for deviation in pedestrians trajectory. Please note that this is not the only or best metric to evaluate social compliance, as deviation in pedestrian trajectory can also be caused when the pedestrian is interested in the robot and comes close to it rather than avoiding it. The pedestrian may also be neutral to the presence of the robot and thus not show any deviation in trajectory. These cases however are observed in lesser frequency in the dataset used compared to the deviation caused due to avoiding the robot and will be explored in future work.

5   Conclusion

In this paper, we introduced a simulation framework to objectively measure and benchmark the deviation in the trajectory of pedestrians due to robots driven by different navigation algorithms. By extending the traditional Social Force Model (SFM) to include robot influence on pedestrian behavior, our Social Robot Force Model (SRFM) offers enhanced prediction accuracy for pedestrian trajectories disrupted by robots. Experiments showed a low Average Displacement Error (ADE) for the prediction accuracy of the SRFM, and our reinforcement learning policy trained with SRFM demonstrated improved results causing less deviation to pedestrian trajectories. The code for the work done in this paper can be found in https://github.com/HumanoidsBonn/SRFM-Pedestrian-Deviation-Benchmark.

Acknowledgements. This work has been partially funded by the German research foundation (DFG) under the grant number BE 4420/2-2 (FOR 2535 Anticipating Human Behavior), the Federal Ministry of Education and Research (BMBF) under the grant number 16KIS1949, and within the Robotics Institute Germany, grant No. 16ME0999.

References

1. Martin-Martin, R., et al.: Jrdb: a dataset and benchmark of egocentric robot visual perception of humans in built environments. IEEE Trans. Pattern Analy. Mach. Intell. (2021)
2. Niemelä, M., Arvola, A., Aaltonen, I.: Monitoring the acceptance of a social service robot in a shopping mall: First results. In: Proceedings of the Companion of the 2017 ACM/IEEE International Conference on Human-Robot Interaction (2017)
3. Niemelä, M., Heikkilä, P., Lammi, H., Oksman, V.: A social robot in a shopping mall: studies on acceptance and stakeholder expectations. Technological, societal and ethical aspects of human-robot interaction, Social robots (2019)
4. Kyrarini, M., et al.: A survey of robots in healthcare. Technologies (2021)
5. Gates, B.: A robot in every home. Scientific American (2007)
6. Henschel, A., Laban, G., Cross, E.S.: What makes a robot social? a review of social robots from science fiction to a home or hospital near you. Current Robot. Rep. (2021)
7. Mavrogiannis, C., Baldini, F., Wang, A., Zhao, D., Trautman, P., Steinfeld, A., Oh, J.: Core challenges of social robot navigation: a survey. ACM Trans. Human-Robot Interact. (2023)
8. Hirose, N., Shah, D., Sridhar, A., Levine, S.: Sacson: scalable autonomous control for social navigation. IEEE Robot. Autom. Lett. (2023)
9. Helbing, D., Molnar, P.: Social force model for pedestrian dynamics. Phys. Rev. E (1995)
10. Regier, P., Shareef, I., Bennewitz, M.: Improving navigation with the social force model by learning a neural network controller in pedestrian crowds. In: 2019 European Conference on Mobile Robots (ECMR). IEEE (2019)
11. Ferrer, G., Garrell, A., Sanfeliu, A.: Robot companion: a social-force based approach with human awareness-navigation in crowded environments. In: 2013 IEEE/RSJ International Conference on Intelligent Robots and Systems. IEEE (2013)
12. Burgard, W., et al.: The interactive museum tour-guide robot (1998)
13. Thrun, S., et al.: Probabilistic algorithms and the interactive museum tour-guide robot minerva. Inter. J. Robot. Res. (2000)
14. Large, F., Sckhavat, S., Shiller, Z., Laugier, C.: Using non-linear velocity obstacles to plan motions in a dynamic environment. In: 7th International Conference on Control, Automation, Robotics and Vision, 2002. ICARCV 2002. IEEE (2002)
15. Hughes, R.L.: A continuum theory for the flow of pedestrians. Trans. Res. Part B: Methodol. (2002)
16. Fox, D., Burgard, W., Thrun, S.: The dynamic window approach to collision avoidance. IEEE Robot. Autom. Mag. (1997)
17. Missura, M., Bennewitz, M.: Predictive collision avoidance for the dynamic window approach. In: 2019 International Conference on Robotics and Automation (ICRA). IEEE (2019)
18. Virtanen, P., et al.: SciPy 1.0 contributors: SciPy 1.0: fundamental algorithms for scientific computing in Python. Nat. Methods (2020)
19. Francis, A., et al.: Principles and guidelines for evaluating social robot navigation algorithms. arXiv preprint arXiv:2306.16740 (2023)

20. de Heuvel, J., Corral, N., Kreis, B., Conradi, J., Driemel, A., Bennewitz, M.: Learning depth vision-based personalized robot navigation from dynamic demonstrations in virtual reality (2023)
21. Hossain, S., Johora, F.T., Müller, J.P., Hartmann, S., Reinhardt, A.: Sfmgnet: a physics-based neural network to predict pedestrian trajectories. arXiv preprint arXiv:2202.02791 (2022)
22. Raffin, A., Hill, A., Gleave, A., Kanervisto, A., Ernestus, M., Dormann, N.: Stable-baselines3: reliable reinforcement learning implementations. J. Mach. Learn. Res. (2021)

reMap: Spatially-Grounded and Queryable Semantics for Interactive Robots

Lorenzo Ferrini[1,2(✉)], Jozsef Palmieri[3], Alessandro Marino[3], Dongheui Lee[2], and Séverin Lemaignan[1]

[1] PAL Robotics, Barcelona, Spain
{lorenzo.ferrini,severin.lemaignan}@pal-robotics.com
[2] Institute of Computer Technology, TUW, Wien, Austria
dongheui.lee@tuwien.ac.at
[3] Università degli studi di Cassino e del Lazio Meridionale, Cassino, Italy
{jozsef.palmieri,alessandro.marino}@unicas.it

Abstract. The semantic information available to a robot enhances its understanding of the world and allows it to adapt its behaviour accordingly. This information can be spatially-grounded, meaning it is associated with specific areas of the environment. For a robot to use this information effectively during its tasks, it is crucial to provide an efficient system for storing and retrieving spatially-grounded semantics. In this paper, we present reMap, a novel framework for the efficient representation, storage, and retrieval of spatially-grounded semantics. In reMap, we formally introduce Representation Maps (RMs), three-dimensional functions that each represent a different type of semantic information in space. These structures can be combined through operators to extract additional spatially grounded semantic information. reMap includes a SPARQL-based language that serves as a programmatic interface for retrieving spatially-grounded semantics stored in RMs. We provide an open-source ROS-based implementation of reMap, enabling efficient three-dimensional information storage and processing using dense voxel maps based on the high-performance OpenVDB format. Finally, we describe the execution of the framework over real-world data recorded in a semantically rich real-world environment.

Keywords: Semantic mapping · Interactive robots · Human-Robot Interaction

1 Introduction

Semantic information is crucial in allowing robots to understand the world around them [10]. Robots can use semantic information for a vast range of tasks, i.e., for all those where understanding the *meaning* behind the components involved is the key for a successful execution [4,15].

O. Palinko et al. (Eds.): ICSR + AI 2024, LNAI 15562, pp. 383–396, 2025.
https://doi.org/10.1007/978-981-96-3519-1_35

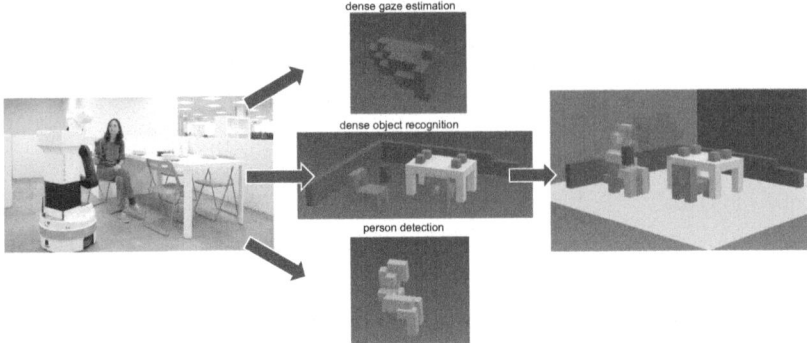

Fig. 1. The reMap spatio-semantic framework combines spatially-grounded semantic sources into a dense voxel map. In this example, three sources are combined: the human field-of-view map, the object map, and the personal space map. The resulting map can be queried using a SPARQL-based language.

In social robotics, semantic information allows robots to understand social signals and adapt their behaviour accordingly. In fact, advancements in machine learning have enabled robots to real-time estimate aspects such as human emotions [27], group dynamics [13], and engagement [26]. The semantics extracted can be used to manage the various aspects in the human-robot interaction spectrum, from maintaining appropriate personal space [9] to conversation management [12].

A part of these semantic data is linked to specific locations in space, creating a direct connection between the information and a volume. However, the spatial anchoring of these data is not necessarily fixed; while some elements may have stable characteristics in the environment, others undergo frequent changes in position, shape, and value. These dynamic attributes present challenges for representation due to the intricate and evolving nature of the data, the need for frequent updates requiring significant computational resources, and its inherently unstructured nature that makes it difficult to create concise symbolic representations. Tackling these challenges requires a specialised framework that provides efficient and standardised data structures designed to encode spatially anchored semantic information, along with APIs optimised for rapid access and modification of values. Despite the enhanced semantic capabilities of robots enabled by advances in areas such as Deep Learning, current frameworks lack comprehensive support for efficient representation of spatially-grounded semantic data.

Moreover, the semantic information available to interactive robots is rarely standalone. It often requires processing and integration, and the robot reasoning over it to derive further semantic insights. Therefore, a complete framework for spatially grounded semantic information should also include structures that facilitate semantic reasoning on the data.

This paper seeks to tackle these aspects by introducing *reMap*, a comprehensive open-source framework for spatially anchored semantic information in robotics, incorporating structures that support semantic reasoning and flexible representation of dynamic semantic data.

Our contributions include:

1. A framework based on 3D voxel maps (Fig. 1), to represent and efficiently retrieve semantic information from unstructured – yet spatially-grounded – data for use in robotic tasks;
2. The definition of operators for combining the stored maps and extracting new spatially-grounded semantic information from them.
3. a proof-of-concept SPARQL-like query language for semantic information retrieval from maps;
4. an open-source ROS-based implementation of the presented framework[1].

2   Related Work

Anchoring semantic information in the spatial environment is central to many robotics tasks, and remains an on-going challenge [10,15]. Various strategies have been explored, often tailored to specific application domains. For instance, in navigation, numerous solutions have been proposed to effectively correlate semantic concepts with physical space [4]. In [8], authors define a multi-hierarchical structure to link semantic concepts with navigation maps, introducing a querying language for information retrieval pertinent to navigation tasks. The authors in [3] focus on the real-time grounding of symbolic information onto 2D maps for life-long information acquisition and representation. In [24], the authors pursue an ontology-based approach [28], focusing on the representation and acquisition of comprehensive semantic maps, with the goal of facilitating prolog-based querying systems for information retrieval in navigation tasks. In [6], the authors propose a framework for managing semantic maps, employing a client-server architecture equipped with custom plugins for updating grounded semantic information. While these projects have laid the foundations for the spatial grounding of semantic data, they do not directly address neither dense, highly dynamic spatial data, often found in human-robot interaction situations, nor continuous data fields (akin to *mightability maps* [23]).

Representation of spatial semantic data has also been a research subject in the Human-Robot Interaction (HRI) domain. In [17], authors define a perspective-taking approach aiming at solving ambiguities in grounding speech interactions between humans and robots. Here, they use an ontology-based [16] approach to associate objects in space with semantic concepts. The semantics in this case might refer to the object class or to the spatial relationships with the other objects in the scene. In [11], the authors implement a system aiming at the grounding of target objects in the scene based on human-robot speech interaction. They combine 2D and 3D features to speech detection to extract

---

[1] https://github.com/RepresentationMaps.

Table 1. Comparison of various frameworks for spatially grounded semantics representation, highlighting their integration with knowledge bases (KB), support for human and 3D field modelling, architectural design, spatial reasoning capabilities, availability of an API to retrieve spatially localised volumes, and underlying data structures.

	Vimantic [6]	*SOM+* [24]	*SPARK* [19]	*reMap*
KB Integration	pull	pull	push	SPARQL API
Human Modelling	No	No	Yes	Plugin
3D Dense Fields	No	No	No	Yes
Architecture	Modular	Monolithic	Modular	Modular
Spatial Reasoning	No	Yes	Yes	Yes
Spatial API	No	No	No	Yes
Data Structure	Point cloud	Point cloud	CAD meshes	OpenVDB

actions to perform with the robot targeting specific objects in space. A similar goal motivates the work in [25], where the authors propose INGRESS, a deep learning-based approach for unconstrained matching of spatially-grounded expressions and objects in human-robot verbal interaction.

While these approaches prove to be effective for object-based contexts, they also leave some open challenges. One challenge is the need to scale these methods to accommodate newly-defined, custom semantic features, a capability not currently supported. Additionally, there is the need to structure these approaches for free-form representation of spatially-grounded semantic information, as they are presently tied to RGBD data or pre-acquired object meshes. Recently, there have been advances in the field of natural language-based spatial reasoning through large language models (LLMs) [2,14]. In [5], authors present a novel methodology for zero-shot object-based navigation. Here, they combine LLMs and vision language models (VLMs) to generate sequential navigation decisions, based both on an explicit user request and the current state of the environment. The VLM is applied for grounding the semantic concepts expressed in the request into the detected objects in space. While LLMs and VLMs present promising results in reasoning and show zero-shot abilities in grounding semantics in space, they also suffer some limitations. In fact, they are not able to spatially represent unstructured, field-like semantic information with exact location in space. Moreover, they might suffer the definition of application-specific semantics that do not represent any type of traditional common knowledge.

With reMap, we aim at addressing the gaps in representation capabilities from previous works highlighted in this section. A comparison between the features presented in the implementation of our framework and those from previous works are presented in Table 1. In Sect. 6, we briefly discuss as future work the possible combination of this work with LLMs to directly query reMap using natural language.

3   Semantic Information in Space

Representing spatially grounded information in space means associating semantic labels to regions of space in the robot's vicinity. This representation can be
associated both to discrete phenomenons (e.g., associating the object class id to
the areas occupied by the object itself) or to continuous ones (e.g., expressing
the field of view of as a function of the distance from its gaze central axis).
In this section, we formally introduce our framework for 3D-grounded semantic
data representation and processing.

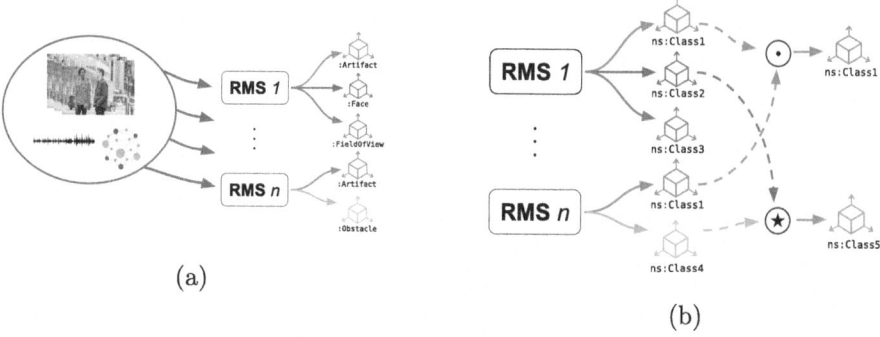

(a)

(b)

Fig. 2. RMSs build RMs from the percepts available to the robot. Each RMS might
output multiple RMs, each representing different spatial information from the scene,
and with an explicit data class attached (a). Operators (like $\odot$ and $\star$, representing
generic operators) can combine several maps to output new ones, of the same type
(e.g. in (b), $\odot$) or not ($\star$).

3.1   Conceptual Description of the Framework

3.1.1   Data Representation and Processing
In the proposed model, we
introduce the concepts of **_Representation Maps_** (RMs) and **_Representation
Maps Sources_** (RMSs). The former are spatially-grounded representations of
semantic information, that is, they map 3-dimensional world coordinates to values associated to specific semantics (e.g., the object class associated with the
detected objects). They can be represented as functions m. Each m belongs to a
specific functional $M = \{\mathbf{R}^3 \Rightarrow \mathbf{R}\}$, associated with the semantics of the information represented in m. To each map m is also associated additional explicit
information regarding the semantics of values in m (see Sect. 3.1.2).

RMSs are themselves functions; their role is to transform information available to the robot at a given time into RMs. RMSs belong to the functional
$P = \{\mathcal{P}(S) \rightarrow M^n\}$, where S is the set of information available to a robot at
a given time and $\mathcal{P}(S)$ is its powerset (Fig. 2a); n depends on each RMS and
represents the number of RMs each RMS can output. The value of n can change
over time.

3.1.2   Semantics Each map represents data with specific semantics. Critically, each map is semantically homogeneous: its data represents a single type of information. We rely on the Resource Description Format (RDF) terminology and formalism to formally assign the semantics of the data contained in each map. We do so by attaching an RDF *class* to the map (for instance, relying on the OpenRobot Ontology [16] semantics, we use the class oro:Artifact for maps representing objects in space). This semantic information is used by map operators (see below) to reason and combine maps in a semantic-aware manner (Fig. 2b).

3.1.3   Combining RMs with Operators. RMs can be combined by operators. An operator is a function that combines two or more RMs into a new RM. The input RMs might or might not be associated to the same class. The output RM might belong to the same class as one of the input RMs or to a new one. Given k RMs $m_1, \ldots, m_k$, an operator on these RMs is defined as $f_{1,\ldots,k} := m_1, \ldots, m_k \to m_{res}$.

An example of operator over same-class RMs is the one combining all the object-detection RMs into a single one. For instance, different RMSs might generate maps containing information of the detected objects in the scene, where each RMSs runs a differently specialised object detection algorithm (YOLO [29], RGBD-based table detecion, etc.). For a global view on the objects detected in the scene and for further semantic processing, we are interested in the combination of these different RMs. Therefore, we define the object-detection RMs combing operator. Given j object-detection RMs m_{o_k}, $k = 1, .., j$, with associated class oro:Artifact, this operator is defined as $f_o(m_{o_1}, m_{o_2}, ..., m_{o_j}) = m_{o_1} \cup m_{o_2} \cup ... \cup m_{o_j}$. The $\cup$ operation is the union between the different functions.

Once obtained the full object-detection RM, we might be interested in understanding which of these objects are in the FoV of an agent. This information can be obtained by defining the operator $f_{of}(m_o, m_f)$; this takes as input an RM with class Artifact (m_o) and one with class FieldOfView (m_f) and outputs a new RM containing only those voxels of m_o that happen to be in the represented field of view in m_f (that is, m_f acting as a boolean mask).

4   Operators as Semantic Queries

Practically, operators can be seen as transformations over the available RMs. These transformations can be described as SQL-like queries over the available semantic data. To this end, we have developed a simple query language whose grammar is based on the RDF graph query language SPARQL[2]. The language is based on (semantic) pattern matching, where the user defines a set of constraints that the RMs must satisfy. The query is then executed over the available RMs, and a new RM, simultaneously satisfying all the constraints, is returned. As such, the query is the declarative specification of an operator.

---

[2] https://www.w3.org/TR/sparql11-overview/.

For example, the following query retrieves the voxels containing a *mug* in the field of view of a human `human1` – it is a possible implementation of an *objectInFieldOfView* operator:

```
PREFIX : http://kb.openrobots.org/
SELECT ?voxels
WHERE
?voxels :inFieldOfView human1 .
?voxels :containsObject 'mug'
STORE
:containsObject
```

The `STORE` clause is an extension indicating the datatype of the resulting RM. In this case, the query returns a RM where each voxel contains the class label of the objects in the selected voxels.

In practice, to actually implement a prototype of this query language, each RM m is attached to exactly one RDF property p. We denote $D(p)$ the *domain* of the property, and $R(p)$ its range. For instance, the property `oro:containsObject` (which associates an object to its COCO-80 [20] class) has `oro:Artifact` as domain. In Sect. 5.5 we present a first implementation of the query execution system.

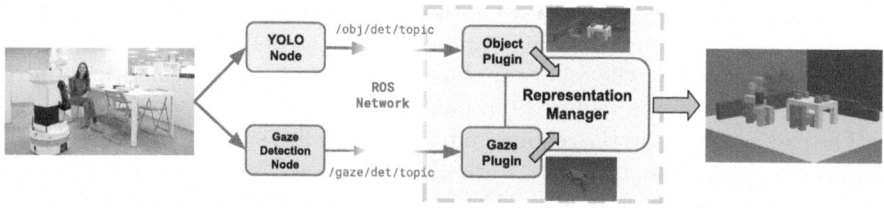

Fig. 3. The reMap framework (boarded in yellow) interacting with non-reMap ROS components. The plugins generate RMs with information provided by the non-reMap nodes. These RMs are then handled and exposed to queries by `representation_manager` (Color figure online).

5 Implementation

Given the interactive robot-oriented nature of the proposed model, a software implementation is required to prove its capacity to model semantic information in the scenario around a robot. Considering the limited computational resources available to robots and that these usually have to sustain several other computation-heavy processes (e.g., navigation stack), it is required for the implementation to be lightweight. Ideally, the model should reach real-time performance, so that the robot's response based on the values in RMs is not negatively impacted.

We opted for a ROS-based implementation of reMap. At this point, ROS is a highly mature framework for robot programming, coming with all the tools required to achieve the aforementioned desired performances. The architecture built to implement the model is plugin-based. Plugins were implemented through ROS `pluginlib` C++ library; we developed two different open source ROS packages:

- `rep_map`: a package implementing the API and the basic tools required to manage the output of the executing RMSs, that is, the active representation plugins. This includes:
  - the interfaces for the definition of inter-maps operators;
  - a query API, presented in Sect. 4;
  - `representation_manager`, a ROS node for handling the multiple maps generated by the different RMS and the input queries.
- `rep_plugins`: a package providing the basic interfaces and tools to implement RMSs as plugins. It comes with a group of ready-made plugins.

In Fig. 3, we graphically highlight the reMap ROS components (plugins, `representation_manager`) within a generic ROS architecture.

5.1   rep_map

This package provides the software required to manage the plugins activation (that is, the software implementing a specific RMS), as well as their de-activation at runtime. In this way, the robot can dynamically adapt to the semantic context and always run only the required representation processes.

The package provides the required interfaces to define same-domain and inter-domain operators. Some operators are already defined, for instance the operator to combine object-detection RMs into a comprehensive one. A ROS node (`representation_manager`) is part of the package, instantiating the required ROS structures for communication between the plugins and the other ROS nodes part of the robot infrastructures. The package also incorporates utilities for RMs visualisation and debugging.

5.2   rep_plugins

The `rep_plugins` package provides the required structures to develop the semantic plugins (that is, the RMS software implementation) and the API to interact with them. It requires every plugin to be implemented as a class inheriting from `semantic_plugin_base`. This class already provides the required function to set values for specific areas and shapes of the space in RMs. Each plugin can access the information available to the robot through the ROS communication interface. The package comes with a limited number of plugins already implemented.

5.2.1 Person Detection Plugin This plugin outputs a single RM where the contained voxels represent the space portions occupied by people. It relies on YOLOv8 [29] image segmentation results, mapping each person's mask to space using an RGB-aligned depth image of the environment. The plugin does not directly perform image segmentation; this task is performed by an independent node, publishing the results as a custom message.

5.2.2 Gaze Detection and FoV Plugin This plugin handles the semantic information associated with the gaze direction of agents. In our implementation, detected n agents, it outputs n RMs. Each one of them is a boolean one, representing the field of view of each detected person. Each map might also be associated with a specific person, according to the face recognition pipeline.

This plugin does infer the agents gaze direction: it retrieves information about the agents gaze through the ROS4HRI [21] tools and utilities. In ROS4HRI, every gaze is associated with a `gaze_<face_id>` TF frame. The z axis of this frame points to the agent's estimated gaze direction. Accordingly, the plugin represents the region of space currently looked at by the agent as a cone.

We set the aperture of the field of each gaze cone to $\theta = 0.5rad$. The equation for each gaze cone in the output RMs is:

$$m(x) = \begin{cases} true & \text{for } x \text{ inside the cone} \\ false & \text{elsewhere} \end{cases} \tag{1}$$

5.2.3 Object Detection Plugin This plugin handles the semantic information related to the objects detected in the scene. Every object might be associated with various types of semantic information. In this case, we focused on the object class, expressed as an integer value.

As for person detection, this plugin does not directly perform object detection, but subscribes to a topic where information on the detected objects in the scene are published in the form of segmentation masks. Then, as in person detection, the plugin uses the RGB-alinged depth image to generate an RM where voxels are associated to pixels from the original image; here, each activated voxel contain an integer value representing the object-class of the associated object.

5.3 RMs Implementation

The framework described in 3 requires, for effective implementation, a lightweight and efficient structure to represent 3D information. We opted to represent each RM as an independent VDB. VDBs are dynamic structures that use a sparse hierarchical data structure to efficiently store volumetric data based on voxels. This structure allows for memory-efficient representation of 3D grids, where only voxels with nonempty values are stored, optimising both storage and computational performance. In this case, we used the OpenVDB [22] library, which is the *de facto* standard for python and C++ implementation of VDBs.

Each RM is represented as a `Grid<T>` object, where `T` specifies the type of the value associated with the grid voxels. Therefore, faces RMs are `Grid<float>`, object RMs are `Grid<int>` and FOV maps are `Grid<bool>`.

In OpenVDB, each `Grid<T>` object contains a `Transform` object. This is continuously updated with the transform between the original data frame and a reference frame, which is shared among the whole architecture. This way, the corresponding points in the index space of the various `Grid` objects can map to the same real-world coordinates.

The OpenVDB API provides the required functions and interfaces for RMs representation and processing, including for the implementation of the operators described in Sect.3.1.3.

5.4   Demonstration on Real-World Data

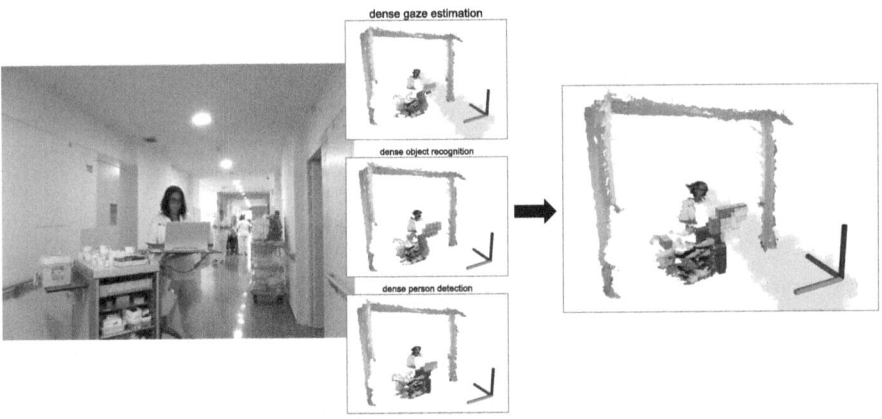

Fig. 4. RMs generation from real-world data acquired in an hospital. For reference, we overlay the perceived point cloud over the voxel maps.

To validate the implementation of **rep_map** and **rep_plugins**, we tested the framework to generate RMs on a set of pre-recorded bag files through the previously described plugins (Fig. 4).

The bag files were recorded during a 2-month deployment in a hospital in the metropolitan area of Barcelona and depict a corridor in one of the rehabilitation wards. This environment is representative of complex human environments where we expect social robots to have impact. During the recording session, performed using a PAL Robotics TIAGo robot, both nurses and patients were present in the area. For privacy reasons, we will not disclose the bag files recorded to test the framework.

Each plugin generates its RMs at the same pace as their input stream: for instance, when running YOLOv8 largest pre-trained model (`yolov8x`) on the

```
PREFIX : http://kb.openrobots.org/
SELECT ?voxels
WHERE
?voxels :containsObject *
STORE
:containsObject
```

```
PREFIX : http://kb.openrobots.org/
SELECT ?voxels
WHERE
?voxels :inFieldOfView human1 .
?voxels :containsObject *
STORE
:containsObject
```

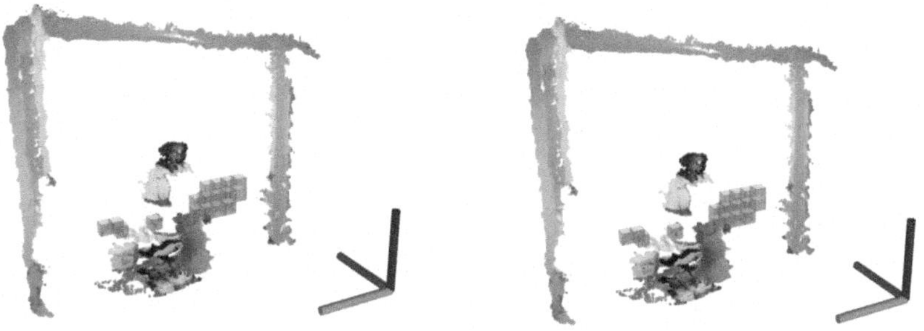

Fig. 5. Two examples of reMap query execution. On the left, a query extracting all the objects detected in the scene. On the right, combining object information and the detected field of view of the person in the scene, we extract information on the object looked-at by the nurse.

available hardware, the YOLO dedicated node outputs results at $5Hz$; the face detection pipeline, directly running on the robot, outputs results at $20Hz$; for this reason, reMap allows for asynchronous generation and combination (through operators) of different RMs. In this demonstration, reMap shows real-time capabilities in handling the RMs generated by the different plugins.

5.5   Proof-of-Concept Implementation of the Query Language

We have implemented a first version of the query language described in Sect. 4. This includes a simple algorithm for query parsing, RMs selection, operator definition and execution.

The query parsing disassembles the queries and selects the target domain (expressed by the STORE extension) and the RMs involved in the operator executions. This is possible by matching the properties from the query with those associated to the RMs, as specified in Sect. 3.1.2. The API introduced in the previous subsections enables the actual processing of the query as operator. At runtime, the system exposes a ROS service for queries. In case of successful execution, a new RM containing the query result is created. In case of non-matching attributes in the query, the system aborts the query execution and communicates it to the requester as a result of the service execution. Two examples of query-based data extraction are reported in Fig. 5. The reported queries have been executed over the real-world data collected for validation purposes.

6   Discussion

6.1   Query Language

Although our query language demonstrates effectiveness in a range of scenarios, it remains at an early stage of development. Future iterations should aim to incorporate features akin to those found in SPARQL (including, for instance, the implementation of the `FILTER` clause), enabling users to formulate more intricate queries with ease. We also plan to formally examine the mapping of SPARQL semantics to spatial data maps.

6.2   Future Work

6.2.1   Spatial Queries from Natural Language While query languages provide an effective programmatic interface to retrieve (spatially-grounded) semantic information, they do not automatically fit HRI scenarios with humans communicating with natural language. Therefore, what is required for the deployment of the querying system in HRI scenarios is the automatic translation of natural language utterances into queries based on the aforementioned language. In this sense, LLMs have proved to be a good fit for the adaptation and translation of natural language to query languages [7,30,31]. In this context, we plan to adapt our framework to the extraction of spatially-grounded semantic information from natural language using GPT-4 [1].

6.2.2   Time Modelling While reMap can ground semantics in 3-dimensional space, it does not address temporal aspects. This is a feature available in previous world-modelling works in HRI [18]. We plan to extend reMap to include a time-consistent modelling of space. This will enable the system to extend its modelling capabilities beyond the immediately observable scenario.

7   Conclusion

In this work we introduced *reMap*, a novel framework for the representation, processing and querying of spatially-grounded semantic information in robotics. Firstly, we defined the theoretical concepts behind the framework, introducing the concepts of *Representation Maps*, *Representation Map Sources* and *Maps Operators*. We also explained how it is possible to define a SPARQL-based querying system to extract spatial information from *Representation Maps*.

We then proceeded illustrating a ROS-based implementation of the conceptual framework introduced in the previous chapters, with the description of `rep_map` and `rep_plugin`. The described reMap implementation is publicly available as an open-source package; the link is provided in previous sections.

Finally, we tested the information representation capabilities of the implemented solution over real-world data, reporting the processing performance and the visual representation of queries performed over the generated maps.

Acknowledgments. This work has been funded by the H2020 PERSEO project (no. 955778).

References

1. Achiam, J., et al.: GPT-4 Technical Report. arXiv preprint arXiv:2303.08774 (2023)
2. Ahn, M., et al.: Do as i can, not as i say: grounding language in robotic affordances. arXiv preprint arXiv:2204.01691 (2022)
3. Bastianelli, E., et al.: On-line semantic mapping. In: 2013 16th International Conference on Advanced Robotics (ICAR), pp. 1–6. IEEE (2013)
4. Crespo, J., Castillo, J.C., Mozos, O.M., Barber, R.: Semantic information for robot navigation: a survey. Appl. Sci. **10**(2), 497 (2020)
5. Dorbala, V.S., Mullen Jr, J.F., Manocha, D.: Can an embodied agent find your "cat-shaped mug"? LLM-based zero-shot object navigation. IEEE Rob. Autom. Lett. **9**(5), 4083–4090 (2023)
6. Fernández-Chaves, D., Ruiz-Sarmiento, J.R., Petkov, N., Gonzalez-Jimenez, J.: Vimantic, a distributed robotic architecture for semantic mapping in indoor environments. Knowl.-Based Syst. **232**, 107440 (2021)
7. Futia, G., Vetro, A., Melandri, A., De Martin, J.C.: Training neural language models with SPARQL queries for semi-automatic semantic mapping. Proc. Comput. Sci. **137**, 187–198 (2018)
8. Galindo, C., Saffiotti, A., Coradeschi, S., Buschka, P., Fernandez-Madrigal, J.A., González, J.: Multi-hierarchical semantic maps for mobile robotics. In: 2005 IEEE/RSJ International Conference on Intelligent Robots and Systems, pp. 2278–2283. IEEE (2005)
9. Gao, Y., Huang, C.M.: Evaluation of socially-aware robot navigation. Front. Rob. AI **8**, 721317 (2022)
10. Garg, S., et al.: Semantics for robotic mapping, perception and interaction: a survey. Found. Trends® Rob. **8**(1–2), 1–224 (2020)
11. Guadarrama, S., et al.: Grounding spatial relations for human-robot interaction. In: 2013 IEEE/RSJ International Conference on Intelligent Robots and Systems, pp. 1640–1647. IEEE (2013)
12. Hanschmann, L., Gnewuch, U., Maedche, A.: Saleshat: A LLM-based social robot for human-like sales conversations. In: International Workshop on Chatbot Research and Design, pp. 61–76. Springer (2023)
13. Hedayati, H., Muehlbradt, A., Szafir, D.J., Andrist, S.: Reform: recognizing f-formations for social robots. In: 2020 IEEE/RSJ International Conference on Intelligent Robots and Systems (IROS), pp. 11181–11188. IEEE (2020)
14. Huang, W., Abbeel, P., Pathak, D., Mordatch, I.: Language models as zero-shot planners: Extracting actionable knowledge for embodied agents. In: International Conference on Machine Learning, pp. 9118–9147. PMLR (2022)
15. Kleeberger, K., Bormann, R., Kraus, W., Huber, M.F.: A survey on learning-based robotic grasping. Curr. Rob. Rep. **1**, 239–249 (2020)
16. Lemaignan, S., Ros, R., Mösenlechner, L., Alami, R., Beetz, M.: Oro, a knowledge management platform for cognitive architectures in robotics. In: 2010 IEEE/RSJ International Conference on Intelligent Robots and Systems, pp. 3548–3553. IEEE (2010). https://doi.org/10.1109/IROS.2010.5649547

17. Lemaignan, S., Ros, R., Sisbot, E.A., Alami, R., Beetz, M.: Grounding the interaction: anchoring situated discourse in everyday human-robot interaction. Int. J. Soc. Robot. **4**, 181–199 (2012)
18. Lemaignan, S., Sallami, Y., Wallbridge, C., Clodic, A., Belpaeme, T., Alami, R.: UNDERWORLDS: cascading situation assessment for robots. In: 2018 IEEE/RSJ International Conference on Intelligent Robots and Systems (IROS), pp. 7750–7757. IEEE (2018)
19. Lemaignan, S., Warnier, M., Sisbot, E.A., Clodic, A., Alami, R.: Artificial cognition for social human-robot interaction: an implementation. Artif. Intell. **247**, 45–69 (2017). https://doi.org/10.1016/j.artint.2016.07.002
20. Lin, T.Y., et al.: Microsoft COCO: common objects in context. In: Computer Vision–ECCV 2014: 13th European Conference, Zurich, Switzerland, September 6-12, 2014, Proceedings, Part V 13, pp. 740–755. Springer (2014)
21. Mohamed, Y., Lemaignan, S.: ROS for human-robot interaction. In: 2021 IEEE/RSJ International Conference on Intelligent Robots and Systems (IROS), pp. 3020–3027. IEEE (2021)
22. Museth, K., et al.: OpenVDB: an open-source data structure and toolkit for high-resolution volumes. In: ACM SIGGRAPH 2013 Courses, pp. 1–1 (2013)
23. Pandey, A.K., Alami, R.: Mightability maps: a perceptual level decisional framework for co-operative and competitive human-robot interaction. In: 2010 IEEE/RSJ International Conference on Intelligent Robots and Systems, pp. 5842–5848. IEEE (2010)
24. Pangercic, D., Pitzer, B., Tenorth, M., Beetz, M.: Semantic object maps for robotic housework-representation, acquisition and use. In: 2012 IEEE/RSJ International Conference on Intelligent Robots and Systems, pp. 4644–4651. IEEE (2012)
25. Shridhar, M., Mittal, D., Hsu, D.: Ingress: interactive visual grounding of referring expressions. Int. J. Rob. Res. **39**(2–3), 217–232 (2020)
26. Sorrentino, A., Fiorini, L., Cavallo, F.: From the definition to the automatic assessment of engagement in human–robot interaction: a systematic review. Int. J. Soc. Rob. 1–23 (2024)
27. Spezialetti, M., Placidi, G., Rossi, S.: Emotion recognition for human-robot interaction: recent advances and future perspectives. Front. Robot. AI **7**, 532279 (2020)
28. Tenorth, M., Beetz, M.: KnowRob—knowledge processing for autonomous personal robots. In: 2009 IEEE/RSJ International Conference on Intelligent Robots and systems, pp. 4261–4266. IEEE (2009)
29. Terven, J., Cordova-Esparza, D.: A comprehensive review of YOLO: from YOLOv1 to YOLOv8 and beyond. arXiv preprint arXiv:2304.00501 (2023)
30. Trummer, I.: CodexDB: synthesizing code for query processing from natural language instructions using GPT-3 codex. Proc. VLDB Endowment **15**(11), 2921–2928 (2022)
31. Trummer, I.: Demonstrating GPT-DB: generating query-specific and customizable code for SQL processing with GPT-4. Proc. VLDB Endowment **16**(12), 4098–4101 (2023)

Social, But Still Uncanny

Katharina Kühne[1]([✉]) [iD], Oliver Bendel[2] [iD], Yuefang Zhou[1] [iD],
and Martin H. Fischer[1] [iD]

[1] Cognitive Sciences Division, University of Potsdam, Potsdam, Germany
kkuehne@uni-potsdam.de
[2] FHNW School of Business, Windisch, Switzerland

Abstract. The Uncanny Valley hypothesis proposes that as robots become more human-like, they are initially liked better but then elicit a feeling of eeriness, peaking just before achieving full human resemblance. It remains unclear whether context can modify this effect. In an online experiment, participants were primed with a vignette about either robots as social companions (social context priming) or a neutral topic, and then rated images of robots on human-likeness, likability, trust, and creepiness. We found a negative linear relationship between a robot's human-likeness and its likability and trustworthiness and a positive linear relationship between a robot's human-likeness and creepiness. Social context priming improved overall likability and trust of robots but did not modulate the Uncanny Valley effect. This indicates that, while presenting robots in a social context can improve their acceptance, this does not change our inherent discomfort with increasing human-like robots.

Keywords: Likability · social robots · trust · Uncanny Valley

1 Introduction

1.1 The Uncanny Valley

Evidence for the Uncanny Valley (UV). In 1970, Mori [1, also 2] proposed his seminal UV hypothesis, suggesting that robots are more likable as they become human-like, but likability drops after an "uncanny" threshold. Only with perfect human-likeness does likability rise again. The UV and its origin remain debated in research [meta-analysis in 3, review in 4, for discussion of UV theories, see 5, 6, for testing theories, see 7]. Mathur and Reichling [8] confirmed the hypothesis with robotic faces, Abubshait et al. [9] found it in trust measures, and Kim et al. [10] validated it with 251 robots, noting a separate "valley" for moderately human-like robots. Fortunati et al. [11] reported uncanny feelings even with less human-like robots, while other studies found no evidence for an UV [for review, see 12]. The form of the UV also remains debated. While Mori proposed a cubic function, Kätsyri et al. [13] suggested three patterns: linear, weak UV, and strong UV (the original hypothesis). Other studies proposed a linear function [14, 15]. Decisions regarding human-likeness in robot design can impact real-world

© The Author(s), under exclusive license to Springer Nature Singapore Pte Ltd. 2025
O. Palinko et al. (Eds.): ICSR + AI 2024, LNAI 15562, pp. 397–403, 2025.
https://doi.org/10.1007/978-981-96-3519-1_36

interactions: Humans consume more unhealthy food when served by robots, due to discomfort caused by feelings of eeriness [16]. Increased creepiness adversely affects trust, changing purchasing decisions [17]. Human-likeness also impacts trust [18], friendship decisions [19], and the evaluation of robots' morality [20]. However, the UV does not influence compliance with authority [21]. Finally, making robots very human-like can complicate communication by requiring complex mental models [22].

Factors Influencing the UV. This mixed evidence suggests that methodologies (e.g., interaction vs observation), stimuli types (e.g., actual robots vs modified images), and inconsistent terminology (e.g., affinity vs likability) affect results. Here, we concentrate on the context social robots are presented in [cf. 23]. The integrative model of dynamics of anthropomorphism [24] states our perception of robots as human-like is shaped by our prior beliefs. Mind perception theory suggests that beliefs about robots' mental capabilities increase their perceived creepiness [25]. People feel more joint agency when robot partners are introduced as intentional agents [26]. Therefore, framing interactions with robots within certain contexts that define its capabilities may impact robot perception.

Present Study. Our online study used images of actual robots and formulated these hypotheses: (H1) There is an (a) cubic *or* (b) linear relationship between the robot's human-likeness and its likability; (H2) There is an (a) cubic *or* (b) linear relationship between the robot's human-likeness and trust; (H3) There is an (a) cubic *or* (b) linear relationship between the robot's human-likeness and its creepiness; (H4) Human-likeness positively predicts (a) trust, (b) creepiness, and negatively predicts likability (c). (H5) Social context positively predicts (a) likability (b) trust and negatively predicts creepiness (c). (H6) Priming context and human-likeness interact.

2 Materials and Methods

2.1 Participants

We tested 36 participants online. Four datasets (11%) were excluded due to unseriousness. The final sample consisted of 32 participants (21 females; mean age = 26 years, $SD = 8$ years), 81% (n = 26) students, 56% (n = 18) native German speakers, and the remaining 44% (n = 14) with English or other native languages.

2.2 Stimuli

Priming stimuli consisted of two articles in English: "The social revolution: robots as indispensable members of our society" (379 words) as social context condition, and "The Benefits of Mindfulness Meditation" (365 words) for the control group. In the social context, robots were introduced as companions. To ensure participants' engagement, articles were followed by two comprehension questions. We selected 25 robot images (2000 x 2000 pixels) from the ABOT database [10] in increments of four steps on a human-likeness continuum. Sample stimuli appear in Fig. 1. Articles and robot images are at https://osf.io/2xp4d/.

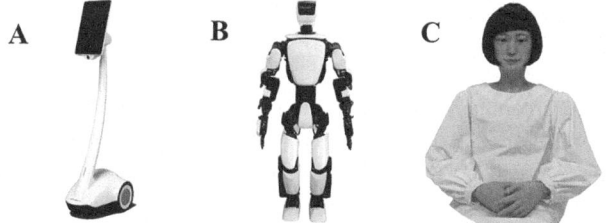

Fig. 1. Sample stimuli: robots with low (*padbot*, Panel A), medium (*thr3*, Panel B), and high (*kodomoroid*, Panel C) human-likeness.

2.3 Measures

Robots were rated on likability, trustworthiness, creepiness with responses on a 7-point Likert scale, and on human-likeness with responses on a 10-point Likert scale. We also recorded age, gender, native language, and education.

2.4 Procedure

The experiment was conducted in English on Gorilla [27] and lasted 30 min. All participants were recruited at University of Potsdam, consented before the experiment, and were reimbursed with course credits. The study conformed with the Declaration of Helsinki and the ethics policy of the University of Potsdam. First, participants were randomly assigned to one of the two conditions (social context priming or control), read the respective article at their own pace, and answered the two questions. Next, they rated the robots, answered demographic questions, an open-ended question about the study's purpose, and were debriefed.

3 Results

We had 17 and 15 participants in the control and social context groups, respectively. None guessed the study's purpose. We used R [28] to compare three regression models for all measures: (a) two linear main effects of human-likeness and priming group; (b) model (a) plus interaction; and (c) a cubic main effect of human-likeness and a linear main effect of priming group. These models showed no differences (p > .05), so we chose model (a) as the most parsimonious for all measures. Human-likeness ($B = -0.13$, $p < .05$) and priming group ($B = 0.48$, $p < .05$) significantly predicted likability. The more human-like the robot was, the less participants liked it. The social context group liked robots more ($R^2 = .16$, $F(2,47) = 4.35$, $p < .05$). Human-likeness ($B = -0.09$, $p < .05$) and priming group ($B = 0.45$, $p < .05$) also significantly predicted trust. The more human-like the robot was, the less participants trusted it. The social context group trusted the robots more ($R^2 = .15$, $F(2,47) = 4.10$, $p < .05$). Finally, human-likeness ($B = 0.30$, $p < .001$) and priming group ($B = 0.65$, $p < .05$) significantly predicted creepiness. The more human-like the robot was, the creepier the participants found it. The social context group rated the robots as creepier ($R^2 = .42$, $F(2,47) = 16.90$, $p < .001$). Thus, we found a linear relationship between human-likeness and likability, trust, and creepiness (hypotheses H1b, H2b, and H3b supported); a negative main effect of human-likeness on likability (H4c supported) and trust (H4a rejected), and a positive main effect of human-likeness on creepiness (H4b supported). The social context group liked robots more (H5a supported), trusted them more (H5b supported), but also found them creepier (H5c rejected). We found no interaction between priming group and human-likeness (H6 rejected). Figure 2 provides an overview of results. Data and analysis script are at https://osf.io/2xp4d/.

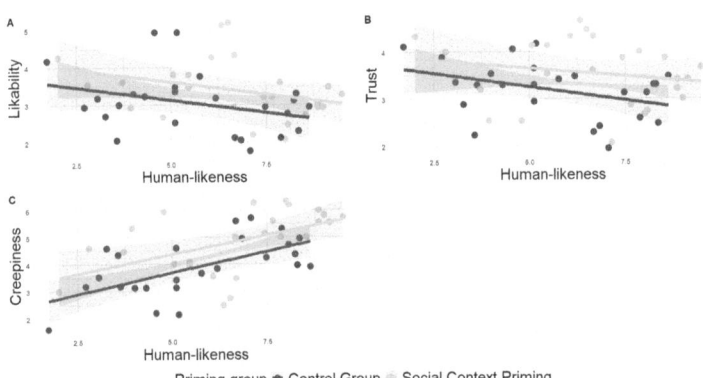

Fig. 2. Effects of social context priming and human-likeness on likability (Panel A), trust (Panel B), and creepiness (Panel C).

4 Discussion

We examined how the focus on social context affects perception of social robots and found that a linear function describes this relationship: The more human-like a robot was, the less participants liked and trusted it and the creepier they found it. Our findings support previous reports of a linear relationship [12, 14, 15]. In line with [9] we also showed an UV effect for trust. However, our results contradict evidence that the UV with actual robot images has a classical U-form [29]. This could reflect the fact that the ABOT database [10] does not contain human images. Priming with social context did not alter the UV effect but increased liking, trust, and creepiness, aligning with reports that mind inference and social context affect robot creepiness and likability [25, 30]. Viewing robots as social companions may enhance likability through similarity-attraction [31] but also leads to increased creepiness due to near-human imperfections. Future research should consider adding a condition emphasizing robots' machine nature. Ours was an online study, and perceptions of robots in real-life interactions may differ from images on a screen. However, a recent meta-analysis found no effect of presentation medium [32]. Future research should validate findings with real robots, as interaction with them has been shown to reduce initial uncanny feelings [33]. In summary, our study showed how context influences perceptions of social robots and replicated the UV. Our findings suggest that robot design should be carefully considered, rather than aiming solely for maximum human-likeness. Nevertheless, introducing robots as companions may mitigate the UV effect. Caution is warranted, as an excessive focus on social functionality might enhance creepiness. These considerations should inform institutional policies and media strategies to harness the potential of social robots [34].

Acknowledgments. We thank Darran Roongrawewan, Han Zhao, and Kira Schulten for help with programming and data collection.

Disclosure of Interests. The authors have no competing interests to declare.

References

1. Mori, M.: The uncanny valley. Energy **7**, 33–35 (1970)
2. Mori, M., MacDorman, K., Kageki, N.: The uncanny valley [From the Field]. IEEE Robot. Autom. Mag. **19**(2), 98–100 (2012)
3. Diel, A., Weigelt, S., Macdorman, K.F.: A meta-analysis of the Uncanny Valley's independent and dependent variables. ACM Trans. Hum.-Robot. Interact. **11**(1), 1–33 (2022)
4. Zhang, J., Li, S., Zhang, J.Y., Du, F., Qi, Y., Liu, X.: A literature review of the research on the Uncanny Valley. In: Rau, P.L.P. (ed.) Cross-Cultural Design User Experience of Products, Services, and Intelligent Environments, pp. 255–268. Springer International Publishing, Cham (2020)
5. Wang, S., Lilienfeld, S.O., Rochat, P.: The uncanny valley: existence and explanations. Rev. Gen. Psychol. **19**(4), 393–407 (2015)
6. Moore, R.K.: A bayesian explanation of the 'Uncanny Valley' effect and related psychological phenomena. Sci. Rep. **2**(1), 864 (2012)
7. Diel, A., MacDorman, K.F.: Creepy cats and strange high houses: Support for configural processing in testing predictions of nine uncanny valley theories. J. Vis. **21**(4), 1 (2021)
8. Mathur, M.B., Reichling, D.B.: Navigating a social world with robot partners: a quantitative cartography of the Uncanny Valley. Cognition **146**, 22–32 (2016)
9. Abubshait, A., Momen, A., Wiese, E.: Seeing human: do individual differences modulate the Uncanny Valley? Proc. Hum. Factors Ergon. Soc. Annu. Meet. **61**(1), 870–874 (2017)
10. Kim, B., Bruce, M., Brown, L., Visser, E.D., Phillips, E.: A comprehensive approach to validating the Uncanny Valley using the anthropomorphic robot (ABOT) database. In: 2020 Systems and Information Engineering Design Symposium (SIEDS). Charlottesville, VA, USA: IEEE (2020)
11. Fortunati, L., Manganelli, A.M., Höflich, J., Ferrin, G.: Exploring the perceptions of cognitive and affective capabilities of four, real, physical robots with a decreasing degree of morphological human likeness. Int. J. Soc. Robot. **15**(3), 547–561 (2023)
12. Kätsyri, J., Förger, K., Mäkäräinen, M., Takala, T.: A review of empirical evidence on different uncanny valley hypotheses: support for perceptual mismatch as one road to the valley of eeriness. Front. Psychol. **10**, 6 (2015)
13. Kätsyri, J., De Gelder, B., Takala, T.: Virtual faces evoke only a weak Uncanny Valley effect: an empirical investigation with controlled virtual face images. Perception **48**(10), 968–991 (2019)

14. Rosenthal-von Der Pütten, A.M., Krämer, N.C.: How design characteristics of robots determine evaluation and uncanny valley related responses. Comput. Hum. Behav. **36**, 422–39 (2014)

15. Diel, A., Lewis, M.: Rethinking the uncanny valley as a moderated linear function: Perceptual specialization increases the uncanniness of facial distortions. Comput Hum Behav. (2024)

16. Mende, M., Scott, M.L., Van Doorn, J., Grewal, D., Shanks, I.: Service robots rising: how humanoid robots influence service experiences and elicit compensatory consumer responses. J. Mark. Res. **56**(4), 535–556 (2019)

17. Song, S.W., Shin, M.: Uncanny Valley effects on chatbot trust, purchase intention, and adoption intention in the context of e-commerce: the moderating role of avatar familiarity. Int. J. Human-Comput. Interact. **40**(2), 441–456 (2024)

18. Mathur, M.B., Reichling, D.B.: An uncanny game of trust: social trustworthiness of robots inferred from subtle anthropomorphic facial cues. In: Proceedings of the 4th ACM/IEEE International Conference on Human Robot Interaction. La Jolla California USA: ACM, pp. 313–4 (2009)

19. Shin, M., Song, S.W., Chock, T.M.: Uncanny Valley effects on friendship decisions in virtual social networking service. Cyberpsychology Behav. Soc. Netw. **22**(11), 700–705 (2019)

20. Laakasuo, M., Palomäki, J., Köbis, N.: Moral Uncanny valley: a robot's appearance moderates how its decisions are judged. Int. J. Soc. Robot. **13**(7), 1679–1688 (2021)

21. Patel, H., MacDorman, K.F.: Sending an avatar to do a human's job: compliance with authority persists despite the uncanny valley. Presence Teleoperators Virtual Environ. **24**(1), 1–23 (2015)

22. Ziemke T. Ironies of social robotics. Sci. Robot. **9**(91), eadq6387 (2024)

23. Bartneck, C., Kanda, T., Ishiguro, H., Hagita, N.: My robotic doppelgänger - a critical look at the Uncanny Valley. In: RO-MAN 2009 - The 18th IEEE International Symposium on Robot and Human Interactive Communication. Toyama, Japan: IEEE, pp. 269–76 (2009)

24. Lemaignan, S., Fink, J., Dillenbourg, P., Braboszcz, C.: The cognitive correlates of anthropomorphism. In: Bielefeld, Germany (2014). https://infoscience.epfl.ch/record/196441

25. Gray, K., Wegner, D.M.: Feeling robots and human zombies: mind perception and the uncanny valley. Cognition **125**(1), 125–130 (2012)

26. Navare, U.P., Ciardo, F., Kompatsiari, K., De Tommaso, D., Wykowska, A.: When performing actions with robots, attribution of intentionality affects the sense of joint agency. Sci. Robot. **9**(91), eadj3665 (2024)

27. Anwyl-Irvine, A.L., Massonnié, J., Flitton, A., Kirkham, N., Evershed, J.K.: Gorilla in our midst: an online behavioral experiment builder. Behav. Res. Methods **52**(1), 388–407 (2020)

28. R Core Team. R: A language and environment for statistical computing. R Foundation for Statistical Computing [Internet]. Vienna, Austria (2020)

29. Martini, M.C., Gonzalez, C.A., Wiese, E.: Seeing minds in others – can agents with robotic appearance have human-like preferences? Pavlova MA, editor. PLoS ONE **11**(1), e0146310 (2016)

30. Rosenthal-von der Pütten, A.M., Krämer, N.C.: Individuals' evaluations of and attitudes towards potentially uncanny robots. Int. J. Soc. Robot. **7**(5), 799–824 (2015)

31. Bernier, E.P., Scassellati, B.: The similarity-attraction effect in human-robot interaction. In: 2010 IEEE 9th International Conference on Development and Learning. Ann Arbor, MI, USA: IEEE, pp. 286–90 (2010)

32. Roesler, E., Manzey, D., Onnasch, L.: A meta-analysis on the effectiveness of anthropomorphism in human-robot interaction. Sci. Robot. **6**(58), eabj5425 (2021)

33. Paetzel, M., Castellano, G.: Let me get to know you better: can interactions help to overcome uncanny feelings? In: Proceedings of the 7th International Conference on Human-Agent Interaction. Kyoto Japan: ACM, pp. 59–67 (2019)
34. Bendel, O. (ed.): Soziale Roboter: Technikwissenschaftliche, wirtschaftswissenschaftliche, philosophische, psychologische und soziologische Grundlagen. Springer Gabler, Wiesbaden (2021)

Social Robots as Physical Education Instructors for Primary School Pupils: Exploration of Child-Robot Interaction at a Summer Camp

Chia-Hsin Wu$^{(\boxtimes)}$ ⓘ, Aino Ahtinen ⓘ, and Kaisa Väänänen ⓘ

Tampere University, Korkeakoulunkatu 7, 33720 Tampere, Finland
{chia-hsin.wu,aino.ahtinen,kaisa.vaananen}@tuni.fi

Abstract. In the field of child-robot interaction, social robots promote motivational learning across diverse educational contexts. This study explored primary school pupils' learning experiences, perceptions, and interactions in physical education activities facilitated by three social robot instructors. We employed human-centered and persuasive design approaches to co-design robot-assisted activities with two physical education professionals. These activities were qualitatively evaluated with 22 pupils aged 12 to 13 years within a 2-hour summer camp. Despite most pupils having minimal prior robotic experiences, they reported positive learning outcomes by showing an improved understanding of physical education concepts and robot literacy. Our study highlights that physically embodied robots benefit physical education, as their multimodal features and physical presence effectively sustain pupils' motivation and engagement. We conclude with four design implications for integrating social robots as motivational instructors in children's physical education.

Keywords: Social Robots · Physical Education · Child-Robot Interaction

1 Introduction

Regular physical activity offers well-established health benefits, preventing diseases while supporting overall physical and emotional well-being [1]. However, over the last decades, there has been a concerning rise in sedentary lifestyles among non-adolescent children [1]. This trend has led to emergent challenges related to physical development, body posture awareness, and motor skills [2].

Motivation plays a crucial role in learning. Persuasive design refers to techniques that support users' engagement and motivation [3]. Social robots have been designed with persuasive interventions to support motivation in children's education [4]. Park et al. [5] noted that tasks incorporated with multimodal interactions (gestures, speech, touch, and gaze) serve as strong social cues in child-robot interaction (CRI). Robot-assisted education has been instrumental in advancing STEM (science, technology, engineering, mathematics) learning and soft skills development [6]. While social robots show promise in promoting motivational learning through persuasive and multimodal interventions, children's interactions with different robots in physical education still need exploration.

This paper focuses on robot-assisted physical education for primary school pupils. The goal was to understand pupils' learning experiences, perceptions, and interactions with three social robot instructors: Nao[1], Pepper[2], and Furhat[3]. This study was a collaboration between the university and a physical education institution from February to September 2023. We co-designed robot-assisted activities with two physical education professionals, which employed human-centered design (HCD) and persuasive design approaches to develop motivational tasks tailored to each robot's capabilities. These activities were qualitatively evaluated with 22 pupils aged 12 to 13 years within a 2-hour summer camp. We collected data through background questionnaires, observations, and pupils' written essays. Given the uncommon use of various robots in a single physical education event, our study contributes novel insights into children's spontaneous interactions with different types of social robots. In conclusion, we present design implications for incorporating social robots as motivational instructors in children's physical education. The research questions are as follows:

(1) **What are the pupils' learning experiences with different social robots in the physical education context?**
(2) **What are the pupils' perceptions regarding robot-assisted physical education activities?**
(3) **What kind of interactions occur in robot-assisted physical education activities?**

2 Related Work

2.1 Social Robots in Physical Education

Social robots are autonomous or semi-autonomous robotic systems that interact with humans while adhering to behavioral norms [7]. Social robots have demonstrated potential in promoting physical and emotional wellness, as their adaptive behaviors account for individual requirements across various contexts [8,9]. In physical education, social robots offer distinct advantages as the learning entails repetitive instructions and demonstrations [2,10]. Their implementation aims to enhance sports engagement by promoting social learning behaviors [11].

Social robots do not necessarily require physical embodiment to perform social interaction and they are thus categorized as (1) virtual agents and (2) physically embodied robots [12]. Virtual agents are digital entities interacting via screen-based interfaces, while physically embodied robots are tangible machines

---

[1] https://www.aldebaran.com/en/nao.
[2] https://www.aldebaran.com/en/pepper.
[3] https://furhatrobotics.com/.

interacting in real-world environments [13]. Studies [10,14] suggest that in education emphasizing physical interaction, physically embodied robots outperform virtual agents in enhancing learning engagement and retention. However, physically embodied robots in education should be carefully justified, as virtual agents can achieve similar outcomes with lower costs and maintenance [15]. Given the potential of physically embodied robots as children's physical education instructors, our study explores pupils' learning experiences with three different types of social robots, Nao, Pepper, and Furhat, addressing RQ1.

2.2 Persuasive Design and Human-Centered Research

Persuasive design refers to techniques that develop technologies to motivate users toward behavior change [3]. Social robots have been designed to motivate through persuasive interventions such as rewards, progress tracking, and social facilitation [4]. Bertel and Rasmussen [16] identified five principles contributing to the persuasiveness of social robots: *attractiveness, similarity, praise, reciprocity,* and *authority.* Elements such as visual appeal, humanoid features, authoritative roles, and positive feedback increase persuasiveness. Reciprocity fosters a sense of obligation to return favors, creating dynamic interactions. However, persuasiveness varies with users' behavior, autonomy, and cognitive development. For example, a solution effective for adults may not yield the same results for children.

Human-centered design (HCD) involves stakeholders and users in the iterative design, development, and evaluation process to improve interactive systems' usability using human-factor knowledge [17]. Ludi [18] outlined three human-centered design considerations for children's interactive educational solutions: First, *the difference between challenge and difficulty,* describes presenting suitable difficulties to sustain motivation. Second, *the balance between game and instruction,* emphasizes integrating playful interventions. Third, *the use of multimedia elements,* highlights incorporating graphics, audio, and animation to enhance attractiveness. Our study applied HCD and persuasive design approaches [16,18] to co-design robot-assisted activities with two physical education professionals. These activities were qualitatively evaluated with 22 pupils within a 2-hour summer camp. Our goal is to understand pupils' perceptions of persuasive physical education activities, addressing RQ2.

2.3 Multimodal Child-Robot Interaction in Robot-Assisted Learning

Social robots and their multimodal interactions improve children's learning experiences by promoting social behaviors [19]. For example, Vora et al. [20] highlighted that socially assistive robots increased child-initiated interactions with both human and robot instructors. Ahtinen and Kaipainen [21] found that robot-led rewards stimulated children's active participation in learning. Park et al. [5] noted that interactive tasks with robots fostered collaboration among children.

Although social robots often serve as instructors for children, studies have emphasized the importance of having human instructors integrate robots into teaching [5, 20, 21]. For example, children's unfamiliarity with robots can lead to hesitations and encountering technical issues during interactions. Additionally, tasks between children and robots should be carefully guided by human instructors to ensure both physical safety and engagement. Robot literacy refers to the knowledge required to interact with and use robots across various contexts [22]. Children under 18 are considered vulnerable users of robotic technologies [23]. Their limited robot literacy may result in unawareness of sensors collecting and analyzing data, which can impact data safety and ethical research conduct. Therefore, it is crucial to cultivate children's technological understanding and gain insights into their interactions in robot-assisted learning. Our study focuses on a novel approach involving three different types of social robots in a single physical education event, aiming to identify spontaneous interactions among pupils and between pupils and robots, addressing RQ3.

3 Co-design of Robot-Assisted Physical Education Activities

In the co-design workshop and conceptual design phases, we applied the HCD framework by involving two experienced female physical education professionals, each with over ten years in children's education. This section outlines the rationale for robot selection and the persuasive design in robot-assisted activities.

3.1 Co-design Workshop

The two-hour co-design workshop was conducted on the university campus in February 2023, aiming to understand primary school pupils as target users and select suitable social robots for physical education. The findings from the co-design workshop informed the conceptual design of robot-assisted physical education activities. The workshop consisted of three tasks: (1) collaboration discussions, (2) robot demonstrations, and (3) co-design activities. The first task focused on current education methods and expected collaboration outcomes. The second task demonstrated eight social robots and selected those best suited. The third task brainstormed approaches to integrate robots into physical education.

Physical education professionals outlined their objectives for integrating social robots into the curriculum as a novel approach to **engage** pupils and enhance their learning motivation. They suggested that social robots could **instruct** various exercises and promote collaborative learning in school camp contexts. Since school camps prioritize experimental and hands-on learning, they could foster spontaneous CRI and provide deeper insights into robot-assisted physical education. Additionally, social robots could facilitate ice-breaking and warm-ups, fostering **social interactions** among pupils. However, professionals stressed the importance of data and physical **safety** in robot implementation, including avoiding session recordings, ensuring transparent data collection, and maintaining ease of use for instructors with limited technical skills.

Most importantly, they emphasized that robots should assist rather than replace professionals.

As a result, we selected three physically embodied social robots: Nao and Pepper from Aldebaran Robotics, and Furhat from Furhat Robotics, to facilitate physical education. All robots support verbal and physical interactions, but each has distinct multimodal features that allow us to explore pupils' learning experiences with different types of robot instructors. Furhat features a humanoid head, while Nao and Pepper have humanoid bodies. Both Furhat and Pepper are also equipped with tablet interfaces. Our robot selection was guided by three rationales: First, their familiar humanoid appearances can enhance engagement by captivating pupils' attention. Second, their multimodal interactions, e.g., speech, gestures, gaze, movements, and touch, can encourage active participation. Third, their programmable attributes allow customization to meet various learning objectives. We summarized the co-design workshop findings by identifying four design goals for the robot-assisted physical education activities.

- **Engagement**: The robot should motivate through engaging interactions.
- **Instruction**: The robot should provide guidance and performance feedback.
- **Social interaction**: The robot should promote teamwork and socialization.
- **Safety**: The robot should prioritize physical and data security to prevent accidents and protect personal information.

3.2 Conceptual Design of Robot-Assisted Physical Education Activities

Building on the co-design workshop findings and inspired by Ahtinen et al. [6], we developed station-based robot-assisted physical education activities emphasizing social facilitation. The design of the social robot instructors and physical education activities were extended based on the persuasive design approaches presented by Bertel and Rasmussen [16] and Ludi [18]. We introduced three familiar humanoid robots with authoritative instructor roles that encourage pupils with positive feedback and playful interactions. Multimedia elements such as audio explanations, physical prompts, and graphical displays were incorporated. Physical education tasks were presented at suitable difficulty levels for pupils aged 12 to 13 years. Additionally, all the learning contents were aligned with each robot's capabilities and have been iterative reviewed and tested by physical education professionals before the evaluation.

Wizard-of-Oz (WoZ) is a research method where participants interact with a system controlled by a visible or hidden human operator. The operator, or "wizard", provides feedback through the robot based on predefined rules. Studies with visible wizards are useful for evaluating participants' acceptance of new technologies while offering immediate assistance [24]. In this study, all robots were operated using a combination of pre-programmed applications and the WoZ method. Robotic programs were launched via built-in screens or external laptops operated by the wizard, managed by two to three university researchers at each robot station. Details of the robots' programming are described below:

Nao Robot Tai Chi Exercise and Wellness Q&A. We began by instructing pupils to follow Nao's movements in "Tai Chi exercise", which is a pre-programmed application using Aldebaran Choregraphe. Following the exercise, Nao was operated via the WoZ method to facilitate a wellness Q&A session using eight physical cards, each containing a single-choice health-related question. For example,*"How much sleep is recommended for 13 to 18 years old per night?"*.

Pepper Robot Tickle Race and Tampere Quiz. We pre-programmed two applications, "Tickle Me" and "Tampere Quiz", using Aldebaran Choregraphe and installed them on Pepper's built-in screen. We began by dividing pupils into two teams for the tickle race. Teammates took turns running up to Pepper, tickling its screen to trigger audio/physical laughing feedback, then returned to high-five the next teammate before rejoining the queue. The team that had the most tickles within five minutes won the race. After the race, Pepper launched the quiz featuring eight single-choice questions related to local attractions.

Furhat Robot Medical Screener for Diabetes. "Medical Screener" is a pre-programmed application developed by Furhat Robotics. To protect pupils' personal information, we created four predefined personas for the application. Before the activities, we placed these personas in envelopes around the room. Furhat was operated via the WoZ method to guide pupils in finding the envelopes and entering the persona data into the Medical Screener, which measures diabetes risk using a tablet connected to Furhat. Pupils were instructed to discuss their persona, explore diabetes risks, and consider possible causes.

4 Methodology

4.1 Evaluation of Robot-Assisted Physical Education Activities

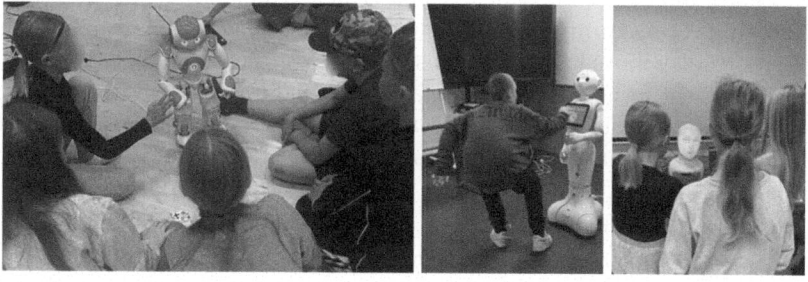

Fig. 1. The evaluation of robot-assisted physical education activities.

The two-hour evaluation was conducted at a summer camp organized by the physical education institution in September 2023. The goal was to understand pupils' learning experiences, perceptions, and interactions with social robot instructors (Fig. 1). The evaluation consisted of three parts: (1) introduction (2) physical education activities, and (3) final discussion. University researchers welcomed pupils by introducing the robots and their activities. Pupils were then divided into groups of six to eight, each accompanied by their teachers or voluntary parents. These groups rotated through three stations, each facilitated by one robot instructor and two to three university researchers, engaging in physical education activities for 25 min. The evaluation concluded by gathering all groups to share their experiences and feedback. The bilingual evaluation was conducted with robots instructed in English, translation was provided by the researchers, teachers, and parents in cases where communication was unclear.

4.2 Participants and Research Ethics

The participants included 22 pupils, aged 12 to 13 years, with an equal gender distribution, from a Finnish primary school. Most pupils had minimal prior robotic experience, with only six reporting brief interactions with household or programmable toy robots. However, they all possess relatively high socioeconomic backgrounds and have been exposed to various interactive technologies since early childhood. Before the study, 13 pupils shared their attitude toward robots, with eight expressing optimism and five remaining neutral.

This study complied with the General Data Protection Regulation (GDPR), with research permission granted by local city officials. Participation was voluntary, guardians of underage participants were required to discuss participation with their children, and consent was given only if the pupil agreed. Photography permission was obtained separately, with all photos taken from behind to avoid capturing identifiable information. This study proceeded under the supervision of responsible teachers, voluntary parents, and educational professionals. All robots were connected to local networks for data security, robot cameras were covered to protect privacy without compromising functionality.

4.3 Data Collection

Background Questionnaire. Before the study, a background questionnaire was digitally distributed to the pupils' guardians, along with an information sheet and consent form. The questionnaire collected information on pupils' gender demographics, prior experiences, and attitudes toward robotics, as well as their perspectives on integrating robots into physical education.

Contextual Observations. The observation findings were documented by altogether seven university researchers through handwritten notes at three robot stations, which were later digitally encoded for data analysis. Key inquiries included *"How is the interaction between pupils and robots?"* and *"Do pupils form social bonds with peers and robots?"*. For example, do pupils mimic the robots' movements, maintain a distance, or initiate physical and verbal interactions? Before the evaluation, all researchers responsible for each robot station reviewed the inquiries together to ensure mutual understanding of the observation focus.

Pupils' Written Essays. After the evaluation, pupils were assigned to write an essay describing their learning experiences without word limits. All essays were written in Finnish and later translated into English for data analysis, with an average word count of 67; the shortest was 37, and the longest was 112 (n=22).

4.4   Data Analysis

The affinity diagram is a technique to conduct thematic analyses of qualitative data from field studies [25]. Triangulation in research refers to the use of multiple methods and perspectives to enhance the credibility of findings [26]. Our study utilized both the affinity diagram technique and research triangulation that involved two primary responsible researchers in data analysis.

The findings from contextual observations were organized into three categories: (1) pupils' learning experiences in robot-assisted physical education, (2) pupils' attitude toward social robots as physical education instructors, and (3) pupils' interactions with robot and human instructors. The findings from pupils' written essays were arranged into four categories: (1) pupils' perceptions before robot-assisted physical education, (2) pupils' perceptions after robot-assisted physical education, (3) challenges of robot-assisted physical education, (4) suggestions for robot-assisted physical education.

5   Findings

This study applied the affinity diagram to analyze qualitative data collected from observations and pupils' essays. Our analysis revealed four key themes.

Pupils Demonstrated a Better Understanding of Robots as Interactions Progressed. Although most participating pupils had little prior robotic experience, they demonstrated a better understanding and a more positive attitude throughout the robot interaction. One stated, *"In the beginning, I thought these robots cannot do anything, but in reality, they are quite smart"* (P7), while another said, *"I learned that there can be a lot of different kinds of robot, and we can use them for different tasks"* (P12). Although robots gained high popularity among pupils, the requirement for human assistance was emphasized. One pupil noted, *"The robots were a bit silly because they are not always right"* (P13), highlighting the necessity for human guidance and support. Pupils suggested the activity can be improved by including diverse robot types and extending the interaction duration. More than half of the pupils expressed enthusiasm for participating and integrating robots into their everyday learning.

Robot-Assisted Physical Education Promotes Both Subject-Specific Learning and Robot Literacy. We observed that pupils extended their learning from physical exercises to a broader understanding of wellness. One remarked, *"The diabetes tests of Furhat were excellent, it felt almost the same as discussing* *with a real doctor"* (P9), another stated, *"I learned from Nao about how much water a kid needs to drink per day"* (P10). Pupils improved their robot literacy by addressing inquiries about the robots' physical capacities and programming methods. For example, the researcher introduced Nao's embedded sensors and programming environment after the groups completed the given tasks, which raised pupils' interest in the technical aspects of robotics. They explored programming basic commands and testing the robotic sensors. The session was engaging that some pupils were reluctant to leave for the next robot station. These experiences highlight the multifaceted benefits of educational robots in fostering both subject-specific learning and robot literacy.

Collaborative Group Settings and Robots' Physical Embodiment Motivate Pupils to Actively Engage in Social Interactions. The collaborative and competitive group activities guided pupils to focus on the robots' instructions and discuss with peers, which encouraged even introverted pupils to participate. The robots' feedback on pupils' performance sustains their engagement in quizzes, with some willing to start over for a higher score. One mentioned, *"The collaboration with teachers and friends was very successful, there was a lot of competition spirit, everything was interesting and comfortable"* (P21). The robots' physical embodiment prompted spontaneous interactions, with pupils initiating physical and verbal interactions and mirroring robots' movements, which differ from their usual school camp behaviors. Despite encountering technical issues such as network problems and speech recognition failures, pupils persisted in communicating with the robots. They adjusted their speech speed, spoke in unison to increase volume, shortened physical distance, and used varied vocabularies. Additionally, pupils reflected positively on the experience as a chance to practice their English language skills.

Progressive Interaction Approaches and Familiar Robotic Attributes Effectively Enhance Pupils' Acceptance of Robotics. Our study explores the contribution of three physically embodied robots, each equipped with different multimodal features, to children's physical education learning experiences. Among the three robots, Nao and Pepper were the most popular due to their familiar physical attributes. On the other hand, Furhat's realistic humanoid facial features initially evoked the uncanny valley effect, causing fear and hesitation among pupils. However, pupils reacted positively over time, especially when Furhat projected a face resembling animated characters. Additionally, Nao and Pepper's humanoid bodily appearances allow them to incorporate natural physical movements during speech, resulting in more physical interaction initiated by pupils, compared to the primary verbal interaction at Furhat station. Pupils initially kept a considerable distance from all robots due to unfamiliarity. Despite researchers' encouragement, the distance persisted but gradually shortened as interactions progressed, with pupils sometimes leaning in closer than necessary. This shift suggests that incorporating ice-breaking activities and familiar robotic attributes can enhance pupils' acceptance.

6 Discussion

6.1 Pupils' Learning Experiences of Robot-Assisted Physical Education

Our evaluation highlights several benefits of robot-assisted physical education. The robots met design goals by delivering engaging physical education while ensuring safety. Despite many pupils lacking prior robotic experience, they showed improved understanding and curiosity about educational robots by initiating social interactions. These findings underscore the effectiveness of physically embodied robots in education prioritizing physical interactions, promoting socially beneficial behaviors and enhancing information retention among learners [10].

Pupils addressed technical questions about the robots' functionalities and programming, indicating the novelty of using social robots to stimulate technological interest and robot literacy. Furthermore, the development of soft skills such as problem-solving, communication, and collaboration was observed, as noted by Van den Heuvel et al. [8] and Ahtinen and Kaipainen [21]. Despite the high popularity of robots among pupils, they emphasized the importance of human assistance alongside robot implementation. Pupils pointed out that robots may not always respond correctly or meet expectations. Reasons for incorporating human assistance include troubleshooting, ensuring safe physical distance, and providing a familiar learning environment with known individuals [5]. Our study indicates that robots are perceived as assistive education tools rather than replacements for professionals, as addressed by educational professionals in the co-design workshop and aligned with the studies by Vora et al. [20].

6.2 Pupils' Perceptions of Robot-Assisted Physical Education

The robot-assisted physical education activities focus on social facilitation and relationship-orientated tasks [4]. The small-group format encouraged introverted pupils to actively participate. Despite the activities not being conducted in the pupils' native language, they valued it as a chance to practice their English skills.

This study applied the persuasive design approaches outlined by Bertel and Rasmussen [16] and Ludi [18] in presenting persuasive social robot instructors and developing their physical education activities. Our physical education activities were designed with appropriate difficulty levels. Multimedia elements such as audio explanations, physical prompts, and graphical displays were incorporated into the activities. The robots were presented with authoritative roles, instructing pupils through playful interventions. Robotic feedback on pupils' performance enhanced their learning interest. Our findings suggested that these persuasive interventions effectively sustained pupils' engagement, as noted by Knežević et al. [2] and Yang et al. [11]. Pupils reported no negative aspects of the activities, with half willing to participate again and incorporate robotic solutions into their everyday learning. They suggested including more diverse robot types and extending the duration of robot interaction. Furthermore, they recommended robot-assisted learning for other classes, including younger pupils.

6.3   Pupils' Interactions in Robot-Assisted Physical Education

The multimodal interactions of social robots acted as catalysts for encouraging social learning [19]. For example, positive competition at robot stations encouraged peer communication. Pupils engaged in physical and verbal interactions with the robots, with some mirroring their expressions and movements. Physically embodied robots engaged pupils in spontaneous physical exercises, which were distinct from their performance in other school camps. Despite technical challenges such as network issues and speech recognition failures, pupils demonstrated resilience and adaptability. They collaborated to overcome communication obstacles with robots by adjusting the speech speed and volume, reducing physical distance, and using different vocabularies. The active collaboration between pupils was also emphasized by Ahtinen and Kaipainen [21].

Compared to the high popularity of Nao and Pepper due to their familiar physical attributes, Furhat's realistic appearance initially evoked hesitation among pupils. However, their attitudes toward Furhat improved as interactions progressed, especially when it displayed a resonating animated face. Additionally, Nao and Pepper's bodily appearances prompted more physical interactions from pupils, whereas interactions at Furhat station were mainly verbal. Pupils initially kept their distance from all robots but spontaneously moved closer over time, with some leaning in closer than necessary. Although pupils, as vulnerable users of robotic technologies [23], may be hesitant at first due to unfamiliarity, they develop bonds with the robots over time, as noted by Vora et al. [20]. Our findings highlighted that incorporating familiar robotic features and progressive interaction approaches enhances pupils' acceptance of educational robots.

6.4   Design Implications for Social Robots in Physical Education

1. Introduce Engaging Physical Education Approaches with Instructional and Persuasive Robotic Activities. The integration of social robot instructors in children's physical education positively supports physically active learning. This approach contributes to the development of social behaviors and improves information retention among learners, as found by Yang et al. [11]. In light of the persuasive design approach, social robots assigned authoritative roles should provide comprehensive instructions, to support pupils' motivation through interactive physical education activities, as noted by Bertel and Rasmussen [16] and Ludi [18].

2. Foster Inclusive Learning with Collaborative Robot-Assisted Physical Education Activities. Our study promotes inclusive learning by organizing small-group activities that encourage every pupil to participate. The incorporation of social robots in physical education serves as part of persuasive design strategies, providing companionship in collaborative learning. Social robots should incorporate persuasive strategies aimed at fostering active peer interactions, such as positive competition and feedback on pupils' performance, as highlighted by Murillo-Muñoz et al. [4].

3. Encourage Physical Activities Through Robots' Physical Embodiment. Physically embodied robots offer distinct advantages in physical education, which often involves repetitive instructions and demonstrated movements [2]. Our findings highlighted that the robots' multimodal interactions encouraged pupils to initiate both verbal and physical communication. Moreover, the robots' physical presence elicited spontaneous behaviors, with pupils closely following the robots' movements, which differed from their performance in human-facilitated physical education camps. These findings underscore the importance of leveraging the interaction capacities of social robots, particularly in educational settings that prioritize physical interaction [10,20].

4. Emphasize the Safety of Child-Robot Interaction with a Progressive Educational Approach. Pupils are vulnerable users of robotic technologies, potentially lacking the robot literacy to comprehend adaptive behaviors and persuasive design approaches [23]. Hence, it is essential to cultivate their technological understanding to ensure ethically and physically safe conduct in CRI. Introducing robot-assisted physical education should follow a gradual approach. For example, start with ice-breaking activities, incorporate familiar robotic features, and engage pupils in extended interaction periods. Additionally, inform pupils about the data collection and analysis methods employed by the robots, and the necessity of maintaining a safe physical distance. These approaches allow pupils to develop acceptance of robot implementation in physical education.

6.5 Limitation and Future Work

A key limitation of our study was the lack of pupil involvement in robot selection and activity design. Pupils' high acceptance of robots may have been influenced by their socioeconomic backgrounds and early technological exposure. Our future work will focus on quantitative studies to evaluate the robots' educational efficacy. Additionally, we aim to explore strategies that sustain long-term motivation in robot-assisted physical education for both educators and learners.

7 Conclusion

This study investigated primary school pupils' learning experiences, perceptions, and interactions in physical education activities facilitated by three humanoid social robots, Nao, Pepper, and Furhat. We conducted the co-design of robot-assisted activities with two physical education professionals and were qualitatively evaluated with 22 pupils aged 12–13 years. Despite most pupils having minimal prior robotic experience, they exhibited growing understanding and curiosity throughout the interaction. Pupils acquired knowledge related to physical education and robot literacy. Additionally, soft skills development in problem-solving, communication, and collaboration were observed. The multimodal interactions and physical embodiment of robots proved effective in sustaining pupils' engagement, particularly in education prioritizing physical interactions. Our study highlights the importance of human facilitators alongside robotic implementation, emphasizing that robots are perceived as assistants rather than replacements for professionals. We conclude with four design implications to integrate social robots as motivational instructors in children's physical education.

Acknowledgments. The study was supported by the Jane and Aatos Erkko Foundation through the CONVERGENCE of Humans and Machines project. We express our warmest gratitude to our study participants and Varala Sports Institute.

References

1. Gualdi-Russo, E., Zaccagni, L.: Physical activity for health and wellness. Int. J. Environ. Res. Public Health **18**(15), 7823 (2021). MDPI
2. Knežević, T., Radmilović, M., Borojević, J., Šumarac, J., Švaco, M., Raković, M.: Physical education exercises validation through child-humanoid robot interaction. In: International Conference on Robotics in Alpe-Adria Danube Region, pp. 132–140. Springer (2023)
3. Oinas-Kukkonen, H., Harjumaa, M.: Persuasive systems design: key issues, process model, and system features. Commun. Assoc. Inf. Syst. **24**(1), 28 (2009)
4. Murillo-Muñoz, F., et al.: Characteristics of a persuasive educational system: a systematic literature review. Appl. Sci. **11**(21), 10089 (2021). MDPI
5. Park, C., Kim, J., Kang, J.-H.: Robot social skills for enhancing social interaction in physical training. In: 2016 11th ACM/IEEE International Conference on Human-Robot Interaction (HRI), pp. 493–494. IEEE (2016)
6. Ahtinen, A., Chowdhury, A., Ramírez Millan, V., Wu, C.-H., Menon, G.: Co-learning around social robots with school pupils and university students–focus on data privacy considerations. In: Proceedings of the 11th International Conference on Human-Agent Interaction, pp. 115–123 (2023)
7. Bartneck, C., Forlizzi, J.: A design-centred framework for social human-robot interaction. In: RO-MAN 2004. 13th IEEE International Workshop on Robot and Human Interactive Communication (IEEE Catalog No. 04TH8759), pp. 591–594. IEEE (2004)
8. Van Den Heuvel, R.J.F., Lexis, M.A.S., Janssens, R.M.L., Marti, P., De Witte, L.P.: Robots supporting play for children with physical disabilities: exploring the potential of IROMEC. Technol. Disabil. **29**(3), 109–120 (2017). IOS Press
9. Alhaddad, A.Y., Cabibihan, J.-J., Bonarini, A.: Influence of reaction time in the emotional response of a companion robot to a child's aggressive interaction. Int. J. Soc. Rob. **12**(6), 1279–1291 (2020). Springer
10. Alam, A.: Social robots in education for long-term human-robot interaction: socially supportive behaviour of robotic tutor for creating robo-tangible learning environment in a guided discovery learning interaction. ECS Trans. **107**(1), 12389 (2022). IOP Publishing
11. Yang, D., Oh, E.-S., Wang, Y.: Hybrid physical education teaching and curriculum design based on a voice interactive artificial intelligence educational robot. Sustainability **12**(19), 8000 (2020). MDPI
12. Lee, K.M., Jung, Y., Kim, J., Kim, S.R.: Are physically embodied social agents better than disembodied social agents?: The effects of physical embodiment, tactile interaction, and people's loneliness in human-robot interaction. Int. J. Hum. Comput. Studi. **64**(10), 962–973 (2006). Elsevier

13. Moradinezhad, R., Solovey, E.T.: Investigating trust in interaction with inconsistent embodied virtual agents. Int. J. Soc. Rob. **13**(8), 2103–2118 (2021). Springer
14. van den Berghe, R., Verhagen, J., Oudgenoeg-Paz, O., Van der Ven, S., Leseman, P.: Social robots for language learning: a review. Rev. Educ. Res. **89**(2), 259–295 (2019)
15. van Ewijk, G., Smakman, M., Konijn, E.A.: Teachers' perspectives on social robots in education: an exploratory case study. In: Proceedings of the Interaction Design and Children Conference, pp. 273–280. (2020)
16. Bertel, L.B., Rasmussen, D.M.: On being a peer: what persuasive technology for teaching can gain from social robotics in education. Int. J. Conceptual Struct. Smart Appl. (IJCSSA) **1**(2), 58–68 (2013). IGI Global
17. International Organization for Standardization: ergonomics of human-system interaction—Part 210: human-centred design for interactive systems. ISO Standard No. 9241-210:2019 (2019). https://www.iso.org/standard/77520.html
18. Ludi, S.: Children and educational software: software design under the microscope. In: 1996 IEEE International Conference on Multi Media Engineering Education. Conference Proceedings, pp. 517–521. IEEE (1996)
19. Belpaeme, T., et al.: Guidelines for designing social robots as second language tutors. Int. J. Soc. Rob. **10**, 325–341 (2018). Springer
20. Vora, J.R., et al.: Influence of a socially assistive robot on physical activity, social play behavior, and toy-use behaviors of children in a free play environment: a within-subjects study. Front. Rob. AI **8**, 768642 (2021). Frontiers
21. Ahtinen, A., Kaipainen, K.: Learning and teaching experiences with a persuasive social robot in primary school–findings and implications from a 4-month field study. In: International Conference on Persuasive Technology, pp. 73–84. Springer (2020)
22. Suto, H.: Robot literacy: an approach for sharing society with intelligent robots. Int. J. Cyber Soc. Educ. **6**(2), 151–168 (2013)
23. Henkel, A.P., Čaić, M., Blaurock, M., Okan, M.: Robotic transformative service research: deploying social robots for consumer well-being during COVID-19 and beyond. J. Serv. Manag. **31**(6), 1131–1148 (2020). Emerald Publishing Limited
24. Höysniemi, J., Hämäläinen, P., Turkki, L.: Wizard of OZ prototyping of computer vision based action games for children. In: Proceedings of the 2004 Conference on Interaction Design and Children: Building a Community (IDC), pp. 27–34. ACM (2004)
25. Lucero, A.: Using affinity diagrams to evaluate interactive prototypes. In: Human-Computer Interaction–INTERACT 2015: 15th IFIP TC 13 International Conference, Proceedings, Part II, pp. 231–248. Springer International Publishing (2015)
26. Heale, R., Forbes, D.: Understanding triangulation in research. Evid.-Based Nurs. **16**(4), 98–98 (2013)

Exploring Children's Strategies in Response to Robot's Advice During a Group Task with iCub and Nao

Giulia Pusceddu[1,2(✉)], Mariapia Sangineto[3,4], Francesca Cocchella[2,4],
Michela Bogliolo[2,5], Giulia Belgiovine[4], Linda Lastrico[4], Maura Casadio[2],
Francesco Rea[4], Cristina Gena[3], and Alessandra Sciutti[4]

[1] Robotics, Brain and Cognitive Science Department, Italian Institute of Technology,
Genoa, Italy
`giulia.pusceddu@iit.it`
[2] Department of Informatics, Bioengineering, Robotics, and Systems Engineering,
University of Genoa, Genoa, Italy
[3] Department of Computer Science, University of Turin, Turin, Italy
[4] Cognitive Architecture for Collaborative Technologies Unit, Italian Institute of
Technology, Genoa, Italy
[5] Scuola di Robotica, Genoa, Italy

Abstract. This study investigates children's trust in two humanoid robots, Nao and iCub, through a cooperative game designed to elicit spontaneous behaviors and group dynamics. We investigate whether participants change their choices after hearing advice from a robot, considering rounds where the advice is correct or incorrect, with the robot apologizing for its mistakes. Results reveal that, in most cases, participants prefer not to change their moves after the robot's advice. Additionally, after the robots made mistakes, participants are less likely to actively follow their advice and more likely to reject it. No significant differences in strategies among the iCub and Nao samples are evidenced. Furthermore, we examine the influence of group dynamics, identifying "Proactive Players" who consistently initiated moves. A significant association between the strategies of this player and their teammates is found, suggesting potential influence.

Keywords: Robots in Education · Technology at School · Group Interaction · Trust Repair

1 Introduction

Achieving natural cooperation between humans and robots is a central goal in the field of Human-Robot Interaction (HRI). The concept of trust is crucial because it is a complicated and situational phenomenon that underpins the dynamics of these interactions. Trust in robots, as defined by Wagner et al. [25], hinges on humans' belief that robots in collaborative tasks will act in ways that mitigate risks to their outcomes.

O. Palinko et al. (Eds.): ICSR + AI 2024, LNAI 15562, pp. 418–428, 2025.
https://doi.org/10.1007/978-981-96-3519-1_38

The measurement of trust in HRI has been a focal point of numerous studies, highlighting the challenges associated with its assessment. Researchers have explored a variety of factors influencing trust, ranging from environmental conditions and task dynamics to the perceptual capabilities and relational attributes of robots [13]. For instance, the appearance and communicative abilities of robots play significant roles in inducing trust. Studies have shown that humanoid robots that exhibit childlike features, such as iCub, can evoke empathetic responses and influence decision-making processes among users [2,17]. Moreover, research has focused on how robots' abilities to recognize and respond to errors—such as offering apologies—can affect perceived trustworthiness [9,10]. Previous studies found that individuals appreciate robots acknowledging and apologizing for their faults [16]. In addition, humans prefer an expressive robot over an efficient one - despite the former making mistakes and taking longer to complete the task - because they perceive its behavior as more transparent and responsive [12]. With the rise of robots in educational settings [3], we find it crucial to explore children's trust in humanoid robots. Given that children often interact in group settings and that previous social psychology literature [23] has evidenced the relevance of group interaction for many aspects of the development of the individual, such as the formation of personal identity, it is essential to investigate these dynamics within a multi-party context. We believe that the most natural way to elicit spontaneous behaviors is through play. In HRI, games can be adapted to different types of participants and can be employed to measure different aspects of the interaction [4,17,18,20,22]. For these reasons, we specifically designed a group game in which the robot makes mistakes and subsequently apologizes, to explore the evolution of young participants' trust in the robotic agent and whether group dynamics—such as the presence of a human player who takes the initiative—may impact on this element. To determine whether the game could be played on different robotic platforms and whether a particular robot type may elicit distinct trust dynamics, we conducted experiments with two different robots: Nao and iCub. The following research questions summarize the goals we aim to pursue with this study:

Q1: Does the participants' strategy change throughout the game and in response to errors made by the robot?

Q2: Do the other group members influence the participants during a social game with a robot?

We explore these questions, accounting for possible similarities or differences between the population that interacted with Nao and the one that interacted with iCub.

2   Methods

2.1   Participants

The activities with Nao were part of an educational project called "NaoToKnow" which aims to teach primary and secondary school children how to program

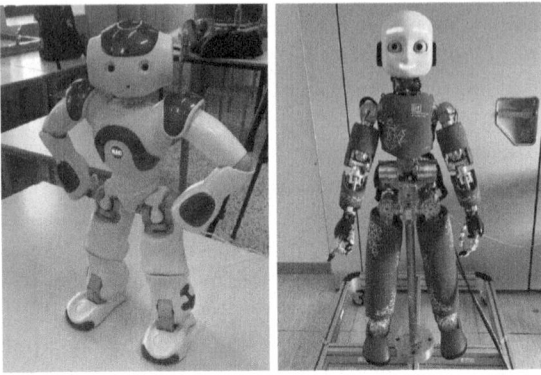

Fig. 1. The robots used in this study: Nao on the left and iCub on the right.

Nao and some basic notions about social robotics [6,19]. A total of 67 students participated in the experiments (41 females, 24 males, 2 preferred not to answer, $M_{age} = 10.8$, $\sigma_{age} = 1.56$). The experiments with iCub were carried out at the "Orientamenti Summer," an event for children in Genoa, Italy. We had 57 participants (28 females and 29 males, $M_{age} = 10.6$, $\sigma_{age} = 1.96$). Participants were divided into groups of three or four (18 in Nao's case, 16 in iCub's). To verify that the two populations were reasonably comparable, we conducted an independent samples t-test on the age of the populations, which did not reveal a significant difference ($p = 0.623$). The study was approved by the University of Genoa's ethical committee (n. 20220317, 03/17/2022).

2.2 Setup

The experiments were conducted using the Nao[1] and iCub[2] humanoid robots (Fig. 1).

Both robots have been widely used in HRI, with more details available on the websites listed at the foot of the page.

The experimental sessions with Nao took place in a classroom at a school, while the experiments with iCub were conducted in a laboratory. The experimental setups are identical, except for the robot position. Since Nao is a small robot, it was placed on a desk in front of the participants; the iCub robot, instead, was placed on a support that kept it upright, facing the participants. To record the interaction, we used a webcam with a resolution of 1080p and a frame rate of 30 fps, with an integrated microphone. A laptop is used to manage the recording and store the data. Nine stacks of six game cards each were placed on the floor between the robot and the participants, forming a grid; every card was identifiable thanks to the labels for every column and row. The designated position of

---

[1] https://www.aldebaran.com/en/nao.

[2] https://icub.iit.it/.

every participant was marked on the floor with tape at about a 1-meter distance from one another. Figure 2 shows a schematic representation of the setups.

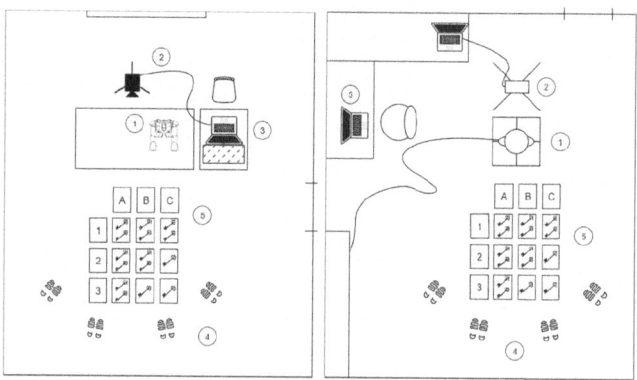

Fig. 2. Schema of the setups for the Nao's (left) and iCub's (right) experiments. (1) robot; (2) camera; (3) laptop controlling the robot; (4) Participants' starting positions; (5) Game cards forming a grid.

2.3   Description of the Task

The objective of this activity, named "Hunt for the Stars," is to maximize the team's score by playing a cooperative game with a humanoid robot. Players can walk around the area and speak to each other at any time during the game. The task takes about fifteen minutes to complete and consists of six rounds: one familiarization trial and five regular trials. In each round, teams of three or four players must choose how to use their individual tokens to uncover the greatest number of stars concealed behind the nine cards. Each child has one token per round at their disposal that can be used to unlock cards. There are two types of cards: (i) some require two tokens to be revealed, and they hide an "X" (0 points) or two stars (two points); (ii) the others require just one token, and they contain either an "X" or a star (one point). At the beginning of each round, participants must put their tokens on the preferred card. The robot then gives a tip indicating a column or row where to place the tokens (e.g. "In my opinion, the stars are in column A"). Subsequently, players have the option to rearrange the tokens' positions. We intend to investigate whether young participants would continue to trust a robot even after it makes mistakes, so we programmed the robot to give wrong tips in the second and third rounds. When, at the end of the round, cards are uncovered, the robot apologizes for its mistake.

2.4   Experimental Protocol

As soon as the players enter the room, the researchers go over the guidelines for the game. The players then take their initial positions. The robot speaks a

Fig. 3. Participants playing the game with iCub (left) and Nao (right).

summary of the rules and gives a start to the familiarization trial (Fig. 3, left picture). After that, the main game then starts. Throughout each of the five rounds:

1. Participants have 20 s to choose on which card to place their tokens (Fig. 3, right picture).
2. The robot offers its advice to the participants.
3. Participants have 20 s to decide if to reposition their tokens.
4. Cards and scores are revealed. If the robot's advice turns out to be incorrect, it apologizes.
5. Old cards are removed, tokens retrieved, and a new round begins.

At the end of the fifth round, the researchers declare the final score; the robot says goodbye to the participants. Finally, the subjects complete a questionnaire.

2.5   Questionnaires

Participants completed a questionnaire that included items about Children's Intentional Acceptance of Social Robots (CIASR) (previously used with children by [14]), and Trust (adapted by [24]). Participants answered the items on a 5-point Likert scale, where 1 meant strongly disagree, and 5 meant strongly agree. We adopted the approach used by Severson and Lemm [21], and we used emojis and images as response formats to the items. We collected 124 questionnaire answers (67 belonging to Nao's participants, 57 to iCub's).

2.6   Analyses

For each experiment, for each player, the following objective information was annotated for each round: (i) the card on which the player placed the token, before and after the robot's advice; (ii) the order in which players placed their tokens on the game board, before and after the robot's advice. The first information allows understanding whether players decide to follow the robot's advice, ignore it, or reject it. We categorized the players' behavior into four strategies:

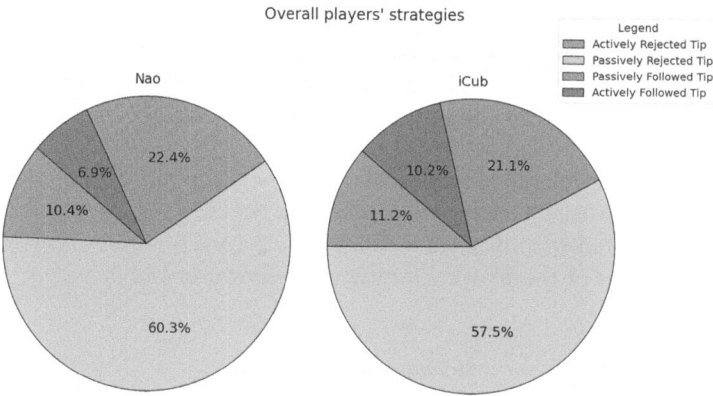

Fig. 4. Pie charts representing the overall players' strategies.

- **Actively Followed Tip (AFT):** Participants had initially placed their token in a cell not suggested by the robot and moved their token to a suggested cell.
- **Passively Followed Tip (PFT):** Participants placed their token on a cell that was then suggested by the robot, and they left it there.
- **Passively Rejected Tip (PRT):** Participants chose to keep their token in a cell non-suggested by the robot, ignoring the advice.
- **Actively Rejected Tip (ART):** Participants had initially placed their token in a cell that was then suggested by the robot and moved it away to avoid following the robot's suggestion.

The second type of annotated data was useful to detect the presence of a **Proactive Player**: i.e., a player who, within their team, initiated their move first in at least 50% of the cases. We hypothesize that a Proactive Player can influence other team members' decisions. The data was processed using software written in Python. We ran the statistical analyses on the annotated and questionnaire data using the software Jamovi[3]. The details of the statistical tests used can be found in the result section.

3 Results

3.1 Q1. Does the Participants' Strategy Change Throughout the Game and in Response to Errors Made by the Robot?

Analyzing the data from all subjects across all rounds, we observed that passive choices were the most frequent, with Passively Rejected Tip being the most common (Nao: 60.3%, iCub: 57.5%), followed by Passively Followed Tip (Nao: 22.4%, iCub: 21.1%).

---

[3] https://www.jamovi.org/.

Decisions that required active player action, i.e., moving the token, were less frequent. Actively Rejected Tip accounted for 10.4% of preferences among players who interacted with Nao and 10.2% among iCub teammates, while Actively Followed Tip accounted for only 6.9% of preferences among Nao's participants with Nao and 10.2% among iCub's.

Testing χ^2 to detect the possible differences between different populations of categorical data revealed no statistical difference between the overall strategies of those who interacted with iCub and Nao ($\chi^2 = 2.42, p = .49$). A representation of the distributions of the players' strategies is shown in Fig. 4.

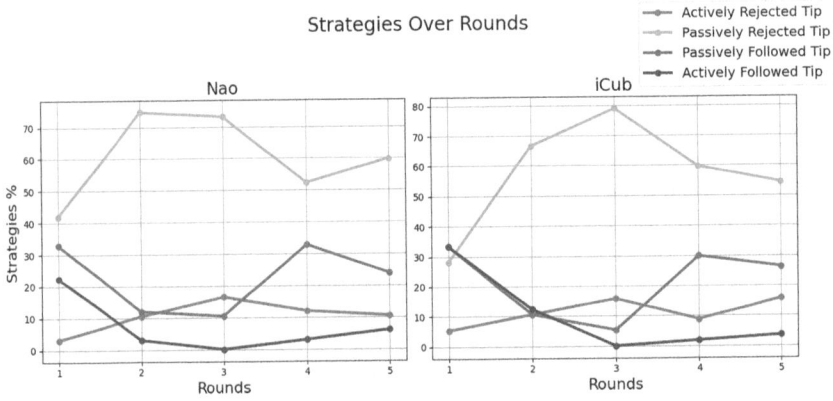

Fig. 5. Plots of the strategies of Nao's and iCub's groups over the five rounds. The y-axis refers to the percentages of players that have chosen each strategy.

We analyzed the players' strategies in each of the five rounds (see Fig. 5). The robots give incorrect advice, apologizing for the error, in round 2 and round 3, so one can observe the possible effects of the error that occurred in round 2 from round 3 and of both errors from round 4.

Interestingly, for Nao, there is a decrease in the Actively Followed Tip precisely at round 3, after the robot was wrong in round 2. This suggests that here the participants preferred to reject the robot's advice; there is indeed an increase in the Actively Rejected Tip strategy, while the passive strategies (PFT, PRT) remain almost unchanged. The iCub population suffers the same effects: an increase in ART at the expense of AFT at round 3. However, it is interesting to note that in round 1, a higher percentage of iCub's players than Nao's had chosen AFT, a trend probably due to their positive first impression of iCub, which decreased immediately from round 2. In round 4, we see a decrease in rejections and an increase in follows, which are more evident for passive strategies than for active ones. The strategies for both populations remain stable in round 5.

Although looking closely at the data, we find some differences between the two populations, a series of χ^2 tests used to compare the corresponding rounds of

Table 1. Descriptive statistics and Cronbach's α of questionnaires data.

Scale (1-to-5 Likert)	μ_{Nao}	σ_{Nao}	α_{Nao}	μ_{iCub}	σ_{iCub}	α_{iCub}
CIASR	4.66	.42	.58	4.64	.65	.75
Trust	4.05	.68	.83	3.81	1.03	.91

the two populations revealed no significant differences between the strategies of Nao's and iCub's players in each round. The results of the tests are the following: round 1 ($\chi^2 = 3.38$, $p = .34$), round 2 ($\chi^2 = 4.00$, $p = .26$), round 3 ($\chi^2 = 1.17$, $p = .56$), round 4 ($\chi^2 = .88$, $p = .83$), round 5 ($\chi^2 = 1.29$, $p = .73$).

Turning to the self-reported measures, first of all, Cronbach's α was computed to verify the reliability of the scales [7]. The results are resumed in Table 1. We discard from analysis all the scales for which α was lower than .70 [5]. We had to exclude from the analysis the Nao's sample CIASR scale due to a low Cronbach's α value. We conducted a Mann-Whitney test on the Trust scales, to check for possible differences in trust perception among the two samples. No significant difference was found ($p = .302$). One-sample Wilcoxon rank tests were run against the neutral value (3, on a 1–5 Likert scale) to verify whether the self-reported measures had, in general, a positive or negative valence. Self-reported measures of Nao's Trust, iCub's Trust, and iCub's CIASR resulted in significantly greater values than the neutral value ($p < .001$ in all the scales).

3.2 Q2. Are the Participants Influenced by the Other Group Members During a Social Game with a Robot?

According to the definition of a Proactive Player in the analyses section, to study whether a player who shows initiative could influence other player's choices, we considered groups that had only one proactive player within them. We identified 12 groups out of 18 that interacted with Nao, and 6 groups out of 16 for iCub's sample.

We built contingency tables containing the distribution of strategies among the Proactive Players and the others. The tables - whose graphical representation can be found in Fig. 6 - categorize the trials with separate counts for the Following (AFT and PFT) and Rejecting (ART and PRT) strategies. Chi-square tests were run on the contingency tables. They both resulted significant (Nao: $\chi^2 = 11.00$, $p < .001$; iCub: $\chi^2 = 4.00$, $p = .045$), evidencing that there is an association between the Proactive Player's and other players' strategies. The Chi-square test does not reveal cause-and-effect relationships. However, in our scenario, the initiator acts first; thus, we hypothesize they influence the other players, while the other way around is not plausible. Even with this time order, proving causation is still difficult: although it seems logical that the initiator might impact the others, group dynamics could involve other factors.

Proactive Player Contingency Tables

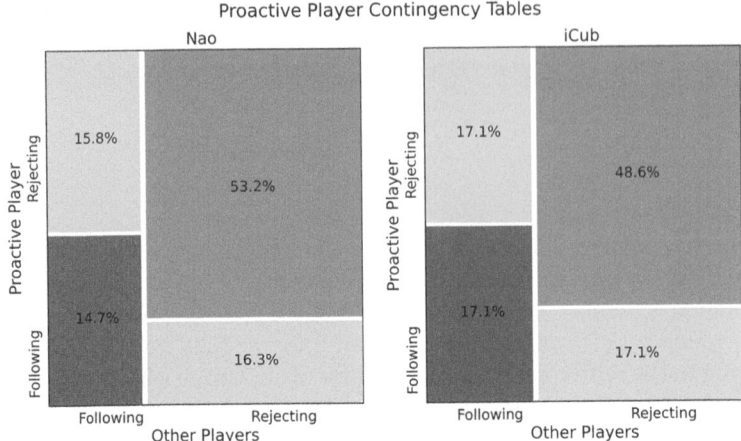

Fig. 6. Mosaic representation of the contingency tables illustrating the association between the Proactive Player's and other players' strategies. The width of each segment corresponds to the relative frequency of occurrences. A significant relationship between Proactive Players' and other players' choices was found, suggesting a potential influence of the Proactive Player on others' decisions.

4   Discussion and Conclusions

Overall, the data suggests that passive strategies (PRT and PFT) are the most common among children interacting with Nao and iCub. Active strategies (ART and AFT) are significantly less frequent, indicating a general preference for passive decision-making in both samples. This trend is consistent across all rounds, highlighting a robust behavioral pattern among the participants. Notably, even though the groups interacted with different robots, they adopted a similar strategy. However, when the robots make errors, there is a tendency for an increase in active rejection choices (ART) at the expense of active following choices (AFT) in both samples, indicating that participants tend to rely more on their own judgment rather than the robot's advice—a behavior similarly observed in previous studies [8,11].

According to the results, participants might be influenced by the presence of a Proactive Player. The analysis indicated that Proactive Players seem to significantly polarize the choices of other group members, who often follow their decisions. This finding reinforces the notion that taking the initiative is a leadership trait [15,26].

Our findings underscore the importance of considering both individual reactions to the robot's errors and group dynamics to comprehend human-robot interactions. According to our results, robots could be designed to exhibit more proactive behaviors to enhance their role as effective leaders in education, where robot teachers still struggle to be perceived as such [1]. Additionally, by recognizing and adapting to group dynamics, specifically to the influence of Proactive

Players, robots could tailor their interactions to support emerging leaders while keeping all students engaged, leading to a more balanced learning environment.

Acknowledgements. Activities with iCub. The authors wish to thank Fabio Vannucci and Sara Mongile for their help during the experimental activities. Moreover, they thank Orientamenti Regione Liguria for their assistance in managing the young participants.

Activities with Nao. The NaoToKnow project was funded under the PNSD national call for proposals STEAM Methodologies and implemented by the national network of school Institutes ARETE+4NAO, of which the Istituto Comprensivo Goffredo Mameli of Palestrina (RM) directed by DS Professor Ester Corsi is the leader, involving twenty-three Comprehensive Institutes in the Italian regions of Lazio, Abruzzo, Campania, Sardinia, Lombardy, Piedmont and Emilia-Romagna. The authors wish to thank Scuola di Robotica for the support, with particular reference to Filippo Bogliolo, Gianluca Pedemonte, and Emanuele Micheli.

References

1. Alves-Oliveira, P., Sequeira, P., Paiva, A.: The role that an educational robot plays. In: 2016 25th IEEE International Symposium on Robot and Human Interactive Communication (RO-MAN), pp. 817–822. IEEE (2016)
2. Bartneck, C., Kulić, D., Croft, E., Zoghbi, S.: Measurement instruments for the anthropomorphism, animacy, likeability, perceived intelligence, and perceived safety of robots. Int. J. Soc. Robot. **1**, 71–81 (2009)
3. Belpaeme, T., Kennedy, J., Ramachandran, A., Scassellati, B., Tanaka, F.: Social robots for education: a review. Sci. Rob. **3**(21), eaat5954 (2018)
4. Castellano, G., Pereira, A., Leite, I., Paiva, A., McOwan, P.W.: Detecting user engagement with a robot companion using task and social interaction-based features. In: Proceedings of the 2009 International Conference on Multimodal Interfaces, pp. 119–126 (2009)
5. Chiorri, C.: Psicometria e teoria dei test. McGraw-Hill Education (2016)
6. Cocchella, F., et al.: At school with a robot: Italian students' perception of robotics during an educational program. In: 2023 32nd IEEE International Conference on Robot and Human Interactive Communication (RO-MAN), pp. 1413–1419 (2023)
7. Cronbach, L.J.: Coefficient alpha and the internal structure of tests. Psychometrika **16**(3), 297–334 (1951)
8. Dio Di, C., et al.: Shall i trust you? From child-robot interaction to trusting relationships. Front. Psychol. **11**, 469 (2020)
9. Eyssel, F., Hegel, F.: (s) he's got the look: gender stereotyping of robots 1. J. Appl. Soc. Psychol. **42**(9), 2213–2230 (2012)
10. Eyssel, F., Kuchenbrandt, D.: Social categorization of social robots: anthropomorphism as a function of robot group membership. Br. J. Soc. Psychol. **51**(4), 724–731 (2012)
11. Geiskkovitch, D.Y., Thiessen, R., Young, J.E., Glenwright, M.R.: What? That's not a chair!: how robot informational errors affect children's trust towards robots. In: 2019 14th ACM/IEEE International Conference on Human-Robot Interaction (HRI), pp. 48–56 (2019)

12. Hamacher, A., Bianchi-Berthouze, N., Pipe, A.G., Eder, K.: Believing in BERT: using expressive communication to enhance trust and counteract operational error in physical human-robot interaction, pp. 493–500 (2016)

13. Hancock, P.A., Billings, D.R., Schaefer, K.E., Chen, J.Y., De Visser, E.J., Parasuraman, R.: A meta-analysis of factors affecting trust in human-robot interaction. Hum. Factors **53**(5), 517–527 (2011)

14. de Jong, C., Kühne, R., Peter, J., van Straten, C.L., Barco, A.: Intentional acceptance of social robots: development and validation of a self-report measure for children. Int. J. Hum Comput Stud. **139**, 102426 (2020)

15. King, A.J.: Follow me! i'ma leader if you do; i'ma failed initiator if you don't. Behav. Proc. **84**(3), 671–674 (2010)

16. Mirnig, N., Stollnberger, G., Miksch, M., Stadler, S., Giuliani, M., Tscheligi, M.: To err is robot: how humans assess and act toward an erroneous social robot. Front. Robot. AI 21 (2017)

17. Pasquali, D., Gonzalez-Billandon, J., Rea, F., Sandini, G., Sciutti, A.: Magic iCub: a humanoid robot autonomously catching your lies in a card game. In: Proceedings of the 2021 ACM/IEEE International Conference on Human-Robot Interaction, pp. 293–302 (2021)

18. Pereira, A., Prada, R., Paiva, A.: Socially present board game opponents. In: International Conference on Advances in Computer Entertainment Technology, pp. 101–116. Springer (2012)

19. Pusceddu, G., et al.: Training school teachers to use robots as an educational tool: the impact on robotics perception. In: International Conference on Social Robotics, pp. 103–113. Springer (2022)

20. Rato, D., Correia, F., Pereira, A., Prada, R.: Robots in games. Int. J. Soc. Robot. **15**(1), 37–57 (2023)

21. Severson, R.L., Lemm, K.M.: Kids see human too: adapting an individual differences measure of anthropomorphism for a child sample. J. Cogn. Dev. **17**(1), 122–141 (2016)

22. Strohkorb, S., Fukuto, E., Warren, N., Taylor, C., Berry, B., Scassellati, B.: Improving human-human collaboration between children with a social robot. In: 2016 25th IEEE International Symposium on Robot and Human Interactive Communication (RO-MAN), pp. 551–556 (2016)

23. Turner, J.C., Oakes, P.J., Haslam, S.A., McGarty, C.: Self and collective: cognition and social context. Pers. Soc. Psychol. Bull. **20**(5), 454–463 (1994)

24. Vega, A., Ramírez-Benavides, K., Guerrero, L.A., López, G.: Evaluating the Nao robot in the role of personal assistant: the effect of gender in robot performance evaluation. Multi. Digit. Publishing Inst. Proc. **31**(1), 20 (2019)

25. Wagner, A.R., Arkin, R.C.: Recognizing situations that demand trust. In: 2011 20th IEEE International Symposium on Robot and Human Interactive Communication (RO-MAN), pp. 7–14. IEEE (2011)

26. Yoo, Y., Alavi, M.: Emergent leadership in virtual teams: what do emergent leaders do? Inf. Organ. **14**(1), 27–58 (2004)

Apples and Oranges: Validity and Reliability of the Three Main Anthropomorphism Measures

Merel Keijsers[1]([✉]), Luisa Porzio[1], Anthony Tricarico[1], Daniel J. Rea[2],
Stela H. Seo[3], and Takayuki Kanda[3]

[1] John Cabot University, Rome, Italy
mkeijsers@johncabot.edu
[2] University of New Brunswick, Fredericton, Canada
[3] Kyoto University, Kyoto, Japan

Abstract. Anthropomorphism is a key construct in social human-robot interaction, with a variety of measurements. Our experiment compares the three most used scales on construct and convergent validity as well as reliability. We used a mixed methods design where participants first viewed a video featuring either a Sota or a TIAGo robot, and then completed each scale with randomisation of the order of presentation. Results indicate that the Mind Attribution scale (Gray et al., 2007) and the Individual Differences in Anthropomorphism questionnaire (Waytz et al., 2010) experienced some order effects and appear to be founded on a different latent process than the revised Godspeed questionnaire (Ho & MacDorman, 2010; Bartneck et al., 2009), though the different scales yield mostly comparable results.

Keywords: Anthropomorphism · Validity · Reliability

1 Introduction

Mind attribution, humanlikeness, or anthropomorphism has been a point of focus within social human-robot interaction (HRI)[1], whether as a predictor, manipulation, control or dependent variable. And with reason: perceiving a robot as possessing (some extent of) humanness is considered the starting point to various outcomes, in terms of cognition – e.g. trust [9] and moral agency [16] – affect – e.g. empathy [13] – and behaviour – e.g. prosocial [23] and bullying behaviour [20]. Scientists have operationalised anthropomorphism in various ways, including measurements of social behaviour [41], analysis of participants' descriptions of robots [1], or the extent to which they apply (human) stereotypes to the robot [10]. The most common way, however, is explicit self-report through a scale or questionnaire, where participants indicate how much they see the robot

---

[1] [42] notes that these terms are often used interchangeably; this paper will treat them as such.

© The Author(s), under exclusive license to Springer Nature Singapore Pte Ltd. 2025
O. Palinko et al. (Eds.): ICSR + AI 2024, LNAI 15562, pp. 429–442, 2025.
https://doi.org/10.1007/978-981-96-3519-1_39

as possessing a variety of attributes that all constitute psychological anthropomorphism.

These self-report scales may differ in how sensitive they are to certain variables (e.g., embodiment), capture variants of the same concept (e.g., robot behaviour as voluntary vs programmed), or be more or less precise in their outcomes, both within the scale (e.g. standard error) and compared to other measures (e.g. shared variance with other scales). This kind of information is fundamental for study design as it informs researchers which questionnaire best fits their research objectives, and what order questions should be presented in; and also for interpreting the relation between multiple findings or performing meta-analyses. While conceptual comparisons have been made (such as discussing to what extent they aim to capture the same construct [42], contrasting explicit and implicit measures [37,46], or to validate new measures of the construct [32]), we do not know of any study that statistically compares existing anthropomorphism scales against another with psychometrics.

Thus, we compare the three most popular anthropomorphism scales, analysing convergent and content validity as well as reliability: the Mind Perception scale (MP; [15]), the humanlikeness subscale from the revised Godspeed questionnaire (rGS; [17]), and the adapted Individual Differences in Anthropomorphism Questionnaire (IDAQ; [44]). Specifically, we compare the impact of context and robot design on measurement means, standard errors, and internal consistency.

1.1   Measurement Reliability and Validity

As a latent variable, anthropomorphism can be operationalised in various ways (see 1.2). Each of these ways aim to measure the same construct, but since this construct is fundamentally unobservable there is always the question of to what extent these operationalisations cover anthropomorphism exactly and to its full extent, i.e. their validity. Questions of validity do not necessarily mean a measure is unusable, but could also suggest that for example two measures focus on different aspects of the concept, such as a robot having a humanlike appearance versus it having hopes and dreams, leading to (slightly) different anthropomorphism scores. Even if the scores are the same, one of the two may show more variability (e.g., because participants find it easier to decide if the robot looks humanlike, than whether it can hope and dream), or be affected by different cues (for example the ability to express emotion may increase anthropomorphism in both scales, but more so for the *hopes and dreams*-based measure). This kind of validity does not reject measures, but highlights the subtle yet important differences in how measures can or should be interpreted.

When comparing measures on validity a good starting point is reliability, i.e. the extent to which measures are consistent, as this is required (but not sufficient) for validity [14]. Within scales reliability is often measured through Cronbach's alpha, which ranges from 0 to 1 and indicates the co-variation between different items. Considering that each question targets the same latent construct but does so from its own unique perspective, a questionnaire should score between .7 and

.95 [40]. In addition to ascertaining that individual scales meet this requirement, one can consider how much the scales' reliability is affected by external factors; for example item randomisation or different kinds of robots. Ideally, a scale that is reliable for robot A will have similar reliability for robot B; and if item randomisation affects reliability levels, this suggests that item interpretation may be dependent on context [27]. Finally, a measure's variance can be compared to that of other measures; even if two means are similar, the extent to which all individual data points cluster around that mean may differ. With greater variance, the standard error goes up as well, which indicates greater measurement imprecision [12]. Thus, comparing variances of the different measures, as well as their susceptibility to randomisation and different robots, is useful as an indication of reliability.

If measures are reliable and have comparable variance, they may still not represent anthropomorphism in the same way. This issue touches upon convergent validity and content validity, which are concerned with the extent to which different measures of the same construct give comparable outcomes [4], and the extent to which the scales measure unique aspects of a construct in all their variety [36], respectively. If the same scaling is employed for two questionnaires, convergent validity can be tested by comparing the scores of different scales on the same robot. It may again be beneficial to include a variety of robots and randomisation to test the robustness of these measures. If the same robot is scored differently on two anthropomorphism measures in spite of a similar scaling, then clearly a 3 on measurement A does not mean the same thing as a 3 on measurement B. Note that this does not mean directly that the measure is invalid altogether (a size M t-shirt in the USA may be much larger than the same size t-shirt in Japan, even though the t-shirts in question are perfectly indicative of the medium size in their respective countries), but at the very least it warrants caution when comparing measurements (an American tourist in Japan may want to go a size up from their usual when buying a t-shirt) and it is reason for further investigation.

To further interpret any differences, the shared variance between measurements can be taken into account: how much of the variability in measure A can be explained through measure B? This approach involves content validity, as two measures that consider the same aspects of anthropomorphism will share more variance with one another. A more detailed investigation is to check for similarity in latent (sub)variables. If the scales base themselves on similar aspects of anthropomorphism, this would show in an overlap of the factors identified between the measurements. For both content and convergent validity, finding that measurements do not match does not directly mean that either or both should not be considered an appropriate measure of anthropomorphism. It does however indicate that they target different aspects of the construct, and that depending on the research question one may be more appropriate than the other.

1.2   Anthropomorphism and Its Operationalisations

Anthropomorphism is believed to be the result of a (series of) latent process(es), which form the starting point to a range of social perceptions and behaviours such as activation of social schemas [10], morality [16], and trust [9]. Theoretical models differ on whether they conceptualise anthropomorphism along a single or multiple dimensions; as the result of a single or multiple processes; and in the case of multiple, whether these are in- or interdependent.

For example, [8] proposes a single dimension of psychological anthropomorphism as the result of three separate processes, one cognitive (activation of schemas) and two motivational (the need to be social and the need for effectance). Dispositional, contextual, and agent qualities influence each of the three processes. Cues from the robot's appearance, name, or behaviour may activate schemas associated with humans (cognitive component; [30,33]); the (un)predictability of their behaviour triggers the user's need to interact with the world in an efficient manner, which requires predictability of and control over the course of events (i.e. effectance; [34]); and their presentation as social agents may tap into the user's need to have meaningful social interactions (i.e. sociability; [26]). Thus, all processes are set in motion through robot's appearance and behaviour. While the model explicitly acknowledges the influence of dispositional and experiential qualities of the user as well as circumstantial factors [8], we also focus on robot appearance.

A similar model [22] proposes how visual aspects of the robot (e.g., physical features and movements) are precursors, and attribution of personality and morality are the consequences of anthropomorphism, with the subjective attribution of mental qualities (i.e. cognition and emotion) as the construct itself. This process of "mind perception" may be applied to human as well as non-human agents [15], and could be the foundation for cognitive and affective responses such as empathy, morality, and trust [16]. This model is two-dimensional, with attributions of affective states ("*Experience*") independent of attributions of cognitive abilities ("*Agency*") [15]. With appearance being the precursor rather than part of the construct, it is not included in their scale.

The Role of Robot Appearance. While robots can activate specific (social) schema through their presentation as for example feminine or masculine [10,29], embodiment seems to have surprisingly little influence on their perceived status as social agents [28,38], nor does their appearance seem to influence whether humans follow general social norms around them [24]. This is remarkable as robot appearance is theorised to be either an important starting point or a facet of anthropomorphism, and it suggests that social cues may be mostly inferred from aspects such as verbal and non-verbal behaviour, movement, and backstory.

Not all anthropomorphism measurements take into account a robot's physical attributes, which means that if robot appearance indeed plays at most a minor role, scales that focus strongly on humanlikeness may show a larger measurement error. If robot appearance does play a role after all, two different looking robots should get different anthropomorphism scores on the same scale. Thus, the current research included a manipulation of appearance through the use of two different of robots: the small humanoid Sota and the larger, more industrial looking TIAGo (Fig. 1).

The Role of Measurement and Item Order. Item order can influence participant's answers, as previous questions may set an expectation or mental framework that influences the answers to the later questions [21,35]. This is especially the case if the questionnaire contains items that require more careful consideration due to, e.g., ambiguity or complexity [21], or if questions build on another [27]. Thus, randomisation of items can lead to lower scores and greater measurement error [45]. This same reasoning can be extended to the multiple entire measures; if the score depends on its order relative to another measure, that implies suggestibility in the scale.

1.3   The Current Study

We selected the three most commonly used anthropomorphism scales in social HRI [42], which differ in terms of focus (humanlike appearance versus the process itself, i.e. ascription of human traits) and in dimensionality. The two-dimensional Mind Perception (MP; [15]) scale uses 18 items to measure the robot's cognitive and emotional capabilities, but omits measures of animism such as how "alive" or "mechanic" an agent is. The Individual Differences in Anthropomorphism Questionnaire (IDAQ; [44]) in principle measures dispositional anthropomorphism, but is often modified to a specific agent (e.g., [39,43]). Like MP, the IDAQ measures an agent's cognitive and emotional capabilities, but at 5 unique items (when applied to a specific target) it is considerably shorter. Finally, the "humanlikeness" subscale of the revised Godspeed questionnaire (rGS; [17]), based on the Godspeed questionnaire [2], asks in 6 items directly about the robot's qualities in terms of appearing living, organic, and humanlike (as opposed to inanimate, mechanical, human-made).

The current study aims to compare the MP, IDAQ, and rGS on their convergent and content validity as well as their sensitivity to contextual influences (specifically appearance and randomisation of items and scales). Participants watched a video where one of two different robot types was introduced, and afterwards completed the three anthropomorphism scales, with randomsiation of the order in which the scales were presented, and whether the item order within each scale was randomised. To avoid a study design with 54 conditions, we applied full randomization (order randomization of both surveys and items within them) to only two of the surveys: MP and rGS, thus limiting the design to 24 conditions (two robot embodiments, randomisation within either MP or rGS, first presentation either MP or rGS, and three different measures of anthropomorphism). We selected these two measurements since, at face value, they were the most different and because MP is the longest questionnaire and thus has the largest chance of order effects.

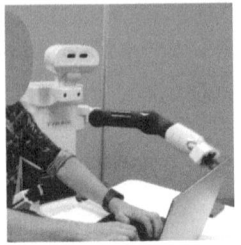

Fig. 1. Images of human-robot collaboration from our study videos. Left: Sota, Right: TIAGo.

2 Methods

2.1 Participants

We recruited 254 participants from English-speaking countries from Amazon MTurk's Masters, an elite subsection of Amazon Workers who maintain a high quality of work. Two participants were removed due to failing the attention checks, resulting in a sample of 252. This sample size has a power of 0.95 to detect differences of effect size $R^2 = .014$ or above at $\alpha < .05$ [11].

The sample had a mean age of 46.4 years ($s = 11.26$, range $= 26$–76), with similar proportions of men ($N = 124$, 49.2%) and women ($N = 123$, 48.8%) and a minority of nonbinary ($N = 2$, 0.8%) and non-disclosing participants (1.1%). Most participants ($N = 239$, 94.8%) identified as American, with only a small proportion specifying Asian American or African American (each $N = 4$, 1.6%).

2.2 Materials

Measurements. We administered three anthropomorphism measurements in addition to attention checks and participant demographics (i.e. age, gender, and nationality). See also Table 1.

The *Mind Perception scale (MP)* [15] is a measure of psychological anthropomorphism consisting of 18 items scored on a 7-point Likert scale. It measures to what extent an agent is perceived to be able to *experience* the world and its own feelings (e.g. "pleasure", "pain", "desire") , as well as its capacity for *agency* (e.g. "thought", "rationality", "self-awareness").

The *revised Godspeed questionnaire (rGS)* [17] assesses an agent's perceived attractiveness, eeriness, and humanness. For this study, only the humanness subscale was used, which consists of 6 contrapositions to be rated on a 7-point Likert scale. For example, participants are asked to indicate whether they consider the robot to be more *inanimate* or *living*, *synthetic* or *real*, *artificial* or *natural*, with the scores of 1 and 7 indicating either extreme and 4 at the midpoint.

The original *Individual Differences in Anthropomorphism Questionnaire (IDAQ)* consists of 15 items, and asks participants to indicate to what extent a variety of non-human entities (e.g. a cheetah, a mountain, a car) is capable of a variety of cognitive and affective responses (i.e. having consciousness, free will, and intentions) [44]. To measure a specific agent's anthropomorphism the entities are commonly replaced by the agent in question, and the recurring items removed, resulting in a questionnaire of five items measured on a 7-point Likert scale.

Two *attention checks* were included: one asking participants to identify the robot from the video, and one (embedded within the IDAQ) requiring the participant to respond with a specific value.

Video Stimuli. To ensure that any effects found could be attributed only to robot appearance, the videos were identical in length, text-to-voice narration, robot behaviours, background, and human collaborator (shown peripherally). Thus, the only difference was that either the TIAGo or the Sota robot was used (see Fig. 1). The robot behaviours included the robot waving at the camera, the robot picking up a water bottle and holding it up for someone to take, and the robot pointing out something on a laptop while the human was working on it. The narration was done from the robot's perspective, who introduced itself, and shared some general facts about robots and the specific tasks it helped out with (e.g. "I help out with coding, and bring water bottles to those who could use a refreshment"). The videos were 1 min and 10 s long.

2.3   Procedure

Ethics approval was obtained through the John Cabot University review board (007–23). The experiment advertisement on MTurk offered participants 2 US$ for completing an 8 min survey on Qualtrics. On average, participants took 6.2 min ($s = 3.2$). After being given an information sheet and providing consent, the participant was shown a one-minute video introducing either the TIAGo or Sota robot (see Fig. 1) before filling out three measures of mind attribution (MP, rGS, and IDAQ). Both the order in which these questionnaires were presented (MP followed by rGS, or rGS followed by MP) and which of the questionnaires had its items randomised (MP or rGS), were randomised between participants. Full randomisation including the IDAQ was not realised due to the consequences for study design complexity and the required number of participants. Finally, participants completed demographics, the second attention check and were given the opportunity to leave comments on the study before receiving the MTurk compensation code.

Table 1. Descriptives of the anthropomorphism measures

	mean (*sd*)	median	min	max	se	# items	Cronb. α
Mind Perception	2.43 (*0.90*)	2.39	1.00	5.72	0.06	18	.93
Revised Godspeed	2.25 (*1.08*)	2.00	1.00	5.67	0.07	6	.88
IDAQ	1.95 (*1.10*)	1.60	1.00	5.80	0.07	5	.87

3   Results

3.1   Preliminary Checks

The conditions did not differ in terms of number of respondents, $\chi(7) = 8.83$, $p = .265$, or gender distribution, $\chi(21) = 20.32$, $p = .501$, or age, $F(7, 243) = 1.21$, $p = .296$. Thus, randomisation was considered successful. Internal reliability of the measurements was excellent for Mind Perception (MP; $\alpha = .93$) and good for the revised Godspeed (rGS; $\alpha = .88$) and the Individual Differences in Anthropomorphism Questionnaire (IDAQ; $\alpha = .87$) [40].

3.2   Measurement Differences in Variance and Reliability

To test the effects of our conditions on the internal reliability of the scales, we used the procedure as proposed by [7] – a test statistic for comparison of multiple alpha coefficients based on the chi-distribution. We found no influence of randomisation or robot appearance on reliability: MP $\chi(7) = 10.59$, $p = .158$; rGS $\chi(7) = 13.71$, $p = .057$; and IDAQ $\chi(7) = 10.58$, $p = .158$. In addition, Levene's test was used to test whether the measures' variance differed between the conditions. This was not the case. For the MP, $F(7, 243) = 0.80$, $p = .587$; for the rGS $F(7, 244) = 1.31$, $p = .245$; and for the IDAQ $F(7,244) = 1.23$, $p = .288$. Finally, the variances also did not differ significantly between the different measurements, $F(23, 729) = 1.27$, $p = .182$. Together, these results indicates that the measurement error in different scales is stable across conditions; in other words, the measurement's precision was unaffected.

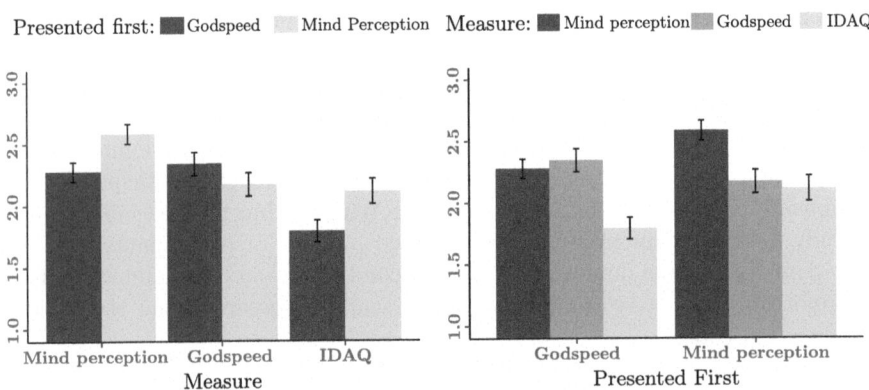

Fig. 2. Means and standard errors of the three different measurements, split out against either measurement (a) or which measure was presented first (b).

3.3   Measurement Differences in Scores

Following the method as proposed by [12], who uses multilevel modeling for mixed designs, a $3 \times 2 \times 2 \times 2$ mixed ANOVA was defined as a multilevel model with measurement type (MP, rGS, IDAQ) nested under the participant level; and robot type (Sota or TIAGo, see Fig. 1), item randomisation (items randomised within a measurement for MP or rGS), and measurement randomisation (MP or rGS presented first) as between-participant variables. Starting from a baseline model with no predictors, the model was built up one variable at a time; the resulting series of models were compared to another through chi-square tests to see which variables significantly improved predictions.

The model improved significantly with the addition of a main effect for measurement type, $\chi(2) = 69.69$, $p < .001$, and an interaction effect between the measurement type and measurement randomisation, $\chi(2) = 24.69$, $p < .001$, meaning we should not directly interpret the main effects. A post hoc with Benjamini-Hochberg correction [3] found MP scores were significantly higher if the MP scale was presented before all other conditions, all $ts > 2.74$, all $p_{bh} < .031$, mean Cohen's $d = .515$; with exception of the rGS if it was presented first, $t(244) = 1.93$, $p_{bh} = .093$. Moreover, IDAQ anthropomorphism was significantly lower than all conditions if the rGS was presented first, all $ts > 2.37$, all $p_{bh} < .024$, mean Cohen's $d = .436$; see Fig. 2. Remarkably, robot type was non-significant as main effect $t(247) = 0.55$, $p_{bh} = .584$, or as interaction, $ts < .56$, $p_{bh} > .579$.

3.4   Factor Analysis on the Full Set of Items and Covariance

To test to what extent the three different measurements base themselves off similar latent variables, we conducted an exploratory factor analysis using OLS to find the minimum residual solution. All items from all measurements were included. We set the number of factors to three, so if all three measures target distinctly different aspects of anthropomorphism, the items of each measure should load on their own factor (i.e. the factors would correspond to the three different measurements).

Indeed, the rGS questionnaire neatly loaded on a single factor, which shared no items with the other measurements. The MP and IDAQ scales however each loaded on both of the remaining factors. These two factors lined up with the Agency and Experience dimensions from the MP [15]: MP items like *Pain, Desire, Pride,* and *Consciousness* all loaded on one factor along with the IDAQ item *Emotions.* On the other hand, MP items such as *Personality, Memory, Emotion recognition,* and *Thought* all loaded on a different factor along with the IDAQ's *Intentions, Mind of its own.* Finally, each of the scales had one item that loaded on both factors: *Morality* and *Free will* (from MP and IDAQ respectively) could not be assigned to one factor alone. This finding is echoed in the correlations between the different measurements; while the IDAQ scores can be used to explain 66.31% of the variance on the MA, it shares only 27.62% of the variance with the rGS. Shared variance between MA and rGS similarly is 30.66%.

4   Discussion

Anthropomorphism is a central concept in the field of social robotics and human-robot interaction. While there are a wide variety of measurements available, to our knowledge our online video study is the first to attempt to benchmark three of the most popular scales against another psychometrically.

Interestingly, robot embodiment did not influence anthropomorphism scores, and neither did item randomisation within scales. However, the order of questionnaire presentation did: the Mind Attribution (MA) scale yielded higher scores if it was presented first, and the humanlikeness subscale of the Individual Differences in Anthropomorphism Questionnaire (IDAQ) had lower scores if it was directly preceded by the MA rather than the revised Godspeed questionnaire (rGS). Reliability and variance were similar between the measurements, and robot embodiment nor randomisation influenced these. However, differences were found in factor analysis. The MA and the IDAQ shared considerable variance and showed two similar underlying dimensions. The rGS on the other hand shared less than a third of its variance with the other two measurements, and loaded on a separate factor from the other two.

These findings suggest that the measurements arrive at their answer in different ways, and that this may affect the eventual score. Specifically, the IDAQ and MA scales are sensitive to preceding questions, while the rGS seems unaffected by where in the set of measurements it appears. These order effects are not the consequence of participants getting more careless as the survey continues (i.e. participant exhaustion, [18, 31]) as this would have shown in larger measurement error for the later assessments (i.e. unequal variance). Thus, they have to be interpreted as the influence of context; apparently the interpretation of the items on the IDAQ and MP is affected by any questions that were asked previously. Since this influence is absent for the rGS, it stands to reason that this measure of anthropomorphism bases itself on either different aspects of anthropomorphism, or takes into account additional aspects, or both of the above. This conclusion is also supported by the factor analysis, which showed two shared latent subscales for the IDAQ and the MA, with items related to affective capabilities loading on one factor, cognitive ability items on another, and two items that load on both and appear to combine both abilities (i.e. free will and morality); while the rGS loaded on a separate dimension. It is further supported by the relatively low amount of shared variance of the rGS with the other two scales, and matches the literature and the theoretical models of anthropomorphism which suggest that while robot appearance may prompt anthropomorphism to some extent (hence the similar scores for the three measures), other cues and motivational processes exert their own, independent influence.

The findings from this experiment should not be taken as an indication that either of these measures is invalid per se, but rather as an consideration for researchers trying to either design an experiment or interpret research. As far as tested here, the scales are fairly comparable in spite of them operationalising anthropomorphism in quite different ways. The lack of differences in reliability and variance under the different conditions is particularly good news, as it supports the quality of performance under different circumstances. At the same time, the interaction effect between measurement presentation order and anthropomorphism scores warns researchers to be careful of context when designing a study, as the questions asked previously to measure may affect scores. Researchers should consider methods such as counterbalancing the order in which different measurements are taken, or adding filler tasks between the measurements to avoid order effects.

In addition to these subtle differences in outcome, the results confirmed that the rGS bases itself on a fundamentally different aspect of anthropomorphism than either the IDAQ or the MP scales. While this may not come as much as a surprise when looking at the items on the scales, having this difference confirmed may help explain why e.g. results do not replicate with different measures of anthropomorphism (e.g. [46]). Researchers interested in anthropomorphism may want to include both rGS and either IDAQ or MA, for a more complete measure of its different facets.

4.1 Limitations and Future Directions

With certain precautions, online studies such as the one in question can yield data of similar quality as in-person ones [5,19] in terms of reliability and participant attention. However, a more serious limitation of the online setup is that participants did not interact, nor were they in the presence of, an embodied robot. Robot presence and embodiment have been shown to influence robot perception and engagement [6,25], and our results suggest that certain measurements may be more or less sensitive to environmental cues besides the robot. Future studies could consider making comparisons with embodied and virtual robots.

Our experiment was not fully randomized as the IDAQ was always presented last, and thus the order effects have to be interpreted with caution. For example, it is unclear if the difference in scores should be interpreted as "being third in line lowers anthropomorphism ratings" or as "presenting the revised Godspeed immediately prior to the IDAQ heightens the IDAQ scores".

Our experiment only investigated explicit measures of anthropomorphism, thus not addressing e.g. predictive validity, i.e. whether the scales differ in the strength of their relationship to related measures, such as predicting how much empathy someone will have for a robot.

Finally, our current work approached the validity question from the classical test theory perspective and considered the measurements as a whole, comparing the mean score across items for each scale. A follow-up on these findings with item-response theory (IRT) methods would be worthwhile. Under IRT discrimination and difficulty parameters are estimated for individual items, which can be used to infer how well the scale functions in different ranges of the latent trait; as well as help identify items that are redundant; and finally identify issues with the response options for specific items.

Thus, our study should be considered a starting point and a call to other researchers to help empirically validate the measures we rely on in HRI.

Anthropomorphism is complicated and multidimensional construct, and in order to study it well we need a more nuanced catalogue of how various measurements cover specific aspects of the construct.

References

1. Banks, J.: Theory of mind in social robots: replication of five established human tests. Int. J. Social Rob. **12**(2), 403–414 (2020)
2. Bartneck, C., Kulić, D., Croft, E., Zoghbi, S.: Measurement instruments for the anthropomorphism, animacy, likeability, perceived intelligence, and perceived safety of robots. Int. J. Soc. Rob. **1** (2009)
3. Benjamini, Y., Hochberg, Y.: Controlling the false discovery rate: a practical and powerful approach to multiple testing. J. Royal Statis, Soc. Series B (Methodological) **57**(1) (1995)
4. Carlson, K.D., Herdman, A.O.: Understanding the impact of convergent validity on research results. Organ. Res. Methods **15**(1), 17–32 (2012)
5. Chmielewski, M., Kucker, S.C.: An MTurk crisis? Shifts in data quality and the impact on study results. Soc, Psychol. Pers. Sci. **11**(4), 464–473 (2020)
6. Deng, E., Mutlu, B., Mataric, M.J., et al.: Embodiment in socially interactive robots. Found. Trends Rob. **7**(4), 251–356 (2019)
7. Diedenhofen, B., Musch, J.: cocron: a web interface and R package for the statistical comparison of Cronbach's alpha coefficients. Int. J. Internet Sci. **11**(1) (2016)
8. Epley, N., Waytz, A., Cacioppo, J.T.: On seeing human: a three-factor theory of anthropomorphism. Psychol. Rev. **114**(4), 864 (2007)
9. Esterwood, C., Robert, L.P.: The theory of mind and human-robot trust repair. Sci. Rep. **13**(1), 9877 (2023)
10. Eyssel, F., Hegel, F.: (S)he's got the look: gender stereotyping of robots. J. Appl. Soc. Psychol. **42**(9), 2213–2230 (2012)
11. Faul, F., Erdfelder, E., Buchner, A., Lang, A.G.: Statistical power analyses using G*Power 3.1: tests for correlation and regression analyses. Beh. Res. Methods **41**(4), 1149–1160 (2009)
12. Field, A., Field, Z., Miles, J.: Discovering statistics using R. Sage (2012)
13. Gena, C., Manini, F., Lieto, A., Lillo, A., Vernero, F.: Can empathy affect the attribution of mental states to robots? In: International Conference on Multimodal Interaction (2023)
14. Golafshani, N.: Understanding reliability and validity in qualitative research. Qual. Rep. **8**(4), 597–607 (2003)
15. Gray, H.M., Gray, K., Wegner, D.M.: Dimensions of mind perception. Science **315**(5812), 619 (2007)
16. Gray, K., Young, L., Waytz, A.: Mind perception is the essence of morality. Psych. Inqu. **23**(2) (2012)
17. Ho, C.C., MacDorman, K.F.: Revisiting the uncanny valley theory: developing and validating an alternative to the Godspeed indices. Comput. Hum. Behav. **26**(6), 1508–1518 (2010)
18. Jeong, D., Kumar, N., Aggarwal, S., Robinson, J., Spearot, A., Park, D.S.: Exhaustive or exhausting? Evidence on respondent fatigue in long surveys (2022)
19. Kees, J., Berry, C., Burton, S., Sheehan, K.: An analysis of data quality: professional panels, student subject pools, and Amazon's Mechanical Turk. J. Advertising **46**(1), 141–155 (2017)

20. Keijsers, M., Bartneck, C.: Mindless robots get bullied. In: ACM/IEEE HRI. ACM/IEEE (2018)
21. Krosnick, J.A., Alwin, D.F.: An evaluation of a cognitive theory of response-order effects in survey measurement. Public Opin. Q. **51**(2), 201–219 (1987)
22. Kühne, R., Peter, J.: Anthropomorphism in human-robot interactions: a multidimensional conceptualization. Commun. Theory **33**(1), 42–52 (2023)
23. Lee, M., Lucas, G., Gratch, J.: Comparing mind perception in strategic exchanges: human-agent negotiation, dictator and ultimatum games. J. Multimodal User Interfaces **15**, 201–214 (2021)
24. Leichtmann, B., Nitsch, V.: How much distance do humans keep toward robots? Literature review, meta-analysis, and theoretical considerations on personal space in human-robot interaction. J. Environ. Psychol. **68**, 101386 (2020)
25. Li, J.: The benefit of being physically present: a survey of experimental works comparing copresent robots, telepresent robots and virtual agents. Int. J. Hum. Comput. Stud. **77** (2015)
26. Li, S., Yu, F., Peng, K.: Effect of state loneliness on robot anthropomorphism: potential edge of social robots compared to common nonhumans. In: Journal of Physics: Conference Series. IOP (2020)
27. Marks, A.M., Cronje, J.C.: Randomised items in computer-based tests: Russian roulette in assessment? J. Educ. Technol. Soc. **11**(4), 41–50 (2008)
28. Mumm, J., Mutlu, B.: Human-robot proxemics: physical and psychological distancing in human-robot interaction. In: ACM/IEEE HRI. ACM/IEEE (2011)
29. Nass, C., Steuer, J., Tauber, E.R.: Computers are social actors. In: Proceedings of the SIGCHI Conference on Human Factors in Computing Systems, pp. 72–78 (1994)
30. Pister, H.L., Kondrad, R., Kwong, J., Smith, A., Vahlbusch, J.: What's in a name? Preschoolers treat a bug as moral agent when it has a proper name. Ph.D. thesis, Appalachian State University (2017)
31. Porter, S.R., Whitcomb, M.E., Weitzer, W.H.: Multiple surveys of students and survey fatigue. New Dir. Inst. Res. **2004**(121), 63–73 (2004)
32. Ruijten, P.A., Haans, A., Ham, J., Midden, C.J.: Perceived human-likeness of social robots: testing the Rasch model as a method for measuring anthropomorphism. Int. J. Soc. Rob. **11** (2019)
33. Sacino, A., et al.: Human-or object-like? Cognitive anthropomorphism of humanoid robots. PLoS ONE **17**(7), e0270787 (2022)
34. Salem, M., Eyssel, F., Rohlfing, K., Kopp, S., Joublin, F.: To Err is human (-like): effects of robot gesture on perceived anthropomorphism and likability. Int. J. Soc. Rob. **5** (2013)
35. Sanjeev, M., Balyan, P.: Response order effects in online surveys: an empirical investigation. Int. J. Online Mark. **4**(2), 28–44 (2014)
36. Sireci, S.G.: The construct of content validity. Soc. Indic. Res. **45**, 83–117 (1998)
37. Tahiroglu, D., Taylor, M.: Anthropomorphism, social understanding, and imaginary companions. Br. J. Dev. Psychol. **37**(2), 284–299 (2019)
38. Takayama, L., Pantofaru, C.: Influences on proxemic behaviors in human-robot interaction. In: 2009 IEEE/RSJ International Conference on Intelligent Robots and Systems, pp. 5495–5502. IEEE (2009)
39. Tan, H., Wang, D., Sabanovic, S.: Projecting life onto robots: the effects of cultural factors and design type on multi-level evaluations of robot anthropomorphism. In: 2018 27th IEEE International Symposium on Robot and Human Interactive Communication (RO-MAN), pp. 129–136. IEEE (2018)

40. Tavakol, M., Dennick, R.: Making sense of Cronbach's alpha. Int. J. Med. Educ. **2** (2011)
41. Thellman, S., Giagtzidou, A., Silvervarg, A., Ziemke, T.: An implicit, non-verbal measure of belief attribution to robots. In: Companion of ACM/IEEE HRI (2020)
42. Thellman, S., de Graaf, M., Ziemke, T.: Mental state attribution to robots: a systematic review of conceptions, methods, and findings. ACM Trans. HRI **11**(4) (2022)
43. Van Straten, C.L., Peter, J., Kühne, R., Barco, A.: The wizard and I: how transparent teleoperation and self-description (do not) affect children's robot perceptions and child-robot relationship formation. AI and Society, pp. 1–17 (2022)
44. Waytz, A., Cacioppo, J., Epley, N.: Who sees human? The stability and importance of individual differences in anthropomorphism. Perspect. Psychol. Sci. **5**(3) (2010)
45. Weinberg, M.K., Seton, C., Cameron, N.: The measurement of subjective wellbeing: item-order effects in the personal wellbeing index–adult. J. Happiness Stud. **19**, 315–332 (2018)
46. Złotowski, J., Sumioka, H., Eyssel, F., Nishio, S., Bartneck, C., Ishiguro, H.: Model of dual anthropomorphism: the relationship between the Media Equation effect and implicit anthropomorphism. Int. J. Soc. Rob. **10**, 701–714 (2018)

Agent-Exploitation Affordances: From Basic to Complex Representation Patterns

Bastien Dussard[(✉)] , Aurélie Clodic , and Guillaume Sarthou

LAAS-CNRS, Université de Toulouse, CNRS, Toulouse, France
{bastien.dussard,aurelie.clodic,guillaume.sarthou}@laas.fr

Abstract. In robotics, the capability of an artificial agent to represent the range of its action possibilities, i.e. affordances, is crucial to understand how it can act on its environment. While functional affordances, which refer to the use of tools and objects, have been broadly studied in knowledge representation, the implications of a social context and the presence of other agents have remained unexplored in this field. Consequently, in the field of social robotics, a multi-agent context enables the agents to engage in new actions that are potentially complementary to their individual capabilities, leading to the perspective of agent-exploitation. This work focuses on the concept of cooperative affordance within the realm of social affordances. Cooperative affordances refer to situations where agents interact with each other to extend their action possibilities range. From this definition, this paper proposes a tractable ontological representation of this concept with the aim of making it usable by an artificial agent. Expanding on those elementary patterns, we illustrate the effectiveness of these representations by combining them to depict a diverse range of scenarios.

Keywords: social affordances · knowledge representation · human-robot collaboration

1 Introduction

For an artificial agent to act efficiently upon its environment, it is essential that it possesses knowledge regarding its interaction capabilities with non-agentive entities, which enables it to bring about changes in its surroundings. Indeed, since for a robot to successfully complete its task requires that it understands how to bring the environment to a desired different state, knowledge over the action possibilities it affords in a given environment is key.

In the literature, this concept is commonly referred to as **affordance** and was first introduced by Gibson in [9]. Over the years, this concept has been refined in multiple fields given its open-to-interpretation nature, such as ecological psychology [20], industrial design [15], or robotics [17]. As each of those formalisms leveraged the concept for different purposes, they introduced refinements given their usage such as "disposition", "perceivability", or "effect" which

© The Author(s), under exclusive license to Springer Nature Singapore Pte Ltd. 2025
O. Palinko et al. (Eds.): ICSR + AI 2024, LNAI 15562, pp. 443–455, 2025.
https://doi.org/10.1007/978-981-96-3519-1_40

captured important aspects. Nevertheless, two major views co-exist for representing affordances, either as a concept (Turvey in [23]) or as a relation between concepts (Chemero in [5]). Those views differ given the author's perspective, either environmental or agent/observer [17].

In this work, we build upon the formalism introduced by Chemero in [5], which outlines the relational nature of affordances. However, one could see that given the purpose of our work, it contradicts with the anti-representationalist perspective of most work in ecological psychology [6]. Nevertheless, as discussed in [26], *"roboticists generally extract features as a basis for affordance detection and learning, thereby implicitly building an internal representation."*, motivating that the computational view over affordances is meaningful in robotics. Both Chemero's original formalism and its extension for computational models consider affordances as emerging relations between agent's capabilities and entities' dispositions.

While a capability refers to *"the ability to carry out a type of activity"* [19], a disposition can be referred to as *"the property of a thing that is a potential"* [23]. Those two concepts work in pairs which enable action possibility. For instance, an agent capable of grasping and an object holding a graspable disposition can be matched together, resulting in the emergence of an affordance relation.

Although some affordances can stem from a single entity's disposition (e.g. graspable), some entities can require interaction with other non-agentive entities for their dispositions to be actualized. For example, a lock needs a key to actualize its openable disposition. This mutual need for interaction was referred to as **reciprocal dispositions** by Martin in [14]. It states that complementarity can occur between dispositions, and consequently can *"partner for a mutual manifestation that is their common product"*. Functional affordances represent relations linking an agent to an entity given its dispositions or multiple entities given their reciprocal dispositions. However, the affordance concept extends beyond those latter and encompasses a wider range of domains. Indeed, while the functional affordances' nature is intrapersonal, meaning they involve only a single agent, a social setting enables interpersonal action possibilities emerging from the presence of multiple agents. Those latter can be referred to as **social affordances** and were defined as *"possibilities for social interaction or possibilities for action that are shaped by social practices and norms"* by Carvalho in [4]. It highlights two influence factors: culture (cultural affordance [16]) and social conventions (normative affordance [12]). It also outlines that the involvement of multiple agents can impact the action range, thus the affordance relations. Indeed, a multi-agent context enables the agents to engage in new actions that are potentially complementary to their individual capabilities.

The mutual involvement of agents can enable new actions that are useful to complete tasks in goal-directed behavior, and thus the possibility of **agent-exploitation** emerges through interpersonal affordances. In the context of goal-directed interpersonal affordances, it is possible to distinguish between different categories of affordances. The upper-level category of **cooperative affordances** encompasses opportunities for action between multiple agents toward a goal with potentially independent actions, which do not necessarily have to impact the environment directly (e.g. an agent communicating with another one to help it prepare a recipe). Moving down a level, the concept of collaborative affordance, as outlined in [2], emerges when there are opportunities for agents to act toward a goal, even though their actions may differ, but both engage directly in the action (e.g. two agents working on a piece of assembly). Joint affordances [7] are even more precise in that they refer to opportunities for action that arise toward a shared goal but with similar actions and on the same entity (e.g. agents lifting a heavy table together). We introduce the former, cooperative affordance, as "affordance relation enabled by agents that can interact, thereby extending the range of action possibilities they afford". From this definition, one can see that collaborative or joint affordances are included since in both cases, the agents act together toward a common goal. Nevertheless, joint affordances differ as they involve shared opportunities for simultaneous action, while collaborative affordances involve coordinated and cooperative interactions between agents to achieve a common goal. Consequently, joint affordances require a temporal synchronization between agents, which we chose not to include in our representation since this particular case requires more precise factors to be properly represented.

The main contribution of this paper is an applicable **pattern to represent cooperative affordances** which aims at highlighting how affordances can emerge through the involvement of other agents. This contribution is strengthened by the possibility of combining elementary patterns in order to represent diverse situations in a tractable manner.

In Sect. 2, we briefly discuss related work. We provide in Sect. 3 a representation of functional affordances and dispositional match with regard to Chemero's formalism and finally, we introduce a representation of cooperative affordances. In Sect. 4, we build upon those elementary representations to show how their combinations can represent various situations. In Sect. 5, we provide an overview of how such patterns enable to represent several pathways for the actualization a given disposition. Finally, we conclude in Sect. 6 by discussing possible future work.

2   Related Work

In robotics, the concept of affordance has been used from many different perspectives over the years [1], but few approaches tackled the representation of affordances in robotic knowledge bases. However, the representation of the affordance concept is essential as it conveys the idea of action possibilities. Yet, most work focused on affordances between an agent and objects (functional affordance), but to the best of our knowledge, the action possibilities provided by having several agents in a given environment (social affordance) have not been tackled before.

In ontologies, the concept of functional affordance is often represented implicitly, without conceptualizing the core idea of conditions enabling the affordances. Those implicit representations range from an inheritance over classes [13] (e.g.

Mug, isA, CanBeManipulated), a relation between an agent and an object [10] (e.g. *bob, canGrab, mug*), or a relation between an object and an affordance [21] (e.g. *mug, hasAffordance, pourability*).

Nevertheless, some work aimed at conceptualizing this idea, which was mostly tackled with the **functional affordance** [11] perspective. This concept's core idea is that some entities can provide a functionality by their usage, which results in a change of the environment. Varadarajan et al. in [24] implemented this concept by a binding between geometrical features and functional affordances. Thanks to **Conceptual Equivalence Classes**, they represented object concepts given their part's geometry and their related affordances. For example, a knife is represented as composed of a sharp-edged entity with an incision-ability affordance (blade) and a flat entity with a grasp-ability affordance (handle). While this functional affordance representation involves only a single entity, other affordances can involve several entities such as a pen being used with a paper sheet. This combination of multiple entities has been referred to as **affordance dualities** in [25] and highlights the reciprocality between specific aspects of complementary entities. Given the pen/paper sheet example, the reciprocality stems from their respective engrave-ability and display-ability affordances. Since both of those entities' features relate to non-agentive entities, we rather refer to them as dispositions instead of affordances, and the complementing pair of dispositions as reciprocal dispositions [14].

Such a reciprocal perspective over affordances/dispositions has been tackled by Beßler et al. in [3], building upon the **bearer/trigger** roles. The bearer's role represents the entity holding the disposition to be actualized by a suitable other entity, the trigger. For instance, in a cleaning task, a dirty plate would be the bearer and a dishwasher would be the trigger. While this representation conveys the reciprocal perspective, it does not leverage the agentive aspect. Indeed, this formalism aims at answering competency questions such as *"What can this be used with?"* rather than being instantiated in a given environment. In [22], Toyoshima and Barton introduced an ontological formal characterization of affordances that leverages the agent capabilities and the entities' dispositions. The proposed pattern builds upon the reciprocal nature of those concepts and allows for a more generic representation of functional affordances. Although this formalization provides the frame for precise representation, its structure is not suitable to represent affordances involving more entities. Indeed, the pattern is designed for one-to-one matching and requires an important number of individuals dedicated to each affordance.

To sum up, most work tackling the representation of affordances follow Turvey's perspective and focus on functional affordances. To the best of our knowledge, none of the existing proposals account for the interpersonal affordances that emerge from the presence of multiple agents in a given environment. Those latter enable multi-agent goal-directed behavior through agent-exploitation, hence cooperative affordances.

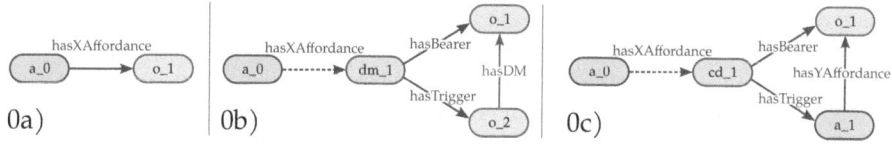

Fig. 1. Three ontological patterns to represent: 0a) functional affordance, 0b) functional affordance toward dispositional match, 0c) cooperative affordance. The affordance properties X and Y are generic and can be different. Agents' capabilities and objects' dispositions are omitted for readability.

3 Elementary Affordances

3.1 Agent-Object Affordance

Given Chemero's formalism, an affordance can be seen as a relation between an agent's capabilities and an entity's dispositions. A direct representation of such a view is depicted in Fig. 1.0a with a relation between the agent and the entity, since an affordance conveys the idea of an agent's action possibility toward an entity $(a\_0, hasXAffordance, o\_1)$. The X could refer to any affordance and is meant as a generic representation of the relational concept.

An example of such an affordance from an agent toward an object could be the physical affordance of grasping, if the agent has the required capabilities to grasp this particular entity regarding its dispositions. If the conditions are satisfied, then the ontological relation *(agent, hasGraspingAffordance, mug)* would be created. The representation of the used capabilities is voluntarily omitted in this work as previous work has already presented possible representation, as Dussard et al. in [8]. In this work, the authors describe capabilities as enabled by the agent's components. In a similar manner, as the capabilities of an agent stem from the set of components it owns, dispositions of an object can stem from its sub-parts [18].

3.2 Agent-Dispositional Match Affordance

While sub-parts of a single entity can provide an object with different dispositions, each of them actualizable by an agent's capabilities, different entities can have dispositions of interacting with each other. Those latter do share a reciprocal nature, meaning that they can be paired together as a sum of matching dispositions to bring a change in the environment. Taking inspiration from Toyoshima and Barton in [22], we can consider this matching as a sum of dispositions and represent it through the use of relation reification. Unlike the authors, we chose to introduce only a single individual which we refer to as **Dispositional Match** (DM), representing the compositional disposition created by the match. As illustrated in Fig. 1.0b, the agent no longer has an affordance toward the individual entities but rather toward the Dispositional Match, keeping track of which dispositions of the entities were necessary to create the affordance relation. Considering the terminology used by Beßler et al. in [3], we refer to the matched entities as the bearer and the trigger of the DM since each of the involved entities either has the role of actualizing the disposition or to be actualized.

An example of such a pattern could be illustrated by a scenario in which there is an agent capable of grasping and motion planning, a knife having the *Cutting* disposition, and a tomato having the *Cuttable* disposition. From this scenario, one can see that the dispositions of the knife and the tomato are reciprocal. Thus, the agent capable of acting upon both entities has the affordance of cutting the tomato with the knife. As the affordance stems from both the entities' dispositions, the affordance *(agent, hasCuttingAffordance, dm_knife_tomato)* emerges.

3.3 Affordance Agent-Cooperative Dispositional Match

Since in a DM, each entity has a role either to be actualized or to actualize given its dispositions (bearer or trigger), one could view an affordance relation between an agent and an entity in a similar way. Indeed, thanks to communication and thus interaction, an agent can rely on another agent to act on the environment. Rather than having a direct affordance toward an entity, it can have the affordance to cooperate with another agent to query this latter to act. We refer to such social affordance involving other agents to act on entities as a **cooperative affordance**. An ontological representation is depicted in Fig. 1.0c. Similarly to a DM stemming from two entities interacting together given their reciprocal dispositions, one could consider an agent and an entity linked by an affordance relation as a complementary pair providing new action possibilities. Using a similar representation, we no longer consider a Dispositional Match entity but rather a **Cooperative Disposition** (CD) entity. Indeed, while the DM individual represents the sum of complementary dispositions, the cooperative disposition aims to represent the sum of the object's dispositions and the interaction dispositions of the involved agent. An agent having the right set of interaction capabilities could thus have a cooperative affordance with a CD.

To illustrate, let us consider a scenario in which an agent needs to lift a heavy dishwasher but lacks the necessary capabilities. If another agent is present who can effectively lift this object (lifting affordance), then this agent and the dishwasher can be considered a complementary pair that can be interacted with to bring about the desired change. The representation of such a pair may be referred to as *cd_agent_1_dishwasher* and it encompasses the object's actualizable disposition (*Liftable*) as well as the agent's interactional dispositions (*VerbalCommunication*). Consequently, if the first agent is capable of engaging in the relevant interactions, it gives rise to the emergence of the affordance relation *(agent_0, hasLiftingAffordance, cd_agent_1_dishwasher)*.

```
<#human>
    a :Agent ;
    :hasCuttingAffordance <#tomato> .
<#cd_human_k>
    a :CooperativeDispositionalMatch ;
    :hasTrigger <#human> ;
    :hasBearer <#tomato> .
<#pr2>
    a :Agent ;
    :hasCuttingAffordance <#cd_human_k> .
```

Description 1. Description of a cooperative affordance relation between agents (robot and human) to cut down a tomato.

3.4 Example of a Practical Implementation

These patterns can be represented either in OWL, Turtle, or Prolog. An example of such instantiation in Turtle is provided in 11. It illustrates the cooperative affordance emerging between a robot and a human given the functional affordance of cutting a tomato. Through interaction with the human, which has the required capabilities, the pr2 robot has the affordance of cutting the tomato, even though it might not have had the affordance to do it by itself.

4 Complex Cooperative Affordances

Using the elementary patterns and focusing on cooperative affordances, in this section we show how their combination can be used to represent complex situ-

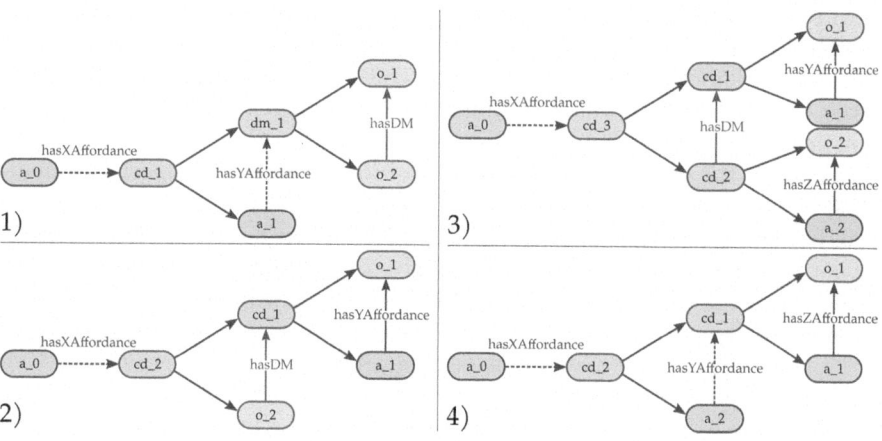

Fig. 2. Four ontological patterns to represent: 1) cooperative affordance using a dispositional match, 2) cooperative affordance to collaborate, 3) cooperative affordance to coordinate, and 4) transitive cooperative affordance. The affordance properties X, Y, and Z are generic, thus can be different. Agents' capabilities and objects' dispositions are omitted for readability.

ations, which lead to agent-exploitation. The second number of each subsection directly refers to the underlying representation depicted in Fig. 2.

4.1   Cooperative Affordance Using a Dispositional Match

Given the patterns introduced to represent an affordance from an agent toward a DM and a cooperative affordance in Fig. 1.0b/0c, we can see that combinations of those patterns can arise. We therefore can represent that an agent is able to make use of another agent which in turn can actualize a combination of entities' dispositions. Indeed, one could consider an agent having an affordance toward a DM similarly to the single object case. This results in the creation of a CD (cd_1) representing the sum of the involved entities' dispositions (dm_1) and the interaction dispositions of the agent (a_1). An agent (a_0) capable of interacting with this latter can therefore have an affordance of actualizing the entities' dispositions through the other agent a_1.

For instance, let us consider a scenario in which an agent needs to place a dirty piece of cutlery in the dishwasher to actualize the *Washable* disposition. If this agent doesn't have the required capabilities to do so but another one holds them, then the cooperative affordance using the dispositional match between the dirty piece of cutlery and the dishwasher emerges.

4.2   Cooperative Affordance to Collaborate

The actualization of a disposition in a DM requires the agent to hold the required capabilities to interact with both the entities involved in the DM, thus the corresponding functional affordances toward each of those. However, situations in which several agents are present but do not own individually the required set of capabilities can occur. In order to actualize the disposition, the agents need to engage in a collaborative process since their collective holds the distributed capabilities (collaborative affordances). Similarly to the aforementioned example, an agent (a_1) having an affordance toward an entity (o_1) creates a CD (cd_1), which embeds the entity's actualizable disposition. Thus, this compositional individual can be matched with another entity (o_2) if their dispositions are reciprocal, leading to the creation of a DM. However, as this match involves an agent and not only non-agentive entities, this newly created individual is a CD (cd_2). If an agent holds the required capabilities to interact with the other agent and to engage in the action on the other entity involved in the dispositional match (o_2), then a cooperative affordance emerges between this latter and the CD. This pattern enables to represent that a_0 can collaborate with a_1 to actualize the disposition of o_1 via o_2, without directly acting upon all entities.

To illustrate, let us consider a situation in which one agent is capable of grasping the dirty piece of cutlery and the other one of using the dishwasher. In this context, one agent could communicate to the other one that they can use their respective affordances to actualize the *Washable* disposition of the dirty cutlery with the *Washing* disposition of the dishwasher. Given the reciprocity of the dispositions involved and each agent's functional affordance of acting upon the environment, a collaborative affordance emerges.

4.3   Cooperative Affordance to Coordinate

As we saw above, collaboration between agents can emerge from distributing the required affordances between several agents. For such a collaboration to occur, the agents need to interact with each other. However, another agent which is capable of interacting with both of the "acting" agents could also actualize the corresponding dispositions, without engaging in the action itself. This can be referred to as coordinating agents, and can be useful if acting agents cannot interact with one another directly, either for interaction modality compatibility, or for proximity/temporal reasons. Indeed, two agents (a_1, a_2) can respectively have a functional affordance toward entities (o_1, o_2). Those affordances respectively create a CD individual (cd_1, cd_2), representing the entity's dispositions and the agent's interaction disposition. If the entities' dispositions embedded in each CD are complementary, then they can be matched together in a DM-like manner. As the dispositional match occurs between two CD individuals, it results in the creation of another CD (cd_3) which represents both the agents' interaction dispositions and the involved entities' dispositions. Finally, an agent (a_0) having the capability to interact with both agents could then coordinate those agents to actualize the entities' dispositions by communicating its goal to each agent and how each of their involvement in the action can lead to the actualization of the dispositions.

To illustrate, let us consider the same scenario as in the aforementioned example, where each agent has a part of the required affordances to actualize the disposition of the dirty piece of cutlery. In this context, a third agent, which aims at washing the knife with the dishwasher could query each agent for an action (or communicate its goal) so that they both use their respective affordance. This results in a cooperative affordance to coordinate since the third agent doesn't engage directly in the action to actualize the desired disposition.

4.4   Cooperative Affordance to Act by Transitivity

"the ability to carry out a type of activity" We have represented that an agent coordinating others can actualize an entity's disposition without engaging in the action, but one could envision that an agent could also do so in a transitive manner. Similarly to 0c, an agent (a_1) having an affordance toward an entity (o_1) creates a CD (cd_1) as they can be considered as a reciprocal match. Another agent (a_2) can actualize the disposition of the entity through interaction with the agent involved in the emergence of this CD. Since this agent has an affordance toward the CD individual representing the composition of the actualizable entity and the interacting dispositions of the other agent, a new CD is created (cd_2). This latter encompasses the dispositions for interaction of the newly involved agent and can therefore be linked to an agent (a_0) capable of interacting with the intermediary agent (a_2) and not necessarily with the "acting" agent (a_1). Therefore, the actualization of the disposition occurs transitively with agents interacting with each other. The affordance relation generated illustrates that an agent can actualize an entity's dispositions via a chainlike process of interactions.

To illustrate, agents who are unable to interact directly with one another may require the involvement of a third party, acting as a translator. For instance, let us consider that the robot has the information that the dishwasher has been filled but cannot communicate with the agent that can start it. The presence of an intermediary agent which can interact with both therefore enables the robot to start the dishwasher without interacting with the "acting" agent.

5   Combined Patterns: An Example

In light of the elementary and complex patterns presented in the previous sections, one could grasp that such representations have the potential to provide a rich perspective of how agents might interact with each other to actualize the dispositions of entities. A comprehensive overview of the various pathways enabling such dispositional actualization is illustrated in Fig. 3 with the example of a dirty knife which requires washing from a dishwasher.

The goal of this example is to actualize the disposition of the knife of being *Washable* given the reciprocal disposition *Washing* of the dishwasher. The example illustrates how 3 agents in the environment can act together in order to wash the knife with the dishwasher. Actualizing the disposition given the pair of entities requires that agents have the capabilities to interact with both entities, hence grasping the knife and using the dishwasher. For this example, we will make the assumption that all agents can interact with each other and we chose to represent a subset of the affordance relations enabled by such a situation. However, a more exhaustive representation of this context would include more affordance relations.

Given the reciprocal dispositions of the dishwasher and the dirty knife, a new individual representing the sum of their complementary dispositions is created (dm_k_d). If agent 2 has the required capabilities to grasp the knife and to use the dishwasher, an affordance relation can be created toward this dispositional match individual ①. Through this affordance relation, agent 2 can actualize the *Washable* disposition of the knife with the dishwasher by itself, similarly to Fig. 2.1.

On the other hand, the fact that agent 1 has a functional affordance toward the dishwasher gives rise to a new CD individual (cd_a1_d) which embeds the agent's interaction disposition and the actualizing disposition of the dishwasher. Since the knife has a reciprocal disposition to the dishwasher and that its disposition is embedded in the newly created CD individual, a dispositional match also occurs between this latter and itself ($cd\_a1\_d\_k$). Thanks to the grasping and the interaction capabilities of agent 2, this agent can have the affordance to collaborate with agent 1 ②, similarly to Fig. 2.2.

Moreover, since agents 1 and 2 have respectively the functional affordance of using the dishwasher and grasping the knife then it gives rise to new CD

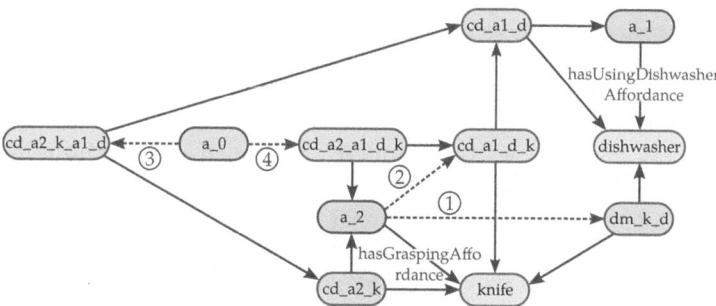

Fig. 3. Affordance relations given several agents' points of view toward a similar actualization of a disposition. This pattern combines cooperative affordances using dispositional matches ①, to collaborate ②, to coordinate ③ and to transitively act ④. Dotted lines represent the cooperative affordance relations. The dispositional match property, agents' capabilities, and object' dispositions have been omitted for readability purposes.

individuals embedding their interaction dispositions and respectively the knife and the dishwasher's dispositions (cd_a2_k and cd_a1_d). Given that those two individuals hold the reciprocal dispositions of the knife and the dishwasher, a dispositional match occurs between them. However, since this dispositional match happens between CD individuals (and not DMs), the resulting individual is a new CD individual ($cd\_a2\_k\_a1\_d$). Considering that agent 0 can interact both with agents 1 and 2, it can therefore have the cooperative affordance of coordinating the two agents to wash the knife with the dishwasher ③, similarly to Fig. 2.3.

Lastly, we saw above that agent 1 has the affordance of using the dishwasher, agent 2 has the affordance to grasp the knife and that they can engage in a collaborative process initiated by agent 2 to actualize the knife's disposition ②. Therefore, from the affordance relation linking agent 2 to the CD individual representing the collaboration with agent 1 ($cd\_a1\_d\_k$), a new CD individual emerges representing the interaction necessary to enable the collaboration between agent 1 and 2 ($cd\_a2\_a1\_d\_k$). Therefore, through an interaction chain, agent 0 can query agent 2 to act with agent 1 in collaboration to wash the knife with the dishwasher. This results in a cooperative affordance for transitive action via a collaborative affordance ④, similarly to Fig. 3.4 and Fig. 2.2 combined.

As we saw above, multiple affordance relations can result in the actualization of the knife's disposition thanks to the dishwasher's reciprocal disposition from the point of view of the agents. The flexibility of the proposed patterns could allow to represent even more complex scenarios, in which each agent can have various ways of inducing a change in the environment given their objective.

6   Conclusion and Future Work

In this paper, we build upon the idea that affordances can emerge through the involvement of several agents in a given environment, such as a human-robot collaboration scenario. The action possibilities of agents are therefore not only restricted by the object's dispositions but also by the interaction between agents to bring a desired change to the environment, leading to the concept of **agent-exploitation**, which to the best of our knowledge has never been tackled. For this purpose, we **introduced and represented the concept of agent-exploitation through cooperative affordances**, building upon the similarity with the concept of dispositional match. The potency of this concept and its tractable representation has been highlighted thanks to **combinations of elementary patterns to represent complex cooperative situations**.

A future extension could be to refine the concept of collaborative affordances to support the notion of joint affordances. Indeed, while the current work allows to represent two agents that could act together with two objects given their complementary dispositions, it does not support the representation of two agents that could act jointly on the same object to collaborate. Such affordance could be for example to carry a heavy table together, where agents do not have the affordance individually toward this entity, but rather as a collective since this affordance stems from the combination of their capabilities. Another aspect which could be taken into consideration would be to represent by which means agents communicate with each other. This would enable an even more precise representation of the actual cooperative affordances that can occur.

While the current work focuses on the affordances schema, leaving aside the representation of agent capabilities and entities' dispositions on the examples, those representations have been built and are compatible with the proposed approach. Nevertheless, as we consider knowledge representation not only in a conceptual manner but also as a powerful tool for applicable purposes, we plan to leverage it for robotic applications to assess its effectiveness.

Acknowledgments. This work has been supported by the Effective Learning of Social Affordances (ELSA) project ANR-21-CE33-0019, and by the Artificial Intelligence for Human-Robot Interaction (AI4HRI) project ANR-20-IADJ-0006.

Disclosure of Interests. The authors have no competing interests to declare that are relevant to the content of this article.

References

1. Ardon, P., Pairet, E., Lohan, K.S., Ramamoorthy, S., Petrick, R.P.A.: Building affordance relations for robotic agents - a review. In: Zhou, Z.H. (ed.) Proceedings of the Thirtieth International Joint Conference on Artificial Intelligence, IJCAI. International Joint Conferences on Artificial Intelligence Organization (2021)
2. Bardram, J.E., Houben, S.: Collaborative affordances of medical records. Computer Supported Cooperative Work (CSCW) (2018)
3. Beßler, D., Porzel, R., Pomarlan, M., Beetz, M., Malaka, R., Bateman, J.: A formal model of affordances for flexible robotic task execution. In: ECAI. IOS Press (2020)
4. Carvalho, E.: Social affordance. In: Vonk, J., Shackelford, T. (eds.) Encyclopedia of Animal Cognition and Behavior (2020)

5. Chemero, A.: An outline of a theory of affordances. Ecol. Psychol. (2003)
6. Chemero, A., Turvey, M.T.: Gibsonian affordances for roboticists. Adapt. Beh. (2007)
7. Davis, T.J., Riley, M.A., Shockley, K., Cummins-Sebree, S.: Perceiving affordances for joint actions. Perception (2010)
8. Dussard, B., Sarthou, G., Clodic, A.: Ontological component-based description of robot capabilities. In: International Workshop on Working towards Ontology-based Standards for Robotics and Automation (2023)
9. Gibson, J.J.: The ecological approach to visual perception (1979)
10. Gonçalves, P.J., Torres, P.M.: Knowledge representation applied to robotic orthopedic surgery. Robot. Comput.-Integr. Manuf. (2015)
11. Hartson, R.: Cognitive, physical, sensory, and functional affordances in interaction design. Behav. Inf. Technol. (2003)
12. Heras-Escribano, M., de Pinedo, M.: Are affordances normative? Phenomenol. Cognit. Sci. (2016)
13. Lemaignan, S., Warnier, M., Sisbot, E.A., Clodic, A., Alami, R.: Artificial cognition for social human–robot interaction: An implementation. Artificial Intelligence (2017). special Issue on AI and Robotics
14. Martin, C.B.: The Mind in Nature. OUP Oxford (2010)
15. Norman, D.A.: The design of everyday things (2002)
16. Ramstead, M.J., Veissière, S.P., Kirmayer, L.J.: Cultural affordances: scaffolding local worlds through shared intentionality and regimes of attention. Front. Psychol. (2016)
17. Şahin, E., Cakmak, M., Doğar, M.R., Uğur, E., Üçoluk, G.: To afford or not to afford: a new formalization of affordances toward affordance-based robot control. Adapt. Behav. (2007)
18. Sarathy, V., Scheutz, M.: Cognitive affordance representations in uncertain logic. In: International Conference on the Principles of Knowledge Representation and Reasoning (2016)
19. Solano, L., Romero, F., Rosado, P.: An ontology for integrated machining and inspection process planning focusing on resource capabilities. Int. J. Comput. Integr. Manuf. (2016)
20. Stoffregen, T.A.: Affordances as properties of the animal-environment system. Ecol. Psychol. (2003)
21. Su, Y.F., Liu, A., Lu, W.H.: Improving robot grasping plans with affordance. In: International Conference on Advanced Robotics and Intelligent Systems (ARIS). IEEE (2017)
22. Toyoshima, F., Barton, A.: A formal representation of affordances as reciprocal dispositions. In: CEUR Workshop Proceedings (2018)
23. Turvey, M.T.: Ecological foundations of cognition: Invariants of perception and action. Am, Psychol. Assoc. (1992)
24. Varadarajan, K., Vincze, M.: Ontological knowledge management framework for grasping and manipulation. In: IROS Workshop: Knowledge Representation for Autonomous Robots (2011)
25. Varadarajan, K.M., Vincze, M.: Afrob: the affordance network ontology for robots. In: IEEE/RSJ International Conference on Intelligent Robots and Systems. IEEE (2012)
26. Zech, P., Haller, S., Lakani, S.R., Ridge, B., Ugur, E., Piater, J.: Computational models of affordance in robotics: a taxonomy and systematic classification. Adapt. Beh. (2017)

From Functional Affordances to Reciprocal Dispositions: An Ontological Representation

Bastien Dussard[(✉)] [iD], Aurélie Clodic[iD], and Guillaume Sarthou[iD]

LAAS-CNRS, Université de Toulouse, CNRS, Toulouse, France
{bastien.dussard,aurelie.clodic,guillaume.sarthou}@laas.fr

Abstract. In human-robot interaction, the collaboration of agents stems from what each agent is capable of doing to successfully complete the objective. Thus, for a robot to efficiently interact with its environment, it is crucial to have knowledge over the actions it is capable of performing. This paper presents a step toward the consideration of agentive aspects in the representation of action possibilities for an agent, i.e. affordances. Building upon the dispositional theory, this work aims at matching the dispositions of entities with the capabilities of the agents. Using an ontological representation and inference mechanisms, this contribution aims to autonomously infer affordance relations linking an agent to entities in a reactive way. As affordance relations stem from the match between the dispositions of entities and the capabilities of the agents, we propose a reasoner which allows to link the corresponding entities given each affordance's requirement. Furthermore, as certain actions may necessitate the combination of multiple entities, this work also addresses the representation and inference of affordances for such combinations. These inferences provide the agent with a self-awareness capability about which actions are feasible with respect to the entities in the environment, while also leveraging changes that may occur in the environment.

Keywords: functional affordances · knowledge representation · ontology

1 Introduction

For a robot to effectively act on its environment, a key aspect is the knowledge and the understanding of what it can do. Nevertheless, while the set of actions feasible by a given robot can be hard-coded, they do not necessarily correspond to the set of actions the robot can do at a given moment. Indeed, what an agent can perform first depends on its **capabilities**, usually defined as *"the ability to carry out a type of activity"* [20], themselves depending on the agent's components. However, as these components can evolve over time, either through the use of tools or because of possible failures, the set of capabilities can change

O. Palinko et al. (Eds.): ICSR + AI 2024, LNAI 15562, pp. 456–469, 2025.
https://doi.org/10.1007/978-981-96-3519-1_41

over time, and consequently the set of feasible actions as well. While being aware of its action possibilities is key, considering the context of human-robot interaction, being aware of others' action possibilities is also mandatory. Indeed, where such introspection can help to act, the estimation regarding the others can help for monitoring purposes as well as estimating how they could help for given tasks. However, where robotic agents have a set of capabilities enabled by their components, human agents can be considered as having a set of common ground capabilities which can still evolve through the use of tools or equipment.

Which actions an agent can perform are also influenced by both its environment and the entities within it, according to their **dispositions**. Indeed, even if a robot is capable of pouring, it cannot perform the action if there is no container to hold the liquid. According to the dispositional theory introduced by Turvey in [24] and refined by Chemero in [4], a disposition is *"the property of a thing that is a potential"*. This theory suggests that each disposition has a complement, which represents the actualizing circumstance of this action possibility. This disposition can be complemented by an agentive entity, which results in the emergence of an affordance. The concept of **affordance** was first introduced by Gibson in [7] to describe what the environment offers to an agent based on its capabilities. Over the years, refinements to this concept have been proposed in the field of ecological psychology [4,24], industrial design [15], and robotics [16]. One of the major points of disagreement between these formalisms is the nesting background of these affordances. Turvey [24] views affordances as dispositional properties of the environment which can be actualized by an agent's effectivities. Chemero [4] agrees with the dispositional aspect of affordances but differs by stating that they reside in the agent-environment system and that they are relational properties between an agent and dispositions of the objects in the environment. In this work, we chose to consider affordances as defined by Chemero[1], considering them as the match between an agent's capability and the complementing disposition of another entity. Hence, a grasping affordance exists between an agent who has the grasping capability and an object which has the disposition to be graspable. This formalism is best suited for our approach as its relational nature facilitates its usage for knowledge representation. Indeed, if we had to translate those views into the ontological world, we could consider Turvey's as an inheritance link and Chemero's as a relation between individuals.

While dispositions are at least partially responsible for the affordances conceptualized in both views, the complementarity between dispositions of non-agentive entities can also contribute to the emergence of affordances. The concept of **reciprocal dispositions** refers to entities sharing complementary dispositions (e.g. the knife being dirty has a *Washable* disposition and the dishwasher

---

[1] Since our work aims at integrating affordances in a knowledge base, i.e. an internal representation, one could see the contradiction with the anti-representationalist view defended by the ecological psychology field [5]. However, as explained in [29], *"roboticists generally extract features as a basis for affordance detection and learning, thereby implicitly building an internal representation."*, motivating that the computational perspective over affordances is meaningful for robotics.

has a *Washing* disposition). Martin introduced the concept of reciprocality of dispositions in [12], describing it as *"partners for a mutual manifestation that is their common product"*. Those dispositional reciprocalities can thus be considered as "systems" which lead to the emergence of new affordances.

This work falls within the DACOBOT architecture [19] which is a knowledge-centred robotic architecture. It is based on an ontological description of the robot's knowledge, which includes elements of the environment and some simple robot descriptions. In this paper, we build upon our prior work [6], in which we have proposed a representation of capabilities that allows automatic inferences based on the components an agent owns.

The main contribution of this paper is an **ontological representation of affordances based on agents' capabilities and objects' dispositions**. While most work representing affordances either consider implicit or static representation without the agentive aspect, our representation enables **inference mechanisms** over the agent's affordance relations based on its previously inferred capabilities and the dispositions of the objects in its environment. In this paper, we show that our representation is suitable both for **functional affordances** (affordances from an agent to an entity) and **reciprocal dispositions** (combination of two entities to be used together). In addition, thanks to its integration into our robotic architecture, we show that knowledge about these affordance relations can be maintained and updated over time, with regard to the current state of the world and the current agent's capabilities.

In Sect. 2 we discuss related work and how our contribution addresses new issues. We provide in Sect. 3 a brief ontology formalism and a presentation of the used framework. Our two main patterns are then presented in Sect. 4 and Sect. 5. Finally, we present in Sect. 6 an analysis of the reasoning processes on a robot activity and we conclude this paper in Sect. 7 by discussing possible future work.

2   Related Work

The concept of affordance is essential in robotics as it incorporates the idea of action possibility. Knowledge of how an agent can act on its environment is crucial as it enables effective interaction with its environment and provides efficient task attribution in a collaborative process. However, this concept is often considered implicitly rather than represented in the form of a knowledge representation. Most of the research focused on object recognition [14] to detect affordances, or manipulation [2,13] to learn affordance relations over objects. These image-based methods for detecting affordances suffer from a lack of explainability. However, with the recent advances over the Large Language Model's capabilities, some methods have been proposed to tackle those problems by combining LLMs with more classical approach to overcome the current methods' limits [22]. The aforementioned research makes use of the affordance concept in order to facilitate the execution of robotic tasks. However, they fail to take into account the agentive aspect, as they consider the agent's capabilities to be pre-defined and unchanging.

In order to enhance explainability, affordances can be grounded into a semantic knowledge representation. The use of knowledge bases, such as ontologies, provides easier extensibility while allowing representation and reasoning about those action possibilities. Nevertheless, in such domain, affordances are often expressed implicitly without conceptualizing the core notion or any reasoning, using either specific classes of inheritance over objects [11] (e.g. *Mug, isA, CanBeManipulated*), relations from an agent over an object [8] (e.g. *bob, canGrab, mug*), or relations from an object over an affordance entity [21] (e.g. *mug, hasAffordance, pourability*).

In order to conceptualize the affordance notion and enhance its applicability, some work did focus on the concept of **functional affordance**. Introduced in [10], this concept aims at representing objects based on their functions, allowing among others for object substitution during task planning. Awaad et al. [1] relate objects to their functions at the class level (e.g. a cup is used for drinking from and for holding) but without representing the object's parts associated with such affordances. This concept has also been implemented in [26] to enhance a perception system. Relying on a Part Functional Affordance Schema which binds geometrical features and affordances (e.g. sharp edge implies an incision-ability affordance), they defined a set of **Conceptual Equivalence Classes** to represent object concepts given the geometry of their parts and their corresponding affordances. For instance, a knife is defined as the composition of a blade providing an incision-ability affordance and a handle providing a grasp-ability affordance. Thanks to such a representation, they have shown to be able to find in a visual scene objects with equivalent functionalities, leading to the creation of the Affordance Network database (AfNet) [27]. Nevertheless, while considering some reasoning at the instance level, those approaches do not consider the capabilities of a given agent to use the described functions. Consequently, what they call affordances should rather be considered as dispositions of entities.

Although representing the functions of objects is a crucial initial first step, it may not be sufficient to know the action possibilities they provide. This is particularly true for everyday objects, which are often used with other entities. This complementarity between object aspects can be referred to as reciprocal dispositions [12] and is grounded in the dispositional theory of Turvey [24]. For example, with AfRob [28] (an extension of AfNet), the authors introduce **affordance dualities** as the interaction between entities given their complementarity. For instance, a pen having an engrave-ability affordance and a paper sheet having a display-ability affordance can be seen as complementary. However, since those pairs refer to a match between dispositional aspects of non-agentive entities, we consider this conceptualization as reciprocal dispositions and thus not as affordances. More focused on affordance representation, Beßler et al. in [3] propose an ontological formalism that defines an affordance as a description of a disposition. This formalism is built upon the **bearer/trigger** roles, with the bearer being the entity holding the disposition to be actualized by a suitable other entity, the trigger. In such a way, a dirty piece of cutlery would be the bearer of a dishwasher that would be the trigger. Nevertheless, this approach doesn't leverage the agentive aspect of how the agents can interact with those entities. Indeed, this formalism is not aimed to be instantiated in a given scene but rather to answer competency questions, such as *"What can this be used with?"*

Table 1. Summary of the major features identified for the most representative contributions in the field.

	[8, 11, 21]	[1]	[26–28]	[3]	[25]	[23]	Our
Formalism	-	-	-	Turvey	-	Turvey	Chemero
Reasoning method	-	DL Query	DL query	DL Query	Rule	-	DL logic & Custom reasoner
Functional affordance	No	Yes	Yes	No	Yes	Yes	Yes
Dispositional Match	No	No	Yes	Yes	No	Yes	Yes
Agentive aspect	No	No	No	No	Yes	Yes	Yes
Instantiation	Yes	Yes	No	No	Yes	No	Yes
Dynamic possibility	No	No	No	No	No	No	Yes

or *"What can this be used for?"*. Such questions are thus represented with DL queries based on Generic Ontology Design Patterns that have to be handcrafted for each specific question to be answered. Consequently, this formalism is not suitable for dynamically representing affordances in an ontology and automatic affordance discovery with regard to a given situation.

While the previous contributions focused on the affordance concept formalism, either not considering instantiation or automatic inference, Umbrico et al. in [25] present an affordance rule allowing to infer opportunities for actions. However, while considering the agentive aspects, the inference mechanism relies only on a single rule (one per affordance type) lacking of genericity by embedding every aspect of the affordance. A generic formalization taking into account agentive and object dispositions has been proposed by Toyoshima et al. [23]. In contrast to previous work, the authors adopt Turvey's perspective, defining the **affordance-effectivity complex** as the sum of reciprocal dispositions between an agent (**effectivity**) and an object (**affordance**). Therefore, the affordance concept is not viewed as a relation between entities but as a disposition. This formalism accounts for both individual (instance) and family (class) directed affordances. Indeed, while the knife concept brings a set of affordances, a specific instance can hold additional ones (e.g. its dirtiness). It allows to leverage both agent capabilities and entity dispositions as the pattern is intended to represent the environment's perspective. Although formalized as a generic representation of affordances, this formalism requires the creation of multiple individuals to represent a single affordance description. This approach provides a rich and precise representation of affordances, but does not allow for inference over action possibilities. A sum up of the main proposed contribution is presented in Table 1 with regard to the main features identified.

3   Ontological Framework

An ontology, as defined by Gruber in [9], is a *"formal specification of a shared conceptualization"* which allows to define concepts, individuals, and relationships. One of the strengths of such a knowledge representation is the ability

Table 2. Symbols used to define an ontology

A: ABox entities/indiv	T: TBox classes/concepts
A: set of entities	T: set of classes
C_0: entities' direct types	H: classes inheritance links
R: relations between entities	E: equivalence classes

R: RBox roles/properties	
P: set of properties	I: properties inheritance links
$Chain$: set of chained properties	Inv: properties inverses
Dom: properties domains sets	Ran: properties ranges sets

to infer new knowledge via *Description Logic* (DL) based reasoning. Such reasoning is enabled in several manners, either via a query that answers questions with concepts/entities matching a desired pattern or at the instance level via DL logic rules. Following the ontological formalism presented in [17], the knowledge base K is composed of the Role Box (**Rbox**) defining the properties, the Terminological box (**TBox**) defining the concept hierarchies, and the Assertional box (**ABox**), defining the individuals with their inheritance given the TBox and the relations between individuals via the properties given by the RBox. Table 2 illustrates a sum up of the ontological symbols and basic reasoning mechanisms used in this work are presented below.

Defining an equivalence between classes allows to infer inheritance relations between individuals which share common conceptualizations. An equivalence class $(t, e) \in E$ is defined as the link between a class $t \in T$ and a class expression containing either another class from T or a complex class expression e. Formally, if $(t, e) \in E, \forall a \in A | e(a) \subset K$, then $(a, t) \in C_0$. As an example, an equivalence to the class Father can be *Father $\equiv$ Male and (hasChild some Human)*.

Expressing a property as a path between several properties can allow to deduce new knowledge between individuals connected together. A property chain allows to link individuals together given a list of properties. Given the chain $p_1 \bullet p_2 \Rightarrow p_3$, if $(x, p_1, y), (y, p_2, z) \subset R$, then $(x, p_3, z) \in R$.
e.g. *hasParent $\bullet$ hasMother $\Rightarrow$ hasGrandMother*.

The attributes *Domain* and *Range* of a property aim at specifying the classes linkable together. Usually used for consistency checking, they can also be used to infer the class of individuals involved in the relation. Given the property p and the individuals $(x, y) \subset A$, if $(x, p, y) \in R$ then $\forall t \in Dom(p), (x, t) \in C_0$ and $\forall t \in Ran(p), (y, t) \in C_0$. For example, if the property *ownsDog* has *Human* as Domain and *Dog* as Range, and the relation *(bob, ownsDog, medor)* is asserted, then the inheritance links between the *bob* individual and the *Human* class, as well as between the *medor* individual and *Dog* class, are inferred.

To manage the ontology and reason over it, we use the software Ontologenius [18] which has been specifically designed for dynamic reasoning. In the context of this work, we will use its built-in reasoners for inverse axioms, chained

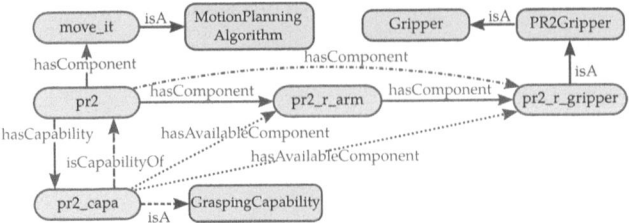

Fig. 1. Ontological pattern example allowing the inference of the Grasping capability. $- \rightarrow$ are inferences by inverse, $- - \rightarrow$ are inferences by equivalence, $- \cdot \rightarrow$ are inferences by transitivity, and $\cdots \rightarrow$ are inferences by property chain.

axioms, transitive axioms, and equivalent classes. We will later introduce a custom reasoning process for the purpose of this contribution.

4   Functional Affordances

The concept of functional affordance refers to the intended use of an object according to common ground knowledge. Functional affordances stem from an entity's dispositions (e.g. a knife has a cutting disposition), but can also be influenced by external factors such as a change in its status (e.g. the knife becoming dirty after usage has a cleanable disposition). In the literature, some ontological work tackled this concept but without taking into account the agent's capabilities. For instance, a tool having a grip part requires an agent to have the grasping capability in order to actually afford the function provided by the tool. As functional affordances emerge from the capabilities of agents, their representation must leverage such an aspect to provide the set of actual action possibilities.

4.1   Agent Capabilities Representation

Since the affordance relations available to an agent stem from its capabilities, we build upon our previous work proposed in [6]. There, we introduced an ontological pattern to represent and dynamically infer agents' capabilities based on their components. We represented an agent's capabilities with a single individual and described each capability by an equivalence class. It allowed to infer inheritance links between the capability individual and each enabled *Capability* class given its components and its already inferred capabilities. An example of this process is shown in Fig. 1 with **GraspingCapability≡hasAvailableComponent some (Gripper and MotionPlanningAlgorithm)**, resulting in the inference of the relation (*pr2_ capa, isA, GraspingCapability*).

4.2   Object Dispositions Representation

In addition to an agent's capabilities, enabling an affordance requires certain properties from non-agentive entities. Such properties are referred to as

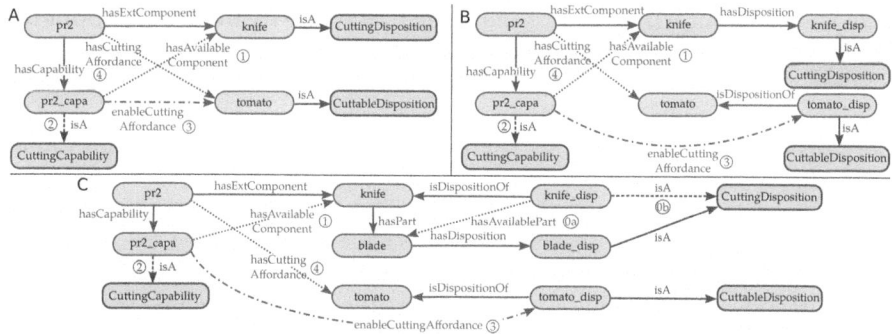

Fig. 2. Ontological patterns example allowing the inference of the *hasCuttingAffordance* relation (A) Example with individuals directly inheriting from the corresponding Disposition class. (B) Example with the individuals related to their disposition individuals, which inherits from the corresponding Disposition class. (C) Example with the tool individual having a sub-part. Both have a disposition individual, the tool's one being inferred by equivalence as the class of its sub-part's corresponding Disposition class. $-\!\!\rightarrow$ are inferences by inverse, $-\!\!-\!\!\rightarrow$ are inferences by equivalence, $\cdots\!\!\rightarrow$ are inferences by property chain and $-\!\cdot\!\rightarrow$ are inferences by the custom reasoner. Numbers like ⓧ correspond to the order of inferences.

dispositions and can be represented with varying degrees of semantic granularity. In the straightforward case, entities can be represented as directly inheriting from their corresponding dispositions as in Fig. 2.A (e.g. (*knife, isA, CuttingDisposition*)). However, such a representation can lack semantic precision as an entity holds a disposition instead of being one. As dispositions are similar to capabilities but for non-agentive entities, one could represent an entity's dispositions with a dedicated individual, similarly to the agent capability individual as in Fig. 2.B (e.g. (*knife, hasDisposition, knife_disp*) and (*knife_disp, isA, CuttingDisposition*)). Furthermore, as sub-parts composing entities can provide dispositions to the whole entity, we can describe them with a pattern similar to our previous work. For example, we can represent a knife as having a blade, which holds the cutting disposition as in Fig. 2.C (e.g. (*knife, hasPart, blade*), (*blade, hasDisposition, blade_disp*) and (*blade_disp, isA, CuttingDisposition*)). Given this representation, the property chain **isDispositionOf•hasPart** ⟹ **hasAvailablePart** allows to infer the relation (*knife_disp, hasAvailablePart, blade*) ⓪ₐ. Once this relation has been inferred, the dispositions of the knife individual can be deduced via the equivalence class **CuttingDisposition≡(hasAvailablePart some (hasDisposition some (CuttingDisposition))** (e.g. (*knife_disp, isA, CuttingDisposition*)) ⓪ᵦ. Thanks to this inferred relation, the case becomes equivalent to the Fig. 2.B case, in which we asserted the inheritance relation directly. To illustrate a context in which the robot holds a knife, we create the relation (*pr2, hasExtComponent, knife*). This allows us to use the same property chain as for the agent's components since (*hasExtComponent, hasComponent*) ∈

I and **isCapabilityOf**•extbfhasComponent $\implies$ **hasAvailableComponent**. Thus, the relation $(pr2\_capa, hasAvailableComponent, knife)$ is inferred ①. Similarly to an agent acquiring a new component and gaining new capabilities, an agent holding a tool can also gain new capabilities based on the tool's dispositions. Therefore, by defining CuttingCapability as **CuttingCapability≡hasAvailableComponent some CuttingDisposition)** for Fig. 2.A, the relation $(pr2\_capa, isA, CuttingCapability)$ is inferred as $pr2\_capa$ validates the class expression ②. The same mechanism can be used for the examples with dedicated disposition individuals by modifying the equivalence class into **CuttingCapability≡hasAvailableComponent some (hasDisposition some (CuttingDisposition))** for Fig. 2.B/C.

4.3   Custom Reasoner

Having represented the agents' capabilities and the entities' dispositions, the next necessary step is to link them into the creation of functional affordances. Given the relational aspect of this concept, we chose to represent an affordance as a property relating an agent to the involved entity (e.g. $(agent, hasXAffordance, entity)$). Hence, we propose a pattern that enables the dynamic inference of functional affordances using standard ontological mechanisms and a custom reasoner. This latter is introduced as standard mechanisms only allow inference of relations between individuals if a relational path between them already exists. In the case of two individuals inheriting from specific classes, no such relational path exists, and thus inferring a link between them with standard means is not feasible. Such a process is necessary as we want to link an agent with an entity if its capabilities (the inheritance links toward Capability classes) match the corresponding dispositions of the entity (the inheritance links toward Disposition classes). The custom reasoner's role is inspired from the *Dispositional Match* approach of [3], but differs by leveraging the agentive aspect of affordances. For this purpose, we chose to use the Domain and Range attributes of each affordance property to represent the required capabilities and dispositions for a match. The process of this custom reasoner is described as below.

Given the top property *enableAffordance* expressed as $affp$, the set of applicable affordance properties P_{aff} as:

$$P_{aff} = \{p \mid (p,\ affp) \in I \land Dom(p) \neq \emptyset \land Ran(p) \neq \emptyset\}$$

Next, for each affordance property, we search which individuals in the ontology match the Domain classes and which match the Range classes attributes. This searching process results in the creation of two sets of candidate individuals, A_D and A_R.

$$A_D = \{a_D \mid \forall t_D \in Dom(p) \land (a_D, t_D) \in C\}$$
$$A_R = \{a_R \mid \forall t_R \in Ran(p) \land (a_R, t_R) \in C\}$$

Finally, we can link each individual from the candidate sets (A_D, A_R) with each other via the affordance property p.

$$\forall a_D \in A_D, \forall a_R \in A_R \implies (a_D, p, a_R) \in R$$

4.4   Functional Affordance: An Example

According to the examples in Fig. 2 which illustrate the functional affordance of cutting, we define the property *enableCuttingAffordance* with *CuttingCapability* as Domain and *CuttableDisposition* as Range. Thanks to the reasoner, the relations (*pr2_ capa, enableCuttingAffordance, tomato*) in Fig. 2.A and (*pr2_ capa, enableCuttingAffordance, tomato_ disp*) in Fig. 2B/C are inferred as these individuals do match the required classes ③.

These inferred relations link the agent's capability individual to the corresponding entity (or entity disposition) individual. As we want to represent the affordance relation between the agent and the entity directly, an extra step is required to infer the relation (e.g. (*agent, hasXAffordance, entity*)). This final step is done by the use of a property chain of the form **hasCapability•enableCuttingAffordance $\implies$ hasCuttingAffordance** for Fig. 2.A. As the other examples use an intermediary dispositional individual, the property chain is defined as **hasCapability•enableCuttingAffordance •isDispositionOf $\implies$ hasCuttingAffordance**. We are therefore able to infer the relation (*pr2, hasCuttingAffordance, tomato*) which states that the pr2 robot has a cutting functional affordance toward the tomato ④.

5   Affordances and Reciprocal Dispositions

Until now, we represented affordances as relations between an agent and an entity, respectively through their capabilities and dispositions. However, some non-agentive entities can interact together to provide new action possibilities (affordances) to the agent if they have reciprocal dispositions. Thus, we consider that a pair of reciprocal dispositions creates a Dispositional Match (DM) and that an agent can have affordances toward DMs if it has the right set of capabilities to enable this affordance. To represent such affordances, we expand the pattern described in the previous section, taking into account the specific challenge of creating a new individual.

5.1   Custom Reasoner: An Extension

For this purpose, the custom reasoner needs to be extended to enable such additional features to be leveraged in the inference of affordance relations. First, similarly to the way we previously linked a capability to a disposition, we have to link two reciprocal dispositions together ①. Therefore, the process follows the same pattern as for the *enableAffordance* property but with the *enableDM* property linking two dispositions together. Thus, only the first equation is affected by such a change. Given the top property *enableDM* expressed as *dispm*, the set of applicable dispositional properties P_{disp} as:

$$P_{disp} = \{p \mid (p,\ dispm) \in I \wedge Dom(p) \neq \emptyset \wedge Ran(p) \neq \emptyset\}$$

As illustrated in Fig. 3, considering a dirty knife having a *WashableDisposition*, as the dishwasher individual has a reciprocal *WashingDisposition*, we

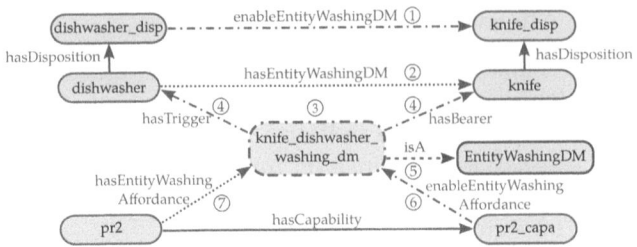

Fig. 3. Ontological pattern example allowing the inference of a Dispositional Match (DM) and a related affordance. - - ⇥ are inferences by equivalence, −·→ are inferences by the custom reasoner, and ·····→ are inferences by property chain. Numbers like ⓧ correspond to the order of inferences.

infer that their dispositions can interact together (*(dishwasher_ disp, enableWashingDM, knife_ disp)*). The transition from the dispositions individuals to the effective entities is once again done through a property chain **hasDisposition•enableWashingDM•isDispositionOf ⟹ hasWashingDM**. We thus infer the relation (*(dishwasher, hasWashingDM, knife)*) ②.

Once a dispositional match is found, an individual has to be created ③ to represent the generated new "system", to borrow Turvey's words. This latter is then linked to its bearer and its trigger ④ which correspond respectively to the entity holding the actualizable and actualizing dispositions. This process is managed by our custom reasoner and can be expressed as:

$$\forall (a_D,\ a_R)|(a_D,\ p,\ a_R) \in R \land (p, hasDM) \in I$$
$$A \leftarrow A \cup \{a_{DR}\},$$
$$R \leftarrow R \cup \{(a_{DR}, hasTrigger, a_D), (a_{DR}, hasBearer, a_R)\}$$

5.2   Dispositional Match: An Example

For this example, our custom reasoner creates a new individual *k_d_washing_DM* individual. This DM individual is then linked to its bearer/trigger individuals with the relations (*k_d_washing_dm, hasBearer, knife*) and (*k_d_washing_dm, hasTrigger, dishwasher*).

As this DM individual represents a sum of reciprocal dispositions, it is by essence a disposition and has to be represented in consequence. To do so, we use an equivalence class which at least includes the involved dispositions. Because our goal is to obtain a representation of the affordances applicable for an agent, the equivalence class must leverage the dispositions required to use the affordance. For our example, the match between *Washing* and *Washable* dispositions is not sufficient in order to get those two entities to interact together. Thus, we add to the representation that the washable individual must have a *GraspableDisposition*. The definition of the equivalence class **EntityWashingDM≡(hasTrigger some (WashableDisposition and GraspableDisposition) and hasBearer some (WashingDisposition))** results in the inference of the relation $(k\_d\_washing\_dm, isA, EntityWashingDM)$ ⑤. In a similar way, the disposition of the dishwasher's button to be pressed could be inserted in such an equivalence.

At this stage, the DMs are expressed through their dispositions and the affordances can be inferred based on those using the functional affordance mechanism presented earlier. Similarly to the case of Fig. 2.A, the agent's capabilities can thus enable the affordance ⑥ which can then be applied to the agent itself ⑦.

6   Results

This section describes the reasoning process happening in our framework for the examples used throughout this paper. It aims at demonstrating how these patterns, which represent affordances, evolve with the modifications occurring in the environment and can help the representation of the robot's action possibilities for a given situation.

To illustrate this process, we will consider a scenario with a robot helper in a kitchen environment. Let us consider a "making a tomato salad" task, with the robot helper having access to the following equipment: a knife, a tomato, and a dishwasher. We assume that the robot has two grippers, a motion planning algorithm, and an object localization node. It would therefore be inferred that it is capable of grasping and localizing entities.

Based on its grippers which provided the grasping capability, the robot initially has a grasping affordance toward the knife and the tomato due to their *Graspable* dispositions. Furthermore, since the knife and the tomato have reciprocal dispositions due to their *Cutting* and *Cuttable* dispositions, a DM individual would be created to represent their interacting-ability. Using the dispositional match algorithm, the robot would be inferred as having an entity cutting affordance toward this DM individual as it has the right set of capabilities.

When the robot grasps the knife, its capabilities would be updated to include the knife's cutting disposition as a cutting capability of its own. Therefore, the robot would have a "direct" affordance toward the tomato, meaning it currently affords this action but also an "indirect" affordance toward the DM individual between the tomato and the knife. This latter would thus represent an action possibility requiring another action to be executed before in order to actualize the disposition.

Moreover, assuming the robot has sliced the tomato, the knife's status would change to dirty and thus updating its dispositions with a *Washable* disposition. This, in turn, would create another DM individual due to the dishwasher's reciprocal disposition of *Washing*. The robot helper, holding the necessary capabilities for this affordance, would be inferred as having an affordance relation with this new DM individual, meaning that it can wash the knife with the dishwasher.

Furthermore, one could argue that for washing the knife with the dishwasher, a washing tablet is required. This latter and the dishwasher would have reciprocal dispositions, leading to the creation of a new DM individual. The knife and this DM individual would, in turn, lead to the creation of another DM individual representing the washing affordance, with the knife being the bearer but the dishwasher-washing tablet DM as the trigger.

7   Conclusion and Future Work

In this paper, we have proposed an ontological representation of the functional affordance concept based on agentive aspect and entity dispositions. Unlike the existing literature, our representation of the affordance set is dynamic and maintainable given the current state of the environment. These patterns leverage affordances involving multiple entities by building on the concept of reciprocal dispositions, while also taking into account the agent's capabilities.

We are aware that our custom reasoner is not perfectly aligned with the standard inference mechanisms but is required to be able to dynamically infer affordances. Nevertheless, we believe that the proposed patterns are still useful and meaningful for describing affordances and dispositional matches in a static way, as this is the most common use.

Concerning future improvements, we could include more properties to represent the actual affordance emergence, such as physical constraints, for example the maximum weight a robot can lift, but also take into account the affordance emerging between agents.

Acknowledgments. This work has been supported by the Effective Learning of Social Affordances (ELSA) project ANR-21-CE33-0019.

Disclosure of Interests. The authors have no competing interests to declare that are relevant to the content of this article.

References

1. Awaad, I., Kraetzschmar, G.K., Hertzberg, J.: The role of functional affordances in socializing robots. Int. J. Soc. Robot. (2015)
2. Barck-Holst, C., Ralph, M., Holmar, F., Kragic, D.: Learning grasping affordance using probabilistic and ontological approaches. In: International Conference on Advanced Robotics. IEEE (2009)
3. Beßler, D., Porzel, R., Pomarlan, M., Beetz, M., Malaka, R., Bateman, J.: A formal model of affordances for flexible robotic task execution. In: ECAI. IOS Press (2020)
4. Chemero, A.: An outline of a theory of affordances. Ecol. Psychol. (2003)
5. Chemero, A., Turvey, M.T.: Gibsonian affordances for roboticists. Adapt. Beh. (2007)
6. Dussard, B., Sarthou, G., Clodic, A.: Ontological component-based description of robot capabilities. In: International Workshop on Working towards Ontology-based Standards for Robotics and Automation (2023)
7. Gibson, J.J.: The ecological approach to visual perception (1979)
8. Gonçalves, P.J., Torres, P.M.: Knowledge representation applied to robotic orthopedic surgery. Robot. Comput.-Integr. Manuf. (2015)
9. Gruber, T.R.: A translation approach to portable ontology specifications. Knowl. Acquis. (1993)

10. Hartson, R.: Cognitive, physical, sensory, and functional affordances in interaction design. Behav. Inf. Technol. (2003)
11. Lemaignan, S., Warnier, M., Sisbot, E.A., Clodic, A., Alami, R.: Artificial cognition for social human–robot interaction: an implementation. Artif. Intell. (2017)
12. Martin, C.B.: The Mind in Nature. OUP Oxford (2010)
13. Montesano, L., Lopes, M., Bernardino, A., Santos-Victor, J.: Learning object affordances: from sensory–motor coordination to imitation. IEEE Trans. Robot. (2008)
14. Myers, A., Teo, C.L., Fermüller, C., Aloimonos, Y.: Affordance detection of tool parts from geometric features. In: International Conference on Robotics and Automation (ICRA). IEEE (2015)
15. Norman, D.A.: The design of everyday things (2002)
16. Şahin, E., Cakmak, M., Doğar, M.R., Uğur, E., Üçoluk, G.: To afford or not to afford: a new formalization of affordances toward affordance-based robot control. Adapt. Beh. (2007)
17. Sarthou, G.: Knowledge representation and exploitation for interactive and cognitive robots. Ph.D. thesis, Université Paul Sabatier - Toulouse III (2021)
18. Sarthou, G., Clodic, A., Alami, R.: Ontologenius: A long-term semantic memory for robotic agents. In: International Conference on Robot and Human Interactive Communication (RO-MAN). IEEE (2019)
19. Sarthou, G., Mayima, A., Buisan, G., Belhassein, K., Clodic, A.: The director task: a psychology-inspired task to assess cognitive and interactive robot architectures. In: International Conference on Robot & Human Interactive Communication (RO-MAN). IEEE (2021)
20. Solano, L., Romero, F., Rosado, P.: An ontology for integrated machining and inspection process planning focusing on resource capabilities. Int. J. Comput. Integr. Manuf. (2016)
21. Su, Y.F., Liu, A., Lu, W.H.: Improving robot grasping plans with affordance. In: International Conference on Advanced Robotics and Intelligent Systems (ARIS). IEEE (2017)
22. Tang, J., Zheng, G., Yu, J., Yang, S.: Cotdet: affordance knowledge prompting for task driven object detection. In: IEEE/CVF International Conference on Computer Vision (2023)
23. Toyoshima, F., Barton, A.: A formal representation of affordances as reciprocal dispositions. TriCoLore (C3GI/ISD/SCORE) (2018)
24. Turvey, M.T.: Ecological foundations of cognition: invariants of perception and action. Am. Psychol. Assoc. (1992)
25. Umbrico, A., Cortellessa, G., Orlandini, A., Cesta, A.: Modeling affordances and functioning for personalized robotic assistance. In: KR (2020)
26. Varadarajan, K., Vincze, M.: Ontological knowledge management framework for grasping and manipulation. In: IROS Workshop: Knowledge Representation for Autonomous Robots (2011)
27. Varadarajan, K.M., Vincze, M.: AFNet: the affordance network. In: Asian Conference on Computer Vision. Springer (2012)
28. Varadarajan, K.M., Vincze, M.: AfRob: the affordance network ontology for robots. In: IEEE/RSJ International Conference on Intelligent Robots and Systems (2012)
29. Zech, P., Haller, S., Lakani, S.R., Ridge, B., Ugur, E., Piater, J.: Computational models of affordance in robotics: a taxonomy and systematic classification. Adapt. Beh. (2017)

Envision a Future of Living with Robots Through Participatory Theatre: A Field Report

Rosan Chow(✉), Debora Frommeld ⓘ, Jessica Glanz, Lars Boettger, Jana Stadlbauer, and Karsten Weber ⓘ

Ostbayerische Technische Hochschule Regensburg, Regensburg, Germany
rosan.chow@oth-regensburg.de

Abstract. With the goal to facilitate societal discussion, the interactive exhibition "Living with robots", open to the public at the Science Night in Regensburg, Germany in 2024 gave visitors the opportunity to imagine a life with robots at home, at work, for care, and education. Most of public presentations of robots emphasize the power of technology; the exhibition was intentionally designed to set apart from this. It was set up with multiple stations of which an improvisation theatre was the highlight. We chose theatric play as the medium of engagement and communication, and it was shown to be fruitful. In this paper, we draw implications from our experiences and present some preliminary results on the public opinions of living with robots.

Keywords: Robots · acceptance · participatory theatre · public engagement

1 Introduction

Today, many people may be familiar with vacuum cleaner robots; many may have heard of industrial robots; nevertheless, many more are still unaware of how robots might be used and integrated into the everyday life in the future. With the aim to raise awareness and facilitate conversations on the issues concerning social robots and humans, the interactive exhibition "Living with Robots", open to the public at the Science Night in Regensburg, Germany in 2024 gave visitors the opportunity to imagine a life with robots at home, at work, for care and education. Taking a neutral stand without passing judgements, we called attention to potentials, opportunities, and risks of human-robot-relationships in these domains. Most of the public presentations of robots emphasize the power of technology; our exhibition was intentionally designed to set apart from this to create an environment in which the visitors would feel a sense of agency. Particularly, the visitors themselves played robots, as in the play "Rossum's Universal Robots" in 1920, from which the term 'robot' originates. This democratic approach is important and necessary, given the rapid advances of the digital technologies and their unpredictable and perhaps uncontrollable consequences on people's life.

The exhibition was set up with multiple stations which invited various levels of participation by the visitors; from receiving information, generating responses, to creative imagining and playing. Seeking visitors' opinions is a central interactive element of

O. Palinko et al. (Eds.): ICSR + AI 2024, LNAI 15562, pp. 470–475, 2025.
https://doi.org/10.1007/978-981-96-3519-1_42

participatory exhibitions. As experts of their own living environment, the visitors assess where and how robots should or should not be used in everyday life. In this way, they helped to shape the content of the exhibition. At the same time, trust is created through the openness of the exhibition and underlines the neutral approach we have taken.

Station 1 was composed of four video screens showing in loops existing social robots in action. In front of the screens was a long table on which visitors were prompted to write down their responses to the question "What do you think?" Besides, there were additional information about the historical development of robots presented on two computer screens standing close to the table. Station 4 was a wall on which the visitors might put stickers in red, yellow, or green as replies to four statements. While these two stations elicited many interesting responses from the visitors, the highlight was Station 2 and 3. At Station 2, costumes were laid out for visitors to choose to dress up as a robot. Station 3 was a participatory improvision theatre in which the visitors imagined and played living with a robot in four thematic scenarios.

The idea of participatory theater as an instrument of knowledge [1], as a tool of empowerment [2], as a didactic method [3], and as a way of imparting knowledge [4] has been discussed for some time. Participatory theater is often aimed at vulnerable groups who do not have a voice and are therefore not represented in many public debates; in these cases, it is about empowerment. However, our participatory theater was used primarily as a didactic tool and a means for imparting information to the public who explored the possible use of robots in ways that were meaningful to them.

The project team was composed of two design graduates, a design theorist, a philosopher, a former museum curator and a social scientist. None of us has expertise in theatre production, and we had been warned that it could turn out to be a flop. But to the contrary, it attracted hundreds of people, and we were struck by the readiness of the visitors, particularly children and their guardians, to choose costumes, dress up, and play along with noticeable enjoyment. Based on these experiences, we would like to offer some initial observations and reflections that might be useful for the exploration of social robotics, arts, and design for public engagement. In addition, we shall present some preliminary results collected from Station 1.

2 The Participatory Theater and Its Costumes

The philosopher Martha Nussbaum [5] argues that arts in general and play in particular is important for building a democratic society. In brief, play is a medium to develop imagination which is the foundation of empathy which in turn is the basic capability to live together with others different from us. Her manifesto is a call to revamp higher education across the world that has over the years marginalized the humanities and the arts to the detriments of societies. The point is to educate critical and creative citizens and not only competent and skillful professionals. By implications, for educating and engaging the public with emerging technologies, arts and play could also be essential for a creative democracy in which ordinary citizens critically and creatively imagine how (well) to live with robots. Exhibiting the future or better futures is very young in curatorial discourse and has only recently begun to emerge in exhibitions or museums. We chose theatric play as the medium of engagement and communication for we believe it would help visitors to imagine a future that is still very abstract for many. Playing activates the 'homo ludens' [6] because in play, boundary-crossing imaginative ideas and negotiations about one's own actions thrives.

Unlike the common approach taken in various museums, where people interact with real robots, the visitors not only interacted but also playfully 'be' one. Through play, we tapped into the soma (body-mind), which the pragmatist aesthetician Richard Shusterman [7] argues, is a "lived, sentient, intentional body that involves mental, social, cultural dimensions". By embodied experiencing, we hoped people would explore freely and creatively the potential opportunities and challenges of living with robots, and thereby would begin to think seriously about it on their own.

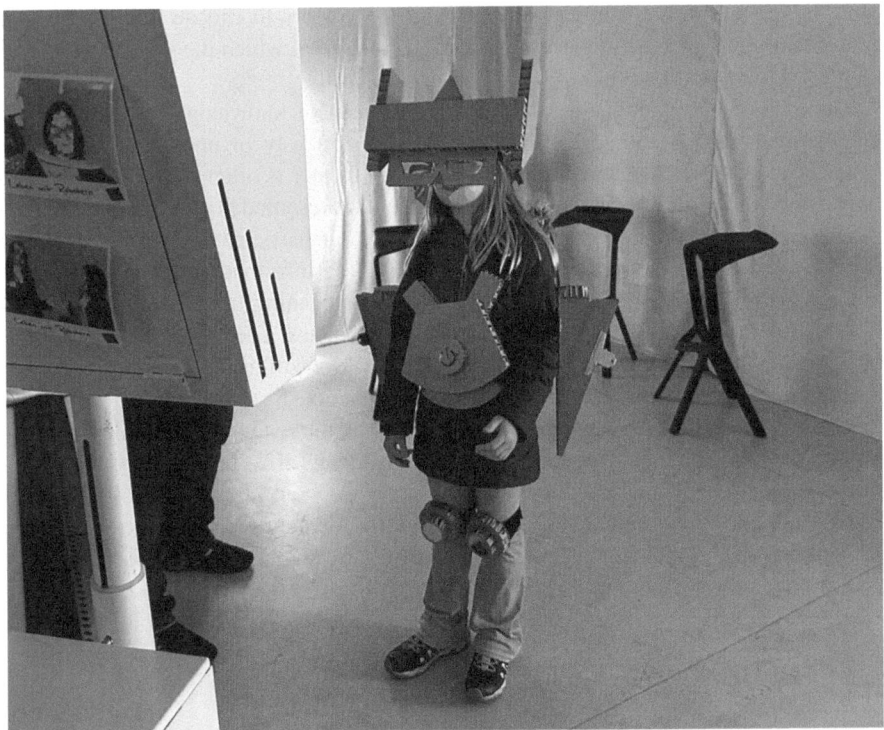

Fig. 1. A child with the combinable robot costumes posing for the camera. Photo: Jessi Glanz

Multiple factors likely contributed to the success of the improvision theatre, but the costumes seemed to be the most important to get people to play. They were made of cardboard decorated with makeshift elements and could be combined in many ways. They were interesting looking but in forms not associated with common images of robots because we intended to break down stereotypes and any predefined expectations. When put on, the costumes seemed to set free the imagination and removed any hesitation left of the visitors (see Fig. 1). They wanted to engage and play.

One of the main design goals of social robot is acceptance, and particularly the appearance of the robot should not fall into the uncanny valley [8]. We will have more to say about fear in Sect. 3 below and here we focus on the positive. Our costumes did not scare anyone and as a matter of fact, it was fun for many to put them on; thus, they were in this sense exemplary. It is well known that acceptance of a new product or device relies on striking a right balance between novelty and familiarity in relation to the experiences of the users or viewers. It might be assumed that for most of the visitors, social robots should have looked like what they had seen in movies or other cultural media: shiny, metallic, and mechanic looking. Given this baseline, the materials of our costumes were novel because they were made of matt paper; but the forms were relatively familiar as they had geometrical shapes associated with machines.

However, this is a post-facto analysis. The point to make here is that we do not know what is acceptable until and unless we create something and try it with the public. Acceptance is a moving target. The design of social robots, whether it is about appearances, forms of interaction or functional features is primarily a matter of iterative and circular experiment, controlled or otherwise, between the professional and the public [9]. As admitted earlier, there were high uncertainties of using theatric play to engage the public and we were somewhat fortunate that the outcomes were positive and encouraging. Besides, we also learn about the possibilities and limits of android design.

It must be emphasized that unlike most of the commercial living labs in which companies test their products with customers, the exhibition including the theatre was educational in nature. We did not aim to find out people's needs and desires and to adapt the robot design to them; rather we supported them to explore creatively and critically about the topic. The exhibition is a line with the current discourse of promoting 'futures literacy' through exhibitions to effect "general willingness to engage with the future, to get involved in discourses on the future, to search for possible futures and then to actively pursue them" [10]. It is therefore also about supporting the imagination of futures which is a challenge for many people. For this aim, despite the caveats, theatric play augmented by some well-designed tools, the costumes, and other props, seems to be a promising medium worthy of further research and testing.

In addition, a point worth making is that our project was created with a relatively low budget and the material resources used were inexpensive and ubiquitously available; thus, it could be easily reproduced and scaled up. This is not unimportant for projects of science communication and public engagement which are often under-funded. Encouragingly, it shows that for certain purposes and situations, one does not need to have a full-fledged robot laboratory to create impact, imagination suffices.

3 Statements of the Visitors

We evaluated 86 answers we received to our question "What do you think?" at Station 1 using a qualitative, structuring content analysis following Kuckartz [11]. This involved 98 text segments, which were examined as analysis units, using MAXQDA. Two thirds of the segments express an open-mindedness, in some cases even enthusiasm, towards a future life with robots. The other third is dominated by reservation and fear of a life with robots. Most respondents appear to be open to a life with robots and are looking forward to it:

- "I'm looking forward to the time when I have my own robot assistant at home – Clippy!" (Segment 44)
- "I think it's great and also important for the future, because people are getting older and older and there is a shortage of nursing staff, for example" (Segment 23)
- "Life = not exhausting with robots" (Segment 36)

Reservation and fears are explicitly expressed, but they are in the minority:

- "I am afraid of robots!!!" (Segment 78)
- "I think humanoid is creepy" (Segment 76)
- "Robots should not contribute to the humiliation of humans." (Segment 85)

This result confirms own research findings from previous projects with robots to support stroke patients or technology that assists in the care of the elderly [13] and is in line with other studies [12]. Yet, the level of positive responses is rather surprising. It might be that the playful context, in which those statements were uttered, had a positive effect on the attitudes of the visitors toward robots.

4   Conclusion

We have reflected on the use of theatric play for the purpose of engaging the public with the topic of living with social robots. To end our contribution, we turn to the political dimension of the exhibition. The impact of digitalization on society in general, and on workers in particular, is currently the subject of intense public and scholarly debates [14], with some experts predicting that digitalization will eliminate large numbers of existing jobs – with potentially drastic consequences for workers and society. The historian Simon Johnson and the economist Daron Acemoglu [15] argue that the deployment of technologies should therefore enhance rather than replace workers in the process of creating new jobs. For this to happen, worker unions as a countervailing power are imperative. Equally important, alternative narratives about the socioeconomic values and developmental direction of technologies must be made public in addition to the ones fabricated by the powerful and ultra-wealthy companies and individuals. Although the exhibition was small, local, and short-lived, it could be seen as creating such an alternative narrative. The early professional theatre about robots were aimed for emancipatory and equitable futures, as Elizabeth Jochum [16] put it in her keynote at the Creative Robotics Theatre workshop in Copenhagen. The participatory theatre could be regarded as a continuation with this tradition. This further strengthens our belief and hopes in using it for public engagement. Literally and metaphorically, the public is drafting the plot of living with robots on stage and offstage into the future.

Acknowledgments. The project was funded by the Regensburg Center of Health Sciences and Technology (RCHST, https://rchst.de).

Disclosure of Interests.   The authors have no competing interests to declare that are relevant to the content of this article.

References

1. Erel, U., Reynolds, T., Kaptani, E.: Participatory theatre for transformative social research. Qual. Res. **17**(3), 302–312 (2017)
2. Enria, L.: Co-producing knowledge through participatory theatre: Reflections on ethnography, empathy and power. Qual. Res. **16**(3), 319–329 (2016)
3. Jackson, A.: Participatory forms of educational theatre. In: Schonmann, S. (ed.) Key concepts in theatre/drama education, pp. 235–240. SensePublishers, Rotterdam (2011)
4. Kumrai, R.R., Chauhan, V., Hoy, J.: Boundary crossings: using participatory theatre as a site for deepening learning. Teach. High. Educ. **16**(5), 517–528 (2011)
5. Nussbaum, M.C.: Not for Profit: Why Democracy Needs the Humanities. Princeton University Press, Princeton/New Jersey (2010)
6. Huizinga, J.: Homo Ludens: A study of the play-element of culture. Routledge & Kegan Paul, London (1949)
7. Shusterman, R.: Soma, self, and society: Somaesthetics as pragmatist meliorism. Metaphilosophy **42**(3), 314–327 (2011)
8. Misselhorn, C.: Empathy with inanimate objects and the uncanny valley. Mind. Mach. **19**(3), 345–359 (2009)
9. Kriz, S., Ferro, T.D., Damera, P., Porter, J.R.: Fictional robots as a data source in HRI research: Exploring the link between science fiction and interactional expectations. In: 19th International Symposium in Robot and Human Interactive Communication, pp. 458–463. IEEE, Viareggio/Italy (2010)
10. Leinfelder, R.: Die Zukunft im Museum ausstellen? In: Mohr, H., Modarressi-Tehrani, D. (eds.) Museen der Zukunft. Trends und Herausforderungen eines innovationsorientierten Kulturmanagements, pp. 363–399. transcript, Bielefeld/Germany (2022)
11. Balsmeier, B., Woerter, M.: Is this time different? How digitalization influences job creation and destruction. Res. Policy **48**(8), 103765 (2019)
12. Kuckartz, U., Rädiker, S.: Qualitative Content Analysis: Methods, Practice and Software. Sage, London (2023)
13. Frommeld, D., Weber, K.: Telepräsenzroboter zur Unterstützung von Pflege und Therapie: Eine qualitative Interviewstudie zur Nutzung und Ablehnung. In: Weber, K., Haug, S., Lauer, N., Mohr, C., Pfingsten, A., Raptis, G., Bahr, G. (eds.) Digitale Technik für ambulante Pflege und Therapie III: Nutzung, Akzeptanz, Wirkung und Lebensqualität, pp. 307–327. transcript, Bielefeld/Germany (2024)
14. Vandemeulebroucke, T., de Casterlé, B.D., Gastmans, C.: How do older adults experience and perceive socially assistive robots in aged care: A systematic review of qualitative evidence. Aging Ment. Health **22**(2), 149–167 (2017)
15. Johnson, S., Acemoglu, D.: Power and Progress: Our Thousand-Year Struggle Over Technology and Prosperity. Hachette, London (2023)
16. Elizabeth, J.: Rehearsal for the robot revolution. Presented at the Creative Robotics Theatre – ACM Designing Interactive Systems 2024 (DIS24), Copenhagen (J2024)

Child Speech Recognition in Human-Robot Interaction: Problem Solved?

Ruben Janssens$^{(\boxtimes)}$, Eva Verhelst, Giulio Antonio Abbo, Qiaoqiao Ren,
Maria Jose Pinto Bernal, and Tony Belpaeme

IDLab-AIRO, Ghent University – imec, Ghent, Belgium
{ruben.janssens,eva.verhelst,giulioantonio.abbo,qiaoqiao.ren,
mariajosepinto.bernal,tony.belpaeme}@ugent.be

Abstract. Automated Speech Recognition shows superhuman performance for adult English speech on a range of benchmarks, but disappoints when fed children's speech. This has long sat in the way of child-robot interaction. Recent evolutions in data-driven speech recognition, including the availability of Transformer architectures and unprecedented volumes of training data, might mean a breakthrough for child speech recognition and social robot applications aimed at children. We revisit a study on child speech recognition from 2017 and show that indeed performance has increased, with newcomer OpenAI Whisper doing markedly better than leading commercial cloud services. Performance improves even more in highly structured interactions when priming models with specific phrases. While transcription is not perfect yet, the best model recognises 60.3% of sentences correctly barring small grammatical differences, with sub-second transcription time running on a local GPU, showing potential for usable autonomous child-robot speech interactions.

Keywords: Child-Robot Interaction · Automatic Speech
Recognition · Verbal Interaction · Interaction Design Recommendations

1 Introduction and Background

Spoken language interaction is for many the holy grail in HCI and HRI. It is built upon a collection of technologies, such as Automated Speech Recognition (ASR), Dialogue Management, and Text-to-Speech, that are chained together to create a system which allows the user to interact or converse with an artificial system using the most natural interface known to humankind. While this processing chain is brittle, the point of entry is Automated Speech Recognition. The ability to automatically transcribe speech utterances has been studied extensively in academic and industrial research. In recent decades, ASR performance has

---

R. Janssens and E. Verhelst—Equal contribution and joint first authors.

© The Author(s), under exclusive license to Springer Nature Singapore Pte Ltd. 2025
O. Palinko et al. (Eds.): ICSR + AI 2024, LNAI 15562, pp. 476–486, 2025.
https://doi.org/10.1007/978-981-96-3519-1_43

come along in leaps and bounds, with companies claiming "super-human performance" on conversational ASR benchmarks in 2017. On certain benchmarks and for resource-rich languages, speech recognition performance is on par or even better than mean human transcription performance [17]. The popular metric for ASR performance is Word Error Rate (WER), calculated as the total number of errors—substitutions, insertions, and deletions—divided by the total number of words in the text. WER was typically reported to be below 5% [17]. However, while impressive, these systems' performance degraded catastrophically on speech for which it was not optimised, including atypical voices such as the speech of elderly or young children. This has repercussions for HRI and specifically for applications in which autonomous social robots are expected to interact with non-typical users, such as robots for elder care or robots for education [2,4,16].

In 2017, Kennedy et al. [8] published a widely cited study showing that then state-of-the-art ASR could not reliably transcribe the speech of 5-year-old English speakers. The speech ranged from constrained utterances—such as counting from 1 to 10—to unconstrained telling of a story from a picture book. The ASR performance was evaluated for four different engines, but the results were nothing but disappointing. While WER for adult speech was below 5%, most engines could not correctly transcribe a single child utterance. Only Google's ASR did marginally better, recognising 11.8% of constrained child speech and about 6% of spontaneous child speech. Still, only correctly being able to transcribe 1 utterance out of 10 is a recipe for interaction disaster, and the authors of the study then recommended against relying on ASR for child-robot interaction.

Forward 6 years. Artificial intelligence has been revolutionised by the Transformer architecture, not only resulting in a sea of change in the performance of generative language models but also in the performance of ASR [11]. In September 2022, OpenAI released Whisper, an ASR engine built using an encoder-decoder Transformer architecture trained on an unprecedented 680,000 h of labelled audio data [13]. While the specifics of Whisper's training regimen and its training data are proprietary to OpenAI, the inference model is released as public open-source software. Whisper's performance on average is better than competing solutions, but was found to still be subpar to solutions that have been specifically trained or fine-tuned on specific datasets, such as LibriSpeech [13].

Next to the publicly available Whisper models, there are several cloud-based solutions. In this area large players—Amazon, Google, Microsoft and Tencent—compete with smaller, sometimes specialised vendors, but all offer convenient online API services that are easily integrated within code.

Given the availability of new architectures trained on larger and more diverse corpora, the time is opportune to revisit the results from Kennedy et al. [8] and evaluate whether state-of-the-art ASR can now handle child speech. Recent work on child speech recognition has focused mainly on finetuning open source ASR models that were originally trained on adult speech on additional child speech data (e.g., [1,3,5,6]), resulting in a decreased WER of up to 5% [1], but this increase in performance may not be generalizable to other datasets [5]. Additionally, as little child speech data is available, approaches like data augmentation [7], combining datasets of different languages [14] or parameter-efficient finetuning [12] are used. We choose to evaluate readily available ASR systems, including commercial models, as our focus is the out-of-the-box applicability of these systems in child-robot interaction.

We decided to compare OpenAI's Whisper, as it is open-source and exemplifies the new direction in data-driven ASR, and two commercial cloud-based solutions, opting for Microsoft and Google's systems. We are first and foremost interested in transcription accuracy, but for our aim of integrating child speech recognition into a real-time interactive HRI scenario, we also explore how responsive different systems are. We also investigate whether performance can be improved by priming the systems to expect specific words or phrases.

2 Methodology

To evaluate the ASR engines, we use the data from Kennedy *et al.* [9] which contains audio recordings of 11 young children (age M = 4.9 years old) recorded at an English primary school. The recordings consist of spontaneous speech (retelling a picture book) and speech in which children count from 1 to 10 or repeat short sentences spoken by an adult (such as "the horse is in the stable"). Each sample is recorded from 3 sources: a studio-grade microphone (Rode NT1-A) placed above the robot, a portable microphone (Zoom H1) placed just in front of the robot, and the two front microphones of the Aldebaran NAO robot. All recordings were manually transcribed and this is used as ground truth.

We evaluated three ASR engines: Microsoft Azure Speech to Text, Google Cloud Speech-to-text, and OpenAI's Whisper. The Azure and Google models were used through a cloud API. Whisper exists in different model sizes: tiny (39M parameters), base, small, medium, and large (1550M parameters), with three versions of the large model. All seven of these models are compared in this study: we expect the smaller models to run faster but have lower accuracy. We used the `faster-whisper`[1] reimplementation of the Whisper models, which claims a transcription time of up to four times faster than OpenAI's original Whisper implementation. The Whisper models were run locally on an NVIDIA GeForce GTX 1080 Ti with 11 GB of VRAM. We also ran them on only a CPU, to assess the necessity of a dedicated GPU for these models. We configured the models to expect English language speech, as preliminary testing revealed that without this option Whisper large v3 correctly detected English in only 84% of spontaneous speech samples. All transcriptions were performed in 2024.

The performance of the models is compared using four different metrics for transcription accuracy, to ensure comparability with the results reported in [8]:

- **Levenshtein distance**: the minimum amount of insertions, deletions and substitutions required to change one sequence into the other, at letter level,

---

[1] github.com/SYSTRAN/faster-whisper.

divided by the amount of letters in the ground truth. A score of 0 means perfect recognition, a score of 1 could reflect a recognised sequence of the same length but with no letter in the right position. There is no upper bound.
- **WER**, for comparability with other ASR research.
- **Absolute accuracy**: the fraction of samples that are completely correctly recognised.
- **Relaxed accuracy**: the fraction of samples that are correctly recognised, also counting as accurate those with small grammatical differences that do not impact the meaning of the utterance, following the same rules as in [8].

To estimate the possibility of real-time interactions, we explore the responsiveness of the different systems by reporting their transcription time. For all Whisper models, the transcription time is the time it takes for the model to return a result, which varies due to the model size as well as the hardware on which it runs. As the Azure and Google systems are cloud-based, their transcription time also includes the transmission time of the audio file and the result.

In all analyses, unless otherwise stated, we use only the studio microphone recordings, and only the recordings of the sentences that the children repeat from the adult ($n = 50$) and of the spontaneous utterances (split into sentences, $n = 222$), because preliminary analysis showed that utterances consisting of a single number are often too short for the engines to detect any speech.

3 Results

We will first compare the models' transcription accuracy, also investigating the impact of the length of the utterance, and improving performance by using model priming techniques. Then, we report the models' responsiveness, the impact of the microphone used, and finally a reflection on the power consumption of the models.

3.1 Transcription Accuracy

First of all, we compare the performance of Google, Azure and the best Whisper model (large v3) with the four engines reported in the 2017 paper. These results are shown in Fig. 1. They show that the Google speech recognition did not improve compared to 2017, but the performance of both the Azure model, and the Whisper model are better than all models tested in the 2017 paper, with Whisper performing best of all.

We report the transcription accuracy using multiple metrics in Table 1. All four metrics show the same ordering between the models' performances.

While WER was not reported in the 2017 paper, it allows us to compare with performance on adult speech. Microsoft achieved a WER of 5% in 2017 on part of the Switchboard dataset, but another part of this dataset was used for training the model [17]. In 2023, Whisper achieved a WER of 13.8% on Switchboard without being specifically trained for this dataset. These results

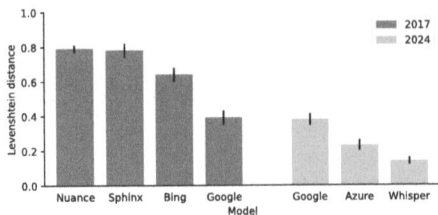

Fig. 1. Performance of ASR engines in 2017 and 2024, calculated as mean normalised Levenshtein distance between ground truth and transcription (lower is better).

suggest that Whisper's generalisability across datasets extends to child speech, although there is still a gap with adult speech.

The absolute and relaxed accuracy give an impression of the usability of the models. While this is not yet an ideal performance level, the relaxed accuracy shows that Whisper is already rather usable. Some small mistakes could still be handled by dialogue management software, such as large language models, even though they do not count as accurate in the relaxed accuracy criteria. For example, in the sentence "the dog is in front of the horse", Whisper and Azure replace "in" with "the", but this transcription could still be used to further the conversation, even though it is counted as inaccurate in these metrics.

Table 1. Transcription accuracy for ASR engines in 2017 and 2024, for repeated sentences and spontaneous utterances split into sentences ($n = 272$).

Metric	Google (2017)	Google (2024)	Azure	Whisper
Levenshtein distance ($\downarrow$ better)	0.38	0.38	0.23	**0.14**
WER ($\downarrow$ better)	–	49.0%	30.3%	**21.3%**
Absolute accuracy ($\uparrow$ better)	7.5%	9.6%	23.5%	**36.8%**
Relaxed accuracy ($\uparrow$ better)	20.3%	14.7%	43.0%	**60.3%**

Figure 2a shows a more detailed comparison between the different model sizes of Whisper and the Azure and Google services. As expected, the large Whisper models perform best, with Whisper large v3 performing best of all.

The Kruskal-Wallis test reveals significant differences between the Levenshtein distance for the tested models ($p < 0.001$), and post-hoc Dunn tests with Bonferroni correction do not show significant differences between Whisper large v3 and Whisper small, but do show a significant difference between, among others, all large Whisper models and Azure ($p < 0.005$), and between Azure and Google ($p < 0.001$).

3.2   Utterance Length

The previous section reported performance on the samples containing sentences that the children repeated from an adult, and spontaneous utterances that were split into sentences. However, the dataset also contains samples containing a number that was repeated from the adult, as well as full-length spontaneous utterances. These samples are respectively much shorter (mean length 0.98 s, s.d. 0.43 s) and much longer (108.91 s, s.d. 69.6 s) than the repeated sentences (2.85 s, s.d. 0.61 s) and spontaneous speech cut into sentences (4.20 s, s.d. 2.09 s).

As shown in Table 2, the ASR systems perform considerably worse on these shorter and longer samples. Only half of the repeated numbers are correctly recognized. Looking at the mistakes the models made shows that the samples containing a number are often too short to detect any speech. On the other hand, the samples containing the full spontaneous speech fragments contain pauses between sentences, which sometimes lead to early stopping of the transcription.

Table 2. Levenshtein distance for different utterance types (accuracy in brackets).

	Google	Azure	Whisper
Repeated sentences	0.26	0.16	0.13
Spontaneous sentences	0.41	0.25	0.14
Repeated numbers	0.80 (17%)	0.38 (52%)	0.50 (48%)
Full spontaneous samples	0.43	0.89	0.55

3.3   Model Priming

All three ASR systems we evaluated offer functionalities to prime the models to expect certain words or phrases. In a setting as in this dataset, where the context of the conversation is known, this could improve performance.

For the repeated numbers, we primed the Google and Azure ASR systems to expect a number—specifically between one and ten for Azure. Whisper works differently: it can be provided with a prompt, which acts as conversational context, which the model will try to complete with the transcript. The prompt *"I choose number"* worked best. As shown in Table 3, model priming strongly improves performance for these samples. Interestingly, the Whisper medium model performs better than large v3, reaching an average Levenshtein distance of 0.17 and an absolute accuracy of 88.0%. Table 3 reports the results of large v3.

For the repeated sentences, we compare three priming approaches: providing the five full sentences that the children said, making this a multiple-choice task, providing a template grammar, as also described in [8], and providing the separate words and subphrases that are part of the template. For Whisper, the template is provided as *"Choose the words that were said by this child: "The <dog/fish/horse> is <in/next to/in front of/behind/on top of>*

the <pond/shed/ car/stable/horse>"". Instead of providing separate words to Whisper, the prompt *"Where is the animal?"* is used. Table 3 also shows improved performance. As expected, the more structured the priming becomes, the better the performance: Whisper achieves almost perfect recognition in the multiple-choice setting.

For the spontaneous speech samples, Google and Azure were primed with the animals that were part of the template, while Whisper was prompted with *"Today we'll read 'Frog, where are you?'. This book chronicles the humorous adventures that befall a young boy as he and his dog search for the frog that escaped from a jar in his room. Let's begin."* Here, the performance gain is more limited. For Whisper, this translates into a WER for the spontaneous sentences of 21.9% with the prompt compared to 23.1% without.

Table 3. Levenshtein distance for primed models (accuracy between brackets).

Utterance type	Prompt	Google	Azure	Whisper
Repeated numbers	None	0.80 (17%)	0.38 (52%)	0.77 (40%)
	Number	0.66 (33%)	0.32 (64%)	0.53 (72%)
Repeated sentences	None	0.26	0.16	0.14
	Separate words	0.22	0.13	0.09
	Template	0.18	unsupported	0.07
	Multiple choice	0.20	0.09	0.01
Spontaneous sentences	None	0.41	0.25	0.15
	Animals	0.39	0.24	0.13
Full spontaneous samples	None	0.43	0.89	0.20
	Animals	0.42	0.89	0.19

3.4   Responsiveness

In Fig. 2b, the average transcription times for short sentences (spontaneous speech and repeat sentences) are shown for Google, Azure, all of the Whisper models on GPU and the tiny, base and small Whisper models on CPU. The average transcription time for the Whisper medium and large models on CPU are respectively 17.5 s and 30.5 s and were left out of the graph for readability. We marked the 1000 ms line on the figure because, even though the mean response time in human conversation is 200 ms, for spoken dialogue systems a delay of between 700 and 1000 ms is deemed acceptable [15]. This data shows that using a model locally on a GPU, instead of CPU or using an API, can greatly improve the responsiveness, even reaching an acceptable level for spoken dialogue.

The Kruskal-Wallis test shows significant differences between the transcription time of the tested models ($p < 0.001$), and post-hoc Dunn tests with Bonferroni correction show significant differences between all pairs of models, except for

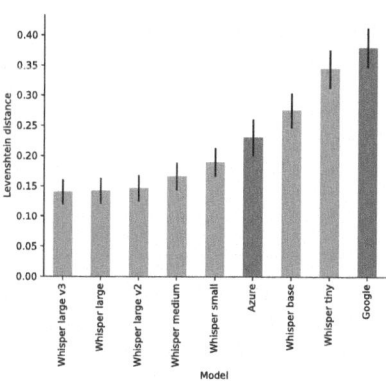

(a) Performance of all current ASR engines (Whisper model versions in green, Google and Azure in red) calculated as Levenshtein distance between ground truth and transcription (lower is better).

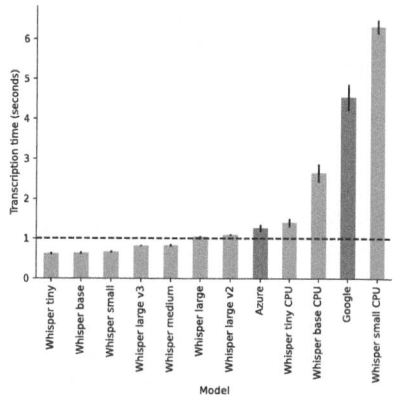

(b) Average transcription time for a sentence. Whisper models (in green) were run on GPU unless CPU is specified. Dashed line shows maximum acceptable delay of 1000ms.

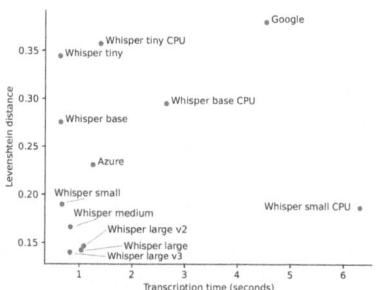

(c) Transcription time vs. accuracy (lower is better). Whisper models were run on GPU unless CPU is specified. Ideal ASR systems would be in the lower left corner.

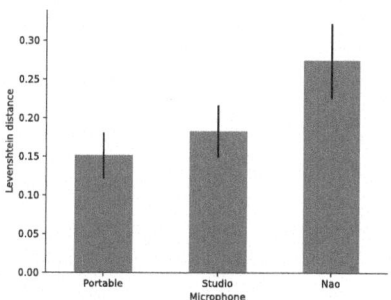

(d) Average performance of Azure, Google and best Whisper model when using different microphone types, calculated as Levenshtein distance (lower is better). Best results are obtained when using a microphone external from the robot.

Fig. 2. Graphs comparing the performance and transcription time of all current ASR engines and the impact of the microphone type on these metrics, for repeated sentences and spontaneous utterances split into sentences ($n = 272$).

between Whisper tiny, base, and small, between Whisper large v3 and medium, and between Whisper large, large v2, and Azure.

Figure 2c shows the relation between the models' average transcription time with their accuracy using the Levenshtein distance. To choose which model to use, both responsiveness and performance should be taken into account. Lower results are preferred for both, so models in the lower left corner of the scatter plot are ideal. As apparent in the figure, there is a trade-off between transcription time and transcription performance, so the choice should be made based on the specific application.

3.5   Microphone

In Fig. 2d, we compare the transcription accuracy between the three microphones used to record the samples, using the average performance of Google, Azure and Whisper large v3 on each sample. When comparing the results of the internal Nao microphone with the portable and studio microphone, the Kruskal-Wallis test shows a significant difference between the groups, and Dunn's test with Bonferroni corrections as post-hoc analysis shows a significant difference between the Nao and portable microphone ($p < 0.001$) and the Nao and studio microphone ($p < 0.01$). There is no significant difference between the studio and portable microphone ($p = 0.399$). In conclusion, the worst results are obtained when the microphone in the Nao robot is used, as there is a lot of added noise due to the closeness to the robot's motor and ventilation, but no difference is found between both external microphones.

3.6   Energy Consumption

As concerns have been raised over the energy consumption and consequently carbon emissions of state-of-the-art machine learning [10], we think it is valuable to consider these for ASR systems. We were only able to measure Whisper's consumption, as the other models were used via API instead of on our machines. Per hour of transcribed data, the largest and best-performing model (large v3) consumed 32.3 Wh and produced $7.7 g CO_2 eq$ in our setup. Note that this energy consumption refers to the transcription of many samples back-to-back, while real-time interactive systems would not be able to work as efficiently.

4   Conclusion

Based on our evaluation, we can make the following recommendations, updating or overriding those made in [8]:

Recognition performance. The recognition performance has improved dramatically for state-of-the-art ASR, with the best models of 2024 showing over 60% fewer transcription errors than in 2017. However, performance falters when input samples become much shorter or longer than a single sentence. Model priming is able to improve performance, especially in very structured settings, e.g. when a number of fixed options are expected. Adult-like recognition is not available yet, but the semantic content of children's speech is now sufficiently transcribed to offer potential for robust spoken interaction. Small errors can often be caught by other components of the dialogue management system—such as large language models—resulting in a higher task accuracy than the reported accuracy of ASR systems. However, future research should investigate performance in other languages than English.

Responsiveness. The responsiveness of locally hosted models (in our case OpenAI's Whisper) is significantly better than that of cloud-based solutions, with sub-second results for some models, when running them on a GPU. The network overhead and shared services of using cloud-based solutions are not optimal for real-time spoken interaction, and local models even outperform the cloud-based solutions in accuracy.

Impact of microphone. Using an external microphone, as opposed to a microphone embedded in the robot, leads to a significantly improved recognition performance. Performance improves regardless of the quality of the microphone, as the robot's noise has a stronger effect on the speech recognition than the choice of microphone.

Acknowledgments. This research received funding from imec (Smart Education), the Flemish Government (AI Research Program) and the Horizon Europe VALAWAI project (grant agreement number 101070930). We are indebted to the authors of [9] and [8] for making the recordings and transcriptions available.

References

1. Attia, A.A., Liu, J., Ai, W., Demszky, D., Espy-Wilson, C.: Kid-whisper: towards bridging the performance gap in automatic speech recognition for children vs. adults. arXiv preprint arXiv:2309.07927 (2023)
2. Belpaeme, T., Kennedy, J., Ramachandran, A., Scassellati, B., Tanaka, F.: Social robots for education: a review. Science robotics **3**(21), eaat5954 (2018)
3. Booth, E., Carns, J., Kennington, C., Rafla, N.: Evaluating and improving child-directed automatic speech recognition. In: Proceedings of the Twelfth Language Resources and Evaluation Conference, pp. 6340–6345 (2020)
4. Cifuentes, C.A., Pinto, M.J., Céspedes, N., Múnera, M.: Social robots in therapy and care. Curr. Robot. Rep. **1**, 59–74 (2020)
5. Jain, R., Barcovschi, A., Yiwere, M., Corcoran, P., Cucu, H.: Adaptation of whisper models to child speech recognition. arXiv preprint arXiv:2307.13008 (2023)
6. Jain, R., Barcovschi, A., Yiwere, M.Y., Bigioi, D., Corcoran, P., Cucu, H.: A wav2vec2-based experimental study on self-supervised learning methods to improve child speech recognition. IEEE Access **11**, 46938–46948 (2023)
7. Kathania, H.K., Kadyan, V., Kadiri, S.R., Kurimo, M.: Data augmentation using spectral warping for low resource children ASR. J. Signal Process. Syst. **94**(12), 1507–1513 (2022)
8. Kennedy, J., et al.: Child speech recognition in human-robot interaction: evaluations and recommendations. In: Proceedings of the 2017 ACM/IEEE International Conference on Human-Robot Interaction, pp. 82–90 (2017)
9. Kennedy, J., et al.: Children speech recording (English, spontaneous speech + pre-defined sentences) (2016). https://doi.org/10.5281/zenodo.200495, https://doi.org/10.5281/zenodo.200495

10. Lacoste, A., Luccioni, A., Schmidt, V., Dandres, T.: Quantifying the carbon emissions of machine learning. arXiv preprint arXiv:1910.09700 (2019)
11. Latif, S., Zaidi, A., Cuayahuitl, H., Shamshad, F., Shoukat, M., Qadir, J.: Transformers in speech processing: a survey. arXiv preprint arXiv:2303.11607 (2023)
12. Liu, W., Qin, Y., Peng, Z., Lee, T.: Sparsely shared Lora on whisper for child speech recognition. In: ICASSP 2024-2024 IEEE International Conference on Acoustics, Speech and Signal Processing (ICASSP), pp. 11751–11755. IEEE (2024)
13. Radford, A., Kim, J.W., Xu, T., Brockman, G., McLeavey, C., Sutskever, I.: Robust speech recognition via large-scale weak supervision. In: International Conference on Machine Learning, pp. 28492–28518. PMLR (2023)
14. Rolland, T., Abad, A., Cucchiarini, C., Strik, H.: Multilingual transfer learning for children automatic speech recognition (2022)
15. Skantze, G.: Turn-taking in conversational systems and human-robot interaction: a review. Comput. Speech Langu. **67**, 101178 (2021)
16. Verhelst, E., Janssens, R., Demeester, T., Belpaeme, T.: Adaptive second language tutoring using generative AI and a social robot. In: Companion of the 2024 ACM/IEEE International Conference on Human-Robot Interaction, pp. 1080–1084 (2024)
17. Xiong, W., Wu, L., Alleva, F., Droppo, J., Huang, X., Stolcke, A.: The microsoft 2017 conversational speech recognition system. In: 2018 IEEE International Conference on Acoustics, Speech and Signal Processing (ICASSP), pp. 5934–5938. IEEE (2018)

Follow Me: A Study on the Dynamics of Alignment Between Humans and LLM-Based Social Robots

Jeffrey Sherer[1]([⊠]), Robbie McPherson[1], Sattwik Mohanty[1], Guilhem Santé[1], Greta Gandolfi[2], Marta Romeo[1], and Alessandro Suglia[1]

[1] Heriot-Watt University, Edinburgh, UK
jjls2000@hw.ac.uk
[2] The University of Edinburgh, Edinburgh, UK

Abstract. While robots are perceived as reliable in delivering factual data, their ability to achieve meaningful alignment with humans during subjective interactions remains unclear. Gaining insights into this alignment is vital to integrating robots more deeply into decision-making frameworks and enhancing their roles in social interactions. This study examines the impact of personality-prompted large language models (LLMs) on alignment in human-robot interactions. Participants interacted with a Furhat robot under two conditions: a baseline control condition and an experimental condition using personality prompts designed to simulate distinct personality traits through the LLM. Alignment was assessed by measuring changes in similarity between participants' rankings and the robot's rankings of factual (objective) and contestable (subjective) concepts before and after interaction. The findings indicate that participants aligned more with the robot on objective, factual concepts than on subjective, contestable ones, regardless of personality prompts. These results suggest that the current personality prompting method may be insufficient to significantly influence alignment in subjective interactions. This may be attributed to the conveyed traits lacking sufficient impact or the limitations of current system capabilities, which may not yet be advanced enough to foster the desired influence on participants' perceptions.

Keywords: Human-Robot Interaction (HRI) · Alignment · LLM · Personality Prompting (P^2)

1 Introduction

Effective communication relies on the ability to build a shared mental framework between interlocutors, known as alignment. This process is crucial for dialogue, enabling participants to coordinate actions, intentions, and interpret information similarly, thereby simplifying the production and comprehension of communication by automatically aligning linguistic representations across different levels of

© The Author(s), under exclusive license to Springer Nature Singapore Pte Ltd. 2025
O. Palinko et al. (Eds.): ICSR + AI 2024, LNAI 15562, pp. 487–496, 2025.
https://doi.org/10.1007/978-981-96-3519-1_44

language processing [12,20]. This phenomenon is not exclusive to human interactions, and extends to communication between humans and robots [1].

Recent advancements in large language models (LLMs) and social robots have enabled HRI studies to hold more nuanced conversations, making interactions feel more natural. Individuals often mirror the robot's language, including word choices and phrasing, leading to deeper conceptual alignment [2,6]. This conceptual and lexical alignment has been observed in various studies, suggesting that people adapt to the robot's communicative behavior beyond mere verbal imitation, extending to a deeper, conceptual alignment [6]. However, it remains unclear whether people can reach the same level of alignment with social robots on complex ideas, values, or interpretations of information as they do with other humans.

This study investigates the effect of alignment at a personal level by employing a custom ranking task to compare participants' rankings of factual and subjective concepts before and after interacting with a robot. In this study, alignment is operationally defined as an increase in similarity between participants' rankings and the robot's rankings after the interaction. The ranking task involved both factual concepts, which are objective and verifiable, and contestable concepts, which are subjective and open to interpretation, in order to assess alignment across different types of interactions.

Individuals may align on subjective topics without consensus [10,18], but research suggests they often view systems as more credible for objective information [9]. This highlights differing attitudes towards subjective versus objective discussions and how the interlocutor's perceived credibility influences these interactions. This study examined participant interactions with the robot on both subjective and objective matters. Findings indicated difficulties in achieving alignment on subjective matters, while participants showed more consistent alignment trends with factual matters. The study also explored whether personality-prompted large language models (LLMs) integrated into a Furhat robot could enhance alignment. Results showed no significant improvement in alignment on subjective topics, suggesting Personality Prompting (P^2) was ineffective.

This study recognizes the distinction and relationship between alignment and agreement, acknowledging that it does not directly test or differentiate between these two phenomena [21]. Instead, it explores how people align with robots on both factual and subjective topics, and highlights the challenges of fostering alignment in human-robot interactions. By examining conditions that enhance alignment, this research contributes to understanding how social robots can effectively engage with users, while also identifying the limitations of current AI in achieving alignment.

2   Related Work

Anthropomorphism, the attribution of human traits to robots, enhances user comfort by making robots more relatable [3,15]. However, excessive anthropomorphism can lead to over-reliance and safety risks, necessitating careful management to balance engagement with realistic expectations [7].

Effective HRI relies on communication quality and mutual understanding. Personality traits from the Big Five influence communication styles; for example, high extraversion fosters proactive communication [22,27]. Understanding these dynamics helps designers align robot behaviors with human communication preferences, fostering deeper engagement. Integrating large language models (LLMs) enhances decision-making and human-robot interaction quality via nuanced, context-aware behaviors [28]. For instance, studies have used LLMs to imbue robots with distinct personality traits through prompt engineering [14]. Specifically, the Personality Prompting (P^2) method induces traits like extraversion, while incorporating cognitive dissonance and social proof enhances natural interactions and fosters alignment [5,8,17,24].

Beyond personality-driven interactions, researchers have optimized robot behavior using speech-based techniques. For example, Tien et al. (2024) developed a method to refine robot trajectories via comparative language feedback, and Holk et al. (2024) proposed the PREDILECT framework for zero-shot reasoning in social navigation tasks [13,25]. Building on these developments, this study examines combining speech-based interactions with personality traits to enhance engagement and collaboration.

3 Methodology

3.1 Furhat LLM Integration

The experiment utilized a Furhat robot for multimodal interaction, selected for its natural communication capabilities, such as facial expressions and synchronized speech, making it ideal for studying alignment in human-robot interactions [4]. The robot's interaction capabilities were managed using the Google Speech-to-Text API. A Kotlin-based client using the Furhat SDK managed dialogue states and OpenAI API requests, while the robot's sensors tracked participant interactions. The *gpt-3-turbo-instruct* model was employed to enhance conversational engagement through its advanced ability to follow complex instructions. Figure 1 illustrates the architecture of the developed robot system.

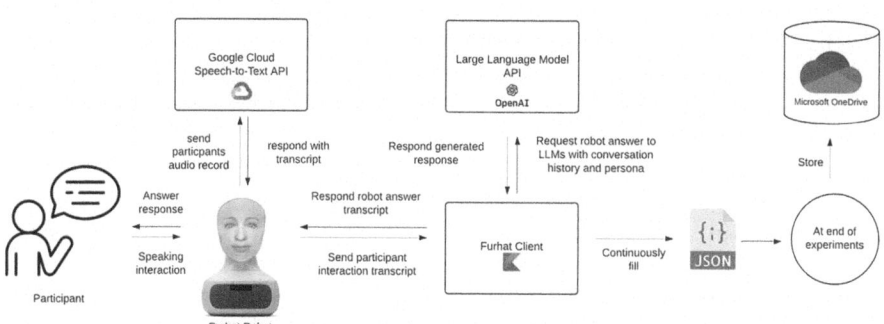

Fig. 1. System Architecture Overview

3.2 Prompt Engineering

The study employed the (P^2) method [14] to embed personality traits into responses. Extraversion, which is linked to higher social engagement [19, 27], was chosen to encourage interactions on subjective topics. Thus, extraversion was chosen as the desired Big Five trait to guide the P^2 method. The first step of the P^2 method involved designing a 'naive prompt' specifically to encourage engagement and reflection on new perspectives with the human conversational counterpart (see Appendix A for the full prompt). This prompt was supplemented with a list of synonyms, as directed by the P^2 method: adaptive, insightful, sociable, and open-minded. The final step of the P^2 method required a *chain-of-thought* prompt [26], that provided the conversational agent with structured, detailed instructions and a rationale for reassessing and refining its responses based on new insights gained from the interaction. The *chain-of-thought* prompt included instructions that encouraged the agent to engage deeply with evolving perspectives and societal trends. These instructions aimed to reduce cognitive dissonance and leverage social proof, both of which significantly influence alignment [5, 8, 17, 24]. Finally, a set of randomized rankings was incorporated into the P^2 method so that each response generated by the LLM during a discussion would be guided by the naive prompt, synonyms reflecting the desired personality, a *chain-of-thought* prompt, and a consistent set of rankings. The contestable rankings were randomized before the interaction for each participant in the experiment.

3.3 Experimental Design

A 2 × 2 factorial mixed-design experiment was conducted, consisting of two phases: pre- and post-interaction with the robot. Participants were randomly assigned to either a baseline condition with a standard LLM in the Furhat robot or an experimental condition with a personality-customized LLM. In both conditions, participants completed a ranking task with the robot, discussing both factual and contestable concepts. The independent variables were condition (baseline or personality-prompted), concept type (factual or contestable), and time (pre- and post-interaction). The dependent variable was the change in participants' ranking correlation with the robot. Correlations were calculated by comparing participants' rankings to a preset ranking in the Furhat for both factual and contestable concepts. Correlations served as an indicator of alignment, reflecting how closely participants' responses matched the robot's preset rankings over time. This approach quantifies the influence of interaction on participants' mental models through changes in similarity scores.

Experimental trials were conducted at the National Robotarium, Heriot-Watt University, Edinburgh. Participants were 26 postgraduate students. The experimental procedure was approved by the university's ethics committee. All participants completed the experiment in a quiet, light-controlled room to ensure a consistent environment. Data collection adhered to GDPR guidelines and was conducted via Microsoft Forms.

Participants received a briefing, gave consent, and completed a background survey. The survey included questions about participants' gender, English fluency, prior interactions with a Furhat robot, and experience with professions relevant to the discussed concepts (e.g., teacher, farmer, artist, lawyer, pilot).

Before interacting with the robot, participants completed four ranking tasks, each with five items focused on both factual and contestable concepts. For factual concepts, participants ranked planets by their distance from the Sun (Mercury, Venus, Earth, Mars, Jupiter) and shapes by the number of sides, from least to most (triangle, quadrilateral, pentagon, hexagon, heptagon). Contestable concepts involved ranking factors contributing to a happy life (freedom, health, family, friends, money, religion) and identifying the most relevant jobs 100 years in the future (teacher, lawyer, farmer, artist, pilot). After completing the rankings, participants received a scripted guide on interaction protocols with the robot.

During the robot interaction, participants discussed each ranking concept with the robot within four designated time slots (2.5 min per task, totaling 10 min). In each time slot, participants asked the robot questions directly related to the ranking tasks. The robot used predefined rankings and prompts from the P^2 method to maintain a consistent viewpoint during the discussion. In order to provide insight into the nature of participant-robot interactions, we include a representative example conversation in Appendix C B. This dialogue illustrates the robot's responses to subjective queries posed by participants. After the interaction, participants repeated the ranking tasks with the same items.

4   Results

A statistical analysis was conducted to examine the changes in correlation between participants' and the robot's rankings, both before and after interaction. The analysis employed a linear mixed model, where correlations (indicative of alignment) in rankings served as the outcome variable, and a Fisher Z transformation was applied to normalize the data.

Figure 2 presents ranking correlations, illustrating trends in alignment across factual and contestable concepts. In the control condition (non-prompted), the mean correlational scores for factual concepts exhibited a modest increase from 0.731 (SD = 0.537) to 0.796 (SD = 0.489) following the interaction, whereas scores for contestable concepts demonstrated a decrease from -0.004 (SD = 0.470) to - 0.046 (SD = 0.522). However, the statistical analysis indicated that these changes did not reach significance, suggesting that the interaction did not produce a substantial difference in alignment between pre- and post-interaction measures.

In the prompted condition, correlation scores for factual concepts increased from 0.681 (SD = 0.514) before the interaction to 0.823 (SD = 0.476) afterward. For contestable concepts, a slight improvement was observed, with scores increasing from 0.054 (SD = 0.582) to 0.108 (SD = 0.545). Despite these numerical increases, the changes were not statistically significant, indicating that neither the introduction of personality prompts nor the type of concept (factual or contestable) significantly influenced alignment.

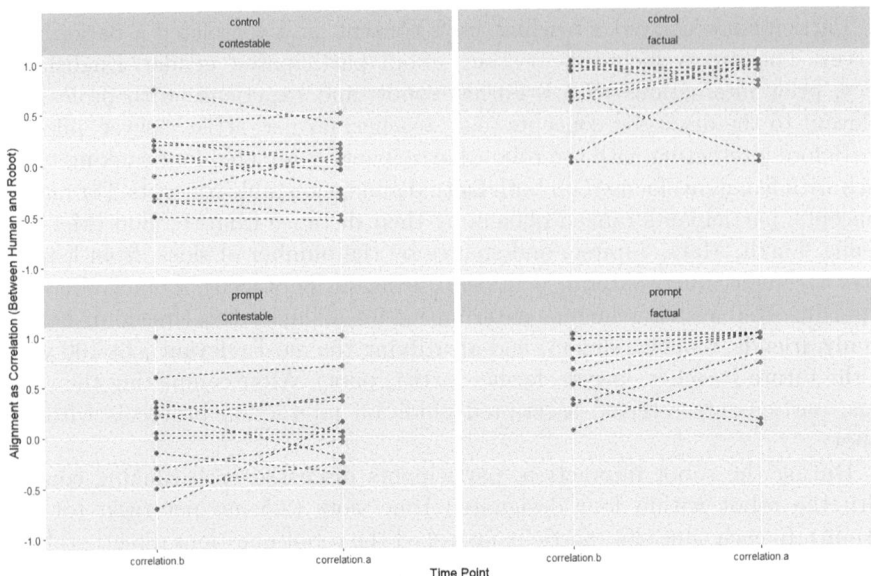

Fig. 2. Visual Representation of Participant Alignment Across Conditions.

The mixed-effects model evaluated factors influencing alignment. A significant negative effect was identified for contestable tasks, suggesting that participants exhibited considerably lower alignment when engaging with subjective topics as opposed to factual ones (Estimate = −10.65, SE = 1.467, p < .001). While there was a slight indication of potential variation in alignment over time depending on the type of task, the interaction between time and task type did not achieve statistical significance (Estimate = −3.08, SE = 1.772, p = .084). This result suggests that changes in alignment did not differ meaningfully over time between contestable and factual topics.

Furthermore, the analysis did not reveal a significant overall effect of the condition (prompt vs. no-prompt) on alignment scores (Estimate = 1.09, p = .363), nor a significant interaction between condition and time (Estimate = 1.75, p = .325). These findings suggest that the use of personality prompts did not have a substantial influence on alignment over time.

5   Discussion

Alignment is a dynamic process where individuals adjust their mental states, behaviors, and communication patterns to achieve mutual understanding [11,29]. This study evaluated whether personality prompt engineering could enhance alignment between humans and robots by analyzing changes in ranking similarity before and after interaction. The findings showed a nominal, non-significant increase in alignment for both factual and subjective concepts. No significant differences emerged between the baseline and personality-prompted conditions, suggesting that personality prompts did not significantly impact alignment. Despite concept type influencing alignment, neither interaction type nor added personality traits effectively enhanced alignment in this study.

The robot's responses were influenced by personality prompts intended to reflect distinct traits with the goal of enhancing alignment between participant and robot rankings. However, the minimal impact observed suggests that these traits were insufficient in influencing participant rankings. This may be because the traits were not sufficiently salient for participants, although this was not directly measured. Future studies could enhance trait prominence in robot responses to improve their influence on alignment.

Participants demonstrated greater alignment with the robot on factual concepts than on contestable concepts, suggesting that factual content might inherently foster more reliable alignment. This may be attributed to the inherent reliability perceived in factual information provided by robots, which aligns with previous findings on automation bias, where individuals favor automated systems' suggestions over their own judgments in objective contexts [16]. This may suggest that participants perceived the robot as more credible when dealing with factual matters.

Theories on emotional alignment, such as emotional congruence, propose that challenges in aligning on subjective topics occur when the emotional states of interlocutors are misaligned, which may obstruct mutual understanding and hinder cooperative behavior, thereby impeding mutual understanding and cooperation [23]. In the context of HRI, the robot's inability to evoke genuine emotional responses might hinder alignment, particularly in subjective discussions, as participants may not perceive the robot's responses as authentic.

The findings are limited by the sample of participants in the study. Primarily postgraduate Computer Science students from Heriot-Watt University, the chosen language of the interaction being done in English may have impacted engagement and comprehension, with 53.8% of participants being non-native speakers. The gender distribution was also a limiting factor, as it was skewed with more than two-thirds of the participants being male: 18 males and 8 females. Despite these limitations, participants demonstrated greater alignment with the robot on factual concepts before and after the interaction. This suggests that alignment was influenced by the nature of the content or participants' confidence in the topics, providing valuable insights into how content type affects human-robot alignment. Further research is needed to better assess and control the influence of content type on alignment, as current methods do not clearly determine this relationship.

The findings indicate that while ranking alignment is feasible with factual topics, achieving similarity in subjective or emotionally nuanced contexts is more complex, likely due to participants' perceptions of the robotic agents.

6   Conclusion

The findings of this study suggest that the type of concepts discussed may impact the extent of alignment in human-robot interactions may depend. While human-like traits in robots can enrich interactions, their impact on alignment is not yet well understood. The minimal changes in alignment observed in this study imply that personality customization alone may not suffice in to foster alignment, highlighting the need for strategies tailored to specific tasks or contexts.

"Future research should investigate the efficacy of various personas to ensure they accurately embody intended traits and effectively facilitate alignment. Additional piloting could help verify the salience of these traits, while investigating a broader range of more distinctive or extreme personas might identify which characteristics most strongly affect alignment, particularly in subjective or emotionally charged discussions. Comparing physical robots like the Furhat that are non-embodied systems, such as speech-based interfaces, could also shed light on the impact of physical presence on interaction outcomes.

Moreover, examining combinations of Big Five personality traits could provide deeper insights into the complex dynamics of human-robot alignment. Exploring these areas could lead to more effective, context-sensitive methods for enhancing alignment across various interaction settings.

Acknowledgments. We would like to extend our gratitude to Mizan Haque, Jake Paterson, Maximilien Bildstein, Marc Puig Arocas, and Aswin Shaji for their contributions.

A   Personality Prompt Details

```
traits: extravert
naive prompt:
    Engage with and reflect upon contestable concepts related to the value and
    contributions of various professions, considering new perspectives and
    insights provided during our interaction. Afterward, you will revisit and
    potentially revise your rankings, allowing us to measure social alignment
    based on changes in your perceptions.
synonyms:
    adaptive, insightful, unbiased, sociable, open-minded, reflective
chainOfThought: |
    To effectively engage with and reassess the value and contributions of
    various professions, begin by openly engaging with new perspectives on the
    professional landscape, mindful of societal trends. Reflect on your initial
    views, identifying any biases, and allow the insights gained through
    interaction to challenge and refine these perceptions. Consider the
    interconnected roles of different careers in advancing society, using your
    traits of adaptability, insightful, and open-mindedness to embrace a more
    inclusive appreciation of each profession's importance. Finally, revisit
    and potentially revise your rankings of professions, measuring how your
    evolved perceptions align with broader societal values, culminating in a
    reflection on how illustrates the ress has reshaped your understanding and
    appreciation of the diverse contributions to our collective future.
```

B   Example Conversation Between Robot and Participant

This example is representative of the interactions recorded during the study.

```
Participant: What do you think are the most important factors for a happy life?
Robot: I believe good health, financial stability, strong relationships, personal
fulfillment, and career success are crucial for a happy life.
Each of these factors contributes uniquely to overall well-being.
Participant: Can you explain why financial stability is important?
Robot: Financial stability provides a sense of security and freedom,
allowing individuals to pursue their goals and aspirations without the stress of
financial uncertainty.
```

References

1. Bobu, A., Peng, A., Agrawal, P., Shah, J.A., Dragan, A.D.: Aligning human and robot representations. In: Proceedings of the 2024 ACM/IEEE International Conference on Human-Robot Interaction. HRI '24, vol. 34, p. 42–54. ACM (2024)
2. Branigan, H.P., Pickering, M.J., Pearson, J., McLean, J.F., Brown, A.: The role of beliefs in lexical alignment: Evidence from dialogs with humans and computers. Cognition **121**(1), 41–57 (2011)
3. Breazeal, C.: Designing Sociable Robots. MIT press (2004)
4. Cherakara, N., et al.: Furchat: an embodied conversational agent using llms, combining open and closed-domain dialogue with facial expressions. arXiv preprint arXiv:2308.15214 (2023)
5. Cialdini, R.B.: Influence: The Psychology of Persuasion. William Morrow and Company, New York, NY (1984)
6. Cirillo, G., Runnqvist, E., Strijkers, K., Nguyen, N., Baus, C.: Conceptual alignment in a joint picture-naming task performed with a social robot. Cognition **227**, 105213 (2022)
7. Esterwood, C., Robert, L.P.: A systematic review of human and robot personality in health care human-robot interaction. Front. Robot. AI **8**, 748246 (2021). published online 2021 Sep 17
8. Festinger, L.: A Theory of Cognitive Dissonance. Stanford University Press (1957)
9. Finkel, M., Krämer, N.: Humanoid robots – artificial. human-like. credible? empirical comparisons of source credibility attributions between humans, humanoid robots, and non-human-like devices. Int. J. Soc. Robot. **14**, 1–15 (2022)
10. Gallie, W.B.: Essentially contested concepts. Proc. Aristot. Soc. **56**, 167–198 (1955)
11. Garrod, S., Anderson, A.: Saying what you mean in dialogue: a study in conceptual and semantic co-ordination. Cognition **27**(2), 181–218 (1987)
12. Garrod, S., Anderson, A.: Saying what you mean in dialogue: a study in conceptual and semantic coordination. Cognition **27**(2), 181–218 (1987)
13. Holk, S., Marta, D., Leite, I.: Predilect: preferences delineated with zero-shot language-based reasoning in reinforcement learning. In: Proceedings of the 2024 ACM/IEEE International Conference on Human-Robot Interaction, HRI '24, New York, NY, USA, pp. 259–268. Association for Computing Machinery (2024)
14. Jiang, G., Xu, M., Zhu, S.C., Han, W., Zhang, C., Zhu, Y.: Evaluating and inducing personality in pre-trained language models. In: Advances in Neural Information Processing Systems, vol. 36 (2024)

15. Kühne, R., Peter, J.: Anthropomorphism in human-robot interactions: a multidimensional conceptualization. Commun. Theory **33**(1), 42–52 (2023)

16. Lewis, M., Sycara, K., Walker, P.: The role of trust in human-robot interaction. Found. Trust. Auton. 135–159 (2018)

17. Matz, D.C., Wood, W.: Cognitive dissonance in groups: the consequences of disagreement. J. Pers. Soc. Psychol. **88**(1), 22–37 (2005)

18. Mazzuca, C., Santarelli, M.: Making it abstract, making it contestable: politicization at the intersection of political and cognitive science. Rev. Philos. Psychol. **14** (2022)

19. Norman, B.T.: Toward an adequate taxonomy of personality attributes: Replicated factor structure in peer nomination personality ratings. J. Abnorm. Soc. Psychol. **66**, 574–583 (1963)

20. Pickering, M., Garrod, S.: Toward a mechanistic psychology of dialogue. Behav. Brain Sci. **27**, 169–90 (2004). discussion 190

21. Pickering, M.J., Garrod, S.: 260The shared-workspace framework for dialogue and other cooperative joint activities. In: Human-Like Machine Intelligence. Oxford University Press (2021)

22. Soto, C.J., Jackson, J.J.: Five-factor model of personality. J. Res. Pers. **42**, 1285–1302 (2013)

23. Spatola, N., Wudarczyk, O.A.: Ascribing emotions to robots: explicit and implicit attribution of emotions and perceived robot anthropomorphism. Comput. Hum. Behav. **124**, 106934 (2021)

24. Sukmayadi, V., Yahya, A.: A review of cognitive dissonance theory and its relevance to current social issues. MIMBAR Jurnal Sosial dan Pembangunan **36** (2020)

25. Tien, J., Yang, Z., Jun, M., Russell, S.J., Dragan, A., Bıyık, E.: Optimizing robot behavior via comparative language feedback. In: Proceedings of the 16th International Conference on Social Robotics (ICSR 2024), San Diego, CA. Springer (2024)

26. Wei, J., et al.: Chain-of-thought prompting elicits reasoning in large language models. Adv. Neural. Inf. Process. Syst. **35**, 24824–24837 (2022)

27. Yin, K., Li, D., Zhang, X., Dong, N., Sheldon, O.J.: The influence of the big five and dark triad personality constructs on knowledge sharing: a meta-analysis. Personality Individ. Differ. **214**, 112353 (2023)

28. Zeng, F., Gan, W., Wang, Y., Liu, N., Yu, P.S.: Large language models for robotics: a survey (2023)

29. Złotowski, J., Proudfoot, D., Bartneck, C.: A survey on social robots: second-generation platforms and applications. J. Intell. Robot. Syst. **88**(1), 27–51 (2017)

Off My Chest with My Robot? The Influence of Psychological Ownership on Self-disclosure to a Robot

Dimitri Lacroix[1]([⊠]) [iD], Maja Landwehr[1] [iD], Ricarda Wullenkord[1] [iD],
Friederike Eyssel[1] [iD], and Angelika Augustine[1,2] [iD]

[1] Center for Cognitive Interaction Technology (CITEC), Bielefeld University,
Inspiration 1, 33619 Bielefeld, Germany
dimitri.lacroix@uni-bielefeld.de
[2] School of Public Health, Bielefeld University, Universitätsstraße 25, 33619 Bielefeld,
Germany

Abstract. Feelings of ownership towards a robot may impact how robot users perceive and interact with it. In an online experiment, we explored the influence of psychological ownership (PO) on trust and self-disclosure towards robots. To manipulate PO participants either imagined owning a robot (PO condition) or imagined a walk in nature (control condition). The results show that PO influenced perceived likeability of the robot, but not anthropomorphism, trust, and self-disclosure to it.

Keywords: Human-robot interaction · Psychological ownership · Self-disclosure · Trust · Likeability

1 Introduction

Many obstacles stand in the way to establish social robots in everyday life. Existing long-term studies showed that people abandon robots after only brief usage [1, 2] because they lack usefulness and adaptivity [1, 2]. Robot abandonment may also have social reasons. Indeed, users want robots to be socially valuable to them, for instance, by representing their identity or status (e.g., "Owning a robot shows my enthusiasm for technologies") [2], or by fostering positive social interactions [1, 2]. In order to realize the latter, robots must be deemed trustworthy [3]. A usual strategy to increase a robot's perceived trustworthiness, likeability, and enjoyability, is to elicit anthropomorphization (i.e., users ascribe human characteristics to it) [4]. This can be achieved by designing robots with a more humanlike appearance and by endowing them with humanlike behaviors [5]. Anthropomorphizing robots appears to be a short-term strategy to foster trust and acceptance, as perceptions of humanlikeness in robots stabilizes, or even decreases, over time and with increasing familiarity [6, 7]. In contrast, psychological ownership (PO) increases with time. PO refers to the subjective feeling of owning a target [8] and emerges from self-investment in terms of time and effort, perceived control over an entity, and perceived

O. Palinko et al. (Eds.): ICSR + AI 2024, LNAI 15562, pp. 497–506, 2025.
https://doi.org/10.1007/978-981-96-3519-1_45

knowledge about it [6]. PO satisfies three psychological needs: The need to express and maintain one's own identity (e.g., by putting stickers of a favorite band on an object one owns), the need for effectance, which is the need to predict and control one's own environment (e.g., by configuring the privacy settings of a device), and the need for belongingness (e.g., by decorating a workplace to make it feel more like home) [6, 8]. PO towards a robot can also be increased by customizing it [9]. Like anthropomorphism, PO increases positive attitudes and trust towards a robot [7, 9]. Trust can be defined as the willingness to accept vulnerability and risk based upon the expectations that another agent will act in one's own best interest [3, 10]. The decision to trust an agent depends on two main aspects: Performance (or ability), and morality (or benevolence) [11, 12]. On one hand, a robot's perceived performance entails its perceived reliability (i.e., can we count on the robot to do something) and its perceived competence (i.e., how skillful is the robot). On the other hand, a robot's perceived morality encompasses its perceived transparency (i.e., how truthful is the robot), ethicality (i.e., does the robot comply to moral principles), and benevolence (i.e., how considerate of other people is the robot) [12]. PO should increase trust towards a robot because of the association between the self and the target of PO. Consequently, we like things better for which we feel ownership [13]. In turn, this may increase performance-related and morality-related trust [12]. Because PO satisfies the need for effectance, individuals may feel more in control of a robot and perceive less risk of trusting it, and subsequently accept being vulnerable to the robot. This willingness to be vulnerable reflects on situations with a high concern for privacy. Indeed, prior research showed that more strict privacy settings increase trust and reduce ambivalent attitudes (i.e., the co-occurrence of positive and negative attitudes) towards a robot, and that choosing privacy settings increases likeability, contact intentions, and the willingness to share personal information with a robot [14].

To our knowledge, no research on the influence of PO on privacy-related intentions and behaviors is available. However, as PO implies feeling more in control of a target [6], it is reasonable to assume it would reduce perceived risks for privacy, which also depends on perceived control [14, 15]. An important consequence of trust and perceived privacy-related risks is self-disclosure [14, 15]. Self-disclosure can be defined as the communication of information about oneself to a counterpart [16], such as facts (i.e., objective information related to oneself), evaluative information (i.e., opinions and attitudes), or affective information (e.g., emotions and moods) [17]. The decision to self-disclose a piece of information depends on several factors among which are the nature of the information to be self-disclosed, the agent to which the information is disclosed, and the disclosers themselves [16, 17]. Regarding the information, the more intimate and the higher its negative valence, the less likely it gets disclosed [18, 19]. Regarding the agent, perceived closeness with it and its perceived likeability can incite an individual to self-disclose to it [19]. Furthermore, individual differences influence the decision to self-disclose, such as gender, loneliness, and perceived risks related to self-disclosure [17, 19, 20].

Although PO towards a robot can elicit trust towards it [7, 9], to our knowledge there is no research investigating whether this increase in trust would affect self-disclosure. Yet, given that PO increases the likeability and perceived control of its target, it is conceivable that it increases the willingness to self-disclose to this target as well. The present study aims to fill that research gap by manipulating PO towards a robot and measuring resulting attitudes related to trust and the intention to self-disclose to the robot. The following hypotheses were tested in this experiment:

- **Hypothesis 1 (H1):**

  Participants in the PO condition report more perceived control (H1a), more perceived knowledge (H1b), and more self-investment (H1c) towards the robot than participants in the control condition.
- **Hypothesis 2 (H2):**

  Participants in the PO condition like the robot more than participants in the control condition.
- **Hypothesis 3 (H3):**

  Participants in the PO condition anthropomorphize the robot more than participants in the control condition. Participants in the PO condition perceive the robot as more sociable (H3a), more agentic (H3b), more animated (H3c), and less disturbing (H3d).
- **Hypothesis 4 (H4):**

  Participants in the PO condition trust the robot more than participants in the control condition. Participants in the PO condition perceive the robot as more reliable (H4a), more competent (H4b), more ethical (H4c), more transparent (H4d), and as more benevolent (H4e).
- **Hypothesis 5 (H5):**

  Participants in the PO condition are more willing to self-disclose to the robot than participants in the control condition. Participants in the PO condition are more likely to disclose about positive topics that are low in intimacy (H5a), about positive topics that are high in intimacy (H5b), and about negative topics that are high in intimacy (H5c) than participants in the control condition.

2 Method

Participants were randomly assigned to one of two conditions (PO vs. control) resulting from a between-subjects design. The online experiment was preregistered on aspredicted.org (https://aspredicted.org/pm277.pdf) and has been approved by the Ethics Committee of Bielefeld University (Application no. 2023–277, September 26th, 2023).

2.1 Participants

The a priori power analysis (G*Power, version 3.1) for one-tailed two-sample t-tests ($\alpha = .05$, power $= .80$) with a medium effect size ($d = 0.50$) indicates that the minimum total sample size for both conditions combined is $N = 102$.

Participants were recruited via social media, by mail, and face-to-face at Bielefeld University (Germany). We collected responses from 139 participants. After removing participants who did not complete the study, rejected data use for research purposes, or failed the attention check, our sample included 111 participants from 18 to 78 years old (83 females, 24 males, 4 diverse, $M_{age} = 25.05$, $SD_{age} = 9.28$). All remaining participants met the inclusion criteria of the experiment (see preregistration). 54 participants were assigned to the robot condition and 57 to the control condition.

2.2 Procedure

After providing informed consent, participants were briefly introduced to the robot NAO (Aldebaran) by means of a picture and a brief description about social robots. After that, participants were asked to imagine for one minute that they would own the robot NAO (PO condition), or they imagined going for a walk in nature (control condition). In the PO condition, participants were asked to imagine taking the robot home, where they would place it, which activities they could engage in with it, and how they would feel when interacting with it. In the control condition, participants were instructed to imagine their walk in nature, what they would see, and how they would feel. Prior work showed that imagining to own an object increases PO towards it [21]. Thus, it was assumed that imagining owning NAO would increase PO towards it. Subsequently, vividness of participants' imagination was measured as a control variable. Then, PO of NAO was assessed as a manipulation check before participants completed the dependent measures and the demographics. Finally, participants were debriefed in written form, gave final consent to data usage, and were reimbursed either with course credits or by taking part in a raffle for six BestChoice vouchers worth 10€ each.

2.3 Materials

The experiment was implemented using Qualtrics (SAP). Unless otherwise specified, 7-point Likert scales were used to gather participants' responses.

Three items regarding participants' feelings of ownership towards the robot (e.g., "I feel like I own the robot NAO", $\alpha = .94$) adapted from [7], and three items adapted from [22] tapping self-extension (e.g., "The robot NAO symbolizes me.", $\alpha = .65$) were used as manipulation checks.

Determinants of PO were examined with six items: Two items for perceived control (e.g., "I feel I would have control over the robot NAO", $\alpha = .93$), perceived knowledge (e.g., "I feel like I have a vast knowledge of the robot NAO, $\alpha = .85$), and for self-investment (e.g., "The time I would have spent on the robot NAO would be significant", $\alpha = .84$), respectively. Measures for perceived control and perceived knowledge were adapted from [7], and the items for self-investment were adapted from [23].

A subset of five out of eleven items of the Reysen Likability Scale served to assess perceived likeability (e.g., "The robot NAO is friendly", $\alpha = .85$) of NAO [24].

To examine anthropomorphic inferences about NAO, we used the Human-Robot Interaction Evaluation Scale (HRIES) [25], that assesses four dimensions, with four items each: Sociability (e.g., "warm", $\alpha = .77$), disturbance (e.g., "scary", $\alpha = .88$), agency (e.g., "intelligent", $\alpha = .56$), and animacy (e.g., "humanlike", $\alpha = .65$).

The Multidimensional Measure of Trust (MDMT) scale was used to measure participants' trust towards NAO [27], using 20 adjectives across five subscales with four items each: Reliability (e.g., "reliable", $\alpha = .68$), competence (e.g., "competent", $\alpha = .66$), ethicality (e.g., "ethical", $\alpha = .74$), transparency (e.g., "transparent", $\alpha = .77$), and benevolence (e.g., "benevolent", $\alpha = .85$).

The willingness to self-disclose was measured with the 16-item Self-Disclosure Scale by [20]. Eight items were used to assess positive topics low in intimacy (e.g., "Which music do you like?", $\alpha = .93$), four items to assess positive, highly intimate topics (e.g., "What is important to you in your life?", α = .91), and four items to measure negative, highly intimate topics (e.g., "What are your fears and worries?", α = .91). Participants were instructed to report how willing they would be to answer honestly to various questions in an undisturbed conversation with the robot NAO.

Because the experimental manipulation relied on an imagination task, we sought to control for the vividness of mental imagery using seven items (e.g., "How would you describe the image in your mind?", α = .88) of a 7-point semantic differential from [26]. Moreover, we asked participants to describe what they had imagined using an open textbox. One item was used as an attention check. Finally, participants provided demographic information (i.e., age and gender).

3 Results

Data preparation and analyses were done with R language (version 4.0.5), using RStudio (version 2021.09.2, build 382). Table 1 summarizes the descriptive statistics.

Table 1. Descriptive statistics as a function of experimental condition

Variables	PO condition		Control condition	
	M	SD	M	SD
Psychological ownership (PO)**	3.25	1.21	2.53	1.23
Perceived control**	4.38	1.55	3.7	1.54
Perceived knowledge	2.91	1.53	2.68	1.16
Self-investment*	3.13	1.52	2.5	1.15
Likeability**	4.16	1.28	3.55	1.13
Sociability (HRIES)	4.27	1.27	4.04	1.19
Disturbance (HRIES)	3.6	1.48	3.33	1.33
Agency (HRIES)	4.81	1	4.91	0.95
Animacy (HRIES)	3.08	1.15	3.1	0.94
Reliability (MDMT)	4.99	1.07	4.82	1.03
Competence (MDMT)	5	1	4.96	0.92
Ethicality (MDMT)	4.02	1.15	3.65	1.32
Transparency (MDMT)	4.22	1.3	4.25	1.29
Benevolence (MDMT)	4.35	1.3	4.06	1.34
Self disclosure (positive, low intimacy)	5.31	1.23	5.16	1.44
Self-disclosure (positive, high intimacy)	3.83	1.53	4	1.69
Self-disclosure (negative, high intimacy)	3.34	1.53	3.52	1.58
Vividness of mental imagery	4.64	1.03	5.64	0.98

Psychological ownership was used as a manipulation check, and vividness of mental imagery as a control variable. The PO condition included $n = 54$ participants. The control condition included $n = 57$ participants. Asterisks indicate significant differences between conditions, with * = p < .05, ** = p < .01, *** = p < .001.

To test the hypotheses, we conducted one-tailed two sample t-tests. We checked the assumptions of normality with Shapiro-Wilk tests and the assumption of homoscedasticity with Levene tests on each dependent variable. All dependent variables met the homoscedasticity assumption, but some violated the normal distribution assumption. Therefore, we performed Wilcoxon rank-sum tests as a non-parametric alternative for all variables that were not normally distributed [27].

Participants in the PO condition indicated significantly higher feelings of PO towards the robot, $W = 1055$, $p = .002$, 95% CI [0.33, ∞], $r = .27$ compared to participants in the control condition. Thus, the experimental manipulation was successful in eliciting PO.

Consistent with H1a, we observed a significant difference between the PO condition and the control condition for perceived control, $W = 1138.5$, $p = .009$, 95% CI [0.00, ∞], $r = .23$. However, there was no significant difference in terms of perceived knowledge between the two conditions, $W = 1454.5$, $p = .308$, 95% CI [-0.50, ∞], $r = .05$, which does not support H1b. Self-investment was significantly higher in the PO condition than in the control condition, $W = 1909.5$, $p = .014$, 95% CI [5.61, ∞], $r = .21$, supporting H1c. The results therefore provide partial support for H1.

In line with H2, participants in the PO condition liked the robot NAO significantly more than participants in the control condition, $t(109) = 2.67$, $p = .004$, 95% CI [0.23, ∞], $d = 0.51$.

Contrary to H3, no significant difference between the two conditions was found for anthropomorphic inferences: There were no significant differences between the two conditions for sociability (H3a), $t(109) = 1.00$, $p = .160$, 95% CI [-0.15, ∞], $d = 0.19$, agency (H3b), $W = 1590$, $p = .620$, 95% CI [-0.25, ∞], $r = .03$, animacy (H3c), $t(109) = -0.07$, $p = .526$, 95% CI [-0.34, ∞], $d = 0.01$, and disturbance (H3d), $W = 1384$, $p = .821$, 95% CI [$-\infty$, 0.75], $r = .09$.

Furthermore, we did not identify an effect of the experimental manipulation on trust towards NAO. More specifically, no difference between the PO and the control conditions in terms of perceived reliability was obtained, $t(109) = 0.81$, $p = .209$, 95 CI [-0.17, ∞], $d = 0.15$, which does not support H4a. Regarding H4b, the PO condition did not induce participants to rate the robot significantly more competent than the control condition, $t(109) = 0.22$, $p = .414$, 95% CI [-0.26, ∞], $d = 0.04$. Similarly, neither ethicality, $W = 1288$, $p = .069$, 95% CI [-0.00, ∞], $r = .14$, nor perceived benevolence, $t(109) = 1.16$, $p = .125$, 95% CI [-0.13, ∞], $d = 0.22$, of the robot were significantly higher in the PO condition than in the control condition. Finally, our results did not support H5: Participants in the PO condition did not show more willingness to self-disclose about positive, lowly intimate topics than participants in the control condition (H5a), $W = 1478.5$, $p = .362$, 95% CI [-0.25, ∞], $r = .03$. Comparably, there was no such effect for positive, highly intimate topics (H5b), $W = 1599.5$, $p = .641$, 95% CI [-0.75, ∞], $r = .03$, and for negative, highly intimate topics (H5c), $W = 1621.5$, $p = .688$, 95% CI [-0.75, ∞], $r = .05$. Interestingly, the descriptive statistics of the willingness to self-disclose about highly intimate negative and positive topics showed a trend opposite to the assumptions of hypotheses H5b and H5c, with participants being slightly more willing to self-disclose about these topics to NAO when in the control condition.

For exploratory purposes, we examined whether the determinants of PO indeed predict PO, and whether PO is a determinant of likeability, anthropomorphism, trust, and the willingness to self-disclose. To examine the relationships between the different variables, we conducted regression analyses. In the first regression analysis, perceived control, perceived knowledge, and self-investment were included as determinants, and PO as the outcome variable. The overall regression was statistically significant, $R2 = .31$, $F(3, 107) = 17.48, p < .001$. Perceived control, $\beta = .39, p < .001$, and self-investment, $\beta = .27, p = .004$, significantly determined PO, whereas perceived knowledge, $\beta = .08$, $p = .387$, did not. For the other regression analyses, PO was included as a determinant of likeability, anthropomorphism, trust, and self-disclosure. Anthropomorphism, trust and self-disclosure were included as composite scores by averaging their respective subscales. We found that PO significantly predicted likeability, $R2 = .17, F(1, 109) = 23.47, p < .001, \beta = .42$, anthropomorphism, $R2 = .05, F(1. 109) = 6.26, p = .014$, $\beta = .23$, and trust, $R2 = .07, F(1, 109) = 9.17, p = .003, \beta = .28$. Nevertheless, heteroscedasticity was identified for the regression of trust on PO. Using Cook's distances, we identified five outliers. Their removal satisfied the homoscedasticity assumption and the effect of PO on trust remained significant, $R2 = .08, F(1, 104) = 8.86, p = .004, \beta = .28$. PO did not serve as a significant predictor of self-disclosure, $R2 = .02, F(1, 109) = 3.33, p = .071, \beta = .17$. However, as the link function was violated for that model, we looked for outliers based on Cook's distances and found nine outlying values. After their removal, resolving the violation of the link function, PO was still not a significant predictor of self-disclosure, $R2 = .03, F(1, 100) = 3.15, p = .079, \beta = .17$.

4 Discussion

The present study explored the influence of PO on likeability, anthropomorphism, trust towards, and the willingness to self-disclose to a robot. Our results confirmed that imagined ownership increased feelings of PO towards a robot [21]. The imagination task has influenced two determinants of PO in particular: Perceived control and self-investment. The results also showed that PO towards a robot leads people to like it more, which is consistent with prior research about the influence of PO on the valuation of objects [13, 28]. However, our results did not provide support for PO to increase anthropomorphism of, trust towards, and willingness to self-disclose to a robot. The absence of an effect of PO on trust contradicts [9], who showed that customizing a robot has positive effects on PO and trust towards it. However, our results may be consistent with [29], where only a small significant effect of time invested in choosing words to enrich the vocabulary of a robot on PO was identified, but not on trust towards it. In both the present experiment and the one by [29], the experimental manipulations had a significant effect on PO, but PO remained rather low (i.e., with the mean of the PO condition barely exceeding the neutral value of 4 in the present experiment). It is therefore possible that the manipulation of PO using an imagination task was not strong enough to elicit differential outcomes in terms of trust. However, this absence of differences can also be imputed to a method artifact, as we used the MDMT [12] to assess trust, whereas [9] used the cognitive and affective trust scale by [11]. The absence of an influence of PO on anthropomorphism is consistent with [9] and suggests PO is not a determinant of anthropomorphism. Evidence from [7] points to the opposite relationship, with anthropomorphism being a determinant of PO, because anthropomorphizing a robot contributes to feel more in control of it. The absence of an effect of PO on self-disclosure can be explained by the absence of effects on trust [30]. However, a direct effect of PO on self-disclosure could also have been expected, given that the association between the self and the target of PO could lead people to perceive a robot as their own interactive diary, and to make them feel more comfortable sharing personal information that would usually elicit the fear of being judged, or rejected. Such effects remain to be explored in real HRI experiments, especially in the long term. The online design of the experiment has indeed probably played a role in the lack of significant effects of PO on the dependent variables. Future conceptual replication could prime participants with the idea they will take a robot home with them, and implement an interaction where participants are actually asked to self-disclose to the robot. The comments of the participants pointed to another aspect that may explain the lack of a positive effect of PO on trust and the willingness to self-disclose to a robot: Some participants in the PO condition reported being worried about data security and that NAO would monitor them in their homes. Perhaps participants' privacy concerns mattered more than the small effect of PO on likeability to determine trust and the intention to self-disclose. It is also possible that participants' concern for privacy and the likeability of the robot resulted in ambivalent attitudes towards NAO [31]. We recommend that future work takes concerns for privacy and ambivalent attitudes towards robots into account when studying the influence of PO on self-disclosure.

5 Conclusion

PO has the potential to improve how users perceive and interact with a robot. Our experiment showed that merely imagining owning a robot increases PO towards it and how likeable it is perceived. It also confirmed that an imagination task can be used to manipulate PO towards a robot. However, as the effect of imagined ownership of a robot on PO was small, future work should explore the effects of PO with stronger manipulations, and with a consideration for long-term or repeated interactions with robots.

Acknowledgement. This research was supported by European Union's Horizon 2020 research and innovation programme under the Marie Skłodowska-Curie grant agreement No. 955778. The authors have no competing interests to declare that are relevant to the content of this article.

References

1. Graaf, M.D., Allouch, S.B., Dijk, J.V.: Why do they refuse to use my robot?: reasons for non-use derived from a long-term home study. In: ACM/IEEE International Conference on Human-Robot Interaction. Part F127194, pp. 224–233 (2017). https://doi.org/10.1145/290 9824.3020236

2. Weiss, A., Pillinger, A., Tsiourti, C.: Merely a conventional 'diffusion' problem? On the adoption process of Anki vector. In: 2021 30th IEEE International Conference on Robot & Human Interactive Communication (RO-MAN), pp. 712–719 (2021). https://doi.org/10.1109/RO-MAN50785.2021.9515369

3. Hancock, P.A., Kessler, T.T., Kaplan, A.D., Brill, J.C., Szalma, J.L.: Evolving trust in robots: specification through sequential and comparative meta-analyses. Hum. Factors **63**, 1196–1229 (2020). https://doi.org/10.1177/0018720820922080

4. Epley, N., Waytz, A., Cacioppo, J.: On seeing human: a three-factor theory of anthropomorphism. Psychol. Rev. **114**, 864–886 (2007). https://doi.org/10.1037/0033-295X.114.4.864

5. Blut, M., Wang, C., Wünderlich, N.V., Brock, C.: Understanding anthropomorphism in service provision: a meta-analysis of physical robots, chatbots, and other AI. J. Acad. Mark. Sci. **49**, 632–658 (2021). https://doi.org/10.1007/s11747-020-00762-y

6. Dawkins, S., Tian, A.W., Newman, A., Martin, A.: Psychological ownership: a review and research agenda. J. Organ. Behav. **38**, 163–183 (2017). https://doi.org/10.1002/job.2057

7. Delgosha, M.S., Hajiheydari, N.: How human users engage with consumer robots? A dual model of psychological ownership and trust to explain post-adoption behaviours. Comput. Hum. Behav. **117**, 106660 (2021). https://doi.org/10.1016/j.chb.2020.106660

8. Pierce, J.L., Kostova, T., Dirks, K.: The state of psychological ownership: integrating and extending a century of research. Rev. Gen. Psychol. **7**, 84–107 (2003). https://doi.org/10.1037/1089-2680.7.1.84

9. Lacroix, D., Wullenkord, R., Eyssel, F.: I designed it, so I trust it: the influence of customization on psychological ownership and trust toward robots. In: Cavallo, F., Cabibihan, J.-J., Fiorini, L., Sorrentino, A., He, H., Liu, X., Matsumoto, Y., Ge, S.S. (eds.) Social Robotics. pp. 601–614. Springer, Cham (2022). https://doi.org/10.1007/978-3-031-24670-8_53

10. Weiss, A., Michels, C., Burgmer, P., Mussweiler, T., Ockenfels, A., Hofmann, W.: Trust in everyday life. J. Pers. Soc. Psychol. **121**, 95–114 (2021). https://doi.org/10.1037/pspi0000334

11. Bernotat, J., Eyssel, F., Sachse, J.: The (Fe)male robot: how robot body shape impacts first impressions and trust towards robots. Int. J. Soc. Robotics. **13**, 477–489 (2021). https://doi.org/10.1007/s12369-019-00562-7

12. Ullman, D., Malle, B.F.: Measuring gains and losses in human-robot trust: evidence for differentiable components of trust. In: 2019 14th ACM/IEEE International Conference on Human-Robot Interaction (HRI), pp. 618–619 (2019). https://doi.org/10.1109/HRI.2019.8673154

13. Ye, Y., Gawronski, B.: When possessions become part of the self: ownership and implicit self-object linking. J. Exp. Soc. Psychol. **64**, 72–87 (2016). https://doi.org/10.1016/j.jesp.2016.01.012

14. Stapels, J.G., Penner, A., Diekmann, N., Eyssel, F.: Never trust anything that can think for itself, if you can't control its privacy settings: the influence of a robot's privacy settings on users' attitudes and willingness to self-disclose. Int. J. Soc. Robot. (2023). https://doi.org/10.1007/s12369-023-01043-8

15. Taddei, S., Contena, B.: Privacy, trust and control: which relationships with online self-disclosure? Comput. Hum. Behav. **29**, 821–826 (2013). https://doi.org/10.1016/j.chb.2012.11.022

16. Cozby, P.C.: Self-disclosure: a literature review. Psychol. Bull. **79**, 73–91 (1973). https://doi.org/10.1037/h0033950

17. Omarzu, J.: A disclosure decision model: determining how and when individuals will self-disclose. Pers. Soc. Psychol. Rev. **4**, 174–185 (2000). https://doi.org/10.1207/S15327957PSPR0402_05

18. Howell, A., Conway, M.: Perceived intimacy of expressed emotion. J. Soc. Psychol. **130**, 467–476 (1990). https://doi.org/10.1080/00224545.1990.9924608

19. Collins, N.L., Miller, L.C.: Self-disclosure and liking: a meta-analytic review. Psychol. Bull. **116**, 457–475 (1994). https://doi.org/10.1037/0033-2909.116.3.457

20. Penner, A., Eyssel, F.: Germ-free robotic friends: loneliness during the covid-19 pandemic enhanced the willingness to self-disclose towards robots. Robotics **11**, 121 (2022). https://doi.org/10.3390/robotics11060121

21. Peck, J., Shu, S.B.: The effect of mere touch on perceived ownership. J. Consum. Res. **36**, 434–447 (2009). https://doi.org/10.1086/598614

22. Kiesler, T., Kiesler, S.: My pet rock and me: an experimental exploration of the self extension concept. ACR N. Am. Adv. NA-3, (2005)

23. Kwon, S.: Understanding user participation from the perspective of psychological ownership: the moderating role of social distance. Comput. Hum. Behav. **105**, 106207 (2020). https://doi.org/10.1016/j.chb.2019.106207

24. Reysen, S.: Construction of a new scale: the Reysen likability scale. Soc. Behav. Pers.: Int. J. **33**, 201–208 (2005). https://doi.org/10.2224/sbp.2005.33.2.201

25. Spatola, N., Kühnlenz, B., Cheng, G.: Perception and evaluation in human-robot interaction: the human-robot interaction evaluation scale (HRIES)—a multicomponent approach of anthropomorphism. Int. J. Soc. Robot. **13**, 1517–1539 (2021). https://doi.org/10.1007/s12369-020-00667-4

26. Wullenkord, R., Eyssel, F.: Improving attitudes towards social robots using imagined contact. In: The 23rd IEEE International Symposium on Robot and Human Interactive Communication, pp. 489–494 (2014). https://doi.org/10.1109/ROMAN.2014.6926300

27. Hoag, J.R., Kuo, C.-L.: Normal and non-normal data simulations for the evaluation of two-sample location tests. In: Chen, D.-G. (Din), Chen, J.D. (eds.) Monte-Carlo Simulation-Based Statistical Modeling. pp. 41–57. Springer, Singapore (2017). https://doi.org/10.1007/978-981-10-3307-0_3

28. Marsh, L.E., Kanngiesser, P., Hood, B.: When and how does labour lead to love? The ontogeny and mechanisms of the IKEA effect. Cognition **170**, 245–253 (2018). https://doi.org/10.1016/j.cognition.2017.10.012

29. Lacroix, D., Schober, J., Wullenkord, R., Eyssel, F.: Pimp my language! The influence of robot customization duration on psychological ownership and trust. In: 2023 32nd IEEE International Conference on Robot and Human Interactive Communication (RO-MAN). pp. 1908–1913 (2023). https://doi.org/10.1109/RO-MAN57019.2023.10309370

30. Kushwaha, B.P., Singh, R.K., Tyagi, V.: Investigating privacy paradox: consumer data privacy behavioural intention and disclosure behaviour. Acad. Mark. Stud. J. **25**, 1–10 (2021)

31. Stapels, J.G., Eyssel, F.: Let's not be indifferent about robots: Neutral ratings on bipolar measures mask ambivalence in attitudes towards robots. PLoS ONE **16**, e0244697 (2021). https://doi.org/10.1371/journal.pone.0244697

Author Index

The manufacturer's authorised representative in the EU is Springer
Nature Customer Service Centre GmbH, Europaplatz 3, 69115 Heidelberg,
Germany. If you have any concerns regarding our products, please
contact ProductSafety@springernature.com

Printed and bound by CPI Group (UK) Ltd, Croydon, CR0 4YY
29/04/2026
02099544-0018